Professor Elizabeth Stanley is an established, internationally recognised scholar in the areas of state crime, human rights, incarceration, and social justice. Her work is highly regarded for its originality, quality, and social impact. Her books include: *Human Rights and Incarceration* (edited collection, Palgrave, 2018); *State Crime and Resistance* (edited collection, Routledge, 2013); and *Torture, Truth and Justice* (Routledge, 2009). Her monograph *The Road to Hell* (Auckland University Press, 2016) contributed to the 2018 establishment of a Royal Commission into Abuse in Care in New Zealand. She held a prestigious Rutherford Discovery Fellowship from 2014 to 2019, and is director of the Institute of Criminology, and deputy head of the School of Social and Cultural Studies, at Te Herenga Waka – Victoria University of Wellington.

Dr Trevor Bradley is a senior lecturer at the Institute of Criminology, Te Herenga Waka – Victoria University of Wellington, where he teaches courses on policing and crime prevention. His ongoing programme of research focuses on plural policing in Aotearoa New Zealand, which incorporates private policing, security, and various citizen-led policing bodies. Recent projects have included an international research collaboration on intelligence-led policing, as well as work on volunteer community policing in New Zealand. His recent publications include a new edition of the book *Introduction to Criminological Thought* (Edify, 2019), as well as various articles on governance failures and poor standards in the New Zealand private security industry. In 2020, he co-authored articles on policing during the Covid-19 pandemic.

Dr Sarah Monod de Froideville is a lecturer at the Institute of Criminology, Te Herenga Waka – Victoria University of Wellington. Her current research is broadly centred on harms to the environment in the New Zealand context, with a specific focus on (1) water-related harms and water security, (2) historical pollution, and (3) exploitative human–animal relations embedded into contemporary New Zealand culture. She also has an ongoing interest in the intersections between media representations, crime, and youth justice, stemming from her past work on moral panics in relation to young people. Early papers and her monograph *Making Sense of Moral Panic: A framework for research* (Palgrave, 2017) paid close attention to the changing shape of panics in neoliberal societies focused on preventing risk.

The Aotearoa Handbook of Criminology

Edited by
Elizabeth Stanley,
Trevor Bradley,
and Sarah Monod de Froideville

AUCKLAND
UNIVERSITY
PRESS

First published 2021

Auckland University Press
University of Auckland
Private Bag 92019
Auckland 1142
New Zealand
www.aucklanduniversitypress.co.nz

© Elizabeth Stanley, Trevor Bradley, Sarah Monod de Froideville, and the contributors, 2021

ISBN 978 1 86940 939 5

A catalogue record for this book is available from the National Library of New Zealand

This book is copyright. Apart from fair dealing for the purpose of private study, research, criticism or review, as permitted under the Copyright Act, no part may be reproduced by any process without prior permission of the publisher. The moral rights of the authors have been asserted.

Book design by WordsAlive Ltd
Cover design by Kalee Jackson
Cover image by Brendan Kitto

This book was printed on FSC® certified paper

Printed in China by Everbest Printing Investment Ltd

Contents

1 Introduction:
   Criminological Transformations   01
   Elizabeth Stanley, Trevor Bradley, and Sarah Monod de Froideville

PART ONE: CRIME KNOWLEDGE, CRIME POLITICS   07

2 Representing Crime:
   Shaping Understandings, Building Hegemony   09
   Fairleigh Gilmour

3 Counting Crime and Victims:
   The Case of 'Volume Crime'   21
   Trevor Bradley

4 Researching Crime and Criminal Justice:
   Funding, Politics, and Ethics   34
   Antje Deckert

PART TWO: CRIMES   47

5 Crimes of Intoxication:
   Unsettling the Alcohol/Drugs–Crime Link   50
   Fiona Hutton

6 Sexual Violence:
   The Logic of Patriarchy   61
   Jan Jordan

7 Responding to Intimate Partner Violence:
   Connecting Law, Language, and Supports   73
   Ang Jury, Natalie Thorburn, and Ruth Weatherall

8 Cybercrime and Cyber-harm:
   Exploring Young People's Sharing of Intimate Images   84
   Claire Meehan

9	Hate Crime, Racism, and Islamophobia: 'This Is Exactly Who We Are' *Daniel Botha and Scott Poynting*	94
10	Environmental Harm: Clean and Green, or Brutal and Contaminated? *Sarah Monod de Froideville and Moorea Smithline*	107
11	White-collar Crimes: Culpability, Causes, and Control *Simon Mackenzie*	119
12	Ignoring State–Corporate Crimes: The Case of the Pike River Mine Disaster *Elizabeth Stanley and Sally Day*	131

PART THREE: CRIMINAL JUSTICE — 143

13	Penal Populism: Its Life and Death *John Pratt and Jordan Anderson*	147
14	Policing: Past, Present, and Future *Trevor Bradley, Elizabeth Stanley, and Angus Lindsay*	159
15	Crime Prevention: Exploring Conventional Practices *Russil Durrant*	176
16	Ngā Kōti o Aotearoa / New Zealand Courts: Building Māori-focused Approaches, Developing Therapeutic Justice *Khylee Quince*	188
17	Sentencing: From Parity to Problem-solving *James C. Oleson*	200
18	The Youth Justice System: A Site of Evolution and Reform *Nessa Lynch*	213
19	Community Sentences: Expanding a System of Control and Surveillance? *Anita Gibbs*	225
20	Restorative Justice: The 'Land of the Long White Lie' *Juan Marcellus Tauri*	239
21	Hyper-incarceration: Inequality and Imprisonment *Liam Martin*	250

22	Rehabilitation: Risks, Needs, and Building Good Lives *Russil Durrant and Joanne Riley*	264
23	(Re)Integration: Recentring Strengths in Communities *Alice Mills and Cinnamon Lindsay Latimer*	276
24	Prison Abolitionism: Philosophies, Politics, and Practices *Ti Lamusse and Tracey McIntosh*	289

PART FOUR: DIFFERENTIAL EXPERIENCES — 303

25	Victimology: From Criminality to 'Victimity' and the Problem of Victim Blame *Rebecca Stringer*	306
26	Police Racism: The Responsibilities of Police Leadership *Kim Workman*	317
27	Rangatahi Māori, Samoan Talavou, and Youth Justice: Challenging the Monoculture through Decolonising Practices *Tamasailau Suaalii-Sauni, Juan Marcellus Tauri, Robert Webb, Arapera Blank-Penetito, Naomi Fuamatu, Fa'afete Taito, and Salevao Faauuga Manase*	331
28	Mental Health and Crime: A Critical Review *Bruce M. Z. Cohen*	345
29	Neuro-disabilities and Criminal Justice: Time for a Radical Rethink *Anita Gibbs*	358
30	Gangs: The Politics and Political Management of the 'Gang Problem' *Jarrod Gilbert*	370
31	Decriminalising Crimes: The Case of Sex Work *Lynzi Armstrong*	383
32	Deportations: Sorting Citizens across Borders *Elizabeth Stanley*	394

CONTRIBUTORS — 407

INDEX — 413

1

Introduction
Criminological Transformations

Elizabeth Stanley, Trevor Bradley, and Sarah Monod de Froideville

Criminological perspectives – like the concerns of crime and justice – are always in a process of transformation. This is nowhere more apparent than in Aotearoa New Zealand, where criminology has consolidated from its 1970s introduction at the Institute of Criminology, Victoria University of Wellington, to become an integral feature of teaching and research at most New Zealand universities. As this handbook shows, the discipline that has emerged is one which is led largely by critical, decolonising and feminist perspectives – something that places New Zealand criminology at odds with dominant disciplinary approaches taken across other neoliberal states, including settler-states.

From the outside, it might be thought that this progressive disciplinary development has mirrored national policies and practices to crime problems. Internationally, New Zealand is often regarded as a place of innovation and imaginative approaches to combating crime. One example is the youth justice system, often described as 'world leading' for its emphasis on diverting young people from the criminal justice apparatus, its focus on restorative justice and the involvement of whānau in formal proceedings. The development of specialised courts, such as Rangatahi Courts, is another. That our police do not *yet* routinely carry firearms on their person also sets New Zealand apart from almost all other nations.

Yet these approaches distract from some uncomfortable truths. Criminal justice issues in New Zealand are highly politicised, sensitive to the demands of populist lobby groups, and sensationalised by a news media dominated by commercial interests. In turn, New Zealand has also built intensely negative and socially harmful responses to crimes and criminal justice. This can be seen in many examples, from the entrenched use of imprisonment as a tool of colonial control and repression, to the limited protections afforded to women and children bearing the brunt of 'family' and sexual violence, to the reticence to criminalise multiple harms committed by powerful individuals and institutions. In short, official responses to crime have emerged in highly contradictory ways. While there are signs of progressive ventures, the overwhelming sense is of a crime and criminal justice landscape that reflects and embeds wider structural relations of inequality, and which fails to alleviate pain, violence, and harm at individual, family, or community levels.

Critics from academic, social, legal, and even government quarters have been instrumental in drawing attention to these entrenched problems, yet often to muted responses. In 2018, the newly elected Labour government launched several criminal-justice related initiatives – including an advisory group, Te Uepū Hāpai i te Ora, that reported on the profound need for transformative approaches to crimes and social harms. Whether we will see substantive shifts resulting from the group's recommendations is another matter. Many of Te Uepū's recommendations mirrored those from Moana Jackson's 1988 report *The Maori and the Criminal Justice System: A new perspective: He whaipaanga hou*. Despite Jackson's astute and evidence-based critique of New Zealand's monocultural system and its role in disproportionately criminalising Māori communities, few changes if any have been implemented over the following four decades. In the same way, other landmark reports – such as *Puao-Te-Ata-Tu / Daybreak* (1989) or *Te Ara Hou / The New Way* (1989), which sought to challenge the racism, discrimination, and inequities of criminal and welfare systems – began to gather dust almost as soon as they were published. More recent critical commentaries around issues such as detaining young people in police cells, inhumane treatments and conditions in prisons, or police pursuits of fleeing drivers have also been met with limited actions for improvements in practice. Suffice to say, from the mid-1980s there has been a troubling trajectory in New Zealand's political leadership of dismissing expertise and evidence in favour of quick-fix, often populist policies that have exacerbated problems at significant expense. It is not incidental that this approach has coincided with an acceleration of a neoliberal agenda that has also dominated justice-sector thinking.

The need to respond to these troubling issues is joined by new concerns, including whether New Zealand can respond to the criminal justice implications emerging from the crises of climate change and the Covid-19 pandemic. These are already exacerbating problems – such as unprecedented economic and psychological strain, conflicts around resources, escalations in family violence, fears regarding the normalisation of policing 'special powers', or the exclusionary capacities of enhanced border controls – that are critically important to address. It is vital that our future criminologies and our social, political, and legal actions engage with the local manifestations of these and other global harms and insecurities.

THIS COLLECTION

The *Aotearoa Handbook of Criminology* is the first comprehensive collection of readings from criminologists and practitioners based in the 'land of the long white cloud'. We offer it as a resource that outlines the foundations of crime and justice settings alongside critical, decolonising, and feminist perspectives on criminological ideas and practices. The ensuing chapters are keenly attuned to the representations, politics, laws, policies, and practices of crime and control, and sensitive to how gender, ethnicity, class, age, ability, and sexuality intersect across these in unique ways.

While this is a substantive collection, there are important omissions. The need to develop a tight collection has meant that many scholars we admire are not featured. Some vital criminological considerations – such as the rise of surveillance technologies, the development of privatised criminal justice responses, or diverse theorisations of crime, among other areas – are absent. There are also areas that need to be strengthened within New Zealand's criminology, not least to ensure the prioritisation of Māori and Pasifika ways of conceptualising and responding to crime and justice. The persistent hyper-incarceration of tangata whenua, and the discriminatory practices of policing, prosecution, and sentencing that precede it, require urgent and ongoing attention. Notwithstanding these concerns, the chapters in this first volume are vigorous, enticing, and intensely thought-provoking. They invite you to expand your criminological imaginations and to reassert new ways of thinking about and creating solutions for the multiple harms that are endured in New Zealand and beyond.

The chapters: A thematic introduction
The chapters are divided into four distinct sections: Part One focuses on crime knowledge, Part Two on crime types, Part Three on criminal justice, and Part Four on differential experiences of crime and justice. We provide a fuller overview of all the chapters in the introductions to each part. However, in bringing these works together, we identified four themes that are worthy of further reflection here. These relate to: (1) the representations and constructions of crimes, offenders, and victims; (2) the limits of regulation and justice measures, including how seemingly progressive shifts can increase controls over marginalised populations; (3) the significant harms that endure in criminal justice spheres, including from official responses to crime; and (4) the ongoing need for decolonising and transformative shifts to our criminal justice system and wider society. These four broad themes reflect the nature of the criminology currently being undertaken in New Zealand, and they also underline the significant problems that New Zealanders must work through to attain more effective and relevant responses to crime and justice.

With regard to the first theme, contributors to this volume demonstrate time and again how distorted constructions serve to marginalise and criminalise specific communities. Diverse groups – including drug users, young people using mobile technologies for sexual expression, gang members, those with mental illness, sex workers, and non-citizens, among others – are regularly targeted with distorted and exaggerated versions of their identities and activities (see chapters by: Hutton; Meehan; Cohen; Gilbert; Armstrong; Stanley). These depictions are personally harmful and create stigmatising associations. Moreover, such misrepresentations in the news media and across government and academic discourses reflect entrenched relations of power that can lead to ineffective and unjust policies and practices (a point also evidenced by: Gilmour; Bradley; Deckert; Gilbert).

These representations can embed a perceived need for state controls over those who are officially regarded as 'risky' or problematic. Risk-focused criminal justice approaches tend to shift the focus from contexts of deprivation or discrimination to the potential of individuals to cause harm to others. They rely on the idea that harm can be prevented by measuring, predicting, and controlling 'risky' populations, a point that serves to legitimise intensified practices of surveillance and control of individuals and communities. Such rationalities are evident right across criminal justice practices, including in crime prevention, community sentences, offender rehabilitation, and mental health treatments, and even in relation to the exclusionary restrictions on borders and citizenship (see: Durrant; Gibbs; Durrant & Riley; Cohen; Stanley). These risk rationalities are moulded to fit, and they fuel racist, ableist, and sexist discourses while downplaying the intrinsically political nature of criminal justice that serves capitalist, settler-society interests.

Misrepresentations and negative constructions are directed not just to offenders or 'risky' others. Constructions of victims and the offences against them can also serve to normalise victimisation, or hide the conditions under which harms and violence occur. This emerges in many different ways. It can be seen in the narratives that encourage victim blaming, as well as the representations of sexual violence that explicitly and implicitly defend male entitlement to women's bodies (see chapters by Jordan or Stringer, for example). It is also apparent, as Botha and Poynting demonstrate, in the political discussions that denied the hate crimes experienced by Muslims in the wake of the March 2019 Christchurch mosque massacres.

From these discussions, it is clear that criminologists have to be persistently attentive to power differentials and the ways in which images and discourses are powerful conduits for renewing structural inequalities, including reinforcing the legacies of settler colonialism. It is also necessary to consider and challenge dominant constructions. That is, these representational forces are powerful but they are not fixed, a point all too clearly illustrated in Armstrong's exploration of the decriminalisation of sex work.

Dominant constructions give rise to a second substantive theme: that legal and regulatory frameworks often fail to protect populations. Criminal justice interventions can both reflect and embed inequalities. Indeed, even practices that appear progressive may increase controls over marginalised populations. Contributors illustrate how policing (Bradley et al.; Workman), crime prevention (Durrant), courts (Quince; Oleson; Lynch; Gibbs), restorative measures (Tauri), correctional practices (Gibbs; Martin; Lamusse & McIntosh), and even rehabilitative, treatment, and reintegrative processes (Mills & Latimer; Durrant & Riley; Cohen) are underpinned by structural, institutional, and sociocultural settings that revolve around inequitable 'race', class, age, ability, sexuality, and gender relations. Under these conditions, every feature of criminal justice – including the use of discretion, offence recording, diversions, plea bargaining, surveillance, punishments, or other interventions – is filtered through dominant power relations in a settler-state. Those who are less powerful often suffer from a lack of protection.

The chapters in this handbook show us, then, that New Zealand's criminal justice apparatus is intrinsically unjust in its perpetuation of violence, disadvantage, and colonial controls. Inequitable situations are exacerbated further when we consider how the New Zealand state also fails to secure effective protections or punishments for many other egregious harms. Part of the problem here links to the skewed constructions in which criminality is not even seen. For example, racist hate crimes, white-collar crimes, state–corporate crimes, crimes against animals and ecosystems, digital crimes, and family violence crimes are often ignored completely, or explained away under different terminology that removes criminalising associations as they become redefined as 'accidents', 'disasters', 'one-off events', or 'personal conflicts' (see: Bradley; Jury et al.; Meehan; Botha & Poynting; Monod de Froideville & Smithline; Mackenzie; Stanley & Day). Criminal acts are, in turn, normalised, or made socially and legally permissible. This can be seen in the lax oversight and monitoring of institutions, the denial and disregard of complaints, and a 'light touch' (and often voluntary) regulatory system that enhances a landscape of impunity. These approaches enable serious offenders to evade accountability for their wrongful deeds. They also reveal that the 'crime problem' that is regularly narrated by political and media commentators tells us more about dominant practices of criminalisation, policing, or prosecution than it does about the true extent of violation and suffering that stems from offensive behaviours.

These concerns plug into the third theme around the nature, extent, and impact of harms and victimisation. Criminological (as well as political and social) attention has, historically, served to actively silence some victims of crime, or to blame them for their circumstances and the crimes against them. This has been most obvious in the mass gendered harms associated with family violence, interpersonal violence, and sexual violence (see: Gilmour; Jordan; Jury et al.; Stringer; Armstrong). Under patriarchal conditions, those who are victimised and stigmatised are additionally burdened with the task of preventing their victimisation. The true nature of this extensive societal violence and how its impacts seep across our communities, across generations, is downplayed.

A minimisation of victimisation is also apparent in the treatment of other groups, including those harmed by the 'crimes of the powerful' noted above. It is rare, for example, to see official agencies funnel any justice attention to climate crises, industrial pollution, species harms, or the violence that ensues from the consolidation of border securities (Monod de Froideville & Smithline; Stanley). From official representations, such global crimes often appear to have no victims. Further, there is limited consideration of how the impacts of these crimes (their physical, economic, psychological, or emotional harms) far outstrip those that ensue from acts that normally constitute the 'crime problem' (see: Mackenzie; Bradley). A similar minimisation of victimisation is also apparent in the mass harms generated by new technologies. Through digital media, gendered and racist harms can be perpetuated on national and global scales (see: Gilmour; Meehan; Botha & Poynting). Transnational victimisations are changing the crime landscape in complicated ways, and we do not yet have useful or respectful responses to identify those victimised through online spheres, or to prevent, punish, or repair these types of crimes (Durrant).

Such problems dovetail with the fact that, as inferred above, many of our traditional formal interventions also create systemic and institutional harms. These are embedded through racist strategies (among others, see: Bradley et al.; Workman; Suaalii-Sauni et al.; Tauri), as well as by the neoliberal consolidation of penal populism (Pratt & Anderson), but have also been given a new lease of life through risk-based rationalities and their associated technologies that present as neutral but perpetuate bias (Cohen; Stanley). The multiple system harms in operation are wide-scale and devastating in their long-term impacts. Consider the ramifications, for example, of the hyper-criminalisation of those with mental illness (Cohen) or the hyper-incarceration of Māori communities (Martin; Lamusse & McIntosh). These experiences remind us that while significant harms result from criminal victimisation, they also emerge from many official responses to that victimisation.

In many ways, then, our current approaches to 'crime' are damaging, failing, and counter-productive. This leads us to our final theme of the book, which involves two separate, though related, issues of significant importance for change: the decolonisation and transformation of justice responses. Currently a great deal of work, and much critical commentary, is focused on ways to decolonise and transform all facets of New Zealand's prevailing system of injustice. While various chapters reflect on the potential to achieve meaningful decolonisation and/or transformation, they also present clear warnings about how difficult it can be to fundamentally alter the balance of power, and how even seemingly progressive shifts can result in the further embedding of inequalities. There is a need for attentive Māori-centred action to fulfil Te Tiriti o Waitangi obligations through criminological research (see, e.g.: Deckert; Monod de Froideville & Smithline; Suaalii-Sauni et al.) as well as through criminal justice organisations and programmes (e.g., Quince; Lamusse & McIntosh; Workman). Such actions also have to be honest. Many transformative policies and processes have in fact expanded the state's reach into Māori and Pasifika communities by a dual process of co-option and indigenisation (Tauri; Suaalii-Sauni et al.). Decolonising justice can emerge only from Indigenous-led and ethical community justice alternatives, and must be attentive to the legacies and realities of a colonial society that has perpetuated intergenerational disadvantage and trauma (Mills & Latimer).

Decolonising imperatives link with wider initiatives to fundamentally transform criminal justice institutions, policy, and practice. Many reforms are already apparent in New Zealand – such as the development of a more diverse judiciary, together with the development of 'problem-solving' courts or Māori-focused courts (like the Matariki Court or Ngā Kōti Rangatahi) that are changing the cultural dynamics of justice (Oleson; Quince). While these courts are gaining in popularity, they are not without their issues, not least that they can bring more people into the system through a criminalisation of social problems.

Alongside these reformist measures, there are many in New Zealand who are working towards truly transformative responses to 'crime', including the ways in which society is structured to make certain responses appear as necessary or correct. Contributors to this handbook regularly reflect on the need to prioritise person-centric, relationship-based, socially engaged, culturally safe, and life-improving responses to harms and violence (Jury et al.; Gibbs; Durrant & Riley). They also remind us that truly transformative responses will require radical actions (see Hutton; Lamusse & McIntosh; Armstrong; Stanley) – to decriminalise, build stronger social, economic, and cultural rights, challenge exclusionary (real or metaphorical) borders, and abolish the conditions that make so many of our harmful criminal justice responses even possible.

CONCLUSION

Taken together, the chapters in this handbook present a troubling recognition of multiple failings around crime and justice in Aotearoa New Zealand and beyond. While there are undoubtedly useful and protective responses to crimes and harms across many areas, there remain significant gaps in knowledge, policy, and practice. Further, the 'crime problem' is highly politicised, and official responses are frequently led by emotion or institutional strategic intent rather than by evidence or community need.

Under these conditions, criminal justice frames are largely led by short-term political gains that have served only to reproduce and sustain settler-colonial conditions, and which have entrenched inequitable power relations in terms of 'race', class, gender, sexuality, age, ability, legal status, and species. Despite the continual deployment of new laws, strategies, policies, and frameworks for the criminal justice sector over the past few decades, discriminatory and harmful practices have been maintained and, in some respects, consolidated.

For criminology thinkers, there is a great deal to unpack, think through, and act on. We hope that this collection will assist you in propelling future improvements to how we define crime, how we prevent it, and how we can respond in much better ways to those who are victimised by crimes and wider harms. Further, given the many problems highlighted around our official responses, we encourage you to think and act beyond the dominant frames of criminal justice. After all, the chapters in this handbook repeatedly demonstrate the need to use criminological knowledge and imaginations to propel decolonising, feminist, critical, and socially just knowledge and transformations as a means to reinvigorate safety and well-being across all our communities.

Mā te rongo, ka mōhio. Mā te mōhio, ka mārama. Mā te mārama, ka mātau. Mā te mātau, ka ora.

Part One

Crime Knowledge, Crime Politics

Part One reflects on how knowledge about crime is extensively mediated through media narratives and political agendas, as well as through institutional strategies and policies. The three chapters illustrate how criminological data is intensely skewed towards official versions of the 'crime problem'.

The first chapter, by Fairleigh Gilmour, explores the fundamental concerns of how 'crimes' are represented in media. By unpacking significant theoretical concepts that underpin news production – such as hegemony, news values, and moral panics – she demonstrates how representations of crime and violence reflect entrenched relations of power in Aotearoa New Zealand, and inevitably serve ideological and political functions. Primary definers set the boundaries (and increasingly write the scripts) for crime news, an issue that ensures the public hold narrow views of what constitutes the crime problem and what is made possible as solutions. Drawing on diverse examples – from Grace Millane's tragic murder to moral panics about young offenders and Māori offenders – Gilmour illustrates how news production and values are structured through age, class, race, and gender relations. Still, there may be signs of change: given the rise of digital and social media in the New Zealand landscape, as elsewhere, new technologies are changing the media–crime nexus in diverse and complicated ways.

Trevor Bradley's chapter on counting crime presents a sobering account of the ways in which official data also rarely accounts for the realities of crime and victimisation in New Zealand. The concerns of official reporting and recording have long been of interest to criminologists, not least as they demonstrate how official statistics offer an inherently biased perspective. Bradley shows the fundamental deficiencies of statistics collated by New Zealand Police (NZP), which have a particular emphasis on 'volume crimes' (offences such as burglary, property crime, shoplifting, vehicle crime, and criminal damage). In doing so, he demonstrates how NZP statistics inevitably fuel populist debates and misdirect efforts to certain offences or populations of offenders while failing to respond to long-established serious crimes (such as intimate partner violence) or to new cybercrimes (such as online fraud or identity thefts) that pose significant risk to the public. He concludes that we should dismiss NZP statistics in any assessment of crime risks and decisions on how to prevent or reduce criminal activities.

The chapter by Antje Deckert considers the nature of crime and criminal justice research in New Zealand, and provides a critical analysis of the research landscape that has emerged. She shows the sometimes strained intersections between academics and the policy sector, and highlights some of the problems (such as academic struggles to access full, quality data; the government's disregard of research evidence; access and censorship issues; and the limited nature of independent research funds) that researchers face. Deckert also shows how orthodox researchers have often maintained the status quo in shaping debates on crime, or on who can be seen as offenders or victims. This critique is especially relevant in terms of the need for criminology to respect and prioritise Indigenous world views, knowledges, and epistemologies. Thus, she highlights the need for academics to more fully revolve their activities around ethical practices, fulfil their obligations to Te Tiriti o Waitangi, and work towards decolonising research methodologies.

2

Representing Crime
Shaping Understandings, Building Hegemony

Fairleigh Gilmour

Crime is a staple of traditional and digital media in Aotearoa New Zealand, and most New Zealanders obtain the majority of their crime information from the news media (Ministry of Justice, 2016). However, representations are changing and becoming increasingly violent, graphic, and sensationalised. This chapter explores some of the key theoretical concepts – including hegemony, news values, and moral panics – that have been used to analyse media representations of crime, and will discuss these concepts in terms of the New Zealand setting. This chapter will also unpack how depictions of crime and violence in the New Zealand media are structured through gender, class, race, and age relations of power. Finally, this chapter will discuss how digital and social media have changed the media–crime nexus in complex ways.

McGregor's (2017) research demonstrates that crime news constitutes a significant proportion of hard news, and that this proportion is increasing over time, and coverage has changed, particularly in terms of source. Due to the lack of resourcing of news departments, there is less investigative journalism in New Zealand, rendering police sources more powerful and limiting story range (McGregor, 2017). Furthermore, journalistic reliance on a limited number of sources (and their failure to engage with advocacy, academic, or Māori sources) results in a failure to scrutinise criminal justice institutions or hold them accountable (Boyle & Stanley, 2019).

The dominant role of violent crime in the news media often translates into elevated concerns around crime in the community. In New Zealand, most people believe that crime is increasing, particularly at a national level (Ministry of Justice, 2016), while over time we are seeing a gradual drop in crime. What we see in the media about crime is therefore not reflective of reality (insofar as we can know the 'reality' of crime through crime statistics and victimisation and offending surveys), but rather offers a 'distorted' image of the crime picture (Bradley & Walters, 2019).

THE POLITICAL ECONOMY OF NEWS MEDIA PRODUCTION

Since the media do not present us with an undistorted reality of crime, some scholars of crime and the media have asked: How can we make sense of which crimes are reported and how these crimes are framed? One approach is to draw from Marxist conceptualisations of news media production, which acknowledge not only that media representations of crime are not representative of actual crime statistics, but also that the media are *ideological* and serve the interests of the powerful. That the news media may be seen to serve the ends of a dominant elite can be understood in two key ways. First, in terms of an analysis of the political economy of news production; that is to say, *who owns and produces the news*. News media are shaped by: the size of the media companies, their limited number, the wealth of their owners, their profit-driven approach, and journalistic reliance on government and business 'experts' to frame news (Herman & Chomsky, 1988). These factors all shape the quality and content of the news media that we receive. Second, through the understanding that the media operate in such a way as to make the interests of the ruling class seem natural or commonsense. Values and beliefs are fundamental to reproducing class relations (Gramsci, 1971), and the media play a key role in manufacturing consent and reproducing hegemony.

Prior to the late 1980s, New Zealand had significant publicly owned media. However, the late 1980s and early 1990s saw a restructuring and deregulation of the broadcast media (Comrie, 1999). By the 1990s, New Zealand had, and today continues to have, one of the most deregulated media systems in the world (Transparency International, 2013). While deregulation was argued to increase choice, competition for advertising has destroyed programme ranges. News programming has become more entertainment-based, and there has been a waning of serious discourse about public affairs and stories about politics, economics, or industrial news (Atkinson, 1994; Comrie, 1999). Long-form journalism, which allows for complex analysis and social critique, has suffered a 'slow death' (Barton, 2016). New Zealand has thus followed a global pattern whereby deregulation has worked to stymie range and limit the extent to which reporting is in the public interest.

Media is often perceived to be fundamental to democracy, serving the Habermasian notion of the 'public sphere' (Habermas, 1989), a space where citizens can debate key issues of the day: a place for both discussion and dissent. Yet in the contemporary era, we are perhaps losing some of our liberty to dissent. The constraints to our liberty no longer necessarily inhere in legal limits to publication (what we would term censorship) but rather in the increasingly limited corporate ownership of news media. Certainly in New Zealand, there is a duopoly of news media ownership: in 2018, the NZME and Fairfax conglomerates owned an estimated 89.3 per cent of market share (Myllylahti, 2018). The aggressive liberalisation of the news media thus poses a challenge to its role in maintaining the public sphere of a genuine democracy (Hope, 1996).

The reproduction of the interests of the powerful in the news cannot be reduced, however, to media ownership. Rather, the structures of news production, its time constraints, and the requirement for accredited – and thus seemingly impartial – information, means that there is an overreliance on powerful voices in the media, who get to be the 'primary definers' of social events (Hall et al., 1978). In terms of crime news, the relationship between police and the media has often been described as 'symbiotic', given that journalists often have to rely on police for sources, while police rely on journalists for a positive image (Ericson, Baranek, &

Chan, 1989). This mutually beneficial relationship limits the tendency to seek out alternative viewpoints on a given crime. However, McGregor (2017) has argued more recently that we need to reconceptualise this notion of symbiosis in the contemporary New Zealand setting. Due to the decrease in funding for newsrooms and journalistic endeavours, police press releases are increasingly reproduced in the news media, giving police the power to set the agenda for understanding crime news and delimiting the potential for critical discussion (McGregor, 2017).

Gramsci's concept of hegemony signals that while those in power may sometimes rule through coercion, just as important is the process through which civil society deploys ideas and values in order to persuade the subordinate class that the existing system is acceptable or natural. In this way, the values and norms that support the system which allows the ruling class to rule end up becoming universal. How might this help us explain representations of crime in the media? The media tend to focus on street crimes (generally crimes of the poor and powerless) while crimes of the powerful (such as corporate crime, state crime, white-collar crime) tend to attract far less media attention (Barak, 1988). Furthermore, in discussing crime, the media tend to ignore broader political, economic, or social issues that might be influencing crime, in favour of focusing on discourses of individual pathology or deviance.

One study that explores the ideological function of news media in New Zealand is Havemann's (1991) analysis of violent crime in three major newspapers: the *New Zealand Herald*, the *Waikato Times*, and the *Dominion*. He noted:

> All three newspapers ran stories about random, 'senseless' violence, stories which pander to the fear underlying the 'law and order' discourse. Stories about senseless violence apparently sell newspapers. But they also aid and abet a government anxious to distract attention from its economic and social policies (p. 55).

In particular, Havemann found news media to be reluctant to discuss marginalisation, unemployment, increasing wage inequality, or the impacts of colonisation (or the government policies that were exacerbating any of these issues) as possibly playing a role in increasing crime rates. In this way, individuals are blamed for all crime problems, while systemic issues are overlooked. The result is that we are encouraged to see crime as an individualist issue, to support law-and-order politics, and to envisage crime as 'street crime' while not worrying about the crimes of the powerful.

NEWS VALUES

As we have already noted, the media do not provide an accurate portrayal of crime. While neo-Marxist interpretations help explain the ideological underpinnings of mass media production, another body of work that helps us make sense of mediated representations of crime involves the concepts of newsworthiness and news values. These concepts elaborate on why some stories are chosen over others: what is it that makes a story 'newsworthy'? The concept of news values was developed by Galtung and Ruge (1965), whose study of Norwegian newspapers identified a system by which news items were selected and prioritised for publication. Their ideas were revisited by Chibnall (1977), who, drawing from a Marxist framework, explored the 'law and order' focus of news media and unpacked some of the (often unwritten) codes and rules that shape journalistic practice and how newsrooms report on crime. Jewkes (2011) redeveloped news values with a specific focus on crime news. She argues that what all the news values have in common is their reliance on a 'broadly right-wing consensus' (p. 62). The media frame crime stories such that they can call for a tough-on-crime approach: more police, more prisons, and tougher sentencing as a response to crime. In this way, broader social causes and socio-economic factors can be dismissed and politicians can be seen to be 'doing something' about crime (see also Pratt & Anderson, chapter 13 this volume). Harcup and O'Neill (2017) have revisited news values to emphasise the impact of social media: audiences are no longer passive consumers and the shareability of a news item on social media is increasingly important.

Wright Monod (2017a), whose approach will be outlined in this section, draws from empirical research in the contemporary New Zealand setting and describes nine values:

- *Violence* is a staple of crime news and violent crime is over-represented in the news media.
- The news value of *proximity* relates to how near or relevant an event will be to a presumed audience. It can be spatial – local minor crime incidents might be featured in the regional press, but not in the national papers. However, the notion of proximity can also be cultural and relate to the presumed audience of the media. For example, victims who are Pākehā and middle class are more likely to be reported on in the media.
- The news value of *risk* refers to the fact that crime news reports encourage the public to fear for their personal safety. While most violent crime is committed by someone known to the victim, stranger violence is over-represented in the news media. This makes violent victimisation seem random, unpredictable, and ready to strike at any time.
- A sense of the *extraordinary* is a dominant crime news value: bizarre or unusual cases are more newsworthy.
- *Personification*, or reporting on individuals, describes how complex social explanations of crime are ignored and individual stories are preferred. The crimes of famous and/or powerful individuals are particularly attractive for these purposes.
- A further crime news value is *emotion*, particularly if there are related images that evoke strong feelings.
- Connectedly, *spectacle* is a crucial news value, with images and videos increasingly central to news reporting.
- Any news story involving *children* becomes instantly more newsworthy. As victims, children are presented as innocent and sympathetic. As offenders, children represent the future, and their deviant behaviour can be interpreted as symptomatic of a broader moral decline.
- Finally, *shareability* relates to the likelihood that the story will be shared on social media.

We can see these patterns operating broadly in the New Zealand context. The recent murder of British backpacker Grace Millane, for example, received significant media attention. A stranger murder involves *violence* and is rare enough in New Zealand to be *extraordinary*. Millane was photogenic, and the use of her picture throughout media reporting provided *spectacle*. Her father, who was frequently interviewed, was eloquent and sympathetic, adding to the cultural *proximity* of the case – he was readily relatable to a presumed middle-class Pākehā audience. The story was often subject to *personification*, with a focus on the individuals involved in the case, specifically Millane and her family. The details of the case and the impact on Millane's family provoked strong *emotion* in the audience. That Millane was attacked by a relative stranger meant that the element of *risk* was apparent.

The media coverage on the Millane case is noticeably more substantial than that of another murder which happened only a few days earlier. An elderly man in Petone, Francis Tyson, was murdered and decapitated by his neighbour. In the six months following their deaths, there were 1644 stories about Millane in New Zealand newspapers, compared to 28 about Tyson.[1] The Tyson case, while extremely violent and confronting, was not as newsworthy as the death of Millane. Tyson was not photogenic. He knew the offender. He was a drug dealer, a fact that lessened the cultural proximity to a presumed middle-class readership and also made the case much harder to simplify into the binaries of innocent victim and evil offender that facilitate personification. Thus, while both cases were violent and tragic, Tyson's murder did not meet as many of Wright Monod's news values, lessening media interest in reporting on the case.

MORAL PANICS IN THE NEW ZEALAND PRESS

An important framework for analysing crime in the news is Cohen's formulation of the 'moral panic', which helps us understand the relationship between media representations, public reactions, and policy shifts. Cohen's 1972 book *Folk Devils and Moral Panics* explored a disproportionate reaction in the UK media to some fairly minor seaside confrontations between young people from two subcultures – mods and rockers – in the mid-1960s. For Cohen (1972), a moral panic occurs when:

> A condition, episode, person or group of persons emerges to become defined as a threat to societal values and interests; its nature is presented in a stylized and stereotypical fashion by the mass media; the moral barricades are manned by editors, bishops, politicians and other right-thinking people; socially accredited experts pronounce their diagnoses and solutions (p. 9).

Key elements of a moral panic are therefore: the identification of a specific group as deviant; the use of simplified, symbolic language to describe them; the rise of 'moral entrepreneurs' who discuss the problem; and a resulting 'crackdown', usually taking the form of hastily constructed (and thus rarely evidence-based) policy. Key to the concept is the disproportionality of the panic: the degree of concern is in no way proportionate to objective levels of harm.

Cohen was also concerned with how labelling and punishing particular groups can exacerbate marginalisation and actually increase deviant activity through a 'deviancy amplification spiral'. Some groups are more frequently targeted by moral panics. Jewkes (2011, p. 76) suggests that those most likely to be targeted include: young working-class men; those whose behaviour breaks conventional worker norms (such as strikers); those who dress or present themselves outside the norms (such as punks or gang members); and people who fail to conform to traditional conservative family ideals (single mothers on welfare, for example). Hall et al. (1978) meanwhile highlighted the development of moral panics in response to social anxieties around young men from ethnic minorities.

Shuker et al.'s (1990) historical analysis identifies several moral panics in New Zealand. The first is the 1920s concern over 'larrikinism'. At this time, political worries about the treatment of children led to the Child Welfare Act in 1925 and the establishment of a Child Welfare Branch in the Education Department. The new child welfare officers brought increased attention to youngsters seen as neglected or 'out of control'. There was a corresponding rise in the number of neglected children and street kids, and these young people were presented as a threat to public order. However, there is little evidence of actual deterioration in youth behaviour. A panic concerning youthful immorality emerged in the Lower Hutt region in the 1950s. Concerns around supposed misbehaviour by young people in the region led to an inquiry which 'frothed over teenage "milk bar gangs", seedy sex in darkened picture theatres and underage "orgies"' (Brickell, 2012, p. 95). The Hastings Blossom Festival Affray in 1960 was much exaggerated in the media. What was described as a 'riot', a 'mob' of 'thousands' of 'vicious youths', was in fact a minor incident in which a few people were fighting and no one was injured.

The use of specific terms to describe youth subcultures – in 1950s New Zealand, non-conformists were called 'bodgies' (male) and 'widgies' (female) – also marked the symbolic construction of these 'folk devils'. Similarly, the Queen Street riot of 1984 received widespread press attention and resulted in the Local Government Amendment Act, which gave local authorities greater discretionary power to ban liquor from public venues. There was a broader social context to the riot, including catalysts such as the 1981 Springbok tour, the introduction of centralised policing, and the alienation of youth, particularly Māori and Pasifika youth. However, the dominant media narrative relied heavily on official accounts of the affray and focused on negative discussions of the rioters.

Each of the moral panics explored by Shuker et al. (1990) occurred during a time in New Zealand's history that can be understood as a 'boundary crisis'. They were times of rapid social change during which social anxieties became fixated on specific threats in an attempt to re-establish social order. Moral panics thus seem to be a key feature of the New Zealand news, with a particular focus on young people at times of significant social change. These moral panics demonise youth, who are presented simultaneously as at risk and as pathologically deviant. Both historical and contemporary analyses (Shuker et al., 1990; Wright, 2010; Wright Monod, 2017a) indicate that while more liberal explanations for youth justice issues do appear in the media, it is conservative, individualised interpretations of youth crime that remain dominant.

RACE IN THE NEWS MEDIA

The New Zealand news media generally present Māori in a negative light (Coxhead, 2005), and frame issues, including crime, as divorced from social context and especially from the impacts of colonisation (McCreanor et al., 2014). A key issue is race-tagging: the unnecessary use of racial or ethnic references in negative media reporting. Kernot (1990), for example, showed that media crime reports used race labels such as 'Māori', 'Pacific Islander', or 'Polynesian' up to four times as often as labels such as 'Pākehā', 'European', or 'Caucasian'. McCreanor et al.'s study indicated not only that newspaper representations of Māori strongly associated Māori people with crime, but also that the primary sources of information for crime stories were overwhelmingly Pākehā, with iwi and independent Māori voices rarely given the space to comment. Deckert's (2019) analysis of media representations of Māori women offenders demonstrates a gendered dimension to racialised representations of crime in the New Zealand press: stories about Māori women were significantly more likely to take an unfavourable tone than stories about Pākehā women.

Drawing from Cohen's conceptualisation of moral panic, Beddoe (2014) explores the construction of 'feral families' as contemporary folk devils, arguing that the media construct 'feral families' as welfare dependent, prone to violence and predominantly Māori. A key focus of negative media reporting in the contemporary era is around child abuse, which is often presented as a 'Māori problem', despite the fact that family violence in New Zealand cuts across class and ethnic lines (Wilson & Webber, 2014). Maydell's (2018) study examined the coverage of serious child abuse in New Zealand newspapers and found that the dominant construction of child abuse was as a 'Māori issue'. Eschewing an analysis of the risk factors that cut across ethnic groups (such as poverty, unemployment, and substance abuse issues), media reporting focused on the personalities of the perpetrators and their supposedly innate characteristics. Wright Monod (2017b, p. 352), meanwhile, explores how, when Māori children are themselves offenders, affective images are used to evoke emotion in readers, distorting perceptions of crime and inviting audiences to read these children as 'inherently criminogenic'. These negative media representations impact on Pākehā–Māori relationships and on how Māori see themselves, and they undermine the potential for equality and justice in society (Barnes et al., 2012; McCreanor et al., 2014).

DIGITAL MEDIA, CITIZEN JOURNALISM, AND ONLINE HARASSMENT

One of the most striking features of the contemporary media landscape is how quickly it is changing. The percentage of New Zealanders for whom social media is a major source of crime news has increased from 23 per cent in 2013 to 45 per cent in 2016; young people are particularly likely to use social media as a main source of information (Ministry of Justice, 2016). Some commentators suggest that the rise of digital media exacerbates the detrimental impacts of deregulation. Edwards (2016, p. 55), echoing Wright Monod's (2017a) news value of 'shareability', notes that alongside the slashing of newsroom staff numbers, there is now a 'clickbait approach to news', neither of which is 'good for democracy'.

There are additional complexities to the relationship between digital media and democratic discourse. It is not simply that people increasingly receive their news online; everyday citizens also increasingly produce news. As Baudrillard (1981/2019) argues, the traditional press does not offer any meaningful form of reply from the audience to the primary definers. Thus, rather than authentic communication, there is a 'monopoly of speech' held by social elites. New forms of media can be interpreted as a re-democratisation of information production. One important aspect of this is citizen journalism, defined by Goode (2009) as:

> a range of web-based practices whereby 'ordinary' users engage in journalistic practices. Citizen journalism includes practices such as current affairs-based blogging, photo and video sharing and posting eyewitness commentary on current events (p. 1288).

The growth in citizen journalism has been facilitated by technological advances (particularly the proliferation of smart phones) and the development of an interactive media environment (Mythen, 2010). To what extent, however, has the advent of citizen journalism allowed non-hegemonic ideas to be circulated with greater ease? It has positive impacts: democratising journalism, pluralising the number of voices heard, and enabling new technologies. But it also has been critiqued. There is unequal access to digital media, as well as the potential to embed populist forms of news presentation that erode the quality of available information and undermine democratic society by enabling the spread of false information (Mythen, 2010; Tilley & Cokley, 2008).

Citizen journalism has been argued to increase police accountability, with police abuses being caught on mobile phones, including recent instances in New Zealand (see also *New Zealand Herald*, 2017). A combination of technologically empowered citizens who produce information that challenges official accounts of events and a media environment where there is a market for anti-establishment news (Greer & McLaughlin, 2010) may change perspectives on police and protest, with implications for how police will maintain legitimacy in this evolving media environment. The online sharing of information can thus be interpreted as contributing to the accountability of public institutions and the maintenance of the kind of public sphere necessary for genuine democracy. The digital era, however, has also allowed for the proliferation of harmful online content, cyberbullying, and the sharing of harmful images.

One of the most extreme recent examples of the use of digital technology to underpin (or further publicise) criminal behaviour was the 2019 Christchurch mosque shootings in which the assailant livestreamed the attacks to Facebook using a GoPro (see Botha & Poynting, chapter 9 this volume). The first-person shooter perspective, alongside the click-bait style language of the shooter's (now suppressed) manifesto, suggests that social media saturation was a key goal. Facebook claims to have caught 1.2 million of the 1.5 million uploads in the 24 hours after the shooting before they made it to users' newsfeeds (Klonick, 2019), but has not shared how many people viewed, commented on, reacted to, or shared the 300,000 copies that made it online (Harwell, 2019). In the aftermath, there has been significant debate around how the use of digital platforms to spread extremist views and hate speech can be limited and how this regulation ought to occur. While successive New Zealand governments have acknowledged the complexities posed by the increasing dominance of digital media platforms, efforts at regulation have remained piecemeal and fragmented across different government departments (Mason & Errington, 2019; Thompson, 2019).

SOCIAL MEDIA AND ONLINE COUNTER-PUBLICS

This chapter previously touched on the concept of the public sphere as a key aspect of an authentic liberal democracy. This notion of the public sphere has also been used to explore the development of social media and how it has expanded opportunities to contribute to public discourse. Fraser's (1992) critique of the Habermasian notion of the public sphere points out that it has often operated in such a way as to be exclusionary. The rise of social media has opened up opportunities for many previously excluded groups – what Fraser called 'subaltern counterpublics' – to flourish. For example, while women were historically excluded from the public sphere in the Habermasian sense, new forms of media have allowed women and girls to form 'counter-publics' through which to develop alternative narratives of violence and victimisation.

Online space might expand the possibilities for harassment, but it also allows people to resist and respond to harassment in novel ways and subvert the dominant narratives that underpin it (Vitis & Gilmour, 2016). While sexual harassment is a key issue online, online space also affords opportunities to challenge gendered violence. For example, in their qualitative interviews with New Zealand young people, Sills et al. (2016) found that while rape culture was a significant issue for participants in online space, social media simultaneously afforded them opportunities to seek out a feminist education and to engage in and develop safe online spaces in which rape culture could be contested. Young people were thus able to 'access and participate in an alternative – networked and collective – cultural space' that 'resourced them with the support, knowledge, and tools to critically respond to rape culture' (Sills et al., 2016, pp. 948–949).

There are also negative outcomes from the growth of 'counter-publics' online. While online activism often advocates for racial justice and challenges dominant constructions of crime, there are also counter-publics that foster divisiveness, disunity, and even criminal behaviour. The online space can just as well be used to foster political, racial, or gender-based violence. Meanwhile, regulating the online space poses serious questions in terms of freedom of expression, civil liberties, and surveillance. Both the capacity to regulate the online environment and the question of responsibility remain. In the case of the Christchurch video, Facebook struggled to remove uploads, and technology-based efforts to find and remove it were imperfect (Perrigo, 2019). It is also unclear how nation-states can effectively regulate global issues, and what role the major corporations – such as Facebook and Twitter – can, will, and should play in regulating dangerous and/or criminal behaviours online.

CONCLUSION

This chapter has explored some of the major theoretical approaches to understanding crime and the media within the contemporary Aotearoa New Zealand context. While many of these approaches are useful for examining crime news, the complexity of this study also needs to be acknowledged. As Greer (2010) argues: 'Media are fantastically diverse. Understanding media, therefore, requires a diversity of theoretical, methodological and epistemological approaches' (p. 9).

While the deregulation of the New Zealand media has seen an increasingly limited media ownership, and there is significant evidence of deeply racialised, gendered, classed, and aged crime reporting in the New Zealand press, the advent of new and digital media offers a counterpoint to hegemonic news media. However, as this chapter has demonstrated, digital media should not be understood as a panacea. While they offer us diverse voices about crime and justice, they also open up new challenges, not least in terms of how we will regulate and respond to virtual domains.

STUDY QUESTIONS

- In this chapter, we explored Cohen's 'moral panic' concept. Think of a contemporary moral panic in the New Zealand context – how did this panic develop?

- What are some key ways in which the media shape our understanding of crime and the criminal justice system?

- What are some negative and positive impacts of digital media on our understanding of crime and criminal justice?

FURTHER READING

Bradley, T., & Walters, R. (Eds.). (2019). *Introduction to criminological thought* (3rd ed.). Auckland, New Zealand: Edify.

McGregor, J. (2017). Crime, news, and the media. In A. Deckert & R. Sarre (Eds.), *The Palgrave handbook of Australian and New Zealand criminology, crime and justice* (pp. 81–94). Cham, Switzerland: Palgrave MacMillan.

Sills, S., Pickens, C., Beach, K., Jones, L., Calder, D. O., Benton-Greig, P., & Gavey, N. (2016). Rape culture and social media: Young critics and a feminist counterpublic. *Feminist Media Studies, 16*(6), 935–951. doi:10.1080/14680777.2015.1137962

NOTES

1 Based on Factiva database findings, full name as search term.

REFERENCES

Atkinson, J. (1994). The state, the media and thin democracy. In A. Sharp (Ed.), *Leap into the dark: The changing role of the state in New Zealand since 1984* (pp. 146–177). Auckland, New Zealand: Auckland University Press.

Barak, G. (1988). Newsmaking criminology: Reflections on the media, intellectuals, and crime. *Justice Quarterly, 5*(4), 565–587. doi:10.1080/07418828800089891

Barnes, A. M., Borell, B., Taiapa, K., Rankine, J., Nairn, R., & McCreanor, T. (2012). Anti-Māori themes in New Zealand journalism – toward alternative practice. *Pacific Journalism Review, 18*(1), 195–216. doi:10.24135/pjr.v18i1.296

Barton, C. (2016). Anatomy of a redundancy: The suffocation of long-form journalism in New Zealand. In E. Johnson, G. Tiso, S. Illingworth, & B. W. Bennett (Eds.), *Don't dream it's over: Reimagining journalism in Aotearoa New Zealand* (pp. 144–164). Christchurch, New Zealand: Freerange Press.

Baudrillard, J. (1981/2019). *The political economy of the sign*. London, UK, & New York, NY: Verso.

Beddoe, L. (2014). Feral families, troubled families: The spectre of the underclass in New Zealand. *New Zealand Sociology, 29*(3), 51–68. Retrieved from https://search.informit.com.au/documentSummary;dn=898659386951932;res=IELFSC

Boyle, O., & Stanley, E. (2019). Private prisons and the management of scandal. *Crime, Media, Culture, 15*(1), 67–87. doi:10.1177/1741659017736097

Bradley, T., & Walters, R. (Eds.). (2019). *Introduction to criminological thought* (3rd ed.). Auckland, New Zealand: Edify.

Brickell, C. (2012). Moral panic or critical mass? The queer contradictions of 1950s New Zealand. In H. Bauer & M. Cook (Eds.), *Queer 1950s. Gender and sexualities in history* (pp. 94–114). London, UK: Palgrave MacMillan.

Chibnall, S. (1977). *Law-and-order news: An analysis of crime reporting in the British press*. London, UK: Tavistock Publications.

Cohen, S. (1972). *Folk devils and moral panics: The creation of mods and rockers*. London, UK: MacGibbon and Kee.

Comrie, M. (1999). Television news and broadcast deregulation in New Zealand. *Journal of Communication, 49*(2), 42–54. doi:10.1111/j.1460-2466.1999.tb02792.x

Coxhead, C. (2005). Māori, crime and the media: The association of Māori with crime through media eyes. *Yearbook of New Zealand Jurisprudence, 8*(2), 264–299. Retrieved from https://search.informit.com.au/documentSummary;dn=490633008404674;res=IELNZC

Deckert, A. (2019). Indigeneity matters: Portrayal of women offenders in New Zealand newspapers. *Crime, Media, Culture, 16*(3), 1–21. doi:10.1177/1741659019873771

Edwards, B. (2016). Journalism and democracy. In E. Johnson, G. Tiso, S. Illingworth, & B. W. Bennett (Eds.). *Don't dream it's over: Reimagining journalism in Aotearoa New Zealand* (pp. 55–65). Christchurch, New Zealand: Freerange Press.

Ericson, R. V., Baranek, P. M., & Chan, J. B. L. (1989). *Negotiating control: A study of news sources*. Toronto, Canada: University of Toronto Press.

Fraser, N. (1992). Rethinking the public sphere: A contribution to the critique of actually existing democracy. In C. Calhoun (Ed.), *Habermas and the public sphere* (pp. 109–142). Cambridge, MA: MIT Press.

Galtung, J., & Ruge, M. H. (1965). The structure of foreign news: The presentation of the Congo, Cuba and Cyprus crises in four Norwegian newspapers. *Journal of Peace Research, 2*(1), 64–91. doi:10.1177/002234336500200104

Goode, L. (2009). Social news, citizen journalism and democracy. *New Media & Society, 11*(8), 1287–1305. doi:10.1177/1461444809341393

Gramsci, A. (1971). *Selections from the prison notebooks of Antonio Gramsci* (Q. Hoare & G. N. Smith, Trans & Ed.). New York, NY: International Publishers.

Greer, C. (2010). *Crime and media: A reader*. London, UK: Routledge.

Greer, C., & McLaughlin, E. (2010). We predict a riot? Public order policing, new media environments and the rise of the citizen journalist. *British Journal of Criminology, 50*(6), 1041–1059. doi:10.1093/bjc/azq039

Habermas, J. (1989). *The structural transformation of the public sphere: An inquiry into a category of bourgeois society* (T. Burger & F. Lawrence, Trans.). Cambridge, MA: MIT Press.

Hall, S., Critcher, C., Jeferson, T., Clarke, J., & Roberts, B. (1978). *Policing the crisis: Mugging, the state and law and order*. London, UK: MacMillan.

Harcup, T., & O'Neill, D. (2017). What is news? News values revisited (again). *Journalism Studies, 18*(12), 1470–1488. doi:10.1080/1461670X.2016.1150193

Harwell, D. (2019, March 20). Fewer than 200 people watched the massacre live online. This group pushed it to millions. *New Zealand Herald*. Retrieved from https://www.nzherald.co.nz/nz/news/article.cfm?c_id=1&objectid=12214612

Havemann, J. (1991). Doing violence to the news in New Zealand. *Australian Journalism Review, 16*(1), 45–56.

Herman, E. S., & Chomsky, N. (1988). *Manufacturing consent: The political economy of the mass media.* New York, NY: Pantheon Books.

Hope, W. (1996). A short history of the public sphere in Aotearoa/New Zealand. *Continuum: Journal of Media & Cultural Studies, 10*(1), 12–32. doi:10.1080/10304319609365721

Jewkes, Y. (2011). *Media and crime* (2nd ed.). London, UK: Sage Publications.

Kernot, B. (1990). Race-tagging: The misuse of labels and the Press Council. In P. Spoonley & W. Hirsh (Eds.), *Between the lines: Racism and the New Zealand media* (pp. 53–55). Auckland, New Zealand: Heinemann Reed.

Klonick, K. (2019, April 25). Inside the team at Facebook that dealt with the Christchurch shooting. *New Yorker.* Retrieved from https://www.newyorker.com/news/news-desk/inside-the-team-at-facebook-that-dealt-with-the-christchurch-shooting

Mason, C., & Errington, K. (2019). *Anti-social media: Reducing the spread of harmful content on social media networks.* Retrieved from https://www.privacyfoundation.nz/wp-content/uploads/2019/05/Anti-Social-Media-Report.pdf

Maydell, E. (2018). 'It just seemed like your normal domestic violence': Ethnic stereotypes in print media coverage of child abuse in New Zealand. *Media Culture & Society, 40*(5), 707–724. doi:10.1177/0163443717737610

McCreanor, T., Rankine, J., Moewaka Barnes, A., Borell, B., Nairn, R., & McManus, A.-L. (2014). The association of crime stories and Māori in Aotearoa New Zealand print media. *Sites: A Journal of Social Anthropology and Cultural Studies, 11*(1), 121–144. doi:10.11157/sites-vol11iss2id240

McGregor, J. (2017). Crime, news, and the media. In A. Deckert & R. Sarre (Eds.), *The Palgrave handbook of Australian and New Zealand criminology, crime and justice* (pp. 81–94). Cham, Switzerland: Palgrave MacMillan.

Ministry of Justice. (2016). *Public perceptions of crime 2016 – survey report.* Retrieved from https://www.justice.govt.nz/assets/Documents/Publications/20161130-Final-PPS-report.pdf

Myllylahti, M. (2018). *New Zealand media ownership 2018.* Auckland, New Zealand: AUT Research Centre for Journalism, Media and Democracy (JMAD). Retrieved from https://www.aut.ac.nz/__data/assets/pdf_file/0013/231511/JMAD-2018-Report.pdf

Mythen, G. (2010). Reframing risk? Citizen journalism and the transformation of news. *Journal of Risk Research, 13*(1), 45–58. doi:10.1080/13669870903136159

New Zealand Herald. (2017, April 28). Claims of police brutality after footage emerges of man allegedly pepper sprayed in Porirua. Retrieved from https://www.nzherald.co.nz/nz/news/article.cfm?c_id=1&objectid=11847213

Perrigo, B. (2019, March 15). 'A game of whack-a-mole'. Why Facebook and others are struggling to delete footage of the New Zealand shooting. *Time.* Retrieved from https://time.com/5552367/new-zealand-shooting-video-facebook-youtube-twitter/

Shuker, R., Openshaw, R., & Soler, J. M. (1990). *Youth, media and moral panic in New Zealand: From hooligans to video nasties.* Palmerston North, New Zealand: Department of Education, Massey University.

Sills, S., Pickens, C., Beach, K., Jones, L., Calder, D. O., Benton-Greig, P., & Gavey, N. (2016). Rape culture and social media: Young critics and a feminist counterpublic. *Feminist Media Studies, 16*(6), 935–951. doi:10.1080/14680777.2015.1137962

Thompson, P. A. (2019). Beware of geeks bearing gifts: Assessing the regulatory response to the Christchurch call. *The Political Economy of Communication, 7*(1), 83–104. Retrieved from https://www.polecom.org/index.php/polecom/article/view/105

Tilley, E., & Cokley, J. (2008). Deconstructing the discourse of citizen journalism: Who says what and why it matters. *Pacific Journalism Review, 14*(1). Retrieved from https://search.informit.com.au/documentSummary;dn=171212093914631;res=IELNZC

Transparency International. (2013). *Integrity Plus 2013: New Zealand national integrity system assessment*. Retrieved from https://www.transparency.org.nz/docs/2013/Integrity-Plus–2013-New-Zealand-National-Integrity-System-Assessment.pdf

Vitis, L., & Gilmour, F. (2016). Dick pics on blast: A woman's resistance to online sexual harassment using humour, art and Instagram. *Crime, Media, Culture, 13*(3), 335–355. doi:10.1177/1741659016652445

Wilson, D., & Webber, M. (2014). *The people's report: The people's inquiry into addressing child abuse and domestic violence*. Auckland, New Zealand: The Glenn Inquiry. Retrieved from https://nzfvc.org.nz/news/first-glenn-inquiry-report-released

Wright, S. (2010). *Angel faces, killer kids and appetites for excess: Reapproaching moral panic*. Unpublished doctoral thesis, Victoria University of Wellington, Wellington.

Wright Monod, S. (2017a). *Making sense of moral panics: A framework for research*. Cham, Switzerland: Palgrave Macmillan.

Wright Monod, S. (2017b). Portraying those we condemn with care: Extending the ethics of representation. *Critical Criminology, 25*(3), 343–356. doi:10.1007/s10612–016–9348–1

3

Counting Crime and Victims
The Case of 'Volume Crime'

Trevor Bradley

In 2018, the Ministry of Justice administered the first sweep of the New Zealand Crime and Victims Survey (NZCVS).[1] One significant, albeit predictable, finding was the considerable difference in the amount of crime reported to it and the number of victimisations recorded by New Zealand Police (NZP) for the same period.[2] Overall, just 23 per cent of crimes captured by the survey had been reported to NZP. Such significant discrepancies between survey and police 'counts' of crime are hardly a new discovery. Since 1996, New Zealand surveys have consistently recorded a much higher incidence of crime than have the police, and have thereby revealed the extent to which NZP statistics fail to represent the reality of crime and victimisation.[3,4] It is interesting to question, then, why NZP statistics, despite their obvious deficiencies, continue to enjoy privileged 'Tier 1' status.[5]

Criminology has long been aware of the pitfalls of police-recorded crime (Biderman & Reiss, 1967), and that most crime goes unreported, undetected, and unrecorded (Bradley & Walters, 2019; Patrick, 2014). As a result, police statistics can mislead public perceptions of risk (New Zealand Crime and Safety Survey [NZCASS], 2015) and supply a questionable evidence base for developing policy and strategy (Sherman, 2013). Moreover, unconventional offences that are much less likely to be reported and/or detected are especially under-represented. For example, cybercrimes are rarely reported, despite their exponential growth (NZCVS, 2018, p. 114; Meehan, chapter 8 this volume), and there is no official ANZSOC offence classification to accommodate them (Bradley & Walters, 2019, p. 26).[6] NZP statistics therefore offer an inherently biased sample of crime and criminality (Reiner, 2016, p. 108). A more abstract, though no less important, problem revolves around the fact that every attempt to count crime (victim surveys included) is bedevilled by the problem of how it is defined. As Fogg (2014, para. 12) noted, there is 'no such thing as a definitive measure of crime, because there is no such thing as a single definition of crime'. In confining the definition of crime to acts prescribed by the Crimes Act 1961, police statistics replicate and help sustain the view that it is crimes like burglary, car theft, and individual acts of violence that constitute the crime problem while ensuring the limited profile of the 'typical' offender is maintained.

Contrary to soundbite media reporting and political rhetoric, then, NZP crime statistics do not represent a full picture of crime and victimisation. As administrative data, these statistics require critical interpretation to make better sense of what they actually measure (Hope, 2013, p. 39). With this in mind, this chapter seeks to illustrate the fundamental deficiencies of NZP statistics by framing discussion around 'volume crime': a convenient, if flawed, term for a selection of conventional high-incidence offences that constitute the bulk of recorded crime (Brown & Smith, 2018). Volume crimes are at the forefront of public and political concern (Leask, 2017b; Sachdeva, 2016) and provide a useful frame for critical analyses for two reasons. First, looking at volume crime highlights the very limited capacity of NZP to supply reliable measures of the conventional offences that dominate political and media discourse. It illustrates how NZP statistics present an unreliable index of risk and help justify misdirected prevention and reduction efforts aimed at the 'usual suspects'. Second, the restricted range of traditional volume crimes also highlights the limited jurisdiction of police statistics. That is, in being confined to a handful of conventional, terrestrial offences the current composition of volume crime underlines the failure of NZP to account for a range of new volume crimes that pose even greater risks to public safety.

The chapter consists of three sections. The first unpacks the concept of volume crime and the range of conventional offences encapsulated by it. The political salience and public sensitivity surrounding conventional volume crime and the disproportionate attention it continues to receive are discussed. From here, the second section draws on a subset of high-volume conventional offences reported to the NZCVS/NZCASS and reported to and recorded by NZP. In comparing the discrepant totals in both, this section illustrates the extent to which police statistics, in New Zealand and overseas, significantly under-represent conventional volume crime. To further highlight this routine under-representation, comparable survey and police data on intimate partner violence (IPV) will also be reviewed. Finally, the third section switches attention to online fraud and identity theft. These 'new', unconventional volume crimes rarely feature in NZP statistics, despite their significant impact and consequences. As a result, the official statistics paint an unreliable, misleading picture of the types of crime from which a growing proportion of society, comprising individuals and institutions, is clearly at risk (Cross, 2018).

VOLUME CRIME: THE CONVENTIONAL PICTURE

Volume crime is a term most commonly used to refer to those offences reported to or detected by police in large numbers and which are, in turn, disproportionately represented in recorded crime (see Brown & Smith, 2018, p. 5). Predictably, NZP employs a similar definition. As NZP's national manager: prevention (NMP) explained, 'Police uses the term volume crime to describe the bulk of cases dealt with,' and referred to burglary, assault, shoplifting, vehicle crime, and criminal damage as examples.[7] However, if volume crime describes the 'bulk of cases dealt with', then a range of other offences – including IPV and 'family harm' (which demand 41 per cent of a frontline officer's time [New Zealand Family Violence Collective, 2017]), sexual violence, and cybercrimes – ought to be included, but are not.

Volume crime is a term familiar to most police organisations, and one to which their publics are also highly attuned. Reported increases and decreases in volume crimes often shape public perceptions of and satisfaction with police performance (Ludwig et al., 2017). Volume crime is often a key theme of populist, law-and-order campaigns, given that political parties recognise its salience with the public. New Zealand media and politicians display a keen sensitivity to conventional volume crime. For example, burglary has long been the focus of media attention, a key theme of which has been an inadequate police response (Leask, 2017b).[8] The public, too, have fixated on these offences. The final NZCASS (2015, p. 34) asked respondents to identify which crimes posed particular problems in their neighbourhood. Almost 70 per cent selected burglary. In the run-up to the 2014 general election, New Zealand First promised greater protection to homeowners, farmers, and shopkeepers who shoot to kill intruders (New Zealand Herald, 2014). An apparent 'surge' of property crime in 2016 (Weekes, 2017) led political parties from across the spectrum to offer populist 'solutions', including mandatory minimum jail time for 'three-strike' burglars (Kirk, 2016). Aware of the potential electoral impact, the police minister attempted to reassure an anxious public by announcing that henceforth all burglaries would be attended by police within 48 hours (Tait, 2016). Police effectiveness in reducing burglary was the subject of no fewer than 10 separate reviews between 2000 and 2006 (Chetwin, 2005; Office of the Auditor General, 2006).

NZP continues to prioritise conventional volume crimes.[9] Its NMP confirmed that most police districts have volume crime managers and specialist volume crime 'squads'. Reducing volume crime is a key pillar of the current NZP Four Year Plan (NZP, 2017), and is among the anticipated outcomes of the 1800 police officers promised by the 2017 coalition government (Baird, 2019). In August 2018, Waitematā Police launched a new Precision Targeting Team focused on burglary and robbery (NZP, 2018a), while Operation Pencil targets volume vehicle crime in Auckland City (NZP, 2018b). New anti-burglary initiatives, including an NZP-led target hardening project – Locks, Lights and Lines of Sight – and a Corrections-led treatment programme for convicted burglars, have also helped maintain the focus on conventional volume crime (*Stuff*, 2019). The ongoing attention that volume crimes receive from government, police, and media helps sustain public perceptions that it is offences like burglary, assault, and vehicle theft that pose the greatest risk.

Underestimating the scale of conventional volume crime

As noted above, conventional volume crime is regularly underestimated in New Zealand. Comparing the counts of a subset of offences reported to and recorded by both NZP and the NZCASS (2015, p. 116) illustrates the extent to which NZP statistics routinely under-represent volume crime. The subsets of burglary and assault will be compared here because they represent household and personal offences and because they have the highest incidence rate of all offences captured by the NZCASS.

Overall, the NZCASS (2015, p. 117) captured a total of 1.9 million offences, 817,000 (43 per cent) of which were made up of 'Burglary', 'Theft from Vehicle/Vehicle Interference', 'Assault', and 'Robbery'. Of these, 36 per cent (n=294,120) were *reported* by victims to police and, revealing the size of the 'grey figure' in respect to these offences, just 47 per cent (n=137,000) were *recorded* by police.

As shown in Table 3.1, 41 per cent of burglaries captured by the NZCASS were also reported to police (p. 106), while just 48 per cent (n=40,000) of these were recorded by police (p. 122). The under-representation of 'Assault' is even more pronounced. From the 500,000 incidents captured by the NZCASS, just under 25 per cent (n=124,000) were reported to police (p. 106) and of these just 26 per cent (n=32,000) were recorded by police (p. 122). While the NZCASS captured over 700,000 assaults and burglaries, only 72,000, or around 10 per cent of known incidents, were included in the official police count.

Table 3.1.
Burglaries and Assaults in NZCASS (2015) and Police Recorded Crime

	Reported to NZCASS (2015)	Reported to Police	Recorded by Police
Burglary	203,000	83,000 (41%)	40,000
Assault	500,000	124,000 (24.8%)	32,000

Source: NZCASS (2015)

A similar pattern is evident in the NZCVS (2018). Comparing the number of burglaries and assaults reported to both the NZCVS and police with the number recorded by police for the same period illustrates the extent to which NZP statistics continue to under-represent conventional volume crime.

Table 3.2.
Burglaries and Assaults in the NZCVS (2018) and Police Recorded Crime

	Reported to NZCVS (2018)	Reported to Police	Recorded by Police (2017)
Burglary	312,000	114,600 (36%)	60,285
Robbery & Assault	230,305	64,485 (28%)	54,105

Source: NZCVS, 2018

As shown in Table 3.2, 312,000 burglaries were captured by the NZCVS (2018, p. 29), just over a third (*n*=114,660) of which were reported to police (p. 114). A search of the NZP 'Unique Victims (Demographics)' data set (which counts individual victims once, even if they were victims of multiple 'incidents') for the period covered by the NZCVS revealed that just 60,285 were recorded by police. The 'Victimisations (Demographics)' data set (which records all incidents of burglary, not the number of victims) recorded 74,735 burglaries.[10]

In the NZCVS (2018, p. 30) assault is not counted as a standalone category but is combined with robbery to form the larger category 'Robbery and Assault (except sexual assault)'. Intimate Partner Violence (IPV) is not included in the NZCVS 'Robbery and Assault' figures, but is counted and reported as a separate offence. In the NZP statistics, however, IPV *is* included with other types of assault (except sexual assault) and recorded as part of the more general category of 'Acts Intended to Cause Injury'. While imperfect, the NZCVS and NZP figures for these offences can be compared when we combine NZCVS data on 'Robbery and Assaults' and IPV, and NZP data on 'Acts Intended to Cause Injury' which 'bundles' together Assaults, IPV, Robbery and associated offences.

As shown in Table 3.2, the NZCVS captured 230,305 incidents of 'Robbery and Assault' (2018, p. 58), 28 per cent (*n*=64,485) of which were reported to police (NZCVS, 2018, p. 115). A search for 'Acts Intended to Cause Injury' within the NZP 'Victimisations (Demographics)' data set for 2017 revealed that police recorded 50,089 non-sexual 'Assaults' (which included incidents of IPV) and 4016 'Robbery, Extortion and Related Offences'; a combined total of 54,105 incidents.

When we combine the NZCVS figures for IPV committed by current partners (*n*=30,000) with incidents of 'Robbery and Assault' *that were reported to police* (*n*=94,485), we find the police statistics under-represent these offences by almost a third (*n*=54,105).[11]

It is often pointed out that victim surveys capture offences that may not be counted by police because of their triviality. This is a valid criticism. Victim surveys often do 'overcount' by including minor offences that, while technically criminal, are often ignored by police because they are either too minor or there is insufficient evidence (Bradley & Waters, 2019, pp. 39–42; Patrick, 2014). One might have assumed, then, that the explanation for much lower quantities of crime recorded by police is because they focus on and record more serious offences.

Both NZCASS and NZCVS analysed reporting patterns based on victim perceptions of seriousness. These show that even 'very serious' offences reported to the survey often go unreported to police and are therefore significantly under-represented in NZP statistics. NZCASS (2015, p. 109), for example, found that of those offences perceived by victims as the 'most serious', including serious assaults and sexual violence, less than half (45.6 per cent) were reported to police. Similarly, the NZCVS (2018, p. 121) found that just 40 per cent of those offences considered by victims to be 'very serious' were reported to police. Therefore, the NZP statistics also supply a deficient account of serious crime, a situation that is not unique to New Zealand (see Slawson, 2018).

ONLINE FRAUD: THE NEW VOLUME CRIME

The NZP statistics provide an incomplete and therefore unreliable measure of conventional volume crimes such as burglary and assault, including IPV. However, the situation is much worse for 'new' volume crimes, such as online fraud, which barely feature at all. In this regard, NZP statistics for crime committed online are particularly deficient.

A large and growing body of research (Button & Cross, 2017; Cross, 2019; Loveday, 2017; Maguire & Dowling, 2013; Treadwell, 2011; Yar, 2013) has documented the revolution, and continued evolution, in networked digital technology that has facilitated new forms of criminal offending. The huge growth of internet penetration (users), a massive expansion of mobile devices, new forms of interaction via social networking (e.g., Facebook, Instagram) and the growth of online shopping and banking have combined to create a vast and growing pool of criminal opportunities (Button & Cross, 2017, pp. 5–6). Simply put, a considerable amount of crime is 'moving off the street and onto the internet' (Muir, 2016, p. 2). The immense potential for online fraud is illustrated by the proportion of the population that now routinely uses online banking. In the UK, half the adult population and 76 per cent of 25–34-year-olds now rely on online banking (Office for National Statistics [ONS], 2013), while New Zealanders make more than 6 million online payments worth a total of $35 billion every day (Edmunds, 2016). Our increasing reliance on Information and Communications Technology (ICT) as well as computer networks has created a 'fraudogenic' environment (Button & Cross, 2017, p. 78) in which 'millions of people are targeted via the internet and related technology every day' (Button et al., 2014, p. 392).

Online fraud is now a 'global problem' (Smith, 2010; Wall, 2007). While fraud itself is hardly new – fraud laws were first established by the Statute of Westminster in 1275 – its move online, and the ability to reach across international borders, means it is now a daily risk faced by those who would not previously have been targeted. Fraud has thus transitioned from a terrestrial white-collar crime to a volume crime affecting millions of individual victims. Indeed, Loveday (2017) contends that cybercrime represents 'the single most critical problem confronting the police' (p. 102). Thus, while it is accepted that volume crime has 'a new profile' and has 'replaced that with which the police have traditionally wrestled' (p. 102), the NZP continue to 'plod along' the same old path and the old terrestrial profile continues to dominate police recorded crime.

Defining cybercrime

Furnell and Dowling (2019, p. 14) suggest that, because of its dynamic and changing nature, debates about cybercrime have been dominated by questions of how to define it. Nonetheless, they identify two broad categories: computer-dependent and computer-enabled crimes. The former refers to offences that can be committed only by using a computer, and includes the spread of malicious 'viruses', 'hacking', and distributed denial of service (DDoS) attacks (Maguire & Dowling, 2013). Computer-enabled crimes, on the other hand, refer to 'old' crimes committed in new ways (Wexler, 2018, p. 4). By using networked computers, old offences such as fraud, deception, and blackmail have increased exponentially in 'scale and reach' (Furnell & Dowling, 2019, p. 14). In the past decade, for example, 'ransomware' – an online attack that blocks computer access until owners pay a ransom – has become a billion-dollar industry. Even police agencies have been victims of these attacks and in some cases have paid the ransom (Wexler, 2018, p. 5). Moreover, in recent years the variety of cybercrimes has expanded, with offences like 'romance scams' and 'sextortion' becoming much more prevalent (Wexler, 2018, p. 17; see also Meehan, chapter 8 this volume).

Estimating online fraud: International experiences

Crime committed online is rarely reported to police and thus rarely appears in police statistics. Wexler (2018) estimates that, in the US, for every online crime that is reported six more are not. However, even a cursory examination of the available international data shows just how ubiquitous online fraud has become. Since 2015 the Crime Survey of England and Wales (CSEW) has included 'cyber-crimes'. Its 2015 'sweep' captured 3.4 million fraud incidents, with 1.9 million (51 per cent) being cyber-related.[12] In comparison, just 621,017 fraud offences, both cyber and non-cyber, were recorded by police for the same period (ONS, 2016, p. 42). The 2019 CSEW for the year ending March 2019 reported an estimated 3.8 million incidents of fraud, an increase of 17 per cent from the previous year (3.3 million incidents), over half of which (54 per cent) were cyber-related (ONS, 2020). Just 608,000 (16 per cent) of all fraud cases were recorded by police for the same period (ONS, 2019). According to a recent report by the National Audit Office (NAO), fraud is now 'the most commonly experienced crime in England and Wales and most of it takes place online' (NAO, 2017, p. 6). Like the number of incidents, the associated losses are enormous. The NAO (2017, p. 8) estimated that, in 2016, individuals in England and Wales lost over £10 billion, while the private sector lost £144 billion. Despite the losses sustained, the police continue to focus on conventional volume crimes in their statistics and practices (*Guardian*, 2017).

A similar situation prevails in Australia. The Australian Bureau of Statistics' (ABS) 'Personal Fraud' report (ABS, 2016) estimated that, in 2015, 1.1 million Australians fell victim to credit-card fraud (much of it committed online) at a cost of A$2.1 billion. A further 126,300 were victims of identity theft, and 449,100 Australians who were exposed to online 'scams' responded by supplying personal information, money, or both. Cross et al. (2016, p. 1) estimate that $8–10 million is sent overseas every month by Australians in response to online scams, while the Australian Competition and Consumer Commission (2018) reported that individuals lost over $340 million to fraud in 2017.

Cybercrime and online fraud in New Zealand

New Zealand was a relative latecomer in collecting evidence on vulnerability to cybercrime. New Zealand victim surveys have been administered for over 20 years, but the 2018

NZCVS (2018, p. 87) was the first to canvass respondents on fraud and cybercrime.[13] Its results show that cybercrime easily 'qualifies' as volume crime in that over 307,000 New Zealanders experienced almost 400,000 incidents of 'Fraud' ($n=206,000$) or 'Cybercrime' ($n=101,000$) over the previous 12 months, just 7 per cent of which were reported to police; the lowest reporting rate of any offence captured by the survey. Illustrating its indiscriminate nature, and underlining the threat posed, the NZCVS (2018) also found no statistically significant difference in cybercrime victimisation 'between women and men, between different age groups, between different ethnic groups (with the exception of Asian people), and between different geographical regions' (p. 88).

Various other sources support the NZCVS results. A 2019 media release from Netsafe – New Zealand's independent, non-profit online safety organisation – reported that New Zealanders lost more to online fraud in 2018 than at any time in Netsafe's 20-year history. Since 2017, reported incidents grew from 8100 to 13,000, while the losses sustained tripled from $10.1 million to $33 million (Netsafe, 2019). Importantly, most of these incidents were reported to Netsafe, not NZP, and are thus excluded from NZP statistics.

A similar pattern is evident in the quarterly reports issued by the Computer Emergency Response Team (CERT), a 'one-stop shop' set up by government in 2017 to monitor, track, and advise on cyber-related incidents. While CERT acknowledges extremely low reporting rates, its 2018 final quarter report noted that cyber-scams and fraud incidents made up almost half of the 1330 reports received – 91 per cent of which were experienced by individuals. This represented an increase of 236 per cent from the third quarter. CERT estimated the losses associated with these incidents at $4.9 million (CERT, 2018, p. 2). Clearly, online fraud is a pervasive issue for New Zealand.

Identity theft is a different but equally high-volume cybercrime, though it often results in fraud. In a press release designed to raise public awareness, the Department of Internal Affairs (DIA) pointed out that each year 130,000 New Zealanders are victims of identity theft, very few cases of which are reported to NZP (DIA, 2019). IDCARE NZ, a non-profit providing free advice to victims, points out that 'by far the number one motivation . . . is accessing your bank account' (Daalder, 2019, para. 10). According to the DIA (2019), identity theft costs the New Zealand economy around $209 million annually.

Finally, a 2018 Research New Zealand survey on internet use found that 79 per cent of adult users in New Zealand had experienced some sort of cyber-security issue, 72 per cent of which were targeted by a 'scam'. It's little wonder the survey also found 75 per cent of New Zealanders believed that cyber-security is a major issue, 44 per cent worry about what happens to their personal data, and 33 per cent do not think the internet is a safe place (Research New Zealand, 2019, p. 3).

NZP statistics on fraud

An examination of NZP statistics – from the 'Recorded Crime Victim Statistics' (RCVS) and 'Recorded Crime Offender Statistics' (RCOS) – quickly reveals the extent to which NZP offender- and victim-related data fails to offer a reliable guide to the extent of online crimes such as fraud.

In the RCVS there is no offence category for fraud-related offences, online or terrestrial, and the few offences that *may be* recorded are accommodated within 'Theft and Related Offences'. A search of these data for 2017 found 136,291 offences: almost half ($n=57,759$) were vehicle-related; 28,097 were 'Theft From Retail Premises'; 45,144 offences related to 'Theft (Except Motor Vehicle)'; and 1674 offences involved 'Theft from Person (Excluding by Force)'.[14]

Although the RCOS does include the offence category 'Fraud, Deception and Related Offences', it is even more deficient than the RCVS. This is because it is offender-focused data, which is always lower than victim data because of the difficulties in identifying offenders. The offences are contained in two separate but related data sets. The first, 'Proceedings (offender demographics)', counts the number of times that police took 'proceedings against' an offender (such as 'court action' or 'formal warning') broken down by offence type. According to these data, there were 3215 proceedings for 'Fraud, Deception and Related Offences' in 2017. Of these, however, 2928 (91 per cent) were for 'Obtaining Benefit by Deception'. A further 183 proceedings were for 'Dishonest Conversation', 85 for 'Forgery of Documents', and only 6 for 'Frauds Not Elsewhere Defined'. The second data set, 'Unique Offenders (demographics)', is similar but counts each offender only once, irrespective of the number of proceedings taken against them. This data set recorded just 1999 proceedings for 'Fraud, Deception and Related Offences' in 2017, 1768 (88 per cent) of which were for 'Obtaining a Benefit by Deception' and just 165 for 'Other Fraud and Deception Offences'.[15] Taken together, these two data sets illustrate the inadequacies of the NZP statistics as a measure of unconventional volume crime, especially when we consider that the NZCVS (2018, p. 87) found that 307,000 New Zealanders had been victims of 'Fraud' and/or 'Cybercrime' over the same period.

Despite overwhelming evidence that growing numbers of New Zealanders are victims of computer-enabled offences, NZP and the media continue to emphasise the threat of conventional terrestrial volume crime, such as assault and burglary. In 2017, the *New Zealand Herald* ran a series of 'special' reports. 'Counting Crime' boldly promised 'the most in-depth look at NZ's crime statistics *ever*' (Leask, 2017a, para. 5, emphasis added). Setting the tone for the narrow range of conventional crimes examined, the first report asked, 'Have you ever wanted to know how safe your street *really* is?' (Leask, 2017a, para. 2, original emphasis). Informed by NZP statistics, its centrepiece was an 'exclusive interactive map' pinpointing where and when crime was happening around the country. The second report detailed retail theft (Hurley, 2017a), while the third focused on burglary (Leask, 2017b) and the fourth on car theft (Leask, 2017c). The fifth focused on assault and claimed to identify the 'most dangerous places in the country' (Hurley, 2017b). Online fraud did not feature, despite presenting significantly higher risks. The image of crime portrayed in these reports reflects the limitations of the police statistics upon which they depend. Reinforcing the message that we are most at risk from crimes like assault and burglary, a media article informing readers of when and where a crime 'was most likely to happen' quoted NZP's chief data scientist: 'So when are people most vulnerable? When they're drunk. When people are out and about as opposed to home and safe' (Huffadine, 2018). Like the statistics that inform it, this assessment of vulnerability neglects the reality that for far too many New Zealanders 'home' is rarely equated with 'safe'.

CONCLUSION

Police statistics reflect both the reporting patterns of victims and the recording practices of police, as well as the offences and offenders targeted by police. Despite the trappings of greater technological sophistication, these basic principles have hardly changed in over a century. A crucial function of official statistics is to supply a reliable index of risk. However, the inability to differentiate virtual from terrestrial crime, and the considerable under-representation of crime online, has exposed the failure of NZP crime statistics to keep pace with and adapt to the new landscape of criminal offending. Such deficiencies call into question their status as 'nationally important' Tier 1 statistics deemed 'essential' for informed government decision-making and the allocation of scarce resources. For offences like online fraud, the police statistics obscure far more than they inform and are thus not fit for this purpose. The volume of online crime also forces a fundamental reconsideration of the constitution of the 'crime problem' and, in turn, the current deployment of prevention and reduction resources.

In New Zealand our attempt to count crime is at an important juncture. The NZCVS has confirmed funding until 2021, but its longer-term future is yet to be determined. Inconsistent political commitment to crime/victim surveys has resulted in their sporadic administration since 1996. Until such commitment, matched with funding, has been made, there is every possibility that such irregularity will continue. Instruments like the NZCVS throw much-needed light over the dark figure of NZP statistics and allow a more accurate assessment of the daily risks we face. We therefore need to wean ourselves off our long-term dependence on police statistics and further invest in alternative methods of counting crime and victims.

STUDY QUESTIONS

- What is volume crime? Is this a useful term or concept, as currently deployed in New Zealand? What should qualify as volume crimes?
- Given the limitations of police statistics, how might we better measure crime committed online?
- Thinking specifically about gender, class, and race, how do NZP recorded crime statistics reflect and help maintain established power relations?

FURTHER READING

Furnell, S., & Dowling, S. (2019). Cyber crime: a portrait of the landscape. *Journal of Criminological Research, Policy and Practice, 5*(1), 13–26. doi:10.1108/jcrpp–07–2018–0021

Patrick, R. (2014). *A tangled web: Why you can't believe crime statistics.* London, UK: Civitas.

Reiner, R. (2016). *Crime.* Cambridge, UK: Polity Press.

NOTES

1. The NZ Crime and Victims Survey (NZCVS) (2018) replaced the NZ Crime and Safety Survey (NZCASS) (2006, 2009 & 2015).
2. See https://www.police.govt.nz/about-us/publications-statistics/policedatanz
3. See the NZ National Survey of Crime Victims 1996, 2001 (Ministry of Justice, 1996; Morris & Reilly, 2003).
4. Incidence refers to estimates of the total number of offences/crimes in a given period. Prevalence refers to the proportion of people or targets (properties or cars) in an area (or population) victimised. Prevalence is used to identify the risk of victimisation (NZCVS, 2018, p. 24).
5. 'Tier 1' statistics are 'NZ's most important statistics, essential to help the Government, business, and members of the public to make informed decisions and monitor the state and progress of New Zealand' (see data.govt.nz, https://data.govt.nz/use-data/showcase/official-statistics/).
6. ANZSOC refers to the Australian and New Zealand Standard Offence Classification, a three-tier hierarchical classification system for categorising different offence types: division, subdivision, and group (see: http://archive.stats.govt.nz/methods/classifications-and-standards/classification-related-stats-standards/offence/classification-and-coding-process.aspx; Bradley & Walters, 2019, p. 26).
7. An OIA request (10 July 2019) asked NZP for the 'official' or 'working' definition of volume crime, to identify offences considered to be 'volume crimes' and identify any specialist units/squads tasked specifically with addressing volume crime.

8   Recent examples of sensational media headlines include 'A burglary reported every 7 minutes' (Weekes, 2017) and 'Cops swamped by 189 burglaries a day nationwide' (Sherwood, 2019).

9   More broadly, volume crime was specifically targeted in the 2002 National Crime Reduction Strategy, and it became a central plank of the 2012 Better Public Services initiative that sought (but did not meet) a 20 per cent reduction in 'total crime' (Bradley & Walters, 2019, pp. 296–297).

10 Fieldwork for the NZCVS was conducted between March and October 2017. To match this the search of NZP victimisation data covered 1 January 2017 to 31 December 2017. The 'Unique Victims (Demographics)' data set counts each victim once, regardless of the actual number of victimisations experienced, while the 'Victimisations (Demographics)' data set counts all incidents of victimisation. See https://www.police.govt.nz/about-us/publications-statistics/data-and-statistics/policedatanz/victimisations-demographics

11 For the 'Victimisations (Demographics)' NZP data set, see https://www.police.govt.nz/about-us/publications-statistics/data-and-statistics/policedatanz/victimisations-demographics. For the 'Unique Victims (Demographics)' data set, see https://www.police.govt.nz/about-us/publications-statistics/data-and-statistics/policedatanz/unique-victims-demographics. In addition to recording far fewer IPV incidents, NZP statistics do not 'count' instances of 'psychological' and 'financial' abuse perpetrated by intimate partners, nor other forms of abuse involving 'coercive control' (personal communication with NZ Family Violence Clearing House, 26 September 2019).

12 In addition, it found that adults experienced 2 million 'computer misuse' incidents, of which 1.4 million were computer virus–related and 0.6 million were incidents of unauthorised access to personal information.

13 The NZCVS categorised fraud and cybercrime as 'non-violent personal offences' but did not define 'cybercrime', nor indicate the types of offences included under that label. It is a reasonable assumption, however, that online fraud would have featured prominently.

14 Some of the offences grouped under the general category 'Theft and Related Offences' are not related to, and thus do not shed light on, the incidence of or reporting rates for fraud. These offences were excluded.

15 Some of these police proceedings were for 'Deceptive Business/Government Practices' but as these are not directly fraud-related they were excluded.

REFERENCES

Australian Bureau of Statistics. (2016). *Personal fraud 2014–2015, 4528.0*. Retrieved from https://www.abs.gov.au/AUSSTATS/abs@.nsf/Lookup/4528.0Main+Features172014–15?OpenDocument

Australian Competition and Consumer Commission. (2018). *Targeting scams: Report of the ACCC on scam activity 2017*. Retrieved from https://www.accc.gov.au/publications/targeting-scams-report-on-scam-activity

Baird, A. (2019, August 20). Where the extra 1800 police will go. *Newshub*. Retrieved from https://www.newshub.co.nz/home/politics/2018/08/where-the-extra-1800-police-officers-will-go.html

Biderman, A., & Reiss, A. J. (1967). On exploring the dark figure of crime. *The Annals of the American Academy of Political and Social Science, 374*(1), 1–15. doi:10.1177/000271626737400102

Bradley, T., & Walters, R. (Eds.). (2019). *Introduction to criminological thought*. (3rd ed.). Auckland, New Zealand: Edify.

Brown, R., & Smith, R. (2018). Exploring the relationship between organised crime and volume crime. *Australian Institute of Criminology: Trends and issues in crime and criminal justice, 565*, 1–15.

Button, M., & Cross, C. (2017). *Cyber fraud, scams and their victims*. London, UK: Routledge.

Button, M., McNaugton-Nicolls, C., Kerr, J., & Owen, R. (2014). Online frauds: Learning from victims why they fall for these scams. *Australian and New Zealand Journal of Criminology, 47*(3), 391–408. doi:10.1177/0004865814521224

Chetwin, A. (2005). *Overview: Research on the effectiveness of police practice in reducing residential burglary*. Wellington, New Zealand: Ministry of Justice. Retrieved from https://www.justice.govt.nz/assets/Documents/Publications/report-10-overview.pdf

Computer Emergency Response Team (CERT). (2018). *Quarterly report highlights*: Q4 1 October – 31 December. Retrieved from https://www.cert.govt.nz/about/quarterly-report/

Cross, C. (2018). Expectations vs reality: Responding to online fraud across the fraud justice network. *International Journal of Law, Crime and Justice, 55*, 1–12. doi:10.1016/j.ijlcj.2018.08.001

Cross, C. (2019). Is online fraud just fraud? Examining the efficacy of the digital divide. *Journal of Criminological Research, Policy and Practice, 5*(2), 120–131. doi:10.1108/JCRPP–01–2019–0008

Cross, C., Richards, K., & Smith, R. (2016). Challenges of responding to online fraud victimisation in Australia. *Australian Institute of Criminology: Trends and Issues in Crime and Criminal Justice, 518*, 1–14. Retrieved from https://aic.gov.au/publications/tandi/tandi474

Daalder, M. (2019, August 28). Identity theft by the numbers. *Newsroom*. Retrieved from https://www.newsroom.co.nz/2019/08/28/776922/identity-theft-by-the-numbers

Department of Internal Affairs. (2019). *Identity theft – what is identity theft?* Retrieved from https://www.dia.govt.nz/Identity---What-is-identity-theft

Edmunds, S. (2016, May 6). New Zealand's top online banking mistakes and how to avoid them. *Stuff*. Retrieved from https://www.stuff.co.nz/business/money/79655096/new-zealands-top-online-banking-mistakes-and-how-to-avoid-them

Fogg. A. (2014, January 16). What is crime? We can't measure it because we haven't defined it. *Guardian*. Retrieved from https://www.theguardian.com/commentisfree/2014/jan/16/what-is-crime-measure-definitions

Furnell, S., & Dowling, S. (2019). Cyber crime: A portrait of the landscape. *Journal of Criminological Research, Policy and Practice, 5*(1), 13–26. doi:10.1108/jcrpp-07-2018-0021

Guardian (2017, June 30). Online fraud costs public billions but is still not a police priority, says watchdog. Retrieved from https://www.theguardian.com/uk-news/2017/jun/30/online-costs-public-billions-but-is-still-not-a-police-priority-says-watchdog

Hope, T. (2013). What do crime statistics tell us? In C. Hale, K. Hayward, A. Wahidin, & E. Wincup (Eds.), *Criminology* (pp. 39–59). Oxford, UK: Oxford University Press.

Huffadine, L. (2018, January 25). Where and when a crime's most likely to happen to you. *Stuff*. Retrieved from https://www.stuff.co.nz/national/crime/100501749/where-and-when-a-crimes-most-likely-to-happen-to-you

Hurley, S. (2017a, June 13). Counting crime: Retail thefts cost country $1.2b. *New Zealand Herald*. Retrieved from https://www.nzherald.co.nz/nz/news/article.cfm?c_id=1&objectid=11870565

Hurley, S. (2017b, June 14). Counting crime: NZ's CBDs our most dangerous places. *New Zealand Herald*. Retrieved from https://www.nzherald.co.nz/nz/news/article.cfm?c_id=1&objectid=11854593

Kirk, S. (2016, February 11). ACT three strikes for burglary bill struck out of Parliament. *Stuff*. Retrieved from https://www.stuff.co.nz/national/politics/76790953/act-three-strikes-for-burglary-bill-struck-out-of-parliament

Leask, A. (2017a, June 12). Counting crime: An in-depth look at offending and victims in New Zealand. *New Zealand Herald*. Retrieved from https://www.nzherald.co.nz/nz/news/article.cfm?c_id=1&objectid=11853739

Leask, A. (2017b, June 15). Counting crime: Burglaries in New Zealand – where, when and how. *New Zealand Herald*. Retrieved from https://www.nzherald.co.nz/nz/news/article.cfm?c_id=1&objectid=11854097

Leask, A. (2017c, June 12). Theft from cars – when, why, how and who. *New Zealand Herald*. Retrieved from https://www.nzherald.co.nz/nz/news/article.cfm?c_id=1&objectid=11853851

Loveday, B. (2017). Still plodding along? The police response to the changing profile of crime in England and Wales. *International Journal of Police Science & Management, 19*(2), 101–109. doi:10.1177/1461355717699634

Ludwig, A., Norton, M., & McLean, I. (2017). *Measuring police effectiveness.* A Gwilym Gibbon Centre for Public Policy working paper. Retrieved from https://www.nuffield.ox.ac.uk/media/1976/2017-02-measuring-police-effectiveness.pdf

Maguire, M., & Dowling, S. (2013). *Cyber crime: A review of the evidence.* Home Office research report, 75, October. London, UK: Home Office. Retrieved from https://www.bl.uk/britishlibrary/~/media/bl/global/social-welfare/pdfs/non-secure/c/y/b/cyber-crime-a-review-of-the-evidence-chapter-1-cyberdependent-crimes.pdf

Ministry of Justice. (1996). *New Zealand National Survey of Crime Victims 1996.* Wellington, New Zealand: Ministry of Justice. Retrieved from https://www.cbg.co.nz/site/cbg/New%20Zealand%20National%20Survey%20of%20Crime%20Victims%201996.pdf

Morris, A., & Reilly, J. (2003). *New Zealand National Survey of Crime Victims 2001.* Wellington, New Zealand: Ministry of Justice. Retrieved from https://www.cbg.co.nz/site/cbg/National_NZ_Survey_Crime-Victims.pdf

Muir, R. (2016, December 8). It's time to face up to the challenge of policing in a digital age [Blog post]. *Police Foundation.* Retrieved from http://www.police-foundation.org.uk/2016/12/its-time-to-face-up-to-the-challenge-of-policing-in-a-digital-age/

National Audit Office. (2017). *Online fraud.* London, UK: Home Office. Retrieved from https://www.nao.org.uk/wp-content/uploads/2017/06/Online-Fraud.pdf

Netsafe. (2019, April 3). *Kiwis lose $33M in 2018 – new approach needed in the fight against online scams.* Retrieved from https://www.netsafe.org.nz/wp-content/uploads/2016/12/33M-record-high-scam-losses-reported-to-Netsafe-in--2018-.pdf

New Zealand Crime and Safety Survey. (2015). *Main findings report – Te rangahau o Aotearoa mō te taihara me te haumarutanga 2014.* Wellington, New Zealand: Ministry of Justice. Retrieved from http://www.justice.govt.nz/assets/Documents/Publications/NZCASS-201602-Main-Findings-Report-Updated.pdf

New Zealand Crime and Victims Survey (NZCVS). (2018). *Key findings report: Cycle 1 (March–September 2018) descriptive statistics.* Wellington, New Zealand: Ministry of Justice. Retrieved from https://www.justice.govt.nz/justice-sector-policy/research-data/nzcvs/resources-and-results/

New Zealand Family Violence Collective. (2017). *Family violence statistics.* Retrieved from https://nzfvc.org.nz/family-violence-statistics

New Zealand Herald (2014, July 18). NZ First's shoot to kill law. Retrieved from https://www.nzherald.co.nz/nz/news/article.cfm?c_id=1&objectid=11295250

New Zealand Police. (2017). *Four year plan 2017/18 – 2020/21: The safest country policing 2021.* Wellington, New Zealand: New Zealand Police. Retrieved from https://www.police.govt.nz/about-us/publication/new-zealand-police-four-year-plan-2017-2021

New Zealand Police. (2018a, August 20). Waitematā to benefit from additional police. *Police News.* Retrieved from https://www.police.govt.nz/news/release/waitemat%C4%81-benefit-additional-police

New Zealand Police. (2018b, July 24). Auckland police target vehicle crime. *Police News.* Retrieved from https://www.police.govt.nz/news/release/auckland-police-target-vehicle-crime

Office of the Auditor General (OAG). (2006). *New Zealand Police: Dealing with dwelling burglary – follow-up audit.* Wellington, New Zealand: OAG. Retrieved from https://www.oag.govt.nz/2006/burglary/docs/burglary.pdf

Office for National Statistics (ONS). (2013). *Internet access – households and individuals, 2013.* Retrieved from http://www.ons.gov.uk/ons/dcp171778_322713.pdf

Office for National Statistics (ONS). (2016). *Crime in England and Wales: year ending Mar 2016.* Retrieved from https://www.ons.gov.uk/peoplepopulationandcommunity/crimeandjustice/bulletins/crimeinenglandandwales/yearendingmar2016

Office for National Statistics (ONS). (2019). *Crime in England and Wales: year ending June 2019.* Retrieved from https://www.ons.gov.uk/peoplepopulationandcommunity/crimeandjustice/bulletins/crimeinenglandandwales/yearendingjune2019

Office for National Statistics (ONS) (2020, March). 'Nature of fraud and computer misuse in England and Wales: year ending March 2019'. Retrieved from https://www.ons.gov.uk/peoplepopulationandcommunity/crimeandjustice/articles/natureoffraudandcomputermisuseinenglandandwales/yearendingmarch2019#trends-in-fraud

Patrick, R. (2014). *A tangled web: Why you can't believe crime statistics.* London, UK: Civitas.

Reiner, R. (2016). *Crime.* Cambridge, UK: Polity Press.

Research New Zealand. (2019). *A report on a survey of New Zealanders' use of social media and opinions on cyber security 2018.* Wellington, New Zealand: Research New Zealand.

Sachdeva, S. (2016, February 20). Police slammed for not doing enough to solve burglaries. *Stuff.* Retrieved from https://www.stuff.co.nz/national/crime/76745138

Sherman, L. (2013). The rise of evidence-based policing: Targeting, testing, and tracking. *Crime and Justice, 42*(1), 377–451. doi:10.1086/670819

Sherwood, S. (2019, September 14). Cops swamped by 189 burglaries a day nationwide. *Stuff.* Retrieved from https://www.stuff.co.nz/national/crime/115744068/cops-swamped-by–180-burglaries-a-day-nationwide

Slawson, N. (2018, February 15). Police failing to record thousands of crimes, including rape. *Guardian.* Retrieved from https://www.theguardian.com/uk-news/2018/feb/15/police-failing-to-record-thousands-of-crimes-including

Smith, R. G. (2010). Identity theft and fraud. In Y. Jewkes & M. Yar (Eds.), *Handbook of internet crime* (pp. 273–301). Cullompton, UK: Willan Publishing.

Stuff. (2019, August 27). Can the burglary rate be reduced? Retrieved from https://www.stuff.co.nz/opinion/115268198/can-the-burglary-rate-be-reduced

Tait, M. (2016, August 29). Police to attend all burglaries. *New Zealand Herald.* Retrieved from https://www.nzherald.co.nz/nz/police-to-attend-all-household-burglaries/NWRJUSKM2EIE5KAX3NITRHWJWQ/

Treadwell, J. (2011). From the car boot to booting it up? Ebay, online counterfeit crime and the transformation of the criminal marketplace. *Criminology and Criminal Justice, 12*(2), 175–191. doi:10.1177/1748895811428173

Wall, D. S. (2007). *Cybercrime: The transformation of crime in the information age.* Cambridge, UK: Polity Press.

Weekes, J. (2017, February 7). A burglary reported every 7 minutes as recorded crime rate jumps. *Stuff.* Retrieved from https://www.stuff.co.nz/national/crime/88971054/a-burglary-reported-every–7-minutes-as-recorded-crime-rate-jumps

Wexler, C. (2018). Crime has been changing, and police agencies need to catch up. *The changing nature of crime and criminal investigations.* Washington, DC: Police Executive Research Forum. Retrieved from https://www.policeforum.org/assets/ChangingNatureofCrime.pdf

Yar, M. (2013). *Cybercrime and society* (2nd ed). London, UK: Sage Publications.

4

Researching Crime and Criminal Justice
Funding, Politics, and Ethics

Antje Deckert

In the period following the Second World War, until the mid-1970s, crime and criminal justice (CCJ) research was largely ad hoc and practitioner-led. Justice officials developed projects on, among other things, correctional psychology, new police promotion methods, indeterminate sentences for habitual criminals, and the nature of the 'crime problem' in Aotearoa New Zealand. Over that period, a handful of scholarly journal articles and monographs were published. Things changed with the 1974 establishment of the Institute of Criminology at Victoria University of Wellington, which provided a major boost to CCJ research. Some of this history, and the development of New Zealand criminology since 1974, has been traced by Rodgers and Stenning (2017). Building on their work, this chapter provides a critical overview of this research landscape. Firstly, it examines researcher access to quality CCJ data and New Zealand research funding, and considers how state controls prevent academics from collaborating with the policy sector. Secondly, the 'control-freak' nature of criminology (Agozino, 2010) itself is examined, showing how orthodox CCJ discourses in policy and academia conspire against the 'criminal other' to maintain the status quo. The third section provides a glimpse into the world of research ethics and researcher obligations under Te Tiriti o Waitangi; this, in turn, leads to the fourth and final section, which outlines some CCJ scholar-activists' decolonising efforts, an issue that is particularly relevant in the neocolonial context of New Zealand.

ACCESS TO CRIME AND JUSTICE DATA

Criminological researchers work on topics of national importance and engage with the activities of central government organisations. As a result, they are also highly dependent on the data and research developed by these groups, as well as from their contracted researchers. For scholars, this inevitably leads to questions such as: How does our CCJ data emerge? What are its limitations? And, whose interests are served in how it is focused?

Next to academic criminology and private research contractors (such as Kaitiaki Research and Evaluations Ltd), the New Zealand Police (NZP), Ministry of Justice (MoJ), Department of Corrections and Te Puni Kōkiri (TPK) have developed their own research agendas, resources, and capacities that prioritise their specific policy needs with respect to CCJ. For example, NZP routinely generates crime statistics that document recorded and resolved offences, and its research reports are concerned with topics such as road safety, public safety, or public perceptions of the police (New Zealand Police, 2019). The MoJ produces annual conviction, sentencing, and three-strikes statistics.[1] It also conducts the New Zealand Crime and Victims Survey (NZCVS) and publishes research reports on various topics, including New Zealand's sex industry and the legal drinking age (Ministry of Justice [MoJ], 2019). Corrections (2019a) generates and publishes quarterly statistics pertaining to New Zealand's remand and sentenced prison population, persons serving a community-based sentence, unnatural deaths in prison, prison escapes, and serious assaults. Since 2013, Corrections has also published an online journal (*Practice: The New Zealand Corrections Journal*), which aims to disseminate knowledge about best practice (Smith, 2013). TPK (2019) has published several research reports that specifically address the impact that CCJ has on Māori. This includes a report on the children with an incarcerated parent, and research on the socio-economic drivers of crime.

However, despite this large volume of CCJ-related data, official statistical reporting is often narrow in scope, sometimes inaccurate, and insufficiently detailed for either use in academic research or the development of effective policies and interventions. For example, Department of Corrections statistics on serious prison-based assaults include both physical and sexual assaults perpetrated either against staff or among incarcerated individuals. However, the official statistics fail to record assaults by staff. Similarly, they do not provide nuanced accounts of the presented data (e.g., to show the different levels of assaults on men and women, or to distinguish between sexual and physical assaults). Further, departmental data can be at odds with that presented through other sources (such as from monitoring bodies like the Ombudsman's Office).

The CCJ policy sector occasionally commissions research from academics and community researchers. One eminent example is Moana Jackson's *The Maori and the Criminal Justice System. A new perspective: He whaipaanga hou* (1988), which exposed racial biases in New Zealand's criminal justice system and explains how they contribute to the sustained excessive incarceration of Māori tāne, wāhine, and rangatahi. Though widely acclaimed, this landmark work did not lead to substantive changes in the treatment of Māori within the CCJ sector.

Why is this so? The limited uptake of academic research by policy-makers may be due to government ministries and departments viewing academic research as not always directed towards government initiatives, or as too critical in nature, or as inadequately addressing policy needs (Smith, 1999). Added to this, steady personal contacts are rare because the policy sector undergoes staff turnover much more regularly than do university departments. Hence, academics can find it difficult to efficiently access decision-makers. More broadly, scholarly jargon does not easily translate into policy language. The policy sector prefers brief research summaries and high levels of certainty with regard to projected outcomes, while academics tend to elaborate on their research findings and limitations. Further, policy workers are risk-averse, seeking to protect the political image of their minister, while academics have a legislated mandate to be the 'critic and conscience' of society, according to the Education Act 1989; they should be free, too, 'to question and test received wisdom, to put forward new ideas and to state controversial or unpopular opinions'. In sum, the relationship between academia and the CCJ policy sector faces multiple challenges (see Gluckman, 2011, 2013, 2017), not least as academics seek research independence, while policy-makers aim for high levels of control.

An illustration of state control mechanisms leading to abuse of power and interference with researcher rights (under the Official Information Act 1982 and Education Act 1989) relates to the case of Jarrod Gilbert in 2015. Gilbert, a sociologist at the University of Canterbury, was denied access to police data after NZP deemed him 'unfit' to undertake research because of his alleged gang affiliations. These claims were based solely on Gilbert's previous research on gangs (Gilbert, 2015a, 2015b; Green Party, 2015). His case exposed the degree of control exercised by NZP via its research 'agreements' with academics when applying for access to police data (an issue that is relevant for other government CCJ agencies). The agreement required researchers to supply police with the final report prior to publication for 'vetting', and included provision for NZP to veto any research findings from being published. NZP also reserved the right to 'blacklist' researchers who breached the agreement, thus blocking access to police resources (data and personnel) for research purposes (Gilbert, 2015b).

Another example, which is ongoing, relates to academics' encumbered access to New Zealand prisons for research purposes. The Department of Corrections' (2019b) Prison Operations Manual fails to identify explicit visitation rights for external researchers, and the Corrections website lacks information on how to request access to prisons and on what grounds the department may deny such requests. To undertake research with any incarcerated person or staff member (including prison staff, probation officers, and head office staff), external researchers must gain consent from the department, and their work will inevitably be judged against departmental interests and be subject to institutional controls. Hence, the CCJ sector has effectively established a research monopoly with regard to their institutions, processes, and people. In comparison, academics in the US and the UK enjoy relatively easy access, which is evidenced by the vast amount of UK/US research literature based on interviews with incarcerated individuals, victims, and CCJ workers.

RESEARCH FUNDING

Any discussions on research funding have to consider where the funds emerge from, but also the political, social, and cultural context in which funds are allocated. There are limited funds for independent criminological work in New Zealand, and there remains some government agency control of the CCJ research agenda through the deployment of funding. This is particularly the case with funding directed from key government sources, such as from NZP, MoJ, Corrections, or TPK.

Historically, CCJ institutions were funded to hold significant researcher capability, but this has been stripped back in the past decade. Within civil society, non-governmental organisations such as JustSpeak rely on fund-raising and the time of their dedicated volunteers. Academics have access to university internal research funding, which constitutes a blend of tax-generated monies and university business income, but they are also encouraged to compete for external research grants.

Most of the larger, multi-year, and prestigious research grants are open to scholars from all academic disciplines and are, therefore, highly competitive (with less than 10 per cent of applicants receiving funding). To name only a few, these grants include the Fulbright New Zealand Scholar Award granted by the US Fulbright Commission, and the Rutherford

Discovery Fellowship, James Cook Fellowship, and Marsden Grant awarded by the Royal Society of New Zealand. Despite their competitive nature, each of the aforementioned grants has funded a large volume of CCJ research, some of it relating to Māori and Pasifika youth justice (see Suaalii-Sauni et al., chapter 27 this volume), rape and objectification (Jordan, chapter 6 this volume), state violence (Stanley, 2016), sex work (Armstrong, chapter 31 this volume), and (re)integration (Mills & Latimer, chapter 23 this volume). Academic criminologists interested in particular niche topics may also be successful in applying for grants administered by the Ministry of Social Development, the Health Research Council, or the Ministry of Business, Innovation and Employment.

Only two New Zealand-based private funding agencies focus solely on CCJ issues. The Law Foundation administers, inter alia, legal research grants and policy project grants. It has, for example, sponsored research on child witnesses (New Zealand Law Foundation, 2019). The Borrin Foundation was established in 2016 at the behest of the late Judge Ian Albert Borrin, who bequeathed $38 million to sponsor impact-focused, philanthropic law and justice research (Borrin Foundation, 2018). The foundation awarded, for example, Moana Jackson a two-year research grant for his study *He Whaipaanga Hou – A New Approach 2018*, which looks to update his ground-breaking 1988 report (qv.) on New Zealand's criminal justice system and Māori people (Borrin Foundation, 2019).

Postgraduate students interested in CCJ issues have access to a variety of university or externally funded scholarships. Like seasoned academics, postgraduates may compete for university grants open to students from all academic disciplines, such as vice-chancellor's scholarships. Some scholarships are reserved for international students, and some are offered by senior academics who have obtained large, multi-year research grants for set master's or PhD topics. Other scholarships seek to remedy some of the inequalities that persist in academia, and hence target specifically women, students with a disability, Māori and Pasifika students, or students who experience financial hardship. Universities tend to allocate a small research fund (often between $500 and $1000) for postgraduate students to conduct fieldwork and attend conferences. Post-doctoral positions, common in other academic disciplines like medicine, are relatively rare in New Zealand criminology. In line with other social sciences, then, CCJ scholars are somewhat stymied by limitations on the availability of independent funding. Beyond this research economy, it is also important to consider the wider political and ideological context in which criminological thinking and research has developed, as this is also crucial in understanding the contemporary New Zealand CCJ landscape. It is to this that the next section turns.

FROM ORTHODOX TO COUNTER-COLONIAL CRIMINOLOGY

Contemporary criminology is largely based on scholarly theories first developed by white men in the eighteenth and nineteenth centuries. These theories sought to address three main problem areas of CCJ: (1) how to best identify and capture people who break the law (criminalistics/forensics); (2) how to treat individuals once they are in custody (administrative and academic penology); and (3) how to explain why crime exists (academic criminology). These three discourses rely on a description of the criminal as 'other', and criminology has a long-standing history of colluding with the state to exercise control over the 'criminal other'.

The discursive process of 'othering' (Said, 1979) gives voice to and glorifies the 'non-criminal self'. It makes the 'non-criminal self' visible while it silences and vilifies the 'criminal other'; rendering the 'criminal other' invisible. Beyond this binary positioning, strategies of discursive othering include silencing the voices of people behind bars and using dehumanising language (Aladaylah, 2010). Discursive constructions of the 'criminal other' as inherently deficient and inferior, and therefore requiring surveillance and control, have established a social hierarchy. That hierarchy – by its very design – excludes the 'criminal other' from access to mainstream criminological discourses in academia, policy, and media. The social hierarchy was established by criminological 'pioneers', like Cesare Lombroso, who misappropriated Darwinist doctrines of biological hierarchy and abused elite access to public discourse.

According to Foucault (1969), discourse is a system of concepts, theories, and practices. This system makes statements about the world it seeks to explain. Through these explanatory statements, the system generates new knowledge and simultaneously limits it. Limitations occur because the system needs to reject contradictory statements that threaten the internal consistency of its ongoing narrative. Hence, criminological discourse in academia, policy, and media determines the scope of CCJ and constructs the identity of the subjects who live within it (as incarcerated people, victims, CCJ professionals, or criminologists). The prevailing criminological discourse (known as mainstream, orthodox, or authoritarian criminology) generates moral, intellectual, and cultural power (Said, 1979; Tauri 2012a; Van Dijk, 2008). It generates power because it legitimates particular versions of reality while excluding alternative ones (Lessa, 2006). Criminological discourse equips those with privileged access to it with the power to legitimate their views on what constitutes criminal behaviour and criminal justice, while excluding alternative competing viewpoints. This is, for example, evident in the New Zealand government's rejection of Moana Jackson's (1988) recommendation that social harms be addressed within a kaupapa Māori-based system of justice. Academics, having control over scholarly criminological discourse, also generate control over distinct social groups – mainly 'victims' and 'offenders'. Privileged access to and the ability to shape criminological discourse also equips academics with the power to describe, define, and limit their reality (Agozino, 2003; Cunneen, 2006; Van Dijk, 2008). In other words, the social elite, including CCJ policy-makers and academics, has the power to establish what passes as truthful knowledge about the 'criminal other' and the nature of our responses to them.

Orthodox criminology focuses most of its discursive power on the subjects it describes – that is, 'the criminal other' (Foucault, 1969). In doing so, it has succeeded in establishing itself as an independent academic discipline, emancipated from its sociological, psychological, medical, and legal heritage. Criminological research completed by New Zealand policy workers remains driven by an empirical, psychological positivist perspective (Department of Corrections, 2019a; MoJ, 2019; personal communication, MoJ, 2018, May 2) and thus remains orthodox in nature. Administrative penologists are bound by the black-letter-law definition of crime. As government employees, they have neither the freedom nor the incentive to question the letter of the law. Therefore, administrative penologists tend to research convicted individuals already under state control, and are mainly concerned with the prospects of reducing reoffending and improving rehabilitation. To reduce reoffending statistics, prison administrators and parole boards rely heavily on empirical predictive tools informed by or based on postivisitic frameworks like the Dynamic Risk Assessment for Offender Re-entry (DRAOR) (Muirhead et al., 2018).

Within academia, orthodox criminologists dictate, expand, and limit thematic frontiers and ideological directions with regard to CCJ (Cohen, 1988). In constant interaction with state CCJ discourses, mainstream academic discourse ensured its own survival by continuing to differentiate the criminal from the non-criminal (Agozino, 2003; Lynch, 2000; Tauri, 2012a; Young, 2011). When academic criminology established itself in the early twentieth century, its promoters aspired for it to be a social *science* that emphasised the application of *scientific* methods in empirical studies of CCJ (Liu, 2009). However, from the late 1950s onwards, many criminologists started to take their gaze off the 'convict' to also capture the 'non-adjudicated criminal' (particularly white-collar crime), and strayed from the black-letter-law definition of crime to also include 'socially injurious acts' (such as environmental harms) in their field of study (Jeffery, 1959, p. 6). As Howard Becker (1967) pointed out, university academics, including criminologists, must decide whose side they are on. But even challenges offered by the various strands of critical criminology and, more recently, zemiology (see, for example, Boukli & Kotzé, 2018; Hillyard et al., 2004), which contest the ontological reality of crime and seek to focus on social harm, nonetheless remain conceptually reliant on the idea of 'crime' as defined by the state.

As can be ascertained from the chapters in this collection, most New Zealand university-based criminologists conduct research under the umbrella of critical, feminist, or decolonising criminology. The fact that the research agenda within the New Zealand CCJ policy sector is dominated by orthodox criminology while academic criminology is largely critical in nature may cause some disconnect between the skill requirements of the policy sector and the level of statistical analysis proficiency that university graduates can offer, for example, in 'fixed effects regression, hierarchical linear modelling, structural equation modelling, cross-lagged panel modelling [and] multi-nominal logistic regression' (personal communication, MoJ, 2018, 2 May). Whether and how to bridge that gap remains under investigation (see, for example, Gluckman, 2011, 2013, 2017).

Orthodox criminologists have received praise for exposing the excessive imprisonment of Indigenous peoples in New Zealand and elsewhere (Clifford, 1984). Yet they have also been criticised for marginalising Indigenous voices and for playing a significant role in producing many of the issues that Indigenous peoples and ethnic minorities face in contemporary Eurocentric criminal justice processes (Agozino, 2003, 2004; Cunneen & Tauri, 2016; Lynch, 2000; Tauri, 2012a, 2012b). Post-colonial theory has done little to alleviate these issues, and can, arguably, serve only as a theoretical framework in situations where the coloniser has entirely retreated from the once-colonised territory (Smith, 1999), and perhaps in cases where the coloniser remains on the territory but the once-colonised people have regained mainstream status. However, when the coloniser remains on the invaded territory and continues to exercise tactics of domination – as is the case in New Zealand – colonialism has not yet ceased. It has merely switched tactics; that is, it now uses neocolonial forms of economic, political, social, and cultural oppression as opposed to physical violence. Agozino (2003) advocates, therefore, for a counter-colonial criminology.

Counter-colonial criminology argues that orthodox criminology rejects Indigenous peoples' world view, knowledges, and epistemologies. This rejection constitutes a negative experience that drives Indigenous peoples away from criminology both as academics and as research participants. To counteract this contemporary trend, criminologists need to respect Indigenous world views, knowledges, and epistemologies (Cunneen & Tauri, 2016; Smith, 1999); employ non-silencing research methods when studying issues that primarily affect Indigenous communities (Deckert, 2015); and pay attention to the excessive incarceration of Indigenous peoples more frequently until this social problem is fully recognised by policy-makers and aptly addressed (Cunneen & Tauri, 2016; Deckert, 2014). Counter-colonial criminologists would also use non-othering language, work to empower Indigenous peoples, and conduct research that meets ethical standards (Brown, 1995; Smith, 1999; Van Dijk, 2008).

RESEARCH ETHICS AND TE TIRITI O WAITANGI

In 1984, three medical researchers employed by the University of Auckland published an article in the high-ranked journal *Obstetrics and Gynaecology*. In 1987, their unethical research conduct was exposed in a *Metro* magazine article which explained that women with precancerous carcinoma in situ of the cervix (CIS), and some with micro-invasive cancer of the cervix or vaginal vault had, without their knowledge, received repeated diagnostic biopsies and cervical smears, but had been left untreated or undertreated in order to study the extent to which these lesions developed into invasive cancer. The result was that many developed invasive cancer and some died (Cartwright Inquiry, 2011, para. 3).

The scandal was followed up by the Cartwright Inquiry (1987–88), so named after its chair, District Court judge Silvia Cartwright.[2] One significant outcome of this inquiry has been that, since 1988, all New Zealand university research proposals involving human and animal participants must undergo a formal ethics review at their host institution (Tolich et al., 2015). Ethically relevant researcher obligations also emerge from Te Tiriti o Waitangi and its principles of partnership, participation, and protection (PPP). These principles were developed by the Royal Commission on Social Policy in 1988 (Hudson & Russell, 2009), the same year the Cartwright Inquiry mandated ethics reviews.

First, the partnership principle commands researchers to ensure that researched individuals and communities are respected, particularly in their right to autonomy. With regard to partnership, researchers should ask themselves how their research design and conduct serves to enhance mutual respect and participant self-determination; how good faith is created between the researcher and participants; how research participants and the researched community will benefit from the research findings; and how the data, information, and knowledge provided by research participants are acknowledged.

Second, the participation principle reminds researchers of the importance of involving the researched community in the design, implementation, administration, and analysis of the research project. With regard to participation, researchers should ask themselves whether participants will inform or influence the research design, the questions asked, and its methods and final analysis; how participants may be involved in fieldwork and information-sharing; and whether the researched community may fulfil a formal stakeholder role.

Third, and finally, the protection principle requires that researchers actively preserve individual and collective rights, including cultural values, norms, and practices, such as language. In regard to protection, researchers should also ask themselves how they actively protect participants from coercion, deception, and harm; how they protect their privacy; how potential power imbalances may be addressed; and how cultural and diversity factors will be respected.

Regarding studies with Māori individuals and communities, kaupapa Māori scholars continue to challenge current research practices, and have provided detailed guidance for ethical research (Hudson & Russell, 2009), which can be structured around three broad themes: respect, control, and reciprocity.

- Respect entails the recognition of Indigenous groups as sovereign entities and respect for their cultural knowledge and traditions.
- Control affirms Indigenous control over involvement of Indigenous groups in research processes and relates to the ability of Indigenous groups to control the extent of their participation in research processes and negotiate what is acceptable.
- Reciprocity involves ensuring there are mutual benefits and that they are realised within Indigenous groups in an equitable manner (p. 62).

Accordingly, Hudson and Russell (2009, p. 67) have suggested revising the PPP principles 'to ensure that issues of reciprocity, equity and benefit-sharing are an explicit part of the negotiation process between researchers and Māori communities'. While research ethics are key to discussions on how to conduct research with Māori communities, such debates represent only the tip of the iceberg that is the decolonisation of CCJ research.

DECOLONISING CRIME AND CRIMINAL JUSTICE RESEARCH

In the academic realm, decolonisation refers to the ongoing process of challenging Eurocentric narratives about the Indigenous 'other' and replacing them with Indigenous-centric narratives to reverse the effects of colonialism and neocolonialism (Said, 1979; Smith, 1999). Academics who work in this area produce Indigenous-centred theories, research outputs, and discourses that are inevitably political. Through their work, these academics become scholar-activists as they shed light on marginalising structures, processes, practices, and discourses, and they advocate, both explicitly and implicitly, for Indigenous self-determination (Agozino, 2016).

Indigenous struggles for sovereignty and efforts to decolonise academia and society, in general, started to occur parallel to the postwar civil rights movement in the US during the 1960s (Smith, 1999). In New Zealand,

> [s]ome of the signposts which have marked this journey include such activities as the Land March of 1974, Waitangi Day protests from 1971, the occupation of Bastion Point (1978) and of Raglan Golf Course (1978), the disruption of the Springbok Rugby Tour (1981), Te Kohanga Reo (1982), the Māori Education Development Conference (1985) and Kura Kaupapa Māori (1986) (Smith, 1999, p. 113).

That Māori were increasingly criminalised and the Māori prison population rose (Robson, 1971) in the wake of aforesaid struggles for Indigenous self-determination appears to be no coincidence. In fact, it is easy to draw parallels to Michelle Alexander's (2010) argument that the mass incarceration of Black people in the US is a contemporary tool for social control. Incarceration is used to subdue racialised minorities. It substitutes its predecessors: slavery and Jim Crow laws. As long as Māori concentrated in rural New Zealand, incarceration was proportionate. However, that changed with the urban drift and protest movements that occurred from the 1960s onwards. These parallels arguably make neocolonialism and decolonisation not only key but central themes for CCJ research in New Zealand.

Many seminal works have been published on the topic of decolonising academia internationally and in New Zealand, especially since the 1990s (see, for example, Pihama et al., 2015; Smith, 1999). Increasingly, some focus on New Zealand CCJ research. Indigenous pioneers in this arena are Moana Jackson (Ngāti Kahungunu and Ngāti Porou), Kim Workman (Ngāti Kahungunu and Rangitāne), Tracey McIntosh (Ngāi Tūhoe), Juan Marcellus Tauri (Ngāti Porou), Robert Webb (Ngāpuhi), Michael Roguski (Te Ātiawa and Tūwharetoa), Khylee Quince (Ngāpuhi , Ngāti Porou, Ngāti Kahungunu), Ani Mikaere (Ngāti Raukawa and Ngāti Porou), and Riki Mihaere (Ngāti Kahungunu).

The latest ground-breaking book on decolonising CCJ research is, no doubt, *Indigenous Criminology* (Cunneen & Tauri, 2016), and there is now a New Zealand-based academic journal, *Decolonization of Criminology and Justice*. Co-edited by Antje Deckert (AUT) and Juan Marcellus Tauri (University of Waikato), it was launched in 2018 and published its inaugural open-access issue in 2019.

Decolonising efforts are also made in support of postgraduate researchers because the 'pedagogy of whiteness ... affects the research supervision process' between Māori postgraduate students and non-Māori faculty staff (Fitzgerald, 2005, p. 34; see also Berryman et al., 2017). For example, the terminology of supervisor/supervision suggests that the relationship between students and faculty staff is primarily one of paternalistic oversight and social control. This is a far cry from research as a collaborative endeavour of equal partners, which is promoted by Indigenous scholars and communities.

CONCLUSION

The history of CCJ research in Aotearoa New Zealand is young. Its most important chapters are likely yet to be written. Unlike in other Western jurisdictions, New Zealand CCJ research is dominated by a critical lens, shared by academics, advocacy groups, and some contract researchers. New Zealand's criminology is, therefore, at the forefront of a decolonising movement in academia, which includes scholar-activism (Agozino, 2016), prison abolition, decarceration, Indigenous criminology, feminism, and anti-criminology. However, despite all the ethical and theoretical advances made, the criminalisation and mass incarceration of Māori people has remained a major social injustice and human rights issue that needs to be urgently addressed (United Nations News Center, 2014). Crime, penal, and social policies based on critical CCJ research will be vital in this ongoing process.

STUDY QUESTIONS

- How does academic criminology contribute to the marginalisation of Indigenous peoples in New Zealand society?
- When and why were research ethics committees introduced at New Zealand universities?
- Explain the three ethical principles that guide criminological research involving human participants in New Zealand, and describe what they entail in practice.

FURTHER READING

Cunneen, C., & Tauri, J. M. (2016). *Indigenous criminology.* Bristol, UK: Polity Press.

Deckert, A., & Sarre, R. (2017). *The Palgrave handbook of Australian and New Zealand criminology, crime and justice.* Cham, Switzerland: Palgrave Macmillan.

Workman, K. (2018). *Journey towards justice.* Wellington, New Zealand: Bridget Williams Books.

NOTES

1 At the time of writing, the Labour government had only recented announced that it would repeal the three-strikes law.

2 The Cervical Cancer Inquiry, aka the Cartwright Inquiry (1987–88), was established following public evidence of the treatment of women with cervical cancer at the National Women's Hospital. Among other elements, the inquiry found long-standing failures in the values and practices of researching clinicians, including not ensuring that patients had informed choice about treatments, and clinician failures to treat the precursors to cancer.

REFERENCES

Agozino, B. (2003). *Counter-colonial criminology: A critique of imperialist reason*. London, UK: Pluto Press.

Agozino, B. (2004). Imperialism, crime and criminology: Towards the decolonisation of criminology. *Crime, Law and Social Change, 41*(4), 343–358. doi:10.1023/B:CRIS.0000025766.99876.4c

Agozino, B. (2010). Editorial: What is criminology? A control-freak discipline! *African Journal of Criminology and Justice Studies, 4*(1), i–xx. Retrieved from https://sta.uwi.edu/conferences/12/icopa/documents/What%20is%20Criminology.pdf

Agozino, B. (2016). *Critical, creative and centered scholar-activism: The fourth dimensionalism of Agwuncha Arthur Nwankwo*. New Haven, Nigeria, Africa: Fourth Dimension Publishing.

Aladaylah, M. (2010). Centering the other: Making the Native visible. *Revista de Divulgação Científica em Língua Portuguesa, Linguística e Literatura, 12*. Retrieved from www.letramagna.com/artigo3_XII.pdf

Alexander, M. (2010). *The new Jim Crow: Mass incarceration in the age of colorblindness*. New York, NY: New Press.

Becker, H. (1967). Whose side are we on? *Social Problems, 14*(3), 239–247. Retrieved from https://www.sfu.ca/~palys/Becker1967-WhoseSideAreWeOn.pdf

Berryman, M., Glynn, T., & Woller, P. (2017). Supervising research in Māori cultural contexts: A decolonizing, relational response. *Higher Education Research & Development, 36*(7), 1355–1368. doi:10.1080/07294360.2017.1325851

Borrin Foundation. (2018). *About us*. Retrieved from www.borrinfoundation.nz/about

Borrin Foundation. (2019). *He whaipaanga hou – A new approach 2018*. Retrieved from https://www.borrinfoundation.nz/project/he-whaipaagna-hou–2018

Boukli, A., & Kotzé, J. (2018). *Zemiology: Reconnecting crime and social harm*. Cham, Switzerland: Palgrave Macmillan.

Brown. (1995). The reproduction of othering. *Feminism & Psychology, 5*(4), 535–538. doi:10.1177/0959353595054014

Cartwright Inquiry. (2011). *Unethical experiment at National Women's Hospital*. Retrieved from www.cartwrightinquiry.com

Clifford, W. (1984). An approach to Aboriginal criminology. *Anglo-American Law Review, 13*(1), 33–51. doi:10.1177/147377958401300103

Cohen, S. (1988). *Against criminology*. New York, NY: Broadway Play Publishing.

Cunneen, C. (2006). Racism, discrimination and the over-representation of Indigenous people in the criminal justice system: Some conceptual and explanatory issues. *Current Issues in Criminal Justice, 17*(3), 329–346. doi:10.1080/10345329.2006.12036363

Cunneen, C., & Tauri, J. M. (2016). *Indigenous criminology*. Bristol, UK: Polity Press.

Deckert, A. (2014). Neo-colonial criminology: Quantifying silence. *African Journal of Criminology and Criminal Justice, 8*(1), 39–60.

Deckert, A. (2015). Criminologists, duct tape and Indigenous peoples: Quantifying the use of silencing research methods. *International Journal of Comparative and Applied Criminal Justice, 40*(1), 43–62. doi:10.1080/01924036.2015.1044017

Department of Corrections. (2019a). *Resources*. Retrieved from www.corrections.govt.nz/resources

Department of Corrections. (2019b). *Visits to prison*. Retrieved from https://www.corrections.govt.nz/resources/policy_and_legislation/Prison-Operations-Manual/Visits-to-prisons

Fitzgerald, T. (2005). Partnership, protection and participation: Challenges for research supervision in Aotearoa/New Zealand. In P. Green (Ed.), *Supervising postgraduate research: Contexts and processes, theories and practices* (pp. 30–47). Melbourne, Australia: RMIT University Press.

Foucault, M. (1969). *The archaeology of knowledge*. London, UK: Routledge.

Gilbert, J. (2015a, November 25). Dr Jarrod Gilbert: The police have deemed me unfit to undertake crime research because I know criminals. *New Zealand Herald*. Retrieved from https://www.nzherald.co.nz/nz/dr-jarrod-gilbert-the-police-have-deemed-me-unfit-to-undertake-crime-research-because-i-know-criminals/PFQGJPFFQTBZP5NPCV6WNEZ5NY/

Gilbert, J. (2015b, November 25). *The Police research contract.* Retrieved from www.jarrodgilbert.com/blog/the-police-research-contract

Gluckman, P. (2011). *Towards better use of evidence and policy formation: A discussion paper.* Auckland, New Zealand: Office of the Prime Minister's Science Advisory Committee. Retrieved from https://www.pmcsa.org.nz/wp-content/uploads/Towards-better-use-of-evidence-in-policy-formation.pdf

Gluckman, P. (2013). *The role of evidence and policy formation and implementation: A report from the prime minister's chief science advisor.* Auckland, New Zealand: Office of the Prime Minister's Science Advisory Committee. Retrieved from https://www.pmcsa.org.nz/wp-content/uploads/The-role-of-evidence-in-policy-formation-and-implementation-report.pdf

Gluckman, P. (2017). *Enhancing evidence-informed policy making: A report by the prime minister's chief science advisor.* Auckland, New Zealand: Office of the Prime Minister's Science Advisory Committee. Retrieved from https://www.pmcsa.org.nz/wp-content/uploads/17–07–07-Enhancing-evidence-informed-policy-making.pdf

Green Party. (2015, November 25). *Police censorship of crime research 'an outrage'* [Press release]. Retrieved from https://archive.greens.org.nz/news/article/police-censorship-crime-research-%E2%80%9C-outrage%E2%80%9D

Hillyard, P., Pantazis, C., Tombs, S., & Gordon, D. (2004). *Beyond criminology: Taking harm seriously.* London, UK: Pluto Press.

Hudson, M. L., & Russell, K. (2009). The Treaty of Waitangi and research ethics in Aotearoa. *Journal of Bioethical Inquiry, 6*(1), 61–68. doi:10.1007/s11673–008–9127–0

Jackson, M. (1988). *The Maori and the criminal justice system: A new perspective: He whaipaanga hou: Part 2.* Wellington, New Zealand: Policy and Research Division, Department of Justice. Retrieved from https://www2.justice.govt.nz/website-documents/maori-and-the-criminal-justice-system-a-new-perspective-p2.pdf

Jeffery, C. R. (1959). Pioneers in criminology: The historical development of criminology. *Journal of Criminal Law and Criminology, 50*(1), 3–19. doi:10.2307/1140864

Lessa, I. (2006). Discursive struggles within social welfare: Restaging teen motherhood. *British Journal of Social Work, 36*(2), 283–298. doi:10.1093/bjsw/bch256

Liu, J. (2009). Asian criminology: Challenges, opportunities, and directions. *Asian Journal of Criminology, 4*(1), 1–9. doi:10.1007/s11417–009–9066–7

Lynch, M. (2000). The power of oppression: Criminology as a science of oppression. *Critical Criminology, 9*(1), 144–152. doi:10.1007/BF02461042

Ministry of Justice (MoJ). (2019). *Research and data.* Retrieved from www.justice.govt.nz/justice-sector-policy/research-data

Muirhead, J., Fortune, C.-A., & Polaschek, D. (2018). Risky business: Evaluating the dynamic risk assessment for offender re-entry for use with New Zealand youth. *Practice: The New Zealand Corrections Journal, 6*(2), 81–86. Retrieved from https://www.corrections.govt.nz/resources/research_and_statistics/journal/volume_6_issue_2_november_2018/risky_business_evaluating_the_dynamic_risk_assessment_for_offender_re-entry_for_use_with_new_zealand_youth

New Zealand Law Foundation. (2019). *Legal research publications.* Retrieved from https://www.lawfoundation.org.nz/?page_id=2568

New Zealand Police. (2019). *Publications and statistics.* Retrieved from https://www.police.govt.nz/about-us/publications-statistics

Pihama, L., Tiakiwai, S.-J., & Southey, K. (2015). *Kaupapa Rangahau: A reader: A collection of readings from the Kaupapa Rangahau workshop series.* Hamilton, New Zealand: Te Kotahi Research Institute.

Robson, J. L. (1971). Penal policy in New Zealand. *Australian and New Zealand Journal of Criminology, 4*(4), 195–207. doi:10.1177/000486587100400402

Rodgers, J., & Stenning, P. (2017). A short history of New Zealand Criminology. In A. Deckert & R. Sarre (Eds.), *The Palgrave handbook of Australian and New Zealand criminology, crime and justice* (pp. 17–32). Cham, Switzerland: Palgrave Macmillan.

Said, E. (1979). *Orientalism*. New York, NY: Vintage Books.

Smith, L. T. (1999). *Decolonising research methodologies: Research and Indigenous peoples.* Dunedin, New Zealand: University of Otago Press.

Smith, R. (2013). Editorial. *Practice: The New Zealand Corrections Journal, 1*(1), 2. Retrieved from https://www.corrections.govt.nz/__data/assets/pdf_file/0010/11413/COR-Practice-Journal-Vol1-Iss1-May13-WEB.pdf

Stanley, E. (2016). *The road to hell: State violence against children in postwar New Zealand.* Auckland, New Zealand: Auckland University Press.

Tauri, J. (2012b, March 10). Control freaks and criminologists [Blog post]. *Indigenous Criminologist.* Retrieved from http://juantauri.blogspot.co.nz/2012/03/control-freaks-and-criminologists.html.

Tauri, J. M. (2012a). Indigenous critique of authoritarian criminology in Australasia. In K. Carrington, M. Ball, E. O'Brien, & J. M. Tauri (Eds.), *Crime, justice and social democracy: International perspectives* (pp. 217–233). London, UK: Palgrave Macmillan.

Te Puni Kōkiri. (2019). *Ō mātou mōhiotanga: Our research and publications.* Retrieved from www.tpk.govt.nz/en/a-matou-mohiotanga

Tolich, M., Bathurst, R., Deckert, A., Flanagan, P., Gremillion, H., & Grimshaw, M. (2015). One size does not fit all: Organisational diversity in New Zealand tertiary sector ethics committees. *Kōtuitui: New Zealand Journal of Social Sciences Online, 11*(1), 23–35. doi:10.1080/1177708 3X.2015.1035732

United Nation News Center. (2014, April 8). High rate of Māori in prison among concerns as UN experts wrap up New Zealand visit. Retrieved from https://news.un.org/en/story/2014/04/465682-high-rate-maori-prison-among-concerns-un-experts-wrap-new-zealand-visit

Van Dijk, T. (2008). *Discourse and power.* New York, NY: Palgrave Macmillan.

Young, J. (2011). *The criminological imagination.* Cambridge, UK: Polity Press.

Part Two

Crimes

The eight chapters that form Part Two cover foundational ideas and debates about crime in Aotearoa New Zealand. Importantly, while these chapters include discussions of offence categories that are the 'bread and butter' of media or political constructions of crime, they also expand our thinking on harms and violence that are often overlooked – including, for example, cybercrimes, hate crimes, crimes against the environment, white-collar crime, and state–corporate crimes. These crimes, while largely hidden from popular narratives, cause far more harm to populations than many commonly identified crime problems.

The chapter by Fiona Hutton focuses on crimes that are regularly at the forefront of discussions: crimes of intoxication, aka those crimes connected to alcohol, illicit drugs, and other substances. She critically explores the arguments on the assumed links between 'drugs' and crime, highlighting how debates are often confused by mythical representations of drug users or drug problems that are accompanied by a lack of evidence-based approaches to the criminalisation of drugs. Drawing on results from the New Zealand Arrestee Drug Use Monitoring Study, Hutton shows how alcohol – a legal drug – causes arrestees the most problems. She also presents useful critiques of these types of studies; for example, do such studies just present us with an indicator of who is policed? After all, most drug users engage with drugs recreationally without any ensuing difficulties. While substances may have associations with certain types of offending, a *causal* relationship cannot be established.

From here, the collection turns to concerns of violence. Jan Jordan's chapter on sexual violence revolves around the logic of patriarchy. She demonstrates how patriarchal thinking has permeated our structures, institutions, and sociocultural practices. Male control over womens' bodies (as well as over law, politics, economy, power) has underpinned the history of rape. While rape laws have changed, the cultures and attitudes that reinforce and condone rape have not. Jordan highlights these realities by reflecting on five different themes in relation to New Zealand examples: (1) the male act of possession of women's bodies and lives; (2) the power of men's control over women, such as through threats, attacks, or psychological coercion; (3) masculine entitlement, dovetailed with double standards over sexual lives; (4) the objectification of women's bodies, dehumanising women as 'objects' awaiting male 'use'; and (5) the silencing of women's voices, to protect men from accusations and ensure male impunity. She demonstrates the urgent need for New Zealanders to dismantle the rape culture that supports patriarchal constraint in women's lives.

Arguments to institutionally dismantle patriarchy are reiterated in a chapter on intimate partner violence (IPV), a long-standing problem that has increasingly become a focus for research, policy, and criminal justice actors. Ang Jury, Natalie Thorburn and Ruth Weatherall explore how agencies have responded to this systemic problem in New Zealand. Drawing on experiential accounts, they detail the physical, sexual, psychological, emotional, spiritual, and economic nature of IPV. They show how women are overwhelmingly targeted by this violence, with Māori women being disproportionately victimised. Victims can experience a pattern of social entrapment, the repercussions of which are long-lived and socially damaging. Of course, women (and especially Māori and Pasifika women) have led significant activism, bringing legal changes and safety provisions. Yet, despite these advances, numerous issues remain. For example, criminal justice actors are reticent to criminalise IPV; they tend to dismiss or blame victims, and draw on notions of 'family conflict' to minimise the patterns of controlling behaviours that result in deadly outcomes. At the same time, victims find that there are multiple barriers to accessing limited support services. Ultimately, to ensure an end to IPV, its gendered nature must be confronted, and concerns of justice must be addressed, including the development of resources and services so victims can rebuild their lives.

Another area of offending that is gendered in its nature and impacts relates to cybercrimes. Claire Meehan's chapter shows how cybercrimes create new challenges for responding to victimisation, not least as these under-reported crimes are often transnational, extensive in reach, and extremely harmful. Meehan details the rise of 'sexting', and examines perceptions and responses to young people involved in these activities. Current responses in New Zealand struggle to appreciate the nuances of sexting behaviours when determining whether an act is criminal, harmful, or consensual, not least as sensational reporting has conflated consensual sexting between young people with panics about child exploitation. Such representations have led to the criminalisation of teens for consensual activities. At the same time, sexting can also be connected to image-based sexual abuse. Here, victim-blaming attitudes are common and there is limited appreciation of the ways in which sexting is linked to significant cyber-harms and cyber-victimisations. There is a pressing need for much more research in the area, and to change the ways we report on and represent cybercrimes.

The next chapter reflects on an event in which the offender used the internet as a means to further perpetuate violence and harms: the 2019 Christchurch mosque killings. Daniel Botha and Scott Poynting reflect on these horrific shootings in relation to the nature of the racism, Islamophobia, and hate crimes that have long existed in New Zealand. Prime Minister Jacinda Ardern received worldwide acclaim for her response to the killings. A significant element of the political narrative was to cast the shootings as an aberration in a society that was otherwise inclusive, diverse, and non-racist. A common message in the days that followed was 'this is not New Zealand'. This line was at odds with the abuse, violence, and harassment experienced by Muslims for many years. After considering the nature of Islamophobia and hate crimes in New Zealand, Botha and Poynting illustrate the 'permission to hate' that was operationalised through New Zealand's weak legislation, lax oversight, muted monitoring, and political denials of complaints. They argue that hate crimes – including those based on racism, Islamophobia, transphobia, and homophobia – have been normalised.

Another area in which mass harms are normalised, on national and global levels, is that of environmental harms. Anthropocentrism has led to a climate crisis, and to unprecedented levels of industrial agriculture and plastic use, all of which is affecting human populations, animals, and environments in unprecedented ways. Sarah Monod de Froideville and Moorea Smithline's chapter exposes the nature of environmental harms in New Zealand, and reflects on the value of green criminology to understand them. After first exploring an ecojustice perspective in criminology, they use a species-justice lens to analyse and challenge the harms inherent in New Zealand's horse-racing industry. They follow with an overview of the nature and scale of industrial pollution affecting freshwater and land. Given the intersections between colonisation and environmental harms, they reflect on the need for an indigicentric eco-philosophy that focuses on kinship relations between people and land to be developed within green criminology.

With a brief history of white-collar crime, from colonial atrocities to the waves of corporate collapses and scandals, Simon Mackenzie demonstrates the devastatingly serious problem of white-collar crimes in New Zealand. He shows how the massive physical, economic, psychological, and emotional harms caused by white-collar crimes far outstrip those that ensue from acts that are normally presented as the crime problem. Yet these crimes are often explained away through language of 'accidents' or 'disasters', and offenders regularly evade accountability. Drawing on varied examples from across New Zealand, Mackenzie unpacks explanations for white-collar crime at micro, meso, and macro levels of social organisation. He also demonstrates the difficulties of securing successful criminal justice responses or regulatory frameworks. The official capacity to identify and deal with these crimes in New Zealand is severely stretched, and we require new legislative instruments, criminal justice capacity, and clear-sighted research to identify the crimes of the powerful and protect the public from harms.

The last chapter in Part Two concerns the related harms and issues that ensue from state–corporate crimes. Elizabeth Stanley and Sally Day reflect on the concept of agnosis, or organised ignorance-making, to consider how these crimes are hidden, and rarely criminalised or punished. They engage one example of state–corporate crime in New Zealand, the Pike River Mine disaster, to show how ignorance-making contributed to mass fatalities and numerous other harms for workers, their families, and communities. While individual actions are illuminated, they reflect on how structural conditions and institutional actions (such as the emphasis on financial benefits; government rollbacks on regulation; and failures of accountability) led to the disaster and to ongoing impunity. Yet, as the families and campaigners for Pike River demonstrate, widespread denials and distortions of knowledge can be vigorously challenged, triggering crises for states and corporations. The question remains how, over the long term, states and corporations reconfigure their relationships in ways that normalise inequitable structural and social relations, and minimise regulations or oversight of harmful industries, once more.

5

Crimes of Intoxication
Unsettling the Alcohol/Drugs–Crime Link

Fiona Hutton

It is generally agreed that intoxication relates to 'the aim of artificially inducing a change in one's consciousness' (Becker, 1967, p. 164), and that people use intoxication, via a variety of substances, to 'manage, maintain or change the experience of the self in the world' (Bancroft, 2009, p. 5). In relation to crime, however, intoxication is often viewed through the lens of illicit or illegal drugs. For example, illicit drugs such as heroin or methamphetamine and their associated intoxications are blamed for causing crime, and those who use illicit drugs are often seen as criminal and dangerous. Theoretical developments such as Goldstein's (1985) Tripartite Framework (TPF) have helped to embed the idea that illegal drug use causes crime.[1] However, critics such as Stevens (2007, 2011) and Seddon (2000) argue that the TPF is unsupported by evidence and that the link between illegal drugs and crime has been exaggerated. Similarly, there is no clear causal connection between the use of alcohol and crime (Langenderfer, 2013; Parker, 1993). If there were a causal connection between alcohol and crime, we might expect that the large numbers of those who consume alcohol regularly in countries such as Aotearoa New Zealand would also be regularly committing crime; this is clearly not the case.

This chapter explores some of the arguments related to the 'drugs–crime link', including those related to the ADUM/NEW-ADAM studies. It assesses the ways that the drugs–crime relationship has been examined, and highlights criticisms of assumed links between 'drugs' and crime. The discussion also explores the criminalisation of intoxication, often related to marginalised and vulnerable groups. From here, the focus shifts to alcohol and some of the arguments related to alcohol and violence in particular, as well as the criticisms of attributing a causal relationship between alcohol and crimes of violence.

Although the use of psychoactive substances to alter states of consciousness has a long history (Hutton, 2020; Walton, 2001), anxieties about how intoxication intersects with offending have intensified over the past two decades. The identification of particular ways of consuming alcohol (such as the much-debated 'binge' drinking) and other drugs has problematised our understanding of drug use and crime.[2] For example, binge drinking (itself a problematic concept; see Herring et al., 2008) is often associated with particular populations such as young people or Indigenous groups (Hutton & Wright, 2015). Similarly, the use of synthetic cannabis by certain marginalised groups has caused widespread concern, although an effective policy response is yet to be forthcoming (Hutton, 2020).

Theoretical developments, such as the normalisation thesis (Hutton, 2010; Parker et al., 2002), which suggests that drug use has become more widespread and normal, have reflected increasing concerns about young people's use of illicit drugs (see Duff, 2005; Parker et al., 2002). Anxieties about drug consumption and its connections with disorder and crime have been exacerbated by the development of the neoliberal night-time economy (NTE), with its widening repertoire of spaces and places to consume alcohol and other drugs (Hutton, 2009). Young people inhabiting the burgeoning NTE of Westernised nations have subsequently found their drinking practices keenly scrutinised by regulatory bodies and journalists, with young women and Māori often criticised in New Zealand (Griffin et al., 2013; Hutton et al., 2016; Hutton & Wright, 2015; Measham, 2006). The diversity of (sub)cultural drinking and drug-taking practices, and *who* is criminalised for doing *what*, is often missed in the drugs–crime debates.

'DRUGS', INTOXICATION, AND CRIME

The drugs–crime debate is embedded in societies that have well-developed 'cultures of intoxication', where intoxication via *some* substances by *some* groups is encouraged and celebrated. That some people who use drugs (PWUD) are stigmatised as problematic is intensified by the drugs–crime link, while the intoxications (both legal and illegal) by more privileged groups are normalised and encouraged.

The supposed drugs–crime connection is a complex debate, not least because it is often taken for granted that 'drug' use causes crime. In many ways this is related to the images and ideas that are constructed about 'drug users' in society. People who use illegal drugs like cannabis, ecstasy, heroin, or methamphetamine are constructed in stereotypical ways: as criminal and unpleasant (Taylor, 2008). The public often get ideas about drugs and their users from mainstream media, and therefore popular ideas are based on sensationalised reports of drug users engaging in violent acts (Alexandrescu 2014, 2019).[3] Thus, how the 'drugs–crime link' is considered depends on a number of important factors, such as how drugs are defined. As noted above, when people refer to 'drugs', they are often referring to illicit or illegal substances, despite the wide variety of drugs in society (many of which, such as alcohol, tobacco, and caffeine, are legal).

A variety of drugs in New Zealand are illegal and subject to punishment laid out in the Misuse of Drugs Act 1975 (MDA). Drugs are classified in categories A, B, or C according to the (alleged) harm that they cause, with the most severe penalties reserved for Class A drugs. Methamphetamine, for example, is a Class A drug, and cannabis is a class C drug.[4] This has led to the *bifurcation* of drugs, with some drugs and their users being viewed as problematic and criminalised under the MDA 1975 while other drugs, such as alcohol, are legal and viewed as socially acceptable. This has a bearing on the drugs–crime connection debate, because, when the 'problem' of 'drugs' is raised, people automatically think of illicit drugs as being the problem. This affects how both drugs and crime are viewed, and more importantly it also affects official responses to drugs, drug users, and crime.

Many international commentators view current drug laws as outdated and unfit for purpose, arguing that drug use should be treated as a health and social problem rather than a criminal one.[5] Some jurisdictions are also reforming their drug laws, recognising that they do not effectively tackle the problems related to drug use, and they often create more harms than they solve (see for example, Global Commission on Drug Policy, 2018). Portugal decriminalised the use of all drugs in 2001, and since 2012 the District of Columbia and 11 US states have legalised the recreational use of cannabis. Uruguay legalised their cannabis market in 2017, with Canada following suit in October 2018. (New Zealand held a referendum on legalising cannabis in 2020, with the 'no' vote prevailing by a slender margin.) Responses to illegal drugs in some countries have therefore changed quite dramatically and will affect how the drugs–crime link is viewed in these jurisdictions.

Despite these widespread reforms, Stevens (2007, p. 80) argues that 'the assumption is often made that the use of an illicit drug sometime in the past is enough to relate people's offending to drugs'. In this respect, the drugs–crime link is often accepted uncritically and at face value. Yet, as the European Monitoring Centre for Drugs and Drug Addiction outlines:

> The relationship between drugs and crime is neither simple nor linear. Nor is it universal: many repeat offenders are not involved in drug use and many dependent drug users do not commit any crimes (other than drug use/possession, where it is criminalized) (EMCDDA, 2007, p. 1).

There is therefore significant doubt on the assertion that drug use *causes* crime, despite a *causal* relationship being assumed. This assumption of a causal relationship is often related to the types of crimes that are associated with illegal drug use. The crimes that are linked to drugs are often referred to as 'volume crime' (see Bradley, chapter 3 this volume), such as burglary or thefts from cars, shops, pharmacies, or other premises. Other kinds of crimes that are reported less frequently to police (such as major fraud or sexual violence) are not seen as being linked to illegal drug use. In addition, crimes that happen away from Westernised nations that are linked to drugs or the prohibition of drugs are not seen as 'drug-related crime'. As examples: the 2006 destruction of opium crops by the Burmese government, that led to mass displacement and hunger; the extrajudicial killings of drug users, drug dealers, and farmers in Thailand (Stevens, 2011); and the extrajudicial killings of drug users in the Philippines (over 8000 to date) that have intensified under President Rodrigo Duterte, who has encouraged people to kill drug users. These are not the kinds of crimes that people think of when they hear the phrase 'drug-related crime', as the latter are 'taken to mean . . . the crimes that happen at street level, committed by "deviant" members of the "dangerous classes"' (Stevens 2007, p. 79). Understandings and definitions of 'drug-related crime' are important in these debates, and this chapter now turns to a closer examination of what is meant by 'drug-related crime'.

'DRUGS' AND CRIME: DEFINITIONS

Defining drug- or substance-related crimes is more complicated than it would first appear. There are three main types of 'drugs–crime' offences that are commonly referred to in debates about drug use and crime.

Firstly, there are *substance- or drug-defined crimes*: these are actions involving substances that are specifically mentioned and defined by legislation as criminal (Buchanan, 2008, p. 255). In the New Zealand context, these are crimes that are specified as such under the MDA 1975, such as possession of cannabis or methamphetamine. For example, approximately 5000 New Zealanders each year receive convictions for possession of cannabis (New Zealand Drug

Foundation, 2019). Substance- or drug-defined crime can also be broadened out to encompass legal drugs. For example, people can be criminalised for driving with excess blood alcohol. Substance-defined crimes are also regarded as being socially constructed: certain drugs are defined as illegal not because of evidence of harm, but because 'as a political community we have come to treat some substances differently from others, depending on *who* uses them, *how* and for *what*' (Bancroft, 2009, p. 8, emphasis added). For example, cannabis, an illegal drug, is less harmful than alcohol and tobacco, legal drugs that cause significant amounts of harm (Nutt et al., 2007). Therefore, factors other than the harmfulness of drugs often affect whether drugs and their users are viewed as dangerous and in need of control.

Secondly, there are *substance- or drug-influenced crimes*: these are crimes of intoxication that are committed when a person is 'under the influence', or intoxicated by a substance. Substance-influenced crimes are more difficult to measure than substance-defined crimes because they require an assessment that the offender was under the influence at the time the crime was committed, and that intoxication played some part in the commission of the offence (Buchanan, 2008, p. 256).

Thirdly, there are *substance- or drug-related crimes*: these are crimes that are not committed while under the influence, but are somehow connected to and/or motivated by substance use. A typical example would be a drug user who steals from a shop in order to fund their drug habit. These crimes require an assessment that the person is a substance user, and that the crime was in some way related to their substance use (Buchanan, 2008, p. 256). Though these definitions may appear clear-cut, the reality is more complicated. An examination of the New Zealand Arrestee Drug Use Monitoring (NZ-ADUM) study demonstrates these complexities.

The New Zealand Arrestee Drug Use Monitoring Study

The New Zealand Arrestee Drug Use Monitoring (NZ-ADUM) study was developed to track trends in alcohol and other drug use among police detainees (those who had been arrested). Studies such as these have also been used in other countries to track trends in drug use among detainees.[6] They are often cited as 'evidence' that drug use causes crime, which is then used to justify harsher penalties for drug users under the criminal justice system (Stevens, 2007). So what do these kinds of studies tell us about drug use and crime?

In 2016, the NZ-ADUM detainees named three drug types as largely responsible for their substance use-related problems: alcohol (78 per cent), methamphetamine (33 per cent), and cannabis (32 per cent) (Wilkins et al., 2017). In 2016, 6 per cent of detainees reported that they were using methamphetamine prior to their arrest, but 28 per cent reported that they had been drinking alcohol prior to their arrest. This prompts the question: why the focus on illegal drugs? After all, alcohol appears to be the issue here, rather than the more widely demonised methamphetamine. In New Zealand, 16 per cent of detainees also reported using cannabis prior to their arrest (Wilkins et al., 2017), and cannabis was the drug most often found in urine tests of detainees in the UK (as cited in Stevens, 2007, p. 81). However, the use of cannabis is widespread: globally it is the most common illegal drug used. For example, in New Zealand nearly one in two adults (49.0 per cent) had used 'any [illicit] drugs' for recreational purposes in their lifetime, equating to about 1,292,700 people. The majority (1,224,600 people) had used cannabis, with 46.4 per cent of all people aged 16–64 years having used it in their lifetime (Ministry of Health [MoH], 2010a). The UN's World Drug Report (UNODC, 2017) also notes that in 2015 there were an estimated 183 million 'past year' cannabis users – people who had used cannabis in the previous 12 months. Alcohol is another widely used drug, with 79 per cent of New Zealand adults stating that they used alcohol in the past year in 2017/2018.[7] So is the NZ-ADUM (as well as other global studies) simply picking up the recreational use of drugs like cannabis and alcohol that are *unrelated to offending behaviour*? The same could also be asked of the other drugs registered in detainees' urine samples: are they causing crime, or do they reflect 'normal' use of drugs, both legal and illegal, by detainees?

Further complicating the issue is that many of the detainees in the NZ-ADUM and studies elsewhere have myriad issues that affect their lives, such as mental health issues, social disadvantage, and unemployment (Wilkins et al., 2017). There are also equity issues inherent in the criminal justice system which affect the NZ-ADUM. Some groups, such as Māori, are overpoliced and over-represented in drugs and other arrest and conviction statistics (New Zealand Drug Foundation, 2019; Tauri & Webb, 2012; Webb, 2009). These interrelated issues complicate discussions on drugs and crime even further, as it becomes difficult to single out drug use as the causal factor in someone's offending behaviour. It also means that particular groups become the focus of the drugs–crime debate, with those that experience multiple disadvantages being singled out and blamed for crime.

Criticisms of the NZ-ADUM and other global studies

The New Zealand Arrestee Drug Use Monitoring (NZ-ADUM) study was developed to track trends in alcohol and other drug use among police detainees in New Zealand. These kinds of studies have also been used in other countries, such as the US (Arrestee Drug Abuse Monitoring program, ADAM), the UK (New English and Welsh Arrestees Drug Abuse Monitoring, NEW-ADAM), and Australia (Drug Use Monitoring in Australia, DUMA). However, scholars have argued that the relationship between using drugs and committing crime (if there is one) is dynamic, so it changes, fluctuates, and varies over time. Someone's drug use may vary in its relevance to any offending behaviours they may engage in, and this may change as people age or their wider circumstances change. Studies exploring the drugs–crime connection, such as the NZ-ADUM, have typically looked at offending patterns in specific populations such as those in prisons or among police detainees. This, it is argued, exaggerates the drugs–crime link because

- offenders who use drugs are more likely to be arrested, and
- those who use drugs and are arrested are a small minority of drug users (Stevens, 2011, p. 35).

A further criticism of such studies is that the drugs–crime link intensifies the stigma that PWUD face, making it more difficult for those with addictions to seek help, and deepening the divide between those who use illegal drugs and 'normal' society (Lloyd, 2013). As noted above, studies like the NZ-ADUM capture the drug use of very specific populations: often those who are vulnerable, stigmatised, and likely to come into contact with criminal justice agencies; and as Stevens (2007, p. 83) notes, 'Figures from people who have been caught up in the CJS [criminal justice system] should not be extrapolated to the much larger population of unknown offenders.' Additionally, only certain types of offending are caught in this net – in debates about the drugs–crime link there is a notable absence of discussions about white-collar crime and drugs, for example.

The NZ-ADUM/NEW-ADAM studies are also criticised for providing a narrow view of the complex relationships between drugs and crime (EMCDDA, 2007), as they often focus on 'either just one specific or a few general types of drug-misuse and crime' (Bennett & Holloway, 2005 p. 102), leading to the assumption that drug users are all the same and are affected by drugs such as alcohol, heroin, or methamphetamine in similar ways. But research noting that, for instance, heroin may be linked to particular crimes like shoplifting cannot be widened out to apply to all other forms of drug use (Stevens, 2007). Addiction to or dependence on expensive illegal drugs as the driver for acquisitive crime is not supported by research (Seddon, 2000). Only a small minority of drug users (globally, approximately 13 per cent) suffer from addiction to illegal substances (UNODC, 2019). The vast majority of people who use illegal drugs do so recreationally in ways that cause minimal harms to themselves, their families, and communities (MoH, 2010b; UNODC, 2019). Therefore, focusing on the minority of users who suffer from problems related to addiction skews the argument and inflates the drugs–crime connection (Stevens, 2011). As Bennett and Holloway (2005) also note, drugs vary substantially in their cost, addictive properties, and effects on users, so any relationship to crime will also vary substantially (see also Seddon, 2000).

As detailed above, viewing drug use and any relationship to crime in the context of other social, cultural, and environmental factors is also crucial. Underlying factors such as inequality and deprivation often produce both problematic drug use and crime, and thus qualify as causal links (Hammersley et al., 1989; Stevens et al., 2005). Substances do not have universal criminogenic properties, and wider environmental and individual factors affect how the use of particular substances impact on behaviours (EMCDDA, 2007). For example, recent studies demonstrate that drug-related violence is likely to increase when drug law enforcement is applied (Werb et al., 2011).

Therefore the links between drug use and crime are dependent on many interrelated social, cultural, and environmental factors. As Bean (2008, p. 48) notes: 'One of the main problems in establishing a causal link is that many drug users are not offenders, and the vast majority of drug-using incidents neither cause nor accompany criminality.'

ALCOHOL INTOXICATION AND CRIME

Alcohol intoxication has a strong association with pharmacologically induced crime, and violence in particular (EMCDDA, 2007). The New Zealand Police (NZP) estimate that about one-third of apprehensions involve alcohol, and that half of serious violent crimes are related to alcohol (MoH, 2010b). Approximately one-third of all recorded violent offences and family violence incidents in 2007/2008 were committed when the offender had consumed alcohol prior to the offence. In an analysis of calls to police conducted from January 2008 to December 2012, 38,929 calls (approximately 7700 per year) related to alcohol in Wellington city alone (NZP, 2013).[8] Alcohol is a significant factor in family and domestic violence both in New Zealand and worldwide (Boles & Miotto, 2003; Family Violence Death Review Committee, 2016; Langenderfer, 2013).

As with the NZ-ADUM, criticisms can be applied here: just because alcohol is present, or the offender has been drinking before being apprehended or involved in a crime, it does not necessarily mean that their offending is caused by alcohol. For example, if someone were arrested for a violent crime after consuming two bottles of beer, or one glass of wine, would we consider that alcohol had *caused* their offending behaviour? Alcohol is related to various kinds of offending, but is it a direct cause of crime?

Social and cultural context and expectations about behaviours while drinking or intoxicated play a part in how people think or expect they should behave after consuming alcohol (Room, 2005; Savic et al., 2016). For some Westernised nations a 'culture of intoxication' has been identified, and is characterised by 'letting go' within the context of the NTE, leading to a focus on the drinking practices of particular, visible groups, such as young people (Hutton et al., 2013). Alcohol is also seen as a drug that impairs people's self-control in contexts that would normally inhibit them from disorderly, violent, or criminal acts. It can also affect people's perceptions of the meanings of others' actions or behaviours, leading to aggression and conflict (Parker, 1993). It could be argued that these result from the way that alcohol is used, rather than the pharmacological effects of the substance itself. It is also important to note that the risk of becoming both a perpetrator or a victim of crime may increase when drugs such as alcohol enter the equation (EMCDDA, 2007).[9] Therefore alcohol may be involved or associated with some people's offending and victimisation, but it is not a causal factor.

Heavy drinking and drunkenness are often associated with enactments of masculinity and, in Graham and Wells' (2003) study, young men referred to drinking alcohol as 'drinking testosterone by the glass' (p. 551). Therefore aggression and violence could be a product of the enactment of masculinity, rather than of the substance itself. While young men's drinking is often seen as problematic, it is young women who have become the focus of concerns around youth 'binge' drinking. Feminist scholars have noted the tensions inherent in the neoliberal NTE for women (Griffin et al., 2013; Hutton et al., 2016). Within the hypersexualised NTE young women walk a fine line between being drunk, but not too drunk, and keeping within the boundaries of acceptable femininities. Stepping outside of these boundaries invites censure and unwanted attention from their male counterparts (Griffin et al., 2013). Constructions of femininity and masculinity (as well as other social variables) affect drinking practices and levels of harm, as well as how these drinking practices are responded to and controlled.

Criticisms of the alcohol–crime link

Although alcohol is strongly associated with some forms of crime, e.g., crimes of disorder, an association is not a *causal* relationship. Scholars are therefore reluctant to name alcohol as a causal factor in offending behaviour (Coomber et al., 2013). As with the illegal drug–crime link, alcohol-related crime may be the result of many interrelated factors. Alcohol use is influenced by social and cultural norms governing pleasure, socialising, and fun, as well as factors such as poverty, unemployment, boredom, peer pressure, use of illicit drugs, or mental health concerns.

More nuanced explanations for criminal activity are required. There is some evidence that people who commit alcohol-related violent crime are already of a violent disposition before they use alcohol (or other drugs) (Coomber et al., 2013). Research also commonly indicates that methamphetamine is an aggravating factor in, rather than a cause of, domestic violence, for example. Those who are predisposed to being violent and aggressive may find this impulse aggravated by alcohol or other drugs (Dowling & Morgan, 2018).

In conclusion, as with illegal drugs, it could be argued that alcohol has an association with some types of criminal offending, but a *causal* relationship cannot be established. That is not to say that alcohol plays no part in some criminal behaviour, but that wider factors are often more important when exploring the causes of violent and other criminal offending. It should also be noted that some groups' violence and use of alcohol comes under more scrutiny than others. There is little discourse in these debates about crimes of the powerful in relation to alcohol, while less powerful populations have their leisure pursuits keenly scrutinised. Furthermore, the vast majority of drinking (and other drug-using) occasions happen peacefully, pleasurably, and without significant harms to the user or others.

CONCLUSION

The best that can be concluded is that, as yet, a causal relationship has not been established between either alcohol or illegal drugs and crime. How 'drugs' are defined is an important consideration in these debates. The social construction of some substances as illegal affects how substance-defined crimes are counted, targeted, policed, and punished. Similarly, peoples' levels and means of intoxication (i.e., *who* has become intoxicated through using *which* drugs) are also important factors. Intersectionality is also pertinent here, as the use of alcohol or other drugs is affected by age, social class, gender, ethnicity, sexuality, and so on. Drug and alcohol practices are shaped by historical, cultural, and social mores that often privilege dominant groups. This leads to inequities both in the criminal justice system and in society as a whole.

Studies such as the NZ-ADUM often exaggerate the drugs–crime link by focusing on particular marginalised populations. Police detainees in particular will have a number of other issues that intersect with their drug use at the time of arrest, such as poverty, unemployment, and mental health problems (Wilkins et al., 2017). Therefore, a causal relationship between illegal drugs and crime should not be inferred, particularly as not all those who use drugs commit crime, and illicit substances alone do not have universal criminogenic properties.

Similar arguments are related to the use of alcohol and its link to crime, especially violent crime: multiple interconnected factors are at play in the act of drinking alcohol and becoming intoxicated, so the social, cultural, and environmental context is significant in considering offending behaviours. Intersectionality is again important in these arguments, given that particular groups find their drinking and other drug-taking practices under scrutiny more than others.

In summary, the relationship between both illegal drugs and alcohol and crime is 'complex and intricate' (Seddon, 2000, as cited in Stevens et al., 2005, p. 3). Studies have yet to establish a causal connection. The way that drugs are defined and responded to in contemporary society has reinforced and inflated the drugs–crime connection – a situation that needs to be critically interrogated and urgently rectified (Hutton, 2020).

STUDY QUESTIONS

- How does the social construction of 'drugs' affect the drugs–crime debate?
- List three criticisms of the NZ-ADUM/NEW-ADAM studies.
- What are some of the difficulties in measuring the 'drugs–crime link' in relation to illegal drugs and/or alcohol?

FURTHER READING

Lyons, A., & Kersey, K. (2020). Alcohol and intoxication. In F. Hutton (Ed.), *Cultures of intoxication: Key issues and debates* (pp. 17–44). London, UK: Palgrave Macmillan.

Stevens, A. (2011). *Drugs, crime and public health: The political economy of drug policy* (Chapter 3). Abingdon, UK: Routledge.

Werb, D., Rowell, G., Guyatt, G., Kerr, T., Montaner, J., & Wood, E. (2011). Effect of drug law enforcement on drug market violence: A systematic review. *International Journal of Drug Policy*, 22(2), 87–94. doi:10.1016/j.drugpo.2011.02.002

NOTES

1. The TPF offers three explanations for the drugs–crime link: psycho-pharmacological, economic-compulsive, and systemic (Goldstein, 1985).
2. Binge drinking refers to drinking a large amount of alcohol to intoxication in one sitting. It is sometimes referred to as heavy episodic drinking or hazardous drinking. For discussion, see Herring et al. (2008).
3. In New Zealand, William Bell shot and killed three people at an Auckland RSA (Returned and Services Association) in 2003; in the same year, Antonie Dixon attacked his long-term partner and her friend and went on to kill a stranger on the street. Both men were cited as intoxicated by drugs such as methamphetamine, which was directly linked to their crimes. Yet, there were clearly other factors involved in these cases.

4   See Nutt et al. (2007, 2010) for a critique of how drugs are classified under current drug legislation.
5   See, for example, Health Not Handcuffs, https://www.healthnothandcuffs.nz
6   See the US (Arrestee Drug Abuse Monitoring program, ADAM), the UK (New English and Welsh Arrestees Drug Abuse Monitoring, NEW-ADAM), and Australia (Drug Use Monitoring in Australia, DUMA) studies.
7   See Alcohol.org.nz, *Key facts about drinking*, https://www.alcohol.org.nz/sites/default/files/documents/Key-facts-about-drinking-in-New-Zealand.PDF
8   Wellington city has a population (including surrounding suburbs) of approximately 400,000 people.
9   It is, however, important to note here that intoxication is often used unjustly to blame female survivors of sexual violence for their victimisation. In such cases, the presence of alcohol is often used to excuse male perpetrators of sexual violence, and to blame and vilify female victims of sexual violence for stepping outside the boundaries of acceptable feminine behaviour.

REFERENCES

Alcohol.org.nz. (2019). *Key facts about drinking in New Zealand*. Retrieved from https://www.alcohol.org.nz/sites/default/files/documents/Key-facts-about-drinking-in-New-Zealand.PDF

Alexandrescu, L. (2014). Mephedrone, assassin of youth: The rhetoric of fear in contemporary drug scares. *Crime, Media, Culture, 10*(1), 23–37. doi:10.1177/1741659013511975

Alexandrescu, L. (2019). Streets of the 'spice zombies': Dependence and poverty stigma in times of austerity. *Crime, Media, Culture, 16*(1), 97–113. doi:10.1177/1741659019835274

Bancroft, A. (2009). *Drugs, intoxication and society*. Cambridge, UK: Polity Press.

Bean, P. (2008). *Drugs and crime*. Cullompton, UK: Willan Publishing.

Becker, H. (1967). History culture and subjective experience: An exploration of the social bases of drug-induced experiences. *Journal of Health and Social Behaviour, 8*(3), 163–176. doi:10.2307/2948371

Bennett, T., & Holloway, K. (2005). Disaggregating the relationship between drug misuse and crime. *Australian and New Zealand Journal of Criminology, 38*(1), 102–121. doi:10.1375/acri.38.1.102

Boles, S. M., & Miotto, K. (2003). Substance abuse and violence: A review of the literature. *Aggression and Violent Behavior, 8*(2), 155–174. doi:10.1016/S1359–1789(01)00057-X

Buchanan, J. (2008). Understanding and engaging with problematic substance use. In S. Green, E. Lancaster, & S. Feasey (Eds.), *Addressing offending behaviour: Context, practice and values* (pp. 246–264). Cullompton, UK: Willan Publishing.

Coomber, R., McElrath, K., Measham, F., & Moore, K. (2013). *Key concepts in drugs and society*. London, UK: Sage Publications.

Dowling, C., & Morgan, A. (2018). Is methamphetamine use associated with domestic violence? *Trends and Issues in Crime and Criminal Justice, 563*. Canberra, Australia: Australian Institute of Criminology. Retrieved from https://aic.gov.au/publications/tandi/tandi563

Duff, C. (2005). Party drugs and party people: Examining the 'normalization' of recreational drug use in Melbourne, Australia. *The International Journal of Drug Policy, 16*(3), 161–170. doi:10.1016/j.drugpo.2005.02.001

European Monitoring Centre for Drugs and Drug Addiction (EMCDDA). (2007). *Drugs and crime – a complex relationship*. Retrieved from http://www.emcdda.europa.eu/system/files/publications/470/Dif16EN_85000.pdf

Family Violence Death Review Committee. (2016). *Fifth report: January 2014 to December 2015*. Wellington, New Zealand: Family Violence Death Review Committee. Retrieved from https://www.hqsc.govt.nz/assets/FVDRC/Publications/FVDRC–5th-report-Feb–2016–2.pdf

Global Commission on Drug Policy. (2018). *Regulation: The responsible control of drugs*. Retrieved from https://www.globalcommissionondrugs.org/wp-content/uploads/2018/09/ENG-2018_Regulation_Report_WEB-FINAL.pdf

Goldstein, P. (1985). The drugs/violence nexus: A tripartite framework. *Journal of Drug Issues, 15*(4), 493–506. doi:10.1177/002204268501500406

Graham, K., & Wells, S. (2003). 'Somebody's gonna get their head kicked in tonight!' Aggression among young males in bars – a question of values? *British Journal of Criminology, 43*(3), 546–566. doi:10.1093/bjc/43.3.546

Griffin, C., Szmigin, I., Bengry-Howell, A., Hackley, C., & Mistral, W. (2013). Inhabiting the contradictions: Hypersexual femininity and the culture of intoxication among young women in the UK. *Feminism and Psychology, 23*(2), 184–206. doi:10.1177/0959353512468860

Hammersley, R., Forsyth, A., Morrison, V., & Davis, J. (1989). The relationship between crime and opioid use. *British Journal of Addiction, 84*(9), 1029–1043. doi:10.1111/j.1360-0443.1989.tb00786.x

Herring, R., Berridge, V., & Thom, B. (2008). Binge drinking: An exploration of a confused concept. *Journal of Epidemiology and Community Health, 62*(6), 476–479. doi:10.1136/jech.2006.056721

Hutton, F. (2009). New Zealand. In P. Hadfield (Ed.), *Nightlife and crime: Social order and governance in international perspective* (pp. 293–305). Oxford, UK: Oxford University Press.

Hutton, F. (2010). Kiwis, clubs and drugs: Club cultures in Wellington, New Zealand. *Australian and New Zealand Journal of Criminology, 43*(1), 91–111. doi:10.1375/acri.43.1.91

Hutton, F. (Ed.). (2020). *Cultures of intoxication: Key issues and debates*. London, UK: Palgrave Macmillan.

Hutton, F., Wright, S. (2015). 'You don't ditch your girls': Young Māori and Pacific women and the culture of intoxication. *Critical Public Health, 25*(1), 101–119. doi:10.1080/09581596.2014.946886

Hutton, F., Wright, S., & Saunders, E. (2013). Cultures of intoxication: Young women, alcohol, and harm reduction. *Contemporary Drug Problems, 40*(4), 451–480. doi:10.1177/009145091304000402

Hutton, F., Griffin, C., Lyons, A., Niland, P., & McCreanor, T. (2016). 'Tragic girls' and 'crack whores': Alcohol, femininity and Facebook. *Feminism & Psychology, 26*(1), 73–93. doi:10.1177/0959353515618224

Langenderfer, L. (2013). Alcohol use among partner violent adults: Reviewing recent literature to inform intervention. *Aggression and Violent Behavior, 18*(1), 152–158. doi:10.1016/j.avb.2012.11.013

Lloyd, C. (2013). The stigmatization of problem drug users: A narrative literature review. *Drugs: Education, Prevention and Policy, 20*(2), 85–95. doi:10.3109/09687637.2012.743506

Measham, F. (2006). The new policy mix: Alcohol, harm minimization, and determined drunkenness in contemporary society. *International Journal of Drug Policy, 17*(4), 258–268. doi:10.1016/j.drugpo.2006.02.013

Ministry of Health (MoH). (2010a). *Drug use in New Zealand: Key results of the 2007/08 New Zealand Alcohol and Drug Use Survey*. Retrieved from https://www.health.govt.nz/publication/drug-use-new-zealand-key-results-2007-08-new-zealand-alcohol-and-drug-use-survey

Ministry of Health (MoH). (2010b). *Alcohol quick facts*. Retrieved from https://www.health.govt.nz/system/files/documents/publications/alcohol-factsheets.pdf

New Zealand Drug Foundation. (2019). *The state of the nation: A stocktake of how New Zealand is dealing with the issue of drugs*. Wellington, New Zealand: New Zealand Drug Foundation. Retrieved from https://www.drugfoundation.org.nz/assets/uploads/2019-uploads/Policy-pages/State-of-the-Nation-2019.pdf

New Zealand Police (NZP). (2013). *Calls to Police related to alcohol: Wellington City*. Wellington, New Zealand: New Zealand Police. Retrieved from https://www.police.govt.nz/sites/default/files/publications/calls-to-police-wellington-city-2008-2012.pdf

Nutt, D., King, L., & Phillips, D. (2010). Drug harms in the UK: A multicriteria decision analysis. *The Lancet, 376*(9752), 1558–1565. doi:10.1016/S0140-6736(10)61462-6

Nutt, D., King, L., Saulsbury, W., & Blakemore, C. (2007). Development of a rational scale to assess the harm of drugs of potential misuse. *The Lancet, 369*(9566), 1047–1053. doi:10.1016/S0140-6736(07)60464-4

Parker, H., Williams, L., & Aldridge, J. (2002). The normalization of 'sensible' recreational drug use: Further evidence from the North West England Longitudinal Study. *Sociology, 36*(4), 941–964. doi:10.1177/003803850203600408

Parker, R., N. (1993). The effects of context on alcohol and violence. *Alcohol Health and Research World, 17*(2), 117–122. Retrieved from https://search.proquest.com/docview/1474321340?pq-origsite=primo

Room, R. (2005). Multicultural contexts and alcohol and drug use as symbolic behaviour. *Addiction Research and Theory, 13*(4), 321–331. doi:10.1080/16066350500136326

Savic, M., Room, R., Mugavin, J., Pennay, A., & Livingston, M. (2016). Defining 'drinking culture': A critical review of its meaning and connotation in social research on alcohol problems. *Drugs: Education, Prevention and Policy, 23*(4), 270–282. doi:10.3109/09687637.2016.1153602

Seddon, T. (2000). Explaining the drug–crime link: Theoretical, policy and research issues. *Journal of Social Policy, 29*(1), 95–107. doi:10.1017/S0047279400005833

Stevens, A. (2007). When two dark figures collide: Evidence and discourse on drug-related crime. *Critical Social Policy, 27*(1), 77–99. doi:10.1177/0261018307072208

Stevens, A. (2011). *Drugs, crime and public health: The political economy of drug policy*. Abingdon, UK: Routledge.

Stevens, A., Trace, M., & Bewley-Taylor, D. (2005). *Reducing drug related crime: An overview of the global evidence*. Beckley Foundation Drug Policy Programme, Report Five. Retrieved from https://beckleyfoundation.org/wp-content/uploads/2016/04/BF_Report_05.pdf

Tauri, J. M., & Webb, R. (2012). A critical appraisal of responses to Māori offending. *The International Indigenous Policy Journal, 3*(4), 1–16. doi:10.18584/iipj.2012.3.4.5

Taylor, S. (2008). Outside the outsiders: Media representations of drug use. *Probation Journal, 55*(4), 369–387. doi:10.1177/0264550508096493

UNODC (United Nations Office on Drugs and Crime). (2017). *World drug report 2017*. Retrieved from https://www.unodc.org/wdr2017/index.html

UNODC (United Nations Office on Drugs and Crime). (2019). *World drug report 2019*. Retrieved from https://wdr.unodc.org/wdr2019/prelaunch/WDR19_Booklet_2_DRUG_DEMAND.pdf

Walton, S. (2001). *Out of it: A cultural history of intoxication*. London, UK: Hamish Hamilton.

Webb, R. (2009). Māori, Pacific peoples and the social construction of crime statistics. *MAI Review, 3*, 1–4. Retrieved from https://ndhadeliver.natlib.govt.nz/delivery/DeliveryManagerServlet?dps_pid=FL1479483

Werb, D., Rowell, G., Guyatt, G., Kerr, T., Montaner, J., & Wood, E. (2011). Effect of drug law enforcement on drug market violence: A systematic review. *International Journal of Drug Policy, 22*(2), 87–94. doi:10.1016/j.drugpo.2011.02.002

Wilkins, C., Prasad, J., Romeo, J. S., & Rychert, M. (2017). *Recent trends in illegal drug use in New Zealand, 2006–2016: Findings from the Illicit Drug Monitoring System*. Auckland, New Zealand: Social and Health Outcomes Research and Evaluation (SHORE), College of Health, Massey University. Retrieved from https://static1.squarespace.com/static/59152c88b8a79bdb0e644f2a/t/5aea1fad88251bcbe3817dfc/1525292989357/IDMS+report+2016.pdf

6

Sexual Violence
The Logic of Patriarchy

Jan Jordan

> *From seduction to rape, from rape to seduction, an easy and endless patriarchal loop.*
> —Taslitz, 1999, p. 57

Rape is arguably the most complex and challenging of all crimes. It is one of the most serious offences on our statute books, yet also the least often reported to police. And despite growing social movements and increased media coverage, myths and falsehoods still mask its realities.

Until 1985, rape in Aotearoa New Zealand was defined exclusively as penetration of a vagina by a penis, so was restricted to heterosexual acts performed by a man against a woman. This definition failed to recognise the use of other sexually assaultive objects (such as fingers or bottles), or the penetration of other orifices (such as the mouth or anus), so failed to recognise the possibilities of men being raped or women being sexual aggressors. Feminist lobbying, supported by Institute of Criminology research (Young, 1983), highlighted such problems with how rape was responded to within the justice system, and this led to legislative change. The 1985 changes created one umbrella term, 'sexual violation', divided into two categories: 'rape', as previously defined, and 'unlawful sexual connection', covering all other forms (Sullivan, 1986). The criminal penalties for both were made the same to signify that each could be similarly injurious to victims. Legal changes also removed what had previously been a husband's automatic defence to allegations of rape made by his wife (Jordan, 2004). This was viewed as a radical move by some, one challenging a major cornerstone of gender inequality – no longer did marriage give men what effectively amounted to a licence to rape their wives.

At the time of this book's publication, these legal changes have been in effect for only 35 years. This is but the blink of an eye when viewed in the context of the long history of patriarchal thinking that has shaped the structures and institutions of contemporary societies. In this chapter I begin by sketching the history of rape, arguing that we cannot fully understand sexual violence today without an appreciation of its past. The ways in which the history of rape reflects the history of women under patriarchy will be explored through five key themes: (1) the act of possession, (2) the power of control, (3) male entitlement, (4) the objectification of women's bodies, and (5) the silencing of women's voices. The overall argument attests that, while rape laws may have changed, the culture and attitudes reinforcing and condoning acts of rape have not. The chapter concludes with a call for persons of all gender identities to challenge the beliefs and practices that perpetuate the high levels of sexual violence that continue to exist, and to work together to prevent rape.

Before continuing, I need to clarify that I will focus here on *women's* experiences of rape. The reasons for this emphasis stem from the high prevalence of women as rape victims in tandem with the even higher prevalence of men as rape offenders. I acknowledge the growing awareness of adult male sexual victimisation as well as the increased risks of rape faced by members of gender-minority groups. The critical theoretical approach I apply here recognises the structural gender inequalities within which all acts of sexual violence occur, and that patriarchy's legacy is felt more widely than the limitations of this chapter allow room to explore.

PATRIARCHY

Researchers largely agree that at least since prehistorical times virtually all societies have been defined by gender hierarchies that placed women in a subordinate position to men (Bennett, 2006; Lerner, 1986). Women's inferior status was underlined in Adrienne Rich's definition of patriarchy, which she described as a 'familial-social, ideological, political system... in which the female is everywhere subsumed under the male' (as cited in Eisenstein, 1983, p. 5).

Radical feminist thinkers of the 1970s women's movement applied the concept of patriarchy when seeking to explain the ubiquity of women's social inequality and its links with sexual violence (Millett, 1970). Susan Griffin's 1971 article 'Rape: The All-American Crime' maintained that 'rape is not an isolated act that can be rooted out from patriarchy without ending patriarchy itself' (Griffin, 1975, p. 39). The growing revelation of how common experiences of rape were for women fuelled anger over both its incidence and the societal tolerance that accompanied it. Up to that point, popular discourses around rape had framed it largely from male perspectives, legitimating rape as an inevitable outcome arising from forceful male sexual urges (Franklin, 1984) and blaming women's allegedly inviting behaviours (Amir, 1967). As the silence surrounding rape was broken, it became less tenable to maintain the view that rape was a rare event perpetrated by oversexed, mentally disturbed strangers. Now that women were speaking out, the picture was broadening to include all manner of men connected in all kinds of ways to those they victimised. The implicit question within this realisation was: how can we make sense of an act this terrible being so overwhelmingly common?

Terms such as patriarchy, sexism, and misogyny were useful as feminists grappled to name and understand the prevalence of men's violence against women (Brownmiller, 1999; Griffin, 1975). Social resistance to feminism encouraged a retreat from using such confronting terms, and, as gains were made in gender equality, some conservatives maintained we now lived in a post-patriarchal, post-feminist era. Such optimism has recently been questioned as wave after wave of revelations of sexual violence became public, #MeToo being the most high-profile example (Keller et al., 2018).

As the twenty-first century progresses, recognition of patriarchy's cultural embeddedness and relevance to understanding violence against women has had a resurgence (Hunnicutt, 2009). Whereas once some men reacted as if women using the term 'patriarchy' were accusing individual men of their personal oppression (Johnson, 1997), understanding its systemic nature now enables greater recognition of its role in shaping contemporary gender relations. In describing this, Allan Johnson (1997) points out:

> To live in a patriarchal culture is to learn what's expected of us as men and women, the rules that regulate punishment and reward based on how we behave and appear. These rules range from laws that require men to fight in wars not of their own choosing to customary expectations that mothers will provide child care, or that when a woman shows sexual interest in a man or merely smiles or acts friendly, she gives up her right to say no and control her own body (p. 86).

The related concept of misogyny has also made a comeback; depictions of it as an individual psychological malaise are challenged in favour of recognising it as 'a natural and central manifestation of patriarchal ideology' (Manne, 2018, p. 21). Likewise the term 'rape culture' has reappeared as a more universally accepted shorthand for the ways in which rape is normalised within our society (Harding, 2015). To better understand how rape is responded to in the current climate, the next section provides a brief history of the origins of our rape laws.

PATRIARCHAL THINKING AND RAPE

The earliest laws on rape were designed to right a wrong committed by one man against another man (Brownmiller, 1999). Since the woman was not viewed as a person in her own right, she could not be recognised as the victim (Clark & Lewis, 1977). It was the man who owned her – her father or her husband – who had been wronged. His property had been interfered with, its value reduced, and he was the injured party. This is not simply a curious historical relic; it is a window enabling us to see how the history of rape illustrates the logic of patriarchy.

The hierarchy of power that placed men in positions of dominance over women circumscribed the lives of women in profound ways. Men held a monopoly on political and legal power, resulting in the dominance of male subjectivities in our laws and institutional structures (Bennett, 2006). Male control extended from public to private spheres, with violence towards wives accepted as a necessary means for keeping them under control (Faith, 1993). Explanations for rape typically drew on notions developed from criminology and sexology emphasising the 'naturalness' of male force and female compliance: 'Rooted in the sexual instinct of women we find a delight in roughness, violence, pain and danger' (Ellis, 1948, p. 95, as cited in Gavey, 2019, p. 19).

An inherent suspicion of women's voices prevailed (Taslitz, 1999). Women who accused men of rape had long been depicted as liars, with Chief Justice Hale's edict from 1736 enduring for 250 years in the form of a 'corroboration warning' to jurors to bear in mind the frequency of false rape accusations before determining a man's guilt or innocence (Burt, 1991; Easteal, 1998).

Such beliefs and practices were common when the protest movements of the 1960s and the human rights movements they inspired erupted on to the social landscape. One important development for women involved the spawning of consciousness-raising groups which challenged the social isolation that had dominated the postwar expansion of suburbia (Dann, 1985; Gavey, 2019). The silence surrounding rape began to be broken, exposing patriarchal beliefs that had persisted for centuries. The next sections focus on five strands of patriarchal thinking, examining the thought processes involved, and illustrating each with specific examples drawn from New Zealand rape cases.

The act of possession – 'You're mine'

As a woman owned and possessed by her husband, historically a wife was expected to be submissive at all times (Easteal, 1998). The notion of women being men's property leaves its legacy today. In contemporary Western marriages, a father may still walk his daughter down the aisle to 'give' her away to the man who will be her husband, and whose surname she will now adopt.

Our laws around marital rape reflect this notion of wives 'belonging' to men. For 250 years European, American, and Australasian courts followed Hale's (1736, as cited in Bennice & Resick, 2003, p. 229) decree: 'the husband cannot be guilty of a rape committed by himself upon his lawful wife, for by their mutual matrimonial consent and contract the wife have given up herself in this kind unto her husband, which she cannot retract'. Such thinking was reinforced by Blackstone's (1975, as cited in Bennice & Resick, 2003, p. 229) unities theory, which stipulated that '[h]usband and wife are legally one person. The legal existence of the wife is suspended during marriage, incorporated into that of her husband.' As noted earlier, marital rape was not recognised as unlawful until 1985 in New Zealand, and 1991 in Australia and England.

Law changes seldom equate to substantive behavioural changes. Men treating 'their' wives and partners as if they owned them, or believed they should, remains a familiar strand within our society. This has been particularly recognised in research on family violence (Dobash & Dobash, 1992), but less well acknowledged is the reality that a large proportion of the relationships featuring physical violence will also be characterised by sexual violence (Fanslow & Robinson, 2004), with the sexual violence component typically the hardest for victims to disclose.

Example

In 2019 public controversy erupted when the private letters of one of New Zealand's much-loved poets, James K. Baxter, were published. A letter penned in 1960 provoked considerable reaction for its insights into Baxter's sexual relationship with his wife, celebrated Māori poet Jacquie Sturm. He recounted how, when his previous attempts to engage her in sex failed, he managed to succeed through rape: 'Sex relations with wife resumed. This at least gives some common ground to stand on to clear up difficulties. Achieved by rape. . . . She seems ten times happier in herself. But it looks as if each new act will have to repeat the rape pattern.' He also noted: 'In the act she can and does co-operate once it has begun,' and wondered if men tried too hard to be civilised, 'whereas our wives secretly equate love and violence' (Matthews, 2019, p. 12).

A woman was prompted by the publicity to write her own account of what she could now name as a rape incident experienced when visiting Baxter's Whanganui commune in her youth (Lewis, 2019). Other accounts suggest she may have been one of many (Matthews, 2019). In an earlier letter from 1958, Baxter referred to his 'total inability to keep my fly buttoned' and 'a tendency to rape most hostesses at most parties I went to', adding that these problems 'made life at home impossible' (as cited in Matthews, 2019, p. 12). Finding life at home 'impossible' motivated Baxter to rape his wife, the woman he felt sexually entitled to possess without guilt. Jacquie Sturm's great-grandson commented he was 'sickened' about the letters, adding: 'The letters confirm Baxter as a deeply sexist and patriarchal figure, which can now no longer be ignored or brushed off in deference to his reputation or his literature. . . . Rape is rape. It wasn't acceptable then, or now' (McDonald, 2019, para. 22). His comments implicitly recognise that marital rape not being recognised in law as a crime at the time in no way absolves Baxter of acting as if her owned her.

The power of control – 'I can make you'

The issue of consent typically lies centre-stage in rape allegations. Our existing laws place the onus of proof on the alleged victim, who must demonstrate her lack of consent to a court. Did she say no? Did she mean no? Did she fight back? How hard did she fight? This emphasis places her behaviour under scrutiny while the different acts used against her by the offender remain less visible, unexamined.

There are many tools men can use to make a woman do what they want. These include the exertion of what is often their superior strength to pin a woman down and render her rape-able. Having two or more guys present increases the chances of 'success' further. Threatening to maim or kill her, or her children or others close to her, is also a favoured way of securing her 'co-operation'. Using alcohol or other drugs to make her 'easy' is a further popular strategy; penetrating a body already comatose or sleeping even easier. These are some of the more obvious ways in which control can be exerted, with many psychological forms of coercion equally controlling (Stark, 2007).

Consent is a highly contested and problematic concept. Expectations that women should 'just say no' ignore the gendered power differential that exists between men and women in patriarchal societies (Taslitz, 1999). When an Italian judge ruled that a woman could not have been raped because the tightness of her jeans would have made it impossible for a man to remove them without her co-operation (*Guardian*, 1999), he ignored the fear that may have effectively forced this woman to co-operate. The fear of their attackers has also resulted in women accepting lifts home from men who have just raped them, or agreeing to subsequent sexual acts, with such behaviours gradually being understood and accepted, in some quarters at least, as counter-intuitive evidence (Jordan & Mossman, 2019; Seymour et al., 2014).

Example
Recently, New Zealand cricketer Scott Kuggeleijn stood trial following allegations that he had raped a young woman he met at a bar. She referred to heavy drinking and memory loss, and later recalled having texted 'help' to a friend but being too incapacitated to answer a call from that person. She described Kuggeleijn being in her flat and remembered being pinned down while he held her arms above her head as he raped her (Preston, 2016). Accounts from that night by both parties suggest she said no to sex but, after sleeping, he persisted. He said, 'I tried [having sex] twice, like she might have said "no, no" a few times but it wasn't dozens of times' (Duff, 2019a, para. 6). His defence lawyer maintained, 'A reluctant consent is still a consent,' while Kuggeleijn was quoted in court as having told his friend she 'loved penis' and 'was really getting into it' (*New Zealand Herald*, 2017).

The jury at the first trial could not agree to a majority verdict, so a second trial was held, at the end of which Kuggeleijn was declared not guilty. What angered many commentators was the way New Zealand Cricket responded, failing to call this player's behaviour into account and instead lamenting the potential harm such publicity might do to his future career. Cricket broadcaster Nakul Pande spoke out in protest: 'By saying next to nothing to address Kuggeleijn's actions, and continuing to select him, New Zealand Cricket have publicly chosen to either entirely ignore the questions of consent, appropriate sexual behaviour and misogyny, or subordinate them to cricketing concerns' (Pande, 2019).

From what has been published about this case, we can see some of the complexities surrounding consent. The accused believed that his right to determine the sexual outcome outweighed the victim's reluctance and refusals – he kept trying, consistent with definitions of hegemonic masculinity emphasising the importance of male sexual 'success' (Gavey, 2019). She tried to resist, while incapacitated by heavy drunkenness, but was described in court as finally relenting. While, if true, this may muddy legal definitions of consent, it demonstrates a situation of unequal control where the male's subjectivities ultimately were awarded greater recognition.

Masculine entitlement – I need it, I want it, I'll have it

The legacy of women being viewed as belonging to men has been evident also in male attitudes expressing an entitlement to women's bodies. Not only is sex with 'their' woman viewed as men's right, but access to sex per se has been defined as an essential aspect of heterosexual masculine identity (Franklin, 1984). While evolutionists often link this to the pragmatics of procreation and paternity, the theoretical lens of hegemonic masculinity enables identification of the socially constructed ideals surrounding maleness (Connell, 1995; Kimmel, 1993).

The rhetoric of men's compelling sexual needs was historically used to encourage dutiful sex in wives as well as to justify male recourse to prostitutes, mistresses, and concubines. This reflected the double standard of morality that essentially judged sex-seeking males as studs while condemning sex-seeking females as whores. The heterosexual pornography so easily available in contemporary internet society is dominated by recurrent depictions of men sexually 'having' women any time, anywhere, any way the men please (DeKeseredy & Corsianos, 2016). Sex is presented as a conquest, and women the tools men use to demonstrate their masculinity. The following example features a group of young men who, in adopting this approach to sex, raped multiple young women and yet were never held to account.

Example

In November 2013 a media story broke about a group of young Auckland men, calling themselves the 'Roast Busters', who had been boasting on Facebook about how successful they were in getting young women drunk before raping them (Field & Maas, 2013). They named and shamed the girls online, girls as young as 13–14 years old, while the young men were typically 16–18 years old. During the media furore this case provoked, many commentators raised questions about why these girls were not at home and why they were out drinking, with few asking why these young men chose to sexually exploit girls made vulnerable by alcohol.

Statements made by the boys indicated they viewed sexual conquest as an essential feature of heteronormative masculinity. One claimed: 'My first actual roast for the Roast Busters was bad, it was fun, I felt like the man' (*Newshub*, 2013). Another insisted the girls gravitated towards them like sexual magnets. He said: 'A true roast is where you know you are going there intentionally to roast this female. We don't choose a roast, the roast chooses us. We have girls hitting us up to "hang out with us". They know what we're like; they know what they're in for' (*Newshub*, 2013, para. 9).

The arrogance and sexual entitlement displayed by the Roast Busters reflects more normative attitudes consistent with contemporary masculinity. Researchers Michael Flood and Bob Pease concluded, after reviewing youth studies conducted in the United States, Britain, and New Zealand:

> For many boys and girls, sexual harassment is pervasive, male aggression is normalized, there is constant pressure among boys to behave in sexually aggressive ways, girls are routinely objectified, a sexual double standard polices girls' sexual and intimate involvements, and girls are compelled to accommodate male needs and desires in negotiating their sexual relations (Flood & Pease, 2009, p. 129).

Linked to the notion of male sexual entitlement are notions of objectification and silencing, evident in the ideal woman being the silent object who brokers no resistance. The next two sections explore these complementary concepts.

The objectification of women – 'Any body/hole will do'

The social process of turning a subject into an object serves to dehumanise the subject and to emphasise the object's use value. The objectification of women's bodies contributes to an environment within which how a woman looks becomes her central defining characteristic – all other accomplishments are secondary. In a curious irony, at the same time as feminist activism has reduced the gender gap in such areas as equal pay and challenged men's use of violence, the role models for young women have become increasingly sexualised. Commentators have asked, is this the new sexual empowerment, or is it the old objectification in twenty-first-century guise?

Feminist media analysts have long drawn attention to gendered differences in 'ways of seeing' (Berger, 1977). Throughout much of Hollywood's film history, movies have been controlled by male directors portraying women primarily as 'eroticized objects' (Deveraux, 1990, p. 341). The notion of the female body existing to be looked at begs the question, looked at by whom? In reflecting on these issues, Ann Kaplan (1986) argued: 'Men do not simply look; their gaze carries with it the power of action and possession that is lacking in the female gaze' (p. 231).

The 'male gaze' (Mulvey, 1975) often operates in tandem with the previous attitudes outlined. Sex work provides a case in point. In some brothels a man views a line-up of women's bodies, selects the one he wants to possess and, licensed through the paying of a fee, has sex with her. Her existence as an object for his sexual pleasure erases the need to consider her subjective experience of their interaction – it is simply irrelevant.

The history of the objectification of women's bodies can be linked in the crudest way to a woman being viewed and valued primarily as a hole awaiting male penetration. Such a perspective reflects social constructions of masculinity that emphasise male conquest over mutual connection (Kimmel, 1993). This notion also links to accounts of women's bodies being viewed as interchangeable, their individual subjectivities at best secondary, at worst irrelevant, to their sexual use value. In the following example the objectifying of the victim's body precipitated acts that left her deeply shamed and humiliated – until she challenged her attacker in court.

Example
In 2019 a Hawke's Bay jury found two men accused of rape, Jason Trembath and Joshua Pauling, not guilty by a 11–1 verdict. The victim in this case had not reported to the police. She had been so intoxicated on the night in question that she had little recall of the events until three months later when police showed her a photo. It featured Pauling straddling her, smiling as he performed a sexual act while giving a 'Hang 10' signal. When shown this image, she began shaking uncontrollably and was unable to manage being interviewed by detectives until the next day. The image was new to her, but not to the many men who had already viewed it. For three months it had been displayed on the Taradale Cricket Club's premier team's closed Facebook page (Sharpe, 2019). Trembath had also sent it to work colleagues and other cricket friends (McLeod, 2019). It was only when questioned about a host of indecent assaults performed by Trembath on other women that finally one cricket club member decided to front up about the photograph. The jury were not told about these, for fear of prejudice. Only after declaring the men not guilty did they learn that Trembath had pleaded guilty to 11 charges of indecently assaulting women joggers. In the victim's words, 'I was asked about my high heels and how my bodysuit could be undone easily to have sex but Trembath couldn't be portrayed as someone who had sexually assaulted 11 women' (Duff, 2019b).

The objectification of this young woman was evident in multiple ways. They used her body as a sexual prop for male bonding on the night, before bragging about their exploits to male peers. It was not only Trembath and Pauling who objectified this woman, but all the men who viewed this image and said nothing.

The belief that women's bodies exist for male pleasure is a message regularly endorsed in contemporary media forms. Pornography depicts a changing array of anonymous women whose worth is primarily defined as receptacles for men. This includes acts of oral penetration when the female throat is stuffed too full of maleness to speak: a symbolic metaphor for the silencing of women.

The silencing of women – 'Shut up, bitch'

Accompanying the objectification of the body has been the silencing of women's voices. In the context of rape there is a long history of women being silenced in order to protect men from accusation or, should a woman report her perpetrator, to render her words unbelievable (Jordan, 2004; Kelly, 2010; Wheatcroft & Walklate, 2014). When research on false rape complaints is considered, the findings prove the belief that most women lie about rape to be no more than a myth; unfortunately, as observed by Brown and Horvath (2009), myths such as these 'become part of a self-supporting system whereby the absence of convictions supports the belief that women falsify claims or men's behaviour does not justify the charge' (p. 332).

Dismissing women's rape allegations as lies and false testimony remains commonplace today, as evidenced in former US president Donald Trump's responses to his many accusers. To deflect attention from the nature and content of the women's accusations, he has sought to silence them through ridicule and shame (Manne, 2018). The example below involves the most high-profile rape case in New Zealand's recent history, and demonstrates some of the many difficulties women face in struggling to have their allegations of rape spoken and believed, particularly when the perpetrators are men of status.

Example
When a teenager was raped by three older police officers, the latter relied on her silence ensuring they would get away with it. They also relied on the silence of a 'bro-code' protecting them from being narked on by other police. Years later, when Louise Nicholas eventually took these men to trial, she experienced further silencing processes (Nicholas, 2007). On the first day in court, one of the accused arrived in full police regalia, an overt attempt to speak his status to the jury while diminishing hers (Dewes, 2006). The defendants were permitted to produce character witnesses attesting to their integrity; she, by contrast, was portrayed as 'a maggot-lying bitch' (*New Zealand Herald*, 2007a). The jury were permitted to hear only an edited account of relevant events – they were not told that two of the accused were already serving prison terms for very similar rapes, nor made privy to the knowledge that multiple cases existed involving further victims (*New Zealand Herald*, 2007b). The not-guilty verdict that came at the end of the trial was expected to silence the victim forever. Three strong women turned this outcome around: Prime Minister Helen Clark called for a Commission of Inquiry into Police Conduct; Dame Margaret Bazley (2007) conducted it and mandated a series of changes for New Zealand Police to adhere to; and Louise Nicholas herself chose to work with the police and became an advocate for other victim/survivors of rape. None of these women would be silenced.

PATRIARCHY IS NOT DEAD

The five themes explored above all derive from the patriarchal thinking emerging from centuries of structural gender inequalities. While feminist resistance and activism have challenged these inequalities, particularly since the 1970s, the gains won have benefited individual women but not changed the fundamental structure of gendered power.

In the past decade, public awareness of the high prevalence of sexual violence has grown. Data from the New Zealand Crime Victims Survey (NZCVS) 2018 indicates 192,500 incidents of sexual violence occurred in a 12-month period, with 80 per cent of the adult victims being women (NZCVS, 2018). Rape today is recognised as the most under-reported of all crimes, the reasons for victim reluctance being many and varied (Bourke, 2007; Kelly et al., 2005). Prominent factors include high levels of victim self-blame and shame along with fear of the consequences, as well as fear and mistrust of the justice system (Kingi & Jordan, 2009). Such fear is not misplaced. The majority of those who report their rapes to the police find their case proceeds no further than the investigative stage, with the evidential threshold set too high and/or their lack of credibility viewed as a barrier to successful prosecution (Jordan & Mossman, 2019). For the small numbers whose cases do proceed to trial, their experiences of court processes are degrading and harmful (Kingi & Jordan, 2009), amounting to what one Australian court observer termed a form of 'state-sanctioned violation' (van de Zandt, 1998, p. 125). The chances of seeing their attacker convicted are abysmally low – a New Zealand study determined that only 13 per cent of reported rapes resulted in the offender's conviction, and then most usually as a result of a guilty plea (Triggs et al., 2009). Juries, it seems, persist in believing false accusations are rampant and good men the victims of vexatious liars.

Hopes have been expressed that the tide is turning. The growing popularity of feminism and young women's recent embracing of it using social media have been acclaimed by many as positive digital activism (Keller et al., 2018; Powell & Henry, 2017), but can by no means be interpreted as signifying patriarchy is now dead. The hate speech and vitriolic attacks directed at feminist bloggers and tweeters soon put the lie to that theory (Powell & Henry, 2017), with rape threats commonly uttered by those who feel under threat (Keller et al., 2018) and the most extreme anger expressed in shooting rampages (Manne, 2018).

CONCLUSION

In this chapter I have argued that the history of the crime of rape is a microcosm for the history of women under patriarchy. It should also be the incentive for women, men, and all gender identities to work together to dismantle rape culture and the constraints of traditional sexual stereotyping. While beyond the scope of this chapter to explore, masculinity under patriarchy is a straitjacket of oppression confining men's emotionality in ways similar to how Victorian corsets constricted women's bodies. Such constraints can silence male rape victims (Javaid, 2016); similarly, the dominant heterosexual binary within patriarchy obscures recognition of the high rates of sexual victimisation experienced by those of minority gender-identities (Kingi & Jordan, 2009). While redefining rape laws and achieving legal reforms are important goals to strive for, success in achieving them will always depend on the extent to which equality, respect, and justice are the dominant governing principles throughout a society. For Aotearoa New Zealand, where the more recent history of colonisation sits within the history of patriarchy, the realities of equality, respect, and justice may seem like distant and elusive goals. Ensuring we keep these in our vision, however, will keep us on the path to true gender equality for all, where no one needs to exert power over others through the crime of rape.

STUDY QUESTIONS

- Explain how, and in what ways, patriarchy remains socially embedded.
- Identify the contexts within which women's voices about sexual violence are silenced.
- In what ways are women's bodies objectified in contemporary media forms?

FURTHER READING

Gavey, N. (2019). *Just sex? The cultural scaffolding of rape*. Hove, UK: Routledge.

Manne, K. (2018). *Down girl. The logic of misogyny*. New York, NY: Oxford University Press.

Powell, A., & Henry, N. (2017). *Sexual violence in a digital age*. London, UK: Palgrave Macmillan.

REFERENCES

Amir, M. (1967). Victim precipitated forcible rape. *Journal of Criminology, Criminal Law and Police, 58*(4), 493–502. doi:10.2307/1141908

Bazley, Dame M. (2007). *Report of the Commission of Inquiry into Police Conduct (Vol. 1)*. Wellington, New Zealand: Commission of Inquiry into Police Conduct. Retrieved from https://www.parliament.nz/resource/0000055162

Bennett, J. (2006). *History matters: Patriarchy and the challenge of feminism*. Philadelphia, PA: University of Pennsylvania Press.

Bennice, J., & Resick, P. (2003). Marital rape: History, research, and practice. *Trauma, Violence, and Abuse, 4*(3), 228–246. doi:10.1177/1524838003004003003

Berger, J. (1977). *Ways of seeing*. London, UK: British Broadcasting Corporation & Penguin Books.

Bourke, J. (2007). *Rape: Sex, violence, history*. Emeryville, CA: Shoemaker & Hoard.

Brown, J., & Horvath, M. (2009). Do you believe her and is it real rape? In M. Horvath & J. Brown (Eds.), *Rape: Challenging contemporary thinking* (pp. 325–342). Cullompton, UK: Willan Publishing.

Brownmiller, S. (1999). *In our time: Memoir of a revolution*. New York, NY: Dial Press, Random House.

Burt, M. (1991). Rape myths and acquaintance rape. In A. Parrot & L. Bechhofer (Eds.), *Acquaintance rape: The hidden crime* (pp. 26–40). New York, NY: John Wiley.

Clark, L., & Lewis, D. (1977). *Rape: The price of coercive sexuality*. Toronto, Canada: The Women's Press.

Connell, R. (1995). *Masculinities*. Berkeley, CA: University of California Press.

Dann, C. (1985). *Up from under: Women and liberation in New Zealand 1970–1985*. Wellington, New Zealand: Allen & Unwin/Port Nicholson Press.

DeKeseredy, W., & Corsianos, M. (2016). *Violence against women in pornography*. New York, NY: Routledge.

Devereaux, M. (1990). Oppressive texts, resisting readers and the gendered spectator: The new aesthetics. *The Journal of Aesthetics and Art Criticism, 48*(4), 337–347. doi:10.2307/431571

Dewes, H. (2006, April 1). From teen tearaway to top cop. *Dominion Post*.

Dobash, R. E., & Dobash, R. P. (1992). *Women, violence and social change*. London, UK: Routledge.

Duff, M. (2019a, January 18). NZ Cricket should end its shameful silence on Scott Kuggeleijn. *Stuff*. Retrieved from https://www.stuff.co.nz/sport/cricket/109964652/nz-cricket-should-end-its-shameful-silence-on-scott-kuggeleijn

Duff, M. (2019b, May 13). Is our rape trial system fair? *Dominion Post*.

Easteal, P. (1998). Rape in marriage: Has the licence lapsed? In P. Easteal (Ed.), *Balancing the scales: Rape, law reform and Australian culture*. Leichhardt, Sydney, Australia: Federation Press.

Eisenstein, H. (1983). *Contemporary feminist thought*. Boston, MA: G. K. Hall.

Faith, K. (1993). *Unruly women: The politics of confinement and resistance*. Vancouver, Canada: Press Gang Publishers.

Fanslow, J., & Robinson, E. (2004). Violence against women in New Zealand: Prevalence and health consequences. *New Zealand Medical Journal, 117*(1206), 1–12. Retrieved from https://researchspace.auckland.ac.nz/bitstream/handle/2292/4673/15570342.pdf?sequence=1

Field, M., & Maas, A. (2013, November 7). Rape complaint against Roast Busters in 2011. *Dominion Post*.

Flood, M., & Pease, B. (2009). Factors influencing attitudes to violence against women. *Trauma, Violence, and Abuse, 10*(2), 125–142. doi:10.1177/1524838009334131

Franklin, C. (1984). *The changing definition of masculinity*. New York, NY: Plenum.

Gavey, N. (2019). *Just sex? The cultural scaffolding of rape*. Hove, UK: Routledge.

Griffin, S. (1975). Rape: The all-American crime. In L. G. Schultz (Ed.), *Rape victimology* (pp. 19–39). Springfield, IL: Charles C. Thomas Publications.

Guardian. (1999, February 16). Women when in Rome. . . Retrieved from https://www.theguardian.com/world/1999/feb/16/gender.uk

Harding, K. (2015). *Asking for it: The alarming rise of rape culture and what we can do about it*. Boston, MA: Da Capo Press.

Hunnicutt, G. (2009). Varieties of patriarchy and violence against women: Resurrecting 'Patriarchy' as a theoretical tool. *Violence Against Women, 15*(5), 553–573. doi:10.1177/1077801208331246

Javaid, A. (2016). Male rape, stereotypes, and unmet needs: Hindering recovery, perpetuating silence. *Violence and Gender, 3*(1), 7–13. doi:10.1089/vio.2015.0039

Johnson, A. (1997). *The gender knot: Unraveling our patriarchal legacy*. Philadelphia, PA: Temple University Press.

Jordan, J. (2004). *The word of a woman? Police, rape and belief*. Houndmills, UK: Palgrave Macmillan.

Jordan, J., & Mossman, E. (2019). *Police sexual violence file analysis report: Women rape and the police investigation process*. Wellington, New Zealand: Institute of Criminology, Victoria University of Wellington.

Kaplan, E. A. (1986). Is the gaze male? In M. Pearsall (Ed.), *Women and values: Readings in recent feminist philosophy* (pp. 230–241). Belmont, CA: Wadsworth.

Keller, J., Mendes, K., & Ringrose, K. (2018). Speaking 'unspeakable things': Documenting digital feminist responses to rape culture. *Journal of Gender Studies, 27*(1), 22–36. doi:10.1080/09589236.2016.1211511

Kelly, L. (2010). The (in)credible words of women: False allegations in European rape research. *Violence Against Women, 16*(12), 1345–1355. doi:10.1177/1077801210387748

Kelly, L., Lovett, J., & Regan, L. (2005). *A gap or a chasm? Attrition in reported rape cases*. Home Office Research Study 293. London, UK: Home Office Research, Development and Statistics Directorate. Retrieved from https://www.politieacademie.nl/kennisenonderzoek/kennis/mediatheek/PDF/45316.pdf

Kimmel, M. S. (1993). Invisible masculinity. *Society, 30*(6), 28–35. Retrieved from https://link.springer.com/content/pdf/10.1007/BF02700272.pdf

Kingi, V., & Jordan, J. (with T. Moeke-Maxwell & P. Fairbairn-Dunlop). (2009). *Responding to sexual violence: Pathways to recovery*. Wellington, New Zealand: Ministry of Women's Affairs. Retrieved from https://women.govt.nz/sites/public_files/pathways-to-recovery-pdf_0.pdf

Lerner, G. (1986). *The creation of patriarchy*. Oxford, UK: Oxford University Press.

Lewis, R. (2019, April 20). The darkness and the light. *Dominion Post*, p. 8.

Manne, K. (2018). *Down girl: The logic of misogyny*. New York, NY: Oxford University Press.

Matthews, P. (2019, April 20). Baxter and rape: Now what? *Dominion Post*, p. 12.

McDonald, J. (2019, February 15). My nana, Jacquie Sturm. *Spinoff*. Retrieved from https://thespinoff.co.nz/books/15-02-2019/baxter-week-my-nana-jacqui-sturm/

McLeod, R. (2019, May 17). Club has to wear its tolerance for intimate photo on Facebook. *Dominion Post*.

Millett, K. (1970). *Sexual politics*. New York, NY: Ballantine Books.

Mulvey, L. (1975). Visual pleasure and narrative cinema. *Screen, 16*(3), 6–18. doi:10.1093/screen/16.3.6

Newshub. (2013, November 3). Facebook teen sex shaming exposed. Retrieved from https://www.newshub.co.nz/nznews/facebook-teen-sex-shaming-exposed–2013110317

New Zealand Crime and Victims Survey (NZCVS). (2018). *Key findings*. Wellington, New Zealand: Ministry of Justice. Retrieved from https://www.justice.govt.nz/justice-sector-policy/research-data/nzcvs/

New Zealand Herald. (2007a, March 4). Police sex case: 'Why would I lie about this, why would I make this up?' Retrieved from https://www.nzherald.co.nz/nz/news/article.cfm?c_id=1&objectid=10426900

New Zealand Herald. (2007b, August 11). The Louise Nicholas saga – out of the shadows. Retrieved from https://www.nzherald.co.nz/nz/news/article.cfm?c_id=1&objectid=10457065

New Zealand Herald. (2017, February 21). Scott Kuggeleijn rape trial: Alleged victim enjoyed the sex, cricketer tells court. Retrieved from https://www.nzherald.co.nz/nz/scott-kuggeleijn-rape-trial-alleged-victim-enjoyed-the-sex-cricketer-tells-court/VE453RIXVGPVFY5Z7RQF4QYGRU/

Nicholas, L. (2007). *Louise Nicholas: My story*. Auckland, New Zealand: Random House.

Pande, N. (2019, October 30). *New Zealand's silence on Scott Kuggeleijn is deafening*. [Blog post]. Retrieved from https://www.nakulpande.com/blog/new-zealand-silence-on-scott-kuggeleijn-defeaning

Powell, A., & Henry, N. (2017). *Sexual violence in a digital age*. London, UK: Palgrave Macmillan.

Preston, N. (2016, July 26). Northern districts cricketer's trial: Complainant tells court she has lost friends over process. *New Zealand Herald*. Retrieved from https://www.nzherald.co.nz/nz/news/article.cfm?c_id=1&objectid=11681703

Seymour, F., Blackwell, S., Calvert, S., & McLean, B. (2014). Counterintuitive expert psychological evidence in child sexual abuse trials in New Zealand. *Psychiatry, Psychology and Law, 21*(4), 511–522. doi:10.1080/13218719.2013.839930

Sharpe. M. (2019, May 11). Rape complainant will never forget shock of seeing the Facebook photo that triggered trial. *Stuff*. Retrieved from https://www.stuff.co.nz/national/crime/112617156/rape-complainant-will-never-forget-shock-of-seeing-the-facebook-photo-that-triggered-trial

Stark, E. (2007). *Coercive control: How men entrap women in personal life*. New York, NY: Oxford University Press.

Sullivan, Ginette (1986). *Rape crisis handbook: Counselling for sexual abuse*. Wellington, New Zealand: Rape Crisis Centre.

Taslitz, A. E. (1999). *Rape and the culture of the courtroom*. New York, NY: New York University Press.

Triggs, S., Mossman, E., Jordan, J., & Kingi, V. (2009). *Responding to sexual violence: Attrition in the New Zealand criminal justice system*. Wellington, New Zealand: Ministry of Women's Affairs. Retrieved from https://women.govt.nz/sites/public_files/responding%20to%20sexual%20violence%20attrition-pdf.pdf

van de Zandt, P. (1998). Heroines of fortitude. In P. Easteal (Ed.), *Balancing the scales: Rape, law reform and Australian culture* (pp. 124–142). Leichhardt, Sydney, Australia: Federation Press.

Wheatcroft, J., & Walklate, S. (2014). Thinking differently about 'false allegations' in cases of rape. *International Journal of Criminology and Sociology, 3*, 239–248. doi:10.6000/1929–4409.2014.03.20

Young, W. (1983). *Rape study: A discussion of law and practice (Vol. I)*. Wellington, New Zealand: Institute of Criminology and Department of Justice.

7

Responding to Intimate Partner Violence
Connecting Law, Language, and Supports

Ang Jury, Natalie Thorburn, and Ruth Weatherall

Clare met her abuser when she was 19. She described the first few months of her relationship as 'idyllic, everything you would have wanted or hoped for'. Within a few weeks, however, he started to control whom she spent time with, and insisted on having access to her mobile phone and her computer. When he discovered she had talked to friends about social events that did not include him, he became enraged and demanded that she not go out without him. A few weeks after that, he hit her for the first time. He apologised and appeared genuinely mortified at his behaviour, telling her she was the most important part of his life and that he would never hurt her again. Two months later, the physical abuse resumed. This time, he blamed her for the violence, and cut off her access to shared bank accounts. He accused her of cheating and demanded that she quit her job to 'prove' she was not being unfaithful with someone at work. He digitally monitored her whereabouts, and in one of the subsequent episodes of violence he strangled her. She survived and tried to leave, but found that the attacks were too unpredictable and the frequency of unwanted contact from him after leaving exhausting and distressing. She applied for a protection order, but he contested it, and it was eventually declined after she lost all her savings on lawyers' fees. She returned to the relationship.

Unfortunately, Clare's story is far from unusual. Family violence is a widespread issue in Aotearoa New Zealand. In fact, the rates of family violence are generally acknowledged to be one of the highest of all OECD countries (Kahui & Snively, 2014). This chapter gives an overview of family violence (specifically intimate partner violence) in New Zealand, and explores some of the complexities in working toward a robust criminal justice response. First, the chapter introduces family violence and discusses what family is, who is a victim, what the individual, social, and economics implications are, and how society has responded to the issue. Next, the chapter outlines the ways that lawmakers have created a framework for the criminal justice system to respond to family violence. The chapter concludes by exploring some contemporary issues facing the criminal justice system, helping services, and victims when laws and policies are put into practice.

OVERVIEW OF FAMILY VIOLENCE AND INTIMATE PARTNER VIOLENCE

As a term, 'family violence' includes a range of different types of violent relationships, such as intimate partner violence (IPV), child maltreatment and neglect, and elder abuse. All forms of violence have significant harmful consequences for individuals, families, and whānau. This chapter focuses on forms of family violence that are perpetrated against an intimate partner (any person with whom the victim has been in a romantic or sexual relationship). Intimate partner violence is commonly thought of in terms of physical and sexual violence, such as hitting or strangling a partner, or rape. However, helping agencies and justice actors now recognise that emotional and psychological abuse are just as, if not more, common (Fanslow & Robinson, 2011). Examples of emotional or psychological abuse include repeatedly telling a partner they are worthless, unlovable, or a bad partner or parent. Some helpers are even recognising spiritual or economic abuse as part of IPV. Spiritual abuse can include stopping someone from practising their religion, or belittling their beliefs. Economic abuse includes taking someone's money or stopping them from going to work (Jury et al., 2017).

There are a number of different perspectives on the causes of IPV (Ali & Naylor, 2013). An important one emphasises the role of gender stereotypes (Diemer, 2015; Johnson, 2005). Neave (2015) explains this by saying IPV's 'causes are deeply embedded in community attitudes about gender, and about what is and what is not legitimate and appropriate between intimate partners and within families' (p. 9). Gender stereotypes influence who is most likely to become a victim or a perpetrator of violence, and which tactics are used to abuse the victim. Although IPV occurs in all types of partnerships, it is overwhelmingly perpetrated by men against women, which is reflected in both police apprehension statistics and in protection order statistics (see the New Zealand Family Violence Clearinghouse [NZFVC] site for latest data). Of the IPV-related deaths between 2009 and 2015, 98 per cent involved a situation in which a woman was the primary victim of a male partner (Family Violence Death Review Committee [FVDRC], 2016). In spite of these findings, there has been criticism of the role of gender in IPV (Ali & Naylor, 2013). However, the FVDRC (2017) notes that when intent and magnitude of the violence are considered, gender stereotypes do play an important role. Accordingly, understanding the role of gender in IPV is important for all justice actors.

Who is a victim of IPV?

Although many people have stereotypes in their minds about who is likely to be impacted by IPV, it affects people across all income brackets, educational levels, and ethnicities. Women are particularly at risk: one in three ever-partnered women are subject to physical or sexual violence in their lifetime, and one in two experience emotional or psychological abuse (Fanslow & Robinson, 2011). Nevertheless, there are other factors that contribute to an increased likelihood of victimisation. For example, the colonial history of New Zealand has contributed immensely to rates of violence in Māori communities. The violence of colonisation contributed to widespread intergenerational trauma, the introduction of patriarchal belief structures, negative stereotypes, displacement from whenua (land), and disconnection from traditional family structures of whānau, hapū, and iwi in indigenous communities. Balzer and McNeill (1988) describe the harmful transmission of negative beliefs about Māori through colonisation as an 'invasion of Māori consciousness' which undermined mana. The authors also point out that negative gender stereotypes about women were also introduced as part of colonisation; prior to the arrival of Pākehā, wāhine Māori had strong status in the community and were active participants in formal affairs alongside men. Understanding the harmful ongoing effects of colonisation is integral to understanding why Māori are disproportionately more likely to become victims or perpetrators of IPV or family violence. Additional risks exist for people with disabilities, transgender people, older adults, and queer/takatāpui people.

What are the impacts of IPV?

The impacts of intimate partner violence and family violence are immense and wide-reaching in their individual, social, and economic dimensions. These dimensions often intersect to form a pattern of social entrapment, a process through which victims become isolated and fearful (and sometimes even destructive) but are repeatedly met with unhelpful responses from institutions. The constraints to self-determination that victims face may result from coercive control (e.g., not being allowed to be in contact with support people), unresponsive systems (e.g., dismissive or inadequate responses to disclosures), and structural disadvantages (such as racism or ableism). These collective conditions of social entrapment become almost impossible to unravel (FVDRC, 2016; Tolmie et al., 2018). Accordingly, many victims suffer harmful effects on their mental and physical well-being (Krug et al., 2002). Similarly, children are negatively impacted by IPV, particularly as it often co-occurs with child abuse and neglect (Hamby et al., 2010). Some children experience social, developmental, emotional, and behavioural challenges as a result of IPV, which can affect their development and participation in education.

Such individual impacts have negative flow-on effects for society. Intimate partner violence against women acts as a barrier to gender equality, such as by disrupting women's careers. Similarly, there are extensive economic costs associated with family violence; estimates range between $4.1 billion and $7.0 billion annually (Kahui & Snively, 2014). The most significant economic costs relate to addressing or dealing with victims' pain, harm, or death. Moreover, economic costs are associated with particular institutions, such as law enforcement. For instance, in 2016, there were 118,910 family violence investigations by the New Zealand Police, amounting to 41 per cent of frontline police officers' time (NZFVC, 2017). Clearly, the impacts of IPV are extensive and have warranted a sustained response from communities and the government.

What has been the grassroots response to IPV?

In Aotearoa New Zealand, women's refuges and Rape Crisis centres have emerged in response to violence against women since the 1970s, as they have around the world (Htun & Weldon, 2012). Women's movements both provided material support for women, such as shelters or advocacy, and fostered changes in social attitudes and stereotypes about women (Cook, 2011). Māori and Pasifika women have been especially influential in these movements, particularly in terms of raising recognition of how they were affected both by stereotypes about women and colonisation. These Māori and Pasifika activists influenced women's organisations to incorporate Te Tiriti o Waitangi training and to build decolonising practices and structures into their organisations and movements (Huygens, 2001; National Collective of Independent

Women's Refuges Inc. [NCIWRI], 2015). NCIWRI and Te Ohaaki-a-Hine – National Network for Ending Sexual Violence Together, for example, have both adopted a two-whare model and have committed to 'power-sharing' where Māori and Tauiwi (non-Māori) have equal representation and say in how the organisation is run. In this way, these movements have influenced public discussion around the issue and have significantly shaped the legislative response (Else, 1993; NCIWRI, 2015). The legal changes are the focus of the next section of this chapter.

FAMILY VIOLENCE LAW

The first step toward robust legislation against family violence came with the Domestic Protection Act 1982. The Act included non-violence orders (where the perpetrator was required to leave the house for 24 hours) and non-molestation orders (whether the perpetrator was barred from stalking or entering property). However, the legislation was limited to separated couples and did not apply to situations where the couple was living together. Shortly afterward, the Victims of Offences Act 1987 gave victims of violence the rights to health, welfare, and legal assistance (Swarbrick, 2011b). The Domestic Protection Act 1982 was later replaced by the Domestic Violence Act 1995 due to a growing recognition of the shortfalls in police implementation of protection for victims. This new Act included sexual and psychological abuse in the definition of domestic violence, and included perpetrators causing or allowing children to witness abuse as domestic violence (Swarbrick, 2011b). At the time the Act was considered by anti-violence advocates to be a leap of progress as it had more of a focus on consequences for perpetrators. Furthermore, under the 1995 Act, non-violence and non-molestation orders were replaced by protection orders. The latter applied to victims whether or not they were living with the perpetrator, and these orders were automatically permanent until legally challenged (Swarbrick, 2011a), providing significantly longer periods of protection for victims.

The growing recognition among justice actors of the emotional and social harm caused by IPV in the early 2000s led to further legislative changes. The Victims' Rights Act 2002 replaced the Victims of Offences Act. The 2002 Act was further amended in 2014 to strengthen agencies' responsiveness to victims of IPV by granting victims access to victim treatment and services (NZFVC, 2015). The Domestic Violence Act 1995 was also subject to further reform in 2008, giving police the ability to issue short-term safety orders on the spot and strengthening the penalties for breaching a protection order. It is worth noting, however, that these safety orders do not carry a criminal penalty for breaches, which limits their effectiveness. Also in 2008, the Family Violence Death Review Committee was established to identify trends and patterns between family violence deaths and to propose opportunities for intervention. Based on its findings, the committee makes recommendations for improving family violence policy and practice (Health Quality and Safety Commission New Zealand, 2019).

Between 2010 and 2019, another wave of legal reform responded to the modern environment with three key changes. First, the Harmful Digital Communications Act 2015 made non-consensual recording, possession, or distribution of intimate images and video illegal, and criminalised online harassment. Examples include the sharing of nude images or films of sex acts without consent (see Meehan, chapter 8 this volume). Second, the Domestic Violence (Victims' Protection) Act 2018 gave victims of family violence the right to short-term flexible working conditions, and up to 10 days of paid leave to manage the impacts of victimisation. Victims now have the right, for instance, to temporarily vary their work location or hours in order to attend court proceedings, or access help services such as counselling. The third reform, the Family Violence Amendments Act 2018, introduced three new offences: strangulation, assault on a family member, and coercion to marry. The Act also gave police and other justice actors the ability to track repeat offenders and increase their sentences. Additionally, the Family Violence Act 2018, which replaced the previous Domestic Violence Act in July 2019, introduced a large number of changes in an attempt to strengthen helping service responses by increasing co-ordination between these services.

CONTEMPORARY ISSUES

The above section outlined the criminalisation of family violence and tracked the development of legislation that provides the framework for today's criminal justice system. Aotearoa New Zealand evidentially has a well-developed criminal justice framework for responding to physical and sexual abuse in the context of family violence. Despite this significant progress, there continue to be gaps both in the framework itself and in relation to the enactment (the 'on-the-ground' responses) of justice actors. The first relates to the perceived and actual gaps in the legislative framework. The second reflects the complexities of developing a robust response to family violence by the criminal justice system.

Limitations of the criminal justice system

Despite the comprehensive legislation for responding to physical and sexual family violence in New Zealand, many of the behaviours that are included in the scope of family violence are not criminalised. Examples of non-criminalised abusive behaviour include: psychological abuse, economic abuse, and coercive control. Coercive control is a pattern of abusive behaviour that limits a person's freedom and is criminalised in the UK and parts of Australia. While reporting of these forms of violence will strengthen an application for a protection order, acts of stalking, economic abuse, and psychological abuse are all technically legal acts (McEwan et al., 2009). For example, one Women's Refuge client who had left the relationship continued to be subjected to violence from her abusive ex-partner. During this time, her abuser had been relentlessly contacting her in person, over the phone, and via various social media platforms. This was not prosecuted, despite her being able to give evidence of the digital contact, on the basis that the in-person contact was not overtly threatening (and this could not be evidenced). The lack of criminalisation of psychological abuse, economic abuse, and coercive control while a relationship is ongoing and after it has formally ended is a significant gap in the protective legislation.

Advocates argue that decision-making in the criminal justice system needs to be more consistent, such as through granting protection orders where there is coercive control, and applying the penalty for all breaches of such orders (Jury et al., 2017; Jury et al., 2018). The legislation can be strengthened by following the lead of other countries in criminalising non-physical forms of abuse. Current legislation could serve justice actors more effectively if different laws were integrated. For example, coercive control that spans offences under the Crimes Act and the Harmful Digital Communications Act may be more easily addressed if there is greater recognition of the nature of family violence.

Complexities of enacting family violence legislation

Comprehensive family violence legislation does not necessarily lead to New Zealand victims feeling confident to report abuse, nor to any certainty that perpetrators of violence will be justly convicted (Tolmie & Gavey, 2010). There are a number of factors that may prevent victims from seeking help from justice actors, and may likewise prevent the same justice actors adequately working with perpetrators. Many of these factors are related to harmful social attitudes about intimate partner violence, and pervasive gender stereotypes (particularly relating to parenting) that negatively affect women. This section covers two of these complexities in depth: (1) the language used by justice actors in responding to victims, and (2) the support that can be provided to victims of IPV to ensure they can once again participate fully in society.

The legislation provides the framework for justice actors, but doesn't determine how they actually work with victims in practice. Unfortunately, many victims have felt persecuted or dismissed by justice actors and as though adequate justice was never received. Relatedly, family violence remains significantly under-reported, with most acts of IPV never being communicated to the police (Fanslow & Robinson, 2010). One common reason for not reporting violence is that women are afraid of a negative response from justice actors and other institutions, such as their children's schools (Jury et al., 2018; Rhodes et al., 2011; Roguski, 2012). Social workers, family violence specialists, and researchers have noted that the language used by justice actors can inadvertently make victims feel responsible for IPV and for violence happening to their family (Richardson, 2008; Richardson & Wade, 2009). Importantly, these experts have pointed out that when justice actors fail to consider the full context, negative impacts are more likely to occur (Blacklock & Phillips, 2015; Jury et al., 2018).

IPV occurs in a society that is still influenced by outdated and harmful gender stereotypes (National Council of Women New Zealand, 2018). These stereotypes can influence how justice actors and other helping services respond to victims. In an ideal scenario, justice actors and helping services would recognise straightaway that IPV often involves coercive control. The long-term impacts of coercive control mean that victims can find it difficult to leave a relationship with abusers because abusers make victims feel dependent on the relationship or anxious about surviving outside of it (Roguski, 2012; Tolmie & Gavey, 2010). In situations like this, victims can feel like they can't report violence, that they will be blamed for the violence or for not leaving, or that they will be negatively judged for the ways they cope with violence (Jury et al., 2019).

Accordingly, it is important for justice actors to think carefully about how their language can influence who is considered to blame for abuse. Wilson et al. (2015, p. 28), for instance, outline how justice actors can use phrases such as 'It was just ongoing domestics' or 'She did not appear to be able to take protective action for herself and her daughter' in their notes about IPV. This kind of language helps to exculpate the perpetrator. A better way to phrase those notes would have been 'He had a long history of using violence against her' or 'His violence continued to affect the safety of her and her child'. Although the legislative framework has shifted to focus more directly on perpetrators, justice actors have not necessarily made this shift in their practice.

The use of language in this way is also a problem in the Family Court. Mothers are frequently blamed for harm caused to their children because of their partners' abusive behaviour (Stark, 2012; Woolson Neville, 2013). In a recent example of this, a Women's Refuge client called police to report that her ex-partner had turned up at her house despite the protection order she had in place. Several months earlier, she had returned to the relationship, believing it to be safer for the children if she was always present during their interactions with their father rather than risk them being alone with him while he was drinking, as had happened during their separation. Although separated at the time of the police call-out, police interpreted her reluctance to give a formal statement (a decision based on fear that he would seek to punish her if he faced criminal consequences) as an unwillingness to create safety for her children, and removed them from her care that same day, commenting that she 'needs to start putting the children first'. This made her feel unwilling to call the police in future, and did not lead to safety for the children nor recognise that she had, in fact, been putting their safety first. Accordingly, we now turn our attention to what support is made available for victims, how the criminal justice system can empower or restrict victims, and what other support might be needed.

Support for victims

Perpetrators of IPV often intentionally isolate victims from their core support network: their friends, families, and workplaces (Johnson & Johnson, 2013; Levendosky et al., 2004). In their isolation, victims can feel afraid of losing access to their income, their house, or other relationships if they attempt to access the support that they need. Furthermore, many victims are not often asked about their experiences of violence in any setting other than direct contact with justice actors, which makes it difficult for them to ask for help from other potential places of support, such as workplaces (Elliot et al., 2005; Kohl & Macy, 2008). As a consequence, victims can feel like they cannot talk about their experiences or that they are not worthy of support from lawyers, police, or victim services. Unfortunately, justice actors sometimes demonstrate a lack of understanding about how the barriers created by victimisation impact on help-seeking behaviours (Roguski, 2012; Tolmie & Gavey, 2010). Accordingly, in spite of a robust legislative framework, if victims do not feel able to access help, and justice actors do not actively remove barriers to accessing help, victims are unlikely to receive the supports they need, or to receive justice.

In response to these feelings and encounters, specialist anti-violence services have created a framework of 'empowerment' for victims, so that justice actors work to actively remove barriers for victims who seek help. The concept of empowerment must be understood in the context of victims' feelings of isolation or worthlessness, and their fears of losing necessities such as housing, rather than simply suggesting that victims need to 'self-manage' their safety (Beddoe & Keddell, 2016; Wilson et al., 2015). The latter view has the impact of reducing a complex social problem to a set of expectations of what one individual 'should' do to keep safe. Empowerment must be understood as a collective set of actions on behalf of justice actors, helping services, and victims that both supports victims to access help *and* reduces the barriers (Coombes et al., 2009; FVDRC, 2014; Kasturirangan, 2008; Morgan et al., 2008). For instance, the principle of empowerment would lead a justice actor to recognise that if victims do not feel comfortable or confident in discussing abuse with a lawyer, they should be able to access support to guide them through the process (Levendosky et al., 2004). In broader practice, therefore, justice actors need to find ways to assist victims in overcoming negative feelings in order to access welfare, housing, education, employment, social engagement, and, ultimately, justice (Davies & Lyon, 2014; Kulkarni et al., 2012).

To illustrate: one Women's Refuge client reported that she had returned to an abuser because she could not find a way to survive financially outside of the relationship while also caring for her two children. She was afraid of losing access to her income and didn't know what to do. The Women's Refuge advocate explained that there were legal orders the victim could apply for which would allow her to remain in her house, or keep furniture, and stop the abuser from consistently showing up at her address. Following the principle of empowerment, the advocate then supported the victim to get financial aid and find a lawyer who could help her secure these protection orders. Here, the advocate has recognised that they needed more information to know what support was available through the criminal justice system and in accessing practical, financial, and material help. This action is consistent with the principle of empowerment and ensures that the victim is aware of her choices (and feels able to access them) other than returning to the relationship (Goodman et al., 2018).

When other justice actors also follow the principle of empowerment, victims can more easily overcome the social barriers that prevent them from accessing the right support through the criminal justice system. However, to be truly empowering, we must first attend to unravelling both the individual and structural dimensions of social entrapment that have circumscribed victims' capacities to act (Tolmie et al., 2018). Asking important questions about how this web has been woven can guide our actions and help us to avoid unintentionally perpetuating oppression. For instance, we can ask 'How is the abuser's violence impeding the victim's freedom to make decisions or constraining what decisions she can make?' followed by 'How have organisations' responses to her and her family further dictated which choices she can make? What have they led her to believe about what help is (un)available?' and 'What social conditions have contributed to her entrapment? Where can we see the cumulative impacts of sexism, colonisation, racism, classism, heterosexism, and ableism?' Attending to these questions then opens up the possibility of true empowerment.

CONCLUSION

In the beginning of this chapter, you were introduced to Clare, a victim of intimate partner violence. Although Clare attempted to seek help through the criminal justice system, the response was ultimately unhelpful and she returned to the abusive relationship. In her story we can see that there was a legislative framework and justice actors Clare could access, but in practice the response did not lead to a justice outcome. Clare could not access safety through the criminal justice system and ultimately saw no alternative but to return to the relationship. After reading this chapter, however, you will be aware that the outcome for Clare could have been dramatically different if both the legislative framework were strengthened and justice actors changed how they enacted the legislation. For example, Clare would have benefited from integrated legislation, the criminalisation of coercive control, and justice actors who followed the principle of empowerment. There are many other women like Clare, and the criminal justice system and the practices of justice actors can continue to be improved to better support victims to receive justice.

In this chapter, we have looked at the relatively robust legislative framework of the criminal justice system. This was the current system that Clare accessed. However, as her story illustrates, there continue to be gaps in the legislation. The legislative framework needs to be continually updated to respond to a changing modern environment and all forms of IPV. For example, updating the legislation to integrate different laws and expanding current legislation to include offences such as coercive control would improve the response of the criminal justice system. Such changes would have helped Clare receive the right support. As we have explored in the chapter, and is evident in Clare's story, the legislative framework is only a basis. Justice actors must practise the legislation consistently and with recognition of the impacts of gender stereotypes on IPV. Language and empowerment are two important principles that can help justice actors ensure that their responses to IPV are helpful for victims. In order for the violence against a victim to end, victims must have confidence that the justice system will hold the abuser accountable, that they will be supported to access help, and that, ultimately, they will gain the ability to rebuild their lives with support, resource, and hope through the justice system.

STUDY QUESTIONS

- Discuss the significance of gender for understanding and responding to IPV.
- Describe two different hypothetical cases of IPV. What barriers to justice exist for the victims in each case?
- To what extent should we focus on a robust justice system as the key response to tackling IPV in New Zealand?

FURTHER READING

Fanslow, J., & Robinson, E. (2004). Violence against women in New Zealand: Prevalence and health consequences. *The New Zealand Medical Journal, 117*(1206), 1–12.

Fitz-Gibbon, K., Walklate, S., McCulloch, J., & Maher, J. (Eds.). (2018). *Intimate partner violence, risk and security: Securing women's lives in a global world*. London, UK: Routledge.

Tolmie, J., Smith, R., Short, J., Wilson, D., & Sach, J. (2018). Social entrapment: A realistic understanding of the criminal offending of primary victims of intimate partner violence. *New Zealand Law Review, 2*, 181–217.

REFERENCES

Ali, P. A., & Naylor, P. B. (2013). Intimate partner violence: A narrative review of the feminist, social and ecological explanations for its causation. *Aggression and Violent Behavior, 18*(6), 611–619. doi:10.1016/j.avb.2013.07.009

Balzer, R., & McNeill, H. (1988). *The cultural facilitators of family violence*. Wellington, New Zealand: Family Violence Prevention Coordinating Committee (FVPCC), Department of Social Welfare.

Beddoe, L., & Keddell, E. (2016). Informed outrage: Tackling shame and stigma in poverty education in social work. *Ethics and Social Welfare, 10*(2), 149–162. doi:10.1080/17496535.2016.1159775

Blacklock, N., & Phillips, R. (2015). Reshaping the child protection response to domestic violence through collaborative working. In N. Stanley & C. Humphreys (Eds.), *Domestic violence and protecting children: New thinking and approaches* (pp. 196–213). London, UK: Jessica Kingsley Publishers.

Cook, H. (2011). Women's movement – the women's liberation movement. In *Te Ara – The Encyclopaedia of New Zealand*. Wellington, New Zealand: Ministry for Culture and Heritage. Retrieved from https://teara.govt.nz/en/photograph/27912/challenging-racism

Coombes, L., Morgan, M., Blake, D., & McGray, S. (2009). *Enhancing safety: Survivors' experiences of Viviana's advocacy at the Waitakere Family Violence Court*. Palmerston North, New Zealand: Massey University.

Davies, J., & Lyon, E. (2014). *Domestic violence advocacy: Complex lives/difficult choices*. Thousand Oaks, CA: Sage Publications.

Diemer, K. (2015, July 22). To change attitudes to family violence, we need a shift in gender views. *Conversation*. Retrieved from https://theconversation.com/to-change-attitudes-to-family-violence-we-need-a-shift-in-gender-views-44718

Elliott, D., Bjelajac, P., Fallot, R. D., Markoff, L. S., Reed, B. G., Gatz, M., . . . Taylor, J. (2005). Trauma-informed or trauma-denied: Principles and implementation of trauma-informed services for women. *Journal of Community Psychology, 33*(4), 461–477. doi:10.1002/jcop.20063

Else, A. (1993). *Women together: A history of women's organisations in New Zealand/Ngā rōpu wāhine o te motu*. Wellington, New Zealand: Historical Branch, Department of Internal Affairs & Daphne Brasell Associates Press.

Family Violence Death Review Committee (FVDRC). (2014). *Fourth report: January 2012 to December 2013*. Wellington, New Zealand: Health Quality and Safety Commission New Zealand. Retrieved from: https://www.hqsc.govt.nz/assets/FVDRC/Publications/FVDRC-4th-report-June-2014.pdf

Family Violence Death Review Committee (FVDRC). (2016). *Fifth report: January 2014 to December 2015*. Wellington, New Zealand: Health Quality and Safety Commission New Zealand. Retrieved from https://www.hqsc.govt.nz/assets/FVDRC/Publications/FVDRC-5th-report-Feb-2016.pdf

Family Violence Death Review Committee (FVDRC). (2017). *Fifth report data: January 2009 to December 2015*. Wellington, New Zealand: Health Quality and Safety Commission New Zealand. Retrieved from: https://www.hqsc.govt.nz/assets/FVDRC/Publications/FVDRC-FifthReportData-2017.pdf

Fanslow, J. L., & Robinson, E. M. (2010). Help-seeking behaviors and reasons for help seeking reported by a representative sample of women victims of intimate partner violence in New Zealand. *Journal of Interpersonal Violence, 25*(5), 929–951. doi:10.1177/0886260509336963

Fanslow, J. L., & Robinson, E. M. (2011). Sticks, stones, or words? Counting the prevalence of different types of intimate partner violence reported by New Zealand women. *Journal of Aggression, Maltreatment and Trauma, 20*(7), 741–759. doi:10.1080/10926771.2011.608221

Goodman, L., Epstein, D., & Sullivan, C. (2018). Beyond the RCT: Integrating rigor and relevance to evaluate the outcomes of domestic violence programs. *American Journal of Evaluation, 39*(1), 58–70. doi:10.1177/1098214017721008

Hamby, S., Finkelhor, D., Turner, H., & Ormrod, R. (2010). The overlap of witnessing partner violence with child maltreatment and other victimizations in a nationally representative survey of youth. *Child Abuse and Neglect, 34*(10), 734–741. doi:10.1016/j.chiabu.2010.03.001

Health Quality and Safety Commission New Zealand. (2019). *Family Violence Death Review Committee: About us: Background.* Retrieved from https://www.hqsc.govt.nz/our-programmes/mrc/fvdrc/about-us/background/

Htun, M., & Weldon, S. L. (2012). Civic origins of progressive policy change: Combating violence against women in global perspective, 1975–2005. *American Political Science Review, 106*(3), 548–569. doi:10.1017/S0003055412000226

Huygens, I. (2001). Feminist attempts at power sharing in Aotearoa: Embracing herstory or significant learning towards treaty-based structures. *Feminism and Psychology, 11*(3), 393–400. doi:10.1177/0959353501011003010

Johnson, M. P. (2005). Domestic violence: It's not about gender – or is it? *Journal of Marriage and Family, 67*(5), 1126–1130. doi:10.1111/j.1741-3737.2005.00204.x

Johnson, N. L., & Johnson, D. M. (2013). Correlates of readiness to change in victims of intimate partner violence. *Journal of Aggression, Maltreatment and Trauma, 22*(2), 127–144. doi:10.1080/10926771.2013.743939

Jury, A., Thorburn, N., & Burry, K. (2018). *'There was no other way out': Exploring the relationship between women's experiences of intimate partner violence and their self-harm, suicidal thoughts, and suicide events.* Wellington, New Zealand: National Collective of Independent Women's Refuges Inc.

Jury, A., Thorburn, N., & Burry, K. (2019). *'Relentless, not romantic': Intimate partner stalking in Aotearoa New Zealand.* Wellington, New Zealand: National Collective of Independent Women's Refuges Inc.

Jury, A., Thorburn, N., & Weatherall, R. (2017). 'What's his is his and what's mine is his': Financial power and economic abuse in Aotearoa. *Aotearoa New Zealand Social Work, 29*(2), 69–82. doi:10.11157/anzswj-vol29iss2id312

Kahui, S., & Snively, S. (2014). *Measuring the economic costs of child abuse and intimate partner violence to New Zealand.* Wellington, New Zealand: MoreMedia Enterprises.

Kasturirangan, A. (2008). Empowerment and programs designed to address domestic violence. *Violence Against Women, 14*(12), 1465–1475. doi:10.1177/1077801208325188

Kohl, P. L., & Macy, R. J. (2008). Profiles of victimized women among the child welfare population: Implications for targeted child welfare policy and practices. *Journal of Family Violence, 23*(1), 57–68. doi:10.1007/s10896-007-9139-2

Krug, E. G., Dahlberg, L. L., Mercy, J. A., Zwi, A. B., & Lozano, R. (2002). *World report on violence and health.* Geneva, Switzerland: World Health Organization. Retrieved from https://www.who.int/violence_injury_prevention/violence/world_report/en/full_en.pdf

Kulkarni, S. J., Bell, H., & Rhodes, M. D. (2012). Back to basics: Essential qualities of services for survivors of intimate partner violence. *Violence Against Women, 18*(1), 85–101. doi:10.1177/1077801212437137

Levendosky, A. A., Bogat, G. A., Theran, S. A., Trotter, J. S., von Eye, A., & Davidson, W. S. (2004). The social networks of women experiencing domestic violence. *American Journal of Community Psychology, 34*(1–2), 95–109. doi:10.1023/B:AJCP.0000040149.58847.10

McEwan, T. E., Mullen, P. E., & MacKenzie, R. (2009). A study of the predictors of persistence in stalking situations. *Law and Human Behavior, 33*(2), 149–158. doi:10.1007/s10979-008-9141-0

Morgan, M., Coombes, L., Te Hiwi, E., & McGray, S. (2008). *Accounting for safety: A sample of women victims' experiences of safety through the Waitakere Family Violence Court.* Palmerston North, New Zealand: Massey University.

National Council of Women New Zealand. (2018). *Gender equal.* Retrieved from https://genderequal.nz/

National Collective of Independent Women's Refuges Inc. (NCIWRI) (2015). *Our story: Working for women past, present and future.* Retrieved from: http://bnc.xel.mybluehost.me/wp-content/uploads/2015/11/Our-Story1.pdf

Neave, M. (2015). *Opening statement: Royal Commission into Family Violence.* Melbourne, Australia: Global.

New Zealand Family Violence Clearinghouse (NZFVC). (2015, January 7). *Victims of crime legislation comes into effect.* Retrieved from https://nzfvc.org.nz/news/victims-crime-legislation-comes-effect

New Zealand Family Violence Clearinghouse (NZFVC). (2017). *Data summaries 2017: Snapshot.* Retrieved from https://nzfvc.org.nz/sites/nzfvc.org.nz/files/Data-summaries-snapshot-2017.pdf

Rhodes, K. V., Ditcher, M. E., Kothari, C. L., Marcus, S. C., & Cerulli, C. (2011). The impact of children on legal actions taken by women victims of intimate partner violence. *Journal of Family Violence, 26*(5), 355–364. doi:10.1007/s10896-011-9370-8

Richardson, C. (2008). A word is worth a thousand pictures: Working with Aboriginal women who have experienced violence. In L. R. Ross (Ed.), *Feminist counselling: Theories, issues and practice* (pp. 122–148). Toronto, Canada: Women's Press.

Richardson, C., & Wade, A. (2009). Taking resistance seriously: A response-based approach to social work in cases of violence against Indigenous women. In J. Carrière & S. Stregna (Eds.), *Walking this path together: Anti-racist and anti-oppressive child welfare practice* (pp. 193–216). Winnipeg, Canada: Fernwood.

Roguski, M. (2012). *Understanding the impact of the Family Violence Interagency Response System (FVIARS) on Women's Refuge clients: An exploratory study.* Wellington, New Zealand: Kaitiaki Research and Evaluation.

Stark, E. (2012). Looking beyond domestic violence: Policing coercive control. *Journal of Police Crisis Negotiations, 12*(2), 82–86. doi:10.1080/15332586.2012.725016

Swarbrick, N. (2011a). Domestic violence – law and policing changes – 1980s and beyond. In *Te Ara: The Encyclopaedia of New Zealand.* Wellington, New Zealand: Ministry for Culture and Heritage. Retrieved from https://teara.govt.nz/en/domestic-violence/page-4

Swarbrick, N. (2011b). Victims of crime – supporting victims, 1970s and 1980s. In *Te Ara – the Encyclopaedia of New Zealand.* Wellington, New Zealand: Ministry for Culture and Heritage. Retrieved from https://teara.govt.nz/en/ephemera/26847/victims-of-offences-act-pamphlet

Tolmie, J. E., & Gavey, N. (2010). Is 50:50 shared care a desirable norm following family separation? Raising questions about current family law practices in New Zealand. *New Zealand Universities Law Review, 24*(1), 136–166. Retrieved from https://researchspace.auckland.ac.nz/handle/2292/9560

Tolmie, J., Smith, R., Short, J., Wilson, D., & Sach, J. (2018). Social entrapment: A realistic understanding of the criminal offending of primary victims of intimate partner violence. *New Zealand Law Review, 2*, 181–217. Retrieved from https://researchspace.auckland.ac.nz/handle/2292/45885

Wilson, D., Smith, R., Tolmie, J., & de Haan, I. (2015). Becoming better helpers: Rethinking language to move beyond simplistic responses to women experiencing intimate partner violence. *Policy Quarterly, 11*(1), 25–31. doi:10.26686/pq.v11i1.4529

Woolson Neville, D. (2013). *Experiences of advocacy: Situating experiences of contemporary women's advocates within the feminist movement to end violence against women.* Unpublished master's thesis, Unitec Institute of Technology, Auckland, New Zealand. Retrieved from http://hdl.handle.net/10652/2131

8

Cybercrime and Cyber-harm
Exploring Young People's Sharing of Intimate Images

Claire Meehan

The internet is so entrenched in our lives we cannot imagine living without it. It has become one of the main ways we communicate, socialise, and live. Internet access has developed from dial-up connections on burdensome desktop computers to laptops and smart technology on wireless devices. This access has given rise to social media, with use amongst young people growing exponentially. The most popular social media platforms are Facebook, Instagram, YouTube, and Snapchat (Pew Research Center, 2019). Research by the Office of Communications (2013) suggests that time spent online varies from 15 hours per week to up to 10 hours per day 'internet multitasking'. This evolution has not only made our communications with each other faster and more direct, it has also changed the very nature of how and what we communicate – we produce and share daily excerpts and photos of our lives frequently. Given all of this relatively new technology, there is an increasing convergence of online and offline environments. Within these environments the risks of harm are numerous, including addiction to the internet itself (Kuss & Lopez-Fernandez, 2016).

While the growth and popularity of the internet has facilitated many positives, such as connectivity, support, and digital friendships, the internet can also negatively impact on individuals and their friends, peers, and communities. On an individual level, scholars (see Langlais et al., 2020; Wiederhold, 2016) have considered how 'likes' and 'shares' on social media posts can affect a person's self-esteem. Some have highlighted how social media has become increasingly performative, curated, commodified, and even narcissistic (Dobson, 2015; Stuart & Kurek, 2019). The internet has reshaped the meaning of 'friends' and friendship, going beyond face-to-face relationships and blending one's online and offline lives. Coupled with a culture of 'sharing', this new form of communication has enabled new types of and new responses to traditional, or 'terrestrial', crime.

The reach of technology means cybercrime regularly makes news headlines. Dramatic reporting, alongside misinformation and the conflation of crime and harm, has created cyber-panics, resulting in calls for proactive and punitive regulation to protect users, particularly young people. The ways in which many teens communicate and share their lives online have also come under close scrutiny, invoking a need to understand and appreciate the role of the internet in youth culture. This chapter addresses the changing definitions of and accompanying issues related to cybercrime in order to examine young New Zealanders' sharing of intimate images and messages. In doing so, it examines current responses to cybercrime and highlights the importance of definitions and understandings of cybercrime when initiating these responses.

CYBERCRIME AND CYBER VICTIMS

Until the mid-2000s, cybercrime was viewed as 'any violations of criminal law that involve a knowledge of computer technology for their perpetration, investigation, or prosecution' (US Department of Justice, 1989, p. 2). This evolved to include 'harmful acts committed from or against a computer or network' (OECD, 2002, p. 1). Definitions of cybercrime have been reimagined in this century. Prior to 2000, the majority of definitions included little reference to victims of cybercrime. It is only recently that definitions of cybercrimes have gradually expanded to cover victimisation of human beings (Wall, 2007). In 2001 the Convention on Cybercrime included crimes against children. This put an end to the belief that cybercrimes were solely hacks or e-commercial attacks. Across Aotearoa New Zealand, Australia, the US, Canada, and the UK, conversations between the public, media, policy-makers, and academics attempt to understand the emotional motivations and implications of cybercrime. In sum, there are ongoing challenges around defining, understanding, and responding to cybercrime and victimisation.

As with terrestrial crime, definitions of cybercrime remain fraught with complexities. At its narrowest interpretation, crime is an infraction of criminal law. At its broadest, it might encompass social harms and deviancies beyond criminal law. The varying degrees of overlap between 'terrestrial' and 'cyber' crime, and the latter's online and offline effects, compound these complexities. As a result, and though cybercrime has become part of our everyday vocabulary, it lacks a clear definition among agencies tasked with policing it. As Grabosky pondered in 2001, is cybercrime merely 'old wine in new bottles', or something else? Nevertheless, cybercrime has become a hot topic in academic and public domains, and with good reason – in the vast expanse of cyberspace, new and distinctive forms of criminal activity have emerged, demanding a new criminological understanding which will be gained only through research and communication. Thus, the importance of robust definitions is exceedingly clear when it comes to resourcing, media coverage, public discourse, prevention, law, and policy responses.

Cybercrime has also added complex dimensions to understanding victimisation. Awareness of the risk of victimisation via digital means (for example, on phones and tablets, social media, and photo sharing apps) is thought to have increased the vulnerability of some children and teens (Salter et al., 2013). Cybercrime is often under-reported generally, and some types of cybercrime (for example, the sharing of intimate images without a person's consent) and their impacts are highly gendered (Ringrose et al., 2013). The response has shifted from the traditional police to non-governmental organisations and private corporations such as cybersecurity firms. Certain responses from the justice system to these types of crime have resulted in secondary victimisation – in which, for instance, victims of online romance scams or image-based sexual abuse are blamed for the offences against them.

Cybercrime is unique in that offenders need not be physically proximate with their victims, and it can be transnational (Brenner, 2004; Wall, 2012). The internet gives offenders access to a potentially large victim pool and increases their opportunity for committing certain types of crime – for example, phishing, where a bogus email requests a user's personal data, such as a password or login. If you cast the net wide enough someone will bite – that is, if you send enough emails, someone will respond and fall prey to the scam. Using technology can thus increase the number of 'crimes' a person or organisation can commit in a specific timeframe, and several people can be victimised with the same effort. It is also important to note that in many instances, committing cybercrime, unlike traditional terrestrial crime, requires systems knowledge, rather than technical knowledge. In cyberspace, value is often attached to an idea or information, rather than to tangible property (Wall, 2012), and tools (such as worms and viruses) can be purchased from those with the skills to create them.

CYBERCRIME, CYBER-HARM, AND SEX IN NEW ZEALAND

Cybercrime in New Zealand is prevalent and growing. The Anti-Phishing Working Group, an industry body, estimated that cybercrime cost New Zealand almost $257 million in 2017 (*Radio New Zealand*, 2018). Online safety organisation Netsafe (2019a) recorded 13,000 instances of online scams and fraud and $33 million in losses in 2017. Reports of scams and fraud have drastically increased from 2017, when 8100 reports were made (*Radio New Zealand*, 2018). As well as financial harm, victims can experience psychological harm, feel frustrated and embarrassed, or lose confidence in using digital technology to make payments or connect with others.

When thinking about cybercrime, we often imagine a financial crime, rather than interpersonal harm. While the financial aspect of scams makes it easier to categorise them as a cybercrime, rather than a cyber-harm, it is exposure to sexual content which remains a priority for parents. Netsafe has found that while parents have a range of concerns about the potential online risks their children face, two of the top three relate to sexual content: their child sharing nudes of themselves, and seeing sexually explicit content (Netsafe, 2018, 2019b).

'SEXTING': SHARING INTIMATE IMAGES AND MESSAGES

'Sexting', a relatively new concept, often carries significant negative connotations, especially with regard to young people. The term – a portmanteau word created by the media from a conflation of the phrase 'sexy texts' (Crofts et al., 2016) – is deliberately introduced here in quotation marks, given that New Zealand teens do not use it; instead, they use language such as 'nudes', 'nudies', 'dick pics', and 'naked pics' to describe their experiences (Netsafe, 2017, p. 9). As such, the term 'sexting' does not capture the scope of context and motivations surrounding these behaviours. Nonetheless, it will be used in this chapter to refer to 'any practices relating to sending, receiving, requesting or being asked for self-generated nude, semi-nude or sexually suggestive text messages using a digital device' (p. 9).

Teenage sexting is often conflated with child exploitation material (commonly referred to as child pornography) and the grooming of children online. This confusion is evident in an Australian parliamentary debate from 2010 in which sexting is deemed to be an 'unhealthy' expression of childhood sexuality, which requires 'penalties' to 'suppress it' (see Lee et al., 2013, p. 37). It is presented as deviant behaviour which requires paternalistic intervention in order to 'save young people from themselves' (Döring, 2014). The threat of the online paedophile, actively trawling the internet in an attempt to initiate sexual relationships with children, is also highlighted. In the years since the topic was broached in the Australian Parliament, little has advanced in terms of how we understand young people creating and sharing intimate images. When teen sexting is discussed only within a framework of perceived risk, the scope for critical discussion is lost.

In New Zealand, we have witnessed amplified concern about teenagers engaged in sexting. Inflammatory statements such as 'Kiwi children and teenagers posting sexually explicit images or footage of themselves online – including children as young as 6' (Jones, 2017) represent parents' worst fears. The reality is that for many of today's young people, engaging with explicit material is more normal than often realised. In New Zealand, 4 per cent of teens say they have sent nude or nearly nude content of themselves in the past 12 months. The percentage nearly doubles among 17-year-olds (7 per cent) (Netsafe, 2017). These findings suggest that teens find themselves part of a culture of sharing nudes; but whether they are active, passive, or peripheral participants (Netsafe, 2017), only a minority of teens sext, and of these few are harmed by the behaviour (Salter et al., 2013). Yet sensationalised media reporting continues to shape public perceptions. For example, on Vodafone's Digi-Parenting website, the most frequently viewed page instructs parents on how to stop their child sexting (Vodafone, 2016a, 2016b). This is reflective of the wider attitudes and opinions around teens, technology, and sex.

Gendered dimensions to sexting

Assumptions around sexting tend to focus on girls as the protagonists and boys as passive recipients (Draper, 2012). This is problematic as, generally, there is little evidence to suggest girls send more sexts than boys (Hinduja & Patchin, 2012; Lenhart, 2009; Strohmaier et al., 2014). By creating the narrative that girls are more proactive, mainstream media play into a wider moral panic about teenage girls and sexualisation. From this perspective, girls who sext are victims of a hyper-sexualised popular culture and in need of protection (Karaian, 2012). However, as Hasinoff (2015) argues, this approach fails to take into account female autonomy and the possibility that sexting may be part of normal sexual expression.

The framing of sexting as a teenage girl problem also becomes particularly interesting when boys are involved in sexting incidents. For boys, sexting generally touches on the legal consequences. For example, overseas headlines frequently refer to boys receiving sexts and then being charged under child pornography laws (Emm, 2016; Hill, 2016; Miller & Hirschkorn, 2010). In cases where boys send sexts, they are seen as 'boys being boys'. For example, early in 2017 the local soap opera *Shortland Street* had an episode in which a teenage boy, Harry, sent an intimate picture to his girlfriend. His dad discovered the picture and the episode ended with the now infamous line 'Please, tell me that is not your penis'. Maxine Fleming, a producer on the show, said: 'It is a comedy story, but like all good comedy there's a truth at the core of it, and it is social commentary' (*New Zealand Herald*, 2017, para. 11). While media commentary on the show did offer advice on how to keep teens safe online, it is difficult to imagine a sexting story where a female protagonist would be portrayed in such a light-hearted way.

Image-based sexual abuse

When discussing the sharing of intimate images or messages, it is important to differentiate between consensual sexting and image-based sexual abuse. Albury et al. (2013) outline a typology of sexting that distinguishes naked or semi-naked images, contextual images, joke images, and inoffensive sexual images – all shared consensually – from offensive and unethical sexual pictures which are semi-naked or naked images either produced consensually and shared without consent, or produced and shared without consent. In 2019, 5 per cent of 1001

New Zealand adults surveyed by Netsafe reported being affected by image-based sexual abuse. Although young adults (particularly those under 30) were more likely to report being affected, the research showed that the issue spans generations, with instances of abuse being reported by those 70 years and older (Netsafe, 2018, 2019b). Typical reports from adult women tend to involve an ex-partner trying to maintain control, for blackmail purposes or as retaliation for her leaving the relationship. Sometimes these cases are part of a wider pattern of family violence (*Radio New Zealand*, 2018; see Jury et al., chapter 7 this volume). Men were more likely to report that the most common reasons for the abuse was as a joke or for extortion. Men were also more likely to report intimate content being shared by a stranger, or by someone who they know well but is not an ex-partner.

Research shows that 35 per cent of New Zealanders are unfamiliar with the law around image-based sexual abuse (Netsafe, 2018, 2019b). Netsafe's director of operations, Helen O'Toole, says that victim-blaming attitudes from supporting agencies and individuals can also dissuade people from seeking help. As the material is often created and initially shared consensually within an intimate relationship (Franks, 2015), some victims report that they've felt to blame directly, or that blame has been insinuated in some way. Some are told that they shouldn't have sent the intimate content in the first place, or that they should stop using social media (Netsafe, 2019b). This is reflected in Citron and Franks' (2014, p. 367) findings that victims are often 'shooed away' by police, who see the victims to blame for 'choosing' to share their intimate images. This is reflective of many types of cybercrime where police, as well as the public, do not fully understand the resulting harms, which include bullying, loss of employment, mental health impacts, and suicide attempts.

While many media reports do highlight the harms caused by image-based sexual abuse, victim-blaming is prevalent. (One of the most notorious cases in New Zealand is that of the 'Roast Busters'; see Jordan, chapter 6 this volume.) An enduring theme in the media is the 'stupidity' of the victim, with little to no analysis of the actions or accountability of the offender, particularly with regard to changing legislation. Observations such as 'another law designed to protect individuals from their own stupidity' (*Daily Mail*, 2013) and 'you can't legislate away stupidity' (*CNN*, 2013) have appeared in the UK and US. These themes are affirmed through the views of media-chosen 'expert opinions', such as US attorney Anahita Sedaghatfar, who expressed the view that 'you can't go and pose like you're some *Playboy* model . . . then you say "government, government, help me, save me from my stupidity"' (Fox News, 2014). This coincides with media reporting in New Zealand, where young people who sext have been described as 'giddy' (*Stuff*, 2015) and 'naïve' (Moir, 2011) and at risk of becoming 'addicted' (Hunt, 2016). Such responses present the problem as victim naïveté rather than sexualised violence, adding to the confusion around consensual/non-consensual sharing of intimate images, motivations, and resultant harms.

Legal responses to consensual and non-consensual sharing of intimate images

Under New Zealand's Harmful Digital Communications Act 2015, image-based sexual abuse can be an offence even if the intimate content was initially sent consensually (or created consensually with another person). Penalties for the offence can be a fine of up to $50,000 or up to two years' jail for an individual. Forty-eight (91 per cent) of the criminal prosecutions under the Act in 2017/18 were for image-based sexual abuse incidents. Netsafe, the approved agency under the Act, received almost 3000 complaints of personal harm caused by digital communications in 2018.

For consensual sharing, especially for teens, the legal responses become murkier. Some jurisdictions (for example, Australia, Canada, the US, and the UK) have used legislation aimed at combatting child exploitation material to prosecute young people who have sent intimate images consensually and/or non-consensually. This has been criticised as being punitive, criminalising children and young people (Crofts & Murray, 2013). Some scholars, such as Calvert (2009) and Ryan (2010), argue that child pornography laws should be used to protect young people, rather than criminalise them for participating in actions that may be viewed as normal within a youth sharing culture and sexual development or exploration. When victims are held accountable for the actions of those who have shared their images non-consensually, they may become reluctant to contact police, particularly if they risk prosecution themselves.

Legal responses to sexting in New Zealand have so far been restricted to incidents where harm has been caused to the victim due to a third party sharing intimate images non-consensually. Prior to the Harmful Digital Communications Act, offenders could be charged with distributing objectionable material, but application of censorship legislation was limited, as the remit only included incidents where the victim did not consent to the creation of the initial image (*Stuff*, 2010). It is important to note that while sexts sent by young people could be deemed objectionable material, New Zealand Police have so far only prosecuted harmful incidents that involve children.

Challenging the dominant narrative: sexting and beyond

Teen sexting remains a contentious topic. Academic scholars and practitioners have yet to agree on a definition of sexting, partly due to the various behaviours around creating, sending, receiving, or disseminating an intimate image. Teen sexting highlights how difficult it can be to differentiate between harm, crime, and deviance (as is true for many types of cybercrime).

Rather than present a solely legal response, efforts have been made to challenge the narrative of sexting as inherently negative. In 2015, for instance, the satirical comedian John Oliver ran a story on online harassment, including 'revenge porn', on the HBO show *Last Week Tonight* (2015). While he centred the debate on the online harassment of females, by focusing on women whose images were sent without consent, Oliver highlighted how the framing of sexting often fails to take into account the wider context of victim-blaming and rape culture.

Teenagers, too, are challenging commonly held assumptions. For example, *Teen Vogue*'s column 'UnSlut' has dedicated several columns to sexting and distinguishes between consensual and non-consensual forms of the behaviour (Lindin, 2016). The column also challenges society's expectations of teenage girls, with one article aptly titled 'How to Get Your Parents to Stop Slut Shaming You'. In New Zealand, *Em*, a website aimed at helping teenage girls combat sexual assault, also challenges the dominant narratives on sexting (see *Em*, 2017). Referring to the non-consensual sharing of images, the website maintains that the fault lies not with the creator but with the distributor. By creating space for these narratives and listening to teens it may be possible to create a new, more nuanced framework through which to view sexting. What we do know is that young people themselves rarely get to talk about what they think of 'sexy' media.

CONCLUSION

While cybercrime has become part of our everyday vocabulary, it still lacks a clear definition even among agencies tasked with policing it. Nevertheless, cybercrime has become a hot topic in academic and public domains, and with good reason – in the vast expanse of cyberspace, new and distinctive forms of criminal activity have emerged which demand new criminological understandings. This chapter set out to examine perceptions and responses to young people sexting within changing understandings of cybercrime, cyber-harm, and cyber-victimology.

It is clear that current responses in New Zealand and elsewhere struggle to appreciate the nuances in actions and motivations in behaviours when determining whether an act is criminal, harmful, or consensual.

The framing of cybercrime as far-reaching and ubiquitous distorts our understanding of it. Sensationalised coverage of youth culture, including young people's sharing of images and messages, has created a number of myths around internet use that reinforce a culture of fear about crime and harm; they include the erroneous conflation between consensual sexting between young people and child exploitation material. As with the social construction of 'terrestrial' crime, cybercrime is framed as a prevalent, dramatic, and even catastrophic type of crime – one that lawmakers and enforcers are helpless to deal with. This fear is compounded by the gap that has emerged between our knowledge of what cybercrime entails, its prevalence, and the risk to our young people. We need to close the gap by continuing our research in this area, keeping the public informed, and being aware of how we report on and represent cybercrime, cyber-harm, and internet use.

STUDY QUESTIONS

- Should our definitions of cybercrime include cyber-harm?
- Why do you think there is a gendered dimension to sexting?
- Why is it important to move beyond a mainly legal response to teen sexting?

FURTHER READING

Crofts, T., Lee, M., McGovern, A., & Milivojevic, S. (2016). *Sexting and young people*. Houndmills, UK: Palgrave Macmillan.

Dobson, A. S., & Ringrose, J. (2016). Sext education: Pedagogies of sex, gender and shame in the schoolyards of *Tagged* and *Exposed*. *Sex Education, 16*(1), 8–21. doi:10.1080/14681811.2015.1050486

Yar, M., & Steinmetz, K. F. (2019). Cybercrime and society. 3rd ed. London, UK: Sage Publications.

REFERENCES

Albury, K., Crawford, K., & Byron, P. (2013). *Young people and sexting in Australia: Ethics, representation and the law*. Sydney, Australia: ARC Centre for Creative Industries and Innovation/Journalism and Media Research Centre, University of New South Wales. Retrieved from https://core.ac.uk/download/pdf/30677128.pdf

Brenner, S. W. (2004). Cybercrime metrics: Old wine, new bottles? *Virginia Journal of Law and Technology, 9*(13), 1–52. Retrieved from https://www.yumpu.com/en/document/read/3486067/old-wine-new-bottles-virginia-journal-of-law-and-technology

Calvert, C. (2009). Sex, cell phones, privacy, and the First Amendment: When children become child pornographers and the Lolita Effect undermines the law. *Common Law Conspectus: Journal of Communications Law and Policy, 18*(1), 1–66. Retrieved from https://scholarship.law.edu/cgi/viewcontent.cgi?article=1446&context=commlaw

Citron, D., & Franks, M. (2014). Criminalizing revenge porn. *Wake Forest Law Review, 49*, 345–391. Retrieved from https://digitalcommons.law.umaryland.edu/cgi/viewcontent.cgi?article=2424&context=fac_pubs

CNN. (2013, August 29). *Making 'revenge porn' illegal* [YouTube post] (comment 14). Retrieved from https://www.youtube.com/watch?v=qm8FQnOnXQw

Crofts, T., Lee, M., McGovern, A., & Milivojevic, S. (2016). *Sexting and young people*. Houndmills, UK: Palgrave Macmillan.

Crofts, T., & Murray, L. (2013). 'Sexting', children and child pornography. *Sydney Law Review 35*(1), 85–106. Retrieved from http://www.austlii.edu.au/au/journals/SydLRev/2013/4.html

Daily Mail. (2013, November 16). 'Revenge porn' victims seek new law to make the act of posting sexually explicit images online with permission illegal. Retrieved from http://www.dailymail.co.uk/news/article–2507953/Revenge-porn-victims-seek-law-make-posting-explicit-images-illegal.html

Dobson, A. S. (2015). *Postfeminist digital cultures: Femininity, social media, and self-representation*. New York, NY: Palgrave Macmillan.

Döring, N. (2014). Consensual sexting among adolescents: Risk prevention through abstinence education or safer sexting? *Cyberpsychology: Journal of Psychosocial Research on Cyberspace, 8*(1), 1–18. doi:10.5817/CP2014–1–9

Draper, N. R. (2012). Is your teen at risk? Discourses of adolescent sexting in United States television news. *Journal of Children and Media, 6*(2), 221–236. doi:10.1080/17482798.2011.587147

Em. (2017). *Pics and betrayal*. Retrieved from https://www.dearem.nz/empathise-archive/2017/episode–1-sxt-pics-and-betrayal

Emm, D. (2016, June 29). Sexting and its consequences. *Huffington Post UK*. Retrieved from http://www.huffingtonpost.co.uk/david-emm/sexting_b_10713694

Fox News. (2014, April 22). *Anahita Sedaghatfar on* Fox News's 'Cavuto' *debating legality of revenge porn* [YouTube post], at 2:03. Retrieved from https://www.youtube.com/watch?v=ShszA95xQTo

Franks, M.A., (2015). *Drafting an effective 'revenge porn' law: A guide for legislators*. Available at SSRN 2468823.

Grabosky, P. N. (2001). Virtual criminality: Old wine in new bottles? *Social and Legal Studies, 10*(2), 243–249. doi:10.1177/a017405

Hasinoff, A. A. (2015). *Sexting panic: Rethinking criminalization, privacy, and consent*. Urbana, IL: University of Illinois Press.

Hill, K. (2016, April 12). 'Sexting' the same as child pornography in the courtroom, Limestone Coast police say. *ABC News*. Retrieved from http://www.abc.net.au/news/2016–04–12/sexting-the-same-as-child-porn-in-the-courtroom-say-police/7318940

Hinduja, S., & Patchin, J. W. (2012). *School Climate 2.0: Preventing cyberbullying and sexting one classroom at a time*. Newbury Park, CA: Corwin Press.

Hunt, T. (2016, February 8). Sexting like 'drug addiction' for Kiwi teens, with kids as young as 11 taking part. *Stuff*. Retrieved from http://www.stuff.co.nz/national/health/76672892/sexting-like-drug-addiction-for-kiwi-teens-with-kids-as-young-as–11-taking-part

Jones, N. (2017, August 8). Sexually explicit material of Kiwi youngsters going online weekly, police warn. *New Zealand Herald*. Retrieved from http://www.nzherald.co.nz/nz/news/article.cfm?c_id=1&objectid=11899811

Karaian, L. (2012). Lolita speaks: 'Sexting,' teenage girls and the law. *Crime, Media, Culture, 8*(1), 57–73. doi:10.1177/1741659011429868

Kuss, D. J., & Lopez-Fernandez, O. (2016). Internet addiction and problematic internet use: A systematic review of clinical research. *World Journal of Psychiatry, 6*(1), 143–176. doi:10.5498/wjp.v6.i1.143

Langlais, M. R., Seidman, G., & Bruxvoort, K. M. (2020). Adolescent romantic relationship–oriented Facebook behaviours: Implications for self-esteem. *Youth and Society, 52*(4), 661–683. doi.org/10.1177/0044118X18760647

Last Week Tonight. (2015, June 21). *Online harassment:* Last Week Tonight with John Oliver *(HBO)* [YouTube video file]. Retrieved from https://www.youtube.com/watch?v=PuNlwYsz7Pl

Lee, M., Crofts, T., Salter, M., Milivojevic, S., & McGovern, A. (2013). 'Let's get sexting': Risk, power, sex and criminalisation in the moral domain. *International Journal for Crime, Justice and Social Democracy, 2*(1), 35–49. doi:10.5204/ijcjsd.v2i1.89

Lenhart, A. (2009). *Teens and sexting: How and why minor teens are sending sexually suggestive nude or nearly nude images via text messaging.* Washington, DC: Pew Research Center. Retrieved from https://pdfs.semanticscholar.org/2619/47313cb03400a1b1c04a9816fa1ee0a4c3bf.pdf?_ga=2.113682639.910237552.1580518949-1154062498.1580103073

Lindin, E. (2016). Unslut [Ongoing column series]. *Teen Vogue*. Retrieved from https://www.teenvogue.com/tag/unslut

Miller, M., & Hirschkorn, P. (2010, June 5). 'Sexting' leads to child porn charges for teens. *CBS News*. Retrieved from http://www.cbsnews.com/news/sexting-leads-to-child-porn-charges-for-teens/

Moir, J. (2011, July 14). 'Sexting' craze not in NZ schools. *Stuff: Taranaki Daily News*. Retrieved from http://www.stuff.co.nz/taranaki-daily-news/news/5281320/Sexting-craze-not-in-NZ-schools

Netsafe. (2017). *Teens and 'sexting' in New Zealand: Prevalence and attitudes.* Retrieved from https://www.netsafe.org.nz/wp-content/uploads/2017/12/SEXTING-NZ-Report-Dec-7-2017.pdf

Netsafe. (2018). *New Zealand teens and digital harm.* Retrieved from https://women.govt.nz/sites/public_files/NZ-teens-and-digital-harm_statistical-insights_2018.pdf

Netsafe. (2019a). $33 million lost to scams and fraud. Retrieved from https://itbrief.co.nz/story/33-million-lost-to-scams-fraud-netsafe-says-nz-isn-t-doing-enough-to-stop-it

Netsafe. (2019b). Image based abuse report. Retrieved from https://www.netsafe.org.nz/image-based-sexual-abuse-survey-2019/

New Zealand Herald. (2017, February 19). Shortland St 'penis-gate' episode goes global. Retrieved from https://www.nzherald.co.nz/entertainment/news/article.cfm?c_id=1501119&objectid=11803464

Office of Communications (Ofcom). (2013). *Children and parents: Media use and attitudes report.* London, UK: Office of Communications. Retrieved from https://www.ofcom.org.uk/research-and-data/media-literacy-research/childrens/children-parents-oct-2013

OECD (Organisation for Economic Co-operation and Development). (2002). *OECD guidelines for the security of information systems and networks: Towards a culture of security.* Paris, France: OECD Publishing. Retrieved from http://www.oecd.org/sti/ieconomy/15582260.pdf

Pew Research Center (2019). *Social media fact sheet.* Retrieved from https://www.pewresearch.org/internet/fact-sheet/social-media/

Radio New Zealand. (2018, April 3). Kiwis lose $33M in 2018 – new approach needed in the fight against online scams. *Radio New Zealand*. Retrieved from https://www.rnz.co.nz/news/national/386203/kiwis-lose-33-million-as-online-scam-successes-increase

Ringrose, J., Harvey, L., Gill, R., & Livingstone, S. (2013). Teen girls, sexual double standards and 'sexting': Gendered value in digital image exchange. *Feminist Theory, 14*(3), 305–323. doi:10.1177/1464700113499853

Ryan, E. (2010). Sexting: How the state can prevent a moment of indiscretion from leading to a lifetime of unintended consequences for minors and young adults. *Iowa Law Review, 96*(1), 357–383. Retrieved from https://heinonline.org/HOL/Page?handle=hein.journals/ilr96&div=12&g_sent=1&casa_token=&collection=journals

Salter, M., Crofts, T., & Lee, M. (2013). Beyond criminalisation and responsibilisation: Sexting, gender and young people. *Current Issues in Criminal Justice, 24*(3), 301–316. doi:10.1080/10345329.2013.12035963

Strohmaier, H., Murphy, M., & DeMatteo, D. (2014). Youth sexting: Prevalence rates, driving motivations, and the deterrent effect of legal consequences. *Sexuality Research and Social Policy, 11*(3), 245–255. doi:10.1007/s13178-014-0162-9

Stuart, J., & Kurek, A. (2019). Looking hot in selfies: Narcissistic beginnings, aggressive outcomes? *International Journal of Behavioural Development, 43*(6), 500–506. doi:10.1177/0165025419865621

Stuff. (2010, November 13). Naked photo sends jilted lover to jail. Retrieved from http://www.stuff.co.nz/national/crime/4341191/Naked-photo-sends-jilted-lover-to-jail

Stuff. (2015, December 16). Sexually abusive behaviours in New Zealand secondary schools on the rise. Retrieved from http://www.stuff.co.nz/national/crime/75115344/sexually-abusive-behaviours-in-new-zealand-secondary-schools-on-the-rise

US Department of Justice (1989). *Computer crime: Criminal justice resource manual*. Retrieved from https://www.ncjrs.gov/pdffiles1/Digitization/118214NCJRS.pdf

Vodafone. (2016a, February 9). *Sexting is now as concerning for Kiwi parents as cyberbullying* [Media release]. *Vodafone: News: Community*. Retrieved from https://news.vodafone.co.nz/article/sexting-now-concerning-kiwi-parents-cyberbullying

Vodafone. (2016b). *Staying safe online: Sexting*. Retrieved from https://www.vodafone.co.nz/why-vodafone/family/digi-parenting/safety/sexting/

Wall, D. (2007). *Cybercrime: The transformation of crime in the information age*. Cambridge, UK: Polity Press.

Wall, D. S. (2012). The devil drives a Lada: The social construction of hackers as cybercriminals. In C. Gregoriou (Ed.), *Constructing crime: Discourse and cultural representations of crime and 'deviance'* (pp. 4–18). London, UK: Palgrave Macmillan.

Wiederhold, B. K. (2016). Low self-esteem and teens' internet addiction: What have we learned in the last 20 years? *Cyberpsychology, Behavior, and Social Networking, 19*(6), 359. doi:10.1089/cyber.2016.29037.bkw

9

Hate Crime, Racism, and Islamophobia
'This Is Exactly Who We Are'

Daniel Botha and Scott Poynting

On 15 March 2019, an anonymous user posted to the online message board 8chan a declaration of his intent to attack those whom he labelled 'invaders'. The post contained various weblinks to a 'manifesto', an ideological diatribe about the supposed displacement of the European 'race' and an exterminist call to arms. The user, since identified as the man charged with terrorism and murder in the Christchurch mosque shootings, posted a link to his Facebook page, where he livestreamed the atrocity (Wakefield, 2019).

Over the 17 minutes of the livestream, viewers witnessed a terror event in real-time. The terrorist – who had decorated his (legally purchased) semi-automatic weapons with white-supremacist symbols, references to significant far-right attacks, and tributes to idolised terrorists – travelled first to the Al Noor Mosque in the Christchurch suburb of Riccarton, where he gunned down worshippers who had gathered for Friday prayers, before driving to a second target, the Linwood Islamic Centre, to continue his attack. In total, 51 worshippers were murdered (*ABC News*, 2019) and a further 49 injured (*New Zealand Herald*, 2019). Within 21 minutes of the first emergency calls, the lone gunman had been intercepted on his way to a third possible target and arrested by New Zealand Police (NZP) (Truebridge, 2019). Later, as stunned New Zealanders engaged in collective mourning, the public and political responses to the Christchurch shootings displayed appropriate condemnation of the killings and the hatred that inspired them, compassionate condolence for the bereaved and their communities, and a political pragmatism that identified the immediate issue as gun control.

The day after the attack, Prime Minister Jacinda Ardern announced changes to New Zealand's gun laws, effectively banning the sale and supply of semi-automatic weapons like those used in the Christchurch attack (Fitzgerald, 2019). On 14 June 2019, the accused – 28-year-old white Australian Brenton Tarrant – appeared in Christchurch District Court via audiovisual link and pleaded not guilty to 51 charges of murder, 40 of attempted murder, and 1 of engaging in a terrorist act.[1] He changed his plea to guilty the following March and, in August 2020, was sentenced to life imprisonment without parole.

This chapter challenges the popular wisdom that, prior to the horrendous mass murder of March 2019, anti-Muslim hate crime was totally unprecedented in Aotearoa New Zealand. It considers the antecedents in such hate crime that the state has failed to deal with. It sets contemporary Islamophobia in the context of the history of white settler-colonialist racism and present-day 'Western' imperialism. It reviews New Zealand's well-intentioned legislation against hate crime, exploring how this functions, while also noting its lack of effectiveness. Hate crime is shown in effect to be indulged and enabled by the state, within a global order that produces and marshals anti-Muslim racism.

THE POLITICAL MANAGEMENT OF WHITE SUPREMACY AND ISLAMOPHOBIC VIOLENCE

Ardern's leadership – especially her compassionate engagement with the terrorist's targets, the Muslim community – was immediately lauded in New Zealand and internationally. Soon, images of the prime minister dressed in a hijab circulated widely online, and international commentators quickly noted the stark comparison between Ardern's response to violent white supremacism and that of other notable leaders. United States president Donald Trump, for example, had once responded to a white supremacist murder at Charlottesville's 2017 'Unite the Right' rally by attributing avoidable violence by right-wing hate groups against anti-racist counter-protesters to 'both sides' (Coaston, 2019, para. 1). Ardern, by contrast, was prompt and emphatic in deploring the Christchurch shooter's ideology as well as the crime. 'We are a proud nation of more than 200 ethnicities, 160 languages, and amongst that diversity we share common values,' Ardern (2019) said in her first televised broadcast on 15 March. She continued:

> And the one [value] that we place currency on right now is our compassion and the support for the community of those directly affected by this tragedy and secondly, the strongest possible condemnation of the ideology of the people that did this. You may have chosen us, but we utterly reject and condemn you (paras. 11–12).

In many ways, New Zealand's responses to the events in Christchurch – swift, sweeping gun reform; an emphasis on inclusion and diversity; rebukes of extremism, Islamophobia, and white supremacy; and calls to de-platform hate speech online – deserve the approbation they received at the time.

Yet a problematising of the nature and prevalence of racism and hegemonic whiteness in New Zealand emerged, even as the prime minister – and the nation – responded as admirably as they did to the Christchurch attacks. As Ardern emphasised New Zealand's diversity in her 15 March public address, she simultaneously perpetuated many of the myths about New Zealand values that have paradoxically allowed the type of hatred, racism, and Islamophobia inherent in atrocities like Christchurch to persist. Providing the reassurance many in New Zealand needed at the time, Ardern (2019) asserted:

> For those of you who are watching at home tonight and questioning how this could have happened here, we, New Zealand, we were not a target because we are a safe harbour for those who hate. We were not chosen for this act of violence because we condone racism, because we're an enclave for extremism; we were chosen for the very fact that we are none of these things, because we represent diversity, kindness, compassion, a home for those that share our values, a refuge for those who need it. . . . I am not going to let this change New Zealand's profile (paras. 10, 14).

Ardern's words present the Christchurch shootings as exogenous, totally discrepant, and 'unprecedented', and uphold New Zealand's preferred profile as 'non-racist', 'inclusive', and 'diverse'. This sentiment was echoed when social media users posted their well-intentioned tributes to the victims of the shootings, using a well-rehearsed line, declaring, 'This is not New Zealand' (*New Zealand Listener*, 2019, para. 1).

Such a 'narcissistic self-view' (Ghumkhor, 2019, para. 4), we argue, is emblematic of a complacent form of national self-congratulation that has its origins in the country's colonial history. It is one vested in denial: an insistence that 'racism' and 'hate' are features of 'other' places, not New Zealand. This 'non-racist' self-image is borne from a colonial myth-making project, which positioned New Zealand as a country with the 'greatest' race relations in the world. The fraudulent construction of this patently false national identity was premised on a project of collective amnesia, and, as O'Malley and Kidman (2017) argue, it is undermined by New Zealand's position as a colonial society. Yet, instead of openly dealing with these colonial atrocities – the invasion and theft of Māori land, for example – New Zealanders were instead encouraged to believe that state-imposed racist violence during the New Zealand Wars was the basis of a 'fairer', more 'racially equitable' society (O'Malley & Kidman, 2017). As Brawley (1993) points out, New Zealand did not make the undiplomatic error of Australia by calling its immigration policy the 'White New Zealand' Policy, but that is what it was, just the same, until the 1960s, being more or less coterminous with the 'White Australia' policy.

Such colonial legacies are evident today in the uncomfortable silence – if not outraged denialism – that characterises many public conversations about race 'relations' in New Zealand. Writing in the wake of 15 March, Associate Professor Khylee Quince, director of Māori and Pacific advancement at Auckland University of Technology, critiqued the 'this is not us' narrative, in her comments to the media at the time, as 'misguided and naïve' (as cited in Ryan, 2019, para. 7). 'You have not listened to minority peoples, to Indigenous peoples, to immigrant peoples, who have been saying, in the case of Māori for more than 180 years, this is exactly who we are and you just don't want to face that' (para. 8). Similarly, it could be argued that a history of white-settler-colonialist denial in New Zealand, and its contemporary lack of resolution, has led to ongoing anti-immigrant racism, and above all racism against Muslim immigrants. Such denialism, we argue, was evident in Jacinda Ardern's response at the time. The prime minister's rhetoric carefully presents 'New Zealand' as the 'target' that was 'chosen' by the killer. It was not. New Zealand was the site of the attack; the target was New Zealand Muslims. Ardern's speech of 15 March – notwithstanding the hijab and hugs of the following fortnight – consisted of 671 succinct and precisely chosen words, not one of which was 'Muslim'.

New Zealand Muslims had voiced their concerns about the potential of such an attack for years prior. Indeed, just six days before the Christchurch shootings, ActionStation (2019) released a report documenting experiences of hate, abuse, and harassment online. Further, the imam at the Deans Avenue Mosque – one of the targets in the Christchurch attack – had reported suspicious behaviour at the mosque to police just three weeks prior, but was not taken seriously (*Stuff*, 2019). This is a commonly reported experience of complainants about hate crime (or sub-crime) incidents internationally. In addition, Anjun Rahman (2019), spokesperson for the

Islamic Women's Council of New Zealand (IWCNZ), wrote in an article for *Radio New Zealand* that the IWCNZ had made several complaints directly to various government agencies about the issues New Zealand Muslims faced on a daily basis. Such complaints included meetings with the New Zealand Security Intelligence Service in 2016, the Department of Prime Minister and Cabinet in 2017, the Department of Internal Affairs in 2017, and written correspondence and advocacy to the State Services Commission (Rahman, 2019). Despite these warnings, the IWCNZ received little funding. In this complicit complacency of the nation, however – in the refusal to 'see' racist vilification and racist hate incidents as a problem – the Christchurch mosque attacks can be seen as consonant with New Zealand's history.

Nor is it as if hate crime only surfaced in the public's consciousness in the aftermath of March 2019. The 'we' of 'this is not New Zealand' could have listened more to Muslim victims of hate crime, harassment, and vilification after 9/11.[2] In the wake of the September 2001 airliner attacks in the US, over 50 anti-Muslim incidents were reported in New Zealand, including Muslims being threatened on the street or receiving abusive phone calls and hate mail, and mosques being vandalised (Neville, 2005). Anti-Muslim attacks have continued since that time. In 2004, for instance, a group of skinheads in Wellington abused and attacked a group of Somali young people (Human Rights Commission [HRC], 2004; *New Zealand Herald*, 2004). Yet much of the ongoing Islamophobic violence goes unreported or is inadequately recorded. According to the HRC, it is 'not always possible to obtain disaggregated data across complainants and complaint types' as 'the information is either not provided or cannot be easily obtained', making it difficult to identify 'who complains, where they complain and what they complain about' or any emerging patterns (HRC, 2010, p. 33). Moreover, as the HRC observes, 'the Police do not keep separate statistics relating to ethnicity for reported racial offences, treating them as complaints alongside others relating to offences under the Summary Offences and Crimes Acts' (HRC, 2019, p. 2).

After the London transport bombings on 7 July 2005, there was a further spike in anti-Muslim hate crime in New Zealand, just as there was in Britain, Australia, and elsewhere. The HRC (2005, p. 56) reported an 'unprecedented number of prosecutions and convictions' for racially motivated crime that year. One such case involved two young men with affiliations to the New Zealand extreme right-wing group National Front who systematically vandalised six mosques in Auckland, smashing up to 20 windows at each building and spray-painting 'R.I.P. London' across them, causing approximately $14,000 worth of damage (Neville, 2005). They were convicted and sentenced in November 2005 to one year's imprisonment and ordered to pay $5000 in reparations on seven charges of intentional damage. They were also sentenced to six months' prison, to be served concurrently, for carrying and presenting an imitation M16 rifle. The motivation of the offenders was strikingly prescient of that of the Christchurch terrorist. One of the youths had sent a text message after the 7 July London attacks saying: 'The war has begun on the sand-niggers who blew up London . . . we should retaliate' (*New Zealand Herald*, 2005). In sentencing, Judge Thomas Everitt said he viewed the attacks as acts of racial hatred: 'It was an outrageous desecration of religious buildings, motivated by racial hatred and corrupted politics . . . I didn't accept this was misguided behaviour. This was a high level of offending' (*New Zealand Herald*, 2005). This *was* New Zealand, and it was 14 years before the Christchurch atrocity.

ISLAMOPHOBIA AS RACISM

Islamophobia is 'a type of racism that targets expressions of Muslimness or perceived Muslimness' (All Party Parliamentary Group on British Muslims, 2018, p. 11). According to the Muslim Council of Britain (2018):

- Islamophobia is a form of racism;
- Islamophobia is more than just anti-Muslim hatred or bigotry; and
- Islamophobia does not incorporate criticism of Islam as a faith, but some people may hide behind 'criticism of Islam' when engaging in Islamophobia.

As with most modern racisms, Islamophobia arises from colonialism: it is rooted in empire. Kumar (2012, pp. 41–60) identifies five 'myths' about Islam that have become hegemonic in the present-day 'US-led empire': that 'Islam is monolithic'; that 'Islam is a uniquely sexist religion'; that Muslims are 'incapable of reason and rationality'; that Islam is 'inherently violent'; and that 'Muslims are incapable of democracy and self-rule'.

Kundnani (2016, p. 1), drawing upon Hall et al. (1978), designates Islamophobia as a 'lay ideology' or 'common sense' which sets the horizon of intelligibility of public discussion and popular understanding about Islam – and terrorism – in the contemporary West. Understandings beyond these horizons are rendered irrelevant to the 'debate', or inconceivable. The ideological elements of Islamophobia include: 'Muslims are prone to terrorism'; 'Muslims are *extremists*'; 'Muslim men engage in *oppression* of women, children and minorities'; 'Muslims engage in *infiltration*'; and 'Muslims are *sexually dysfunctional*', leading to sexual predatoriness, 'grooming' and rape by Muslim men, and the 'demographic threat' of giving birth to 'too many children' by Muslim women in nations to which they have immigrated (Kundnani, 2016, pp. 3–4, original emphasis).

Islamophobia is endemic in Western states, including neighbouring Australia. Hussein and Poynting (2017) show these various ideological elements of Islamophobia in discursive play leading to the anti-Muslim Cronulla riots in Sydney in 2005, and how this ideology has become normalised or mainstream across popular culture in Australia. Anti-Muslim ideology underpinned the mass racist violence at Cronulla, despite media and political protestations (notably by Prime Minister John Howard) that Australia is not racist and that the violence was not 'us.' At Cronulla, the 'Other' being vilified and violently attacked was labelled by ethnic and national origin or descendancy, and at the same time as Muslim. The anti-Islam hatred or deprecation is part of a package of othering that functions identically to racisms associated with national or ethnic origin; these categories run seamlessly into each other in the confused and incoherent – but consequential – ideology of racism.

The Christchurch murderer declared a 'war' on Muslims in a disturbed parody of the West's 'war on terror'. A sort of white (European) supremacism, opposing immigration and exhorting ethnic cleansing, pervades the 74 incoherent pages of his online 'manifesto'.[3] In it, he professes not to be anti-Muslim – as long as Muslims stay in 'their place', which is not 'Europe'. For him, 'Europe' takes in New Zealand and Australia. European and white are synonymous. Indigenous people do not appear in this account. The 'invaders' of 'our lands' are Muslims. Their 'vipers' nests' must be burned, and non-European children who are in 'our lands' must be killed. The killer is fixated upon the non-white others outbreeding 'us' and effecting 'white genocide' – a by-now standard Islamophobic trope and one similarly colouring the 'manifesto' of that other mass killer, Anders Breivik, whose motivations and crimes inspired the Christchurch killer, he proclaims.[4]

As Morgan and Poynting (2012) pointed out in the case of Breivik, it would be erroneous to reduce these utterances to the ravings of a madman. They pervade contemporary Western societies, though often parading in apparently more acceptable form. One need not look very far to find evidence of such attitudes in New Zealand. In 2011, survey research from Victoria University of Wellington's Centre for Applied Cross-cultural Research found that 51 per cent of the 302 participants agreed that Muslims had customs that were 'not acceptable' in New Zealand (Centre for Applied Cross-cultural Research, 2011). Complementary attitudinal research echoes these findings, with results from the 20-year longitudinal New Zealand Attitudes and Values

Study indicating that Muslims experience higher levels of prejudice compared to other ethnic groups and lower levels of 'warmth' (Hawi et al., 2019; Highland et al., 2019). Far from being confined to the political extreme, Islamophobic sentiment is now a mainstay feature of many online platforms including Facebook and Twitter (ActionStation, 2019), and – as we argue later in this chapter – it is emboldened by mainstream politicians and other influential agents. Before coming to this, we need to review the legislative framework around hate crime in New Zealand.

HATE CRIME

'Hate crime' is a contested concept, not only because of disputes over what constitutes a crime, but also because of the varied meanings of 'hate' in this context, and differences over its role in causation. The term appears to have originated in the US in the 1980s, during awareness campaigns and advocacy for criminal justice policy aimed at reducing crimes that victimise racialised, ethnic, and religious minorities, and those who are 'othered' because of their sexuality. We may define hate crime as a type of crime, paradigmatically threatening or humiliating or violent, in which the victims are selected – or understand that they are – because they belong to a group that is the subject of prejudice, bias, or hatred on the part of the perpetrator(s). It is thus a form of crime perpetrated against those who are 'different' from those who hold themselves as arbiters of difference, and who can exercise power to do so (Poynting, 2017). Perry (2001) deploys the Gramscian notion of hegemony in asserting that violent sanctions against perceived deviance, and measures to put the presumed inferior in 'their place', are constituted in social relations of inequality, and function to reproduce those social relations:

> Hate crime [is] usually directed towards already stigmatised and marginalised groups. As such, it is a mechanism of power and oppression, intended to reaffirm the precarious hierarchies that characterise a given social order. It attempts to recreate simultaneously the threatened (real or imagined) hegemony of the perpetrator's group and the 'appropriate' subordinate identity of the victim's group (p. 10).

The social order in question will invariably pertain to a particular social (and often physical) space, in which the belonging of the victimised group is challenged – often violently. The victims are perceived as being 'out of place' (Douglas, 1966), and must either be 'put back in their place' or removed. It can be argued, therefore, without too much hyperbole, that all hate crime is a form of 'cleansing', such as 'ethnic cleansing', or other such exterminism.

Hate crime 'sends a message to the entire group to which the victim belongs that they are "different" and that *they* "don't belong"' (Hall, 2005, p. 4). Levin and McDevitt (2002) note that 'hate crimes . . . target not only a primary victim, but everyone in the victim's group' (p. 6). The rationale for conceptualising 'hate crime' as a distinct form of crime, then, becomes clear; it not only is intended to recognise the individual traumatic experiences of those subjected to hate, but also serves as a useful 'moral category' that engenders communal compassion towards *all* who identify with the targeted characteristic (Mason, 2007, p. 249).

HATE CRIME LEGISLATION IN NEW ZEALAND

Following the widespread implementation of hate crime legislation in common law countries, New Zealand introduced a penalty enhancement provision for hate crime in section 9(1)(h) of the Sentencing Act 2002. The Act allows for augmentation of sentences where offenders are found to have committed the offence either partly or wholly because of hostility towards a group of persons who have 'an enduring common characteristic', such as race, colour, nationality, or religion (Brown, 2004, p. 593; Ip, 2005; Mason & MacIntosh, 2014, p. 652; Roberts, 2003, p. 266). Under New Zealand's hate crime legislative framework, an offender is officially charged under the Crimes Act 1961 (for existing crimes such as assault or murder), and it is only at sentencing that any 'hateful' element to the crime is considered as an 'aggravating factor'. Those found to be motivated by hate in the commission of their crime receive a penalty enhancement, such as a longer prison sentence.

In addition to the above, elements of hate crime and hate speech are referenced in other anti-discrimination laws. For example, while no specific offence for 'hate' is enshrined in the Crimes Act 1961, sections 66 and 311(2) make it unlawful to incite any other person to commit a criminal offence, whether that be a threat of violence, criminal nuisance, or public disorder. The Human Rights Act 1993 forbids discrimination on the basis of characteristics such as sexual orientation, marital status, religious belief, skin colour, race, disability, and so on. In addition, section 61(1) of the Human Rights Act 1993 prohibits the publication of any material 'likely to excite hostility against or bring into contempt any group of persons in or who may be coming to New Zealand on the ground of colour, race, or ethnic or national origins of that group of persons'. Section 131(1) of the same Act outlines the maximum penalties for those found guilty of incitement of hostility on the grounds of skin colour, race, or ethnic or national origins: imprisonment for a term not exceeding three months or a fine not exceeding $7000.[5]

'SOMEWHAT CURSORY' APPROACHES TO HATE CRIME

Despite there being no specific hate crime offence in the Crimes Act, the existing literature on New Zealand hate crime laws seems to suggest that the country's sentence enhancement provisions are comparatively strong. International experiences with prosecuting hate crime are marred by restrictive evidential thresholds, which generally require proof of *hate-based* motivation. In New Zealand, however, the wording of the Sentencing Act requires proof of an offender's *hostility* towards an enumerated group (Mason & McIntosh, 2014). Furthermore, where more restrictive hate crime provisions often require proof of *full hate-motivation* towards a subordinated group, the Sentencing Act stipulates that an offender need only be *partially motivated* by *hostility* (Ip, 2005; Roberts, 2003). Theoretically, then, the liberal application of legal terminology such as *hostility* and *partial motivation* provides for a sentencing framework that has a 'wide reach but limited effect' (Ip, 2005, p. 580) – and, indeed, scholars have argued that the sentencing provisions within New Zealand's legislation are superior to that of Canada (Roberts, 2003) and Australia (Mason & McIntosh, 2014).

Relatively strong sentencing enhancement provisions aside, the country's approach to responding to hate crime has come under near-consistent fire from human rights advocates, the HRC, the United Nations, and many of the targets of hate crime, who have insisted for decades – despite extremely low rates of prosecution – that hate-based violence and aggression are pertinent problems in New Zealand and inform the everyday experiences of the country's marginalised. In fact, even when New Zealand's politicians were apparently drafting legislation to get 'tough on crime', hate was added to the list of aggravating factors only as an afterthought; section 9(1)(h) was introduced at the select committee stage in response to a public submission from a gay rights advocate, Callum Bennachie. The submission received the support of gay Labour MP Tim Barnett, who wanted to address the prevalence of anti gay attacks in New Zealand (Brown, 2004). The irony here is palpable; the Sentencing Act 2002, written largely in response to populist demands to 'get tough' on violent crime, had not originally conceived hate crime – generally characterised by behaviour designed to *violently* demote the very *humanity* of its victims – as worthy of inclusion. At best, this approach to hate crime can only be described as 'somewhat cursory' (Brown, 2004, p. 593).

This cursory political approach to hate crime is exemplified again when considering the state's near-constant denial of the significance of hate in the country. Despite the collection of data on hate crime arguably being the *first* step nation-states should take in effectively combating hate crime, there is little information about the extent of racially and religiously motivated crime. New Zealand Police does not routinely collect data on religious or racially motivated crime (HRC, 2019), and academics interested in this area have to make do with self-report studies and media reports. Although the Christchurch shootings resulted in the minister of justice, Andrew Little, announcing that a review of New Zealand's hate crime law would be fast-tracked, and NZP announced that it would be reviewing its recording practices (Duff, 2019), it is worth noting that this sudden burst of action came after decades of inaction.

The HRC had urged the New Zealand government to collect hate crime data as early as 2004 (HRC, 2019), and the United Nations (UN) Committee on the Elimination of Racial Discrimination had echoed these calls on no fewer than two occasions (Committee on the Elimination of Racial Discrimination, 2007, 2017). Furthermore, the HRC made similar recommendations to recording practices in 2009; the government of the day agreed in principle with the recommendations, but said that a more robust system of recording hate crime was 'not a priority' (HRC, 2019, pp. 1, 10). Starved of any reliable data, the HRC collected media reports of racially or religiously motivated crime as part of its annual reports on race relations, but – perhaps indicative of the state's attitudes towards race relations more generally – these reports were discontinued in 2013 due to 'chronic lack of resources caused by the Government's long-term cap on funding' (HRC, 2019, p. 1). The Islamophobic attacks reported in the media included hate mail, parcels of pork, and physical assaults.

Thus, the New Zealand state's response to hate crime – its lacklustre consideration of hate in the drafting of the Sentencing Act 2002, its disregard of persistent recommendations from international authorities, and NZP's poor history of keeping adequate records of crimes potentially motivated by hate – are all indicative of a state apparatus in deep denial. Indeed, even some of the responses to the Christchurch terror attacks were rooted in this proclivity to favour the rhetoric which sought to preserve – as Ardern openly stated – New Zealand's 'profile'. This 'profile' as a seemingly egalitarian country with amicable 'race relations' is predicated on New Zealand's colonial history, part of a carefully constructed (Pākehā) national self-identity that continually fails to see, let alone dismantle, white privilege based on colonialist theft. Yet, state negligence in adequately legislating for, and responding to, hate crime is one thing; its role in emboldening and permitting harmful narratives about 'othered' minorities is another.

PERMISSION TO HATE

That the state should be less than effective in reducing hate crime should not surprise us when we consider the part played by agents of the state in actually encouraging it. Noting that hate crime requires an 'enabling environment' to sustain it, Perry (2001) shows how the state is implicated in maintaining such an environment. It confers 'permission to hate' by normalising hate speech, by failing to legislate effectively against bias-motivated crime, by neglecting to police hate crime diligently (including taking complaints seriously), by populist trafficking in the rhetoric of 'othering', and even by itself perpetrating, and thus modelling, bias-motivated violence (pp. 179–223).

Islamophobic and anti-immigrant sentiment is evident is some high-profile statements made by leading New Zealand politicians. In 2005, during an infamous speech entitled 'The End of Tolerance', foreign minister and leader of the New Zealand First party Winston Peters disparaged the 'moderate face' that 'the New Zealand Muslim community have been quick to show', asserting that it was 'hand in glove' with 'a militant underbelly': 'Underneath it all the agenda is to promote fundamentalist Islam. Indeed these groups are like the mythical Hydra – a serpent underbelly with multiple heads capable of striking at any time and in any direction' (Peters, 2005, paras. 41–44). In 2015, racist provocateur-blogger Cameron Slater (who was then influential, especially in right-wing circles, via his *Whale Oil* website, and had exercised a notoriously symbiotic relationship with leading National Party figures, including 2011–14 justice minister Judith Collins) wrote of Islam: 'religion of peace? No way, it is a death cult and we should kill them before they kill us' (Slater, 2015, para. 11).

The state also affords permission to hate through its failure to appropriately monitor those actively engaged in hate-motivated behaviour. Soon after Christchurch, a number of revelations would indicate that radical white supremacy was not even on the government's radar; writing for *Radio New Zealand*, Patterson (2019) reported that not one public document from the Security Intelligence Service or the GCSB – New Zealand's two main intelligence agencies – mentioned any threat posed by white supremacists. After conducting a cursory look through New Zealand's Hansard record from 2003 to 2019, Coughlan (2020) identified *one* reference to white supremacy. Furthermore, after announcing a high-level inquiry into whether security agencies could have done more to detect a potential far-right terror attack (Patterson, 2019), the prime minister admitted that, prior to Christchurch, New Zealand's intelligence community had been caught in a 'traditional approach to terrorism that would not necessarily have picked up the ideology that New Zealand has experienced on 15 March' (O'Brien, 2019, para. 5). Again, observers of these albeit significant reactive developments should be aware that New Zealand's sudden burst of action occurred in the *wake* of predictable and precedented terrorism. This suggests that the New Zealand state's continued denial and lack of careful attention to hate crime does too little to counteract it effectively. This situation should not, and must not, prevail in the aftermath of the 15 March white supremacist shootings.

CONCLUSION

In this chapter, we sought to problematise some of the pervasive public narratives that emerged in response to the 2019 Christchurch terror attacks. Specifically, we contrasted the notion that the attacks represented an 'aberration', an 'unprecedented' 'blemish' on Aotearoa New Zealand's otherwise faultless 'profile', with a more critical reading of the state's historical responses to hate crime, Islamophobia, and racism. The 'this is not us' narrative is, indeed, an aspirational one. And yet, for the people living in New Zealand whose everyday empirical realities are informed by racism, Islamophobia, homophobia, transphobia, hate, and intolerance, the rhetoric of 'this is not us' remains symptomatic of the state's long history of governing by denial (Asquith, 2014).

The aspiration for a New Zealand where hate crime is not endemic is a worthy one, and the steps taken to date towards eradicating hate crime are worthwhile, if as yet too few and too small. If Perry (2001) is right that hate crime is directed against already othered and subordinated groups and functions to reassert social hierarchies and the place of the dominant within these, then the struggle to eliminate hate crime depends on movements to overturn social hierarchy, dominance, and the attendant othering.

STUDY QUESTIONS

- Why do some criminologists favour conceptualising 'hate crime' as a moral/symbolic concept, as opposed to simply a legal category? What are the merits of such an approach?
- What is meant by the term 'permission to hate'? How is it evident in New Zealand?
- Is Islamophobia a form of 'racism'? How does Islamophobia compare and relate to racism directed towards other groups?

FURTHER READING

Mason, G., & Asquith, N. (2019). Islamophobia within the hate crime framework. In D. Iner (Ed.), *Islamophobia in Australia (Vol. II)*, (pp. 18–26). Sydney: Charles Sturt University & ISRA.

Kundnani, A. (2014). *The Muslims are coming! Islamophobia, extremism and the domestic war on terror.* London, UK, & New York, NY: Verso.

Poynting, S. (2020). 'Islamophobia Kills'. But where does it come from? *International Journal for Crime, Justice and Social Democracy, 9*(2), 74–87. doi: 10.5204/ijcjsd.v9i2.1258

NOTES

1. The authors wish to acknowledge Prime Minister Ardern's powerful denunciation of the (alleged) terrorist in Parliament on 19 March in which she vowed to give the shooter 'nothing. . . . Not even his name'. Yet as he is (rightly) named in open court proceedings, and throughout the national and international media, it would seem unduly coy to omit his name here.
2. The following instances draw, with permission, upon Mason and Poynting (2006). The authors of this chapter wish to acknowledge the work of Dr Victoria Mason on this.
3. The rest of this section is taken from Poynting (2019).
4. That the Christchurch shooter's manifesto was partially designed to 'bait' media outlets, politicians, and academics into finding meaning in the memes and in-jokes published in the document is outside the scope of this chapter. It is, however, important to acknowledge that treating the entire manifesto as a 'joke' lacking ideological content stands in stark contrast with the ideological intent behind the shooter's actions. In other words, the 'manifesto' is both an example of trolling *and* a serious attempt to disseminate far-right ideology.
5. The authors would like to thank Dr Alice Tregunna for her assistance in 2013 in reviewing current hate crime and hate speech laws in New Zealand.

REFERENCES

ABC News. (2019, March 17). Christchurch shooting death toll rises to 50 after one more victim discovered at mosque. Retrieved from https://www.abc.net.au/news/2019-03-17/christchurch-shooting-death-toll-rises-to-50-new-zealand/10909288

ActionStation. (2019). *The people's report on online hate, harassment and abuse.* Retrieved from https://peoplesharassmentreport.com

All Party Parliamentary Group on British Muslims. (2018). *Islamophobia defined: The inquiry into a working definition of Islamophobia / anti-Muslim hatred.* Retrieved from https://appgbritishmuslims.org/publications

Ardern, J. (2019, March 15). 'We were chosen because we represent diversity' – Jacinda Ardern on Christchurch terrorist attack. *Spinoff*. Retrieved from https://thespinoff.co.nz/news/15-03-2019/we-were-chosen-because-we-represent-diversity-jacinda-ardern-on-christchurch-terrorist-attack/

Asquith, N. L. (2014). A governance of denial: Hate crime in New Zealand and Australia. In N. Hall, A. Corb, P. Giannasi, & J. Grieve (Eds.), *The Routledge international handbook on hate crime* (pp. 174–189). London, UK: Routledge.

Brawley, S. (1993). 'No "white policy" in NZ': Fact and fiction in New Zealand's Asian immigration record, 1946–1978. *New Zealand Journal of History, 27*(1), 16–36. Retrieved from http://www.nzjh.auckland.ac.nz/document/?wid=744&page=1&action=null

Brown, C. (2004). Legislating against hate crime in New Zealand: The need to recognise gender-based violence. *Victoria University of Wellington Law Review, 35*(3), 591–608. doi:10.26686/vuwlr.v35i3.5702

Centre for Applied Cross-cultural Research. (2011). *Attitudes toward Muslim immigrants*. Retrieved from https://www.victoria.ac.nz/cacr/research/migration/attitudes-toward-muslim-immigrants

Coaston, J. (2019, April 26). Trump's new defense of his Charlottesville comments is incredibly false. *Vox*. Retrieved from https://www.vox.com/2019/4/26/18517980/trump-unite-the-right-racism-defense-charlottesville

Committee on the Elimination of Racial Discrimination. (2007). *Report of the Committee on the Elimination of Racial Discrimination*. Retrieved from https://www.refworld.org/pdfid/473424062.pdf

Committee on the Elimination of Racial Discrimination. (2017). *Concluding observations on the combined twenty-first and twenty-second periodic reports of New Zealand*. Retrieved from https://tbinternet.ohchr.org/Treaties/CERD/Shared%20Documents/NZL/CERD_C_NZL_CO_21–22_28724_E.pdf

Coughlan, T. (2020, January 2). Time to recall MPs' anti-migrant rhetoric. *Newsroom*. Retrieved from https://www.newsroom.co.nz/2019/03/18/493288/time-to-recall-mps-anti-migrant-rhetoric#

Douglas, M. (1966). *Purity and danger: An analysis of concepts of pollution and taboo*. London, UK: Routledge & Kegan Paul.

Duff, M. (2019, March 30). Hate crime law review fast-tracked following Christchurch mosque shootings. *Stuff*. Retrieved from https://www.stuff.co.nz/national/christchurch-shooting/111661809/hate-crime-law-review-fasttracked-following-christchurch-mosque-shootings

Fitzgerald, K. (2019, March 16). Christchurch terror attack: 'Our gun laws will change' – Jacinda Ardern. *Newshub*. Retrieved from https://www.newshub.co.nz/home/politics/2019/03/christchurch-terror-attack-our-gun-laws-will-change-jacinda-ardern.html

Ghumkhor, S. (2019, March 20). The hypocrisy of New Zealand's 'this is not us' claim. *Aljazeera*. Retrieved from https://www.aljazeera.com/indepth/opinion/hypocrisy-zealand-claim–190319104526942.html

Hall, N. (2005). *Hate crime*. Cullompton, UK: Willan Publishing.

Hall, S., Critcher, C., Jefferson, T., Clarke, J., & Roberts, B. (1978). *Policing the crisis: Mugging, the state and law and order*. Houndmills, UK: Palgrave Macmillan.

Hawi, D., Osborne, D., Bulbulia, J., & Sibley, C. G. (2019). Terrorism anxiety and attitudes toward Muslims. *New Zealand Journal of Psychology, 48*(1), 80–89. Retrieved from https://www.psychology.org.nz/journal-archive/Hawi–80–89.pdf

Highland, B. R., Troughton, G., Shaver, J., Barrett, J. L., Sibley, C. G., & Bulbulia, J. (2019). Attitudes to religion predict warmth for Muslims in New Zealand. *New Zealand Journal of Psychology, 48*(1), 122–132. Retrieved from https://www.psychology.org.nz/journal-archive/NZJP-Issue–481.pdf

Human Rights Commission (HRC). (2004). *Together we grow / Te ranga tahi: Race relations report 2004*. Aotearoa New Zealand: HRC.

Human Rights Commission (HRC). (2005). *Tūi tūi tuituiā: Race relations in 2005*. Aotearoa New Zealand: HRC.

Human Rights Commission (HRC). (2010). *Human rights in New Zealand 2010*. Aotearoa New Zealand: HRC.

Human Rights Commission (HRC). (2019). *It happened here: Reports of race and religious hate crime in New Zealand 2004–2012*. Retrieved from https://www.hrc.co.nz/files/1515/6047/9685/It_Happened_Here_Reports_of_race_and_religious_hate_crime_in_New_Zealand_2004–2012.pdf

Hussein, S., & Poynting, S. (2017). 'We're not multicultural, but . . .'. *Journal of Intercultural Studies, 38*(3), 333–348. doi:10.1080/07256868.2017.1314254

Ip, J. (2005). Debating New Zealand's hate crime legislation: Theory and practice. *New Zealand Universities Law Review, 21*(4), 575–597.

Kumar, D. (2012). *Islamophobia and the politics of empire*. Chicago, IL: Haymarket Books.

Kundnani, A. (2016). Islamophobia: Lay ideology of US-led empire. Retrieved from http://www.kundnani.org/draft-paper-on-islamophobia-as-lay-ideology-of-us-led-empire/

Levin, J., & McDevitt, J. (2002). *Hate crimes revisited: America's war on those who are different*. Boulder, CO: Westview Press.

Mason, G. (2007). Hate crime as a moral category: Lessons from the Snowtown case. *Australian and New Zealand Journal of Criminology, 40*(3), 249–271. doi:10.1375/acri.40.3.249

Mason, G., & MacIntosh, K. (2014). Hate crime sentencing laws in New Zealand and Australia: Is there a difference? *New Zealand Law Review 2014*(4), 647–709.

Mason, V., & Poynting, S. (2006). *Terrorism 'in our backyard': The experiences of ethnically targeted communities of state anti-terrorism measures in Australia and Aotearoa/New Zealand since 11 September 2001*. Paper presented to the XVI World Congress of the International Sociological Association, University of South Africa, Durban, 27 July.

Morgan, G., & Poynting, S. (2012). Introduction: The transnational folk devil. In G. Morgan & S. Poynting (Eds.), *Global Islamophobia: Muslims and moral panic in the West* (pp. 1–14). Farnham, UK: Ashgate Publishing.

Muslim Council of Britain. (2018, November 27). *Muslim Council of Britain welcomes the definition of Islamophobia released by the APPG on British Muslims* [Press release]. Retrieved from https://mcb.org.uk/press-releases/mcb-welcomes-definition-of-islamophobia-by-the-appg-on-british-muslims/

Neville, S. (2005, July 11). R.I.P. tolerance: Backlash hits NZ mosques. *Dominion Post*, p. 1.

New Zealand Herald. (2004, August 11). Arrest follows attacks on Somalis in Wellington. Retrieved from https://www.nzherald.co.nz/nz/news/article.cfm?c_id=1&objectid=3583688

New Zealand Herald. (2005, November 30). Teen vandals get year for mosque attacks. Retrieved from https://www.nzherald.co.nz/nz/news/article.cfm?c_id=1&objectid=10357690

New Zealand Herald. (2019, May 3). Christchurch mosque attacks: 51st victim dies after surgery. Retrieved from https://www.nzherald.co.nz/nz/news/article.cfm?c_id=1&objectid=12227479

New Zealand Listener. (2019, March 20). If 'This is not New Zealand', let us show it.

O'Brien, T. (2019, May 15). Jacinda Ardern admits New Zealand's been too focused on Islamic extremism. *Newshub*. Retrieved from https://www.newshub.co.nz/home/politics/2019/05/jacinda-ardern-admits-new-zealand-s-been-too-focused-on-islamic-extremism.html

O'Malley, V., & Kidman, J. (2017). Settler colonial history, commemoration and white backlash: Remembering the New Zealand Wars. *Settler Colonial Studies, 8*(3), 298–313. doi:10.1080/2201473X.2017.1279831

Patterson, J. (2019). No mention of right-wing extremist threats in 10 years of GCSB and SIS public docs. *Radio New Zealand*. Retrieved from https://www.rnz.co.nz/news/political/385173/no-mention-of-right-wing-extremist-threats-in-10-years-of-gcsb-and-sis-public-docs

Perry, B. (2001). *In the name of hate: Understanding hate crimes*. New York, NY: Routledge.

Peters, W. (2005, July 28). The end of tolerance. *Scoop Parliament*. Retrieved from https://www.scoop.co.nz/stories/PA0507/S00649.htm

Poynting, S. (2017). Hate crime. In A. Brisman, E. Carrabine, & N. South (Eds.), *The Routledge companion to criminological theory and concepts* (pp. 301–305). London, UK: Routledge.

Poynting, S. (2019, March 17). Terrorism has no religion. *Criminology Collective*. Retrieved from: https://www.criminologycollective.nz/2019/03/17/terrorism-has-no-religion/

Rahman, A. (2019). Islamic Women's Council repeatedly lobbied to stem discrimination. *Radio New Zealand*. Retrieved from https://www.rnz.co.nz/news/on-the-inside/384911/islamic-women-s-council-repeatedly-lobbied-to-stem-discrimination

Roberts, J. V. (2003). Sentencing reform in New Zealand: An analysis of the Sentencing Act 2002. *Australian and New Zealand Journal of Criminology, 36*(3), 249–271. doi:10.1375/acri.36.3.249

Ryan, H. (2019, March 31). Kiwi Muslims hope the fight against Islamophobia continues after non-Muslims take off their headscarves. *BuzzFeed News*. Retrieved from https://www.buzzfeed.com/hannahryan/new-zealand-islamophobia-racism-christchurch

Slater, C. (2015, October 29). The only solution is to kill them before they kill us. *Whale Oil*. Retrieved from https://www.whaleoil.net.nz/2015/10/the-only-solution-is-to-kill-them-before-they-kill-us/

Stuff. (2019, May 13). Police ignored reports of suspicious behaviour in Christchurch mosque, imam claims. Retrieved from https://www.stuff.co.nz/national/christchurch-shooting/112689676/police-ignored-reports-of-suspicious-behaviour-in-christchurch-mosque-imam-claims

Truebridge, N. (2019, March 20). Gunman stopped on way to third attack – Police Commissioner Mike Bush. *Stuff*. Retrieved from https://www.stuff.co.nz/national/christchurch-shooting/111425523/gunman-stopped-on-way-to-third-attack--police-commissioner-mike-bush

Wakefield, J. (2019). Christchurch shootings: Social media races to stop attack footage. *BBC News*. Retrieved from https://www.bbc.com/news/technology-47583393

10

Environmental Harm
Clean and Green, or Brutal and Contaminated?

Sarah Monod de Froideville and Moorea Smithline

Crimes against the environment can be remarkably significant in their scale when compared to more conventional criminal acts. However, until the emergence of 'green criminology', few criminologists had paid them much attention. In this chapter we outline what a green criminological perspective entails and illustrate how it can be employed to examine environmental harm in Aotearoa New Zealand.

Green criminology might seem an odd area of study in a country that markets itself as 'clean and green'. Absent from the promotion materials, however, are: polluted waterways from intensified dairy farming (Foote et al., 2015; Joy, 2018); the highest extinction rate of indigenous species in the world (Toki, 2018); unknown levels of chemical use in agriculture, horticulture, and industry (Hancock, 2018); a plethora of animal welfare issues (SAFE for Animals, n.d.); the highest per capita emissions of greenhouse gases from agriculture in the Organisation for Economic Co-operation and Development (OECD, 2017); and contaminated land from legacy waste (Ministry for the Environment, 2018). The notion that New Zealand is a '100 % PURE' environment is, as one commentator puts it, 'pure puffery' (*Stuff*, 2017). Furthermore, there is no integrated regulatory framework to deal with pressing environmental issues (Environmental Protection Authority, 2017).

This chapter begins with an outline of green criminology and the eco-justice approach to the study of environmental harm. We then adopt a species justice lens to develop an understanding of harm and victimisation in the horse-racing industry, before taking a brief look at the issue of industrial pollution. We then touch on the relationship between colonisation and environmental destruction and consider how a Māori world view can facilitate eco-justice. Finally, we draw the chapter to a close with a proposal that criminologists (green and otherwise) are uniquely positioned to contribute new understandings about environmental harm.

GREEN CRIMINOLOGY

'Green criminology' is an umbrella term used to describe the critically engaged study of environmental crimes and harms: their causes and effects; the responses by governments and environmental groups (such as SAFE, Greenpeace, and the World Wide Fund for Nature); the representations of environmental crimes and harms across diverse media platforms; the protests erected against issues; and more. Emerging in the early 1990s, the field has expanded and diversified with increasing pace over the past decade. Newly developed areas of specialisation include environmental victimisation (see Hall, 2017, 2018; Spapens et al., 2016; White, 2018a); green cultural criminology (Brisman & South, 2014); visual green criminology (Natali, 2016); climate change criminology (White, 2018b); and *blue* criminology (research focused on water-related harm) (Brisman et al., 2018).

Green criminology focuses on the study of environmental *harm*. While prohibited acts are part of the green criminological remit, much environmental suffering results from activities that are 'awful but lawful' (Passas, 2005, p. 771). Much of it is lawful because it serves humankind and is premised on the idea that the Earth is a resource for us to use (Beirne & South, 2007). Assessing the potential for injury from environmental harm – that is, the *risk* of harm – is critical for developing policies to prevent environment-related victimisation. Such harms tend to be slow to materialise, they are diffuse in their impact (Hall, 2013; Williams, 1996), and there can be problems locating the starting point or offender (for example, consider the development of cancer from earlier exposure to carcinogenic pollutants). Therefore, a focus on assessing risk is particularly important in green criminological research.

Other concepts central to green criminological work firmly sit outside of the mainstream criminological lexicon. One of these is *anthropocentrism*, a term referring to the ways by which human beings place themselves and their needs at the centre of everything they do. Green criminologists, along with other scholars, argue that our anthropocentrism is inherently harmful to our planet and the beings we share it with. It is our anthropocentrism that has precipitated the rise of fossil fuel use, the industrialisation of agriculture, and the urbanisation of over half of the human population, which is now affecting the Earth in unprecedented ways (Stromberg, 2013). The concept of anthropocentrism also helps to draw our attention to the everydayness of environmental destruction in our consumer-driven, throwaway culture by problematising our 'need' for bottled water or holidays in faraway places. All of us are guilty of committing everyday acts contributing to *ecocide* (Agnew, 2013), a term that refers to the wholesale destruction of ecosystems in a given territory (Higgins et al., 2013).

An eco-justice framework is employed by some green criminologists to identify and examine harm. For example, White and Heckenberg (2014) explain that environmental harm can be conceptualised through three lenses. First, a legal lens considers harm to have occurred when a law prohibiting an activity to do with the environment is breached. For example, dumping rubbish on public land is illegal and carries a maximum penalty of $30,000 in New Zealand under the Litter Act 1979. Second, an ecological lens considers harm via a biological measure of well-being. Here, harm occurs when a measure falls short of established benchmarks for indicating the health of a plant, an ecosystem, a non-human animal, or a human being. Such benchmarks might be found in 'state of the environment' reports, veterinary books, and medical journals. Alternatively, and third, an eco-justice lens considers harm to have occurred when *rights* have been breached. However, these are not the same rights as those encoded in the United Nations rights' charters or the New Zealand Bill of Rights. Rights under an eco-justice lens relates to three different eco-philosophies that consider the nature of the relationship between human beings and the wider environment. An anthropocentric eco-philosophy prioritises human beings over and above all other environmental phenomena; a biocentric eco-philosophy considers human beings as one among many animal species; and an ecocentric eco-philosophy makes no distinction between human beings and any other life form. Following this, environmental justice is anthropocentric insofar as it focuses on the right of all human beings to have access to environmental resources such as drinking water and food, as well as equal protection from polluted sites; species justice is biocentric in that it is concerned with non-human animals and their right to live as sentient beings; and ecological justice is ecocentric as it seeks the protection of ecosystems, via rights, to remain undisturbed.

Depending on the case in question, combinations of these three eco-justices may be held at the same time. Protecting the rights of freshwater ecosystems (thus securing ecological justice), for example, can also help to protect the rights of human beings to have access to clean drinking water (securing environmental justice). In fact, a fundamental part of ensuring that drinking water is clean and safe to drink is protecting the health and well-being of our freshwater sources (Hammond, 2018). Rights can also come into tension with each other. The situation regarding New Zealand's Kaimanawa horses provides a good illustration of such tension. Kaimanawa horses are a wild herd that have roamed parts of the country since 1876 and are now found mainly on the central volcanic plateau in the North Island. Since 1989 the Department of Conservation has conducted a biennial muster to reduce the impact of the horses' grazing and trampling on areas where rare indigenous grasses struggle to survive (Department of Conservation, 2006). While the department can rehome many of the horses in each muster, those that cannot be accommodated are killed. A species justice lens would argue for the protection of the rights of the horses to live as sentient beings and let them remain on the plateau. However, an ecological justice lens would argue that protecting the rights of the horses results in a breach of the rights of the plateau's ecosystems to remain undisturbed.

Despite such tensions, an eco-justice perspective enables green criminologists to render visible the harms that humankind has normalised and made routine, and therefore rarely acknowledges. In the next section we adopt a species justice lens to consider the victimisation of another group of horses in New Zealand: racehorses.

RACEHORSES, HARM, AND THE NEW ZEALAND HORSE-RACING INDUSTRY

The phrase 'rugby, racing and beer' is often used as a shorthand to describe the main recreational pursuits of New Zealanders, across generations. Horse racing arrived with the European settlers, and racing events quickly became a favourite way to mark a wide range of occasions. Often races were held simply because the opportunity to do so arose (Mountier, 1993). Perhaps part of the popularity of 'the races' was that everyone could participate, whereas rugby and beer-drinking were male-dominated activities. Today, horse racing appears as much a part of the cultural landscape as it ever was, if the industry's recorded profit of $1.65 billion in 2018 is anything to go by. We would like to think that this would not remain the case if consideration to the suffering of racehorses for human entertainment were undertaken.

The most popular type of racing both in New Zealand and globally is flat racing (where two or more horses gallop between two set points along an oval track) (McManus, 2013). Flat racing, and the sub-code of jumps racing (where racers jump obstacles along the track), are both forms of thoroughbred racing (New Zealand Thoroughbred Racing [NZTR], 2018a); the two categories of jumps racing are steeplechasing, involving large brush fences, and hurdling, with smaller baton-hurdle fences (NZTR, 2018a). Harness racing, like flat racing, occurs on oval racetracks. However, instead of a mounted jockey, the horse pulls a driver who sits in a two-wheeled cart known as a sulky (Harness Racing New Zealand [HRNZ], 2018). Standardbreds are used for harness racing, with their gait variation – a trot or a pace – determining which race class they compete in (HRNZ, 2018). Unless otherwise indicated, we will use 'horse racing' to refer to all three types of racing.

Racehorses typically begin training at between 18 and 20 months of age, and at the age of two to three they are considered by the horse-racing industry to be in the peak of their racing career (Battuello, 2018; Willoughby, 1975). However, a horse does not reach full skeletal maturity until around the age of six (Bennett, 2008; Willoughby, 1975). Bones, joints, tendons, and ligaments are placed under considerable strain during intensive training and competing, so, at a young age, racehorses are predisposed to long-term and potentially fatal musculoskeletal injuries (Battuello, 2018; Willoughby, 1975; Wilsher et al., 2006). The racing industry describes a horse's experience of debilitating harm from such injuries as 'wastage' to reflect the losses that occur during days out of training, missed racing opportunities, and consequential financial loss through veterinary care and reduced income from race winnings (Battuello, 2018; Wilsher et al., 2006).

The nature of physical injuries sustained on race day varies from minor scrapes through to those considered to be 'wastages'. Whipping racehorses is commonplace and, although NZTR requires whips to be padded to absorb the impact of the whip as it makes contact with the horse (*Horsetalk*, 2012), visible signs of localised trauma and tissue damage on the horse have been found in over 80 per cent of rider–horse interactions (McGreevy et al., 2012). Moreover, horses are most likely to be whipped on the side of their body between the ribs and the hip (known as the flank), where their skin is thin and sensitive to pain.

Most serious injuries are sustained during jumps-racing events. At such an event in 2016, three horses fell and were subsequently euthanised (Walters, 2016). These three deaths were described in the media as 'incidents' and 'unfortunate events' (Walters, 2016, paras. 2, 4). From a species justice perspective, a more appropriate term for these deaths would be 'theriocide', which acknowledges the horse has been killed at the hands of humans (Beirne, 2014; Sollund, 2017). There were 17 recorded theriocides in the 2018–19 racing season (Adams, 2019). Racing also increases horses' blood pressure, putting multiple tiny blood vessels under stress, which can potentially lead to exercise-induced pulmonary haemorrhage (EIPH), or bleeding in the lungs. Horses have been known to suffer massive internal bleeding and choke to death as a result (Mundy, 2000). To manage this possible outcome, the industry administers diuretics to increase urination in the horses (which in turn lowers their blood pressure).

Racehorses suffer substantial stress during racing and training, which can manifest in several ways. Bell's (2006) research found that 89.9 per cent of thoroughbreds suffered from equine gastric ulcer syndrome, for example. 'Stereotypic behaviours' such as cribbing, where a horse bites onto a solid object and sucks in air, and locomotive behaviours, such as a horse weaving their head back and forth over the stable door and stall-walking, serve as psychological coping mechanisms (Lesté-Lasserre, 2016; Strickland, 1997). These kinds of behaviours are not seen in wild horses, like the Kaimanawa horses mentioned earlier, but appear between six months and two or three years of age among racehorses; a period that coincides with the peak of intensive training and competing (Lesté-Lasserre, 2016). Horses who exit the race industry due to injury and/or behavioural issues may not be suitable for rehoming or use in other riding disciplines. These 'unwanted' racehorses often end up being sold to a slaughterhouse. In this way, the horse's owner can squeeze the last bit of money out of them before life ends with a bullet. Considering that there are 120,000 horses in New Zealand, over one-third of which are thoroughbreds and standardbreds, it is likely that a significant proportion of the recorded 892 horses killed in New Zealand abattoirs in 2016 were ex-racehorses (Ministry for Primary Industries, 2018).

While New Zealand has quite extensive animal welfare provisions relative to other countries, the 'rights' of animals to live as sentient beings in accordance with species justice remain unprotected (Francione, 1995). Instead, welfare policies adhere to an anthropocentric system that protects our interests, as animal 'owners'. Our animal welfare policies also engage in what Flynn and Hall (2017) call hierarchical speciesism, whereby species are ordered by how important, sentient, human-like, or 'cute' they are (known as the 'Bambi effect' – see Ferreday, 2011). There are stricter protections for those more prominent on the hierarchy (see, for example, section 30B of the Animal Welfare Act 1999). Interestingly, and disturbingly, the unique circumstances of some animals are provided for (such as animals used in research), while the circumstances of others, like racehorses, are not. Clearly, it did not occur to legislators to consider that the horse-racing industry would be harmful to the animals who are forced to live within it.

The industry itself does have some rules pertaining to horse welfare. Penalties are handed to jockeys or drivers who breach whip regulations, and these typically consist of monetary fines and/or disqualifications from racing for various lengths of time (HRNZ, 2017; NZTR, 2018b). However, evidence suggests that these penalties are factored by competitors into the costs of racing. Fines are small compared to race stakes, which may well be hundreds of thousands. Lucrative stakes on race day may also incentivise stakeholders to do whatever necessary to secure a win, including inflicting physical and psychological harm against the racehorse (Hibbard, 2014). Unfortunately, pressure to win may only be intensified in future, with then Racing Minister Winston Peters having announced in August 2018 that the aim is to double the racing prize pool to $100 million per annum (Anderson, 2018; Tourelle, 2018). High-performing jockeys also receive favourable treatment from the media, irrespective of whether they have breached racing rules or not. Jockey Emily Farr, for example, was described in a news article as a 'talented rider' who 'put in a top day's work' at the 2017 National Jumps Day. This was despite being fined $300 for excessively whipping in one race, and a further $500 for the same breach just a few races later (Ryan, 2017).

Collectively these examples illustrate that a racehorse's 'value' extends only to the point of their profit-making potential. Established racing stallions and mares may be further exploited by breeders to produce race-winning offspring – for a time – after their retirement from racing (Feinn, 2018). However, for the majority of horses who finish their racing career – including those who were perhaps deemed too slow to start it – experiences of victimisation may continue outside of the racing sector (Feinn, 2018). What is more, there are minimal formalised guidelines or policies holding owners, breeders, and trainers to account for their horses' futures; consequently, racehorses are at risk of being sold or given away to unvetted and potentially unsafe homes. In our assessment, it is unlikely that without significant public outcry either the industry or the government will make a genuine effort to address any of the harms that racehorses suffer at any stage of their lives (see Ruggiero & South, 2013). The New Zealand horse-racing industry's $1.65 billion contribution to GDP, combined with the government's $39 million from industry-related gambling taxes, amounts to a substantial pool of money (IER, 2018).

Species justice adopts a rights-based approach towards human interactions with non-human animals and protections that goes beyond the humane treatment of non-human animals provided for in animal welfare laws (Francione & Charlton, 2010; White & Heckenberg, 2014). A species justice perspective holds that non-human animals have a right to a life that is meaningful to them, irrespective of the value placed on that life by anyone else (Francione, 1995). From this critically engaged position, not only does horse racing interfere with horses' sentience, but also their physical and/or psychological suffering is an embedded part of the horse-racing industry (Battuello, 2018; Cao, 2010). Regardless of the fact that there are bodies governing horse racing within New Zealand that strive to take ethics and racehorse welfare seriously, it cannot be denied that racehorses would not experience the harms we have outlined above were it not for the industry's very existence. From a species justice perspective, then, the only appropriate response is for the immediate criminalisation of running horses in racing events, followed by the timely abolition of all sectors of the industry (Battuello, 2018).

INDUSTRY AND ENVIRONMENTAL HARM IN AOTEAROA NEW ZEALAND

Understanding harm to our planet and its inhabitants cannot be separated from capitalist industrial processes. As Lynch et al. (2013) explain, industry harvests its raw materials from the environment (land, oil, timber, for example) to produce goods for the global market. As capitalism is an economic system oriented around the pursuit of profit, corporations under capitalism are continually harvesting raw materials from the environment because they are striving to expand their operations to produce more goods to sell. However, environmental sustainability is possible only with conservation (Lynch et al., 2013). Corporate growth under capitalism therefore goes hand in hand with the escalation of environmental destruction. What we focus on in this section, however, is another way that production processes create harm: through by-products that are returned to the environment as waste. Contamination from industrial waste can devastate ecological well-being, and in turn lead to significant harms to other life forms.

Freshwater pollution

In Aotearoa New Zealand, freshwater pollution is our most pressing environmental problem. Seventy-four per cent of our freshwater fish species are endangered, a higher proportion than in any other country in the world (Joy et al., 2019). Ninety per cent of lowland waterways fail bathing standards, and 40 per cent of our lakes are eutrophic (containing excess nutrients). The worst offender over the past two decades has been intensified dairy farming (Joy, 2014). Excess nutrients from fertiliser and urine from cows seep through soil into waterways, critically disturbing ecosystem well-being (Foote et al., 2015). Freshwater ecologist Mike Joy links these problems back to the arrival of European settlers (Joy, 2014). Since then, approximately 90 per cent of the country's wetlands (which filter and remove waste from water) has been drained to make way for agriculture, and a comparable proportion of vegetation (i.e., native forest cover) has been removed. Intricate and complex ecosystems, which performed crucial hydrologic and biological functions to keep waterways healthy, have been all but destroyed.

Freshwater pollution breaches not only ecosystem rights to remain undisturbed, but also human rights to have access to environmental resources. Compliance with drinking water standards in New Zealand is remarkably poor compared to the United Kingdom or European countries, with 10 times the rate of transgressions of water quality. It is therefore unsurprising that New Zealand is estimated to have one of the worst levels of waterborne diseases in the developed world (Ball, 2007). Figures from the Ministry of Health's (2017) water quality report 2015/16 show that about 20 per cent of New Zealanders between 2009 and 2016 received water from potentially contaminated water supplies. Specifically, 92,000 were at risk of bacterial infection, 681,000 at risk of protozoal infection, and 59,000 at risk from the long-term effects of exposure to harmful chemicals.

The state of our freshwater was illuminated in August 2016, when there was a mass outbreak of gastroenteritis in the small town of Havelock North. One-third of the town's 14,000 residents were estimated to have become ill; 45 people were admitted to hospital, and 4 died (Department of Internal Affairs, 2017). Some who fell ill developed Guillain-Barré syndrome, and others, including children, suffered reactive arthritis. A government inquiry concluded that faecal matter had contaminated the water supply after a period of heavy rain, and that it was a 'culture of complacency' on behalf of parties responsible for overseeing the drinking water system that was to blame (Department of Internal Affairs, 2017). Unless freshwater sources begin to be respected in accordance with eco-justice it is likely that more crises like the one in Havelock North will occur.

Contaminated land

The Ministry for the Environment's 'Hazardous Activities and Industries List' (HAIL) currently identifies 19,568 contaminated sites nationwide (Ministry for the Environment, 2016a). Regional councils hold information relating to confirmed sites, with some projecting that the actual figure will be three times this (Ministry for the Environment, 2016b). Part of the problem is that many sites have since moved into private hands. Film director Peter Jackson's Stone Street Studios, for example, is located at the site of the former Miramar Gasworks, which is listed as one of the ministry's 10 areas requiring urgent clean-ups (Ministry for the Environment, 2018). Who would have imagined that the same studio that stunned the world with epic scenes of New Zealand's untouched landscapes in the Lord of the Rings film trilogy sits atop a fusion of hazardous by-products, such as polyaromatic hydrocarbons and benzene from historical processes of gasification?

Some contaminated sites on the HAIL registry are decommissioned landfills. On Houghton Bay beach, in Wellington, a pipe can be seen releasing water from a stormwater system. Sitting on top of the stormwater system is a landfill that was operative from the 1950s to the 1970s. The water turns orange at times because it is contaminated with leachate, which regularly seeps out from the old landfill. The contaminated water flows out into the bay, which in 2009 became part of a marine reserve. The bay is also regularly used by surfers. On some days the pungent chemical odour of landfill gas can be detected from the beach near the pipe, from the sports fields that now cover the landfill, and from various spots around the suburb of Houghton Bay. Continued exposure to landfill gas can cause respiratory problems, fever, eye irritation, and joint and muscular pain, as well as increased cancer risk (Nair et al., 2019). According to Wellington City Council, which does not measure the gas, the landfill poses little in the way of risk to human health (R. Hon, personal communication, 31 July 2019).

ENVIRONMENTAL HARMS, COLONISATION, AND MĀTAURANGA MĀORI

The beginnings of Aotearoa New Zealand as we know it today involved the violent acquisition of land from Māori by the British Crown through war and confiscation. Wynyard (2017) explains that, during colonisation, lands are not just stolen from Indigenous peoples but also stripped of their flora and fauna to make way for agriculture and the building of townships. In New Zealand, alongside the draining of wetlands, millions of hectares of native bush were felled and transformed into pasture, irrevocably destroying ancient ecosystems. The destruction of the environment was part of the devastation of Māori, too, because in Te Ao Māori (the Māori world), specific lands, mountains, and rivers form part of kinship relations, as tūpuna (ancestors). As land shifted to Pākehā control, the ancestral relations between Māori and features of the environment were disregarded by settlers.

The significance of the relationship between Māori and the environment can be seen in the case that resulted in the Te Awa Tupua (Whanganui River Claims Settlement) Act 2017.

The Whanganui River was given legal personhood in the Act, meaning that in law it has the same rights, powers, duties, and liabilities as a human citizen. The river has two guardians, one from Whanganui iwi and one from the Crown, who are required to act on the river's behalf to ensure its well-being in accordance with its official status as a person. Green criminologists in other contexts have heralded this development as an exemplary piece of environmental legislation (White, 2018a). While they are not wrong, what they miss in their assessments is that the Act was the outcome of the longest-running legal case in New Zealand's history, taken against the Crown by Whanganui iwi for colonial grievances (Hutchison, 2014). Among these was the Crown's assuming of river control and subsequent obstruction of Whanganui iwi's access to the river. In other words, the Act does not recognise Whanganui iwi and the river as intricately intertwined as whānau, a connection that was ravaged by colonisation. Instead, it represents a compromise on behalf of Whanganui iwi to reach an agreement with the state with respect to governing the river. If the river had been returned to Whanganui iwi instead, traditional practices of kaitiakitanga (guardianship) could have been restored. Perhaps, then, green criminologists could respond to the iwi's compromise by envisioning and adopting an *indigecentric* eco-philosophy that centres traditional kinship structures between Indigenous peoples and the land, and endorses their right to practise kaitiakitanga within those relationships. An indigecentric eco-philosophy would align with anthropocentric, biocentric, and ecocentric eco-philosophies and their related eco-justices, insofar as the rights of people, non-human animals, and ecosystems that are part of a whakapapa (genealogy) would be protected.

Green criminologists in New Zealand are uniquely positioned to contribute innovative ways of doing research, especially given our responsibility to incorporate Te Tiriti o Waitangi into research. Treaty obligations involve actively partnering with Māori, consulting with iwi and institutional Māori advisors, and incorporating mātauranga Māori (Māori knowledge) perspectives into our research design. In turn, drawing on mātauranga Māori can demonstrate the value of Indigenous world views in enhancing understandings about environmental harm and advancing the realisation of rights endorsed by an indigecentric eco-philosophy.

CONCLUSION

The criticality of green criminology stimulates a more profound enquiry into the nature and prevalence of environmental harm, irrespective of whether the activity leading to the harm is institutionalised, socially accepted, and legal (Fitzgerald & Pellow, 2014; Sollund, 2015). By doing so, it demonstrates how many of our everyday practices – past, present, and future – can be linked to harms to other forms of life on our planet. We envisage an Aotearoa New Zealand-situated green criminology that is known for its decolonising and methodologically innovative scholarship. That said, all criminologists, whether here or overseas, have a significant task ahead as the impacts of climate change intensify and affect every area of our work. The importance of a green criminology, in fact, moves far outside the boundaries of our discipline at this critical time on earth.

STUDY QUESTIONS

- Identify three harms against the environment, and discuss the tensions (if any) between environmental, species, and ecological eco-justices in relation to these.
- Create a 'species hierarchy' of non-human animals in Aotearoa New Zealand. Critically discuss the reasoning behind your ranking.

- We all commit 'everyday acts of ecocide' against the environment. List your offences, compare them with others, and together consider whether the value they each bring to your lives outweighs the harm they enact.

FURTHER READING

Brisman, A., & South, N. (2014). *Green cultural criminology: Constructions of environmental harm, consumerism, and resistance to ecocide*. Abingdon, UK: Routledge.

Sollund, R. (2008). Causes for speciesism: Difference, distance and denial. In R. Sollund (Ed.), *Global harms. Ecological crime and speciesism* (pp. 109–130). New York, NY: Nova Science Publishers.

White, R., & Heckenberg, D. (2014). *Green criminology: An introduction to the study of environmental harm*. Abingdon, UK: Routledge.

REFERENCES

Adams, J. (2019, August 15). The dark side of horse racing. *Spinoff*. https://thespinoff.co.nz/society/15-08-2019/the-dark-side-of-horse-racing/

Agnew, R. (2013). The ordinary acts that contribute to ecocide: A criminological analysis. In N. South & A. Brisman (Eds.), *Routledge international handbook of green criminology* (pp. 58–72). Abingdon, UK: Routledge.

Anderson, I. (2018, August 31). Number of race tracks look set to reduce as Winston Peters releases the Messara report. *Stuff*. Retrieved from https://www.stuff.co.nz/sport/racing/106702745/number-of-race-tracks-look-set-to-reduce-as-winston-peters-releases-the-messara-report

Animal Welfare Act 1999, https://www.mpi.govt.nz/legal/legal-overviews-legislation-standards/animal-welfare-legislation/#B

Ball, A. (2007). *Estimation of the burden of water-borne disease in New Zealand: Preliminary report*. Wellington, New Zealand: Ministry of Health. Retrieved from https://www.health.govt.nz/system/files/documents/publications/water-borne-disease-burden-prelim-report-feb07-v2.pdf

Battuello, P. (2018). *Horseracing wrongs*. Retrieved from https://horseracingwrongs.com/

Beirne, P. (2014). Theriocide: Naming animal killing. *International Journal for Crime, Justice and Social Democracy, 3*(2), 49–66. doi:10.5204/ijcjsd.v3i2.174

Beirne, P., & South, N. (Eds.). (2007). *Issues in green criminology: Confronting harms against environments, humanity and other animals*. Cullompton, UK: Willan Publishing.

Bell, R. J. W. (2006). *Equine gastric ulcer syndrome in New Zealand racehorses*. Unpublished Master's thesis, Massey University, Palmerston North, New Zealand. Retrieved from https://mro.massey.ac.nz/handle/10179/4997

Bennett, D. (2008). *Timing and rate of skeletal maturation in horses, with comments on starting young horses and the state of the industry*. Retrieved from http://www.equinestudies.org/ranger_2008/ranger_piece_2008_pdf1.pdf

Brisman, A., McClanahan, B., South, N., & Walters, R. (2018). *Water, crime and security in the twenty-first century. Too dirty, too little, too much*. London, UK: Palgrave Macmillan.

Brisman, A., & South, N. (2014). *Green cultural criminology: Constructions of environmental harm, consumerism, and resistance to ecocide*. Abingdon, UK: Routledge.

Cao, D. (2010). Animals' place in legal theory: Introduction to the species issue on animals' place in jurisprudence. *International Journal for the Semiotics of Law, 24*(3), 255–257. doi:10.1007/s11196-010-9180-y

Department of Conservation. (2006). *Kaimanawa wild horses plan*. https://www.doc.govt.nz/about-us/science-publications/conservation-publications/threats-and-impacts/animal-pests/kaimanawa-wild-horses-plan/

Department of Internal Affairs (2017). Government inquiry into Havelock North drinking water. *Report of the Havelock North drinking water inquiry: Stage 1.* Retrieved from https://www.dia.govt.nz/Government-Inquiry-into-Havelock-North-Drinking-Water

Environmental Protection Authority. (2017). *Briefing to the incoming ministers.* Retrieved from https://www.epa.govt.nz/news-and-alerts/latest-news/briefing-to-incoming-ministers/

Feinn, L. (2018, August 6). What really happens to racehorses after they're done racing? *Thedodo.* Retrieved from https://www.thedodo.com/close-to-home/triple-crown-racehorse-retirement

Ferreday, D. (2011). Becoming deer: Nonhuman drag and online utopias. *Feminist Theory, 12*(2), 219–225. doi:10.1177/1464700111404288

Fitzgerald, A. J., & Pellow, D. (2014). Ecological defense for animal liberation: A holistic understanding of the world. *Counterpoints, 448,* 28–48. Retrieved from https://www.jstor.org/stable/42982376?seq=1#metadata_info_tab_contents

Flynn, M., & Hall, M. (2017). The case for a victimology of nonhuman animal harms. *Contemporary Justice Review, 20*(3), 299–318. doi:10.1080/10282580.2017.1348898

Foote, K., Joy, M., & Death, R. (2015). New Zealand dairy farming: Milking our environment for all its worth. *Environmental Management, 56*(3), 709–720. doi:10.1007/s00267–015–0517-x

Francione, G. L. (1995). *Animals, property and the law.* Philadelphia, PA: Temple University Press.

Francione, G. L., & Charlton, A. (2010). Abolitionist approach to animal rights. In M. Bekoff (Ed.), *Encyclopedia of animal rights and animal welfare* (Vol. 1, pp. 1–5). Santa Barbara, CA: Greenwood Press.

Hall, M. (2013). *Victims of environmental harm: Rights, recognition and redress under national and international law.* Abingdon, UK: Routledge.

Hall, M. (2017). Exploring the cultural dimensions of environmental victimization. *Palgrave Communications, 3*(1), 1–10. doi:10.1057/palcomms.2017.76

Hall, M. (2018). Environmental victimisation: Corporate villainy or state connivance? *Radical Criminology,* 1929–7904. Retrieved from http://eprints.lincoln.ac.uk/id/eprint/15918/

Hammond, V. (2018). New Zealand freshwater management – a public health perspective. In M. Joy (Ed.), *Mountains to sea: Solving New Zealand's freshwater crisis* (1st ed., pp. 54–64). Wellington, New Zealand: Bridget Williams Books.

Hancock, F. (2018, April 24). Mapping New Zealand's chemical romance. *Newsroom.* https://www.newsroom.co.nz/2018/04/23/106027?slug=mapping-new-zealands-chemical-romance

Harness Racing New Zealand. (2017, November 24). *Use of the whip regulation.* Retrieved from https://www.hrnz.co.nz/news/use-of-the-whip-regulation/

Harness Racing New Zealand. (2018). *About standardbreds.* Retrieved from https://www.hrnz.co.nz/industry-information/getting-started/about-standardbreds/

Hibbard, S. (2014, November 4). Talk to the animals: The truth about horse racing. *New Zealand Herald.* Retrieved from https://www.nzherald.co.nz/lifestyle/news/article.cfm?c_id=6&objectid=11352939

Higgins, P., Short, D., & South, N. (2013). Protecting the planet: A proposal for a law of ecocide. *Crime, Law and Social Change, 59*(3), 251–266. doi:10.1007/s10611–013–9413–6

Horsetalk. (2012, March 21). Study finds welfare issues around padded whips. Retrieved from https://www.horsetalk.co.nz/2012/03/21/study-finds-welfare-issues-around-padded-whips/

Hutchison, A. (2014). The Whanganui River as a legal person. *Alternative Law Journal, 39*(3), 179–182. doi:10.1177/1037969X1403900309

IER (2018). *Size and scope of the New Zealand racing industry.* Retrieved from https://www.rita.org.nz/sites/default/files/documents/NZ%20Racing%20Size%20and%20Scope%202018%20Full%20Report.pdf

Joy, M. K. (2014). New Zealand's freshwater disaster. *New Zealand Science Review, 71*(4), 97–103.

Joy, M. (Ed.). (2018). *Mountains to sea: Solving New Zealand's freshwater crisis* (1st ed.). Wellington, New Zealand: Bridget Williams Books.

Joy, M. K., Foote, K. J., McNie, P., & Piria, M. (2019). Decline in New Zealand's freshwater fish fauna: Effect of land use. *Marine and Freshwater Research, 70*(1), 114–124. doi:10.1071/MF18028

Lesté-Lasserre, C. (2016, October 11). Equine stereotypies: Vice or coping mechanism? *The Horse*. Retrieved from https://thehorse.com/18866/equine-stereotypies-vice-or-coping-mechanism/

Lynch, M. J., Long, M. A., Barrett, K. L., & Stretesky, P. B. (2013). Is it a crime to produce ecological disorganization? Why green criminology and political economy matter in the analysis of global ecological harms. *British Journal of Criminology, 53*(6), 997–1016. doi:10.1093/bjc/azt051

McGreevy, P. D., Corken, R. A., Salvin, H., & Black, C. M. (2012). Whip use by jockeys in a sample of Australian thoroughbred races – an observational study. *PLoS One, 7*(3), 1–6. doi:10.1371/journal.pone.0033398

McManus, P. (2013). *The global horseracing industry: Social, economic, environmental, and ethical perspectives*. Abingdon, UK: Routledge.

Ministry for Primary Industries. (2018). *New Zealand horses slaughter statistics to June 2018*. Retrieved from https://www.mpi.govt.nz

Ministry for the Environment. (2016a). *Hazardous activities and industries list (HAIL)*. Retrieved from https://www.mfe.govt.nz/land/hazardous-activities-and-industries-list-hail#hail-web

Ministry for the Environment. (2016b). *Interim review of the National Environmental Standard for Assessing and Managing Contaminants in Soil to Protect Human Health: Summary report*. Retrieved from http://natlib-primo.hosted.exlibrisgroup.com/NLNZ:NLNZ:NLNZ_ALMA21273558350002836

Ministry for the Environment. (2018). *Contaminated sites remediation fund priority list*. Retrieved from https://www.mfe.govt.nz/more/funding/contaminated-sites-remediation-fund/csrf-priority-list

Ministry of Health. (2017). *Annual report on drinking-water quality 2015–2016*. Retrieved from https://www.health.govt.nz/publication/annual-report-drinking-water-quality–2015–2016

Mountier, M. (1993). *Racing women of New Zealand*. Wellington, New Zealand: Daphne Brasell Associates.

Mundy, G. D. (2000). Equine welfare. Racing. *Journal of American Veterinary Medical Association, 216*(8), 1243–1246.

Nair, A. T., Senthilnathan, J., & Nagendra, S. M. S. (2019). Emerging perspectives on VOC emissions from landfill sites: Impact on tropospheric chemistry and local air quality. *Process Safety and Environmental Protection, 121*, 143–154. doi:10.1016/j.psep.2018.10.026

Natali, L. (2016). *Visual approach for green criminology: Exploring the social perception of environmental harm*. London, UK: Palgrave Macmillan.

New Zealand Thoroughbred Racing (NZTR). (2018a). *Types of racing*. Retrieved from https://loveracing.nz/nztr/racing-info/types-of-racing

New Zealand Thoroughbred Racing (NZTR). (2018b). *Using whips in racing*. Retrieved from https://loveracing.nz/welfare/using-whips-in-racing

Organisation for Economic Co-operation and Development (OECD). (2017). *OECD environmental performance reviews: New Zealand 2017*. OECD Publishing. doi:10.1787/9789264268203-en

Passas, N. (2005). Lawful but awful: 'Legal corporate crimes'. *Journal of Socio-Economics, 34*(6), 771–786. doi:10.1016/j.socec.2005.07.024

Ruggiero, V., & South, N. (2013). Green criminology and crimes of the economy: Theory, research and praxis. *Critical Criminology, 21*(3), 359–373. doi:10.1007/s10612–013–9191–6

Ryan, T. (2017, October 2). Emily Farr hit twice for excessive use of whip. *Stuff*. Retrieved from https://www.stuff.co.nz/sport/racing/97449176/emily-farr-hit-twice-for-excessive-use-of-whip

SAFE for Animals. (n.d.). *Take action*. SAFE | For Animals. Retrieved from https://safe.org.nz/take-action/

Sollund, R. A. (2015). *Green harms and crimes: Critical criminology in a changing world*. Basingstoke, UK: Palgrave Macmillan.

Sollund, R. (2017). Doing green, critical criminology with an auto-ethnographic, feminist approach. *Critical Criminology, 25*(2), 245–260. doi:10.1007/s10612–017–9361-z

Spapens, A. C., White, R. D., & Huisman, W. (2016). *Environmental crime in transnational context global issues in green enforcement and criminology*. Abingdon, UK: Routledge.

Strickland, C. (1997, September 1). Focus on discipline: Harness racing. *The Horse*. Retrieved from https://thehorse.com/14779/focus-on-discipline-harness-racing/

Stromberg, J. (2013, January). What is the Anthropocene and are we in it? *Smithsonian Magazine*. Retrieved from https://www.smithsonianmag.com/science-nature/what-is-the-anthropocene-and-are-we-in-it-164801414/

Stuff. (2017, July 17). New marketing campaign 100% Pure New Zealand puffery. Retrieved from https://www.stuff.co.nz/the-press/opinion/94781950/editorial-100-pure-new-zealand-puffery

Toki, N. (2018, February 5). Why the survival of NZ's wildlife is in our hands. *Spinoff*. Retrieved from https://thespinoff.co.nz/science/05-02-2018/why-the-survival-of-nzs-wildlife-is-in-our-hands/

Tourelle, G. (2018, August 31). Famous Kiwi holiday racecourses among 20 slated for closure. *Stuff*. Retrieved from https://www.stuff.co.nz/sport/racing/106715262/famous-kiwi-holiday-racecourses-among-20-slated-for-closure

Walters, L. (2016, June 8). Tragic raceday ends in three horses being euthanised. *Stuff*. Retrieved from https://www.stuff.co.nz/sport/racing/80841364/tragic-raceday-ends-in-three-horses-being-euthanised

White, R. (2018a). Green victimology and non-human victims. *International Review of Victimology*, 24(2), 239–255. doi:10.1177/0269758017745615

White, R. (2018b). *Climate change criminology*. Bristol, UK: Bristol University Press.

White, R., & Heckenberg, D. (2014). *Green criminology: An introduction to the study of environmental harm* (1st ed.). Abingdon, UK: Routledge.

Williams, C. (1996). An environmental victimology. *Social Justice: A Journal of Crime, Conflict and World Order*, 23(4), 16–40. Retrieved from https://www.jstor.org/stable/29766973?seq=1#metadata_info_tab_contents

Willoughby, D. (1975). *Growth and nutrition in the horse*. New York, NY: Barnes.

Wilsher, S., Allen, W. R., & Wood, J. L. (2006). Factors associated with failure of thoroughbred horses to train and race. *Equine Veterinary Journal*, 38(2), 113–118. Retrieved from https://www.ncbi.nlm.nih.gov/pubmed/16536379

Wynyard, M. (2017). Plunder in the promised land: Māori land alienation and the genesis of capitalism in Aotearoa New Zealand. In A. Bell, V. Elizabeth, T. McIntosh, & M. Wynyard (Eds.), *A land of milk and honey? Making sense of Aotearoa New Zealand* (pp. 13–25). Auckland, New Zealand: Auckland University Press.

11

White-collar Crimes
Culpability, Causes, and Control

Simon Mackenzie

It is a popular misconception that white-collar crime is less serious than other types of crime. In economic terms it is much more serious. The losses caused in merely one of the major financial scandals in a given year can outpace the total of *all* financial loss caused by blue-collar crime (Friedrichs, 2010). Of course, extensive economic harm is not the only measure of seriousness. We should also consider the physical and emotional harms caused by white-collar crimes, and these also outstrip blue-collar crime. Consider things like: workplace health and safety infringements, many of which negligently or recklessly cause serious injury and death (Tombs & Whyte, 2007); the emotional traumas of white-collar crime victimisation though the myriad scams, frauds, and consumer abuses that permeate late modern capitalist markets (Mackenzie, 2010); the psychological as well as the financial harms when hundreds or thousands of employees lose their pension savings as their company collapses due to criminal mismanagement (Friedrichs, 2004); the legacy of death and disability caused by the negligence that causes massive toxic pollution, like at the Union Carbide plant in Bhopal (Pearce & Tombs, 2012) or the nuclear reactor at Chernobyl (Smith & Beresford, 2005). The list goes on; white-collar crime is a devastatingly serious social problem. It is therefore one of the more enduring puzzles of the criminal justice system that white-collar crime continues to be treated as a less serious threat to the health, well-being, and integrity of society than blue-collar crime.

The definition of white-collar crime is not settled. Does white-collar crime need to involve socially powerful offenders, or are certain *types* of crime inherently white-collar? In practice, most white-collar criminologists use a balance of offender- and offence-based considerations in setting the boundaries of the concept. There is a core of agreement that white-collar crime '(1) occurs in a legitimate occupational context; (2) is motivated by the objective of economic gain or occupational success; and (3) is not characterised by direct, intentional violence' (Friedrichs, 2010, p. 5).

In 1939, Edwin Sutherland used his presidential address to the American Sociological Society to issue a call for more attention to the white-collar criminal, based on his research on the 70 largest US manufacturing, mining, and mercantile corporations (Sutherland, 1940). Reviewing all of the legal decisions issued against these major companies, many of which were household names, he concluded that 97 per cent of them were recidivists, having two or more criminal, civil, or administrative tribunal decisions made against them (Sutherland, 1949). Since then, the study of white-collar crime has grown considerably within criminology, with much of the research being conducted in the US and Europe, some in Australia, and very little in New Zealand. In that respect, as well as being a survey of what is known about the current landscape of white-collar crime in New Zealand, this chapter will include some discussion of key theoretical positions in the wider international literature. This should allow us to see both how the New Zealand experience fits with extant causal and regulatory theories, and how we can build on that base of understanding with further case study research here. The chapter will focus on white-collar crimes that are not green or state–corporate crimes, because those two subjects are given their own treatment in this handbook (see Monod de Froideville & Smithline, chapter 10, and Stanley & Day, chapter 12 this volume). It will be obvious, though, that many state crimes are white-collar, and many green crimes and environmental harms are committed by corporations or more generally are the externalities of late modern capitalist business activities.

A BRIEF HISTORY OF WHITE-COLLAR CRIME IN NEW ZEALAND

White-collar crime in Aotearoa New Zealand has a long history. In fact, contemporary bicultural New Zealand is founded on white-collar crime. Before the arrival of colonial settlers, land was held by Māori as customary land, in which everyone had a common interest. British colonisation, and the exploitative land deals that deprived Māori of significant areas of the country, is a large-scale example of white-collar crime. It was accompanied by smaller-scale examples as hustlers took advantage of the opportunities arising to ply a variety of fraudulent techniques: land-grabbing, misleading investors, and selling land that they didn't own (Hunt, 2001).

The crimes of colonialism aside, the history of commerce in New Zealand has been characterised especially in more recent decades by regular waves of corporate collapses and scandals. In the 1970s these included big names like Securitibank and JBL. Often these corporate collapses involved white-collar crime, as directors tried to trade their way out of debt, which can involve making false representations to new investors about the insolvent state of the business. This was the case, for example, with JBL, which at the time was the biggest corporate collapse in New Zealand's history: company officials were charged after advertising for new investors, whose funds went straight towards attempts to pay down the failing company's debt balance, rather than being put into new investment vehicles (Birchfield, 1972).

In the 1980s, the 'Rogernomics' era of rapid deregulation and market liberalisation by the Labour government provided a new context of opportunity for white-collar crime. During this era of rapid change, lax regulation of financial crimes like money laundering and insider trading in New Zealand allowed corporate greed and irresponsibility to flourish. For example, Equiticorp was a merchant and investment bank which between its inception in 1984 and the global sharemarket crash of 1987 made its chairman, Allan Hawkins, $360 million in personal wealth, placing him as the second most wealthy New Zealander at the time (Thornton, 2006). By 1991 he was bankrupt, owing over $600 million personally, with Equiticorp owing creditors $3.5 billion; and in 1992, after 18 months of investigation by the Serious Fraud Office (SFO), he was at the centre of what at the time was the longest and most costly criminal trial in New Zealand's history (Sturt, 1998). Along with many other similar but less high-profile cases, the interest of Equiticorp's officials in enriching themselves at the expense of the company and others dimmed the glow of the free-market reforms of the 1980s, which had been heralded as unleashing the great Kiwi spirit of entrepreneurialism. That the wild and unlawful excesses of free-market capitalism have to be held in check by controls exerted by effective regulation is a lesson that has been learned the hard way in New Zealand, as elsewhere.

White-collar crime cases continued throughout the 1980s, 1990s, and early 2000s, with another notable upturn during the global financial crisis (GFC) that began in 2007. In the GFC, many New Zealand finance companies came under severe financial pressure, and a considerable number took to illegal means in their attempt to survive, falsifying accounts and issuing fake prospectuses in order to obtain loans from unsuspecting creditors. The list of finance companies that collapsed during the crisis, resulting in prosecutions for fraud, is full of organisations that at the time were household names. Bridgecorp went down owing $460 million to 14,500 investors; its CEO was charged with 18 counts of fraud and sentenced to nearly seven years in jail (see *R v Petricevic*).[1] Viaduct Capital and Mutual Finance were two companies that went into receivership in 2010, owing investors $7.8 million and $9.3 million, respectively. Their directors were charged for misleading investors and using false statements in their prospectus to channel investor funds towards saving failing commercial enterprises owned by the directors (see *Bublitz v R*).[2] South Canterbury Finance owed $1.58 billion when it went into receivership in 2010, with criminal charges for fraud by the SFO following (Lee, 2019).

THE EXTENT OF WHITE-COLLAR CRIME IN NEW ZEALAND

Despite this long history of white-collar crime in New Zealand, punctuated by famous cases during significant periods of financial turmoil, we still do not know the true extent of the problem. The SFO announced its intention in 2011 to produce the first ever 'costs of economic crime' report for the country. A draft of that report, obtained by *Radio New Zealand* in 2012, estimated the overall cost of financial crime to New Zealand at up to $9.4 billion a year (SFO, 2012). In 2013, the *New Zealand Herald* obtained an updated version of the draft report through a freedom of information request, in which the figure had been reduced to '$300 million of "detected financial crime"' (Nippert, 2014, para. 15). The report was never released by the SFO, due to concerns about its methodology. There has not been any systematic attempt since to estimate the overall annual cost of economic crime in New Zealand.

The unpublished draft SFO report contained estimates of fraud in various sectors of the economy, which clearly should be treated with caution, given the report was never publicly released – but they are nonetheless interesting in what they suggest about the overall scale of the fraud problem in New Zealand. For ACC, the fraud estimate was 8–11 per cent of total entitlements paid, and it included fraud by providers, 'which includes over-servicing and phantom billing', and fraud by clients who made fake or inflated claims (SFO, 2012, p. 22). In the health sector, the SFO estimated the total cost of health fraud, detected and undetected, at $359 million (p. 25).

In PricewaterhouseCoopers' (PwC) 2018 Global Economic Crime and Fraud Survey, 51 per cent of New Zealand organisations reported having experienced economic crime. The report notes that 'this figure seems high – aren't we a reasonably honest lot in New Zealand?' (PwC, 2018, p. 1). Indeed, we are reputed to be so, regularly ranking at or very near the top of

Transparency International's Corruption Perceptions Index. As the SFO's director remarked in 2012, however, that index is a measurement of perceptions only, not of reality, and he refers to an SFO survey he organised in 2011 in which only 37 per cent of the randomly chosen New Zealand respondents thought the country was '"largely free" of serious fraud and corruption' (Birchfield, 2012, pp. 58–60). Nonetheless the popular stereotype of our honest country contributes to the muted political and public desire to see white-collar crime as a priority issue.

RESPONSIBILITY FOR ACCIDENTS

It is important in the study of white-collar crime to look closely at the hidden causes of what many people might consider to be accidents and disasters. Many cases of corporate crime look on the surface like accidents or natural disasters, and certainly the corporations that contributed to the causes will be keen to present them as such. Space Shuttles explode, killing those on board (Vaughan, 1996); earthquakes cause cities to collapse with massive loss of life (Green, 2005); oil tankers crash onto rocks and deep-water drilling apparatus malfunctions, causing environmental damage and economic harm to people's livelihoods in the affected regions (Gill et al., 2011); cars catch fire during road traffic accidents (Strobel, 1980); factories (Pearce & Tombs, 2012) or nuclear power plants (Levi & Horlick-Jones, 2013) leak poison into the atmosphere, delivering a toxic legacy of death and disability to thousands; killer products like asbestos continue to be produced and incorporated into buildings long after the dangers are known (Haines, 2017). Each of these examples of 'accidents' and 'disasters', however, refers to a classic case study of white-collar crime, and in each, individual workers and executives, corporations, and sometimes governments have been implicated in the causes.

The collapse of the CTV building in Christchurch during the 2011 earthquake draws out some of the questions around criminal responsibility in the context of accidents and disasters in New Zealand. The six-storey building had been designed in the 1980s by a consulting engineer firm that delegated the structural design work to an inexperienced junior employee. The building design was flawed; the structural engineering firm had an inadequate system of supervision; construction defects as well as design defects were not picked up on-site; and the council should not have signed it off, although it did. After its completion in 1988, serious structural design flaws were noted in the building as early as 1990. Some remedial work was done, but several subsequent opportunities to strengthen it properly were missed, and in 2011 the collapse killed 115 people, a significant proportion of the 185 who were killed throughout Christchurch in the quake. Despite a Royal Commission report which set out the various failings and responsibilities in detail, in 2017 police announced that they would not be bringing any charges in relation to the CTV deaths, in significant part because of New Zealand's antiquated 'year and a day rule', which barred criminal prosecution for a death a year and a day after the cause. This neutralised the possibility of prosecution where the cause was negligent design and failures of process in the 1980s.

The year and a day rule has now been repealed by the Crimes Amendment Act 2019. The next step in the fight against individual deaths as a result of corporate misconduct is for New Zealand to follow countries like the UK and Australia in enacting a corporate homicide law. This will be an important development in New Zealand, where a corporation cannot currently be prosecuted as a principal for manslaughter. Ex-justice minister Andrew Little sought to introduce a change in law, but it has not yet happened (Blumenfeld, 2018).

EXPLAINING WHITE-COLLAR CRIME

We can think about white-collar crime in terms of explanations at the micro, meso, and macro levels of social organisation. Most white-collar crime theorising has been done at the micro and meso levels, so we will focus on these here. The micro level involves explanations at the level of the individual or 'agent'. Here, for example, we find theories of individual choice. The meso level sits in between the micro and the macro, elevating analysis from the level of the individual, but not becoming so high-level or abstracted as to reach the macro. Meso-level analysis looks at the effects on individuals and groups of the organisational forms in which they conduct business: so we analyse some of the negative effects of corporate culture, or consider issues of organisational deviance as opposed to individual wrongdoing.

The macro is the 'highest' analytical level of sociological affairs, involving major structural considerations like political economy, and the globalisation of trade. Macro-level influences on white-collar crime include regulation and its enforcement, macro-economic normativity, and global anomie (Passas, 1990, 1999, 2000). As well as the organisation providing a (meso-level) context for the actions of (micro-level) individuals, the macro-level context of the organisation provides the landscape within which it must operate and make decisions. A globalised market culture that includes in significant degree the neoliberal tendency towards deregulation and competition sets the pace for multinational market actors. Threats to the profitability of the corporation can seem existential to those directing it, and breaking the law in order to maintain profitability is therefore perhaps something like a survival instinct. Certainly, as we have seen, the history of white-collar crime in New Zealand is full of cases of business leaders committing crime in an attempt to keep their company afloat, often concerned not only with themselves but with the fate of their employees and shareholders as well.

Bearing in mind this macro-level context of global competitive economic relations, coupled with the anomic playing field of an aggressive escape of corporate power that has become increasingly uncoupled from particular geographical or jurisdictional roots, let us look a little more closely at the micro- and meso-level explanations of white-collar crime, beginning with the micro.

Micro-sociology and white-collar crime

White-collar crime involves individual choice. Often this is in the context of exploiting an opportunity that is presented to the offender because of their particular position (Benson & Simpson, 2009). This can range from simply having access to the money in the till and deciding to take it, to having access to the company pension scheme and deciding to loot it. Such is the strength of the relationship between power, a privileged position, and opportunity-based crime that Felson (1994) has suggested white-collar crimes should be renamed 'crimes of specialised access'. The opportunity theory of white-collar crime brings a series of interesting conceptual considerations into the equation alongside the usual basics of *rational choice theory*: that is, high reward, low risk and low effort (Cornish & Clarke, 1986). Thinking about white-collar crimes in terms of the exploitation of opportunity also allows us to consider the emotional 'affects' of situation (i.e., temptation) and the relationship between the 'low effort' aspect of rational choice theory and the benefits of a privileged position in society or an organisation. In other words, the 'effort' involved in much white-collar crime is not overcoming practical obstacles to the commission of the crime, since the opportunity is often there for the taking. Rather, the 'effort' may be emotional or moral, in coming to terms with the breach of trust involved in taking advantage of the opportunity, having been trusted not to.

Another major theoretical consideration at the micro level is *routine activities theory*, which sees crime as likely to occur where a motivated offender meets a suitable target in the absence of a capable guardian (Clarke & Felson, 1993; Cohen & Felson, 1979). Many organisational contexts and business trade relationships lack, internally at least, capable guardians exerting the required disincentive to criminality. The argument for regulation as an effective form of control of white-collar crime, explained below, is in part a response to this question of capable guardianship in competitive business markets.

Personality is the other main explanatory variable at the micro level, although the extent to which the personalities of white-collar criminals differ from non-offenders is not settled. Several studies have suggested high-level executives can possess narcissistic or egotistical traits, be risk-takers, and have a sense of entitlement or invulnerability (Chatterjee & Hambrick, 2007; Graffin et al., 2013). High achievers also sometimes suffer from a 'fear of falling', which can lead them to break the rules in order to maintain their levels of success (Weisburd et al., 1991).

Meso-sociology and white-collar crime

Bridging the micro and the meso levels are techniques of neutralisation (Sykes & Matza, 1957). White-collar criminals justify and excuse their legally and morally wrongful actions by referring to narrative explanations (Benson, 1985; Stadler et al., 2012), including appeals to higher loyalties (e.g., 'for the good of the company'), denial of injury ('nobody got hurt', often seen in insider trading and similar apparent 'victimless' offences), denial of responsibility ('just following orders'), denial of victims ('he should have been wearing proper safety gear'), and condemnation of the condemners ('the regulators were out to make an example of me; everyone was doing it'). These processes of denial are micro level in that they take place in the minds of, and quite clearly influence the actions of, individual agents, but they derive from the meso level as they are not made up on the spot by individuals. They are part of the discursive environment of the institutional, organisational, or market culture and, as such, they are internalised by individuals as part of the normative structure of business life. Sutherland (1949) has explained the wider process of the internalisation of group norms in the context of white-collar crime as differential association. Expanding upon differential association theory, Vaughan (1999) has shown how '"toxic" or "criminogenic" organizational cultures can explain why paradoxically, it is often *conformity* to organizational norms and goals that can explain corporate deviancy' (Van Erp, 2018, original emphasis).

An organisational level of analysis is therefore important because the internal culture of a corporation or other business organisation can affect the behaviour of its officials and employees. The PR representatives of corporations are always keen to portray infringements as being micro-level matters – issues with one or two 'bad apples' in the company – where they are almost always more accurately viewed as meso-level effects of the 'dark side' of organisational culture (Vaughan, 1999). Vaughan has coined the term 'organisational deviance' to draw the distinction between crimes committed by individuals in the context of an organisation, and the deviant aspects of the culture of the organisation itself, which can create ongoing situations that are unacceptably risky. Examples include workplace health and safety hazards (Tombs & Whyte, 2007), the unsafe practices identified at the Pike River Mine (see Stanley & Day, chapter 12 this volume), and, in Vaughan's famous study, the creeping escalation of risk taken on by NASA engineers and managers in the Space Shuttle programme, which ended in disaster not only once but twice (Vaughan, 1996).

Many corporations and other business organisations these days have strongly competitive cultures internally and structure their employee performance goals to reward certain measured indicators of success. This can lead to strain as the goals are interpreted as profitability at all costs, and breaking the law becomes seen as a way to achieve this – a way which may in some cases be legitimated by the impression that the bosses expressly or tacitly approve. This was the case at Enron, a corporate scandal that has now become a classic case study in white-collar crime (McBarnet, 2006). New Zealand has its own comparable examples of organisationally approved cultures of deviance. The South Africa-based insurance company Youi began operations in New Zealand in 2014 and was promptly drawn into a scandal that encompassed its Australian and New Zealand outlets. Sales reps had been signing customers up to policies without their consent: after taking credit-card numbers in order to deliver quotes, they then in fact opened up policies and charged the cards. The reps also altered key policy details without the clients' knowledge or consent in order to deliver more attractive quotes, leaving the customers uninsured because of the misstatements of fact when they came to make a claim. The evidence suggested this was a culture of sharp practice that was encouraged and condoned by managers, and incentivised by performance-based sales commissions (Clement, 2016).

The organisational features of contemporary corporate capitalism can also have the effect of reducing individual feelings of responsibility for overall outcomes, such as where employees consider themselves only to be a cog in the machine of corporate strategy that is driven by the management above. There are various ways in which this dilution of feelings of responsibility might happen. Employees may trust that higher-management actors know more about the situation and are therefore able to make decisions that are justifiable, even though they may not seem so to more junior actors possessed of less fulsome information. Alternatively, employees may simply follow orders – so-called 'crimes of obedience' (Kelman & Hamilton, 1989) – where they perceive those higher up as having the legitimate capacity to instruct them, and see their duty as only to follow, not to question. Trust and obedience can become mixed, forming an amalgam that has been called 'engaged followership' (Haslam & Reicher, 2017), in which employees engage with and buy into the leader's vision, generating a sense of loyalty and mission, and reducing empathy for outsiders.

CONTROLLING WHITE-COLLAR CRIME

A debate continues about how best to control white-collar crime, under the general theme of whether it is better to punish or persuade. In this dichotomy, 'punish' suggests the normal routines of the criminal justice system, while 'persuade' suggests a regulatory approach.

White-collar crime and the criminal justice system

White-collar crimes are hard for the police to detect and investigate. Their complexity can make them time-consuming and expensive for prosecutors to deal with. White-collar offenders are more likely to have the stable family circumstances and employment that will serve them well in a plea in mitigation when being sentenced – and in any case, being closer than conventional street criminals to the social class of the judge, they may elicit some sympathy insofar as they don't present as socially dangerous, nor resemble the typical criminal stereotype. They might also have good, expensive lawyers. There are in fact many reasons why the criminal justice system is not an ideal fit for processing white-collar crime. Nonetheless, proponents of the application of punitive policing strategies to white-collar crime put forward several arguments in favour, including the accusation that it is simply ideology to consider that while street criminals should receive criminal justice, white-collar criminals can be dealt with by an alternative system that is based around negotiation (see the section on regulation below) and which reaches for punishment only as a last, rather than a first, resort (Pearce & Tombs, 1990).

In New Zealand the latest heat in the debate about the application of criminal justice sanctions to white-collar criminals has been around the differences with which two conceptually similar crimes are treated: tax evasion and welfare fraud, both of which involve depriving the state of money. Tax evasion far outweighs welfare fraud in financial terms: in 2013, detected welfare fraud in New Zealand amounted to $26 million, compared to $812 million in detected tax evasion (Marriott, 2017, p. 238). However, tax evasion is committed by offenders who are more affluent and powerful than welfare fraudsters, and the latest research has confirmed that in New Zealand, as elsewhere (Reiman, 1979; Weisburd et al., 1991), tax evaders receive considerably more lenient treatment at the hands of the criminal justice system than welfare fraudsters (Marriott, 2012). In New Zealand 'the likelihood of receiving a custodial sentence for welfare fraud is approximately three times as high as tax evasion, for around one quarter of the quantum of fraudulently obtained funds' (Marriott, 2017, p. 239).

Regulating white-collar crime

Noting the challenges of applying traditional criminal justice processes to white-collar crime, and the apparent relative ease with which powerful and sophisticated actors can evade the full application of the system to their activities, a theory of regulation has been developed which aims to better encourage corporate and business compliance with legal norms. A widely adopted model of regulation is the pyramidal system of control (Ayres & Braithwaite, 1992). In a regulatory pyramid, the most used interventions sit at the wide base of the pyramid. These include warning letters, requests to change behaviour, educational and awareness-raising techniques, and other 'soft touch' interventions. At the top of the pyramid, used only where the early interventions fail, are the more serious penalties, including criminal justice prosecutions and administrative penalties with bite, such as licence revocation where that is relevant to the market in question. Critics of this approach suggest that regulators are frequently underfunded, lack teeth, and may be staffed by industry insiders, who on the one hand know the landscape well but on the other may be too sympathetic to business excuses for wrongdoing, and who on a personal career level may wish to return to industry after they leave the regulatory body. Other critics complain that compliance can become a 'ritual' in organisations where documentary processes are used in a formal rather than a substantive way, to prospectively create for the corporation the excuse that it did all it could, while making it more likely that individual 'bad apples' are scapegoated (Parker, 2013).

In New Zealand there are a variety of criminal justice and regulatory bodies charged with controlling aspects of white-collar crime. In financial crime, the Inland Revenue Department investigates crimes related to tax, which in practice is mainly tax evasion. The Serious Fraud Office investigates higher-level frauds, usually above $10 million, including investment frauds, Ponzi schemes, bribery, embezzlement, and corruption. The Financial Markets Authority investigates crimes such as insider trading and price fixing. It regulates securities exchanges, financial advice, brokering, and trusts. Workplace health and safety in New Zealand is regulated by WorkSafe, a body set up under the WorkSafe New Zealand Act 2013 following recommendations made by the Royal Commission on the Pike River coal mine disaster. WorkSafe enforces the Health and Safety at Work Act 2015.

Consumer fraud in New Zealand is regulated by two main organisations: the Ministry for Consumer Affairs (part of MBIE) and the Commerce Commission. The latter was established under the Commerce Act 1986, and is charged with promoting market competition while prohibiting anti-competitive behaviour by traders, such as misleading or deceptive conduct and the formation of cartels. It applies the Fair Trading Act 1986, using a Braithwaite-style responsive regulation model, which includes warnings and publicity about infringements on its website, and in serious cases taking matters to court. The commission has recently obtained a new weapon to use in its regulation of white collar crime in New Zealand: the Commerce (Criminalisation of Cartels) Amendment Act 2019. This provides that a person who intentionally engages in cartel conduct may be imprisoned for up to seven years. Cartel conduct is an agreement not to compete, and includes price fixing, output restriction, and market allocation. It increases the prices of goods and services for consumers, and cartels can be a barrier to prospective new entrants to a market.

CONCLUSION

Although we cannot currently be precise about the extent of white-collar crime in Aotearoa New Zealand, we can be sure that it is a significant problem. Police and regulatory attention to white-collar crime is growing, but official capacity to identify and engage with the breadth of this type of offending is severely stretched. New legislative instruments are being brought to bear on the problem, like the new cartels law and the possibility of a corporate homicide offence. We can hope that official capacity increases to identify the crimes of the powerful and to protect the public against harms caused by them, and hope too that the research knowledge base on this type of crime in New Zealand continues to grow.

In developing that locally relevant New Zealand evidence base on white-collar crime, we can look to the international literature to frame several key questions that will guide research. What is the true extent of white-collar crime here, and does it – as it appears to do elsewhere – outstrip 'blue-collar' crimes in terms of economic and physical types of harm? Why and how are we conditioned to see white-collar crimes in terms of accidents and disasters as opposed to predictable forms of harm that are foreseeable as part of the self-interested risk-taking behaviour of capitalist enterprise? How can we disrupt deviant organisational cultures within corporations that support – and in some cases incentivise – wrongdoing in the pursuit of profit? Is New Zealand really as uncorrupted as global surveys suggest? And if the resolution to the punish-versus-persuade debate is a matter of striking an appropriate balance, what does that balance look like in terms of law and regulation in New Zealand? These and other key questions can support a research trajectory that tests and applies general themes and theories in the New Zealand context, bringing issues such as opportunity, guardianship, neutralisation, and structural strain to life as we work to build understanding of white-collar crime in New Zealand, and to reduce the widespread harm it causes.

STUDY QUESTIONS

- Does corporate violence differ from other forms of violence that criminologists study?
- How does the meso-level concept of organisational deviance relate to micro-level questions of rational choice, and macro-level questions of social structure?
- Why is so little known about white-collar crime in New Zealand?

FURTHER READING

Barak, G. (2017). *Unchecked corporate power: Why the crimes of multinational corporations are routinised away and what we can do about it*. New York, NY: Routledge.

Friedrichs, D. O. (2010). *Trusted criminals: White collar crime in contemporary society* (4th ed.). Belmont, CA: Wadsworth Publishing.

Van Slyke, S., Benson, M., & Cullen, F. T. (2016). *The Oxford handbook of white-collar crime*. Oxford, UK: Oxford University Press.

NOTES

1. *R v Petricevic* [2012] NZHC 665. HC AK CRI–2008–004–029179. Retrieved from https://www.interest.co.nz/sites/default/files/Bridgecorp%20judgment.pdf
2. *Bublitz v R* [2019] NZCA 364. Retrieved from https://forms.justice.govt.nz/search/Documents/pdf/jdo/25/alfresco/service/api/node/content/workspace/SpacesStore/fd8e8534–2c0d–472f-bb20–2ec85d023062/fd8e8534–2c0d–472f-bb20–2ec85d023062.pdf

REFERENCES

Ayres, I., & Braithwaite, J. (1992). *Responsive regulation: Transcending the deregulation debate*. New York, NY: Oxford University Press.

Benson, M. (1985). Denying the guilty mind: Accounting for involvement in a white-collar crime. *Criminology, 23*(4), 583–607. doi:10.1111/j.1745–9125.1985.tb00365.x

Benson, M. L., & Simpson, S. S. (2009). *White-collar crime: An opportunity perspective*. New York, NY: Routledge.

Birchfield, R. (1972). *The rise and fall of JBL*. Wellington, New Zealand: Fourth Estate.

Birchfield, R. (2012, September 2). The director – cover story: Boards blasé about corruption. *New Zealand Management*, p. 58. Retrieved from https://management.co.nz/article/director-cover-story-boards-blas%C3%A9-about-management

Blumenfeld, S. (2018, June). 'Dying for work: Workplace safety and corporate liability', *Clew'd In: Newsletter of the Centre for Labour, Employment and Work (CLEW), 3*, 4–5.

Canterbury Earthquakes Royal Commission. (2012). *Final Report, Volume 6: Canterbury Television Building (CTV)*. Wellington, New Zealand: Department of Internal Affairs.

Chatterjee, A., & Hambrick, D. C. (2007). It's all about me: Narcissistic chief executive officers and their effects on company strategy and performance. *Administrative Science Quarterly, 52*(3), 351–386. doi:10.2189/asqu.52.3.351

Clarke, R. V., & Felson, M. (1993). *Routine activity and rational choice*. New Brunswick, NJ: Transaction Publishers.

Clement, D. (2016, April 1). Youi in the firing line: Current and former employees detail explosive claims about the culture and conduct of the insurer. *Interest*. Retrieved from https://www.interest.co.nz/insurance/80813/youi-firing-line-current-and-former-employees-detail-explosive-claims-about-culture

Cohen, L. E., & Felson, M. (1979). Social change and crime rate trends: A routine activity approach. *American Sociological Review, 44*(4), 588–608. doi:10.2307/2094589

Cornish, D. B., & Clarke, R. V. (1986). *The reasoning criminal: Rational choice perspectives on offending*. Berlin, Germany: Springer-Verlag.

Felson, M. (1994). *Crime and everyday life*. Thousand Oaks, CA: Pine Forge Press.

Friedrichs, D. O. (2004). Enron et al.: Paradigmatic white collar crime cases for the new century. *Critical Criminology, 12*(2), 113–132. doi:10.1023/B:CRIT.0000040258.21821.39

Friedrichs, D. O. (2010). *Trusted criminals: White collar crime in contemporary society* (4th ed.). Belmont, CA: Wadsworth Publishing.

Gill, D. A., Picou, J. S., & Ritchie, L. A. (2011). The Exxon Valdez and BP oil spills: A comparison of initial social and psychological impacts. *American Behavioral Scientist, 56*(1), 3–23. doi:10.1177/0002764211408585

Graffin, S. D., Bundy, J., Porac, J. F., Wade, J. B., & Quinn, D. P. (2013). Falls from grace and the hazards of high status: The 2009 British MP expense scandal and its impact on parliamentary elites. *Administrative Science Quarterly, 58*(3), 313–345. doi:10.1177/0001839213497011

Green, P. (2005). Disaster by design: Corruption, construction and catastrophe. *British Journal of Criminology, 45*(4), 528–546. doi.org/10.1093/bjc/azi036

Haines, F. (2017). Corporate and white-collar crime. In A. Deckert & R. Sarre (Eds.), *The Palgrave handbook of Australian and New Zealand criminology* (pp. 237–250). Cham, Switzerland: Palgrave Macmillan.

Haslam, S. A., & Reicher, S. D. (2017). 50 years of 'obedience to authority': From blind conformity to engaged followership. *Annual Review of Law and Social Science, 13*(1), 59–78. doi:10.1146/annurev-lawsocsci-110316–113710

Hunt, G. (2001). *Hustlers, rogues and bubble boys: A history of white-collar crime in New Zealand*. Auckland, New Zealand: Reed Publishing.

Kelman, H. C., & Hamilton, V. L. (1989). *Crimes of obedience*. New Haven, CT: Yale University Press.

Lee, C. (2019). *The billion dollar bonfire: How Allan Hubbard and the government destroyed South Canterbury Finance*. Paraparaumu, New Zealand: Projects Resources Ltd.

Levi, M., & Horlick-Jones, T. (2013). Interpreting the Fukushima Daiichi nuclear incident: Some questions for corporate criminology. *Crime, Law and Social Change, 59*(5), 487–500. doi:10.1007/s10611-013-9432-3

Mackenzie, S. (2010). Scams. In F. Brookman, M. Maguire, H. Pierpoint, & T. Bennett (Eds.), *Handbook on crime* (pp. 137–152). Cullompton, UK: Willan Publishing.

Marriott, L. (2012). Tax crime and punishment in New Zealand. *British Tax Review, 5*, 623–656.

Marriott, L. (2017). The construction of crime: The presumption of blue-collar guilt and white-collar innocence. *Social Policy and Society, 16*(2), 237–251. doi:10.1017/S1474746416000063

McBarnet, D. (2006). After Enron will 'whiter than white collar crime' still wash? *British Journal of Criminology, 46*(6), 1091–1109. doi:10.1093/bjc/azl068

Nippert, M. (2014, October 29). Revealed: Fraud figures that they tried to block. *New Zealand Herald*. Retrieved from https://www.nzherald.co.nz/nz/news/article.cfm?c_id=1&objectid=11349645

Parker, C. (2013). The war on cartels and the social meaning of deterrence. *Regulation and Governance, 7*(2), 174–194. doi:10.1111/j.1748-5991.2012.01165.x

Passas, N. (1990). Anomie and corporate deviance. *Contemporary Crises, 14*(2), 157–178. doi:10.1007/BF00728269

Passas, N. (1999). Globalization, criminogenic asymmetries and economic crime. *European Journal of Law Reform, 1*(4), 399–423.

Passas, N. (2000). Global anomie, dysnomie and economic crime: Hidden consequences of neoliberalism and globalization in Russia and around the world. *Social Justice: A Journal of Crime, Conflict and World Order, 27*(2), 16–44.

Pearce, F., & Tombs, S. (1990). Ideology, hegemony, and empiricism: Compliance theories of regulation. *British Journal of Criminology, 30*(4), 423–443. doi:10.1093/oxfordjournals.bjc.a048049

Pearce, F., & Tombs, S. (2012). *Bhopal: Flowers at the altar of profit and power*. North Somercotes, UK: CrimeTalk Books.

PricewaterhouseCoopers (PwC). (2018). *Fraud out of the shadows: Key New Zealand insights from PwC's global economic crime and fraud survey 2018*. Auckland, New Zealand: PwC. Retrieved from https://www.pwc.co.nz/pdfs/2018pdfs/pwc-nz-global-economic-crime-survey–2018.pdf

Reiman, J. H. (1979). *The rich get richer and the poor get prison*. New York, NY: John Wiley & Sons.

Serious Fraud Office (SFO). (2012). *Cost of economic crime draft report: An estimate by the Serious Fraud Office of the total scale of fraud in New Zealand*. Retrieved from https://s3.amazonaws.com/s3.documentcloud.org/documents/1336568/img-x14110421–0001.pdf

Smith, J. T., & Beresford, N. A. (2005). *Chernobyl: Catastrophe and consequences*. Chichester, UK: Praxis Publishing.

Stadler, W. A., Benson, M. L., Copes, H., & Klenowski, P. (2012). Revisiting the guilty mind: The neuralization of white-collar crime. *Criminal Justice Review, 37*(4), 494–511. doi:10.1177/0734016812465618

Strobel, L. P. (1980). *Reckless homicide? Ford's Pinto trial*. Chicago, IL: South Bend Press.

Sturt, C. (1998). *Dirty collars*. Auckland, New Zealand: Reed Books.

Sutherland, E. H. (1940). White collar criminality. *American Sociological Review, 5*(1), 1–12. doi:10.2307/2083937

Sutherland, E. H. (1949). *White collar crime*. New York, NY: Dryden Press.

Sykes, G. M., & Matza, D. (1957). Techniques of neutralisation: A theory of delinquency. *American Sociological Review, 22*(6), 664–670. doi:10.2307/2089195

Thornton, M. (2006). *The political economy of white collar crime in New Zealand: 1972–2000*. Unpublished PhD thesis, Victoria University of Wellington, New Zealand.

Tombs, S., & Whyte, D. (2007). *Safety crimes*. Cullompton, UK: Willan Publishing.

Van Erp, J. (2018). The organization of corporate crime: Introduction to special issue of administrative sciences. *Administrative Sciences, 8*(3). doi:10.3390/admsci8030036

Vaughan, D. (1996). *The Challenger launch decision: Risky technology, culture, and deviance at NASA.* Chicago, IL: University of Chicago Press.

Vaughan, D. (1999). The dark side of organizations: Mistake, misconduct, and disaster. *Annual Review of Sociology, 25*(1), 271–305. doi:10.1146/annurev.soc.25.1.271

Weisburd, D., Wheeler, S., Waring, E., & Bode, N. (1991). *Crimes of the middle classes: White-collar offenders in the federal courts.* New Haven, CT: Yale University Press.

12

Ignoring State–Corporate Crimes
The Case of the Pike River Mine Disaster

Elizabeth Stanley and Sally Day

While much academic and criminal justice attention continues to focus on 'street' crimes, critical scholars have widened the scope of what we regard as crime or who we consider as criminals. Directing our attention to the harms and violence perpetuated by those with political, economic, or sociocultural power, they have been attentive to white-collar crimes (Sutherland, 1949), corporate crimes (Clinard & Quinney, 1973), state crimes (Green & Ward, 2004; Stanley & McCulloch, 2013), and state–corporate crimes (Kramer & Michalowski, 2006). These harms easily surpass all street crimes in terms of their scale and severity and their social, emotional, physical, economic, and environmental costs.

There are rich discussions to be had about the nature of crimes of the powerful in Aotearoa New Zealand, and there is an emerging literature that addresses state crimes and white-collar crimes in this context (see, for example, Mackenzie, chapter 11 this volume; Marriott, 2017; Stanley, 2015). This chapter focuses, however, on the category of state–corporate crime, a concept heavily influenced by the earlier theorising of Edward Sutherland (1949) and Richard Quinney (1964, 1977), but developed by Ron Kramer and Ray Michalowski from 1989. In particular, the chapter reflects on the Pike River Mine 'disaster' (Pike River) as a form of state–corporate crime.

This chapter explores how state–corporate crime emerges under a culture of agnosis, or organised ignorance-making. Following a discussion of how ignorance is politically managed, the chapter shows how, in the Pike River case, the risks of 'disaster' were ignored. Political and corporate workers continually emphasised safety and financial benefits, despite consistent and compelling evidence of dangerous, harmful conditions at the mine. In the context of entrenched neoliberalism, the government minimised regulations or constraints over mining (and other) industries, and this provided space for corporate profiteering that continues to emphasise production over worker safety. Following the explosion, the government and courts have failed to hold the corporation, and even individual managers, to account for the events at Pike River.

This chapter also shows how agnosis can be vigorously challenged. The case of Pike River demonstrates how families, civil society groups, and allies can organise against corporate and government injuries, and challenge widespread state–corporate denials and distortions of knowledge. At the same time, this chapter acknowledges the 'criminogenic ways in which . . . corporations and states . . . react to, and jointly mobilise against, collective threats' to continued corporate advancements for profit (Lasslett, 2014, p. 15). In the short term, civilian resistance can propel significant crises for states and corporations. However, over the long term, states and corporations reconfigure their relationships in ways that normalise inequitable structural and social relations of power, and minimise regulations or oversight of harmful industries.

STATE–CORPORATE CRIMES

Following the Space Shuttle *Challenger* disaster in 1986, Kramer and Michalowksi (2006) reflected on how business and government agencies often take collective decisions and actions to produce mass social harm.[1] They subsequently defined state–corporate crime as

> illegal or socially injurious actions that result from a mutually reinforcing interaction between (1) policies and/or practices in pursuit of the goals of one or more institutions of political governance and (2) policies and/or practices in pursuit of the goals of one or more institutions of economic production and distribution (p. 20).

A fundamental premise of this concept is that criminogenic forces are located in political and economic institutions and in the relationships between them. That is, corporations and governments should not be treated as separate, independent institutions as they operate together within broader sociocultural, economic, and political contexts that frame their operational environment (Kramer & Michalowski, 2006, p. 18). These powerful relationships can orchestrate grave state–corporate harms. As Kramer and Michalowski put it, the '*interactions* between economic and political institutions can generate *deviant* organizational outcomes' (p. 18, emphasis added). Sometimes corporations are directly ordered or given an unspoken 'nod of approval' by government institutions to engage in harmful or criminal acts (state-initiated corporate crime). At other times, government institutions fail to regulate or control corporate harms and violence. This can emerge from direct collusion, or from shared goals such that government institutions choose to not act in ways that may restrain corporations from achieving those goals (state-facilitated corporate crime) (Kramer & Michalowski, 2006). Thus, state–corporate crime emerges out of actions *and* omissions.

Researchers have since engaged with Kramer and Michalowski's concept and framework to analyse diverse organisational horrors, including human rights violations (e.g., Green & Ward, 2004; Lasslett et al., 2015), environmental harms (e.g., MacManus, 2014), and workplace injuries (e.g., Bernat & Whyte, 2016; Tombs, 2004; Tombs & Whyte, 2007). Their studies have shown how state–corporate crimes repeatedly victimise people from disadvantaged groups. They also demonstrate that it often falls to civil society campaigners to name crimes and agitate for legislative change, regulation, compensation, prosecutions, or other just responses (Green & Ward, 2004, 2019).

Noting the lack of regulation or criminal legislation directed to powerful business and state agencies, scholars have frequently engaged the concept of 'social harm' or 'social injuries' to describe state–corporate crimes. After all, crimes consist solely of what actions governments *choose* to criminalise. Given their strategic positioning, corporations mostly enjoy benevolent operating environments, and corporate harms are often immune to criminalisation, even following egregious events (Michalowski & Kramer, 2007). For example, workplace deaths and injuries are heavily sanitised through the language of 'accidents' or 'health and safety' within political, legal, and media discourse. This framing has a powerful impact as it prevents serious harms from gaining social attention (an issue exacerbated by the corporate deployment of public relations units to manage potentially damaging narratives). Moreover, it obscures the wider contexts that underpin safety crimes, such as deregulated labour markets, the casualisation of work, gender and racial discrimination in workplaces, or victim-blaming cultures (Tombs & Whyte, 2007). Using a social harm lens allows us therefore to recognise the invisibility of state–corporate harms and their relative immunity to criminalisation.

The failure of states to adequately regulate corporations or to punish them is also fundamentally connected to the historical conditions of capitalism (Bernat & Whyte, 2016, p. 73), including the ways in which criminal justice systems operate to uphold economic systems of power. For example, Tombs and Whyte (2007) highlight how health and safety legislation (which emerged to protect working-class workers from the dangerous effects of industrialisation within capitalist economies) has been dismantled and weakened by neoliberal governments who support corporate profit procurement. Corporate violence and harms are structurally produced, and workers die or are seriously injured as a result of government supports for capitalist, corporate, and market advancements (MacManus, 2016, p. 786).

These structural relations of power have meant that institutional harms are normalised. To take workplace deaths and injuries as one example: New Zealand has, on average, 50 to 60 injury deaths, 600 to 900 deaths from work-related disease and ill health, and 6000 serious injuries in the workplace every year (WorkSafe New Zealand, 2014, 2016, 2018).[2] In 2017 alone, there were over 27,000 ACC claims for injuries that caused more than a week away from work, and the serious non-fatal injury rate is rising (WorkSafe New Zealand, 2018). Moreover, these statistics are underestimates, as they do not include deaths in the maritime or aviation sectors, nor fatalities due to work-related road crashes. Rebecca Lilley, from Otago University, reported that one in ten workers is injured at work in New Zealand each year and, if all workplace injury deaths were recorded, the fatality rate would be approximately 200 per year (Gibb, 2016). There is 'no comprehensive or reliable data set for monitoring workplace fatal injury rates in New Zealand' (Independent Taskforce on Workplace Health and Safety, 2013, p. 9), and no body of research that explores the wider, indirect, and often 'unseen' impacts of workplace injuries and deaths on families or wider communities. Despite the scale of these harms, they generally fall below the media radar and are not given substantive political attention. Part of the problem lies in how processes of ignorance-making work to defuse corporate or state responsibilities, and make harms appear as a necessary or normal feature of institutional activities.

THE MANAGEMENT OF IGNORANCE

A central element in understanding how state–corporate crimes emerge and are made unaccountable relates to the control of knowledge-making. States and corporations have profound impacts on the production, dissemination, and popular acceptance of knowledge. As dominant gatekeepers and processors of information, they set the boundaries of what is or can be observable, and their disseminated ideas usually downplay injurious activities. As Barton et al. (2018, p. 17, original emphasis) outline, given that 'harms of the powerful originate in, and are perpetrated according to, the priorities and operating cultures of powerful institutions and organisations, accounts *of* them are neutralised within the dominant regimes of truth and sustained by the hierarchies of credibility and influence'.

Such knowledge-building regularly relies on an entourage of experts who may provide scientific, analytical, or legal cover for harmful activities (often relying on technological or professional language that is difficult for non-experts to engage with), or who can minimise negative publicity from particular crises as they emerge (Slater, 2012). Many state institutions and corporations also sustain silence through contracts that prohibit employees from publicising facts that might bring their employers into disrepute. Ignorance-making (or agnosis) is therefore 'buttressed by formal disciplinary procedures and legal obligations, around reputational damage and confidentiality' (Barton et al., 2018, p. 17). Issues of public perceptions can take on more importance than the harms themselves.

Under these conditions, institutions can uphold, maintain, and manipulate ignorance for their own ends (Proctor, 2008), to divert attention from difficult stories or to exploit uncertainty about particular events or identities (Slater, 2012). In this respect, ignorance refers not only to knowledge that is absent, but also to knowledge that has been denied, distorted, dismissed, or hidden (Croissant, 2014; Dossey, 2014). Ignorance can subsequently be created in many ways: 'through media neglect and obfuscation, corporate or governmental secrecy and suppression, document destruction, myriad forms of cultural and political selectivity, inattention and forgetfulness, outright attempts to deceive and mislead (aka lying), and more' (Dossey, 2014, p. 331).

There is also a continuum of ignorance (Barton et al., 2018). While ignorance can be a 'strategic ploy' (Proctor, 2008, p. 8) or a 'rational calculation' (Slater, 2012, p. 960), it can also emerge through a gradual forgetting or as a result of dominant sociocultural, political, economic, or institutional settings that set boundaries on legitimate knowledge (Dossey, 2014). Nonetheless, the impacts of agnosis are far-reaching. While good news is invariably amplified by corporations and governments, problems are regularly covered over, minimised, or deemed to be unusual, one-off cases. Ignorance shields politicians and corporate heads from criticism and blurs the links between organisational responsibilities and harmful outcomes.

Agnosis also operates to minimise or simplify the chronic failings of structural systems of power. Narratives of poor government or dysfunctional corporations can hide larger system crises, such as the systemic flaws in corporate activities within a neoliberal politics. When this occurs, the conditions under which state–corporate crimes emerge go largely unaddressed, even in the midst of compelling evidence (Tombs, 2018). Knowledge management can ensure that economic and political powers are even consolidated. For example, following the global financial crisis of 2007–8, a dominant political response reasserted that recovery depended upon increased freedoms and reduced regulations or 'red tape' for private capital (Tombs, 2018). Still, the ramifications of ignorance-making can be temporarily painful for those corporations or politicians involved in harmful behaviours, and especially so at times of crises. This issue became particularly apparent in New Zealand's Pike River Mine 'disaster', to which this chapter now turns.

THE CASE OF PIKE RIVER

The Pike River coal mine is situated in the West Coast region of New Zealand's South Island, east of the Paparoa Ranges and 45 kilometres north-east from Greymouth. The region has long struggled with limited employment opportunities. Sparsely populated and isolated, and with a strong dependence on mining, forestry, dairying, and some tourism, the West Coast is highly vulnerable to global shifts in coal and dairy prices (Ministry for Primary Industries, 2016). Under these conditions, the Pike River venture was warmly welcomed by local communities when it gained government approval to mine on Department of Conservation land in 2005. Raising the prospect of jobs for between 80 and 150 people, local politicians emphasised the benefits of the 'trickle-down' wealth that would profit the region (Macfie, 2013). *The New Zealand Herald* (Booker, 2006, para. 10) reported 'an economic surge is about to sweep through' the region that would 'revitalise' the port and other trades and services. Then mayor Tony Kokshoorn professed the venture as 'one of the best things to happen to the coast' (Booker, 2006, para. 23) and the *New Zealand Herald* (2010) reported that the mine had 'pumped around $80 million each year into the West Coast economy'.

The conditions at the mine have never been easy. Pike has Mount Hawera to the north, a sharp escarpment to the west, Mount Anderson to the south, and the Hāwera earthquake fault line runs through it. The mine site was established to produce high-quality coking coal, which is internationally sought-after, particularly for steel production. Initial explorations found that Pike was a 'gassy' mine, as the coal contained methane, which is highly flammable when mixed with oxygen (Royal Commission, 2012). Methane levels and ventilation had to be carefully managed for the mine to safely operate. This did not happen.

On the afternoon of 19 November 2010, a large explosion killed 29 men (Royal Commission, 2012).[3] At the time of writing, their bodies remain in the mine. The only two survivors, Daniel Rockhouse and Russell Smith, were impacted by the blast and suffered carbon monoxide poisoning, but managed to walk out of the entry drift (a horizontal passageway providing access to the mine). Further explosions on 24, 26 and 28 November dashed family hopes that other miners might have survived the initial blast.

Following years of campaigning by victims' families, their advocates, and supporters, in 2017 newly elected Labour prime minister Jacinda Ardern pledged that a re-entry of the mine would be conducted with the aim of recovering bodies and collecting evidence. In November 2017, Minister (Responsible for Pike River Re-Entry) Andrew Little announced the creation of the 'Pike River Recovery Agency', a stand-alone government department that would navigate the practicalities of re-entering the mine. In November 2018, the minister announced that a 'single-entry' option via the mine drift had been approved, and the first major task, breaching the 30-metre seal inside the drift, began in May 2019.

As the sections below demonstrate, the Pike River mine disaster is a state–corporate crime. This crime emerged out of government and corporate acts and omissions, and was underpinned by strategic ignorance-making. Despite clear knowledge, warnings, and experiences of multiple dangers, the company repeatedly diverted attention from the significant safety risks at the mine. A culture of production over safety was also enabled by the New Zealand government's withdrawal of regulations for workers' protections. Meanwhile, the Department of Labour (now the Ministry for Business, Innovation and Employment) and the courts failed to hold those most responsible to account. A network of economic and political institutions generated multiple harmful organisational outcomes, including mass deaths.

Ignoring institutional risks

In the wake of the disaster, the Royal Commission on the Pike River Coal Mine Tragedy (hereafter Royal Commission) (2012) revealed a combination of unacceptable circumstances and unprecedented decisions taken at the mine, including but not limited to: inadequate methane drainage; the failure to follow usual industry practice by placing the ventilation shaft below ground; the lack of a dedicated ventilation monitoring officer on site; non-functioning gas sensors; flawed electrical and ventilation designs; malfunctioning and inappropriate machinery; lack of necessary training for workers; an unfit-for-purpose emergency escape shaft; no proper emergency fresh air base underground; and management inaction to multiple warning signals.

These concerns did not just emerge after the disaster. Numerous people acting in various capacities (internal and external to the Pike company) raised safety worries, particularly from the failure of the company to follow expert mining advice or to undertake adequate geological and geotechnical investigations *before starting* mining (Macfie, 2013). The Royal Commission (2012, p. 76) analysed 1083 incident reports made in the short two-year active operation of the mine. These included: reports of a large roof fall in the hydro panel; the collapse of the ventilation shaft; numerous recorded methane spikes, electrical trips, and spark ignitions; and a fire in the mine roof – all amounting to serious hazards that could have caused loss of life (Macfie, 2013). Most incidents were not investigated, and there was a mass of backlogged reports waiting for action at the time of the disaster.

The situation that led to the disaster did not emerge from a lack of knowledge about workplace harms. There was systemic evidence to indicate multiple safety risks, but the company failed to take action. Part of the problem was severe dysfunction within senior management: six different people held the position of mine manager during the period 2009–10, and there was a high turnover among experienced technical staff (Ministry for Culture and Heritage, 2017). At times, those responsible for miners' safety often lacked experience, and some had no prior specific mining experience (Macfie, 2013).

The company downplayed this inconvenient knowledge and represented itself as a progressive workplace. At the 2008 annual general meeting, Chief Executive Gordon Ward stated, 'we specifically employ skilled staff to help us safeguard the environment' (Pike River Coal Limited, 2008, para. 44). The following year, the prime minister John Key and the minister of conservation Tim Groser both sang Pike's praises, commenting on how the mine was 'an example of modern mining practices that had minimal impact on the landscape' and that it had 'set a new environmental standard for mining with a "showcase" development high in the Paparoa Ranges' (Pike River Coal Limited, 2009, pp. 8, 9).

The potential lethality of mining in 'gassy' conditions was continually downplayed, with the company emphasising its expertise and technological prowess in extracting coal in difficult environments and its ability to safely mitigate gas build-ups (Macfie, 2013; Pike River Coal Limited, 2009). Company statements ignored methane gas altogether, or emphasised the rarity of explosions and the manageable levels of gas (Pike River Coal Limited, 2007, 2008, 2009). Concerns about risks were reassured as the company even argued that it could harness and recycle gas to power the mine (Pike River Coal Limited, 2009). In this respect, the company moved from '*being* ignorant, to *acts* of ignoring . . . and the *activity* of generating or maintaining ignorance' within the company and for external audiences (Barton et al., 2018, p. 16, original emphasis).

In these endeavours, the company received supports from experts. Mining consultants, engineers, and geologists were commissioned over the years to produce feasibility and exploration studies to appease doubts from bankers, shareholders, and the Department of Conservation, among others. Any reported weaknesses 'were redefined as strengths' (Macfie, 2013, p. 34) by the company, despite the fact that some experts had made their reservations about Pike 'abundantly clear' and some would not endorse the project (p. 49). Nevertheless, Pike was granted all the council consents and access it required. In short, the ignorance of institutional risks was actively maintained across multiple, complicit organisations.

Ignoring the drive for profit

The Pike company was inevitably focused on profit-making but, like other large-scale mine operations, it was 'bonded' to a location: the West Coast (Lasslett, 2014, p. 180). Mining companies spend significant resources on establishing operations, and they require labourers to productively extract minerals to quickly recoup costs and turn a profit. To assist corporate success, mine managers often push back against political attempts to restrain working practices or to impinge on profit returns. This situational context engenders corporate mining cultures that enforce corporate agreements, protect business interests, and reduce costs (Lasslett, 2014, p. 181). As Macfie (2013, pp. 61, 57) put it, the Pike project ran 'on a shoestring' while the company forecasted returns that no company 'had ever managed to achieve from an underground coal mine'.

With a drive for profit-seeking and financial recoveries through accelerated coal production, the company was stymied by problems of establishing a mine in a volatile area beset with potentially dangerous gas levels as well as a significant earthquake fault-line. Setbacks threatened forecast profits, and the company repeatedly requested funding increases from shareholders to keep the project afloat. Increasing pressure and expectations to reach profit goals created a deep-rooted 'culture of production before safety at Pike River' (Royal Commission, 2012, vol. 1, p. 19).

Ignoring the rise of corporate self-regulation

Beyond its basis in institutional risk-taking for the pursuit of profit, the disaster also developed out of strident neoliberalism that has valorised corporate capital, with a New Zealand government emphasis on creating corporate-friendly regulations. The common refrain is that corporations can be trusted to regulate themselves to remove harmful risks (Tombs, 2018, p. 90). Any onus on the state to monitor private capital is decreed to be 'wasteful', 'intrusive', undermining of corporate 'innovation and competitiveness', and against public interests (Tombs, 2018, p. 90).

In the New Zealand context, systemic mining industry problems are contextualised by a lack of government regulation. The introduction of neoliberal reforms and New Public Management to New Zealand in the 1980s transformed the mining sector.[4] It led to the disestablishment of the specialist coal-mining inspectorate (removing a crucial source of mine safety expertise and monitoring) and the dissolution of protections set out in the Coal Mines Act 1979. This contributed to the creation of a deregulated workplace culture where, at best, health and safety concerns were marginalised and, at worst, vilified. The withdrawal of resources meant that inspectors were prevented from taking proactive steps to ensure worker protections, such that by 2010 there were only two mine inspectors for the entire country (Ministry for Culture and Heritage, 2017).

The government's erosion of corporate regulatory restraints left workers at the site extremely vulnerable to harms, despite all the clear warning signs of disaster. The emphasis on stimulating investment (notwithstanding the limited impact of that on local socio-economic well-being) took precedence. Moreover, given that the nature of corporate activity is largely determined by the decisions of private investors, the government failure to provide clear oversight mechanisms or to facilitate the safe protection of workers led to significant institutional problems as, under these conditions, mine managers were discouraged or unable to take protective actions that might impinge on corporate investments (see Lasslett, 2014). The desire for maximum profit inevitably placed pressures on workers such that they did not fully engage with health and safety measures.

Ignoring injustice and the structural basis of corporate deaths

In the wake of state–corporate crimes, it is tempting to attribute harms and violence to the pathological deficits of specific rogue companies or to individual bad apples who have operated outside the usual norms of institutional rules. In this respect, dominant truths can follow a 'familiar litany' of deficiencies, such as institutional breakdowns, personal bad practice, bullying, poor training, and negative working cultures (Slater, 2012). In many ways, these narratives are important, as corporate and political cultures (as well as policies and working practices) are significantly connected to criminogenic environments.

In the case of the Pike River disaster, three 'defendants' – the Pike River Coal company, mine manager Peter Whittall, and Valley Longwall – have faced charges from the then Department of Labour under health and safety legislation. Valley Longwall International, who lost three employees in the mine, was fined NZ$46,800.[5] Pike River Coal was ordered to pay $110,000 to each of the victims' families and fined $760,000 – however, the company claimed it could not afford this, and pledged to pay just $5,000 to each family (Macfie, 2013, pp. 238–239). Despite contesting the findings of the Royal Commission, Whittall and Pike River Coal offered a voluntary payment of $3.41 million to the families and two survivors (*Osborne and Rockhouse v WorkSafe New Zealand*, 2018).[6] This payment was partly taken into consideration by the Department of Labour, who decided not to proceed with any further charges against Whittall. Bereaved family members Sonya Rockhouse and Anna Osborne sought a judicial review of the decision to drop all charges against the mine manager,[7] but the Court of Appeal upheld the High Court decision to reject a judicial review (Carroll, 2017).[8] For bereaved family members, the court proceedings were an example of 'checkbook [sic] justice' (Carroll, 2017, para. 7), as those most responsible evaded prosecution through monetary payments.[9] These attempts demonstrate how legal processes often fail to provide justice following state–corporate crimes, and how corporate actors circumnavigate accountability.

At the same time, a prioritisation on rogue companies or managers can obscure the economic, political, and sociocultural structural conditions that contextualise how extractive industries operate in harmful ways. The conditions that allow state–corporate harms to occur in New Zealand (including the corporate emphasis on the technological complexities of their industries, the limited state regulations, the political and media support of deep corporate profits, and the impunity towards deaths and injuries) are mirrored across multiple industries.

Challenging ignorance

Many individuals and groups have challenged the organised ignorance that led to the Pike River disaster and to subsequent state–corporate acts that prioritise individualised responses. In the lead-up to the disaster, numerous people spoke against hazardous conditions and the corporate dismissals of concerns (Macfie, 2013; Royal Commission, 2012). Advised by the Engineering, Printing and Manufacturing Union (EPMU), some miners organised a stop-work walkout to protest against unsafe conditions, an incident that resulted in Pike threatening to sue the union (Macfie, 2013, p. 180; Royal Commission, 2012, vol. 2, p. 227). Other outspoken workers did not have their contracts renewed (Macfie, 2013). Following the disaster, and after the decision by state-owned enterprise Solid Energy (who bought the mine) to permanently seal the site, thereby preventing the retrieval of their loved ones' bodies, families organised a human blockade and held a picket line (*Stuff*, 2016). Supported by union representatives (such as the late Helen Kelly), many families have struggled to progress health and safety reforms, in the hope of protecting others from workplace deaths. Some acknowledge that they have become 'fighter[s] for justice' and 'a voice for all of those who suffer the ultimate disempowerment at work' (Macfie, 2018, para. 11).

The Royal Commission (2012) and the Independent Taskforce on Workplace Health and Safety (2013) both found that New Zealand's health and safety systems and regulatory agencies were not fit for purpose. And, in 2013, the government created a stand-alone regulator, WorkSafe New Zealand. WorkSafe has led significant legislative reforms, such as the Health and Safety in Employment Amendment Act 2013, the Worksafe New Zealand Act 2013, the Mines Rescue Act 2013, and the Health and Safety at Work Act 2015. The key change facilitated by these new laws is a shift in focus from recording health and safety incidents to proactively identifying and resolving risks. These legislative shifts are, arguably, merely regaining *some* of the previous regulatory power that was lost when consecutive governments deregulated the workplace. As some families have observed, the new regulations are 'too "watered down" to be truly effective' (van Beyen, 2015, para. 3), and they cannot challenge the dominant neoliberal frame in which local industries operate.

CONCLUSION

It is frequently thought that state–corporate crimes result from the deviant activities of states and corporations. However, most emerge from normalised corporate activities. Working-class, labour-intensive industries – such as mining, forestry, building and construction, farming, and fisheries – have all benefited from deregulated conditions while producing significant injuries and harms among their workers. In this respect, and as shown in the above case, state–corporate crimes do not relate to events that are unforeseeable or unintended. Instead, ignorance-making is undertaken to uphold profitable corporate advancements and to minimise external oversight, even when dangerous risks are discovered. Significant harms are supported through the 'production, dissemination and consumption of false knowledge and false or flawed understandings' (Barton et al., 2018, p. 29). Deaths and serious injuries are frequently concealed and obfuscated to uphold the norms and advantages of corporate elites. In this respect, the study of ignorance-making, or the ways in which knowledge is repackaged and distributed to facilitate structural, institutional, and sociocultural inequalities, is vital to a criminology that seeks to understand the full nature of offending and harmful behaviours.

State–corporate crimes have to be understood in relation to interlinked concerns. First, that the workings of individual corporate entities are contextualised by their relationships within advanced global capitalist economies. For example, corporations, as investors, frequently veto political remits on their restraint and can threaten withdrawal from regions, causing problems for those politicians focused on continual economic growth, investments, and re-election (Lasslett, 2014). As a result, political systems and sociocultural arrangements are positioned to facilitate exploitative or harmful working conditions. Second, that there will be different environments for state–corporate crime as a result of the diverse ways in which capital and investments are advanced (Lasslett, 2014). In the case of Pike River, for example, shareholder pressures on the company to extract coal at speed, despite difficult mining conditions, created prime conditions for disaster. This was worsened through the New Zealand government's failure to adequately regulate the mining industry and ensure sufficient, robust, and enforceable worker protections. Third, that state–corporate crimes cannot be approached in terms of individual or institutional deficiencies or pathologies. In many respects, these crimes adhere to normalised social, political, and economic arrangements that underpin capitalist, neocolonialist, and patriarchal societies. Fourth, that these conditions are upheld through a managed ignorance of inequitable structural and social relations of power. This knowledge management is facilitated by states and corporations, and largely legitimised by public audiences. Fifth, this ignorance-making is, however, liable to rupture, especially in the wake of state–corporate crises. Yet, the resistance to silenced or false knowledge is also apparent at other periods, including those times before significant harms and injuries occur. The lesson for criminologists is to therefore be more attentive to these resistant actions and articulations. Uncovering knowledge arrangements, and unpacking the ways in which agnosis operates, are a vital preventative to state–corporate crimes.

STUDY QUESTIONS

- What do you think would be the most 'just' response to the Pike River survivors and families, following the disaster?
- Identify another New Zealand instance of state–corporate crime. Is it state-initiated or state-facilitated corporate crime? And, how did ignorance-making contribute to this criminal event?
- Should New Zealand have a law for corporate manslaughter? Why? Why not?

FURTHER READING

Barton, A., & Davis, H. (Eds.) (2018). *Ignorance, power and harm: Agnotology and the criminological imagination.* Cham, Switzerland: Palgrave Macmillan.

Michalowski, R. J., & Kramer, R. C. (Eds.) (2006). *State–corporate crime: Wrongdoing at the intersection of business and government.* New Brunswick, NJ: Rutgers University Press.

Tombs, S., & Whyte, D. (2015). *The corporate criminal: Why corporations must be abolished.* Abingdon, UK: Routledge.

NOTES

1. This disaster occurred as a result of the intersecting relationships, decisions, and actions between a business (Morton Thiokol Inc.) and a state-owned/run organisation (NASA, the National Aeronautics and Space Administration).
2. The Royal Commission (2012, vol. 1, p. 15) explained that the rate of workplace fatalities is higher than in the United Kingdom, Australia, and Canada, and worse than the OECD average.
3. There have been 211 deaths from nine separate mine explosions in New Zealand, so these deaths are sadly the latest in a longer list of fatal harms.
4. 'New Public Management' refers to a corporatisation of the public sector. It places private-sector values on the public sector, and sets up a quasi-market structure (e.g., decentralisation and privatisation) where public and private service providers compete with each other. (For an overview of the New Zealand experience see Boston et al., 1991.)
5. Valley Longwall is an Australian company that supplies specialist mining equipment and services to the industry (https://vli.com.au/). In 2008, Pike contracted Valley Longwall to provide in-seam drilling services (Royal Commission, 2012).
6. *Osborne and Rockhouse v WorkSafe New Zealand* [2017] NZSC 175, [23 November 2017]. Retrieved from https://assets.documentcloud.org/documents/4277830/Pike-River-ruling-Anna-Elizabeth-Osborne-and.pdf
7. Sonya Rockhouse lost her son Ben and Anna Osborne lost her husband Milton in the disaster.
8. The Supreme Court of New Zealand has since ruled that it was unlawful to withdraw its prosecution of Whittall in exchange for payments to the victims' families (*Osborne and Rockhouse v WorkSafe New Zealand*, 2018).
9. Then Labour Party president Andrew Little and the Council of Trade Unions introduced a Bill to create a new criminal offence of 'corporate manslaughter'. However, the Bill did not gain support from the prime minister John Key and failed to pass the select committee in 2015.

REFERENCES

Barton, A., Davis, H., & White, H. (2018). Agnotology and the criminological imagination. In A. Barton. & H. Davis (Eds.), *Ignorance, power and harm: Agnotology and the criminological imagination* (pp. 13–35). Cham, Switzerland: Palgrave Macmillan.

Bernat, I., & Whyte, D. (2016). State–corporate crime and the process of capital accumulation: Mapping a global regime of permission from Galicia to Morecambe Bay. *Critical Criminology, 25*(1), 71–86. doi:10.1007/s10612–016–9340–9

Booker, J. (2006, January 13). Black gold fires up the West Coast. *New Zealand Herald*. Retrieved from https://www.nzherald.co.nz/nz/news/article.cfm?c_id=1&objectid=10363608

Boston, J., Martin, J., Pallot, J., & Walsh, P. (1991). *Reshaping the state: New Zealand's bureaucratic revolution*. Auckland, New Zealand: Oxford University Press.

Carroll, J. (2017, February 16). Pike families lose appeal against Whittall charges being dropped. *Stuff*. Retrieved from https://www.stuff.co.nz/national/89488420/pike-families-lose-appeal-against-whittal-charges-being-dropped

Clinard, M. B., & Quinney, R. (1973). *Criminal behavior systems: A typology*. New York, NY: Holt, Rinehart and Winston.

Croissant, J. L. (2014). Agnotology: Ignorance and absence or towards a sociology of things that aren't there. *Social Epistemology, 28*(1), 4–25. doi:10.1080/02691728.2013.862880

Dossey, L. (2014). Agnotology: On the varieties of ignorance, criminal negligence, and crimes against humanity. *Explore: The Journal of Science and Healing, 10*(6), 331–344. doi:10.1016/j.explore.2014.08.011

Gibb, J. (2016, June 16). NZ workplace death rate 'appalling'. *Otago Daily Times*. Retrieved from https://www.odt.co.nz/news/dunedin/nz-workplace-death-rate-appalling

Green, P., & Ward, T. (2004). *State crime: Governments, violence and corruption*. London, UK: Pluto Press.

Green, P., & Ward, T. (2019). *State crime and civil activism: On the dialectics of repression and resistance*. London, UK: Routledge.

Independent Taskforce on Workplace Health and Safety. (2013). *The report of the Independent Taskforce on Workplace Health and Safety He Korowai Whakaruruhau*. Retrieved from http://www.hstaskforce.govt.nz/documents/report-of-the-independent-taskforce-on-workplace-health-safety.pdf

Kramer, R. C., & Michalowski, R. J. (2006). The original formulation. In R. J. Michalowski and R. C. Kramer (Eds.), *State–corporate crime: Wrongdoing at the intersection of business and government* (pp. 18–26). New Brunswick, NJ: Rutgers University Press.

Lasslett, K. (2014). *State crime on the margins of empire*. London, UK: Pluto Press.

Lasslett, K., Green, P., & Stańczak, D. (2015). The barbarism of indifference: Sabotage, resistance and state–corporate crime. *Theoretical Criminology, 19*(4), 514–533. doi:10.1177/1362480614558866

Macfie, R. (2013). *Tragedy at Pike River mine: How and why 29 men died*. Wellington, New Zealand: Awa Press.

Macfie, R. (2018, November 14). A victory for the Pike River families – and for those who live by their labour. *Spinoff*. Retrieved from https://thespinoff.co.nz/politics/14–11–2018/a-victory-for-the-pike-river-families-and-for-those-who-live-by-their-labour/

MacManus, T. (2014). Civil society and state–corporate crime: A case study of Ivory Coast. *State Crime Journal, 3*(2), 200–219. doi:10.13169/statecrime.3.2.0200

MacManus, T. (2016). The denial industry: Public relations, 'crisis management' and corporate crime. *International Journal of Human Rights, 20*(6), 785–797. doi:10.1080/13642987.2016.1156882

Marriott, L. (2017). The construction of crime: The presumption of blue-collar guilt and white-collar innocence. *Social Policy and Society, 16*(2), 237–251. doi:10.1017/S1474746416000063

Michalowski, R. J., & Kramer, R. C. (2007) State–corporate crime and criminological inquiry. In H. Pontell & G. Geis (Eds.), *International handbook of white-collar and corporate crime* (pp. 200–219). New York, NY: Springer.

Ministry for Culture and Heritage. (2017, November 8). *Pike River mine disaster*. Retrieved from https://nzhistory.govt.nz/culture/pike-river-mine-disaster

Ministry for Primary Industries. (2016). *Tai poutini West Coast growth study: Opportunities report*. Retrieved from https://www.mpi.govt.nz/dmsdocument/14098-tai-poutini-west-coast-growth-study-opportunities-report-september–2016

New Zealand Herald. (2010, December 1). Economic impact of Pike River tragedy felt on West Coast. Retrieved from https://www.nzherald.co.nz/business/news/article.cfm?c_id=3&objectid=10691213

Pike River Coal Limited. (2007, October 24). *Managing director's address to annual meeting* [Press release]. *Scoop*. Retrieved from http://www.scoop.co.nz/stories/BU0710/S00362.htm

Pike River Coal Limited. (2008, November 28). *Pike River: AGM – managing director's address* [Press release]. *Scoop*. Retrieved from http://www.scoop.co.nz/stories/BU0811/S00533/pike-river-agm-managing-directors-address.htm

Pike River Coal Limited. (2009). *Annual review 2009: Production ramping-up*. Retrieved from media.abnnewswire.net/media/en/reports_gallery/rpt/ASX-PRC-324781.pdf

Proctor, R. N. (2008). Agnotology: A missing term to describe the cultural production of ignorance (and its study). In R. N. Proctor & L. Scheibinger (Eds.), *Agnotology: The making and unmaking of ignorance* (pp. 1–36). Redwood City, CA: Stanford University Press.

Quinney, R. (1964). The study of white collar crime: Toward a reorientation in theory and research. *Journal of Criminal Law, Criminology and Police Science, 55*(2), 208–214. doi:10.2307/1140749

Quinney, R. (1977). *Class, state and crime: On the theory and practice of criminal justice*. New York, NY: Longman.

Royal Commission on the Pike River Coal Mine Tragedy. (2012). *Royal Commission on the Pike River Coal Mine Tragedy Te Komihana a te Karauna mō te Parekura Ana Waro o te Awa o Pike* (Vols 1 & 2). Retrieved from https://pikeriver.royalcommission.govt.nz/

Slater, T. (2012). The myth of 'broken Britain': Welfare reform and the production of ignorance. *Antipode, 46*(4), 948–969. doi:10.1111/anti.12002

Stanley, E. (2015). Responding to state institutional violence. *British Journal of Criminology, 48*(2). 295–297. doi:10.1093/bjc/azv034

Stanley, E., & McCulloch, J. (Eds.) (2013). *State crime and resistance*. London, UK: Routledge.

Stuff. (2016, December 11). Pike River families take control of mine access road, vow to deny Solid Energy entry. *Stuff online*. Retrieved from: https://www.stuff.co.nz/national/87450166/pike-river-families-take-control-of-mine-access-road-vow-to-deny-solid-energy-entry

Sutherland, E. H. (1949). *White collar crime*. New York, NY: Holt, Rinehart and Winston.

Tombs, S. (2004). Workplace injury and death: Social harm and the illusions of law. In P. Hillyard, C. Pantazis, S. Tombs, & D. Gordon (Eds.), *Beyond criminology: Taking harm seriously* (pp. 156–177). London, UK: Pluto Press.

Tombs, S. (2018). Framing the crisis: Private capital to the rescue. In A. Barton & H. Davis (Eds.), *Ignorance, power and harm: Agnotology and the criminological imagination* (pp. 87–111). Cham, Switzerland: Palgrave Macmillan.

Tombs, S., & Whyte, D. (2007). *Safety crimes*. Cullompton, UK: Willan.

van Beyen, J. (2015, August 15). New health and safety regulations don't go far enough, families say. *Stuff*. Retrieved from https://www.stuff.co.nz/business/71147382/

WorkSafe New Zealand. (2014). *Annual report 2013/2014*. Wellington, New Zealand: New Zealand government. Retrieved from https://worksafe.govt.nz/dmsdocument/968-annual-report-2013-2014

WorkSafe New Zealand. (2016). *Annual report 2015/2016*. Wellington, New Zealand: New Zealand government. Retrieved from https://worksafe.govt.nz/dmsdocument/956-annual-report-2015-2016

WorkSafe New Zealand. (2018). *Annual report 2017/2018*. Wellington, New Zealand: New Zealand government. Retrieved from https://worksafe.govt.nz/dmsdocument/4296-annual-report-2017-2018

Part Three

Criminal Justice

The 12 chapters in Part Three outline the key institutions and processes – the 'nuts and bolts' – that form the basis of Aotearoa New Zealand's criminal justice system. Along the way, authors provide nuanced accounts of the current state of justice. The overall picture is not enamouring. As examples: criminal justice policy has been guided by emotional and political rhetoric that has centralised controls, surveillance, and incarceration to the detriment of other rationalities; criminal justice agencies often respond to victims, offenders, and communities in deeply damaging ways, even creating intergenerational harms; and the fundamental basis of the system – to focus on individualised responses to 'crime' – is ultimately problematic as we do not attend to the social, institutional, or structural contexts of problem behaviours. Together, these chapters illustrate how New Zealand's criminal justice system frequently intensifies dominant power relations. They indicate a need for transformative responses to prevent crimes, harm, and violence, and to provide truly meaningful conditions for reparation and restoration.

The opening chapter, by John Pratt and Jordan Anderson, explores the rise and consolidation of populist approaches to criminal justice in New Zealand. While the period following the Second World War had a relatively benign penal climate, the era from the 1980s heralded a significant rise in punitive legislation, correctional securitisation, and imprisonment rates. Pratt and Anderson reflect on the nature of penal populism, exposing its distinction from related ideas such as authoritarian populism or populist punitiveness. They detail five distinct causes of penal populism in the New Zealand context: the decline of deference; the decline of trust; the rise of global insecurities and anxieties; the influence of the mass media; and the symbolic importance placed on victims of crime. The consequences and costs of these developments have been immeasurable. And, while there might now be a redirection of policy to reduce prisoner numbers, the question remains whether the New Zealand government will have the long-term political will to truly disentangle criminal justice from the emotion and politics of penal populism.

While thinking about penal populism inevitably serves as an overarching ideological context for the criminal justice system, the agency gatekeepers to the system are the police. The chapter by Trevor Bradley, Elizabeth Stanley, and Angus Lindsay focuses on the past, present, and future of policing in New Zealand. They consider the nature of policing in relation to the central concept of legitimacy as well as to colonial policing. In doing so, they highlight three issues which, left unchecked, will erode police legitimacy: (1) the continuing impact of colonialism on police strategies and interactions with Māori; (2) the creeping para-militarisation of New Zealand Police (NZP), most clearly evident in the aggressive policing of protest, as well as the recent deployment of Armed Response Teams (ARTs); and (3) the failure of New Zealand's police to adapt to the evident transformations in criminal offending, including from cybercrimes. While NZP has undoubtedly made positive changes over recent years, across diverse areas, there remains some room for organisational change to ensure that policing moves beyond dominant ideologies of crime and offending.

Part of the policing remit relates to how crime may be prevented. Russil Durrant's chapter considers how crime prevention can be conceptualised and acted upon. Crime prevention potentially encompasses many state activities: from community patrols and education programmes to building design and socially just economic policies. Of course, crime can never be eliminated or fully prevented – only reduced in its nature, scope, or severity. In relation to examples of practice from New Zealand, Durrant considers three different models of crime prevention: (1) developmental models that target individual 'risk factors' for later offending; (2) community models that attempt to change features of disorganised social environments; and (3) situational approaches, which reduce opportunities for crime in the physical environment or in particular situations. He highlights the importance of understanding the effectiveness of these interactions, as well as being attentive to their costs, limitations, and harms. Such careful considerations will be important as we progress to new digitalised methods of crime prevention.

For those who are policed and arrested, the next criminal justice encounter is one with the courts. Developed as a key element of New Zealand's colonial control landscape, the court system is now undergoing significant transformations. Khylee Quince presents a contemporary overview of the courts' hierarchy, as well as of the judges who preside over them. She details the shifts in court practice and the ideas – such as relating to therapeutic jurisprudence or to Māori cultural engagements – that are underpinning developments. Wide reforms are leading to a more diverse judiciary, as well as changes in courtroom practice to make courts more accessible and transparent. Maori-focused initiatives – such as the Matariki Court or Ngā Kōti Rangatahi (Youth Courts) – are changing the cultural dynamics of justice. Meanwhile, other solution-focused courts – dealing with offending by homeless people, or responding to sexual violence or substance use – seek to engage holistic measures to offending. Some initiatives demonstrate positive outcomes. However, as Quince clearly demonstrates, there are multiple areas for attention, particularly if we are to address Māori over-criminalisation, hyper-incarceration, and discrimination.

The activities of the courts are further scrutinised by James Oleson via a conceptual and practical outline of contemporary sentencing. He outlines the goals of sentencing (with particular attention to the philosophies of deterrence, incapacitation, rehabilitation, and retribution), as well as the options available to judges. Oleson examines the problems of sentencing disparity, in which like offenders receive *unlike* punishments as a result of judicial discretion, plea bargaining, or other factors. He considers three solutions that have been engaged to control for disparities: mandatory sentencing, sentencing guidelines, and evidence-based sentencing (using risk-assessment instruments to determine sentences). Further, like Quince, he reflects on the possibilities of alternative problem-solving courts, which embrace disparity in their tailored responses to offenders. While these courts are gaining in popularity, they are not without their problems, not least that they can bring more people into the system through a criminalisation of social problems.

One area in which judicial responses have been particularly innovative relates to the Youth Courts. Nessa Lynch's chapter provides an up-to-the-minute overview of New Zealand's youth justice system. Charting the much-lauded, innovative principles that have underpinned the system over the past 30 years, she explores recent conceptual and practical developments. Lynch highlights how New Zealand pursues contradictory approaches to young people who offend. On the one hand, New Zealand has benefited from innovative approaches in policing and the courts that divert or discharge young offenders, and which propel some family-focused and culturally conscious interventions. On the other hand, New Zealand also has many challenges, such as: the direction of serious young offenders to adult trial procedures and adult sentences; the disproportionate rates of Māori children and young people in the system; and the lack of specifically designed responses for girls, or for children and young people with additional needs. Her chapter makes clear that youth justice responses require further attention and resources to ensure that they can attend to children's well-being and rights.

Returning to the adult system, Anita Gibbs considers the nature of community sentences. She begins with a core question for criminologists: to what extent have community sentences in New Zealand operated as real *alternatives* to prison? Following a historical overview of New Zealand's probation service (and its commitment to befriend, help, and assist offenders), she charts the rise of community sentences that now reflect penal-populist and risk-management approaches. Exploring the different rationales for community sentences, and how these have been operationalised in different sentences, Gibbs considers diverse issues: the disproportionate sentencing of Māori offenders; the rise of surveillance measures; and concerns of effectiveness. In doing so, she notes that recent developments – incorporating sentences such as home detention or intensive supervisions – have increased the intensity of surveillance but brought few rehabilitative gains. The chapter ends with a call for the least restrictive sentences that are person-centric, relationship-based, socially engaged, and life-improving.

One criminal justice intervention that has gained significant prominence – before, during, and after sentencing – is that of restorative justice. Restorative justice (RJ) is regularly depicted as a progressive response to crime and has garnered significant supports in New Zealand and elsewhere on that basis. Juan Marcellus Tauri's chapter provides an overview of the concept and practice of RJ, and he challenges the idea that RJ is an empowering response to 'crime' in doing so. In particular, he argues that RJ has been purposefully misrepresented as a form of Indigenous justice, not least as Māori are regularly dissatisfied with the ways in which RJ practices (such as family group conferences) are run, including their tokenistic use of Māori cultural philosophy and practice. Tauri concludes that RJ has been captured by the state, such that RJ has become a means for settler-colonial governments to retain state control over responsibilising justice system activities that continue to harm Māori alongside other Indigenous peoples.

A further flashpoint for harms against Māori relates to New Zealand's continued vigorous use of prisons as a response to crime. In his chapter, Liam Martin reflects upon recent changes in the area, most notably through the Labour government's goals to reduce the prison population, address social disadvantage, and centralise Te Tiriti obligations. Yet these initiatives unfold in an established context of hyper-incarceration, where prison expansion remains high on the agenda. Martin includes original analyses from investigative surveys, undertaken by the office of New Zealand's Ombudsman, that depict common prison experiences characterised by long periods of cell confinement, idleness, lack of access to work or education, and routine violent victimisation. Drawing on the words of New Zealand (ex-)prisoners to show the lived experience of such dehumanising prisonisation, he explores the intergenerational impacts of cycles of confinement within poor and Māori communities. Along the way, he shows that any lack of freedom progresses well beyond the prison walls.

Staying within the remit of Corrections, Russil Durrant and Joanne Riley explore the concept and practice of rehabilitation. Historically encompassing moral or religious reform, contemporary approaches to reform or rehabilitation reflect psychological and social projects. Durrant and Riley consider two dominant models of rehabilitation in New Zealand: the risk-needs-responsivity model (in which individual risk characteristics are targeted for change) and the good lives model (which takes a strength-based approach to promote psychological well-being). In doing so, they argue for the importance of desistance (moving away from crime) in any rehabilitation efforts. There is now significant diversity in the rehabilitation programmes offered by New Zealand's Department of Corrections. Outlining several initiatives, and their connected evaluation data, Durrant and Riley demonstrate how rehabilitation programmes require authentic responses that are culturally safe, relationally linked, and community-connected. They conclude that while some rehabilitation programmes are effective, there is substantial scope for improvement in the nature and range of services on offer.

The chapter by Alice Mills and Cinnamon Lindsay Latimer considers the concept and practice of (re)integration following imprisonment, an issue that has received relatively little academic attention in New Zealand. Examining several schemes and services, they show that any (re)integration efforts must be aligned to desistance strategies that can facilitate strengths-based approaches. Mindful of how structural inequalities, institutional actions, and social relations often impede opportunities for offenders to thrive following sentences, they spell out how prison experiences intensify barriers to successful reintegration. Mills and Latimer consider how these situations are made even harder for Māori – as any idea of (re)integration is linked to offending behaviours but also to the legacies and realities of a colonial society that has perpetuated intergenerational disadvantage and trauma. Acknowledging recent Correctional efforts to enhance reintegration efforts, they argue that without better opportunities for ex-prisoners to be supported and included in communities, those leaving prison can get locked into a cycle of reincarceration.

The final chapter in Part Three challenges our use of the prison and the wider justice system. Ti Lamusse and Tracey McIntosh set out the general failings of prisons (that they do not rehabilitate, do not deter crime, can cause increases in reoffending, undermine public safety, fail to assist victims, are incompatible with tikanga Māori, entrench inequalities, and create significant pains), and show the fundamental problems of the prison as a response to 'crimes'. They call for abolition, not just in terms of the removal of prisons from New Zealand society, but also as a fundamental struggle for social justice and the abolition of conditions that make prisons even possible. Government advisory groups have called for transformational and decolonising changes to criminal justice. Within this, strategies for prison abolition and the new social institutions and conceptual frames that can render prison unnecessary have to be part of the future.

13

Penal Populism
Its Life and Death

John Pratt and Jordan Anderson

From 1945 up to the end of the 1980s, there was a general consensus in societies such as Aotearoa New Zealand about the direction of penal policy. It was driven by an axis of power that revolved around the government of the day (be it left- or right-leaning) and the criminal justice establishment (law professors, civil servants, senior judges, Department of Corrections representatives, and so on). As a consequence, punishments to the human body largely came to an end (the last execution in New Zealand was in 1957). It was also thought that punishment should not involve excessive use of state power, nor be arbitrary or indefinite, given the revelations of Nazi atrocities in the Second World War; indeed, individual rights should be protected from such excesses. This was one of the reasons why indeterminate prison sentences fell into dramatic decline in this period. By 1981 there were only 11 prisoners serving the indefinite sentence of preventive detention in New Zealand. Furthermore, it was generally thought that imprisonment should be used as a last-resort penal option.

As a result of this somewhat benign penal climate, by 1980 New Zealand had a rate of imprisonment of 83 per 100,000 of population – higher than Australia then (66 per 100,000), but lower than England and Wales (87 per 100,000), the point being that the New Zealand rate was nothing out of the ordinary. Indeed, there were further pressures to reduce the use of imprisonment because it was generally regarded as being too expensive, inhumane, and inefficient. Therefore, in any rational penal system, imprisonment should be used only against those who were a danger to the public. In addition, there was a determination by governments and their advisors to find alternative sanctions to prison; periodic detention (a weekend sanction usually involving scrub-cutting) began to be developed in response to this imperative.

This was also an era when 'public voices' – such as crime victims or those claiming to speak on their behalf – were almost wholly absent from the discourse. Media interest in crime and punishment was also limited, with most news outlets controlled by a very staid New Zealand public broadcasting corporation. The *Report of the Penal Policy Review Committee* (1981), issued by a committee composed of a law professor and representatives of Corrections, the Department of Justice, and New Zealand Police, and chaired by a judge – and which had even redefined its own terms of inquiry (from examining rising crime in this country to considering the way in which the penal system generated more crime) – was meant to signal the future. It advocated, inter alia, further limiting the scope of imprisonment, more use of community sanctions, and the abolition of preventive detention. But rather than serve as a blueprint for the future, this report became an epitaph for an era marked by the emphasis given to correctionalism, welfarism, and its commitment (in theory, if not always in practice) to leniency in response to crime.

Thereafter, far from imprisonment being used minimally, its rate escalated dramatically in this country to 214 per 100,000 of population in 2018. This is still a long way behind the most imprisoning society in the world – the United States, with rates that increased from 220 in 1980 to an all-time high of 755 in 2008. But it means that New Zealand has one of the highest rates of imprisonment in the OECD. And in contrast to the previous emphasis on finding alternatives to custody, New Zealand's recent history has been marked by punitive legislation. One example is the 'three-strikes law' (Sentencing and Parole Reform Act 2010), which is based on similar measures in the US. Another is the provision for public protection orders (Public Safety Act 2014), whereby the courts can impose a form of 'civil detention' (in reality, continuing imprisonment) on some sex offenders coming to the end of a finite prison term – and similar, in terms of consequences, to sexual predator laws in the US. Judges have also been exhorted by both Labour- and National-led coalition governments to make more use of longer prison sentences (Pratt & Clark, 2005). Furthermore, in the fervid, overheated penal atmosphere that came into existence, prison conditions became much more focused on security issues than on rehabilitation, amidst reports of serious overcrowding and extended periods of lockdown (see Martin, chapter 21 this volume).

Much of this change has been driven by the formation of a new axis of penal power: this time between governments and lobby groups, most notably the Sensible Sentencing Trust (SST), often in conjunction with talkback radio hosts and other media personalities. Meanwhile, the influence of the criminal justice establishment has been greatly diminished, and sometimes ignored altogether by government. Needless to say, this great expansion of the custodial sector has come at great financial cost. For example, the New Zealand Treasury (2010) noted that spending on justice doubled between 1994 and 2009 in inflation-adjusted terms, with Corrections absorbing 30 per cent of this total. Furthermore, prison building was projected to cost $915 million over the ensuing decade, with running costs then amounting to $150 million per year.

What is it, then, that has brought about this dramatic transformation in penal policy, practice, and expectations? The phenomenon of penal populism, to which New Zealand has been particularly susceptible, lies behind this. Let us first explain what this phenomenon is, before going on to examine why it should be that New Zealand has been so vulnerable to it. The chapter concludes by suggesting that, although penal populism may now be a declining force in New Zealand, it is nevertheless likely to prove difficult to unravel all the knots that it was able to tie in the punishment tapestry of this country. In particular, there will be no simple reversal to the previous axis of penal power.

WHAT IS PENAL POPULISM?

The term 'populism' represents in various guises the moods, sentiments, and voices of significant and distinct sections of the public: not public opinion in general, but instead those segments which feel that they have been ignored by governments, unlike, in their view, more favoured but less deserving groups. They feel that they have been disenfranchised in some way or another, while government policy seems to benefit less-worthy others. Such segments also speak out against those other sections of society which they judge to have been complicit in allowing this lack of representation to occur, in engineering this marginalisation and disenfranchisement of 'ordinary people' who have usually made no claims on the state other than to be allowed to live their lives.

Penal populism then refers to the way in which criminals and prisoners are thought to have been favoured at the expense of crime victims in particular, and the law-abiding public in general. It feeds on expressions of anger, disenchantment, and disillusionment with the criminal justice establishment. It holds them responsible for what seems to have been the insidious inversion of common-sensical priorities, such as protecting the well-being of law-abiding 'ordinary people' by punishing those whose crimes jeopardise their security.

Penal populism also needs to be distinguished from two other variants of populism that are regularly used to characterise this era. First, authoritarian populism, a phrase coined by Stuart Hall (1979, p. 2) to characterise what he saw as the characteristic mode of governance pursued by Margaret Thatcher in the 1980s in the UK, with its emphasis on neoliberal economics in which individuals are given much greater freedom of choice, but made to take much more responsibility for their actions, particularly law-breaking:

> by this means – first, forming public opinion, then, disingenuously, consulting it – the tendency to 'reach for the law' above is complemented by a popular demand to be governed more strictly from below. Thereby the drift to law and order above secures a degree of popular support and legitimacy amongst the powerless, who see no other alternative (p. 2).

After blaming the previous social democratic trajectory of governance for the ills that the Thatcherite version of neoliberalism was intended to correct, Hall (1988) saw authoritarian populism as attempting to impose 'a new regime of social discipline and leadership from above in a society increasingly experienced as rudderless and out of control' (p. 24). In these respects, it is as if the public have no opinion other than that which is constructed for them (from 'above'). However, changes in the structure of the media, including the use of social media, apart from anything else, have meant that it is no longer possible for governments to act as ventriloquists speaking for an inanimate public. Penal populism thus captures the way in which popular movements beyond government have come to capture the views of 'the people', with governments then running to try and catch up with them.

Second, penal populism should be distinguished from populist punitiveness (Bottoms, 1995): that is, politicians 'tapping into' what is perceived to be the public's punitive stance on crime for their electoral advantage, then throwing it aside as it suits them. Again, the assumption here seems to be that governments speak on behalf of the people, rather than 'with' the people, and are able to change their policies and programmes as it pleases them: as if public opinion is cynically exploited and manipulated at election time and then disregarded. In contrast, penal populism is much more directly tied into perceived public views about crime and punishment as presented on their behalf by forces extraneous to government – law-and-order lobbyists, victims' rights groups, and the like. Politicians have no monopoly of discourse on these matters and can allow themselves to become hostages to whatever fortune this brings.

In New Zealand, this is most clearly seen in the impact of the 1999 non-binding citizens' referendum on law and order. The referendum was initiated by Mr Norm Withers, a Christchurch shopkeeper whose mother had been attacked while minding the business for him. Withers decided he would make use of this new provision of electoral legislation to campaign for greater penal severity.[1] This, he thought, would counter what he perceived to be 'a tide of violent crime in his area' (*Press*, 1997). The subsequent referendum question was written for him by the Christian Heritage Party, a right-wing organisation (whose leader would later be sentenced to a nine-year prison term for sexual offences against minors under the harsher measures this referendum enabled). The referendum asked:

> Should there be a reform of our justice system placing greater emphasis on the needs of victims, providing restitution and compensation for them and imposing minimum sentences and hard labour for all serious violent offences?

Despite the question's intrinsic contradictions and inconsistencies (the 'hard labour' proposal would have meant New Zealand violating the UN Standard Minimum Rules for the Treatment of Prisoners to which it had been a signatory), it received a 92.7 per cent vote in its favour. It was then validated by the Labour-led coalition governments from 1999 to 2005.

The referendum served to justify a cluster of legislation supposedly strengthening victims' rights, restricting parole eligibility, and making provision for longer prison terms. The then minister of justice stated that '[the Victims' Rights Bill] is a vital component of the Government's response to public concerns . . . clearly demonstrated by the response to the referendum at the 1999 general election' (Goff, 2002b). And 'the Sentencing and Parole Reform Bill responds to . . . public support for change, as indicated in the 1999 referendum . . . [which] showed huge public discontent with the state of our sentencing system' (Goff, 2002a). Indeed, in recognition of Withers' standing both inside and outside of Parliament, the justice minister informed him of the details of the latter Bill before these became public knowledge (Venter, 2001, p. 1).

But this was still not the end of the matter. The success and attention given to the referendum generated considerable public and media interest and led to the formation of the Sensible Sentencing Trust (SST) in 2001 by Napier farmer Garth McVicar. In a statement to the media about the SST, McVicar said: 'our main goal is getting tougher sentences for repeat violent offenders . . . for these people life has to mean life' (Booker, 2001, p. 4).

Thereafter, this organisation regularly drew government ministers (who were always ready to provide fervent encouragement) to speak at its conferences, as well as making submissions to government committees on crime control and sentencing issues. On these occasions, McVicar would most likely be accompanied by relatives of particularly high-profile murder victims, to which his organisation (rather than the government's Victim Support) had reached out, welcoming them into its campaigning fold. Their presence, of course, then gave him the moral high ground in such representations. Indeed, for the ensuing decade, McVicar himself was seldom out of the headlines (Bartlett, 2009), continually putting pressure on the government and the criminal justice authorities to further shift their policies towards his demands. He thus took the side of vigilantes in their attempts to prevent sex offenders released from prison settling in their home communities; and campaigned against what he saw as judicial leniency and inept Corrections officials. He, on behalf of the SST, also demanded tougher conditions in prisons, and urged the adaptation of 'three strikes' and an end to parole and so on. In these ways, McVicar and the SST played a leading role in public debate on penal policy for over a decade. Having demonstrated a willingness to respect the referendum and to entertain McVicar's and the SST's demands, governments then found themselves compromised in the development of criminal justice policy.

THE CAUSES OF PENAL POPULISM

What was it, though, that brought penal populism into existence? It represented the coalescence of five diverse forces. These are present to varying degrees in many Western societies but particularly so in New Zealand, which helps to explain why the country has been so vulnerable to this phenomenon. In ideal-type format these are as follows.

The decline of deference

The decline of deference refers to the way in which the values and opinions of elite social groups that used to frame public discourse are no longer accepted without question (Nevitte, 1996). Before the 1980s, it was assumed that establishment figures – in the universities, the civil service, and so on – formed a natural class of government on the basis of their lineage, education, and wealth, and by the positions of power that these characteristics then guaranteed for them. Thereafter, however, those in government or government bureaucracies would no longer be viewed as the social superiors of the rest of society with the exclusive right to pronounce on issues of the day, and would accordingly be challenged by those outside these establishment circles. In New Zealand, however, this body had always had a tenuous hold on power and discourse. The very nature of colonisation determined this (Pratt, 2006). A series of commentators confirmed this characteristic of the culture in this country throughout the nineteenth and twentieth centuries. For example, Herz (1912) reported:

> the people who came out here had to work, and to work hard . . . Is it astonishing that they seek only the things of real and practical value – the things that mean money, or that they own a touch of disrespect for life's other aspect and regard Art, for instance as . . . not absolutely necessary (p. 348).

Similarly, Oliver Duff (1941) wrote of a 'widespread distrust of academic minds . . . mistrust of intellectuals is not a new phenomenon [here]. It runs right through our political history' (p. 82). Thereafter, eminent British scientist Lord Robert Winston (*New Zealand Herald*, 2009) observed that the culture of New Zealanders undervalues thinkers and idolises sports stars: '[In] New Zealand being an intellectual is slightly disadvantageous and is often seen by the press as being something which is not to be celebrated' (para. 3). In other words, for much of its European history, it became a country with little by way of critical scholarship or social analysis.

The neoliberal mode of governance introduced to New Zealand by the Fourth Labour Government (1984–87) had given these anti-elitism and anti-intellectualism characteristics further momentum. First, neoliberalism insisted instead that rewards should go to the enterprising and the hard-working, irrespective of their backgrounds and origins. It had no interest in maintaining the existing status quo. The uncertainties created by freeing the economy from risk controls were to be welcomed, it was claimed, since it was envisaged that opportunities would emerge from this and allow enterprise to succeed amidst the chaos created by the economic reforms that were introduced. Second, elites most usually employed in some prestigious capacity in the public sector were regarded as the enemies of neoliberal reforms, and were thought to use their influence to resist or undermine them. As Sir Roger Douglas (1980, p. 56), architect of the restructuring, complained, 'A bureaucrat, once created, has a life completely independent of his creator.'

Criminal justice officials proved to be particularly vulnerable to these challenges. This was because of their apparent failure to address rising crime rates from the 1950s, while simultaneously giving the impression that they would much prefer to attend to the rehabilitative reform of criminals instead. In so doing, they seemed remote and detached from the concerns of 'ordinary people', the kinds of people that the SST and some politicians (following in its wake) went on to target. The decline in crime from the early 1990s across New Zealand and most other Western societies (Farrell et al., 2014; Zimring, 2012) could not displace the way in which rising crime had by then become a taken-for-granted 'social fact' – to which the establishment had no answer. Attempts by its members to explain that crime was in decline, rather than rising, simply became proof of their own irrelevance and duplicity.

The decline of trust

The New Zealand electorate grew increasingly cynical of politicians' promises and guarantees of better futures when these regularly failed to materialise. Worthy citizens who had followed government advice and invested on the stock market, often for the first time, were likely to have been the ones hurt most when the first of the great post-restructuring economic crashes occurred in October 1987. *The Dominion* (1987) reported on the global effects of this event: 'No market around the world escaped the misery . . . Wall Street's 22.6 per cent fall in the Dow was close to twice that of the 1929 one-day decline that heralded the Great Depression,' also noting that 'in the past, New Zealand had largely been insulated from overseas market fluctuations but that had changed with the increasing internationalism and sophistication of stock dealings' (Pirie, 1987, p. 1). Rather than bring better futures, government policies might only bring disaster to those citizens who had loyally adhered to the directions that governments had been urging them to take. However, politicians themselves, along with their advisors, seldom seem to suffer. When leaving government, they are likely to be offered remunerative directorships, memberships of advisory bodies, and so on. Meanwhile, unemployment in this country increased from 4 per cent in 1986 to 10 per cent in 1992 (Pratt & Clark, 2005).

The country was transformed almost overnight from being one of the OECD's most heavily regulated societies to one of its most deregulated. The consequences of the 1987 crash and the shattered dreams of unparalleled, easy-to-come-by riches contributed to a dramatic decline of trust in the mainstream political parties that had engineered the economic reforms. Support fell to 9 (Labour) and 12 per cent (Conservative) of the electorate respectively in opinion polling in the early 1990s (see Pratt & Clark, 2005). While these figures from the 1990s represent all-time lows, politicians remain at the bottom of preferred professional groups, or close to it. Voter turnout at elections also declined (from 93.7 per cent in 1984 to 74.2 per cent in 2011). This decline of trust in mainstream political parties was simultaneous to a surge of support for the populist, right-wing New Zealand First party, which professed to be anti-establishment and on the side of 'the people'. It promised to place control of New Zealand's resources in the hands of New Zealanders, by restoring faith in the democratic process, alongside 'pragmatic and common-sense representation' and 'putting New Zealand, and New Zealanders, first' (New Zealand First, 2014).

Furthermore, the decline of trust in the existing electoral system was the catalyst for a referendum in 1993 where the public voted heavily in favour of proportional representation over the existing 'first past the post' system. The expectation was that this would bring wider representation in Parliament rather than allow the vested interests of the two main parties to continue to dominate government. This has meant that a party like New Zealand First will often be able to attract a sufficiently disaffected core of the electorate sufficient to take it over the 5 per cent threshold it now needs to gain parliamentary representation. On three occasions since (following elections in 1996, 2005, and 2017), it has become 'kingmaker' in coalition governments (although it fared less well in 2020). Much of this party's success has come through speaking to public anxieties about crime and immigration, and proffering its magical but common-sensical solutions to these problems (more police, tougher sentencing, less immigration). The major parties have then been prepared to accede to these demands to win its support in Parliament (Lacey, 2008), and thereby allow its centrepiece policies on these matters to become part of government policy. Furthermore, the popular appeal of 'law and order' that it had demonstrated encouraged the New Zealand mainstream parties (as in Britain and the US – see Jones & Newburn, 2005) to compete with each other on these terms, again building penal populism into government policy.

The rise of global insecurities and anxieties

From the 1980s, the modern world is thought to have become a much riskier, more threatening place (Beck, 1992), in many ways as a consequence of the same restructuring. If this has brought new possibilities of wealth creation (massive financial dealings can be made in a few seconds because of computer technology) and new opportunities for pleasure, fulfilment, and self-enhancement to everyday life, it has also brought an increased awareness of risks – of terrorism, new kinds of cancers, identity fraud, and so on. New Zealand, because of its geographical isolation and the contingent nature of its export markets, is always likely to have been especially vulnerable to such anxieties. What has then compounded these has been the fragmentation or disappearance of many of the old and familiar symbols of security and stability – the certainty and longevity of employment, and the homogeneity of New Zealand society and family life. The shift from manufacturing to service industries from the mid-1980s has also been accompanied by a dramatic contraction in the former safe haven of public sector employment: from 26 per cent of the workforce in 1980 to 17 per cent in 2017. This has meant that many workers now know only temporary employment in the minimally regulated and unpredictable private sector. They may be reduced to the uncertainties of zero-contract hours or life in the 'gig' economy, neither of which provide any guarantees of a regular and certain income. Meanwhile, a large growth in Asian immigration especially has meant that New Zealand has become a far more ethnically diverse country; also, the nuclear family construct has given way to a variety of cohabiting relationships and many more people living alone.

In this context, concerns and perceptions about crime and disorder, with insufficient punishment and control available to deal with these matters, played an important role in stabilising and remedying what were perceived by many as deficiencies in social capital. Such concerns had the ability to draw anxious sections of the public together against common enemies. By the 1990s, the apparent uncontrolled growth of crime silenced the reality of the consistent decline of crime rates, and became the most obvious and immediate symbol of the inability of governments and their experts to make everyday life more secure.

The influence of the mass media

For much of the twentieth century, public discourse on crime, punishment, and related matters was largely shaped by authoritative sections of the media. Here, the New Zealand Broadcasting Company (NZBC) played this role, performing a public service/education role. However, from the 1980s, changes in technology, the advent of satellite television, and the deregulation of broadcasting brought about a much more diverse and pluralistic set of understandings of the world – at a time when the decline of organic community life meant that individuals were becoming much more reliant on the news media than on friends, family, or work colleagues to inform them about the world. New Zealand moved from being a country with two television channels in 1987, terminating each night around 10 p.m., to one that had over 100 available a decade later, often operating on a 24/7 basis. The rise of social media thereafter (Facebook emerged in 2004; Twitter in 2008) has not only loosened the hold of the establishment on public discourse, but also made it possible for individuals to make and report their own news. These structural changes have also meant that the onset of the fall in crime had little public impact. It was not really newsworthy. Instead, crime continued to be reported as the most obvious and immediate source of risk and danger, rather than the less tangible and less obvious consequences of restructuring, such as the risks attached to playing in the financial market and the growing sense of individual isolation and detachment.

The diversification of the media also meant that news reporting became more simplified, more competitive, more readily available than ever before: a sensational story about crime – its menace, not its decline – would beat off competitors, attract the public, and thereby attract more advertising revenue (see also Gilmour, chapter 2 this volume). Cook's (2002, pp. 140–141) study of *One Network News* between 1984 and 1996 demonstrated that the average length of a news item had been reduced by 20 seconds and the maximum length had fallen from 9 to 4.5 minutes: '[T]he faster paced news is cheaper to produce, requiring less time per item and so less research and background information, and appeals to advertisers who prefer a fast paced programme on many subjects rather than one consisting of lengthy analysis of fewer issues.' The same research also showed that political news had declined while crime news had increased.

Amidst this restructuring, the criminal justice establishment now found itself unable to control the parameters of public debate and knowledge about such matters. On talkback radio programmes, for example, those with grievances about what they saw as the growth of crime, the inadequacies of law enforcement, and over-lenient judges could be given a platform to sound their views, spark debate, even become national figures, however detached from the reality of crime and punishment their opinions were.

The symbolic importance of crime victims

The importance of crime news in this new framework of knowledge also gave much greater emphasis to victims' accounts of their experiences, rather than the detached, objective analysis of experts. In this respect, crime victims were given a new kind of authenticity and authority. In most cases, what happened to them was presented as something that could easily happen to anyone at any time: going to school, journeying home from work, and so on became the starting point for a catalogue of horrors that were then inflicted on these unsuspecting victims, however rare and remote such incidents actually were. In May 2014, having been missing for two days, the mutilated remains of Blesilda (Blessie) Gotingco were found in an Auckland cemetery. The mother of three had been walking the short distance home from a bus stop after work when she was run down by a car, abducted, raped, and murdered by a known sex offender released on an extended supervision order.

When such catastrophes – and it is usually the extremely rare catastrophic crime that makes such headlines – could befall respectable, ordinary citizens in the banality of their everyday life, it was as if what had happened to them became a universal experience and a universal danger. Hearing, reading, watching, and learning about victims' traumas led to demands for more emotive and expressive punishments: punishments that sufficiently reflected public anger and revulsion at such incidents. There were also demands for more opportunities for victims to express their own anger at their suffering, as opposed to the carefully measured tones of courtroom professionals, who usually suppressed all such sentiments. Instead, the Victims' Rights Act 2002 has necessitated a spatial and emotional reorganisation of criminal justice proceedings. This now places victims, rather than their offenders, at the centre of proceedings, going through the detail of their victim impact statements. But when judges still seem swayed by reason rather than the pain of victims when passing sentence (in reality their hands are anyway tied by legal constraints on what they can do), this further divides the criminal justice establishment from victims' or potential victims and their expectations of justice. For the latter, this disjuncture is more evidence of how out of touch such officials are from everyday life: victims' or their representatives' anguish and outrage at the end of such proceedings might then be picked up by eager journalists at the courthouse waiting for just such a sensational story. This can then be written up and presented as yet another betrayal of ordinary people by imperious elites, who are oblivious to the pain of innocents.

CONCLUSION

The consequences of penal populism in New Zealand have been extreme. There has been the enormous economic cost of maintaining such a high level of imprisonment when other government expenditure has been significantly cut back. There have also been dramatic social costs: in 2015, the rate at which Māori were incarcerated was eight times higher than that of Pākehā (ActionStation, 2018). In place of any rational planning for penal development, policy in this era has frequently been driven by scandal, often arising in itself from a deteriorating prison estate brought about by overcrowding or the preoccupation with security; or scandal generated by publicity-seeking law-and-order adventurers and politicians thinking that this was the way to grab votes (Boyle & Stanley, 2019).

There has been very little informed public debate about what should happen to inmates while in prison, or what resources are needed within the prison to help with desistance from crime rather than merely keeping the perimeters of the prison secure. And there has been very little informed public debate about the resettlement of prisoners on release. Instead, isolated incidents have led to legislation and administrative measures that have had a mainly symbolic importance. The Prisoners' and Victims' Claims Act 2005, for example, was passed after a number of prisoners were awarded $310,000 in damages for being held in a 'behaviour control unit', similar to US supermax conditions, for which Corrections had no authority to impose. The ensuing public scandal was about the prisoners recovering damages, rather than Corrections subjecting them to this regime. The legislation allows crime victims or their family to sue prisoners for any windfall the latter might receive (damages, as here, or lottery winnings and the like), and to date has been used only once.

Indeed, the history of Corrections policy over the past 20 years is littered with ad hoc responses to public pressure (often orchestrated by the media and the SST) to one-off, high-profile incidents: the termination of all inmate work outside the prison after one of them escaped to South America; the rejigging of bail laws by the National government in 2014 that has since led to an explosion in the remand population (3000 prisoners on remand in 2018, compared with 1800 in 2012); victims being revictimised as they trudge from court hearing to parole hearing to make their representations, while therapeutic assistance that might previously have been available to them under ACC has been reduced; the abolition of one-third automatic remission for most inmates under the Parole Act 2002, making parole the only opportunity for early release for most, and turning this into a minor industry in its own right; the three-strikes law of 2011, passed amidst great claims by its ACT party devotees about what it would do ('contrary to the predictions from members opposite and from elsewhere, [three strikes] is not the end of justice as we know it. It is not the end of compassion or justice. It is a turning point. It allows us . . . to focus on the children of today's violent offenders and try to ensure that they do not follow their fathers. It is, in fact, a great day for New Zealand justice' [Garrett, 2010]): at the time of writing, no prisoner has yet to be sentenced to a full term that the legislation allows on a third strike. And so it would be possible to continue recording all the 'sound and fury' of uninformed, ill-informed political and public discourse with so little to show for it except a large bill to the New Zealand taxpayer.

How did governments allow themselves to be so easily seduced by the siren voices of the SST and the like? Certainly, proclaiming tough-on-crime measures became a way of attracting publicity and voter attention. At the same time, the prominence of these policies is itself a direct product of the electoral changes that took effect in 1996. As we have seen, MMP (mixed member proportional voting system) has meant that the mainstream parties have been compelled to form governments with minor parties that have strong law-and-order agendas if for no other reason than this gives these smaller parties publicity. But the fact that there had to be changes to the electoral process was in itself indicative of the broader consequences of neoliberal restructuring. These were of such an order – both good and bad – that social cohesion began to dissolve. The only way to restore legitimacy to government was by making these electoral changes. Even so, penal policy was also compelled to play a role in rebuilding cohesion. In so doing, the law-and-order programme performed a very useful function for successive governments. It created a dam in which all the toxic waste created by restructuring could be stored, while the restructuring itself continued to weave its way through the social fabric.

Yet perhaps we are in the process of seeing the end of this particular episode of New Zealand's penal history. The Labour–New Zealand First coalition government of 2005–8 had itself tried to put the brake on penal populism, aware of the 'sorcerer's apprentice' that predecessor governments had created. However, its proposal for a sentencing council and a general reduction in sentences was not given legislative effect and these initiatives have now faded into obscurity. Nonetheless, the election of the Labour-led coalition government in 2017, amidst a wave of popular discontent with the general direction that New Zealand society had been taking, has led to an attempt to redirect penal policy. During the election campaign itself, public concerns were not so much about law and order as high levels of immigration. With the latter more strictly regulated, the government was able to turn its attention to bringing the prison population down – with a target of a 30 per cent reduction (over a period of 15 years). It has been helped in this task by the disappearance of the SST from much of public debate on crime issues, and the appearance of alternative discourses on this, provided by Rethinking Crime and Punishment, and more recently by JustSpeak. The exact reasons for this are beyond the scope of this chapter, although all pressure groups are likely to have a finite life, being very much dependent on charismatic leadership rather than bureaucratic momentum. When the former burns out, this is likely to spell the end for the pressure group.

As it is, in 2018 the government formed Te Uepū Hāpai i te Ora – the Safe and Effective Justice Advisory Group. Although Te Uepū has since been disestablished, following the completion of the reports it was commissioned to produce, it consulted with communities across the country to ascertain 'public views' for 'more effective justice', rather than allow the SST, talkback radio hosts, and the like to claim to be the voice of the public. It also consulted with Māori communities and stakeholders in criminal justice. The publication of *Ināia Tonu Nei*, summarising the discussion at the Hui Māori attended by Māori justice stakeholders in 2019, as well as the reports from Te Uepū, give indications of increasing drive for transformative change. While the government's proposals are yet to be published, the Labour and Green parties at least have made it clear both publicly and privately that the size of New Zealand's prison population is unsustainable, and that the criminal justice system, in their words, is 'broken'.

Some administrative adjustments have already been made to repair it: instructions to interpret the existing bail law less rigidly have already helped to bring the rate of imprisonment down to 188 per 100,000 of population by June 2020. The subsequent election result in October – a landslide victory for Labour and the termination of New Zealand First's presence in Parliament – has provided new opportunities for further reductions, given the way in which the latter had resolutely blocked more widespread penal reform, such as the repeal of the highly symbolic three-strikes law. It remains to be seen whether Labour, perhaps with the support of the Green Party, will feel sufficiently confident to take up this challenge by making further inroads to the level of imprisonment and simultaneously trying to change the penal culture of this society that populism had so distorted. Whatever the outcome of this, it is also clear that the voices of victims will have a role to play in subsequent policy development; as indeed will the voices of Māori communities. The days when the (almost wholly) white, male, liberal establishment, for good or bad, determined the course of penal policy in this country are gone.

STUDY QUESTIONS

- How has penal populism differed under different governments in New Zealand?
- How does the media relate to penal populism in New Zealand and elsewhere?
- How has penal populism contributed to the cycle of hyper-incarceration in New Zealand?

FURTHER READING

Garland, D. (1996). The limits of the sovereign state: Strategies of crime control in contemporary society. *British Journal of Criminology, 36*(4), 445–471. doi:10.1093/oxfordjournals.bjc.a014105

Pratt J. (2007). *Penal populism.* Oxford, UK: Routledge.

Pratt, J., & Miao, M. (2019). The end of penal populism; the rise of populist politics. *Archiwum Kryminologii, 2*(XLI), 15–40.

NOTES

1 The Citizens Initiated Referenda Act 1993 allowed for Citizens Initiated Referenda. Withers' petition brought about the last of a swathe of these non-binding votes that occurred throughout the 1990s.

REFERENCES

ActionStation. (2018). *They're our whānau.* Wellington, New Zealand: ActionStation. Retrieved from https://actionstation.org.nz/downloads/tow-report.pdf

Bartlett, T. (2009). *The power of penal populism: Public influences on penal and sentencing policy from 1999 to 2008.* Unpublished master's thesis, Victoria University of Wellington, New Zealand.

Beck, U. (1992). *Risk society: Towards a new modernity.* London, UK: Sage.

Booker, J. (2001, October 6). Sentencing stand firms. *Press,* p. 4.

Bottoms, A. (1995). The philosophy and politics of punishment and sentencing. In C. Clarkson & R. Morgan (Eds.), *Politics of sentencing reform* (pp. 17–49). Oxford, UK: Oxford University Press.

Boyle, O., & Stanley, E. (2019). Private prisons and the management of scandal. *Crime, Media, Culture, 15*(1), 67–87. doi:10.1177/1741659017736097

Cook, D. (2002). Deregulation and broadcast news content: ONE Network News 1984 to 1996. In J. Farnsworth & I. Hutchinson (Eds), *New Zealand television: A reader* (pp. 139–144). Palmerston North, New Zealand: Dunmore Press.

Dominion. (1987, October 21, p. 15). World sharemarkets crash.

Douglas, R. (1980). *There's got to be a better way! A practical ABC to solving New Zealand's major problems.* Wellington, New Zealand: Fourth Estate Press.

Duff, O. (1941). *New Zealand now.* Wellington, New Zealand: Department of Internal Affairs.

Farrell, G., Tilley, N., & Tseloni, A. (2014). Why the crime drop? *Crime and Justice, 43*(1), 421–490. doi:10.1086/678081

Garrett, D. (2010). Sentencing and parole reform Bill – third reading. *New Zealand Parliamentary Debates, 663*, 11226. Retrieved from https://www.parliament.nz/en/pb/hansard-debates/rhr/document/49HansD_20100525_00000745/sentencing-and-parole-reform-bill-third-reading

Goff, P. (2002a). Sentencing and parole reform Bill – second reading. *New Zealand Parliamentary Debates, 599*, 15451. Retrieved from https://www.beehive.govt.nz/speech/sentencing-parole-reform-bill–2nd-reading

Goff, P. (2002b). Victims' Rights Bill – Justice and Electoral Committee. *New Zealand Parliamentary Debates, 603*, 1318. Retrieved from https://www.beehive.govt.nz/speech/victims-rights-bill-second-reading

Hall, S. (1979). *Drifting into a law and order society*. London, UK: Cobden Trust.

Hall, S. (1988). *The hard road to renewal: Thatcherism and the crisis on the left*. London, UK: Verso.

Herz, M. (1912). *New Zealand*. London, UK: T. Werner Laurie.

Jones, T., & Newburn, T. (2005). Comparative criminal justice policy-making in the United States and the United Kingdom. *British Journal of Criminology, 45*(1), 55–80. doi: 10.1093/bjc/azh067

Lacey, N. (2008). *The prisoners' dilemma*. Cambridge, UK: Cambridge University Press.

Nevitte, N. (1996). *The decline of difference: Canadian value change in cross national perspective*. Peterborough, Ontario, Canada: Broadview Press.

New Zealand First. (2014). *About New Zealand First*. Retrieved from www.nzfirst.org.nz/about

New Zealand Herald. (2009, December 14). NZ undervalues thinkers, UK scientist says. Retrieved from www.nzherald.co.nz/nz/news/article.cfm?c_id=1&objectid=10615379

New Zealand Treasury. (2010). *Justice sector: Information supporting the estimates 2010–11*. Retrieved from https://treasury.govt.nz/publications/ise/justice-sector-information-supporting-estimates–2010–11-budget–2010-html

Penal Policy Review Committee. (1981). *Report of the Penal Policy Review Committee*. Wellington, New Zealand: Ministry of Justice. Retrieved from http://www.nzlii.org/nz/journals/NZLRFOP/1984/237.pdf

Pirie, A. (1987, October 21). 'Horrific' trading shocks dealers. *Dominion*, p. 1.

Pratt, J. (2006). The dark side of paradise: Explaining New Zealand's history of high imprisonment. *British Journal of Criminology, 46*(4), 541–560. doi: 10.1093/bjc/azi095

Pratt, J., & Clark, M. (2005). Penal populism in New Zealand. *Punishment and Society, 7*(3), 303–322. doi:10.1177/1462474505053831

Press (1997, July 8, p. 4). Referendum urged.

Venter, N. (2001, March 16). Tougher sentences include 17 years' non-parole. *Dominion*, p. 1.

Zimring, F. (2012). *The great American crime decline*. New York, NY: Oxford University Press.

14

Policing
Past, Present, and Future

Trevor Bradley, Elizabeth Stanley, and Angus Lindsay

Over the past decade, New Zealand Police (NZP) has progressed through widescale transformation. Policing culture, operational strategies, service delivery, and organisational diversity have all been subject to review and reform processes. The resulting reconfiguration has emphasised a more empathetic, victim-centred, proactive, and preventative service that more closely resembles the increasingly diverse populations it serves.

In some areas, NZP has made 'substantial progress' (Rowe & Macauley, 2017, p. 27) in transforming elements of its occupational culture. As one example, during a major Commission of Inquiry into Police Conduct in 2007 (the 'Bazley Report' – see Bazley, 2007), NZP faced significant criticisms on how it dealt with sexual assault allegations, including those made against police officers (see also Jordan, 2004). Over the following decade, NZP worked to increase organisational diversity, improve ethical leadership, enhance responses to inappropriate behaviour and misconduct, mitigate some of the negative impacts on women in policing, and challenge the traditional 'all boys club' (Jordan & Mossman, 2019; Rowe & Macauley, 2017, p. 4).

These advances are important. Yet, as this chapter shows, significant concerns with New Zealand policing remain. Many issues demand urgent attention – including the prolonged detention of young people in police cells (Children's Commissioner, 2019) and the criminalisation of those with mental health problems by inadequately trained officers (Te Uepū Hāpai i Te Ora, 2019a) – while questions surround the efficacy of our police accountability systems (Buttle & Deckert, 2017). Limited space prevents consideration of many policing-related concerns. This chapter therefore focuses on three issues that provide a window on the past, present, and future of policing in Aotearoa New Zealand. These issues, left unchecked, will erode the legitimacy of and undermine the public's trust and confidence in NZP: (1) the New Zealand context of post-colonialism and its continuing impact on Māori interactions with police, and criminal justice more broadly; (2) the creeping paramilitarisation of NZP, most clearly manifest in the policing of protest and the recent deployment of Armed Response Teams (ARTs); and (3) the failure of NZP to adapt to meet the challenges posed by transformations in criminal offending, and particularly to address victimisations from cybercrimes.

POLICE LEGITIMACY, PROCEDURAL JUSTICE, AND PUBLIC SATISFACTION

According to Martin and Bradford (2019), 'the last two decades . . . have witnessed a "legitimacy turn" within criminology generally and policing particularly' (p. 2). Led by Tyler's (2006, 2017) work on why people obey the law, an extensive body of research has identified that legitimacy is central to effective policing (Mazerolle & Wickes, 2015; Murphy et al., 2009; Sunshine & Tyler, 2003). Citizens who view the police as legitimate are more likely to comply with the law, follow instructions, and co-operate (Tyler, 2006). Hinds and Murphy (2007) found legitimacy to be more effective at fostering compliance and co-operation than the use (or threat) of force or the fear of punishment. Police legitimacy is thus associated with safer police–citizen interactions, enhanced social order, and greater public satisfaction with police (Sunshine & Tyler, 2003; Tyler & Huo, 2002).

Mazerolle et al. (2013, p. 246) detail that the 'primary pathway' to achieving legitimacy 'is through procedural justice'. Procedural justice refers to people's perceptions of whether the treatment they receive from the police is 'fair', regardless of the outcome of public–police interactions and encounters (e,g., arrest or detention). The authors found greater compliance and co-operation, and improved perceptions of police legitimacy, when police employ fair procedures and when citizens are treated with dignity and respect and are allowed a 'voice'.

Particularly relevant in the New Zealand context, Hinds and Murphy (2007, p. 30) note that police legitimacy 'is especially important in diverse and disadvantaged communities' and those in which 'long-term tensions between police and the community are an ongoing source of antagonism and mistrust'. The evidence clearly shows that ethnically diverse and disadvantaged communities, often one and the same in New Zealand, are much less likely to experience procedural justice and that their experience of policing differs markedly from the majority (Te Uepū Hāpai i Te Ora, 2019a). In turn, these communities are less likely to have satisfaction in policing. To achieve the target that '90% of people feel safe and have trust and confidence' (NZP, 2019b, p. 42), NZP first needs to resolve those tensions between police and Māori, halt the creeping process of paramilitarisation and coercive policing, and quickly adapt to meet the challenges posed and reduce the harms generated by diverse forms of online victimisation.

COLONIALISM AND ITS CONTEMPORARY LEGACIES

The historical legacy of colonialism has had a 'dispiriting' impact on Māori interactions with the police and, in turn, with all criminal justice agencies (Mikaere, 2013). Colonisation is a crucial backdrop to the continued exercise of unfavourable police discretion toward Māori. Contemporary patterns of policing interactions with and the criminalisation of Māori (and other groups such as Pasifika and African young people) are grounded in and facilitated through hostile relationships of colonisation (Nakhid et al., 2016; Suaalii-Sauni et al., chapter 27 this volume). The contemporary disproportional criminalisation of Māori also has to be understood against the backdrop of ongoing institutional racism or bias (conscious or otherwise) in policing. As Hill (2008) argued, 'While no modern institutions are entirely divorced from their past . . . this . . . is especially pronounced in the case of the police' (p. 40).

The trauma of colonial policing

The police played a central part in the colonisation of Aotearoa New Zealand. In the early years, provincial police officers were relatively disorganised and poorly paid, had few resources, and were expected to police large geographical areas (Hill, 1997). However, through the nineteenth century, the police in New Zealand became one of the most heavily armed forces in the world. The Armed Police Force (1846) and its 1867 replacement, the New Zealand Armed Constabulary, were intensely militaristic. The latter effected a 'stranger policing stranger' approach to ease officer qualms of using force (Hill, 1997, pp. 10, 11). In short, New Zealand policing was fundamentally shaped by the interests of the British settlers in acquiring land and establishing control: officers facilitated and enforced the dispossession and confiscation of Māori land, and actively repressed those engaged in resistance to colonial authorities (Bull, 2004). As just one example, over 1600 armed constables, naval officers, and settler volunteers raided the Taranaki pacifist settlement of Parihaka on 5 November 1881, to evict over two thousand Māori.[1] On this 'day of plunder', having been greeted by singing children and women offering bread, officers and troops destroyed homes, sacred buildings, crops and livestock; raped women; and imprisoned people without trial and charged them with sedition (Wynyard, 2019).[2]

Following the 'Land Wars', when authorities determined that most areas had been 'tamed' (Hill, 1989), two Acts were passed: the Police Force Act and the Defence Act (1886) split the Armed Constabulary into the standing army and the New Zealand Police Force. Although the latter were now regarded as an independent civilian force, they remained and remain 'an instrument of the Crown' (see the 2008 Policing Act, s. 7(1)). Over the following decades, NZP continued to over-police Māori for revolts against new legislation and policy that placed them in direct conflict with settler interests – from the introduction of the 'dog tax' in the 1890s to the selective establishment of 'dry' alcohol areas across Māori settlements in the 1910s (Bull, 2004). Armed officers also continued to repress those refusing to comply with colonisers' demands. For example, in the 1916 invasion of Maungapōhatu settlement in Te Urewera, officers shot two young men dead, raped local women, and unlawfully imprisoned Tūhoe pacifist Rua Kēnana for objecting to military conscription (Hurihanganui, 2019b). The repressive policing of Māori can be identified by other pinnacle events through the twentieth and twenty-first centuries, such as at Bastion Point,[3] Rūātoki,[4] and Ihumātao (the latter discussed below).

Such events remind us that colonisation is not just a historical event. Rather, settler-states are in a perpetual process of colonisation, with colonial power relations continually developed through new forms, strategies, and practices (Blagg & Anthony, 2019). In this regard, policing remains a crucial mechanism of delivery for discriminatory, inequitable, and traumatising state actions experienced by Indigenous people, and through which settler power relations are performed and upheld (Cunneen & Tauri, 2016). Further, while colonisation appears writ large in particularly dramatic events, it is also maintained through the mundane, everyday realities of policing and surveillance. In New Zealand, Māori have continually been cast as 'threat' (Stanley & Mihaere, 2018), which has resulted in disproportionate levels of Māori removals from family,[5] arrests, convictions, prison sentences, and mental health detention. Conversely, Māori victims have also been under-policed, receiving inequitable forms of protection from state agencies, a practice that has likely fuelled Māori dissatisfaction.

Colonial legacies have profound everyday consequences. Institutionally racist policies create forms of systemic disadvantage that have intergenerational impacts (Human Rights

Commission, 2012, p. 3). For example, the targeting of Māori children by police and social welfare from the 1960s led to thousands being placed into institutions. Here, children were disconnected from their families, education, and cultural ties, and subject to horrifying violence, conditions, and treatments by state workers. These victimisation experiences have underpinned a raft of social problems in New Zealand, including long-term mental health difficulties, problem drug use, and family violence, as well as the consolidation of gangs (see Stanley, 2016). In such situations, as Jackson (1988, pp. 20–21) argues, colonial injustices 'defined' Māori and Pākehā (police) relations, and have 'determined' the contemporary position of Māori.

Recognising these historical realities is important to understanding the contemporary 'stresses' experienced by Māori communities that render young Māori especially vulnerable to the types of offending targeted by police. They are also important to understanding why Māori have held negative perceptions of the police for decades, and why Māori have sought to propel alternative responses to dealing with 'crime' (see Jackson, 1988). The perpetual process of colonisation means that the harms generated by police are part of a living memory. The historical trauma of colonisation is a 'soul wound' (Duran, 2006; Duran & Duran, 1995) that is relived by Indigenous people and transferred across generations with each new event of police oppression (Brave Heart & DeBruyn, 1998).

Responding to the colonial legacy
In recent years, New Zealand Police have undertaken significant steps to reposition their relationships with Māori communities through a succession of new work programmes, appointments, and strategies. There is not the space to address these in detail here, but they include: the development of the Responsiveness to Māori (RTM) framework known as Urupare Whītiki; the introduction of iwi liaison officers in the late 1990s; establishment of a Commissioner's Māori Focus Forum and Māori advisory boards in all police districts; the introduction of new processes such as Te Pae Oranga – Iwi/Community Panels to divert low-level offenders from prosecutions; and the development of initiatives such as the Wall Walk, a workshop that allows officers to understand the decades of colonial victimisations and criminalisation endured by Māori.

The Turning of the Tide (ToT) strategy has underpinned many recent developments. Launched in 2012, ToT formed part of the Policing Excellence programme and sought to reduce Māori 'over-representation' in criminal justice via reductions in first-time and repeat offenders and by greater use of alternatives to prosecution. Yet, as Ashton (2019) recently detailed, 'Their aim to cut first time offenders by 10 per cent failed without shifting the numbers at all, and a goal to slash re-offending actually ended with a modest increase' (para. 5).

In 2019, NZP made an ambitious commitment to reduce Māori reoffending by 25 per cent by 2025 (NZP, 2019a) via a new 'refreshed' strategy, Te Huringa o Te Tai. The strategy rests on three pou (pillars): (1) tuatahi, focused on police staff and their mindset; (2) tuarua, improving existing practice and service delivery; and (iii) tuatoru, developing effective partnerships. Together, these strategic pou look to: enhance the recruitment and retention of Māori officers; reduce bias in staff, policies, and systems; improve service delivery for Māori; develop specific strategies and programmes to support Māori offenders and victims; and build effective partnerships with Māori (where Māori are involved as co-designers, co-workers, and co-owners of new programmes).[6] To achieve this, Te Huringa o Te Tai is also attentive to building mutual 'trust and confidence' to transform the delivery of police services (Nash, 2019; NZP, 2019a). As NZP (2018d) recently affirmed:

> Fundamentally policing has always been, and always will be, about people. . . . We will hold on as strongly as ever to our humanity as a policing service and our values of professionalism, respect, integrity, commitment to Māori and the Treaty, empathy and valuing diversity (p. 5).

Despite this admirable assertion of values, however, criminal justice agencies including NZP have not 'had any demonstrable effect on Māori rates of victimisation, offending, re-offending and imprisonment' (Tauri, 2019, p. 192). Official bodies have recently confirmed the embedded racism of criminal justice agencies (Te Uepū Hāpai i Te Ora, 2019a, 2019b). Further, police continue to face accusations of racial profiling (Te Uepū Hāpai i Te Ora, 2019b) and of using their discretion unfavourably against Māori or Pasifika individuals in arrest or processing (Brittain & Tuffin, 2017; Bush, 2015; Chanwai-Earle, 2018; Jones, 2018; Nakhid et al., 2016).

In 2015, Police Commissioner Mike Bush recognised 'unconscious bias' in the organisation, and NZP (2019a, p. 137) has since developed 'targeted unconscious bias training to key staff'. The commissioner argued, however, that this bias was not the same as racism; rather, 'It's something that everyone inherently has' (Bush, 2015). Still, some continue to see NZP as a place of conscious bias and institutionalised racism (see Workman, chapter 26 this volume). Whatever the basis for differential policing, the end results are real and problematic. As one example: the Independent Police Conduct Authority (IPCA) reports that, across many police districts, a much higher percentage of Pākehā are given pre-charge warnings for eligible arrest than Māori. The IPCA (2016) notes that this might not result from ethnicity per se, but from the 'systematic differences between Māori and non-Māori' (p. 14). The long-term disadvantages and marginalisation faced by Māori will inevitably lead to offending that is differentially policed, while the targeting of Māori will continue to result from negative police perceptions. Under these conditions, it is no surprise to note that satisfaction with and trust and confidence in police remains much lower among Māori (and young people) than the national average (NZP, 2019b, p. 42; NZP, 2018b).

CONCERNS OF COERCIVE POLICING

The second issue for this chapter relates to a 'cultural' development that has received growing public critical attention: the militarisation of New Zealand policing. This issue has serious implications for perceptions of police legitimacy and public confidence. As detailed above, the police in nineteenth-century Aotearoa New Zealand (as in other colonial settings) were a heavily armed force that aggressively imposed order and suppressed resistance (although even in these periods, policing involved contradictory tactics, from suppression through warfare and violent force to 'softer' forms of patrolling, surveillance, and community engagements). Through the twentieth century, the reliance on armed responses dissipated as New Zealand Police established itself as a 'community' focused service with an emphasis on maintaining and regulating order through more peaceful, consensual means.

This consensual model has, of course, never been totally peaceful; it has always been applied alongside coercive and oppositional approaches. Here, we consider two elements of these contradictory practices: the persistent use of targeted repressive policing towards certain protesters, and the recent deployment of Armed Response Teams (ARTs). Both examples indicate an increasing resort to and valorisation of coercive policing, despite the claimed commitment to policing by consent. Introduced without any community consultation, developments such as ARTs raise serious questions about police legitimacy and the disproportionate impacts of aggressive policing on particular groups, especially Māori.

The policing of protest

Aggressive 'public order' policing aimed at protecting political and commercial interests has a long history in New Zealand. Many events – including the Great Strike of 1913,[7] the 1951 waterfront dispute,[8] or the 1981 Springbok tour[9] – have created significant tensions, shaken New Zealanders' perceptions of policing, and underlined the precarity of police legitimacy.

Criminological literature (Baker, 2014; della Porter et al., 2006; Waddington, 2007) has described how recognition of the counter-productive nature of the 'escalated force' policing model of the 1960s–70s led to a progressive shift towards a 'negotiated management' model in the 1990s. However, there are concerns, internationally and in New Zealand, that escalated force policing is returning (Baker & Pillinger, 2019). In New Zealand, this could be identified in persistent claims of heavy policing (including the use of surveillance,[10] police use of force, over-arrests, and unlawful charging) towards peace activists, climate protestors, and those campaigning against the arms trade (Hunt & Stewart, 2017; Lock, 2019; Locke, 2019; *Radio New Zealand* [*RNZ*], 2019c; Stewart, 2018). Activists view such activities as tactics to prevent New Zealanders from exercising democratic rights to protest (*RNZ*, 2017), thus undermining attempts to effect meaningful social, political, and environmental change. They also diminish confidence in the police, a point illustrated in the recent policing at Ihumātao.

In 2019, the peaceful occupation of Ihumātao in Māngere was a site of policing tension. The land, sacred to Māori, had been occupied for over three years, following the move by Fletcher Building to develop the area for housing. In July 2019, police officers sought to evict the group and caused a stand-off. Over the following days, police officers were sometimes praised for their interactions – one 'viral' video shows an officer singing waiata with the 'land protectors'. However, tensions significantly increased in early August when those gathered at the site reported around 100 police officers, and 68 police cars, at the scene (Rosenberg, 2019). Activists claimed officers cut site access, refused the distribution of blankets and food, 'manhandled' females, tasered dogs, and intimidated those present (*Otago Daily Times*, 2019; *RNZ*, 2019b). In response, hundreds more arrived to occupy the site, and two Auckland councillors noted police were 'running roughshod over the prime minister's proclaimed desire to enter peaceful and honest talks' (Webb-Liddall, 2019, para. 19). Following interventions from senior Māori officers, the police presence was de-escalated; their actions were, however, seen to have further ruptured trust between many Māori and the police. A spokesperson for occupation organisers 'SOUL' told reporters 'the police have breached our trust. We no longer have any confidence in the New Zealand police' (*RNZ*, 2019a, para. 26).

There is a widespread belief that government, and by extension police, act as a 'neutral referee between competing social and economic interests' and can be trusted to 'mediate' the ruin 'of the *commons* by big business' (Ward, 2011, p. 319, original emphasis). Yet, this is something of a myth (p. 16). In reality, as New Zealand's own history of colonial policing and the policing of protest attests, 'the police have always protected established power against those who challenge it' (Monbiot, 2020, para. 4). Policing has regularly been 'partisan and politically at the behest of the government' (Baker, 2008, p. 152). This serves as a reminder that when political and commercial interests come under threat, instruments of the Crown such as the police can be relied upon to protect and maintain the status quo. In such circumstances, policing by consent (and legitimate, procedurally just, democratic policing) can often be abandoned in preference for 'non-negotiable' control. All of this raises a question fundamental to police legitimacy: Whose interests are being served?

Armed Response Teams

Community trust and police legitimacy has also come under serious challenge by the October 2019 introduction of Armed Response Teams (ARTs), justified through police claims of changes to the 'threat environment' (NZP, 2019c). The teams were ostensibly cast as a response to the white-supremacist killings of Muslims at prayer in Christchurch in 2019, an event that shocked New Zealanders and to which community police officers responded with professionalism and great bravery (see Botha & Poynting, chapter 9 this volume). Developed without community consultation, the ARTs operated in three communities: Counties Manukau, Waikato, and Canterbury (the former two areas largely populated by Māori and Pasifika people). Equipped with pistols, rifles, and tasers, the three-officer teams engaged in 'preventative patrolling' in 'high-risk' areas and were tasked to respond to incidents of 'significant risk' (Bond, 2019, paras. 5, 30).

There have been stinging criticisms of the ARTs from political, legal, academic, and community quarters. They have encompassed many issues, including those relating to: the disproportionate use of firearms; the normalisation of aggressive responses; reduced community perceptions of safety and trust in the police; and the lack of rationale or evidence for an escalation in police force activities.

First, critics argued that, in line with past experience, NZP will disproportionately use firearms and other tactical weapons against Māori and minority communities (as evidenced elsewhere; see Mummolo, 2018). New Zealand data from January 2009 to January 2019 indicates that 66 per cent of all those shot by police were Māori or Pasifika (McKinnell, 2019). Police Tactical Operations Reporting (TOR)[11] data also shows that Māori were subjected to 'over half of all TOR events' and 'Pacific peoples were also over-represented' in relation to 'the number of offender proceedings and relative to population numbers' (NZP, 2018c, p. 7). As ex-police officer McKinnell (2019, para. 9) highlighted, 'It seems inevitable that ARTs would further exacerbate this phenomenon, without some clearly prescribed intervention or mitigation strategies.' Further, ARTs seemed to be working directly against the spirit and intentions of recently developed NZP strategies for Māori, Pasifika, and ethnic communities (Ashton, 2019). Such arguments are also directed to other groups, such as children and young people subjected to tactical options (Johnston, 2017) and those suffering from mental illness, who also disproportionately experience the application of police force (Mental Health Foundation, 2019).

Second, police militarisation is determined to negatively impact on police behaviours, such that it propels aggressive responses to challenging situations. A UK study on police use of tasers found a 48 per cent higher incidence of police force, and also a doubling of assaults on police when they carried tasers (Barak et al., 2019). That is, weapons carriage increased police aggression (as police are more likely to use those weapons than to resort to de-escalation methods), but also increased public aggression (and could lead to civilians also escalating their use of arms) (Mackenzie et al., 2019). A related point is that militarised responses can quickly become normalised as armed patrols, initially dedicated to 'high-risk' incidents, start to pursue everyday police work (McKinnell, 2019). Indeed, there were local reports that ARTs had been used to arrest those accused of breaching bail conditions for mundane dishonesty offences (Bond, 2019). Another early manifestation of 'mission creep' was that, in the first month of deployment, ARTs 'attended more vehicle stops than any other type of job' (Kitchin, 2020). In response to an Official Information Act (OIA) request, it was revealed that they attended 524 vehicle stops in the Waikato, 82 in Canterbury, and 41 in Counties Manukau. More recent data revealed that in the first five weeks of operation ARTs were deployed 75 times per day, 50 times more often than the Armed Offender Squad in the previous year (Bond, 2020); hardly examples of the 'significant risk' used to justify their establishment.

Third, militarising the police can have wider negative impacts. It can make community members feel less safe, as they sense their area is 'dangerous' or they feel oppressed by the routine presence of heavily armed officers. It increases their risks of being shot or harmed through policing activity (Hurihanganui, 2019a; Mackenzie et al., 2019). And it can fuel long-lived tensions between police and the communities they police. As Mummolo's (2018) work in the US has shown, militarised policing 'fails to enhance officer safety or reduce local crime'; it diminishes public trust in the police and has 'no detectable public safety benefit' (p. 9186).

Fourth, and finally, critics state that there is no clear evidence or rationale for the development of ARTs. Notwithstanding the horrific killings in Christchurch, official data shows that incidents involving firearms have been at relatively stable proportions (about 0.9–0.95 per cent of all reported incidents) for some years (Rākete, 2019a). At the same time, the number of assaults against police officers (with and without firearms) decreased from 2015 to 2018.[12] For relatively low-level assaults, police use 'tactical options' (such as 'empty hand tactics', handcuffs/restraints, spit hoods, OC spray, batons, dogs, tasers, and firearms) in about 0.1 per cent interactions with the public (6910 tactical options at 4398 events).[13] Further, the organisation notes a decrease in the police use of force since 2017 (NZP, 2018c, p. 1). All of this raises questions: What is the New Zealand evidence for a riskier operational environment? And, what guiding rationale led to the development of ARTs? Given that ARTs operated beyond their mandate, and faced strong local opposition, their existence jeopardised police legitimacy. They were disestablished in September 2020.

CHANGING DYNAMICS

So far, this chapter has addressed some of the past and present challenges for New Zealand Police, and highlighted tensions in the capacity of the organisation to secure popular legitimacy. While there are strategies and initiatives to break colonising dynamics between police and Indigenous or other minority communities, contradictory coercive approaches remain.

In Aotearoa New Zealand, 'hardline' policing strategies often gain political and populist approval. The dominant New Zealand political and media approach to policing generally revolves around debates on gangs, drugs, youth offending, burglaries, and firearms (see Bradley, chapter 3 this volume; Cheng, 2019; Graham-McLay, 2020). Law-and-order debates, and the emphasis on 'strengthening' policing and punishments, are a frequent part of political and electioneering strategies (see Pratt & Anderson, chapter 13 this volume). For example, in late 2019, the National Party in opposition vowed to implement 'Operation Raptor' style units to deal with the 'gang problem' (Cheng, 2019). The proposed unit would emulate Strike Force Raptor, a military-style unit that has led a 'zero-tolerance' policing of gangs in New South Wales since 2009 (McCulloch, 2019). The leader of the opposition described the Australian unit as 'devastatingly effective'. However, a former Australian detective claimed it had been a 'disaster' and had not reduced gang members. He suggested a far more effective approach: 'You need this community to trust you so that when things need to be brought into line, the police are able to go in and speak to people' (McCulloch, 2019, para. 13).

Hardline approaches reflect and reiterate NZP's own emphasis on the threat of gangs and organised crime (see Gilbert, chapter 30 this volume; Graham-McLay, 2020). Having developed a Gang Intelligence Centre, police have recently established a key 'target' to remove $500 million in 'cash and assets . . . from gangs and criminals by 2021' (NZP, 2019a, p. 54); although this targeted asset drive is tempered with a note that 'we cannot guarantee the asset yield'.

More generally, in policing briefings (NZP, 2018d) and annual reports (NZP, 2018a, 2019a), the key police operational priorities are identified as organised crime, gangs, reducing family harm, methamphetamine, and youth offending. Other 'high profile' areas include firearms, mental health, and roads. NZP (2018b, p. 7) identifies a 'growing demand' for its services in these areas, with the 'drivers of demand' leading to an 'increasingly complex and time consuming' police environment (NZP, 2018a, pp. 6–7). The organisation now takes a 'Prevention

First' approach to address these drivers, and has been able to expand the workforce (with an additional 1800 officers and 485 non-sworn staff) to meet priorities.

The dynamics of crime that are emphasised in police communications reflect long-established traditional concerns of offending and the 'crime problem'. They rarely engage with new forms of offending, such as cybercrime. Indeed, the nature, dynamics, and threats of cybercrime (or online crime/computer-enabled crime) are not mentioned at all in the 2017 'Briefing to the Incoming Minister' or in many annual reports. In *Transforming Police Service Delivery by 2021*, cybercrime receives just one cryptic mention: 'Digital technologies also present new opportunities for us to invest in what works, from having our staff embedded in communities dealing with complex public safety issues, to being online, where new types of harm continue to emerge' (NZP, 2018d, p. 6).

This omission, and the failure of NZP to adapt and meet the challenges posed by cybercrime and the transformation of criminal offending it represents, is somewhat puzzling. Cybercrime has become a global problem, and is described internationally as the most critical issue confronting police (Loveday, 2017, p. 102). Indeed, it is estimated that around half of all property crime in the developed world now takes place online (*Guardian*, 2019).

In recognition that crime has a new 'profile' (see Bradley, chapter 3, and Meehan, chapter 8 this volume), overseas police organisations have established dedicated cybercrime units and bespoke reporting facilities for victims. Yet, beset by organisational inertia and encouraged by government performance targets and political demands, NZP's priorities remain firmly focused on conventional 'terrestrial' crimes. We anticipate that, as the public become more aware of the extent of their online vulnerability and experience victimisations, NZP will need to quickly adapt to avoid losing the public's trust and confidence. Unless NZP, supported by government, invests the necessary resources to upskill, it also risks becoming an irrelevance in the policing of online crime as victims turn to other bodies, often in the private sector, to resolve their problems (Button, 2020).[14]

The privatisation of cybercrime policing threatens public perceptions of police legitimacy, as citizens are forced to seek out other options. However, given the prohibitive costs of private investigation and resolution, it also means that poor and marginalised communities will be further pushed out from the circle of protection or redress for crimes. Privatisation thus has the potential to create even greater inequities, and thus illegitimacies, in the distribution of policing and protective services.

All of this is not to say that the police have not embraced aspects of the digital world: NZP recently unveiled its first ever 'artificial intelligence officer' (Electronic Lifelike Assistant – ELLA), which will operate in new 'digital kiosks'. Designed for public connections, ELLA and the kiosks form part of NZP's new 'digital services', and the organisation notes that the public will continue to make face-to-face and phone contacts, but many interactions will move online:

> They'll visit our websites, see us on social media and in traditional media, and interact with us online and via email . . . they want the convenience of going online for information and using technology to interact with us . . . (NZP 2018d, pp. 5–6).

New online communication resources follow the 2013 'mobility roll out', when all frontline officers were issued with 'mobile devices' allowing offender details and vehicle registration checks while 'on the beat'. However, if NZP is to retain public trust and confidence, similar investments in the capacity to respond to cybercrime are urgently required.

CONCLUSION

The New Zealand Police are in an era of significant transformation that is informed by the past, present, and future of policing. The organisation needs to meet Te Tiriti o Waitangi obligations and to change the dynamics of colonial policing legacies. This work demands significant cultural shifts to embed different practices of discretion, community engagements, and the facilitation of whānau-, hapū-, and iwi-centred responses to 'crime'. Positive transformations are already in practice. However, these may be threatened by how NZP continues to respond to some Māori communities in more repressive ways (not least in the policing of activism or with those living in communities deemed 'high risk'). These concerns plug into the central issue of policing legitimacy.

Any engagement with legitimacy requires a reflection on the nature of what is policed, and who is policed. It raises questions, such as: To what extent does NZP represent, protect, and serve all New Zealand communities? And, do some 'harms' and 'crimes' in New Zealand go under-policed, leaving us unprotected? As detailed in this chapter, this would appear to be the case if we consider the scale of victimisations from cybercrime. As other chapters in this volume attest, this would also seem to be the case with sexual assaults (see Jordan, chapter 6) and white-collar crimes (see Mackenzie, chapter 11), among other significant forms of violence and harm. Such realities remind us of the need to reflect on how police, among other criminal justice institutions, maintain dominant economic, gendered, and racialised ideologies about the 'crime problem' through everyday policies and practices. This could lead us to pose even larger transformative questions on the role of the police in future societies, and to consider whether we still need 'the police'. It seems, then, that the future of policing will – like its past – be subject to contestation and change.

STUDY QUESTIONS

- What factors are important in the establishment and maintenance of police legitimacy?
- To what extent does NZP currently over-police or under-police certain New Zealand communities? What impact, if any, does this have?
- Should policing be increasingly pluralised? What benefits or drawbacks would this bring for New Zealand communities?

FURTHER READING

Henry, T. K., & Franklin, T. W. (2019). Police legitimacy in the context of street stops: The effects of race, class, and procedural justice. *Criminal Justice Policy Review*, 30(3), 406–427.

Jordan, J., & Mossman, E. (2019). *Police sexual violence file analysis report: Women, rape and the police investigation process.* Wellington, New Zealand: Institute of Criminology, Victoria University of Wellington. Retrieved from http://researcharchive.vuw.ac.nz/handle/10063/8249

Wolffram, H. (2017). A history of policing. In J. Gilbert & G. Newbold (Eds.), *Criminal Justice: A New Zealand introduction* (pp. 183–204). Auckland: Auckland University Press.

NOTES

1 Tohu Kākahi and Te Whiti o Rongomai established the settlement on confiscated land in 1866. In 1878, the government opened the area for European settlement, ignoring previous promises

to mark out reserves for Māori. The following year, Te Whiti ordered the surveyors to be peacefully evicted. Māori at Parihaka began to plough fields and pull up survey pegs; hundreds were arrested for doing so.

2   In October 2019, Te Pire Haeata ki Parihaka (Parihaka Reconciliation Bill) was passed providing a state apology and a commitment to annual events, a contribution to the settlement's development, and to protect the name against commercial exploitation (see http://www.legislation.govt.nz/act/public/2019/0060/latest/whole.html).

3   In 1978, 800 police and army officers forcibly removed and arrested occupiers of Bastion Point, confiscated land at Ōrākei, Auckland. (see Boynton, 2018; Wynyard, 2019).

4   In 2007, hundreds of officers – many in full paramilitary gear – locked down the small Tūhoe settlement of Rūātoki as part of 'Operation 8'. Setting up a roadblock along the 'confiscation line', they detained and photographed adults and children, and arrested Māori sovereignty activists on 'terrorism' charges. On the day, police arrested other environmental and sovereignty activists around New Zealand; however, Rūātoki was the only site where police arrived in such force. NZP has since apologised.

5   A 2019 review of Oranga Tamariki highlighted one particular case when up to 14 armed police were involved in the 'traumatising uplift' of a five-month-old baby from a single mother (Neilson, 2020).

6   Many of these strategies reflect the aims of the 2015 Ethnic Strategy (e.g.: developing police capabilities to work with ethnic communities; being responsive; making evidence-based decisions to improve service delivery; building strong partnerships). This strategy was revised in 2019 (NZP, 2019a, p. 137).

7   The Great Strike of 1913 was a series of strikes between mid-October 1913 and mid-January 1914. In one of New Zealand's most violent and disruptive industrial confrontations, between 14,000 and 16,000 workers went on strike, out of a population of just over 1 million.

8   This saw over 16,000 workers on strikes or lock-outs. The police were given special powers – they broke up meetings, searched houses without warrants, and cordoned off areas to stop relief supplies getting to striking workers. Dick Scott (1952) noted that New Zealand was 'under the iron heel of the police state'.

9   The 1981 Springbok tour protests polarised New Zealand. More than 150,000 people took part in over 200 demonstrations in 28 centres to protest apartheid and the touring South African rugby team (the Springboks). Protesters also used the tour to protest racial discrimination against Māori in New Zealand. To protect the Springboks and rugby-goers, NZP created two special riot squads, the Red and Blue Squads. These police were the first in New Zealand to be issued with full riot gear, and they engaged in heavy-handed and violent tactics. It remains the largest policing operation in New Zealand's history (Yska, 2011).

10 Significant concerns about the use of private security/surveillance companies by government agencies, including the police, led to an inquiry into the use of 'Thompson and Clark' that identified substantive problems (see Martin & Mount, 2018; see also https://ssc.govt.nz/assets/Legacy/resources/Report-of-the-inquiry-into-the-use-of-external-security-consultants-by-government-agencies.pdf). However, this inquiry did not include the police. Following an internal investigation, NZP concluded that it managed 'interactions with external security consultants in a professional and appropriate way' (see https://www.police.govt.nz/news/release/outcome-police-investigation-use-external-security-consultants).

11 Note that this data indicates officers' recording of events where 'tactical options' (e.g., restraints, spit hoods, 'empty hand tactics', OC sprays, batons, dogs, TASERs, firearms) are used. There will be errors in recording.

12 Assaults (without firearms) decreased from 1691 in 2015 to 1598 in 2018, while assaults involving a firearm decreased from 15 in 2015 to 11 in 2018 (with seven assaults causing physical injury for police officers, although it is unclear what these entailed) (Rākete, 2019b).

13 It is also important to note that 'spit hoods' are not officially categorised as a tactical option, even though it often requires 'considerable force . . . by a number of officers to put a hood on'.

A response to an OIA request revealed that police had used spit hoods more than 300 times between 2014 and 2016 (see Heron, 2016).

14 Public dissatisfaction with policing services has led to the emergence of a significant private security industry. It is estimated that the global cyber-security market was worth US$137.85 billion in 2017 and will grow to US$231.94 billion by 2022 (Button, 2020, pp. 45–46).

REFERENCES

Ashton, A. (2019, November 14). The detail – a daily news podcast produced for RNZ by Newsroom: Police Māori strategy a re-turning of the tide. *Radio New Zealand*. Retrieved from https://www.rnz.co.nz/programmes/the-detail/story/2018722027/police-maori-strategy-a-re-turning-of-the-tide

Baker, D. (2008). A tale of two towns: Industrial pickets, police practices and judicial review. *Labour History, 95*, 151–167. doi:10.2307/27516314

Baker, D. (2014). *Police, picket-lines and fatalities: Lessons from the past*. London, UK: Springer Publishing. doi:10.1057/9781137358066

Baker, D., & Pillinger, C. (2019).'These people are vulnerable, they aren't criminals': Mental health, the use of force and deaths after police contact in England. *The Police Journal: Theory, Practice and Principles, 93*(1), 65–81. doi:10.1177/0032258X19839275

Barak, A., Lawes, D., Weinbon, C., Henry, R., Chen, K., & Sabo, H. B. (2019). The 'less-than-lethal weapons effect' – introducing TASERs to routine police operations in England and Wales: A randomized controlled trial. *Criminal Justice and Behavior, 46*(2), 280–300. doi:10.1177/0093854818812918

Bazley, M. (2007). *Report of the Commission of Inquiry into Police Conduct – Te Kōmihana Tirotiro Whanonga Pirihimana* (Vol. 1). Wellington, New Zealand: Commission of Inquiry into Police Conduct. Retrieved from https://www.police.govt.nz/about-us/nz-police/commission-inquiry

Blagg, H., & Anthony, T. (2019) *Decolonising criminology: Imagining justice in a postcolonial world*. London, UK: Palgrave Macmillan. doi:10.1057/978–1–137–53247–3

Bond, J. (2019, November 11). Police Armed Response Team arrest in suburban area raises concerns. *Radio New Zealand*. Retrieved from https://www.rnz.co.nz/news/national/402977/police-armed-response-team-arrest-in-suburban-area-raises-concerns

Bond, J. (2020, March 4). Police's new Armed Response Teams deployed 75 a day. *New Zealand Herald*. Retrieved from https://www.nzherald.co.nz/nz/polices-new-armed-response-teams-deployed-75-a-day/JKN3QQUJSTHFPWYJ2NBJL3GXLU/

Boynton, J. (2018, May 24). Remembering Bastion Pt: 'Straight out of a Nazi war movie'. *Radio New Zealand*. Retrieved from https://www.rnz.co.nz/news/te-manu-korihi/358155/remembering-bastion-pt-straight-out-of-a-nazi-war-movie

Brave Heart, M. Y. H., & DeBruyn, L. M. (1998). The American Indian Holocaust: Healing historical unresolved grief. *American Indian and Alaska Native Mental Health Research, 8*(2), 56–78. doi.org/10.5820/aian.0802.1998.60

Brittain, E., & Tuffin, K. (2017). Ko tēhea te ara tika? A discourse analysis of Māori experience in the criminal justice system. *New Zealand Journal of Psychology (Online), 46*(2), 99–107. https://www.psychology.org.nz/journal-archive/Maori-interactions-with-criminal-justice-system.pdf

Bull, S. (2004). 'The land of murder, cannibalism, and all kinds of atrocious crimes?' Maori and crime in New Zealand, 1853–1919. *British Journal of Criminology, 44*(4), 496–519. doi:10.1093/bjc/azh029

Bush, M. (2015, November 28). *Lisa Owen interviews police commissioner Mike Bush* [Press release]. *Scoop Politics*. Retrieved from https://www.scoop.co.nz/stories/PO1511/S00456/lisa-owen-interviews-police-commissioner-mike-bush.htm

Buttle, J., & Deckert, A. (2017). The police complaints process. In A. Deckert & R. Sarre (Eds.), *The Palgrave handbook of Australian and New Zealand criminology, crime and justice* (pp. 525–539). Cham, Switzerland: Palgrave Macmillan. doi:10.1007/978–3–319–55747–2

Button, M. (2020). The 'new' private security industry, the private policing of cyberspace and the regulatory questions. *Journal of Contemporary Criminal Justice, 36*(1), 39–55. doi:10.1177/1043986219890194

Chanwai-Earle, L. (2018, May 28). Nothing 'unconscious' about racial profiling. *Radio New Zealand*. Retrieved from https://www.rnz.co.nz/national/programmes/voices/audio/2018646720/nothing-unconscious-about-racial-profiling

Cheng, D. (2019, November 26). National's law and order plan: Tough on gangs, murderers and the worst youth offenders. *New Zealand Herald*. Retrieved from https://www.nzherald.co.nz/nz/news/article.cfm?c_id=1&objectid=12288372

Children's Commissioner. (2019, May). *Supporting young people on remand to live successfully in the community*. State of Care Series 7, Office of the Children's Commissioner. Retrieved from https://www.occ.org.nz/publications/reports/supporting-young-people-on-remand/

Cunneen, C., & Tauri, J. M. (2016). *Indigenous criminology*. Bristol, UK: Policy Press.

della Porta, D., Peterson, A., & Reiter, H. (2006). *The policing of transnational protest*. Aldershot, UK: Ashgate Publishing.

Duran, E. (2006). *Healing the soul wound: Counseling with American Indians and other Native peoples*. New York, NY: Teachers College Press.

Duran, E., & Duran, B. (1995). *Native American postcolonial psychology*. Albany, New York, NY: State University of New York Press.

Graham-McLay, C. (2020, January 22). People are fearful: New Zealand police admit gang violence is out of control. *Guardian*. Retrieved from https://www.theguardian.com/world/2020/jan/22/people-are-fearful-new-zealand-police-admit-gang-violence-is-out-of-control

Guardian. (2019, June 3). The *Guardian* view of cybercrime: The law must be enforced. Retrieved from https://www.theguardian.com/commentisfree/2019/jun/03/the-guardian-view-on-cybercrime-the-law-must-be-enforced

Heron, M. (2016, October 11). Spit hoods used more than 300 times in two years. *Radio New Zealand*. Retrieved from https://www.rnz.co.nz/news/national/315413/spit-hoods-used-more-than-300-times-in-two-years

Hill, R. (1989). *The colonial frontier tamed: New Zealand policing in transition, 1867–1886*. Wellington, New Zealand: Historical Publications Branch, Department of Internal Affairs.

Hill, R. (1997). 'The control of both races': The policing of the Wellington settlement, 1840–1853. *Journal of New Zealand Studies, 7*(1), 3–13. doi:10.26686/jnzs.v7i1.394

Hill, R. (2008). Māori, police and coercion in New Zealand history. In D. Keenan (Ed.), *Terror in our midst? Searching for terror in Aotearoa New Zealand* (pp. 39–63). Wellington, New Zealand: Huia Publishers.

Hinds, L., & Murphy, K. (2007). Public satisfaction with police: Using procedural justice to improve police legitimacy. *Australian and New Zealand Journal of Criminology, 40*(1), 27–42. doi:10.1375/acri.40.1.27

Human Rights Commission. (2012). *A fair go for all? Rite tahi tātou katoa? Addressing structural discrimination in public services*. Auckland, Aotearoa New Zealand: Human Rights Commission. Retrieved from https://www.hrc.co.nz/files/2914/2409/4608/HRC-Structural-Report_final_webV1.pdf

Hunt, T., & Stewart, M. (2017, October 10). Police arrest anti-weapons protesters trying to block off Westpac Stadium. *Stuff*. Retrieved from https://www.stuff.co.nz/national/97713861/peace-action-blockades-westpac-stadium-arms-industry-forum

Hurihanganui, T. A. (2019a, October 24). Armed Response Team cops criticism: 'Nothing good can come out of this'. *Radio New Zealand*. Retrieved from https://www.rnz.co.nz/news/te-manu-korihi/401685/armed-response-team-cops-criticism-nothing-good-can-come-out-of-this

Hurihanganui, T. A. (2019b, December 18). Rua Kēnana pardon: 200 descendants gather at Parliament. *Radio New Zealand*. Retrieved from https://www.rnz.co.nz/news/te-manu-korihi/405789/rua-kenana-pardon-200-descendants-gather-at-parliament

Independent Police Conduct Authority (IPCA). (2016). *Review of pre-charge warnings.* Wellington, New Zealand: IPCA. Retrieved from https://www.ipca.govt.nz/site/publications-and-media/2016-reports-on-investigations/?PAGE=1

Jackson, M. (1988). *The Maori and the criminal justice system: A new perspective: He whaipaanga hou, Part 2.* Wellington, New Zealand: Policy and Research Division, Department of Justice. Retrieved from https://www2.justice.govt.nz/website-documents/maori-and-the-criminal-justice-system-a-new-perspective-p2.pdf

Johnston, K. (2017, March 26). Police set dog on 12-year-old hiding in kindergarten. *New Zealand Herald.* Retrieved from https://www.nzherald.co.nz/nz/news/article.cfm?c_id=1&objectid=11825033

Jones, N. (2018, June 8). MP accuses police of racial profiling, 'systematic racism'. *Newstalk ZB.* Retrieved from https://www.newstalkzb.co.nz/news/politics/mp-accuses-police-of-racial-profiling-systematic-racism/

Jordan, J. (2004). *The word of a woman? Police, rape and belief.* London, UK: Palgrave Macmillan.

Jordan, J., & Mossman, E. (2019). *Police sexual violence file analysis report: Women, rape and the police investigation process.* Wellington, New Zealand: Institute of Criminology, Victoria University of Wellington. Retrieved from http://researcharchive.vuw.ac.nz/handle/10063/8249

Kitchin, T. (2020, February 2) New armed police unit conducting more routine traffic stops than any other type of job. *Stuff.* Retrieved from https://www.stuff.co.nz/national/crime/119093912/new-armed-police-unit-conducting-more-routine-traffic-stops-than-any-other-type-of-job

Lock, H. (2019, October 7). Police make arrests after day of climate protests in Wellington. *Radio New Zealand.* Retrieved from https://www.rnz.co.nz/national/programmes/checkpoint/audio/2018716607/police-make-arrests-after-day-of-climate-protests-in-wellington

Locke, K. (2019, January 17). Keith Locke: Spy chief's apology to me reveals scandalous truth about the SIS. *Spinoff.* Retrieved from https://thespinoff.co.nz/politics/17–01–2019/keith-locke-spy-chiefs-apology-to-me-reveals-scandalous-truth-about-the-sis/

Loveday, B. (2017). Still plodding along? The police response to the changing profile of crime in England and Wales. *International Journal of Police Science and Management, 19*(2), 101–109. doi:10.1177/1461355717699634

Mackenzie, S., Bradley, T., & Lindsay, A. (2019, October 24). Cops with guns will make us less safe. *Newsroom.* Retrieved from https://www.newsroom.co.nz/@ideasroom/2019/10/24/874930/cops-with-guns-will-make-us-less-safe

Martin, D., & Mount, S. (2018). *Inquiry into the use of external security consultants by government agencies.* Wellington, New Zealand: State Services Commission. Retrieved from https://ssc.govt.nz/assets/Legacy/resources/Report-of-the-inquiry-into-the-use-of-external-security-consultants-by-government-agencies.pdf

Martin, R., & Bradford, B. (2019). The anatomy of police legitimacy: Dialogue, power and procedural justice. *Theoretical Criminology,* 1–19. doi:10.1177/1362480619890605

Mazerolle, L., Bennett, S., Davis, J. T. M., Sargeant, E., & Manning, M. (2013). Procedural justice and police legitimacy: A systematic review of the research evidence. *Journal of Experimental Criminology, 9*(3), 245–274. doi:10.1007/s11292-013-9175-2

Mazerolle, L., & Wickes, R. (2015). Police legitimacy in community context. *Journal of Contemporary Criminal Justice, 31*(2), 128–131. doi:10.1177/1043986215570780

McCulloch, C. (2019, November 27). Australian ex-cop blasts National's 'Strike Force Raptor' plan. *Radio New Zealand.* Retrieved from https://www.rnz.co.nz/national/programmes/checkpoint/audio/2018724382/australian-ex-cop-blasts-national-s-strike-force-raptor-plan

McKinnell, T. (2019, October 20). Police are trialling new heavily armed units. This ex-cop thinks that's a very dangerous idea. *Spinoff.* Retrieved from https://thespinoff.co.nz/society/20–10–2019/police-are-trialing-new-heavily-armed-units-this-ex-cop-thinks-thats-a-very-dangerous-idea/

Mental Health Foundation. (2019, December 10). *Letter to Minister Nash – Stop armed police trials.* Retrieved from https://www.mentalhealth.org.nz/home/news/article/279/letter-to-minister-nash-stop-armed-police-trials

Mikaere, A. (2013). *Colonising myths – Māori realities: He rukuruku whakaaro*. Wellington, New Zealand: Huia Publishers.

Monbiot, G. (2020, January 22). If defending life on Earth is extremist, we must own that label. *Guardian*. Retrieved from https://www.theguardian.com/commentisfree/2020/jan/22/defending-life-earth-extremist-police-extinction-rebellion

Mummolo, J. (2018). Militarization fails to enhance police safety or reduce crime but may harm police reputation. *PNAS: Proceedings of the National Academy of Sciences of the United States of America, 155*(37), 9181–9186. doi:10.1073/pnas.1805161115

Murphy, K., Tyler, T. R., & Curtis, A. (2009). Nurturing regulatory compliance: Is procedural justice effective when people question the legitimacy of the law? *Regulation and Governance, 3*(1), 1–26. doi:10.1111/j.1748–5991.2009.01043.x

Nakhid, C., Azanaw, L., Essuman, K., Ghebremichael, N., Kamau, M., Kavitesi, T., . . . Puni, E. (2016). *African youth experiences with the police and the New Zealand justice system*. Retrieved from http://www.communityresearch.org.nz/research/african-youth-experiences-with-the-police-and-the-new-zealand-justice-system/

Nash, S. (2019, November 6). *Te Huringa o Te Tai – Police Crime Prevention Strategy* [Speech for police launch of Te Huringa o Te Tai]. Retrieved from https://www.beehive.govt.nz/speech/te-huringa-o-te-tai-police-crime-prevention-strategy

Neilson, M. (2020, February 3). Armed police involved in uplift of Māori baby, Oranga Tamariki inquiry reveals. *New Zealand Herald*. Retrieved from https://www.nzherald.co.nz/nz/news/article.cfm?c_id=1&objectid=12304946

New Zealand Police (NZP). (2018a). *Annual report 2017/2018*. Wellington, New Zealand: New Zealand Police. Retrieved from https://www.police.govt.nz/sites/default/files/publications/annual-report–2017–2018.pdf

New Zealand Police (NZP). (2018b). *New Zealand Police citizens' satisfaction survey: Report for 2017/2018*. Wellington, New Zealand: Gravitas Research and Strategy Ltd. Retrieved from https://www.police.govt.nz/sites/default/files/publications/citizen-satisfaction-survey-report–2018.pdf

New Zealand Police (NZP). (2018c). *Tactical options research report 2018: Report 7*. Wellington, New Zealand: New Zealand Police. Retrieved from https://www.police.govt.nz/sites/default/files/publications/annual-tactical-options-research-report–7.pdf

New Zealand Police (NZP). (2018d). *Transforming police service delivery by 2021: He whakahoutanga ratonga pirihimana i mua i te tau 2021*. Wellington, New Zealand: New Zealand Police. Retrieved from https://www.police.govt.nz/sites/default/files/publications/police-service-delivery.pdf

New Zealand Police (NZP). (2019a). *Annual report 2018/19*. Wellington, New Zealand: New Zealand Police. Retrieved from https://www.police.govt.nz/sites/default/files/publications/annual-report–2018–2019.pdf

New Zealand Police (NZP). (2019b). *New Zealand Police citizens' satisfaction survey: Report for 2018/2019*. Wellington, New Zealand: Gravitas Research and Strategy Ltd. Retrieved from https://www.police.govt.nz/sites/default/files/publications/citizen-satisfaction-survey-report–2019.pdf

New Zealand Police (NZP). (2019c). *Armed Response Team trial* [Press release]. Retrieved from https://www.police.govt.nz/can-you-help-us/armed-response-team-trial

Otago Daily Times. (2019, August 6). Police 'rammed' Ihumātao protestors: Organiser. Retrieved from https://www.odt.co.nz/news/national/police-rammed-ihumatao-protesters-organiser

Rākete, E. (2019a, February 28). Firearms incidence OIA request to New Zealand Police. *FYI.org*. Retrieved from https://fyi.org.nz/request/9722 firearms incidence

Rākete, E. (2019b, October 22). Armed police patrols are a dangerous response to a non-existent problem. *Spinoff*. Retrieved from https://thespinoff.co.nz/atea/22–10–2019/armed-police-patrols-are-a-dangerous-response-to-a-non-existent-problem/

Radio New Zealand (RNZ). (2017, March 24). Protesters win case against police. Retrieved from https://www.rnz.co.nz/news/national/327380/protesters-win-case-against-police

Radio New Zealand (RNZ). (2019a, July 24). Ihumātao protest: Govt will not intervene, PM says. Retrieved from https://www.rnz.co.nz/news/national/395100/ihumatao-protest-govt-will-not-intervene-pm-says

Radio New Zealand (RNZ). (2019b, August 4). Police remove guns from Ihumātao, protesters worried. Retrieved from https://www.rnz.co.nz/news/national/395944/police-remove-guns-from-ihumatao-protesters-worried

Radio New Zealand (RNZ). (2019c, November 26). Police move in on climate activists on board OMV oil ship. Retrieved from https://www.rnz.co.nz/news/national/404131/police-move-in-on-climate-activists-on-board-omv-oil-ship

Rosenberg, M. (2019, July 30). Ihumātao eviction protest: An occupation 150 years in the making. *Stuff*. Retrieved from https://www.stuff.co.nz/national/114534802/ihumtao-eviction-protest-an-occupation–150-years-in-the-making

Rowe, M., & Macaulay, M. (2017). *Review of New Zealand Police's progress in response to the 2007 Commission of Inquiry into Police Conduct*. Wellington, New Zealand: Institute for Governance and Policy Studies, Victoria University of Wellington. Retrieved from http://researcharchive.vuw.ac.nz/handle/10063/8143

Scott, D. (1952). *151 Days: History of the great waterfront lockout and supporting strikes, February 15–July 15, 1951*. Auckland, New Zealand: Wilson Printery Ltd.

Stanley, E. (2016). *The road to hell: State violence against children in postwar New Zealand*. Auckland, New Zealand: Auckland University Press.

Stanley, E., & Mihaere, R. (2018). Managing ignorance about Māori imprisonment. In A. Barton & H. Davis (Eds.), *Ignorance, power and harm: Agnotology and the criminological imagination* (pp. 113–138). Cham, Switzerland: Palgrave Macmillan.

Stewart, M. (2018, June 17). 'Lack of neutrality' present in policing of defence industry expo protest, lawyer says. *Stuff*. Retrieved from https://www.stuff.co.nz/national/104749034/lack-of-neutrality-present-in-policing-of-defence-industry-expo-protest-lawyer-says

Sunshine, J., & Tyler, T. R. (2003). The role of procedural justice and legitimacy in shaping public support for policing. *Law and Society Review, 37*(3), 513–548. doi:10.1111/1540–5893.3703002

Tauri, J. M. (2019). Indigenous perspectives and experiences: Maori, crime control and social harm. In T. Bradley & R. Walters (Eds.), *Introduction to criminological thought* (3rd ed. pp. 183–204). Auckland: Edify.

Te Uepū Hāpai I te Ora. (2019a). *He waka roimata: Transforming our criminal justice system*. Safe and Effective Justice Advisory Group. Retrieved from https://www.safeandeffectivejustice.govt.nz/assets/Uploads/fa55462d44/teuepureport_hewakaroimata.pdf

Te Uepū Hāpai I te Ora. (2019b). *Turuki! Turuki! Move together! Transforming our criminal justice system*. Safe and Effective Justice Advisory Group. Retrieved from https://www.safeandeffectivejustice.govt.nz/assets/Uploads/28ce04fd87/Turuki-Turuki-Report-Interactive.pdf

Tyler, T. R. (2006). *Why people obey the law*. Princeton, NJ: Princeton University Press.

Tyler, T. (2017). Procedural justice and policing: A rush to judgment? *Annual Review of Law and Social Science, 13*(1), 29–53. doi:10.1146/annurev-lawsocsci–110316–113318

Tyler, T. R., & Huo, Y. J. (2002). *Trust in the law: Encouraging public cooperation with the police and courts*. New York, NY: Russell Sage Foundation.

Waddington, P. A. (2007). Policing of public order [Editorial]. *Policing, 1*(4), 375–379. doi:10.1093/police/pam057

Ward, T. (2011). In praise of troublemakers: A history of eco-activism in New Zealand. In L. C. Johnsen & T. Ward (Eds.), *Organic explorer NZ: A sustainable travel guide to New Zealand* (3rd ed., pp. 306–322). New Zealand: Organic Explorer Publishing Co.

Webb-Liddall, A. (2019, August 6). Protectors condemn 'intimidating' increased police presence at Ihumātao. *Spinoff*. Retrieved from https://thespinoff.co.nz/atea/06–08–2019/protestors-condemn-intimidating-increased-police-presence-at-ihumatao/

Wynyard, M. (2019). 'Not one more bloody acre': Land restitution and the Treaty of Waitangi settlement process in Aotearoa New Zealand. *Land, 8*(11), 162–176. doi:10.3390/land8110162

Yska. R. (2011, July 8). Inside the 1981 Springbok tour. *New Zealand Listener*. Retrieved from https://www.noted.co.nz/archive/archive-listener-nz–2011/inside-the–1981-springbok-tour

15

Crime Prevention
Exploring Conventional Practices

Russil Durrant

Everyone should have an interest in preventing crime. Although the nature of the 'crime problem' tends to get distorted in media coverage, and is arguably poorly understood by the general public, there is no doubt that offending causes genuine harm to large numbers of individuals every year. The New Zealand Crime and Victims Survey (Ministry of Justice, 2019), for example, estimates that there were over 1.7 million offences in the year prior to the survey, directly affecting just under a third of all New Zealand adults. Establishing what are the best approaches to reducing crime is, therefore, an important task.

This chapter begins by considering approaches to conceptualising and classifying crime prevention. A brief outline of the importance of evaluating crime prevention approaches is also presented. Crime prevention strategies potentially encompass an enormous range of activities and processes, from preschool intellectual enrichment programmes to improvements in policing strategies. Given that 'crime' itself is an extremely broad and heterogeneous category that encompasses everything from residential burglary to corporate fraud, this is perhaps unsurprising. Although a range of different approaches is considered in this chapter, the focus is primarily on those that target developmental, community, and situational contexts, and thus I shall be mainly concerned with efforts to address 'conventional' criminal activities. For each of these main contexts I will outline the main crime prevention initiatives that have been developed and examine the relevant research that allows us to evaluate how effective these strategies are. Where possible, New Zealand research and examples will be employed. In the final section of this chapter, thought is given to how best to reduce crime in

Aotearoa New Zealand. It is argued that evidence supports a range of approaches, although it is also important to critically reflect on both the benefits and the potential harms of crime prevention efforts.

WHAT IS CRIME PREVENTION?

There is no universal agreement among criminologists about exactly what constitutes 'crime prevention' (Sutton et al., 2014). Much of the debate centres on the *scope* of activities that are seen to be included. Brantingham and Faust (1976) cast the net widely when they suggest that crime prevention involves 'any activity, by an individual or a group, public or private, that precludes the incidence of one or more criminal acts' (p. 284), whereas others prefer a narrower focus by excluding the actions of the criminal justice system (e.g., punishment and sentencing), as these are best viewed as strategies of *controlling* crime (Welsh & Farrington, 2012). Regardless of how the boundaries of 'crime prevention' are drawn, it is clear that there is no realistic chance of *eliminating* crime from society, so the challenge is how we might best *reduce* the nature, scope, and severity of offending in order to lessen the harm that crime causes.

There are various different approaches to classifying crime prevention initiatives in the academic literature. One perspective focuses on the main *contexts* in which crime prevention occurs and outlines four major approaches: developmental prevention, community prevention, situational prevention, and criminal justice prevention (Welsh & Farrington, 2012). Developmental crime prevention involves targeting known *risk factors* for later offending – that is, those characteristics of individuals (e.g., impulsiveness, low empathy, poor social skills, low IQ, poor school achievement) and families (e.g., child abuse and neglect, low parental monitoring, antisocial parents) that are known to be statistically related to an increased risk for offending later in life (Farrington, 2015). The logic of this approach is straightforward: if these factors predict later offending and they can, in some meaningful way, be changed or altered through an appropriate intervention, then future offending should be less likely. Community crime prevention, as its name suggests, looks more broadly at aspects of the wider social context that might facilitate offending (e.g., social disorganisation, community disorder) with the aim of changing features of the social environment in ways that reduce the likelihood of crime. Although community approaches may involve a mix of social and situational strategies there tends to be a local focus on these initiatives, often with input from community members.

Whereas developmental and community crime prevention target features of individuals, families, and communities that may lead to offending, situational crime prevention efforts focus on the *proximal* causes of crime with the aim of changing aspects of the environment in ways that make offending less likely. As such, situational crime prevention efforts focus more on the offence than the offender by removing or reducing opportunities for crime: how might the physical environment be changed to make offences less likely to occur? Finally, criminal justice prevention includes the efforts of the criminal justice system (including the police, the courts, and correctional facilities) that might result in a reduction in offending. In this chapter we will focus on developmental, community, and situational crime prevention approaches.

Before specific approaches to crime prevention are described in more detail, it is worth highlighting the importance of employing appropriate methods of evaluating the effectiveness of such programmes in reducing offending. There are various different types of evaluation that can be undertaken, but *impact*, or *outcome*, *evaluations* provide the crucial information about the effect of the programme on reducing crime. Various methods can be employed to see if the programme is achieving its stated aims of reducing crime, but where possible evaluations should employ experimental designs that compare the impact of the intervention on the group exposed to the programme to a similar control group who are not exposed to the intervention. If offending in the experimental group is statistically lower than in the control group, then we are in a position to claim – albeit tentatively – that the programme does what it promises on the box: it reduces offending. Impact evaluations are also important because they can tell us if the programme is ineffective (and hence might be a waste of resources) or, worse, exposure to the programme *increases* the risk of offending.

Just as some medical interventions have negative – often unanticipated – side effects that need to be monitored, so, too, crime prevention interventions might result in harmful outcomes. As the criminologist Joan McCord (2003) has emphasised: 'Unless social programmes are evaluated for potential harms as well as benefits, safety as well as efficacy, the choice of which social programmes to use will remain a dangerous guess' (p. 17). Though there is strong evidence (explored below) that supports the effectiveness of a wide range of crime prevention programmes, some programmes have been shown to *increase* rather than decrease crime. In one comprehensive review of crime prevention programmes, Welsh and Rocque (2014) found that just over 3 per cent of evaluations indicated that the programme led to an increase in offending. Many of these programmes involved group-based programmes with at-risk adolescents (e.g., scared straight, boot camps), suggesting that these kinds of intervention might foster the development of norms and behaviours that increase the risk of offending (Braga, 2016).

DEVELOPMENTAL AND COMMUNITY CRIME PREVENTION

On the back of longitudinal studies, life course and developmental criminologists have been able to provide a comprehensive list of factors that increase the chances of individuals offending in later life (Farrington, 2015). These *risk factors* are the key targets for various developmental and community crime prevention initiatives (Farrington & Welsh, 2007). There are a very large number of such programmes that vary in terms of the nature and scope of their targets, intensity, core aims (crime prevention vs. other beneficial outcomes), and format (Farrington et al., 2016). The focus in this section, therefore, is on a selection of the more prominent programmes that have been developed with a view to considering their impact on reducing antisocial and criminal behaviour.

One important developmental risk factor for later offending is poor school performance. Children who struggle with school work and have significant problems with numeracy and literacy may be more likely to be truant from school, fail to complete educational qualifications, and subsequently find it hard to gain meaningful employment, making offending a more attractive option. Many programmes, therefore, aim to improve school performance in young children by providing resources that can better prepare them for structured learning environments. One of the best known of these initiatives is the Perry Preschool Project in the United States. This project involved the provision of daily home visits to help foster social and cognitive skills, along with attendance at a preschool programme and group meetings for parents. Participants have now been followed up until the age of 40 and the study has demonstrated a number of positive outcomes, including a reduction in criminal offending (Belfield et al., 2006). Similar positive outcomes have been demonstrated for other preschool enrichment programmes (Farrington & Welsh, 2007), and a good case can be made for investing in such programmes, not only because of the beneficial impact on offending but also for their other positive outcomes (Duncan & Magnuson, 2013).

Whereas the Perry programme and others like it focus on enhancing educational outcomes, other programmes are directed more broadly at social and emotional development and target individual risk factors for later offending, such as poor self-regulation and low empathy (Farrington & Welsh, 2007). These programmes are often specifically targeted at children and adolescents with emerging conduct problems that are affecting their family and school life. Social skills training, for example, involves regular structured sessions that aim to foster self-control, anger management, and other social skills using a variety of methods, including role-playing and modelling. Again, there is good evidence that such programmes have positive outcomes in terms of reducing antisocial and criminal behaviour (Lösel & Beelman, 2005; Schindler & Black, 2015).

Many of the important risk factors for later offending that have been identified in longitudinal research reside in the family environment. These include maternal use of tobacco, alcohol, and other psychoactive substances during pregnancy; birth complications; and early exposure to toxic substances (Fergusson et al., 2015). Key risk factors during early and middle childhood include child abuse and neglect, harsh and/or erratic parenting practices, exposure to family conflict, and low levels of parental monitoring (Farrington, 2015). Many developmental interventions, therefore, focus on addressing these risk factors for later offending. It should be noted, however, that many programmes aim to improve a wide range of outcomes for children and families, and are not necessarily *specifically* directed at reducing offending.

Home visitation programmes typically target 'at-risk' families and provide regular home visits during and after pregnancy by trained social workers and/or health professionals. Typically, such programmes aim to provide a range of resources that relate to ante- and post-natal health, parenting, personal development, and early education. International research suggests that these programmes can be effective in reducing later offending (Olds et al., 1998), and an evaluation of the similar Early Start programme run in Christchurch, New Zealand, indicated that it improved a range of social and health outcomes (Fergusson et al., 2013). In this study, Plunket nurses screened families in the Christchurch area for risk factors for later offending, leading to a sample of 443 families who met the screening criteria. Of these, 220 were randomly assigned to the Early Start programme and the remainder acted as the control group. Both groups were followed up at regular intervals over a nine-year period and were assessed on a variety of measures. Results indicated that those who were exposed to the Early Start programme were significantly less likely to attend hospital for unintentional injuries and were less likely to be exposed to harsh and punitive parenting practices. However, there were no differences in other relevant outcomes, such as parental depression, substance use, or family violence, suggesting that the intervention had the greatest impact on parenting practices (Fergusson et al., 2013).

Indeed, there are also a large number of programmes that focus specifically on improving parenting practices. Examples that have been implemented in New Zealand include the Triple P – Positive Parenting Program, the Incredible Years Basic Parent Programme, and Parent Management Training Oregon (Gluckman, 2018). The general aim of these programmes is to provide parents with appropriate tools and resources to enhance positive parent–child social interactions, encourage the use of effective parenting strategies (e.g., setting limits and rules and enforcing them consistently), and manage problem behaviours without resorting to physical punishment. There is good evidence in the international literature that these programmes can generate positive outcomes, including the reduction of antisocial behaviour (Farrington, 2015).

An evaluation of the Incredible Years Parenting Programme in a New Zealand context was initiated by the Ministries of Education and Health and Social Development involving a sample of 166 parents of children aged three to eight who had been referred to the course because of their children's conduct problems (Sturrock & Gray, 2013). The results indicated a number of positive outcomes, including significant reductions in child conduct problems, an improvement in positive parenting practices, and an overall decline in parent–child conflict. A follow-up study found that these positive outcomes were retained two and half years later, and were similar for Māori and non-Māori families (Sturrock et al., 2014). A recent randomised controlled trial of a culturally adapted version of the Triple P programme for Māori families found a number of positive outcomes for families exposed to the intervention, including a reduction in child behaviour problems, improved parental relationships, and greater parental confidence in managing difficult child behaviours in a constructive fashion (Keown et al., 2018).

Developmental research has highlighted the importance of the school, peer, and wider community contexts in the development of offending. Exposure to bullying in schools, school truancy, association with antisocial peers, and residence in socially deprived neighbourhoods all increase the risk for offending (Farrington & Welsh, 2007). School-based programmes aim to enhance engagement and identification with the school environment to reduce truancy, address problem behaviours such as bullying through dedicated antibullying programmes, and foster relationships with prosocial peers through mentoring and the development of effective strategies for resisting peer pressure (Kim et al., 2015; Ttofi & Farrington, 2012). There are a diverse number of community-based programmes that have been implemented; broadly speaking, they aim to foster and promote social cohesion and collective efficacy in communities by providing opportunities for prosocial activities and through facilitating the involvement of community members in enforcing social norms (Gill, 2016).

Finally, it is worth noting that there are various programmes that aim to address a number of different risk factors that relate to individual, family, school, *and* community environments. For example, multisystemic therapy (MST) is a wraparound treatment programme designed for children and adolescents with serious conduct problems. It is broadly based on the idea that interventions need to address factors that exist across multiple domains. As such, MST involves the development of intensive programmes that are tailor-made to address individual problems in family, school, and community contexts (Henggeler & Schaeffer, 2016). Similarly, Functional Family Therapy (FFT) also targets youth with serious conduct problems by addressing a range of risk factors especially within the family environment. A recent pilot study of FFT in a New Zealand context found that it was effective in reducing conduct problems for both Māori and non-Māori participants (Heywood & Fergusson, 2016).

Evaluating developmental and community prevention programmes

To get a clearer idea of the overall effectiveness of developmental and community crime prevention programmes it is useful to look closely at the results of both systematic reviews and meta-analyses, as they can provide information on a range of outcomes across a large number of studies. A meta-analysis of early family parent training programmes by Piquero et al. (2016) involving 78 evaluations found an overall effect size of 0.37 across the different studies. This means that individuals exposed to the programme were 37 per cent less likely to offend compared to individuals in the control group – a significant reduction. In a comprehensive systematic review of systematic reviews of developmental crime prevention programmes, Farrington et al. (2016) found that effect sizes were uniformly positive, indicating that all of the programmes reviewed were effective. The evidence base for community crime prevention programmes is less clear, although research in this area is hampered by a lack of agreement about just what constitutes community-based intervention (Gill, 2016).

In Table 15.1 some of the advantages and disadvantages of developmental and community-based programmes are outlined. The good news is that many programmes – especially those targeted at individuals and families – are well supported by a large number of methodologically robust evaluations. These crime prevention programmes are thus evidence-based. Although our interest in this chapter is crime prevention, many programmes generate a range of positive outcomes, such as improved health, enhanced mental well-being, and better educational outcomes. Thus, we need to consider the broader implications of these programmes when evaluating their overall merit. Finally, there is good evidence that many developmental crime prevention programmes in particular are cost-effective: in monetary terms the savings accrued outweighed the financial costs of implementing the programme (Welsh & Farrington, 2015).

Table 15.1.
The Advantages and Disadvantages of Development and Community-based Crime Prevention Programmes

Advantages	Disadvantages
Targets known risk factors of offending.	Focus on risk factors may obscure real causes of offending.
Evidence supports effectiveness in reducing crime (especially for individual and family programmes).	Relatively small reductions in offending, and not all programmes show positive outcomes.
Programmes generate other positive outcomes (e.g., education, work).	Risk of negative outcomes (e.g. stigmatisation).
	Expensive to implement.

It is also worth thinking carefully about the potential costs or limitations of developmental and community crime prevention programmes. First, although there is good evidence that these programmes are effective, the overall impact of the programmes tends to be quite moderate, and not all programmes generate positive outcomes in all evaluations. This suggests that there is still work to do in developing more effective strategies for reducing crime. In part, this may be due to the focus on risk factors, which, although reasonable, could direct attention away from the underlying *causes* of offending. More generally, there is scope to develop programmes that focus less on risk or deficits and more on developing strengths and achieving outcomes that are meaningful to individuals, such as the I Have a Dream foundation (see: https://ihaveadream.org.nz/). Substantial care also must be taken in the way that developmental programmes are designed and implemented to avoid negative outcomes. For example, most programmes tend to target at-risk families – typically those who come from deprived backgrounds who may already have children with behavioural problems. There is a possibility here that interventions might stigmatise families, resulting in 'labelling effects' that could lead to undesirable outcomes, including an increase in antisocial behaviour. Finally, although such programmes are cost-effective in the long run, they are relatively expensive to implement, and positive outcomes (especially in terms in reductions in criminal offending) may take many years or decades to realise.

SITUATIONAL CRIME PREVENTION

Situational crime prevention is based on the idea that features of the situation or physical environment can exert a strong influence on whether or not individuals engage in criminal activities, and thus crime can be prevented or reduced by altering aspects of the situation in relevant ways. Three main criminological theories inform situational approaches to crime prevention: *rational choice theory*, routine activities theory, and crime pattern theory. According to rational choice theory, offenders are viewed as rational actors – like everyone else their decision-making is shaped by their subjective evaluations of the costs and benefits of their actions (Cornish & Clark, 2008). For individuals who may be motivated to break the law, any strategy that increases the costs or reduces the benefits of offending is likely, therefore, to reduce crime. For *routine activity theorists*, offending is viewed as the confluence of three key factors: a motivated offender, a suitable target, and the absence of a capable guardian (Felson, 2008). Again, the implications for crime prevention are relatively straightforward: prevention will occur if the environment can be manipulated in ways that reduce the likelihood of these three factors converging in time and space. *Crime pattern theory* also focuses on the routine activities of individuals and how they shape opportunities for offending, although the emphasis is more explicitly placed on how these activity patterns shape the geographical concentration of crime (Brantingham & Brantingham, 2008). Individuals, for example, are more likely to offend in places that they are familiar with, and activity patterns create crime 'hot spots' where offending is more frequent.

These three theoretical approaches suggest several ways in which we might prevent or reduce crime by manipulating aspects of the physical and social environment. First, offending will be less likely to occur if individuals have to exert greater effort to commit crimes. This can be achieved through *target hardening* – for example, by installing locks, encrypted passwords, and other forms of access control. Indeed, according to one influential idea, large shifts in the prevalence of offending can be explained by the development of more effective strategies for making theft more difficult (Farrell et al., 2011). Second, reductions in crime should also be achievable by increasing the *risk* associated with offending – for example, by enhancing surveillance (e.g., closed-circuit television, or CCTV). Unlike developmental and community crime prevention programmes, many situational crime prevention strategies have simply not been subject to methodologically rigorous evaluations of their effectiveness in reducing offending (Bowers & Johnson, 2016). Enough good-quality research has, however, accumulated for some specific strategies, including improved street lighting, and the installation of CCTV (Welsh et al., 2015).

Welsh and Farrington (2008, as cited in Bowers & Johnson, 2016) found that improved street lighting resulted in a 21 per cent reduction in offending in areas where it was implemented. The primary reason for this is likely due to the enhanced natural surveillance that better street lighting affords. Perhaps the most prominent situational crime prevention strategy is also predicated on the idea that better surveillance can reduce crime by increasing the risks of being caught. CCTV cameras in public spaces have become a feature of most Western urban environments, including New Zealand. Indeed, it is estimated that there is approximately one CCTV camera in operation for every 300 individuals in Auckland, an increase in 44 per cent since 2015 (Foxcroft, 2018). The effectiveness of CCTV as a crime prevention strategy has been extensively evaluated. The most recent systematic review of relevant studies, stretching back 40 years, found that the implementation of CCTV is associated with significant, albeit somewhat modest, reductions in offending. However, not all evaluations have generated positive findings and CCTV seems to be more effective in reducing some types of crime compared to others (e.g., property but not violent offending) in some environments but not others (e.g., car parks but not city centres). The effectiveness of CCTV also appears to be enhanced when combined with other prevention measures (Piza et al., 2019).

Evaluating situational crime prevention

Table 15.2 summarises some of the main advantages and disadvantages of situational crime approaches. In a review of systematic reviews, Bowers and Johnson (2016) concluded that 'there is good reason to be optimistic about the effectiveness of situational approaches to reducing crime problems' (p. 123). Certainly, better street lighting and CCTV appear to result in small reductions in certain types of offending. Many situational crime prevention initiatives may also result in other positive outcomes, such as more attractive urban environments. Situational crime prevention initiatives are also relatively cheap and easy to implement, making them attractive options for local and national governments.

There are also several potential disadvantages to situational crime prevention approaches. First, reductions in offending tend to be modest, and many approaches either show no evidence for success or have not been rigorously evaluated. Second, we need to consider the possibility that some initiatives might lead to negative outcomes. For example, crime may be reduced in the target area of the intervention, but simply displaced into other locations. Enhanced surveillance also poses a risk of eroding fundamental human rights (e.g., privacy) (Welsh et al., 2015). Finally, situational approaches tend to be quite limited in scope in terms of the kinds of offences that they target (i.e., mainly property offending) and are less relevant for many sorts of crime.

Table 15.2.
The Advantages and Disadvantages of Situational Approaches to Crime Prevention

Advantages	Disadvantages
Evidence supports some effectiveness in reducing crime (especially for street lighting and CCTV).	Relatively small reductions in offending, and not all programmes show positive outcomes.
Programmes generate other positive outcomes (e.g., more attractive urban environments).	Risk of negative outcomes (e.g. displacement of offending, potential loss of individual rights).
Often easy to implement.	Tend to be effective for a relatively limited range of offences.

CONCLUSION

A thorough overview of the recent history of crime prevention policies in Aotearoa New Zealand is provided by Bradley and Walters (2019). This chapter cannot give a detailed account of the various strategies, policies, and initiatives that have been formulated over the past 30 years, but several key points stand out. First, the complex and multifaceted nature of crime and the heterogeneous character of crime prevention strategies tend to elude effective consolidation under any particular government department as initiatives fall variously in the domains of New Zealand Police (NZP), the Ministry of Justice, the Ministry of Social Development, the Department of Corrections, and the Ministry of Health. Second, unlike offender rehabilitation programmes, which are largely delivered by Corrections, many crime prevention initiatives are privately run. For example, the Triple P programme is run by a private organisation that charges for its services, although it is available at no cost in some areas in New Zealand in partnership with the Ministry of Health. The dramatic growth in private security in New Zealand perhaps best illustrates the role of the private sector in providing crime prevention services (Bradley, 2016). Third, the focus of crime prevention initiatives has undergone a variety of changes over the past couple of decades, and differs depending on the specific organisation that is involved. For example, the most recent iteration of NZP's Prevention First model focuses on six drivers of 'demand': alcohol, youth (rangatahi), families (whānau), roads, organised crime and drugs, and mental health (NZP, 2017), whereas the Ministry of Justice's (2013) Youth Action Plan favours three main strategies: crime prevention through community development, delivering early intervention for those at risk of offending, and reducing opportunities and designing out the immediate precursors to offending.

Based on the research reviewed in this chapter, some mix of developmental, community, and situational crime prevention initiatives is likely to be most effective in reducing crime in New Zealand. The important role of developmental approaches was emphasised in a recent report by the prime minister's chief science advisor (Gluckman, 2018), and certainly these approaches are both well supported in the available empirical literature and tend to generate a number of positive outcomes in addition to reducing crime. However, implementing these programmes in a way that can reach relevant populations, while being mindful of the potential to stigmatise vulnerable groups, remains an ongoing challenge. There also remains substantial scope for further development of strategies to address particular types of offending, especially domestic and sexual violence (e.g., Dickson & Willis, 2017), or crimes by powerful actors.

It is impossible to predict how approaches to crime prevention will develop in the future, but technological advances afford law enforcement agencies a range of new techniques and tools (Tombul & Bekir, 2015). For example, developments in face recognition systems that allow for accurate individual identification, in concert with the spread of CCTV, would potentially provide the police and other government agencies with unprecedented opportunities to monitor the public (Nakar & Greenbaum, 2017). Police in New Zealand do not, at present, have the capacity to run facial recognition software or live CCTV, but there is a clear interest in exploring these possibilities in the future (Pennington, 2019). As with ongoing concerns about access to social media, DNA repositories and other sources of 'big data', as well as further development of CCTV coverage in concert with advances in face recognition systems, raise uneasy questions about our right to privacy. Although all New Zealanders have an interest in reducing the harm caused by crime in society, we should be careful to ensure that the crime prevention efforts do not generate more harm than they aim to reduce.

STUDY QUESTIONS

- What is the main focus of developmental crime prevention approaches?
- What are some of the potential negative outcomes of crime prevention approaches?
- If you were in charge of investing in crime prevention in New Zealand, what are the key approaches that you would implement and why?

FURTHER READING

Farrington, D. P., & Welsh, B. C. (2007). *Saving children from a life of crime: Early risk factors and effective interventions.* Oxford, UK: Oxford University Press.

Sutton, A., Cherney, A., & White, R. (2014). *Crime prevention: Principles, perspectives, and practices* (2nd ed.). New York, NY: Cambridge University Press.

Weisburd, D., Farrington, D. P., & Gill, C. (Eds.). *What works in crime prevention and rehabilitation.* New York, NY: Springer.

REFERENCES

Belfield, C. R., Nores, M., Barnette, S., & Schweinhart, L. (2006). The High/Scope Perry Preschool Programme: Cost–benefit analysis using data from the age-40 follow-up. *Journal of Human Resources, 41*(1), 162–190. doi:10.3368/jhr.xli.1.162

Bowers, K. J., & Johnson, S. D. (2016). Situational crime prevention. In D. Weisburd, D. P. Farrington, & C. Gill (Eds.), *What works in crime prevention and rehabilitation* (pp. 111–135). New York, NY: Springer.

Bradley, T. (2016). Governing private security in New Zealand. *Australian and New Zealand Journal of Criminology, 49*(2), 159–178. doi:10.1177/0004865814538038

Bradley, T., & Walters, R. (Eds.). (2019). *Introduction to criminological thought* (3rd ed.). Auckland, New Zealand: Edify.

Braga, A. A. (2016). The continued importance of measuring potentially harmful impacts of crime prevention programs: The academy of experimental criminology 2014 Joan McCord lecture. *Journal of Experimental Criminology, 12*(1), 1–20. doi:10.1007/s11292-016-9252-4

Brantingham, P., & Brantingham, P. (2008). Crime pattern theory. In R. Wortley & L. Mazzerolle (Eds.), *Environmental criminology and crime analysis* (pp. 78–92). Cullompton, UK: Willan Publishing.

Brantingham, P. J., & Faust, F. L. (1976). A conceptual model of crime prevention. *Crime and Delinquency, 22*(3), 284–296. doi:10.1177/001112877602200302

Cornish, D. B., & Clarke, R. V. (2008). The rational choice perspective. In R. Wortley & L. Mazzerolle (Eds.), *Environmental criminology and crime analysis* (pp. 21–46). Cullompton, UK: Willan Publishing.

Dickson, S., & Willis, G. M. (2017). Primary prevention of sexual violence in Aotearoa New Zealand: A survey of prevention activities. *Sexual Abuse: A Journal of Research and Treatment, 29*(2), 128–147. doi:10.1177/1079063215583852

Duncan, G. J., & Magnuson, K. (2013). Investing in preschool programs. *Journal of Economic Perspectives, 27*(2), 109–132. doi:10.1257/jep.27.2.109

Farrell, G., Tilley, N., Tseloni, A., & Mailley, J. (2011). The crime drop and the security hypothesis. *Journal of Research in Crime and Delinquency, 48*(2), 147–175. doi:10.1177/0022427810391539

Farrington, D. P. (2015). The developmental evidence base: Psychosocial research. In D. A. Crighton & G. J. Towl. (Eds.), *Forensic psychology* (2nd ed., pp. 162–181). Hoboken, NJ: John Wiley & Sons.

Farrington, D. P., Ttofi, M. M., & Lösel, F. A. (2016). Developmental and social prevention. In D. Weisburd, D. P. Farrington, & C. Gill (Eds.), *What works in crime prevention and rehabilitation* (pp. 15–75). New York, NY: Springer.

Farrington, D. P., & Welsh, B. C. (2007). *Saving children from a life of crime: Early risk factors and effective interventions.* Oxford, UK: Oxford University Press.

Felson, M. (2008). Routine activity approach. In R. Wortley & L. Mazzerolle (Eds.), *Environmental criminology and crime analysis* (pp. 70–76). Cullompton, UK: Willan Publishing.

Fergusson, D. M., Boden, J. M., & Horwood, L. J. (2013). Nine-year follow-up of a home-visitation program: A randomised trial. *Pediatrics, 131*(2), 297–303. doi:10.1542/peds.2012–1612

Fergusson, D. M., Boden, J. M., & Horwood, L. J. (2015). From evidence to policy: Findings from the Christchurch Health and Development Study. *Australian and New Zealand Journal of Criminology, 48*(3), 386–408. doi:10.1177/0004865815589827

Foxcroft, D. (2018, March 7). The creep of CCTV: Are cameras invading our privacy or keeping us safe? *Stuff.* Retrieved from: https://www.stuff.co.nz/national/crime/101884182/big-brother-is-watching-cctv-numbers-up-40-per-cent-in-auckland

Gill, C. (2016). Community interventions. In D. Weisburd, D. P. Farrington, & C. Gill (Eds.), *What works in crime prevention and rehabilitation* (pp. 77–109). New York, NY: Springer.

Gluckman, P. (2018). *It's never too early, never too late: A discussion paper preventing youth offending in New Zealand.* Retrieved from https://safeandeffectivejustice.govt.nz/research/never-too-early-never-too-late/

Henggeler, S. W., & Schaeffer, C. M. (2016). Multisystemic therapy: Clinical overview, outcomes, and implementation research. *Family Process, 55*(3), 514–528. doi:10.1111/famp.12232

Heywood, C., & Fergusson, D. (2016). A pilot study of functional family therapy in New Zealand. *New Zealand Journal of Psychology, 45*(3), 954–965. Retrieved from https://www.sspa.org.nz/images/Conference_2017/Functional_Family_Therapy_in_New_Zealand.pdf

Keown, L. J., Sanders, M. R., Franke, N., & Shepherd, M. (2018). Te Whānau Pou Toru: A randomised controlled trial (RCT) of a culturally adapted low-intensity variant of the Triple P – Positive Parenting Program for indigenous Māori families in New Zealand. *Prevention Science, 19*(7), 954–965. doi:10.1007/s11121–018–0886–5

Kim, B. K. E., Gilman, A. B., & Hawkins, J. D. (2015). School and community-based preventive interventions during adolescence: Preventing delinquency through science-guided collective action. In J. Morizot & L. Kazemian (Eds.), *The development of criminal and antisocial behaviour* (pp. 447–460). New York, NY: Springer.

Lösel, F., & Beelman, A. (2005). Social problem-solving programs for preventing antisocial behaviour in children and youth. In McMurran, M., & McGuire, J. (Eds.), *Social problem solving and offending: Evidence, evaluation and evolution*. Chichester, UK: John Wiley & Sons.

McCord, J. (2003). Cures that harm: Unanticipated outcomes of crime prevention programs. *Annals of the American Academy of Political and Social Science, 587*(1), 16–30. doi:10.1177/0002716202250781

Ministry of Justice (2013). *Youth crime action plan, 2013–2023: Summary*. Retrieved from https://www.justice.govt.nz/justice-sector-policy/key-initiatives/cross-government/youth-crime-action-plan/

Ministry of Justice (2019). *New Zealand Crime and Victims Survey: Key findings*. Retrieved from https://www.justice.govt.nz/justice-sector-policy/research-data/nzcvs/resources-and-results/

Nakar, S., & Greenbaum, D. (2017). Now you see me. Now you still do: Facial recognition technology and the growing lack of privacy. *Boston University Journal of Science and Technology Law, 23*(1), 88–122. Retrieved from https://www.bu.edu/jostl/files/2017/04/Greenbaum-Online.pdf

New Zealand Police (NZP). (2017). *Prevention First Āraia i te Tuatahi: National Operating Model 2017*. Retrieved from https://www.police.govt.nz/about-us/publication/prevention-first-national-operating-model–2017

Olds, D., Henderson, C. R., Cole, J. R., Eckenrode, J., Kitzman, H., Luckey, D., . . . Powers, J. (1998). Long-term effects of nurse home visitation on children's criminal and antisocial behaviour: 15-year follow-up of a randomized controlled trial. *Journal of the American Medical Association, 280*(14), 1238–1244. doi:10.1001/jama.280.14.1238

Pennington, P. (2019, August 15). Police open to using facial recognition from Auckland transport CCTV cameras. *Radio New Zealand*. Retrieved from https://www.rnz.co.nz/news/national/396716/police-open-to-using-facial-recognition-from-auckland-transport-cctv-cameras

Piquero, A. R., Jennings, W. G., Diamond, B., Farrington, D. P., Tremblay, R. E., Welsh, B. C., & Gonzalez, J. M. R. (2016). A meta-analysis update on the effects of early family/parent training programs on antisocial behaviour and delinquency. *Journal of Experimental Criminology, 12*(2), 229–248. doi:10.1007/s11292–016–9256–0

Piza, E. L., Welsh, B. C., Farrington, D. P., & Thomas, A. L. (2019). CCTV surveillance for crime prevention: A 40-year systematic review with meta-analysis. *Criminology and Public Policy, 18*(1), 135–159. doi: 10.1111/1745–9133.12419

Schindler, H. S., & Black, C. F. D. (2015). Early prevention of criminal and antisocial behaviour: A review of interventions in infancy and childhood. In J. Morizot & L. Kazemian (Eds.), *The development of criminal and antisocial behaviour* (pp. 433–446). New York, NY: Springer.

Sturrock, F., & Gray, D. (2013). *Incredible Years Pilot Study: Evaluation report*. Wellington, New Zealand: Ministry of Social Development. Retrieved from http://www.incredibleyears.com/article/incredible-years-pilot-study-evaluation-report/

Sturrock, F., Gray, D., Fergusson, D., Horwood, J., & Smits, C. (2014). *Incredible Years follow-up study: Long-term follow-up of the New Zealand Incredible Years Pilot Study*. Wellington, New Zealand: Ministry of Social Development. Retrieved from http://www.incredibleyears.com/article/incredible-years-follow-up-study-long-term-follow-up-of-the-new-zealand-incredible-years-pilot-study/

Sutton, A., Cherney, A., & White, R. (2014). *Crime prevention: Principles, perspectives, and practices* (2nd ed.). New York, NY: Cambridge University Press.

Tombul, F., & Bekir, C. (2015). Police use of technology to fight against crime. *European Scientific Journal, 11*(10), 286–296. Retrieved from https://pdfs.semanticscholar.org/2fc7/a52442780fbd4e0a08a2e757d3e5c3b11b19.pdf?_ga=2.89090523.1364657202.1580103073–1154062498.1580103073

Ttofi, M. M., & Farrington, D. P. (2012). Bullying prevention programs: The importance of peer intervention, disciplinary methods and age variations. *Journal of Experimental Criminology, 8*(4), 443–462. doi:10.1007/s11292–012–9161–0

Welsh, B. C., & Farrington, D.P. (2012). Crime prevention and public policy. In B. C. Welsh. & D. P. Farrington (Eds.), *The Oxford handbook of crime prevention* (pp. 3–19). Oxford, UK: Oxford University Press.

Welsh, B. C., & Farrington, D. P. (2015). Monetary value of early developmental crime prevention and its policy significance. *Criminology and Public Policy, 14*(4), 673–680. doi:10.1111/1745–9133.12167

Welsh, B. C., Farrington, D. P., & Taheri, S. A. (2015). Effectiveness and social costs of public area surveillance for crime prevention. *Annual Review of Law and Social Science, 11*(1), 111–130. doi:10.1146/annurev-lawsocsci–120814–121649

Welsh, B. C., & Rocque, M. (2014). When crime prevention harms: a review of systematic reviews. *Journal of Experimental Criminology, 10*(3), 245–266. doi:10.1007/s11292–014–9199–2

16

Ngā Kōti o Aotearoa / New Zealand Courts
Building Māori-focused Approaches, Developing Therapeutic Justice

Khylee Quince

This chapter provides a brief overview of the structure and hierarchy of the New Zealand courts, the judges who preside over them, and the nature of their role within the broader legal and constitutional framework. It describes recent specialist court developments which demonstrate a shift towards a unique New Zealand court practice, and it draws upon the theory and practice of therapeutic jurisprudence, an approach led by evidence of international best practice as well as calls for justice responses that reflect local challenges and obligations – particularly in relation to the position of Māori in Aotearoa.

In the following discussions, it is necessary to remember that the court system of New Zealand was imposed upon the newly formed nation-state following the signing of Te Tiriti o Waitangi between Māori hapū and the British Crown in 1840, and subsequent declarations of sovereignty that same year. Whilst the concept of a 'court' was foreign to tikanga Māori (Māori custom law), disputes within Te Ao Māori were (and are) heard and settled in the physical setting of the marae, which remains the central forum for all communal matters within Māori communities. There were no independent arbiters of disputes in the Māori legal system; rather, the process was one akin to mediation, with outcomes decided by consensus, sealed with the mana (authority) of rangatira or tohunga (chiefs or experts) (Quince, 2007a).

THE INSTITUTIONS

Courts are tribunals presided over by judges tasked with hearing cases and forming judgments over those matters, in accordance with the laws of the land. They are the forum in which the judiciary operates as one of the three branches of government in the Westminster tradition, along with the executive and Parliament. In New Zealand, there are four courts of general jurisdiction – the Supreme Court, Court of Appeal, High Court, and District Court – and the court system and hierarchy generally replicates the English system from which it derives. The role of the courts is to resolve disputes and review decisions by interpreting, applying, and enforcing the law. They serve to interpret the will of Parliament as stated in statute law, and also to clarify and develop the 'common law', or judge-made law, via application of principles to cases. This common-law system means the decisions of higher courts are binding upon those of equal or lower status in the court hierarchy, under the principle of *stare decisis*.[1]

The District Court of New Zealand is the busiest and largest in the country, comprising 58 courthouses and over 160 judges throughout the nation. The court deals with public and private law cases in criminal, civil, family, and youth jurisdictions, including 95 per cent of all criminal trials.[2] Within the District Court are the divisional Family and Youth Courts, which have their own heads of bench – the principal Family Court judge and the principal Youth Court judge. The Family Court hears matters between individuals, on such issues as the care and protection of children, relationship property, and adoption. The Youth Court is a specialist criminal jurisdiction for young people aged 14–17, for all offences other than homicide and some very serious cases or jury trials (see Lynch, chapter 18 this volume).

Other specialist courts include the Māori Land Court, the Māori Appellate Court, the Employment Court, and the Environment Court. In addition, the New Zealand court system includes a number of tribunals presided over by a chairperson and other judicial officers, who hear specific cases or adjudicate disputes. Tribunals are creatures of statute, whose jurisdiction, process, and power are set out in their enabling legislation.

The High Court is the highest court of first instance, and primarily hears serious criminal cases, and complex civil matters that exceed the lower courts' jurisdiction. Both the High Court and the Court of Appeal have 'inherent' jurisdiction, which means they have the power to adjudicate upon a matter, unless it is specifically denied by statute, or by a rule or other authority. Both also have statutory jurisdiction to hear specific matters, as defined by Parliament.

Finally, the Supreme Court of New Zealand was established in 2004 with the abolition of the right to appeal to the Privy Council in London. The six-member court is presided over by the chief justice and grants leave to appeal to hear cases of significance.

THE JUDICIARY

The human face of the courts is their judges, who are appointed by the governor-general on the recommendation of the attorney-general. For District Court appointments, the attorney-general takes advice from both the secretary for justice and the chief District Court judge. Higher judicial appointments for the High Court, Court of Appeal, or Supreme Court are overseen by the chief justice and the solicitor-general. In the District Court, judges are titled 'judge', while those in the higher courts are titled 'justice'. Judges are protected from political interference, and may only be removed from office on the grounds of significant misconduct. Judges must retire at 70, but may be retained for a further two years on an acting warrant if necessary.

After many decades as the domain of Pākehā men, the judiciary has recently become more diverse, reflecting the changing demographics of law graduates and the legal profession from which those eligible for judicial office are drawn. Three of six of the current Supreme Court judges are women, with one Māori male. Two of the ten Court of Appeal judges are Māori, including one of the two female justices. In the High Court ranks of 47 judges nationwide, 14 are female, with one Māori male presiding. Diversity is also beginning to filter through to the appointment of judges at the District Court level, where in 2019 the balance of gender tipped to a female majority for the first time, and where 27 judges identify as Māori and 5 as Pasifika. In early 2020, an unprecedented 11 Māori were appointed to the court. In 2019, Judge Heemi Taumaunu was named as the first Māori chief District Court judge, an appointment that was widely celebrated not only for His Honour's knowledge and experience of the law, tikanga, and te reo Māori, but also for his explicit intentions to bring about change in the justice system to better reflect a changing and diverse Aotearoa, where the Treaty relationship between Crown and Māori is given appropriate recognition and acknowledgement (see McManus, 2019).

SPECIALIST INITIATIVES

As the profile of the judiciary changes to reflect a more diverse national population and legal profession, so, too, has the way in which courts are going about their business. Change in the make-up of the judiciary is one of the reasons for this, as a more diverse bench brings with it different values, cultural or gender priorities, and practice virtues derived from their lives and backgrounds. In addition, the impetus for reform has also emerged out of growing criticism of the justice system. These criticisms have included dissatisfaction with delays in accessing justice, the complexity of language and court procedure, the lack of direct engagement of victims and offenders, and a focus on retributive outcomes (Chief Victims Advisor to Government, 2019; New Zealand Law Commission, 2004; Te Uepū Hāpai i te Ora, 2019). Much of the recent reform in courtroom practice and procedure has therefore focused on providing a more accessible, more transparent, and less traumatic experience for those who come before the courts; considering more expansive dispositions; and using simplified and more direct communication.

Over the past decade, a number of special initiatives have been developed in the New Zealand court system, without any enabling statutory amendments, and often with no dedicated budget. Some of these initiatives aim to streamline the management of cases and processes, while others operate as 'problem-solving' or 'solution-focused' courts to respond to particular social problems or issues underlying offending behaviours.

MĀORI-FOCUSED INITIATIVES

The crisis in the over-representation of Māori as offenders, victims, and prisoners over the past three decades has provided the impetus for a number of court initiatives aimed at addressing this shameful stain. The push for widespread system changes has resulted in several court-based initiatives that are inclusive of te reo me ngā tikanga Māori (Māori language and law) and which harness the goodwill and commitment of Māori communities.

The Matariki Court

Matariki (also known as Pleiades or Subaru) is the constellation of stars that signals the Māori new year. It is often referenced as a metaphor for aspirations for change. The post-plea criminal court instigated by the late former chief District Court judge Russell Johnson in 2010 is therefore named after these transformative ambitions. The Matariki Court operates in the Kaikohe District Court, under the leadership of Judge Greg Davis, who has whakapapa (genealogy links) to the local community.

A qualifying offender who pleads guilty to their charges may be considered for the Matariki Court. This delays sentencing pursuant to section 25 of the Sentencing Act 2002, to allow for a culturally appropriate rehabilitation programme to be formed and undertaken. The court uses the services of a local iwi provider, Te Mana o Ngāpuhi Kowhao Rau, to work with the offender and their whānau, and to prepare a plan to address any identified issues as they work together. The suspension of sentencing to allow for this process is crucial, as many offenders and their whānau are unsure both of their role and how to engage with the court in sentencing, and they have little to offer by way of mitigation before negotiating the facilitated plan. The plan is regularly monitored by Judge Davis and the kaumātua (elder) panel that forms an essential part of the Matariki Court's framework. As Judge Davis has stated, 'whānau hold a critical piece of the puzzle to assist in reducing Māori crime' (District Court of New Zealand, 2013, para. 4). Whānau engagement enables a better sharing of information and understanding of the offender's life and the context for their offending behaviours. The court includes some tikanga Māori protocols in its operation, such as the use of mihimihi (formal introductions), te reo Māori (Māori language), and inclusion of whānau (extended family). The layout of the courtroom is also reorganised to be less intimidating, enabling offenders to sit with their whānau and supporters. The Matariki Court has yet to be formally evaluated.

Ngā Kōti Rangatahi

The most extensive and wide-reaching initiative in terms of court reforms over the past decade has been the development of Ngā Kōti Rangatahi within the Youth Court jurisdiction of the District Court. Founded as part of the government's 10-year Youth Crime Action Plan in 2008, Ngā Kōti Rangatahi operate without any explicit statutory enablement. They merely shift the physical sitting of the Youth Court to a marae, as enabled in section 72 of the District Courts Act 2016, which provides that 'the Judge may hold a session of the court at a time and place the Judge thinks fit'.

Ngā Kōti Rangatahi fulfil the monitoring function of the Youth Court for those young persons who are deemed suitable and who elect to transfer their proceeding to its process. In the youth justice jurisdiction, the whānau or family group of the young person develop a plan to respond to the offending through the family group conference process. The court therefore performs a monitoring rather than an adjudicatory function, with the core decision-making power vested in the family group (Cleland & Quince, 2014).

Ngā Kōti Rangatahi were developed under the leadership of Judge Hemi Taumaunu, as a Māori-led response to particular issues in the youth justice system affecting rangatahi Māori. The New Zealand youth justice system had achieved a world-renowned success in significantly reducing formal responses to youth offending, and yet had not equally benefited Māori and non-Māori in its first 20 years of operation (Cleland & Quince, 2014). Despite halving the numbers of apprehensions and convictions overall, and maintaining long-term success in reducing recidivism, the profile of the hardcore group (about 15 per cent) of persistent youth offenders had remained static. They were Māori, generally male, with complex multiple needs (Cleland & Quince, 2014). Judge Taumaunu spoke of the desire to address their needs, and also, more generally, to consider and respond to the context of their offending and their cultural identities.

From a Māori perspective, the marae is the centre of a community. It is a repository of knowledge, precedent, and whakapapa, acknowledging genealogical ties and relationships (Quince, 2007b). The Rangatahi Courts harness the commitment, aroha (love, compassion), and manaaki (host responsibilities) of the marae and its people. The judge sits alongside a panel of kaumātua, to provide advice, guidance, and encouragement to the rangatahi participants. If a plan is successfully completed, a young person is eligible to be considered for a section 282 discharge, meaning there is no formal record of their engagement with the court.

OTHER SOLUTION-FOCUSED COURTS

The solution-focused courts are founded upon and operate according to the principles and practices of therapeutic jurisprudence,[3] having regard to the etymology of 'therapy', which derives from the Greek *therapeia*, 'healing'. This philosophy promotes the use of the law's processes, engaging workers as 'therapeutic agents', to address social issues underlying offending behaviours (Wexler, 1990). In practice, the courts often counter the *anti-therapeutic* features of orthodox law and processes, namely their austere physical environments, specialist language, and focus on punishment over treatment, rehabilitation, and reintegration.

Therapeutic jurisprudence emerged from the mental health field, to address the historic tension between the punitive focus of the criminal law and the challenges posed by those offenders presenting with mental disorders. The focus of the approach is to tailor specific interventions for 'offenders'. However, it differs from rehabilitative practice as it usually operates at the adjudicative, rather than the post-adjudicative or sentencing, phase (Brookbanks & Woodward, 2007). It is distinguished from restorative justice in the way that it includes active involvement of the judicial officer and other state agents. One criticism of restorative approaches is that they are most successful for offenders who possess economic, social, and cultural capital (and can navigate through and extricate themselves from justice processes using those resources), but less successful for offenders who have fewer resources at their disposal (Cunneen, 2015). There are significant race and class dimensions to that critique; in Aotearoa, the persons least likely to gain the benefit of restorative approaches include Māori, young people, and those presenting with addictions or mental disorder (Cleland & Quince, 2014).

A therapeutic approach in courtrooms changes justice dynamics – including who is involved, which knowledge is prioritised, modes of communication, potential interventions or outcomes, and timing – ensuring that processes get under way without delay, whilst allowing for sufficient time for interventions to be impactful. Unlike many other court processes, it requires the co-construction of plans (to promote participant 'buy-in'), behavioural contracts, regular monitoring of plan progress, and a less adversarial, more collaborative interdisciplinary environment.

Therapeutic justice demands consistency of personnel – maintaining the same judge and other stakeholder representatives in a matter from start to finish. Philosophically, this affirms the commitment to a relational ethic; i.e., that justice is about people and relationships. Practically, however, this consistency is undertaken for several reasons: it meets a best-practice health model; it is efficient; it ensures clearer oversight and progress of cases; and it minimises frustrations when parties have to re-share the same information at each appearance. This team approach also means that regular review hearings are held, in order to monitor progress and check compliance with any behaviour contract, treatment regime, or agreed conditions. This is aimed at addressing a common issue with rehabilitation regimes or processes where the court stands a matter down for completion of a programme, only to have small issues derail its implementation (such as falling attendance due to problems with transport, or a relapse in drinking or drug-taking).

In terms of professional involvement, therapeutic jurisprudence seeks to use expertise from a variety of fields to achieve its aims. For example, behavioural scientists and psychologists may be engaged to check conversation cues to elicit admissions of responsibility, or to encourage compliance with bail or sentencing conditions. The behavioural science research shows that people are more likely to comply with conditions if they participate in the development of a 'contract', so this strategy might be used to negotiate and enforce conditions such as curfew, non-association with certain persons, or agreements to maintain sobriety (Arrigo, 2004).

Another example is the use of psychological research in relation to pleas and acceptance of accountability. One long-identified issue with the legal process is the role of law in perpetuating cognitive distortions – such that there are only 'guilty' or 'not guilty' parties (an issue that does not always represent the messy realities of harmful events). Legal processes are not really about responsibility or culpability, although we often pretend they are – if you're guilty you did it, and if you're not guilty you didn't. There may be better ways to encourage acceptance of alleged behaviour, such as through direct dialogue between the accused and the judge, or avoiding legal formality by asking the accused to tell the judge in their own words what happened.

In summary, therapeutic jurisprudence balances the backward-looking (retributive) and forward-looking (rehabilitative) approaches of justice. The solution-focused courts reimagine to some extent the degree of state control over justice processes, the consistency of outcomes between cases and offenders, and the nature and extent of party participation.

Te Kooti o Timatanga Hou: The Court of New Beginnings and The Court of Special Circumstances

Two courts in Auckland and Wellington serve to respond to offending underpinned by circumstances of homelessness. Te Kooti o Timatanga Hou – the Court of New Beginnings – was developed as a two-year pilot in 2010 by Judge Tony Fitzgerald at the District Court at Auckland, in response to a request by a homeless advocacy group, Lifewise, to the chief District Court judge. The Wellington equivalent, the Court of Special Circumstances, was established in 2012 under the leadership of Judge Susan Thomas, now presided over by Judges Bill Hastings and Barbara Morris.

Both courts respond to recidivist low-level offending by homeless people in central-city catchments, where that offending is directly linked to the offender's housing status. Charges might include, for example, offences relating to drinking in public, or nuisance-related behaviour. The courts operate as a non-adversarial forum in which multiple agencies are tasked with responding to the legal, social, health, and housing needs of homeless offenders. These agencies work together to develop and monitor a plan to address those issues, while holding participants accountable for their offending. Although the courts operate without any statutory footing and with no dedicated budget from the Ministry of Justice, a coordinator is employed at the shared cost of the agencies involved.

Participants tend to present with complex co-morbid mental health and/or addiction needs that require legal and rehabilitative responses (Auckland Homeless Steering Group, 2012, p. 10). Plans might include assistance in securing identification, accessing welfare benefits, and other social supports, such as helping to reconnect with participants' loved ones or communities.

An independent evaluation of the Auckland court in 2012 reviewed the experience of the 54 homeless participants who engaged with the court during its two-year pilot. The evaluation confirmed a number of positive outcomes, including drops in reoffending rates (66 per cent), nights in prison (78 per cent), and hospital admission rates (78 per cent) (Auckland Homeless Steering Group, 2012, p. 23). Interviewed participants reported better engagement with the court, a more culturally welcoming process, and a friendlier approach. They also reported feeling better about themselves, which allowed them to address their substance abuse issues (pp. 21–22).

Some constructive criticism in the evaluation was directed at the need to strengthen the cultural practices of the court, having regard to the high number of Māori participants. It was recommended that a stronger relationship with kaumātua and Māori service providers be explored, with a view to enabling reconnection of Māori participants with their whānau, hapū, and iwi communities (Auckland Homeless Steering Group, 2012, p. 8).

Sexual Violence Court

A two-year pilot Sexual Violence Court was established in Auckland and Whangārei in December 2016, for all serious sexual violence cases to be heard by a jury, in response to a 2015 Law Commission Report recommendation (New Zealand Law Commission, 2015). The pilot aimed to reduce trial delays for such cases, and to improve the court experience for participants, particularly victims and witnesses. One of the core objectives was to address the criticism that sexual violence trials are often scheduled on 'stand by', meaning they only go ahead if other trials do not. This practice causes significant distress and uncertainty for complainants in such trials, who are being asked to recount particularly distressing experiences in the courtroom (Chief District Court Judge, 2019).

The court developed an intensive and proactive case management process, overseen by dedicated case managers and specially trained jury judges. The judges developed best-practice guidelines for case and trial management. This included setting fixed trial dates much earlier in the process than usual to give witnesses certainty, alongside physical measures such as secure waiting areas for complainants and witnesses. The process also relies upon better co-operation between prosecutors and defence counsel.

A 2019 evaluation of the court confirmed positive outcomes in both quantitative and qualitative measures, including vastly improved timeframes for the resolution of cases (30 per cent faster than average in Auckland and 39 per cent in Whangārei), and complainants reported that the trials were managed in ways that did not re-traumatise them (Allison & Boyer, 2019, pp. 35–39). The evaluation also found that judges were more alert to unacceptable lines of questioning and intervened more frequently to stop such tactics, which is a frequently cited concern for witnesses in sexual violence trials (p. 69).

As a result of these successes, all District Court jury judges are now given the specialist training designed for the pilot, and the best-practice guidelines are to be shared and adopted nationwide. The pilot looks set to be made permanent at the two existing sites, with a view to a rollout across the country, dependent on the required political support and resourcing.

The Alcohol and Other Drug Treatment Court: Te Whare Whakapiki Wairua

The Alcohol and Other Drug Treatment Court (AODTC or Te Whare Whakapiki Wairua – 'the house that uplifts the spirit', a name given by respected kaumātua Sir Pita Sharples) was established as a five-year pilot in 2012, under the guidance of Judges Ema Aitken and Lisa Tremewan at the Auckland and Waitākere District Courts, respectively. These courts aim to respond to offending when alcohol or other drugs are identified as drivers of behaviour, and seek to reduce that offending as well as the consumption of alcohol or drugs, and to reduce imprisonment (Ministry of Justice, 2016, p. 3).

In their development, the AODTCs drew on the best-practice experiences of similar courts in the United States and elsewhere. However, given the high prevalence of Māori engagement, and the need to contextually respond to substance-related offending in Aotearoa, the courts have established a pivotal Pou Oranga position and use tikanga Māori protocols in operations. Pou Oranga literally means a 'post or pole of well-being', or metaphorically support for holistic health, and is the name given to the Māori cultural and spiritual advisor in the AODTC.

Evaluations of the court are positive, particularly in terms of supporting the recovery journeys of participants and the rebuilding of relationships, trusts, and connection with their communities (Ministry of Justice, 2016, p. 107). However, quantitative comparative data, between participants and similarly situated offenders who were processed through the general courts between 2012 and 2017, show that initial significant gains (that graduates were 54 per cent less likely to reoffend and 58 per cent less likely to be reimprisoned in 12 months following disposition) are negligible within two to three years (Thom, 2017).

BOUQUETS AND BRICKBATS FOR THE SPECIALIST COURT INITIATIVES

The generally positive evaluations of the specialist court initiatives demonstrate the benefits of their approaches, which might be summarised as drawing upon the following general principles and practices:

- a co-operative inter-agency approach;
- better consideration of the cultural identity and personal circumstances of offenders;
- better incorporation of tikanga Māori, to varying degrees;
- a more personalised, time-intensive engagement with offenders and their whānau or community;
- regular monitoring and consistency of personnel; and
- processes inclusive of incentives, sanctions, exits, and celebrations of success – including graduation.

These values and virtues underpin evaluations that have generally seen positive quantitative outcomes in terms of lower rates of reoffending, or reoffending to less serious levels (Allison & Boyer, 2019; Auckland Homeless Steering Group, 2012; Ministry of Justice, 2016). Of particular benefit is the qualitative data measuring participant experience and engagement. In the AODTC, for example, participants and whānau described the process as 'inclusive, caring and non-judgmental' (Ministry of Justice, 2016, p. 5). In the Māori-focused initiatives, the opportunity to connect to healthy, functional Māori identities and flourishing communities is transformative and often referenced by participants and their whānau.

Notwithstanding these generally positive evaluations, a number of criticisms have been raised. Inevitably, any non-orthodox processes raise the possibility of infringing upon the fair trial and due process rights of an accused, which are fiercely protected in the ordinary courts. For example, the significant reduction of trial delays in the Sexual Violence Court has resulted in defence counsel raising concerns about their ability to prepare a robust case within the new timeframe, which can be anywhere from four to seven months less than the previous average (Allison & Boyer, 2019, p. 48). Acting Chief Judge John Walker strongly rebutted this claim, stating that 'observing Bill of Rights fair trial rights was a paramount consideration both when designing and during the pilot' (Chief District Court Judge, 2019, para. 18).

The establishment of new pilot initiatives allows for a relatively fast rollout of new responses, but this does leave them vulnerable to being disestablished by a reallocation of resources elsewhere in the sector. While the generally positive evaluations of these initiatives can provide political impetus for their permanent embedding and implementation nationwide, this may not be possible given the widespread current strains on caseload and in supporting required personnel and infrastructure investments. Some commentators have argued that the current pepperpotting of specialist court initiatives has exacerbated the phenomenon of 'postcode justice' as defendants are subject to very different justice processes and outcomes dependent upon their domicile. This is a form of geographical discrimination, often privileging large urban communities (Lunt, 2017). Further, intensive resourcing of pilots, such as the AODTC, can lead to 'inequity of provision' for other clients outside of the process (Ministry of Justice, 2016, p. 4).

A further common criticism is the difficulties posed by the reliance of these specialist initiatives on other agencies to provide effective, timely interventions and to support solution-focused processes and outcomes. The irony of the seeming epiphany that courts are not able to appropriately respond to or address social problems that drive offending behaviours means they are heavily reliant upon others to effectively undertake programmes of sustainable and systemic transformative change. For example, the availability of residential treatment beds, anger management programmes or addictions treatment, or the provision of housing are all matters beyond the control of the courts but are crucial to their operation and success (see Ministry of Justice, 2016, p. 4).

With the exception of the Sexual Violence and Family Violence Courts, low victim engagement remains a concern, too, as it is in restorative justice processes. The specialist forums may be perceived as prioritising the needs of offenders above those of victims, especially when the focus of the court may be drivers of offending such as cultural identity, unstable housing, or substance use, rather than the offending behaviour itself. The provision of clear information and communication with victims about the objectives of the courts, their processes, and the victims' place in them may allay some of those fears and increase victim participation.

At a broader political and social level there is some criticism amongst the Māori community of the 'co-option' of our people, tikanga, and marae by the Crown and the justice system, and that initiatives such as Ngā Kōti Rangatahi (as well as the non-judicially controlled Iwi Justice Panels) reinforce Crown/Western/Pākehā superiority over Māori in our last bastion of private cultural space. These concerns were raised more than three decades ago by prominent Māori legal academic Dr Moana Jackson in his seminal report *The Maori and the Criminal Justice System: A new perspective: He whaipaanga hou*. Jackson (1988) was particularly wary of the possibility of a young Māori person's first marae encounter being one framed around a justice process, risking further alienation from an already strained or disrupted cultural identity. It is particularly challenging for Māori to consider the possibility of law and legal processes being in any way 'therapeutic', having regard to what Māori academic Ani Mikaere (2011) has described as the role of 'law as colonisation's enforcer'. A fairly orthodox Māori analysis would also criticise the perpetuation of a system that focuses on individual culpability, pathologising individuals rather than systemic failure or wrongdoing (see, for example, Webb, 2018).

Finally, here, there is also undoubted tension between the evident programme of change in the courts and judiciary, as outlined in this chapter, and the ever-present concurrent calls from many Māori for more significant reform, including calls for a wholly separate and parallel Māori justice system. Some Māori see the piecemeal reforms of recent years as a state-driven and -controlled means of placating Māori while denying meaningful acknowledgement of and support for tino rangatiratanga (self-determination) as affirmed in Te Tiriti o Waitangi (see Cunneen & Tauri, 2016). These are not mutually exclusive agendas: mainstream courts and their personnel *should* reflect the diverse population of our nation, and *should* operate and deliver access to justice as well as processes and outcomes that similarly reflect the range of values, experiences, and desires of our communities.

CONCLUSION

It would not be an exaggeration to describe the courts, as part of the justice system in New Zealand, as being in a state of flux. The past two decades have seen significant change in the structure and hierarchy of the courts, including the establishment of a new Supreme Court, as a symbol of our maturing as a post-colonial settler state. In addition, in the lower courts a number of specialist initiatives have developed to respond to pressing social and cultural issues – including drivers of crime and the need to better respond to the challenges of negative Māori entanglement in justice as victims and as offenders. Part of that challenge has required the holding up of a mirror to the system, to confront some harsh truths – that the courts are part of a system that has been overwhelmingly monocultural in its founding ethos, traditions, and practice, overseen by judges from similarly un-diverse communities, passing judgment on persons who do not look like them, speak their language, or share their culture, values, or experiences.

The purposeful employment of a more diverse judiciary and the deliberate development of court processes that incorporate tikanga Māori protocols and practices may not go far enough for some in addressing the national shame of Māori over-criminalisation and hyper-incarceration. These are, however, evidence of a shift towards the development of what Justice Joe Williams has called 'Lex Aotearoa' – a unique jurisprudence and set of structures, practices, and processes that are distinctly of this whenua (territory), in its iteration as a post-colonial nation. Williams describes this birthing of a distinctly local legal tradition that weaves together the whakapapa (the genealogical strands of the different legal traditions of its peoples) with 'Kupe's law' (representing the traditions of tangata whenua) and 'Cook's law' (derived from the laws of the colonisers). 'Lex Aotearoa' is their child, conceived from Te Tiriti o Waitangi as their point of contact and consummation (Williams, 2013). The next wero or challenge is to strengthen the legal and political foundations upon which these developments sit, to ensure their stability and long-term viability. To paraphrase Justice Williams, it is our responsibility as 'Aotearoans' to rise up to those demands.

STUDY QUESTIONS

- How does the development of solution-focused courts challenge the orthodox approach to the disposition of legal cases? Are those challenges justified in your view?
- How does the diversification of New Zealand's judiciary contribute to the development of our legal system?
- What sources of law, national and international, support the development of a parallel justice system for Māori in Aotearoa New Zealand?

FURTHER READING

Quince, K. (2015). Therapeutic jurisprudence and Māori. In W. Brookbanks (Ed.), *Therapeutic jurisprudence: New Zealand perspectives* (pp. 347–363). Wellington, New Zealand: Thomson Reuters.

Wexler, D. (1990). *Therapeutic jurisprudence: The law as a therapeutic agent.* Durham, NC: Carolina Academic Press.

Williams, J. (2013). Lex Aotearoa: An heroic attempt to map the Māori dimension of modern New Zealand law. *Waikato Law Review, 21*, 1–34.

NOTES

1 A core aspect of the doctrine of *stare decisis* is that a judge should follow precedent when making a decision, unless there is good reason not to do so.
2 See https://www.districtcourts.govt.nz/
3 Due to space limitations, not all specialist courts are mentioned here. For example, I have not described the operation of the Family Violence Court.

REFERENCES

Allison, S., & Boyer, T. (2019). *Evaluation of the Sexual Violence Court pilot*. Wellington, New Zealand: Gravitas Research and Strategy Limited. Retrieved from https://www.districtcourts.govt.nz/reports-publications-and-statistics/publications/sexual-violence-court-pilot-evaluation-report/

Arrigo, B. (2004). The ethics of therapeutic jurisprudence: A critical and theoretical enquiry of law, psychology and crime. *Psychiatry, Psychology and the Law, 11*(1), 23–43. doi:10.1375/pplt.2004.11.1.23

Auckland Homeless Steering Group. (2012). *A report on the progress of Te Kooti o Timatanga Hou – The Court of New Beginnings*. Retrieved from https://www.lifewise.org.nz/wp-content/uploads/2016/01/homeless-court-evaluation.pdf

Brookbanks, W., & Woodward, K. (2007). Alternatives to the traditional trial process. In J. Tolmie & W. Brookbanks (Eds.), *Criminal justice in New Zealand* (pp. 333–358). Wellington, New Zealand: LexisNexis.

Chief District Court Judge. (2019, August 14). *Sexual Violence Court pilot: Evaluation confirms model reduces trial lead-up times and trauma* [Press release]. *Scoop Politics*. Retrieved from https://www.scoop.co.nz/stories/PO1908/S00195/sexual-violence-court-reduces-lead-up-times-and-trauma.htm

Chief Victims Advisor to Government. (2019). *Strengthening the criminal justice system for victims: Te Tangi o te Manawanui recommendations for reform*. Wellington, New Zealand: Ministry of Justice. Retrieved from https://www.safeandeffectivejustice.govt.nz/news/latest-news/chief-victims-advisor-releases-te-tangi-o-te-manawanui-recommendations-for-reform/

Cleland, A., & Quince, K. (2014). *Youth justice in Aotearoa New Zealand*. Wellington, New Zealand: LexisNexis.

Cunneen, C. (2015). Restorative justice? A critical analysis. In B. Goldsen & J. Muncie (Eds.), *Youth, crime and justice* (2nd ed., pp. 137–156). London, UK: Sage Publications.

Cunneen, C., & Tauri, J. M. (2016). *Indigenous criminology*. Bristol, UK: Polity Press.

District Court of New Zealand. (2013). *Matariki Court: Matariki – huarahi ki te oranga tangata*. Retrieved from www.districtcourts.govt.nz/criminal-court/specialist-criminal-courts/matariki-court

Jackson, M. (1988). *The Maori and the criminal justice system: A new perspective: He whaipaanga hou: Part 2*. Wellington, New Zealand: Policy Research Division, Department of Justice. Retrieved from https://www2.justice.govt.nz/website-documents/maori-and-the-criminal-justice-system-a-new-perspective-p2.pdf

Lunt, L. W. (2017). *Preserving the dignity of the mentally unwell: Therapeutic opportunities for the criminal courts of New Zealand*. Wellington, New Zealand: Fulbright New Zealand/Ian Axford Fellowships in Public Policy. Retrieved from https://www.fulbright.org.nz/wp-content/uploads/2017/08/LUNT-Preserving-the-Dignity-of-the-Mentally-Unwell-Therapeutic-Opportunities-for-the-Criminal-Courts-of-New-Zealand-.pdf

McManus, J. (2019, October 18). *Time for transformation, says Chief Judge Taumaunu*. ADLS [Auckland District Law Society]. Retrieved from https://www.adls.org.nz/for-the-profession/news-and-opinion/2019/10/18/time-for-transformation,-says-chief-judge-taumaunu/

Mikaere, A. (2011). *Colonising myths: Māori realities – he rukuruku whakaaro*. Wellington, New Zealand: Huia Publishers & Te Wānanga o Raukawa.

Ministry of Justice. (2016). *Final process evaluation for the Alcohol and Other Drug Treatment Court Te Whare Whakapiki Wairua*. Auckland, New Zealand: Litmus. Retrieved from https://www.justice.govt.nz/assets/Documents/Publications/FINAL-AODT-Court-final-process-evaluation–20160818.pdf

New Zealand Law Commission. (2004). *Delivering justice for all: A vision for New Zealand courts and tribunals* [NZLC Report 85]. Retrieved from http://www.nzlii.org/nz/other/nzlc/report/R85/R85.pdf

New Zealand Law Commission. (2015). *The justice response to victims of sexual violence: Criminal trials and alternative processes* [NZLC Report 136]. Retrieved from https://www.lawcom.govt.nz/sites/default/files/projectAvailableFormats/NZLC-R136-The-Justice-Response-to-Victims-of-Sexual-Violence.pdf

Quince, K. (2007a). Māori disputes and their resolution. In P. Spiller (Ed.), *Dispute resolution in New Zealand* (2nd ed., pp. 256–294). Victoria, Australia: Oxford University Press.

Quince, K. (2007b). Māori and the criminal justice system. In J. Tolmie & W. Brookbanks (Eds.), *Criminal justice in New Zealand* (pp. 333–358). Wellington, New Zealand: LexisNexis.

Te Uepū Hāpai i te Ora – Safe and Effective Justice Programme Advisory Group. (2019). *He waka roimata: Transforming our criminal justice system*. Wellington, New Zealand: Ministry of Justice. Retrieved from https://www.safeandeffectivejustice.govt.nz/about-this-work/te-uepu-report/

Thom, K. (2017). Exploring Te Whare Whakapiki Wairua: Theory, practice and known outcomes. *New Zealand Criminal Law Review*, 180–193.

Webb, R. (2018). Rethinking the utility of the risk factors and criminogenic needs approaches in Aotearoa New Zealand. *Journal of Global Indigeneity*, 3(1), 1–21. Retrieved from https://ro.uow.edu.au/jgi/vol3/iss1/5/

Wexler, D. (1990). *Therapeutic jurisprudence: The law as therapeutic agent*. Durham, NC: Carolina Academic Press.

Williams, J. (2013). Lex Aotearoa: An heroic attempt to map the Māori dimension of modern New Zealand law. *Waikato Law Review*, 21, 1–34.

17

Sentencing
From Parity to Problem-solving

James C. Oleson

> *'Sentencing involves the imposition of a punishment by a court upon a defendant who has been found guilty of, or confessed to, a violation of the criminal law.'*
> —James C. Oleson (2017, p. 363)

Sentencing is at least as old as the Code of Hammurabi (~1700 BCE) and, for most of this history, punishments were usually corporal and often capital – encompassing amputation, burning, boiling, branding, crucifixion, decapitation, drawing-and-quartering, hanging, poisoning, scarring, and stoning (Oleson, 2002). Many countries still retain corporal/capital punishments: for example, caning is still employed in Singapore, and lethal injection is still imposed in many US states. The use of confinement as punishment is a relatively recent phenomenon, and did not become commonplace until 1750–1850 (Foucault, 1977).

Aotearoa New Zealand does not have a death penalty. Capital punishment was abolished in 1989, which means that the most serious crimes are punished with imprisonment (up to and including life imprisonment). But New Zealand *does* punish many of its crimes with imprisonment, and *does* incarcerate many of its offenders for lengthy terms of confinement. New Zealand authorises preventive detention and also administers a three-strikes law. New Zealand has higher incarceration rates than Anglophone countries like Australia, Canada, England, Ireland, Northern Ireland, Scotland, and Wales (Walmsley, 2019). Māori and Pasifika defendants are disproportionately entangled in the criminal justice system, as both victims and offenders.

This chapter first outlines the goals of sentencing, with particular attention to the philosophies of deterrence, incapacitation, rehabilitation, and retribution. It then briefly describes the kinds of sentence that are available to New Zealand judges. Next, it examines the problem of sentencing disparity – in which like offenders receive *unlike* punishments – and identifies three solutions that have been used to help to control disparity: mandatory sentencing, sentencing guidelines, and evidence-based sentencing. Finally, it describes the emergence of problem-solving courts and discusses the pilot testing of alcohol and other drug treatment courts in New Zealand.

GOALS OF SENTENCING

During sentencing, judges weigh a number of competing objectives, but four goals comprise the philosophical cornerstones: deterrence, incapacitation, rehabilitation, and retribution. The first three are consequentialist in nature, which means they focus upon reducing future crimes. Retribution, on the other hand, is a non-consequentialist, retrospective theory of punishment, focusing on punishment deserved for previous conduct. The consequentialist and non-consequentialist foundations of punishment can be merged, such as through limited retributivism. Here, the upper and lower limits of punishment are set on the basis of retributivism, then a penalty is selected within that range on the basis of utilitarian concerns (Morris, 1982). Often, however, the two approaches to punishment are incongruous; Shaw (1932) pointed to the unavoidable tension between rehabilitation and retribution: '[I]f you are to punish a man retributively, you must injure him. If you are to reform him, you must improve him. And men are not improved by injuries' (p. 184).

Deterrence

Deterrence is based on the assumption that humans seek to maximise pleasure and minimise pain (Beccaria, 1764/1991; Bentham, 1830/2009). In order to induce people to forgo the pleasures of crime (e.g., taking things without payment or consuming fun-but-illegal drugs), the state must enforce the penalties attached to crimes (Zimring et al., 1973). This threat of punishment is sufficient to deter most people from committing crimes. Deterrence comes in two forms: specific and general. Specific deterrence suggests that if an offender commits a crime and is punished, that individual will be less likely to reoffend. General deterrence is based upon the fact that people learn vicariously; a punishment imposed upon one person can also prevent others from breaking the law.

Incapacitation

Incapacitation is based on the fact that punishment can make it difficult (or impossible) for an offender to commit further crimes (Zimring & Hawkins, 1995). Although excluding offenders from society might actually make them worse in the long run, offenders can be incapacitated by spatially removing them (e.g., exiling or confining them) or by physically eliminating their capacity to offend (e.g., severing the hand of a thief or chemically castrating a sex offender). In New Zealand, curfews operate as a mechanism to remove offenders from society. Capital punishment is the ultimate incapacitant: dead offenders never reoffend.

Rehabilitation

Rehabilitation is rooted in the idea of crime as disease or immorality. If people commit crimes because of inherent defects, one way to reduce future crime is to correct the defect, whether that defect is physical (e.g., chemical imbalance), moral (e.g., wickedness), psychological (e.g., criminal thinking), or social (e.g., association with criminal peers). For much of the twentieth century, rehabilitation was the dominant theory of punishment. However, after Martinson (1974) published an influential article that questioned it as ineffective, rehabilitation nearly disappeared (Cullen, 2005). In recent years, however, rehabilitation has enjoyed a renaissance. The model of risk-need-responsivity (Bonta & Andrews, 2016) for identifying and addressing the causes of criminal behaviour is, at root, a rehabilitative one (see Durrant & Riley, chapter 22 this volume).

Retribution

Retribution (sometimes called 'just deserts') suggests that criminals should be punished because they deserve it, regardless of consequence. '*Fiat justitia ruat caelum*' ('May justice be done though the heavens fall'). Hegel (1952) claimed that punishment rebalances things: when criminals violate laws, they take advantage of society; therefore when society punishes those criminals, it reclaims the right of society. Retribution takes two forms. Negative retributivism requires that only the guilty *may* be punished, and then only to the extent they deserve, but does not require that punishments *must* be imposed. Positive retributivism, on the other hand, requires that the guilty *must* be punished, to the full extent of their desert. The view of positive retributivism was famously articulated by Kant (1797/2002), who argued that even if an island society was about to disband, the last murderers lying in its prisons must be put to death. Society not only has a *right* to punish them, but also enjoys an affirmative *duty* to do so.

Other sentencing goals

Although deterrence, incapacitation, rehabilitation, and retribution operate as the principal ends of sentencing, they are not the only objectives. Feinberg's (1965) expressive theory of punishment suggests that sentences communicate moral opprobrium to offenders, relating social attitudes about criminal behaviour. In this vein, sentences reinforce legal norms, enhance respect for the law, and provide catharsis for crime victims. In New Zealand, the Sentencing Act 2002 – a 236-page law – governs sentencing decisions. Section 7 specifies eight discrete goals of sentencing. None of the eight is any more important than the others, and judges are free to draw upon them singly or in any combination. Thus, in New Zealand, sentences are imposed:

- to hold the offender accountable for harm done to the victim and the community by the offending;
- to promote in the offender a sense of responsibility for, and an acknowledgment of, that harm;
- to provide for the interests of the victim of the offence;
- to provide reparation for harm done by the offending;
- to denounce the conduct in which the offender was involved;
- to deter the offender or other persons from committing the same or a similar offence;
- to protect the community from the offender; or
- to assist in the offender's rehabilitation and reintegration.

These goals guide judges in deciding an appropriate sentence for a given offence. Although reparation, victims' rights, and rehabilitation are equally weighted with deterrence and incapacitation, New Zealand's high levels of incarceration might suggest that repressive mechanisms trump restorative ones.

TYPES OF SENTENCES

New Zealand judges are limited by the maximum penalties articulated within the Crimes Act 1961. For example, under the crimes against the person provisions of the Act, the maximum penalty for common assault is one year of imprisonment (s. 196); for kidnapping it is 14 years (s. 209); for rape, 20 years (ss. 128–128B); and the maximum penalty for manslaughter (s. 177) and murder (s. 172) is life imprisonment. Other offence types (e.g., crimes against public order, crimes affecting the administration of law and justice, or crimes against rights of property) also provide maximum punishments.

Within the limits of these maximum penalties, and guided by the eight sentencing goals of the Sentencing Act 2002, judges have the ability to tailor their sentences across a hierarchy of sentences. Section 10A of the Sentencing Act identifies six different, increasingly restrictive levels of sentences (see Gibbs, chapter 19 this volume, for further information on how these sentences are applied in New Zealand):

- Discharge or order the offender to come up for sentence if called on: This can be a discharge without conviction (acquittal); a conviction and discharge (releasing the defendant after documenting the conviction); or an order to come up for sentence if called upon (suspending the sentence).
- Sentences of a fine and reparation: A fine is a financial penalty imposed to achieve the purposes of sentencing (e.g., deterrence), while reparation is the offender's restoration of the victim's loss.
- Community-based sentences of community work and supervision: Imposing a term of hours of community work (usually for hospitals, churches, cultural institutions, local authorities, or in training) or a period of supervision under the authority of a probation officer – people sentenced to community supervision must abide by a set of standard conditions and, depending upon the offender and the offence, can also be subject to special conditions. Community-based sentences usually incorporate elements of reparation, rehabiliation, and incapacitation (via surveillance of the offender by community members or probation officers).
- Community-based sentences of intensive supervision and community detention: Intensive supervision is similar to general community supervision, but involves heightened levels of monitoring (sometimes including electronic monitoring) (Tonry & Lynch, 1996); community detention involves abiding by a set of imposed curfews. Incapacitation is therefore more central.
- Sentence of home detention: House arrest is a still more restrictive form of community detention; the offender must remain in an approved residence for the term of detention, and can leave only in the case of emergency or with a probation officer's approval.
- Sentence of imprisonment: Confinement in a prison for a period of time imposed by the judge, with possible further restrictions on parole eligibility; most prison sentences are determinate (set for a fixed period of years), but some (e.g., life imprisonment or preventive detention) are said to be indeterminate. Prison-based penalties are designed to ensure very high levels of incapacitation and control, though prison officials usually seek rehabilitative goals.

In addition to these basic categories of sentence, judges are free to order defendants to pay for court costs or reparation. They also can issue forfeiture orders, seizing the proceeds of crime. The New Zealand government has identified forfeiture as a particularly important tool in the fight against organised crime. For crimes involving motor vehicles, judges can disqualify offenders from driving and/or confiscate their vehicles. Judges can impose non-association orders (prohibiting offenders from associating either with specific people – 'John Smith' – or with members of a group – 'ex-prisoners' or 'patched gang members') and protection orders (used to protect victims in domestic violence cases). The potential permutations are nearly endless. In crafting appropriate sentences, judges consider the totality of the offending, weigh the interests of the defendant and the victim(s), consider the goals of sentencing, and impose a sentence consistent within the limits of the Crimes Act 1961.

Preventive detention

In some cases, defendants pose 'a significant and ongoing risk' to the safety of the members of the community (Sentencing Act 2002, s. 87(1)). If such defendants are convicted of a qualifying sexual or violent offence, if they were 18 or older at the time of the offence, and if the judge believes they are likely to commit another qualifying offence, these offender can be sentenced to indefinite terms of preventive detention. The prophylactic logic of preventive detention lies closer to that of quarantine than traditional punishment (which is usually, in part, retributive). When imposing sentences of preventive detention, New Zealand judges must also specify minimum prison terms (at least five years).

SENTENCING DISPARITY

New Zealand judges enjoy broad discretion. This allows them to tailor individualised sentences that account for the particular characteristics of the offender and the facts of the crime in what has been called an 'instinctive synthesis' (Edney & Bagaric, 2007, p. 15). This discretion, however, means that two identical defendants, possessing equivalent criminal histories and guilty of identical crimes, could serve different sentences. One offender, sentenced by a merciful judge, might receive probation, while an identical offender, sentenced by a retributivist judge, might receive a prison term (Harrison, 1992; Kramer, 2016). But, because both sentences fall within the terms of the Sentencing Act 2002, neither sentence would be 'wrong'. Of course, even offenders who receive the same nominal sentences ultimately serve subjectively different terms of incarceration (Kolber, 2009).

Disparity becomes especially problematic when impermissible factors influence sentencing decisions. For example, research indicates that parole decisions made when decision-makers are rested (at the beginning of the day or after a meal break) are statistically more favourable than decisions made after reviewing cases without a break (Danzinger et al., 2011). Similarly, even after controlling for legal and relevant non-legal variables, being remanded in custody before trial can, itself, be positively and significantly correlated with conviction, incarceration, and sentence length (e.g., Oleson et al., 2014; Philips, 2012). Socio-economic class produces disparite access to justice, with downstream differences in sentencing. Moreover, indigeneity is an especially important issue in New Zealand criminal justice: Māori constitute about 16 per cent of the general population, but 57 per cent of the adult prison population (Te Uepū Hāpai i te Ora, 2019). Whether this is a function of direct or indirect discrimination remains an unsettled question. In light of such over-representation, Jackson (1988) called for the establishment of a separate criminal justice system for Māori more than three decades ago.

Plea bargaining (charge negotiation) is yet another source of sentencing disparity. Although judges ultimately impose criminal sentences, prosecutors enjoy wide discretion over which charges to file (and which facts to prove). In exchange for guilty pleas, prosecutors may reduce the number of charges against the defendant, charge a less serious crime, or amend the summary of facts upon which the charge is based. Defenders of plea bargaining typically cite its efficiency (e.g., pleas save money and time, and avert the hardships of trials). In practice, New Zealand defendants who plead guilty receive a 'sentencing discount' of approximately 25–33 per cent

(Edney & Bagaric, 2007). However, opponents criticise the unscrutinised nature of such negotiations, arguing that it leads prosecutors (and police prosecutors) to overcharge defendants so they can better negotiate downward. It also leads to the punishment of innocent persons (Blume & Helm, 2014). Finally, because plea bargaining turns upon negotiation skills, not just facts, it leads to disparity. Thus, as Willis (1985) observes, 'the final product after allowing for the guilty plea is not the appropriate sentence according to traditional penological criteria' (p. 143).

Mandatory sentencing

Mandatory sentences (including mandatory non-parole periods) provide one robust method of restricting judicial discretion. Beccaria (1764/1991) and Bentham (1830/2009) both advocated this approach, suggesting that once the law is written, the role of the judge should be limited, so as not to be swayed by personal prejudices. Certainly, mandatory penalties increase certainty, consistency, and transparency in sentencing. Mandatory penalties can operate as either fixed or minimum sentences. Sometimes, a particular penalty is specified for a given crime, such as mandatory life imprisonment for treason in New Zealand. More often, however, mandatory minimum sentences operate as sentencing 'floors'. Judges typically still enjoy the discretion to impose *higher* sentences (up to the limits authorised by law), but cannot impose a sentence *below* the statutory minimum, regardless of the considerations that might prompt them to do so.

Presumptive penalties (mandatories but with safety-valve mechanisms) are another, less rigid means of pursuing uniformity in sentencing. In New Zealand, for example, murder is punished by life imprisonment, unless manifest injustice would result. These presumptive and mandatory sentences are popular with politicians and useful to prosecutors, but they are widely criticised by scholars and jurists (e.g., Tonry, 1992) as blunt and inflexible tools capable of producing unjust outcomes.

'Three-strikes' laws are a form of mandatory sentencing that focuses upon criminal history (enhancing sentences for recidivists). These laws present an interesting jurisprudential puzzle, since increasing penalties on the basis of previous convictions subverts traditional legal prohibitions against double jeopardy (trying defendants who have been acquitted or convicted on the same facts), retroactivity (punishing defendants for conduct that was not criminal at the time), and status crimes (punishing defendants on the basis of group membership, such as race or prior convictions) (White, 2006). That being said, habitual felon laws enjoy a long history, extending back to sixteenth-century England.

In New Zealand, the Habitual Criminals Act 1906 authorised indefinite incarceration of three-time felons, but this law had fallen into disuse by the 1950s. In 2010, however, inspired by California's notorious three-strikes legislation (Zimring et al., 2001) and championed by the Sensible Sentencing Trust, New Zealand introduced a new three-strike regime for 40 qualifying offences. Upon conviction for a qualifying non-murder offence, a first-strike warning is added to the offender's record. Upon a second strike (the final warning), the offender must serve the entire sentence imposed by the judge, without parole. Upon a third strike, the offender must serve the maximum penalty under law, and the judge may impose a lesser sentence only if the failure to do so would result in manifest injustice. Although three-strikes legislation was enacted as a tool to punish the 'worst of the worst', many of the three-strikes crimes that have reached the courts have been middle-of-the-road. Consequently, the defendants sanctioned under New Zealand's legislation closely resemble the general prison population: they tend to be young, male, and disproportionately Māori and Pasifika (Oleson, 2015). In August 2018, the first defendant to receive the maximum penalty under the three-strikes law was sentenced to seven years' imprisonment for stabbing a man in the leg. Leading commentators have concluded that the three-strikes law lacks a sound rationale and fails in its stated purpose (Brookbanks, 2016); at the time of writing, the Labour government has committed to repealing the law.

Sentencing guidelines

Sentencing guidelines are one mechanism to cabin sentencing discretion without resorting to mandatory or presumptive sentences. They assume different forms. One approach is to employ a two-dimensional grid, where one axis identifies the range of offences, from least to most serious, while the other axis identifies the range of criminal history, from those with no criminal record to those with extensive records. At the intersection of the appropriate row and column, judges find the corresponding sentencing range. Judges may choose to depart upward or downward from the specified sentence when special circumstances are present, but, as a general matter, the guideline range is presumed to be the correct sentence. Like mandatory sentences, grid systems enhance predictability and transparency (e.g., reducing regional variation in punishments: see Goodall & Durrant, 2013), but shift discretion from courts to prosecutors and, through their rigidity, produce miscarriages of justice. They can also be complicated, leading to calculation and application errors (Oleson, 2011): the US Federal Sentencing Guidelines grid has 43 offence levels and 6 criminal history categories.

A second approach, adopted most enthusiastically in New South Wales but employed also in New Zealand, relates to the issuance of advisory judgments, usually by courts of appeal, as authoritative guidance for lower courts (Buchanan, 2014). Like grid sentencing, they are intended to improve consistency and predictability while leaving room for individualised justice. These opinions are not binding or formal precedent, but provide reliable information to trial courts. In New Zealand, guideline judgments typically consist of a review of the past sentences imposed for a particular offence. Using these past cases, the Court of Appeal articulates guideline ranges, also identifying common features of the offence to guide trial judges when locating individual cases within the range. Of course, if advisory judgments operate as *de facto* legislation, courts might be overstepping their role and usurping the role of Parliament when they issue guidelines (see *Wong v R*).[1] These considerations, among others, prompted the New Zealand Law Commission (2006) to recommend the formation of a sentencing council, rather than issue piecemeal guidance through the Court of Appeal. That recommendation, however, was not adopted.

Evidence-based sentencing

Some courts are beginning to explore the possibility of algorithmic justice or 'evidence-based sentencing', an actuarial approach that uses risk prediction measures to guide sentencing (Oleson, 2020). Research indicates that statistical assessments generally outperform the clinical judgement of even trained experts (Meehl, 1954). For this reason, risk assessment instruments have become ubiquitous in community corrections, and are frequently used to determine the appropriate conditions of probation or parole. In recent years, judges have asked whether risk instruments might also be employed at sentencing (e.g., Kopf, 2015). Might these instruments provide judges with valuable information, in the way that sentencing guidelines provide judges with relevant indicators? After all, if actuarial instruments can distinguish recidivists from those who will not reoffend, then law enforcement resources can be reinvested elsewhere, improving justice and minimising crime. Artificial intelligence and machine learning might play a role, as well. High-risk individuals might be incapacitated for longer periods and/or provided with interventions that reduce criminal propensities, while low-risk defendants (who can be made worse by excessive supervision: see Lowenkamp & Latessa, 2004) might receive non-custodial punishments. It is a promising ideal, especially to policy-makers told to ensure public safety with declining resources (Oleson, 2011), but critics characterise evidence-based sentencing as 'new profiling' and warn of its potential to mislead, reify bias and disparity, and criminalise poverty (e.g., Hannah-Moffat, 2015; Harcourt, 2015; Starr, 2015). Without question, evidence-based sentencing advances criminal justice one step closer to the 'new penology' (Feeley & Simon, 1992), replacing traditional judicial goals of deterrence and rehabilitation with the actuarial management of 'risky' populations.

Despite criticism from scholars around the world, evidence-based sentencing is attracting serious attention in Australia and New Zealand. In February 2016, the New Zealand justice minister introduced a new initiative in which actuarial models would draw upon Statistics New Zealand's Integrated Data Infrastructure (linking justice, tax, and social benefit information) to forecast recidivism as well as benefit-dependence outcomes during sentencing (Jones, 2016). *Should* judges consider financial costs when sentencing? *Should* reliance on state benefits influence one's punishment? The ethical implications of New Zealand's new actuarial endeavour are profound.

PROBLEM-SOLVING COURTS

As noted above, much of the current innovation in sentencing relates to guiding judicial discretion so that sentences are consistent but simultaneously tailored to the specifics of the defendant and the crime. Mandatory and presumptive sentencing, sentencing guidelines, and information from sentencing councils all attempt to strike that balance. But another parallel evolution in sentencing is taking place. Problem-solving courts are being established in Aotearoa New Zealand, as in other jurisdictions around the world (Oleson, 2016).

During the late 1980s, drug trafficking strained Florida's criminal courts beyond capacity. Dockets were congested, courtrooms were plea-bargaining mills, and prisons were crowded. To address these problems, the first drug court was developed in Dade County in 1989. It centred on a monitoring judge and recast courtroom adversaries as collaborative team members. Teams mobilised to make treatment services available. Random drug-testing of volunteering participants was undertaken frequently, and drug treatment was part of case management. Relapse was understood as inevitable. Graduated rewards and sanctions encouraged progress and inhibited misconduct. Elements of harm reduction, therapeutic jurisprudence (Winick & Wexler, 2003),[2] and procedural justice (Tyler, 1988) were all evident, even if not deliberately incorporated.[3] Volunteers entered the programme prior to pleading; prosecution was deferred while the defendant participated and, if the defendant successfully completed the programme, the prosecution was dropped.

Today, the drug court model has gone mainstream. It is a 'movement'. There are more than 4100 drug court treatment programmes in the United States (National Drug Court Resource Center, 2020). Of course, critics of drug courts have identified problems with the model, including cherry picking (selecting low-risk offenders for programme participation to boost success rates), net widening (forcing defendants who would have otherwise been released with a mere caution or informal sanction to satisfy the onerous requirements of drug court), and failure penalties (subjecting defendants who fail out of drug court to longer sentences than those who did not attempt drug court) (e.g., Justice Policy Institute, 2011). Other critics have condemned drug courts' willingness to approach 'drug use as a crime and as a disease, without coming to grips with the inherent contradictions of those two approaches' (Hoffman, 2000, p. 1477), but these concerns have not prevented drug and problem-solving courts from flourishing. Drug court practitioners have identified 10 key components that are integral to success (National Association of Drug Court Professionals, 2004), and drug courts have been identified as an evidence-based practice, reducing recidivism in adults from approximately 50 per cent to approximately 38 per cent (Mitchell et al., 2012).[4] Despite increased front-end costs, the Washington State Institute for Public Policy (2013) reported that every dollar invested in drug courts saved $3.38 in criminal justice costs.

Thus, in New Zealand, two pilot Alcohol and Other Drug Treatment Courts (AODTCs) were launched in November 2012. The Auckland and Waitākere AODTCs were described by Litmus Limited in three early evaluation reports published in 2014, 2015, and 2016; then, in December 2019, Minister of Justice Andrew Little announced that the AODTCs would be made permanent and augmented by a third, Hamilton-based AODTC. After two years, AODTC participants were approximately 23 per cent less likely to recidivate and 35 per cent less likely to commit a serious crime than matched offenders. These promising initial gains, however, appear to decline over time: after four years, there were no significant decreases (Ministry of Justice, 2019).

There are already other problem-solving courts – drug courts, family violence courts, mental health courts, community justice courts, and homelessness courts – operating across Australia and New Zealand (Richardson et al., 2013). Just as mandatory sentencing, sentencing guidelines, and sentencing councils might enhance parity in the exercise of judicial discretion, so might drug courts serve as a foundation for the incorporation of problem-solving principles into the wider criminal justice system (Freiberg, 2005).

CONCLUSION

It is often said that sentencing is the hardest thing judges do (Oleson, 2011). Finding the appropriate balance between the interests of the defendant, the victim, and society is difficult, and attending to the particular facts of the crime and individual characteristics of the defendant while avoiding disparity can be impossible. Lawmakers have introduced a variety of measures to reduce disparity, including mandatory sentencing, sentencing guidelines grids, and advisory judgments. But these solutions present their own challenges, such as oversimplifying a three-dimensional human being into a point on a two-dimensional grid (Luna, 2005), or compromising the separation of powers by engaging the courts in de facto lawmaking (see *Wong v R*). There are also questions about the propriety of therapeutic courts. Although problem-solving courts, such as New Zealand's AODTCs, are hailed as cost-cutting, evidence-based practices, critics insist that recognition of addiction as a disease is incommensurate with treating it as a crime (Hoffman, 2000).

The future of sentencing is uncertain. Perhaps courts will use MRI brain scans to tailor the subjective experience of punishment to individual offenders (Kolber, 2009). More likely, at least in some jurisdictions, courts will employ risk algorithms to engage in actuarial, evidence-based sentencing (Oleson, 2020). Although most of the variables included in evidence-based sentencing are already included in pre-sentence reports, the explicit incorporation of race, sex, age, class, marital status, and employment status into criminal sentencing decisions raises numerous jurisprudential, practical, and ethical questions.

STUDY QUESTIONS

- Some of the factors that might increase the risk of future crime – for example, poverty, criminal family members, or impulsivity – simultaneously imply a lower level of blameworthiness, since the crime that results is less freely chosen. If a judge believes in both utilitarian and retributive bases of punishment, how can a judge usefully weigh these factors?

- Should New Zealand introduce a system of evidence-based sentencing? Proponents suggest it can eliminate unnecessary punishment and reduce costs, but critics warn about dangers of bias and discrimination.

- Drug courts are recognised as an evidence-based practice, producing substantial reductions in recidivism and therefore criminal justice costs. But critics argue that drug courts are inconsistent with the role of traditional criminal courts. Is it contradictory for judges to treat drug addiction as a disease but, simultaneously, to treat it as a crime?

FURTHER READING

Fuller, L. L. (1949). The case of the speluncean explorers. *Harvard Law Review, 62*(4), 616–645. doi:10.2307/1336025

Tolmie, J., & Brookbanks, W. J. (Eds). (2007). *Criminal justice in New Zealand*. Wellington, New Zealand: LexisNexis.

Von Hirsch, A. (1986). *Past or future crimes: Deservedness and dangerousness in the sentencing of criminals*. Manchester, UK: Manchester University Press.

NOTES

1. *Wong v R* [2001] 207 CLR 584.
2. Therapeutic jurisprudence references the extent to which substantive rules, legal procedures, and the roles of lawyers and judges produce therapeutic (or non-therapeutic) consequences.
3. Procedural justice suggests that the perceived procedural fairness of the government (e.g., trial processes), more than the desirability of ultimate outcomes (e.g., winning a case), leads citizens to accept government authority as legitimate.
4. The 10 key components:
   1. Drug courts integrate alcohol and other drug treatment services with justice system case-processing.
   2. Using a non-adversarial approach, prosecution and defence counsel promote public safety while protecting participants' due process rights.
   3. Eligible participants are identified early and promptly placed in the drug court programme.
   4. Drug courts provide access to a continuum of alcohol, drug, and other related treatment and rehabilitation services.
   5. Abstinence is monitored by frequent alcohol and other drug testing.
   6. A co-ordinated strategy governs drug court responses to participants' compliance.
   7. Ongoing judicial interaction with each drug court participant is essential.
   8. Monitoring and evaluation measure the achievement of programme goals and gauge effectiveness.
   9. Continuing interdisciplinary education promotes effective drug court planning, implementation, and operations.
   10. Forging partnerships among drug courts, public agencies, and community-based organisations generates local support and enhances drug court programme effectiveness.

REFERENCES

Beccaria, C. (1991/1764). *An essay on crimes and punishments* (with a commentary by Voltaire). Birmingham, AL: Legal Classics Library.

Bentham, J. (2009/1830). *The rationale of punishment.* Amherst, NY: Prometheus Books

Blume, J. H., & Helm, R. K. (2014). The unexonerated: Factually innocent defendants who plead guilty. *Cornell Law Review, 100,* 157–191. doi:10.2139/ssrn.2103787

Bonta, J., & Andrews, D. A. (2016). *The psychology of criminal conduct* (6th ed.). New York, NY: Routledge.

Brookbanks, W. J. (2016). Three strikes: New Zealand's experience. *Journal of International and Comparative Law, 3*(2), 249–278. Retrieved from http://www.jicl.org.uk/pdf13/3-2-4.pdf

Buchanan, K. (2014). *Sentencing guidelines: Australia.* Washington, DC: Law Library of Congress. Retrieved from https://www.loc.gov/law/help/sentencing-guidelines/australia.php

Cullen, F. T. (2005). The twelve people who saved rehabilitation: How the science of criminology made a difference. *Criminology, 43*(1), 1–42. doi:10.1111/j.0011–1348.2005.00001.x

Danziger, S., Levav, J., & Avnaim-Pesso, L. (2011). Extraneous factors in judicial decisions. *Proceedings of the National Academy of Sciences, 108*(17), 6889–6892. doi:10.1073/pnas.1018033108

Edney, R., & Bagaric, M. (2007). *Australian sentencing: Principles and practice.* New York, NY: Cambridge University Press.

Feeley, M., & Simon, J. (1992). The new penology: Notes on the emerging strategy of corrections and its implications. *Criminology, 30*(4), 449–474. doi:10.1111/j.1745–9125.1992.tb01112.x

Feinberg, J. (1965). The expressive function of punishment. *Monist, 49*(3) 397–423. doi:10.5840/monist196549326

Foucault, M. (1977). *Discipline and punish: The birth of the prison* (A. Sheridan, Trans.). New York, NY: Viking Press.

Freiberg, A. (2005). Problem-oriented courts: An update. *Journal of Judicial Administration, 14,* 196–219. Retrieved from https://research.monash.edu/en/publications/problem-oriented-courts-an-update

Goodall, W., & Durrant, R. (2013). Regional variation in sentencing: The incarceration of aggravated drink drivers in the New Zealand District Courts. *Australian and New Zealand Journal of Criminology, 46*(3), 422–447. doi:10.1177/0004865813483295

Hannah-Moffat, K. (2015). The uncertainties of risk assessment: Partiality, transparency, and just decisions. *Federal Sentencing Reporter, 27*(4), 244–247. doi:10.1525/fsr.2015.27.4.244

Harcourt, B. E. (2015). Risk as a proxy for race: The dangers of risk assessment. *Federal Sentencing Reporter, 27*(4), 237–243. doi:10.1525/fsr.2015.27.4.237

Harrison, R. (1992). The equality of mercy. In H. Gross & R. Harrison (Eds.), *Jurisprudence: Cambridge essays* (pp. 107–125). Oxford, UK: Clarendon Press.

Hegel, G. (1952/1820). *Philosophy of right* (T. M. Knox, Trans.). Oxford, UK: Clarendon Press.

Hoffman, M. B. (2000). The drug court scandal. *North Carolina Law Review, 78,* 1437–1534. Retrieved from https://scholarship.law.unc.edu/nclr/vol78/iss5/5/

Jackson, M. (1988). *The Maori and the criminal justice system: A new perspective: He whaipaanga hou: Part 2* (Study series 18). Wellington, New Zealand: Policy and Research Division, Department of Justice. Retrieved from https://www2.justice.govt.nz/website-documents/maori-and-the-criminal-justice-system-a-new-perspective-p2.pdf

Jones, N. (2016, February 26). Courts to get high-tech help for sentencing. *New Zealand Herald.* Retrieved from https://www.nzherald.co.nz/nz/news/article.cfm?c_id=1&objectid=11595639

Justice Policy Institute. (2011). *Addicted to courts: How a growing dependence on drug courts impacts people and communities.* Washington, DC: Justice Policy Institute. Retrieved from http://www.justicepolicy.org/research/2217?utm_source=%2fdrugcourts&utm_medium=web&utm_campaign=redirect

Kant, I. (2002/1797). *The philosophy of law* (W. Hastie, Trans.). Union, NJ: Lawbook Exchange.

Kolber, A. J. (2009). The subjective experience of punishment. *Columbia Law Review, 109*, 182–236. Retrieved from https://pdfs.semanticscholar.org/4884/8f180e6060d54ac1221f849aa9adf1d8b232.pdf?_ga=2.242860994.1965472539.1580699677–61367471.1580699677

Kopf, R. G. (2015). Federal supervised release and actuarial data (including age, race, and gender): The camel's nose and the use of actuarial data at sentencing. *Federal Sentencing Reporter, 27*(4), 207–215. doi:10.1525/fsr.2015.27.4.207

Kramer, R. (2016). Differential punishment of similar behaviour: Sentencing assault cases in a specialized family violence court and 'regular sentencing' courts. *British Journal of Criminology, 56*(4), 689–708. doi:10.1093/bjc/azv064

Lowenkamp, C. T., & Latessa, E. J. (2004). Understanding the risk principle: How and why correctional interventions can harm low-risk offenders. *Topics in Community Corrections*, 3–8. Washington, DC: National Institute of Corrections. Retrieved from http://caparc.org/uploads/3/5/2/7/35276822/high_low_risk_article.pdf

Luna, E. (2005). Gridland: An allegorical critique of federal sentencing. *Journal of Criminal Law and Criminology, 96*, 25–106.

Martinson, R. (1974). What works? Questions and answers about prison reform. *Public Interest, 10*, 22–54. Retrieved from https://www.gwern.net/docs/sociology/1974-martinson.pdf

Meehl, P. E. (1954). *Clinical versus mechanical prediction*. Minneapolis, MN: University of Minnesota Press.

Ministry of Justice. (2019). *Alcohol and other drug treatment court quantiative outcomes evaluation 2018–19*. Retrieved from https://www.justice.govt.nz/assets/Documents/Publications/AODTC-Quantitative-Outcomes-Evaluation-June–2019.pdf

Mitchell, O., Wilson, D. B., Eggers, A., & MacKenzie, D. L. (2012). Drug courts' effects on criminal offending for juveniles and adults. *Campbell Systematic Reviews, 8*(4), 1–86. doi:10.4073/csr.2012.4

Morris, N. (1982). *Madness and the criminal law*. Chicago, IL: University of Chicago Press.

National Association of Drug Court Professionals. (2004). *Defining drug courts: The key components*. Washington, US: Bureau of Justice Assistance. Retrieved from https://www.ncjrs.gov/pdffiles1/bja/205621.pdf

National Drug Court Resource Center. (2020). *National drug court database & map*. Retrieved from https://ndcrc.org/wp-content/NDCRC_Court_Map/

New Zealand Law Commission. (2006). *Sentencing guidelines and parole reform* (NZLC Report no. 94). Retrieved from https://www.lawcom.govt.nz/sites/default/files/projectAvailableFormats/NZLC%20R94.pdf

Oleson, J. C. (2002). The punitive coma. *California Law Review, 90*(3), 829–901.

Oleson, J. C. (2011). Risk in sentencing: Constitutionally suspect variables and evidence-based sentencing. *SMU Law Review, 64*, 1329–1404.

Oleson, J. C. (2015). Habitual criminal legislation in New Zealand: Three years of three-strikes. *Australian and New Zealand Journal of Criminology, 48*(2), 277–292.

Oleson, J. C. (2016). HOPE springs eternal: New evaluations of deterrence-based sanctioning. *Criminology and Public Policy, 15*(4), 1163–1183. doi:10.1111/1745–9133.12262

Oleson, J. C. (2017). Sentencing theories, practices and trends. In A. Deckert & R. Sarre (Eds.), *Australian and New Zealand handbook of criminology, crime and justice* (pp. 363–377). Cham, Switzerland: Palgrave Macmillan.

Oleson, J. C. (2020). Evidence-based sentencing. *Oxford bibliographies in criminology*, https://www.oxfordbibliographies.com/page/139

Oleson, J. C., VanNostrand, M., Lowenkamp, C. T., Cadigan, T. P., & Wooldredge, J. (2014). Pretrial detention choices and sentencing. *Federal Probation, 78*(1), 12–18.

Philips, M. T. (2012). *A decade of bail research in New York City*. New York, NY: New York City Criminal Justice Agency.

Richardson, E., Thom, K., & McKenna, B. (2013). The evolution of problem-solving courts in Australia and New Zealand: A trans-Tasman comparative perspective. In R. L. Wiener & E. M. Brank

(Eds.), *Problem solving courts: Social science and legal perspectives* (pp. 185–210). New York, NY: Springer.

Shaw, G. B. (1932). Crude criminology. In *The collected works of George Bernard Shaw* (pp. 173–297). New York, NY: William. H. Wise & Co.

Starr, S. (2015). The new profiling: Why punishing based on poverty and identity is unconstitutional and wrong. *Federal Sentencing Reporter, 27*(4), 229–236.

Te Uepū Hāpai i te Ora (2019). *He waka roimata (vessel of tears): Transforming our criminal justice system*. Retrieved from https://safeandeffectivejustice.govt.nz/assets/Uploads/fa55462d44/teuepureport_hewakaroimata.pdf

Tonry, M. (1992). Mandatory penalties. *Crime and Justice, 16*, 243–273. Retrieved from https://www.journals.uchicago.edu/doi/pdfplus/10.1086/449207

Tonry, M., & Lynch, M. (1996). Intermediate sanctions. *Crime and Justice, 20*, 99–144.

Tyler, T. R. (1988). What is procedural justice? Criteria used by citizens to assess the fairness of legal procedures. *Law and Society Review, 22*, 103–135. doi:10.2307/3053563

Walmsley, R. (2019). *World prison population list* (12th ed.). London, UK: Institute for Criminal Policy Research.

Washington State Institute for Public Policy. (2013). *Prison, police, and programs: Evidence-based options that reduce crime and save money* (No. 13–11–1901). Olympia, WA: Washington State Institute for Public Policy. Retrieved from https://www.wsipp.wa.gov/ReportFile/1396/Wsipp_Prison-Police-and-Programs-Evidence-Based-Options-that-Reduce-Crime-and-Save-Money_Full-Report.pdf

White, A. A. (2006). The juridical structure of habitual offender laws and the jurisprudence of authoritarian social control. *University of Toledo Law Review, 37*(3), 705–745.

Willis, J. (1985). The sentencing discount for guilty pleas. *Australian and New Zealand Journal of Criminology, 18*(3), 131–146. doi:10.1177/000486585801800302

Winick, B. J., & Wexler, D. B. (Eds.). (2003). *Judging in a therapeutic key: Therapeutic jurisprudence and the courts*. Durham, NC: Carolina Academic Press.

Zimring, F. E., & Hawkins, G. (1995). *Incapacitation: Penal confinement and the restraint of crime*. New York, NY: Oxford University Press.

Zimring, F. E., Hawkins, G., & Kamin, S. (2001). *Punishment and democracy: Three strikes and you're out in California*. New York, NY: Oxford University Press.

Zimring, F. E., Hawkins, G., & Vorenberg, J. (1973). *Deterrence: The legal threat in crime control*. Chicago, IL: University of Chicago Press.

18

The Youth Justice System
A Site of Evolution and Reform

Nessa Lynch

In 1989, landmark reforming legislation – the Children, Young Persons, and Their Families Act – established new methods of governing youth justice as well as care and protection in Aotearoa New Zealand. It was a lengthy and complex piece of legislation, invoking sometimes competing theoretical frameworks that draw on welfarism (promoting the welfare of children and young people and 'treating' their problems), a justice approach (providing a proportionate sanction to the offence), and the balancing of the rights, needs, and interests of children, family/whānau, and the state.

The 1989 Act was innovative. It explicitly recognised the centrality of the family when dealing with children and young people in conflict with the law, and established that 'family' could entail wider whānau, hapū, and iwi, or the equivalent in that child or young person's culture. The Act also introduced the concept of the family group conference (where the child or young person, their family/whānau, the victim of the offence, state officials, and other interested parties come together to decide on a plan to respond to offending by that child or young person). The Act established a then-innovative principle that victims' interests should be considered in decision-making, and that victims could participate directly in decision-making through the family group conference. The Act also prioritised informal and non-custodial responses, such as warnings, cautions, and police diversion. Even Youth Court matters were to be resolved without use of formal orders where possible. While most of these features are now mirrored in comparable jurisdictions, at the time they were revolutionary (Morris & Maxwell, 1993). The immediate result was a rapid fall in the numbers of children and young people in court and in custody (Maxwell & Morris, 2010).

On the basis of this legislation, youth justice is a sphere in which New Zealand has had a significant impact on international criminological scholarship. This chapter considers the theory and operation of the system, and begins by tracing its evolution across the past decade. It assesses the distinctive and innovative attributes of the 'New Zealand model' of youth justice, such as the emphasis on diversion, the role of family/whānau, and the inclusion of victims. The chapter argues that new principles introduced in recent reforms significantly increase the complexity of the system. It analyses the diverse and arguably competing theoretical underpinnings of the system and the socio-political context of the key stages in reform. Finally, it outlines some of the contemporary challenges for the youth justice system, which are mirrored in comparable jurisdictions.

REFORMS SINCE 2010

While the course of Aotearoa New Zealand's adult justice system progressed along highly punitive lines from the early 2000s (Pratt & Clark, 2005), the youth justice system has retained many of its progressive features. The principles and operation of the 1989 youth-focused Act remained largely untouched until 2010. The shift came with a National-led government (elected in 2008) that established popular-appeal youth justice reforms as a key plank of its electoral manifesto (Lynch, 2012). From late 2010, the resultant new legislation allowed the prosecution of 12- and 13-year-old children (formerly the approach was purely welfare-based unless in cases of homicide). The reforms also broadened the sentencing powers of the Youth Court, to double the available length of the 'custodial supervision with residence' order and make it easier for serious cases to be transferred to the adult court. Even so, the punitive potential of these reforms was largely tempered, or even resisted, by practitioners, professionals, and judges, with the use of punitive measures such as transfers to the District Court falling, and the new powers to prosecute younger children being seldom used (Lynch, 2019).

Oranga Tamariki – a new direction?

While the overall direction of the youth justice system remained diversionary and tolerant, some aspects remained stubbornly static. The 1989 reforms were intended to address long-standing institutional biases affecting Māori youth. Yet Māori over-representation remains significantly high. Children and young people with a care and protection history steadily progressed into youth justice systems (Stanley, 2017). Mindful of these trends and following public concerns about child abuse, the government commissioned an expert report (Modernising Child, Youth and Family Expert Panel, 2015) to examine the youth justice and care and protection systems. The report recommended major legislative and policy reforms, resulting in the establishment of a new ministry (the Ministry for Vulnerable Children – Oranga Tamariki) in 2017 to oversee a revised model for youth justice and care and protection cases. Due to complaints about its stigmatising title, the name was soon changed to Ministry for Children – Oranga Tamariki, although some Māori decline to use the name Oranga Tamariki, considering that it is not deserved by the organisation. The 1989 Act was significantly reformed in 2017 and 2019, and renamed the Children's and Young People's Well-being Act 1989 or the Oranga Tamariki Act 1989.

The 2019 reforms: Increasingly complex principles

Extensive reforms which took full effect in July 2019 have added new concepts to the already complex 'menu' of principles that decision-makers must consider when exercising powers under the legislation. These include:

- **'Well-being'** – The title of the Act has been changed to centre the concept of well-being (and also to remove the term 'families'). Well-being is said to involve a more holistic analysis of the child or young person's circumstances when compared to the more familiar concept of welfare, but it is a somewhat nebulous concept.
- **Purpose of youth justice** – The new section 4 establishes (or clarifies) the purpose of the youth justice system. However, there are still several somewhat competing concepts. The provision explicitly recognises the rights and interests of victims and aims to prevent and reduce offending – indicating a more 'crime control' focused approach. But best interests and protection of rights are required, indicating a child-centred aspect. Further, accountability and responsibility may suggest a restorative justice approach.
- **Concepts from Te Ao Māori** – The new legislative term 'mana tamaiti' means that decision-makers must recognise the 'intrinsic value and inherent dignity' which is derived from a child or young person's whakapapa and their belonging to whānau, hapū, iwi, or a family group, in accordance with tikanga Māori (Māori customary law and practices) or its equivalent in the child or young person's culture. Mana tamaiti and the child or young person's well-being must be protected by recognising their whakapapa and the whanaungatanga (kinship) responsibilities for their family, whānau, hapū, iwi, and family group. The recognition of Te Tiriti o Waitangi is mandated.
- **Effective and meaningful participation** – Sections 10 and 11 give effect to the child or young person's right to be supported to give their views, and their views must be taken into account in decision-making. This gives effect to Article 12 of the United Nations Convention on the Rights of the Child.
- **Restorative justice** – Restorative justice is now explicitly mentioned in the legislation, and must be considered in family group conference plans. This is probably a crystallisation of existing practice, rather than a new direction.

As these principles are new at the time of writing, it is unknown what the practical effect for decision-makers will be. On a day-to-day basis, decision-makers may already be taking these principles and factors into account, making the changes a crystallisation of elements of existing practice. Conversely, a valid criticism is that where there are so many principles, some competing, there is a lack of a coherent vision for youth justice.

KEY FEATURES OF THE NEW ZEALAND YOUTH JUSTICE SYSTEM

This section explores several noteworthy practices of the youth justice system, including: age parameters; the use of diversion; the role of family group conferences; Youth Court practices and initiatives; and the use of remand and custody for young people.

Graduated liability

One of the fundamental questions which a youth justice system must consider is: from what ages should children be criminally liable, prosecutable, or able to be transferred to the adult justice system? The drawing of age boundaries involves questions of capacity, stage of brain development, or simply political assessments of what is palatable for the public (Nagin et al., 2006). New Zealand has a complex graduated system of age parameters which has developed somewhat haphazardly, rather than from a principled basis.

The age of criminal responsibility (the age from which a child can be considered criminally liable) is 10 years (Crimes Act 1961, s 22). This is in line with comparable jurisdictions (such as England and Wales and some Australian jurisdictions), but has been the subject of criticism by international human rights bodies (United Nations Committee on the Rights of the Child

[UNCRC], 2016). Recent international guidance from the Committee on the Rights of the Child (2019) suggests that brain development evidence supports a minimum age of 14. The low age of criminal responsibility is mitigated somewhat by the legislative distinction between children (those aged 10–14 years) and young persons (those aged 14–18 years). Children are treated differently and separately, with an emphasis on offending being symptomatic of welfare issues, and are also protected by the ancient presumption of *doli incapax* (the requirement to prove that the child knew that what they were doing was wrong or contrary to law). The outcomes and process are diversionary, or referral to the care system. Only in rare and serious cases, such as homicide or other offences of serious violence, will children be prosecuted. Overall, practice largely mitigates the effect of the low minimum age, but, as discussed below, exceptions for serious offending still contravene human rights standards.

At the other end of the scale, the age of penal majority – the age at which the adult criminal justice system begins – was 17 years under the original Act, but this was raised to 18 for most offences from July 2019. As discussed below, young people accused of certain serious offences are still dealt with through adult criminal justice processes.

Diversion

Diversion originally referred to a complete diversion away from the criminal justice system ('doing nothing'). More modern diversion schemes may involve the child or young person completing a significant response to address the offence through informal sanctions and also measures to address the criminogenic needs of the child or young person (McAra & McVie, 2018). Diversion is predicated on avoiding the stigmatising and labelling effects of the formal criminal justice system, particularly the aggregation of children and young persons in conflict with the law, and the harmful effects of formal criminal records (McAra & McVie, 2018).

In New Zealand, 70–80 per cent of children and young people coming to notice are dealt with through diversion (Ministry of Justice, 2019). Diversion in the youth justice system may take many forms, including doing nothing, and informal and formal warnings. In addition, police diversion can encompass alternative actions. This involves the child or young person admitting responsibility for the offence. An agreed plan is then put in place, involving small amounts of reparation or community work, along with elements of the plan designed to address the criminogenic needs of the child or young person. This scheme may be used for minor to moderate offending. There are some examples of partnership with iwi (Henwood et al., 2018), which mirror Te Pae Oranga, an adult diversion scheme involving iwi-run panels.

While warnings are provided for by statute, a somewhat unusual feature of the New Zealand Police diversion scheme is that it is not mentioned in the legislation. It is a discretionary police-operated scheme which hinges from section 208(a) of the Act, which states that 'unless the public interest requires otherwise, criminal proceedings should not be instituted against a child or young person if there is an alternative means of dealing with the matter'. A non-statutory scheme has some benefits. A high level of discretion allows a flexible response to the individualised circumstances of the child or young person. However, there are also dangers in an entirely police-governed process, particularly in transparency, equity of outcome, and ensuring that the due process rights of the child or young person are protected (Hopkins, 2015).

The family group conference

A youth justice family group conference (FGC) is a process where the child or young person, their family/whānau, state officials, and the victim of the offence meet to respond to the alleged or proved offending by the child or young person. The FGC makes decisions and recommendations at all stages of the youth justice system, from decisions whether to charge, to sentencing, to bail and pre-trial custody decisions in the Youth Court. Decisions are made by negotiation between the parties, and unanimous agreement must be reached before FGC recommendations are reported back to the referring agency (the police or the Youth Court).

While the FGC is vital to centralising the family/whānau in decision-making, reviews of its practice and operation have been critical (see Tauri, chapter 20 this volume). A 2004 evaluation (Maxwell et al., 2004) found that the requirement to consult families and victims in relation to preferences for the time and place of the FGC was not always followed. A 2012 review found that 'the process has become overly bureaucratic with a focus on convening conferences at the convenience of Child, Youth and Family, for example convening during working hours and using Child, Youth and Family offices as the only venue' (Child, Youth and Family, 2012, p. 15). This review recommended the reinvigorating of the FGC, while acknowledging that the model provided the best approach for decision-making in both the care and protection and youth justice spheres. The review emphasised training and education for professionals and practitioners.

Of further note is the association of the FGC with a restorative justice approach. While the participatory and reintegrative focus of restorative justice is similar to the rationale behind FGCs (Consedine, 1995), restorative justice was never explicitly mentioned in the 1989 Act. Since July 2019, it has been mandatory for the FGC to consider restorative justice. Concerns have also been expressed about the low rate of victim attendance, which impedes a restorative process and outcome. In many instances of youth offending, the victim is also a child or young person. This creates further complexities in balancing the interests of both groups of children, particularly in applying the best interests standard (Lynch, 2018b).

The Youth Court – problem-solving and innovative?

Only about 20 per cent of children and young people coming to notice will be dealt with through prosecution, with the majority resolved through the Youth Court. In the past decade, the number of children and young people appearing in court has dropped by nearly two-thirds (Ministry of Justice, 2019). This trend is also observed in other jurisdictions (McAra & McVie, 2018). Some have suggested that a move from physical crime to undetected cybercrime (for example, instead of a physical assault, children may now increasingly 'harm' others through digital communication channels) may explain this, while others have suggested that increased security and surveillance (such as making cars much more difficult to break into) can explain the drop in traditional youth crimes (Matthews & Minton, 2018). It might also be explained by changes in frontline practice. A justice sector goal to reduce youth offending by 25 per cent by 2017 may have facilitated the increased use of informal measures on behalf of police officers when dealing with lower-level offending by youth.

The Youth Court is a separate and specialised court which has jurisdiction over most youth offending, except for homicide, very serious cases, and jury trials. Procedure is more informal and participatory than adult courts. Judges are encouraged to communicate directly with the child or young person rather than through their legal representative. The design of the courtroom also has implications for participation. Where the space is smaller and young persons are permitted to sit/stand with their advocates, and with their parent(s) or caregiver(s) nearby, participation is enhanced. The Youth Court's ethos is characterised by therapeutic jurisprudence or the problem-solving court model (Casey et al., 2000). In this model, the court's practice and outcomes are informed by multi-disciplinary teams, such as psychologists, psychiatrists, health professionals, social services, and education. Children and young people appearing in the Youth Court have the right to privacy, which supports automatic name-suppression orders. Media are permitted in the Youth Court, but may not publish any material which identifies the child or young person or anything which would identify them, such as school or whānau names. This reduces stigmatisation, as media coverage can be detrimental to the reintegration of children and young persons (Fitz-Gibbon & O'Brien, 2016; Wright Monod, 2017).

An interesting aspect of New Zealand's youth justice system is that most of its tolerant, innovative, and evidence-based aspects arise from practice rather than legislative prescription (Lynch, 2019; see Quince, chapter 16 this volume). Two examples of this are to be found in the Youth Court jurisdiction. The first is the section 282 discharge. This is an unusual power, which allows for the child or young person to go through the court process (even for moderate to serious offending) and, if the child or young person completes his or her FGC plan successfully, to be discharged completely. This means that not only does the child or young person leave the process with no formal order, but it is also as if the charge was never laid. The benefits of this for the child or young person's reintegration are clear, and it offers an incentive to complete the requirements of the FGC plan. Around half of cases are resolved through this order (Ministry of Justice, 2019).

Another example of innovative judicial practice is the setting up of Ngā Kōti Rangatahi (Youth Courts). This involves a relocation of part of the Youth Court's proceedings to a local marae, where the community of the marae becomes involved in the supervision of the FGC plan (a related initiative, the Pasifika Court, has been established in Auckland). Rangatahi Courts are not a separate justice system for Māori, but rather a relocation of a portion of the court process (Quince, chapter 16 this volume). After an initial Youth Court hearing, and if the child or young person and the family consents, the FGC and the subsequent hearings will take place on the marae. The victim of the offence must also agree, and victims are permitted to participate as in the regular Youth Court process. The initiative has developed on an organic basis, rather than through statutory or policy prescription, but the initiative has found support in its promotion of cultural appropriateness, the primacy of the family in decision-making, and the imposition of community-based sanctions (Taumaunu, 2014).

Remand and custody

Following the 1989 legislative changes, the number of children and young persons in custody has remained relatively low (United Nations, 2019). The maximum custodial sanction available to the Youth Court is six months, and this is in a specific youth justice residence. At present there are four youth justice residences. These residences are small-scale by international standards, and house young people completing 'supervision with residence' orders, those on remand, and a small number of children and young people serving a term of imprisonment. It is widely recognised that custody has harmful effects by 'warehousing' damaged young persons in damaging environments (Lambie & Randell, 2013). Custody disrupts whānau and community links. There is a risk of self-harm, or assaults involving other young persons or staff. The strongest negative effect is that of aggregating serious young offenders, which may cement negative behaviours. Experiences in youth justice custody inevitably provide a conduit to adult prison (Department of Corrections, 2001). These findings were confirmed by the United Nations in a global study on children in detention, in which it was reported that 'depriving children of liberty is depriving them of their childhood' (United Nations, 2019, p. 3). Custody disproportionately affects certain groups. Young people with additional needs are over-represented. In New Zealand, rangatahi Māori make up a majority of young people in custody, which underpins their entry to the 'prison pipeline' (Lambie, 2018a). Further, there is considerable evidence of the abuse and neglect of children and young persons in state custody (Stanley, 2015). These issues have been reported worldwide, and in New Zealand a Royal Commission of Inquiry into Abuse in Care commenced public hearings in late 2019.

An enduring issue is the percentage of young persons on remand who do not receive a custodial outcome when later sentenced (Oranga Tamariki, 2018). This appears to be due to the young person's needs not being able to be met in the community, rather than the risk to public safety. Work is ongoing on supported bail programmes and community remand homes to minimise the harmful effects of placement in residence for short periods (Oranga Tamariki, 2018).

CONTEMPORARY CHALLENGES FOR THE YOUTH JUSTICE SYSTEM

In this section, several challenges for the youth justice system are discussed, including how we might respond to serious offenders, female offenders, or those with additional needs, as well as the increasing contribution of the research into brain development and related questions of responsibility. Most of these challenges are not unique to New Zealand and are mirrored in comparable jurisdictions.

Exceptions for serious offending

The youth justice system can be said to take a tolerant and evidence-based approach to most children and young people coming to notice for offending. Most cases are dealt with in a specialised system with tailored principles, processes, and staffing. Nonetheless, exceptions to jurisdiction remain for serious offending which undermine the largely principled basis of the system. While the 2019 raising of the age of penal majority to 18 for most offences is welcome, 17-year-olds accused of 'schedule 1A' offences (a list of serious offences such as sexual violation and aggravated robbery) remain outside the jurisdiction of the specialised Youth Court. There is also provision for young persons to be transferred to the District Court for sentence for serious offending. All cases of murder and manslaughter are automatically within the jurisdiction of the High Court. Jury trials and some cases involving joint charges with adults are also excluded from the youth jurisdiction. Thus, a significant proportion of children and young persons do not benefit from the protections of a specialised youth justice system.

The implications of being dealt with through the adult system are severe for children and young people. The law change in July 2019 means that at least all under-18s have the right to specialised procedures and protections during the investigation stage, including police questioning and the collection of evidence such as DNA and fingerprints. But where a child or young person falls within one of the exceptions to jurisdiction, they are essentially automatically reclassified from 'child' to 'adult'. James et al. (1998) have described this as a 'conceptual eviction'. Transfer to the adult system means that the child or young person is subject to adult trial procedures, such as the formality of a jury trial. It also means that they are subject to adult sentences, including the presumptive sentence of life imprisonment on conviction of murder (Lynch, 2018a). In all but one of the cases involving children or young persons convicted for murder since the Sentencing Act 2002, the offender has received the sentence of life, with at least a minimum period of imprisonment of 10 years. The use of long sentences, particularly the indeterminate sentence of life for children and young persons, is disproportionate to their youth and stage of brain development, and is in direct contrast with the principles embedded in the 1989 Act.

While there are legitimate interests in public safety and accountability for serious offences (Lynch, 2018a), a better conception would be to emphasise the universality of the children's rights approach: 'all rights for all children all of the time' (Kilkelly, 2019). The promotion of public safety and appropriate accountability is provided for in the Convention on the Rights of the Child, but custody must remain a last resort, and indeterminate sentences are disproportionate for young offenders (UNCRC, 2019).

Disproportionate effect on Māori

Although the challenges in Aotearoa New Zealand's youth justice system are specific, they are also mirrored in other jurisdictions. One issue is cross-cutting: the over-representation of certain groups. Māori are over-represented in the New Zealand youth justice system, and this disproportionate effect is observed at all stages from apprehension to custody (Henwood et al., 2018). A range of factors influence this disproportionality, ranging from the effects of colonialism to the largely monocultural nature of the justice system, bias in decision-making, and the higher rate of adverse life events amongst Māori tamariki and rangatahi (Lambie, 2018b). What is clear is that the causes are complex, and the solutions will be complex and long-term, and must be led by Māori. The report from the Ināia Tonu Nei (2019) hui held in Rotorua made a number of recommendations, including: early interventions that are whānau- and child-centred; the expansion of the Rangatahi Court; more Māori judges; and more support in the first 1000 days of a child's life.

Responding to female offending

Most (approximately eight in ten) children and young people in court are male (Ministry of Justice, 2019). The lower rates of offending among females has been attributed to their stricter informal social controls (Carrington & Pereira, 2009). There have recently been suggestions that female youth offending is increasing in both prevalence and severity. Examination shows that this assumption may be based on an overemphasis on a small number of young females (Lynch et al., 2018). While there are a small number of young female offenders who commit serious and persistent offending, these young women are a highly individualised cohort. Concern has also been expressed around the proportion of young females held on remand, with the assertion that this may be on the ground of welfare rather than risk to public safety. Given that very small numbers of young female offenders are distributed across a wide geographical area, they are unlikely to encounter specifically designed effective reintegration programmes (Lynch et al., 2018). Geographical spread also means that young women are held in custody far away from family and support networks.

Children and young people with additional needs

The justice sector chief science advisor's reports (Lambie, 2018a, 2020) on youth offending noted that this cohort exhibits high levels of vulnerabilities, such as mental illness, learning disability, traumatic brain injury, and foetal alcohol spectrum disorder. Those with neuro-disabilities, for example, struggle with comprehension and concentration, meaning they have reduced ability to understand procedures or follow instructions, and an inability to understand consequences of actions (see Gibbs, chapter 29 this volume). Due to the complexity of bail conditions and court procedures, and the predominance of written information, children and young persons with these conditions are more likely to breach bail and fail to comply (Lount et al., 2018). Behaviours relating to neuro-disability can also be mistakenly interpreted as hostility, acting out, or evidence of guilt (Lynch, 2016).

Increased awareness of such conditions in the youth justice system has led to changes in procedures and supports. One such initiative is the ability to appoint a communication assistant who supports the child or young person during court processes or family group conferences. Trained communication assistants have the expertise to ensure that information is presented in an understandable manner and in appropriate language for the child or young person (Lount et al., 2018). While such measures are to be welcomed, there are wider questions about the culpability of such children and young persons, and the need for approaches to ensure that they are not criminalised in the first place (Gibbs, chapter 29 this volume; Gibbs & Sherwood, 2017).

The next frontier – from youth to emerging adulthood

In recent years, a range of scientific and sociological evidence has demonstrated that young adults (those aged between 18 and 25) have characteristics which support special procedures and mitigation in criminal justice outcomes (Dünkel & Pruin, 2012). New Zealand already recognises young adults as a distinct group in several areas of law, policy, and practice. Comparable jurisdictions have more advanced systems, ranging from treating this group within existing youth justice systems to the establishment of 'third systems' especially for young adults. Brain development evidence provides a basis to justify treating young adults differently from adults. While in previous generations a young adult would be expected to achieve markers of adulthood (such as marriage, children, home ownership, or full-time employment) at the age of 18, or close to this age, this is now much rarer. This bolsters an argument that young adulthood is a distinct period of the life course, where there is societal acceptance that special protective measures are required. In recent comments, the UN Committee on the Rights of the Child (2019) explicitly recognised and approved the application of mitigation and special procedures for young adults, commenting:

> The Committee commends States parties that allow the application of the child justice system to persons aged 18 and older whether as a general rule or by way of exception. This approach is in keeping with the developmental and neuroscience evidence that shows that brain development continues into the early twenties (para. 32).

Reforms that recognise the social and developmental concept of young adulthood are already in place in New Zealand. For example, the care age in New Zealand has recently increased to 21 years, and a young adult is entitled to advice and assistance up to 25 years in certain circumstances (Oranga Tamariki Act 1989, ss. 386AAD and 386A). This recognises that the protections and support given to those in the care of the state must mirror the experience of those of the same age in society. Since much of the adult custodial population is aged in the young adulthood bracket, it is likely we will increasingly see defendants who have a 'triple status'– who have a care and protection order, a youth justice matter, and matters in the adult court. This raises concerns around state and societal responsibility for vulnerable adults.

CONCLUSION

What should be the direction of future reform in the youth justice system? As discussed above, Māori-led responses for Māori children must be a leading principle for reform. It is also vital that children are appropriately engaged in evaluations and reform, as they are the experts in their own lives.

Brain development evidence may be a double-edged sword. Scientific understanding provides stand-alone evidence for protective measures and mitigation for children in conflict with the law. But the evidence around the prevalence of traumatic brain injuries and other neuro-disabilities may also be used to class particular children as particularly risky and justify more restrictive measures. The universality of the requirements for special measures for children must prevail (UNCRC, 2019, para. 28). The basis of a principled response according to children's rights standards is the child's age rather than their level of risk or the seriousness of the offence.

Finally, it is relatively easy for scholars and advocates to critique law, policy, and practice as being non-principled or harmful, but more difficult to work in balancing the various rights and interests inherent in law reform and policy formation. Scholars and advocates for children must ensure that they are involved and engaged in policy and law reform, which should also include critical and independent evaluation. For serious offending cases, this must involve considering the legitimate interests of the public and victims (who may themselves be children).

STUDY QUESTIONS

- For effective youth justice reform — what matters most? Is it law, policy, or practice?
- The science of brain development may be used to support protective measures and mitigation in sentencing for children and young people. Are there any dangers in relying on the science of brain development to inform youth justice policy and practice?
- How should the system respond to very serious offending by children and young people?

FURTHER READING

Cleland, A., & Quince, K. (2014). *Youth justice in Aotearoa New Zealand: Law, policy and critique.* Wellington, New Zealand: LexisNexis.

Lambie, I. (2018). *It's never too early, never too late: A discussion paper on preventing youth offending in New Zealand.* Auckland, New Zealand: Office of the Prime Minister's Chief Science Advisor. Retrieved from https://www.pmcsa.org.nz/wp-content/uploads/Discussion-paper-on-preventing-youth-offending-in-NZ.pdf

Lynch, N. (2019). *Youth justice in New Zealand.* Wellington, New Zealand: Thomson Reuters.

REFERENCES

Carrington, K., & Pereira, M. (2009). *Offending youth: Sex, crime and justice.* New South Wales, Australia: Federation Press.

Casey, P., Rottman, D., Tomkins, A., & Carson, D. (2000). Therapeutic jurisprudence in the courts. *Behavioral Sciences and the Law, 18*(4), 445–457.

Child, Youth and Family. (2012). *Final recommendations on improving family group conferences to achieve better outcomes for New Zealand's most vulnerable children.* Wellington, New Zealand: Ministry of Social Development. Retrieved from https://www.msd.govt.nz/documents/about-msd-and-our-work/publications-resources/evaluation/review-family-group-conferences/improving-family-group-conferences.pdf

Consedine, J. (1995). *Restorative justice: Healing the effects of crime.* Lyttelton, New Zealand: Ploughshares Publications.

Department of Corrections. (2001). *About time: Turning people away from a life of crime and reducing re-offending.* Wellington, New Zealand: Department of Corrections. Retrieved from https://www.corrections.govt.nz/resources/research_and_statistics/about_time

Dünkel, F., & Pruin, I. (2012). Young adult offenders in juvenile and criminal justice systems in Europe. In F. Lösel, A. Bottoms, & D. P. Farrington (Eds.), *Young adult offenders: Lost in transition?* (pp. 11–38). London, UK: Willan Publishing.

Fitz-Gibbon, K., & O'Brien, W. (2016). The naming of child homicide offenders in England and Wales: The need for a change in law and practice. *British Journal of Criminology, 57*(5), 1061–1079. doi:10.1093/bjc/azw042

Gibbs, A., & Sherwood, K. (2017). Putting fetal alcohol spectrum disorder (FASD) on the map in New Zealand: A review of health, social, political, justice and cultural developments. *Psychiatry, Psychology and Law, 24*(6), 825–842. doi:10.1080/13218719.2017.1315784

Henwood, C., George, J., Cram, F., & Waititi, H. (2018). *Rangatahi Māori and youth justice: Oranga rangatahi*. Research undertaken for the Iwi Chairs with the support of the Henwood Trust and the Law Foundation. Retrieved from https://iwichairs.maori.nz/wp-content/uploads/2018/02/RESEARCH-Rangatahi-Maori-and-Youth-Justice-Oranga-Rangatahi.pdf

Hopkins, Z. (2015). *Diverted from counsel: Filling the rights gap in New Zealand's youth justice model*. Wellington, New Zealand: Fulbright New Zealand. Retrieved from https://fulbright.org.nz/publications/diverted-from-counsel-filling-the-rights-gap-in-new-zealands-youth-justice-model/

James, A., Jenks, C., & Prout, A. (1998). *Theorizing childhood*. Cambridge, UK: Polity Press in association with Blackwell Publishers.

Kilkelly, U. (2019). All children, all rights, in all circumstances. In N. Lynch (Ed.), *Children's rights in Aotearoa New Zealand – Reflections on the 30th anniversary of the Convention on the Rights of the Child* (pp. 82–85). Wellington, New Zealand: Law Foundation and Michael and Suzanne Borrin Foundation. Retrieved from https://www.lawfoundation.org.nz/?p=10987

Lambie, I. (2018a). *It's never too early, never too late: A discussion paper on preventing youth offending in New Zealand*. Auckland, New Zealand: Office of the Prime Minister's Chief Science Advisor. Retrieved from https://www.pmcsa.org.nz/wp-content/uploads/Discussion-paper-on-preventing-youth-offending-in-NZ.pdf

Lambie, I. (2018b). *Using evidence to build a better justice system: The challenge of rising prison costs*. Auckland, New Zealand: Office of the Prime Minister's Chief Science Advisor. Retrieved from pmcsa.org.nz/wp-content/uploads/Using-evidence-to-build-a-better-justice-system.pdf

Lambie, I. (2020). *What were they thinking? A discussion paper on brain and behaviour in relation to the justice system in New Zealand*. Auckland, New Zealand: Office of the Prime Minister's Chief Science Advisor. Retrieved from https://www.pmcsa.ac.nz/topics/criminal-justice/

Lambie, I., & Randell, I. (2013). The impact of incarceration on juvenile offenders. *Clinical Psychology Review, 33*(3), 448–459. doi:10.1016/j.cpr.2013.01.007

Lount, S. A., Hand, L., Purdy, S. C., & France, A. (2018). Tough talk: Youth offenders' perceptions of communicating in the youth justice system in New Zealand. *Australian and New Zealand Journal of Criminology, 51*(4), 593–618. doi:10.1177/0004865817740404

Lynch, N. (2012). Playing catch-up? Recent reform of New Zealand's youth justice system. *Criminology and Criminal Justice, 12*(5), 507–526. doi:10.1177/1748895811432013

Lynch, N. (2016). *Neurodisability in the youth justice system in New Zealand: How vulnerability intersects with justice*. Wellington, New Zealand: Faculty of Law, Victoria University of Wellington, in conjunction with Dyslexia Foundation of New Zealand (DFNZ). Retrieved from http://neurodisabilitiesforum.org.nz/wp-content/uploads/2016/05/Neurodisabilities-Forum–2016-Report–1.pdf

Lynch, N. (2018a). Towards a principled legal response to children who kill. *Youth Justice, 18*(3), 211–229. doi:10.1177/1473225418819056

Lynch, N. (2018b). 'The other child': The rights of the child victim in the youth justice system. *International Journal of Children's Rights, 26*(2), 228–250. doi:10.1163/15718182–02602002

Lynch, N. (2019). *Youth justice in New Zealand* (3rd ed.). Wellington, New Zealand: Thomson Reuters.

Lynch, N., Fortune, C., Ward, N., De Bes, F., Shearar, A., Bevan, M., & McGlue, H. (2018). *Young female offenders – focus group report*. Wellington, New Zealand: Unpublished report for the Working Group on Young Female Offenders.

Matthews, B., & Minton, J. (2018). Rethinking one of criminology's 'brute facts': The age–crime curve and the crime drop in Scotland. *European Journal of Criminology, 15*(3), 296–320. doi:10.1177/1477370817731706

Maxwell, G. M., Kingi, V., Robertson, J., Morris, A., Cunningham, C., & Lash, B. (2004). *Achieving effective outcomes in youth justice*. Wellington, New Zealand: Ministry of Social Development.

Maxwell, G. M., & Morris, A. (2010). *Family, victims and culture: Youth justice in New Zealand*. Wellington, New Zealand: Social Policy Agency Rōpū Here Kaupapa and the Institute of

Criminology, Victoria University. Retrieved from https://www.msd.govt.nz/about-msd-and-our-work/publications-resources/research/family-victims-culture/index.html

McAra, L., & McVie, S. (2018). Transformations in youth crime and justice across Europe: Evidencing the case for diversion. In B. Goldson (Ed.), *Juvenile justice in Europe: Past, present and future* (pp. 73–103). London, UK: Routledge.

Ministry of Justice. (2019). *Youth justice indicators summary report August 2019.* Retrieved from https://www.justice.govt.nz/justice-sector-policy/research-data/justice-statistics/youth-justice-indicators/

Modernising Child, Youth and Family Expert Panel. (2015). *Expert Panel final report: Investing in New Zealand's children and their families.* Wellington, New Zealand: Ministry of Social Development. Retrieved from https://www.msd.govt.nz/documents/about-msd-and-our-work/publications-resources/corporate/expert-panel-cyf/investing-in-children-report.pdf

Morris, A., & Maxwell, G. M. (1993). Juvenile justice in New Zealand: A new paradigm. *Australian and New Zealand Journal of Criminology, 26*(1), 72–90. doi:10.1177/000486589302600108

Nagin, D. S., Piquero, A. R., Scott, E. S., & Steinberg, L. (2006). Public preferences for rehabilitation versus incarceration of juvenile offenders: Evidence from a contingent valuation survey. *Criminology and Public Policy, 5*(4), 627–651. doi:10.1111/j.1745-9133.2006.00406.x

Oranga Tamariki. (2018). *Young people remanded into youth justice residences – what are the driving factors? Research study.* Wellington, New Zealand: Oranga Tamariki Evidence Centre Te Pokapū Taunakitanga. Retrieved from https://www.orangatamariki.govt.nz/assets/Uploads/About-us/Research/Latest-research/Young-people-remanded-into-YJ-residences/Young-People-Remanded-into-Youth-Justice-Residences-What-are-the-Driving-Factors.pdf

Pratt, J., & Clark, M. (2005). Penal populism in New Zealand. *Punishment and Society, 7*(3), 303–322. doi:10.1177/1462474505053831

Stanley, E. (2015). *The road to hell: State violence against children in postwar New Zealand.* Auckland, New Zealand: Auckland University Press.

Stanley, E. (2017). From care to custody: Trajectories of children in post-war New Zealand. *Youth Justice, 17*(1), 57–72. doi:10.1177/1473225416669145

Taumaunu, H. (2014). Rangatahi Courts of Aotearoa/New Zealand – an update. *Māori Law Review, 22*(11), 1. Retrieved from https://maorilawreview.co.nz/2014/11/rangatahi-courts-of-aotearoa-new-zealand-an-update/

Te Ohu Whakatika. (2019). *Ināia tonu nei – Now is the time: We lead, you follow*, hui Māori report. Retrieved from https://safeandeffectivejustice.govt.nz/news/latest-news/maoriperspectives-on-justice-report-released/

United Nations. (2019). *Report of the Independent Expert leading the United Nations Global Study on Children Deprived of Liberty* (A/74/136, 11 July 2019). Retrieved from https://digitallibrary.un.org/record/3813850?ln=en#record-files-collapse-header

United Nations Committee on the Rights of the Child (UNCRC). (2016). *Concluding observations on the fifth periodic report of New Zealand* (CRC/NZL/CO/5).

United Nations Committee on the Rights of the Child (UNCRC). (2019). *General Comment No. 24 (2019) on children's rights in the child justice system* (CRC/C/GC/24, 18 September 2019). Retrieved from https://www.ohchr.org/en/hrbodies/crc/pages/crcindex.aspx

Wright Monod, S. (2017). Portraying those we condemn with care: Extending the ethics of representation. *Critical Criminology, 25*(3), 343–356. doi:10.1007/s10612-016-9348-1

ID # 19

Community Sentences
Expanding a System of Control and Surveillance?

Anita Gibbs

Before Europeans settled in Aotearoa New Zealand, we know that Māori had their own systems of justice primarily aimed at reconciliation, compensation, healing, and some retribution, but most definitely *not* exclusion from the community (Jackson, 1988; Ministry of Justice, 2001). These systems incorporated core Māori concepts of tapu, mana, muru, and utu, and allowed relationships to be restored, and compensation to be provided when a harmful act occurred (Ministry of Justice, 2001).[1] Inevitably, with colonisation came formalised systems that introduced European models of justice, and more than 170 years later we are still struggling with the legacy of racial discrimination and monoculturalism across all aspects of criminal justice, including the use and operation of community sentences (Jackson, 1988; JustSpeak, 2012).

Today, community-based sentences can be viewed as 'sanctions and measures which share in common a restriction of the offender's liberty through the imposition of behavioural conditions and/or obligations' (Robinson & McNeill, 2017, p. 869). Around 30,000 people on community sentences are supervised by the Department of Corrections each year in New Zealand; this is well over three times the number of people sentenced to imprisonment. A range of community sentence options are available, from low-tariff monetary penalties to high end intensive supervision or home detention. New Zealand's alternatives to imprisonment have not, for the most part, operated as alternatives, and their use has revealed an increasing intensity of surveillance with few gains in rehabilitation. This chapter explores the development of community sentences and the rationale and use of the available options. It ends with reflections on some of the key issues – including the disproportionate impacts of sentencing on Māori;

the concerns of addressing the complex needs of those on community sentences; the rise of surveillant technologies in sentencing; and considerations of 'success' or rehabilitation – that are having an impact on New Zealand's use and implementation of such sentences.

A BRIEF HISTORY OF COMMUNITY SENTENCES IN AOTEAROA NEW ZEALAND

New Zealand introduced the idea of probation as an alternative to imprisonment in 1886, adopting techniques of befriending, helping, and advising first-time offenders, in the hope that offenders would see the error of their ways and avoid future trouble. The First Offenders' Probation Act 1886 enabled courts to impose alternatives to custody. However, with this introduction of probation (here and overseas), the offender gave their voluntary agreement to the court-ordered sanction. These days, no such voluntary compliance is required, and part of the punishment-in-the-community ethos is the likelihood of more punitive sanctions should an offender breach probation (or other community sentence) conditions (Polaschek, 2017; Robinson & McNeill, 2017).

The 1886 Probation Act also established the duties of unpaid probation officers. These duties, initially to hold first-time offenders to account and to help them to engage in meaningful activities to reduce the likelihood of reoffending, are still in use today for all offenders. Subsequent legislation during the twentieth century established specific roles for probation staff, such as court officer, report writer, and supervision roles; and in 1954, the probation service became a fully professionalised service (with paid staff).

In 1962, periodic detention (PD) was added alongside probation as an alternative to imprisonment. It started out as a weekend detention option for boys and young men, and involved those aged 15 to 20 years turning up to a detention centre on a Friday evening and being engaged in work and rehabilitation activities until Sunday afternoon (Newbold, 2016). PD eventually became a day-only option for males and females until it was abolished in 2002 (Newbold, 2016). PD proved to be most popular with the courts (Deckert, 2020): it satisfied the more controlling and surveillance expectations of sentencing, as well as being reparative in nature. In 1980, another alternative to the imprisonment option, community service, was introduced, and this allowed an offender to undertake community-based work for the benefit of charities or public agencies for between 20 and 200 hours in a given year (Gibbs & King, 2002).

In 1985, the Criminal Justice Act overhauled probation, PD, and community service and converted them to sentences in their own right, rather than alternatives to imprisonment. Probation was renamed 'supervision'. A new sentence, community programme, also emerged. This involved a tailor-made programme for offenders involving education, treatment, and cultural and recreational activities all focused on community reintegration. Offenders were to be placed in the care of sponsors (mentors), community leaders, and cultural organisations. However, the option was rarely taken up, mostly (it was thought) because of its resource implications (Gibbs & King, 2002). It was abolished in 2002.

The impact of penal populism

During the 1980s and 1990s, public confidence in the ability of governments or 'elite' experts to get it right when addressing crime and victimisation began to wane. Media and victims' lobby groups began to demand tougher sentences (Pratt, 2008; Pratt & Anderson, chapter 13 this volume). Penal populism, as this public-driven punitiveness has come to be known, is a key factor behind New Zealand's sharp increases in imprisonment rates. The influence of the crime-obsessed media, victims' rights movements, and politicians' promises to be 'tough on crime' also led to increased punitiveness in community-based sentencing, and to the development of surveillance-oriented penalties. Hence, the Sentencing Act 2002 removed PD, community service, and community programme, and incorporated all of these into a new sentence: community work. Five years later, in 2007, came the introduction of new penalties that laid emphasis on secure containment in the community. These were home detention, community detention, and intensive supervision. Although home detention had been available as an early release from imprisonment option since 1999, the 2007 version was an extension of surveillance to community-based options as well as an attempt to reduce the ever-increasing prison population (Gibbs & King, 2003; Martinovic, 2017). The use of these new penalties enabled private security businesses, like Chubb, 3M, and First Security, to manage the global positioning system (GPS) and electronic monitoring (EM) elements and, in effect, join Corrections staff in their surveillance of offenders.

The continued impact of penal populism has seen the addition of other orders in the community; these include parole and release conditions, extended supervision orders, and post-detention conditions (Department of Corrections, 2018). While these orders are not counted as community sentences, they nonetheless occupy a significant amount of the work of Corrections in communities (Department of Corrections, 2018). Most of these orders have been added as extra surveillance measures since the advent of EM, and are designed to ensure that 'high-risk' offenders are continually tracked and supervised after their prison or home-detention sentence ends. There have been challenges to the impacts of penal populism, with initiatives to reduce the increases in prison numbers and ensure that community sentences are effective (Deckert, 2020). Penal populism is, however, alive and well, as seen in recent headlines from Judith Collins, leader of the National Party, on being tough on gangs (*Otago Daily Times*, 2020).

Rehabilitation programmes and risk

During the 1970s a highly influential review of research by Robert Martinson (entitled 'Nothing Works') impacted ideas about rehabilitation such that it was presumed that treatment programmes to help rehabilitate offenders did not work (Cullen, 2013; see Durrant & Riley, chapter 22 this volume). This led to a period of pessimism in correctional services around the globe and, eventually, to the introduction of research- and evidence-based practices which demonstrated that *some things did work* to reduce reoffending. In New Zealand, Corrections embraced the work of North American researchers Andrews and Bonta, which detailed the factors and programmes leading to reductions in reoffending (Cullen, 2013; Newbold, 2008; Polaschek, 2017; Robinson & McNeill, 2017). From the 1990s, many community sentences have been guided by the principles of risk, need, and responsivity, known as RNR (Cullen, 2013; Ingram, 2013; Newbold, 2008; Polaschek, 2017). These RNR tools are used to tailor recommendations for community sentence packages, and target more intensive interventions. Invariably, these tools have their limitations, and the programmes based on the reasoning and rehabilitation research have had mixed results in reducing reoffending or targeting the appropriate length and type of interventions (MacManus, 2019; Newbold, 2008). An over-reliance on risk predictions has led to overly invasive surveillance or punishments for certain offenders (MacManus, 2019).

In 2006, an Effective Interventions strategy (Burton, 2006; Pratt, 2008) was launched by the minister of justice with an emphasis on reducing reoffending and imprisonment through new community interventions. Using the RNR tools and providing all manner of behavioural-change, tikanga, and cognitive-change courses, the effectiveness strategy paved the way for large increases in community sentences as well as intensified parole and home detention conditions (Department of Corrections, 2018; Office of the Auditor General, 2013). In turn, the numbers of community sentences grew, but the reductions in imprisonment and reoffending did not follow (Deckert, 2020; Department of Corrections, 2017; Newbold, 2016). Despite the growth of rehabilitative programmes, there have been no reductions in people on community or prison sentences.

Back to befriending?

More recently, those working to supervise and support offenders have highlighted an emphasis on relationship-based practice, prosocial modelling, and working alongside offenders to understand their dynamic needs and challenges, as well as to enhance their strengths (Cullen, 2013; Ingram, 2013; Office of the Auditor General, 2013). In particular, probation and prison staff seek to identify and address the main issues for offenders (Department of Corrections, 2018; Ingram, 2013). More effort is being made to support offenders back into employment or education and training, into stable accommodation, into receiving help for 'addictions' and mental health needs, and to connect or reconnect them with their families/whānau and communities (Department of Corrections, 2019a; Office of the Auditor General, 2013). Small-scale examples include supported transitional housing in various locations and training towards secure employment for ex-prisoners (Department of Corrections, 2018).[2] Furthermore, Corrections has recently committed to partnerships with iwi-based services, to implement 'offender-centric' approaches to reduce offending (Department of Corrections, 2019a). Examples include the Tiaki Tangata programme and Te Piki Oranga's Māori Motivational Programme, which encourage offenders' self-determination and provide wraparound community supports (Department of Corrections, 2019a; Office of the Auditor General, 2013).[3] Recent research in New Zealand also supports the importance of helping offenders to re-story their identities, and to get supports at 'turning point' moments in their lives to turn away from offending behaviour (Bowman & Morrison, 2019; Morrison et al., 2019).

RATIONALES FOR COMMUNITY SENTENCES

Community sentences are expected to: restrict offenders, or demand work or actions of them; offer practical benefits to the community; reassure victims and the public; keep offenders accountable; and attempt the rehabilitation of offenders (Gibbs & King, 2002). Few would argue that community sentences today are direct alternatives to custody. Specific rationales that apply include ideas of rehabilitation, reparation, public safety, punishment, and ensuring compliance. Each community sentence is likely to include elements of all of these. The ultimate goal is to reduce reoffending (see below).

Rehabilitation offers the hope of change on the part of offenders, as well as the provision of interventions or treatments that might help offenders change the behaviours, attitudes, or lifestyles that led them to offending (Cullen, 2013; Robinson & McNeill, 2017). Robinson and McNeill (2017) note that 'broader understandings of rehabilitation – as a process of social reintegration into the community or as the removal of criminal labels – have tended to disappear from official discourse' (p. 874). This is in part because in an era of penal populism, offender rehabilitation is about individuals who have now 'chosen' to stop offending. To be rehabilitated is less about reintegration back into communities of support and more about an offender's responsibility to change. Rehabilitation now includes a strong focus on victims, particularly how rehabilitation can, within specific supervision options, ensure that offenders both understand the impacts of their offending on victims and guarantee they will not cause further victimisations. Offenders are to manage their own riskiness; they are solely to blame for their offending choices and will be punished if they choose to reoffend.

The rationale of *reparation* has been a long-standing element of periodic detention, community service, community programme, and community work sentences. Making amends, community pay-back, and, more recently, ideas of restoration and reciprocity are considered normal components to justify community sentences (Robinson & McNeill, 2017). Opportunities for restorative conferences occur before sentencing, and probation staff can undertake victim awareness work within community sentences. Sometimes probation staff also facilitate contact between offenders and victims with a view to offenders undertaking reparation, apology, and reconciliation.

The need for *public safety* as a core component of community sentences fits well with a penal-populist view that the public are in danger from violent offenders who are not being supervised or managed carefully enough during or after their sentences (Newbold, 2016). The media have fuelled the fear of crime for the general public, and this has led to calls for harsher penalties and *punishment* (Deckert, 2020; Pratt, 2008). Corrections have incorporated demands for punitiveness and surveillance into community sentences, yet these moves can be resisted by probation staff (Department of Corrections, n.d.a; Ingram, 2013; Office of the Auditor General, 2013; Robinson & McNeill, 2017). Probation staff work with the tensions of control and care as they always have done since the early days of probation (Gibbs & King, 2002).

The management of community sentences

In order to achieve any of the goals of rehabilitation, reparation, public safety, or punishment, the management of offenders and ensuring their compliance with sentence expectations must occur. To that end, a robust management rationale now accompanies the implementation of all community sentences (Department of Corrections, 2018; Robinson & McNeill, 2017). There are two angles to this rationale: compliance with sentence requirements, and implementing systems to ensure case management integrity (Ingram, 2013; Newbold, 2008; Robinson & McNeill, 2017). The first focus of management is on the offender – offenders are managed in terms of their risk, needs, and capacity to comply with sentence requirements and conditions (Ingram, 2013). The second is focused on enabling different parts of the correctional apparatus to work together, and enabling others involved in the management of offenders (for example, private security firms, or the police) to share and access information quickly to promote consistency and efficiencies.

The Department of Corrections has a clear hierarchy of community sentences which link to the aforementioned rationales (Polaschek, 2017). At the bottom of the hierarchy of sentences, discharges are given and these are the least restrictive. Next are fines and reparation orders, which are viewed as low-severity community options. Discharges, fines, and reparation are not managed by Corrections staff. Then comes standard community work and supervision, managed by Corrections staff. Community work is viewed as a restriction of freedom and reparative in nature, while supervision is viewed as rehabilitative. Enhanced standard community options are community detention (with EM) and intensive supervision; these sentences have increasing elements of restriction and obligations, as well as rehabilitation elements. The final, most severe community option is home detention, which can include post-detention options, so that even when the order finishes offenders may still be supervised and have a curfew. Imprisonment sits at the top of the hierarchy of sentences with its own layers of release and post-custody conditions.

In the next section we explore the components for each kind of community sentence, but the rationales above are the foundation underpinning the day-to-day operation of the sentences.

COMMUNITY SENTENCE TYPES AND TRENDS

There are several types of community sentence, and each operates according to different rationales. Some sentences (like supervision, intensive supervision, and home detention) are focused on rehabilitation but also restriction and surveillance. There are sentences (like community work) with reparative and punishment orientations, and there are sentences focused on movement restrictions, such as community detention. About 45 per cent of convicted offenders receive a community sentence annually, amounting to around 30,000 offenders on community-based orders per year (Department of Corrections, 2018; Polaschek, 2017).[4] This section outlines each community sentence and issues of compliance, reconviction, and costs.

Supervision and intensive supervision

Introduced as a sentence in its own right in 1985, supervision can be imposed on offenders for six months to one year. The standard conditions of supervision include: reporting to see a probation officer at specified times; restrictions on associating with certain people; and restrictions on living and employment arrangements (Department of Corrections, n.d.b). Intensive supervision orders involve the standard conditions plus additional obligations – for example, more contact time with probation officers, further attendance at rehabilitation programmes, or undertaking extra assessments for complex issues (Department of Corrections, n.d.b). Intensive supervision orders run from six months to two years. Probation staff working with offenders on all types of supervision orders will have a plan that focuses on offender's risk levels, their identified needs, and their likely compliance with conditions, as well as the benefits they might gain from participation in additional programmes (such as specific education, employment, or substance misuse treatment programmes). In addition, those on supervision and intensive supervision orders might pay a fine or reparation; they might do community work or be subject to EM as part of their supervision conditions. Probation officers still focus on rehabilitation and developing positive relationships with those subject to supervision in order to promote change and reduce reoffending, yet as they manage the 6500-plus supervision orders alongside home detention orders (c.3000), they are inevitably focused on ensuring public safety and surveillance (Deckert, 2020).

Before the introduction of intensive supervision, as well as the additional conditions post-detention from custody or home detention, the numbers of people on supervision were not high (Gibbs & King, 2002). In terms of sentencing, judges appear to favour the more exacting, specific, and restrictive periodic detention or community service. For example, orders of supervision peaked at 5166 in 1995, then dropped off consistently to around 2000 annually before intensive supervision was introduced in 2007 (Gibbs & King, 2002). Since 2007, both types of supervision order have grown. In 2018, there were 4411 supervision orders and 2498 intensive supervision orders. Together, they formed 11 per cent of the sentences imposed that year (Ministry of Justice, 2019). The introduction of extra restrictions, 'add-on' options, and extensions to supervision and home detention are said to have built judicial confidence in these options, and reassured the public that surveillance and public safety are a priority for Corrections (Department of Corrections, 2018).

Community work

Community work accounts for around 45 per cent of community sentences (Ministry of Justice, 2019; Polaschek, 2017). Community work can involve between 40 and 400 hours of unpaid work of benefit to the community. This takes a variety of forms, from practical tasks like clearing parks, beaches, and tracks to helping out at food banks, schools, and cultural centres. Offenders can use some of their community work hours to undertake additional basic employment and living skills (Department of Corrections, n.d.b; Polaschek,

2017). In the past, unpaid work (in the form of periodic detention and community service) was the 'bread and butter' of community sentencing, being handed out in more than 40 per cent of all sentences, and more than 80 per cent of all community sentences (Gibbs & King, 2002). However, since the introduction of community work in 2002 (and the rise of other sentences like home detention and community detention), the numbers of offenders undertaking unpaid work in the community have reduced significantly. In 2018, 11,990 community work orders were handed out, around 20 per cent of all sentences (Ministry of Justice, 2019).

Home detention
Home detention, the most severe option on the tariff of community sentences, was originally a direct alternative to imprisonment when introduced in 1999. With front-end and back-end options, home detention allowed those sentenced to imprisonment to be given the chance to serve that sentence in the community. Wearing an EM bracelet/anklet enables their movements and location to be continuously monitored through GPS or radio frequency. For judges and parole boards, home detention was popular, and during its first six years of operation over 6000 orders were made (Martinovic, 2017). However, these did not appear to dent the rising prison population. In 2007, home detention was introduced as a community sentence in its own right, with 2982 orders in 2018, amounting to 5 per cent of all sentences (Ministry of Justice, 2019).

Today, home detention is both a punishment and a rehabilitative option (Gibbs & King, 2003). It restricts an offender to a particular address and they are electronically monitored 24 hours a day for at least 14 days and up to one year (Department of Corrections, n.d.b). The rehabilitation component includes seeing probation staff regularly and completing programmes focused on reducing the chances of reoffending. Home detention is considered the most intensive option for support and surveillance; the completion rate is high (89 per cent) and the two-year reconviction rate is low at 38.7 per cent, compared to those being released from prison (60.7 per cent) (Department of Corrections, 2018; Martinovic, 2017).

Community detention
In 2018, there were 4666 sentences of community detention (around 8 per cent of all sentences) (Ministry of Justice, 2019). The curfew, as it is known, has proved exceedingly popular since its introduction in 2007, although it, too, has not had any impact on reducing the prison population. The popular appeal is clearly in its surveillance and its capacity to restrict liberty at specific times and to specific places. Community detention is designed to be punitive and to restrict an offender's movements as well as enforce where an offender resides (Department of Corrections, n.d.b). Community detention would not be feasible without the core element of EM. As with home detention, the offender wears a monitored anklet 24 hours per day, seven days a week while subject to this sentence, although the actual time on curfew is less than for those on home detention. Curfews can be a minimum of two hours per day up to a maximum of 84 hours per week, and sentence lengths are between 14 days and six months (Department of Corrections, n.d.b).

Staff monitoring the EM equipment for both home detention and community detention are called field officers, and they work alongside probation officers to monitor and deal with alerts and absences from expected residence or activities. Also, as part of these sentences, the other occupants and/or sponsors (usually family members) have to agree to certain conditions, and in certain cases may face prosecution if they do not comply with those conditions, even though they are not the offenders (Department of Corrections, n.d.a; Gibbs & King, 2003; Martinovic, 2017). The surveillance web, in the guise of public safety, has ensured that both private agencies and unsuspecting family/whānau and friends have continued to be drawn into helping manage offenders on community sentences (Gibbs & King, 2003).

Compliance and breaches

Under the managerial rationale mentioned earlier, Corrections has a strong focus on ensuring offenders comply with the expectations and conditions of community sentences. This has led to a concerning trend with increased numbers of breaches or failures to comply with the requirements, and a large number of subsequent convictions for 'offences against justice', which is the offence category for breaches. In 2018, for example, there were 36,015 convictions of traffic offending, 17,560 convictions of theft, 14,764 convictions of assault, and a staggering 34,423 convictions of offences against justice (Department of Corrections, 2018). If convicted of a breach, an offender can receive a sentence of imprisonment or additional community sentences or fines (Polaschek, 2017). There are without doubt a considerable number of offenders who breach and who are subsequently fast-tracked to prison.

Reconvictions

Community sentences that have high compliance rates due to their constant monitoring, restrictions, and intensity, such as home detention and community detention, have reasonable two-year reconviction rates, especially compared to those people released from prison sentences. The two-year reconviction rates are: home detention, 38.7 per cent; community detention, 38.6 per cent; supervision, 38.6 per cent; community work, 42.9 per cent; and intensive supervision, 50.9 per cent (Department of Corrections, 2018). This compares with 60.9 per cent for those coming out of prison (Department of Corrections, 2018). Some of the variance will be due to the risk levels of offenders, as well as their needs or ability to comply with the requirements of the sentence they have been given. For example, those on intensive supervision are quite likely to be at a higher risk of committing further offences than those on supervision or other punishments, and they will need extra support. Further attention also has to be given to Māori offenders – those who will more likely face discrimination and inequalities – who have the highest rates of reconvictions (50 per cent) for all community sentences compared to 40 per cent for non-Māori (Department of Corrections, 2019a). We shall return to concerns about Māori below.

Costs

It costs between $199 and $330 per day to look after a person in prison (Department of Corrections, 2018). Community sentences are much cheaper, with home detention being $63 per day, community detention $21, intensive supervision $19, supervision $17, and community work $10 (Department of Corrections, 2018). Hence, community sentences are financially cost-effective when compared with imprisonment.

There are, however, many 'hidden' costs, or burdens. For example, home detention and community detention are highly demanding and problematic, both for offenders and for family members and co-residents (Gibbs & King, 2003; Martinovic, 2017). Research shows that an increased stress or burden is inflicted on family members and others by the intrusive nature of EM and the conditions that offenders have to comply with, thus widening the net of surveillance upon those non-offenders who agree to support their family member under EM (Gibbs & King, 2003; Martinovic, 2017). All community sentences have become increasingly punitive, aligning well with the penal-populist agenda (Robinson & McNeill, 2017). These 'hidden' costs, which are not specifically about finances, are just one example of the factors that need to be considered when looking at the overall effectiveness of community sentences (Mental Health Commission of New South Wales [NSW], 2017).

We now turn to consider the main ongoing issues for those subject to community sentences: the needs of offenders, especially Māori offenders; mass surveillance; and *real* effectiveness.

ONGOING ISSUES

Who is the population and what are their needs?

In June 2019, those on community sentences and orders in Aotearoa New Zealand were 79.8 per cent male, 20.2 per cent female; 47 per cent Māori, 10 per cent Pasifika, and 34 per cent European (Department of Corrections, 2019b). As far as age is concerned, just under 40 per cent are under 30 years, another 31 per cent are aged 30–39 years, and just under 30 per cent are 40 years or over (Department of Corrections, 2019b). Significant numbers of offenders being supervised on community (and prison) sentences have substantial mental health issues, post-traumatic stress disorders, substance dependency, traumatic brain injuries, and neuro-disabilities (see Gibbs, chapter 29 this volume; Indig et al., 2016; Mental Health Commission of NSW, 2017).

Of particular concern is that Māori are three times more likely to receive a community sentence than non-Māori (Department of Corrections, 2019a). Additionally, the health, mental health, and social needs of Māori offenders are all more substantial than those of non-Māori (Department of Corrections, 2019a). The needs and issues of Māori offenders and their whānau are of grave concern to advocacy groups, providers of services, and some members of the current government (Department of Corrections, 2019a; JustSpeak, 2012; Safe and Effective Justice, 2018). Hence, Corrections itself is wanting to change the way it works with offenders both inside prison and in the community (Department of Corrections, 2019a; Office of the Auditor General, 2013). New initiatives include the use of 'navigators' to provide culturally based advocacy, support, and training. Navigators will help identify the broad needs of offenders and their whānau, and liaise with service providers – benefit providers, welfare, health, addictions, mental health, justice providers, and others – to meet these needs. Navigators will come from iwi-based services not governed by Corrections. For example, Te Piki Oranga (a Māori wellness organisation based in the Nelson/Blenheim region) provides navigators to assist with health, welfare, and justice needs.[5] Te Piki Oranga runs iwi community panels specifically to reduce the chances of young offenders ending up in prison or on community sentences. In working more closely with iwi, Corrections is at the early stages of co-design, whereby a wider group of iwi and Māori experts have had genuine input in how to effectively and compassionately manage offenders in prison and on community sentences (Department of Corrections, 2019a).

In addition to initiatives already under way we might do well to follow the Youth Court and youth justice system implementation processes of the Oranga Tamariki legislation (Oranga Tamariki Act 1989), whereby extensive use of family group conferences as well as the use of Rangatahi Courts have consistently reduced the numbers of youth in court or on community sentences or their youth equivalent.[6] Through restorative processes, detailed wraparound plans are made with the 'offender', their family, and their wider supports. Plans are tailored to meet the needs of young people, and are followed up by robust support from statutory professionals (e.g., youth justice social workers) and others (e.g., mental health, education, and cultural support workers). At all stages of the youth justice system, the rationales of restoration, rehabilitation, reparation, accountability, and reducing reoffending apply. Formal punishments are avoided if at all possible, although bail and supervision conditions and restrictions may still apply. It is accepted that young people have high and complex needs in a large majority of cases. Applying a youth justice model to adults undertaking community sentences may ensure the needs of offenders are met at the same as reducing the negative elements of punishment (JustSpeak, 2012; Mental Health Commission of NSW, 2017).

Mass surveillance for surveillance's sake?

In 1985, there were 18,313 community sentences. This rose by 131 per cent over three decades, with 42,353 starts in the 2016/17 financial year (Department of Corrections, 2017). There have been ebbs and flows in the use of community sentences, but the general trend is up. Robinson and McNeill (2017) and Polaschek (2017) note the large numbers of people on community sentences in an era of mass supervision. While crime rates are dropping, there are more people on community *and* prison sentences who are being supervised by Corrections staff, private companies, and the community in general. The mass surveillance of offenders is now a norm in New Zealand. The 2007 Sentencing Amendment Act increased conditions, restrictions, monitoring, and compulsory attendance at rehabilitation courses. These have all added more surveillance options for courts and parole boards to use. We should therefore not be surprised that more control will be exerted on those who are deemed deviant, rather than vulnerable.

New Zealand's rates of electronic monitoring are some of the highest in the world compared to other countries, including Australia, the UK, and the US (Martinovic, 2017). The use of a hierarchy of sentences or tariffs also means that lower-tariff options (such as fines) or less-intrusive community work sentences have declined in favour of higher-tariff options like community detention, home detention, and intensive supervision, with all sorts of conditions (and post-detention conditions) attached to them (Polaschek, 2017). Overall, numbers of those on community sentences have increased, alongside the continued rise of the prison population. This has confirmed that community sentences remain as punishment in the community and not as serious alternatives to incarceration (Gibbs & King, 2003; Robinson & McNeill, 2017). In addition, the number of family/whānau members and co-residents who are also drawn into the web of surveillance through home and community detention expectations has increased (Department of Corrections, n.d.a), and there has been an increase in the private security workforce in the form of those who monitor EM compliance. Questions remain about how this mass surveillance in an era of expanding monitoring technologies will develop. While the current Labour government has repeatedly given strong messages on the need to overhaul New Zealand's criminal justice system, politicians from across the party spectrum have continued to promote messages of tough responses to crime, emphasising the need to alleviate risks, enhance security, and ensure compliance (Fyers, 2018; Safe and Effective Justice, 2018).

CONCLUSION

We know that reconviction rates for those starting community sentences are lower than rates for those who start prison sentences, but we do not really know what particular components of particular sentence options may or may not make a difference. All kinds of benefits may come from undertaking components of rehabilitation, restoration, or restriction while being actively supervised and supported by agencies and other supports. True success does not lie in whether a person is 60 per cent or 40 per cent likely to be reconvicted within two years. That is just one measure. Measuring tangible and less-tangible benefits and outcomes of different community sentence options will always be important, as will understanding the core features of what works to help offenders desist from offending. These core features include: building prosocial relationships and resilience; encouraging people to age out of crime as they are supported to engage in meaningful personal, social, and economic relations; helping people learn from transitions or life events, and viewing such events as opportunities for change; helping to support people's commitment to change; and encouraging people to begin the process of change of their self-narratives and views of their own and others' social and personal identities (McNeill et al., 2005; Mental Health Commission of NSW, 2017).

Real rehabilitation is not about numbers or time spent on community sentences or with whom; real rehabilitation occurs when 'all services in the criminal justice system are recovery-oriented and trauma informed, and support offenders to live meaningful lives, especially through work and education' (Mental Health Commission of NSW, 2017, p. 19). Rehabilitation also happens when offenders can access supports, accommodation, good friendships, and care, and are given the chance to actively participate and flourish in all areas of citizenship and society.

New Zealand's use of community sentences, notably the more restrictive use of EM, has continued to rise with negligible impact on prison rates. Māori and those with multiple health, cognitive, and social needs continue to dominate the client base of Corrections. In order to achieve support and rehabilitation rather than retributive or risk-focused punishments, community sentences should be used as alternatives to imprisonment. They should be engaged in the least restrictive manner, be offender- or person-centric, and attempt to make a positive difference to peoples' lives, to assist desistance from offending.

STUDY QUESTIONS

- How can judges be encouraged to use community sentences as genuine alternatives to imprisonment for people convicted of crimes?
- How can Corrections staff respond sensitively to the needs and experiences of those supervised on community sentences?
- Would using a youth justice system approach help reduce the numbers of those subject to community sentences?

FURTHER READING

JustSpeak. (2012). *Māori and the criminal justice system: A youth perspective*. Retrieved from https://www.justspeak.org.nz/ourwork/maori-and-the-criminal-justice-system-a-youth-perspective

Mental Health Commission of New South Wales. (2017). *Towards a just system: Mental illness and cognitive impairment in the criminal justice system*. Sydney, Australia: Mental Health Commission of New South Wales. Retrieved from https://nswmentalhealthcommission.com.au/sites/default/files/documents/justice_paper_final_web.pdf

Morrison, B., Bowman, J., & Meredith, P. (2019). 'I'm trying to change my ways': The desistance processes of persistent offenders. *Practice*, 7(1), 18–26. Retrieved from https://www.corrections.govt.nz/resources/newsletters_and_brochures/journal/volume_7_issue_1_july_2019/im_trying_to_change_my_ways_the_desistance_processes_of_persistent_offenders

NOTES

1. Tapu acted as a prohibitory mechanism to protect people and places; mana was inherited or earnt status, and personal and collective mana were important; muru was a process for seeking justice and compensation when harm had occurred (Ministry of Justice, 2001). Utu was a means of seeking and restoring balance when harm also occurred, primarily through the giving and receiving of gifts rather than exacting revenge (Ministry of Justice, 2001).
2. See *Northern Advocate*, 2019.
3. See Te Piki Oranga Māori Wellness Services, n.d., and https://forms.justice.govt.nz/search/Documents/WT/wt_DOC_135986487/Tu%20Mai%20te%20Rangi%20W.pdf

4   The other 55 per cent receive sentences of imprisonment, monetary penalties, or discharges, or no sentence imposed (see Ministry of Justice, 2019).

5   Te Piki Oranga Māori Wellness Services, n.d.

6   Ngā Kōti Rangatahi (Rangatahi Courts) are specialised Youth Courts that incorporate Māori processes and concepts – see District Court of New Zealand. (n.d.).

REFERENCES

Bowman, J., & Morrison, B. (2019). 'It's all about the choices I make': Understanding women's pathways to desistance. *Practice, 7*(1), 11–17. Retrieved from https://www.corrections.govt.nz/resources/newsletters_and_brochures/journal/volume_7_issue_1_july_2019/its_all_about_the_choices_i_make_understanding_womens_pathways_to_desistance

Burton, M. (2006, August 18). *Effective interventions and safer communities* [Speech]. Retrieved from https://www.beehive.govt.nz/speech/effective-interventions-and-safer-communities

Cullen, F. (2013). Rehabilitation: Beyond nothing works. *Crime and Justice, 42*(1), 299–376. doi:10.1086/670395

Deckert, A. (2020). Battles and legacies: Reviewing Robson's 1971 article on penal policy in Aotearoa. In R. G. Smith (Ed.). *The changing face of criminology in Australia and New Zealand.* London, UK: Sage.

Department of Corrections. (n.d.a). *Electronic monitoring: Important information for sponsors, family and whanau.* Retrieved from https://www.corrections.govt.nz/resources/newsletters_and_brochures/electronic_monitoring_important_information_for_sponsors%2c_family_and_whanau.html

Department of Corrections. (n.d.b). *Working with offenders: Sentences and orders.* Retrieved from https://www.corrections.govt.nz/working_with_offenders/community_sentences/sentences_and_orders.html

Department of Corrections. (2017). *Corrections volumes report 2016/17.* Retrieved from https://www.corrections.govt.nz/resources/research_and_statistics/corrections-volumes-report/corrections_volumes_report_201617

Department of Corrections. (2018). *Annual report 2017/18.* Retrieved from https://www.corrections.govt.nz/resources/strategic_reports/annual-reports/annual_report_201718

Department of Corrections. (2019a). *Hōkai Rangi. Ara Poutama Aotearoa Strategy, 2019–2024.* Retrieved from https://www.corrections.govt.nz/resources/strategic_reports/corrections_strategic_plans/hkai_rangi.html

Department of Corrections. (2019b). *Community-based sentence and order fact and statistics – June 2019.* Retrieved from https://www.corrections.govt.nz/resources/research_and_statistics/community_sentences_and_orders/community_stats_june_2019.html

District Court of New Zealand. (n.d.). *Taking lessons from the Rangatahi Courts.* Retrieved from http://www.districtcourts.govt.nz/youth-court/publications/taking-lessons-from-the-rangatahi-courts/

Fyers, A. (2018, May 16). 20 years of 'tough on crime' stance sees prison population surge. *Stuff.* Retrieved from https://i.stuff.co.nz/national/crime/103795593/the-impact-of-two-decades-of-being-tough-on-crime

Gibbs, A., & King, D. (2002). Alternatives to custody in the New Zealand criminal justice system: Current features and future prospects. *Social Policy and Administration, 36*(4), 392–407. doi:10.1111/1467-9515.t01-1-00261

Gibbs, A., & King, D. (2003). The electronic ball and chain? The operation and impact of home detention with electronic monitoring in New Zealand. *Australian and New Zealand Journal of Criminology, 36*(1), 1–17. doi:10.1375/000486503764805257

Indig, D., Gear, C., & Wilhelm, K. (2016). *Comorbid substance use disorders and mental health disorders among New Zealand prisoners*. Wellington, New Zealand: Department of Corrections. Retrieved from https://www.corrections.govt.nz/resources/research_and_statistics/comorbid_substance_use_disorders_and_mental_health_disorders_among_new_zealand_prisoners

Ingram, C. (2013). Probation practice: Twenty years on. *Practice, 1*(1), 20–23. Retrieved from https://www.corrections.govt.nz/__data/assets/pdf_file/0010/11413/COR-Practice-Journal-Vol1-Iss1-May13-WEB.pdf

Jackson, M. (1988). *The Maori and the criminal justice system: A new perspective: He whaipaanga hou: Part 2*. Wellington, New Zealand: Policy and Research Division, Department of Justice. Retrieved from https://www2.justice.govt.nz/website-documents/maori-and-the-criminal-justice-system-a-new-perspective-p2.pdf

JustSpeak. (2012). *Māori and the criminal justice system: A youth perspective*. Retrieved from https://www.justspeak.org.nz/ourwork/maori-and-the-criminal-justice-system-a-youth-perspective

MacManus, J. (2019, August 13). Why a pastor who abused children served less prison time than a low-level cannabis dealer. *Stuff*. Retrieved from https://i.stuff.co.nz/national/114692088/why-a-pastor-who-abused-children-served-half-as-much-prison-time-as-a-lowlevel-cannabis-dealer

Martinovic, M. (2017). New Zealand's extensive electronic monitoring application. *Practice, 5*(1), 34–40. Retrieved from https://www.corrections.govt.nz/resources/research_and_statistics/journal/volume_5_issue_1_july_2017/new_zealands_extensive_electronic_monitoring_application_out_on_a_limb_or_leading_the_world.html

McNeill, F., Batchelor, S., Burnett, R., & Knox, J. (2005). *21st century social work: Reducing re-offending: Key practice skills*. Edinburgh, Scotland: Scottish Executive. Retrieved from: https://www.researchgate.net/publication/45243577_21st_Century_Social_Work_Reducing_Re-Offending_Key_Practice_Skills

Mental Health Commission of New South Wales. (2017). *Towards a just system: Mental illness and cognitive impairment in the criminal justice system*. Sydney, Australia: Mental Health Commission of New South Wales. Retrieved from https://nswmentalhealthcommission.com.au/sites/default/files/documents/justice_paper_final_web.pdf

Ministry of Justice. (2001). *He hīnātore ki te ao Māori: A glimpse into the Māori world*. Retrieved from https://www.justice.govt.nz/assets/Documents/Publications/he-hinatora-ki-te-ao-maori.pdf

Ministry of Justice. (2019). *Adults convicted and sentenced: Data highlights for 2018*. Retrieved from https://www.justice.govt.nz/assets/Documents/Publications/adult-conviction-and-sentencing-statistics-data-highlights-v1.1.pdf

Morrison, B., Bowman, J., & Meredith, P. (2019). 'I'm trying to change my ways': The desistance processes of persistent offenders. *Practice, 7*(1), 18–26. Retrieved from https://www.corrections.govt.nz/resources/newsletters_and_brochures/journal/volume_7_issue_1_july_2019/im_trying_to_change_my_ways_the_desistance_processes_of_persistent_offenders

Newbold, G. (2008). Another one bites the dust: Recent initiatives in correctional reform in New Zealand. *Australian and New Zealand Journal of Criminology, 41*(3), 348–401. doi:10.1375/acri.41.3.384

Newbold, G. (2016). *Crime, law and justice in New Zealand*. London, UK: Routledge.

Northern Advocate. (2019, November 19). Forestry training pilot helps 11 Ngāwhā prisoners into jobs. Retrieved from https://www.nzherald.co.nz/forestry/news/article.cfm?c_id=47&objectid=12286138

Office of the Auditor General. (2013). *Department of Corrections: Managing offenders to reduce reoffending*. Retrieved from https://www.oag.govt.nz/2013/reducing-reoffending

Otago Daily Times. (2020, August 11). National promises specialist gang unit. Retrieved from https://www.odt.co.nz/news/decision-2020/tough-crime-national-promises-specialist-gang-unit

Polaschek, D. (2017). New Zealand, Corrections in. In K. R. Kerley (Ed.), *The encyclopedia of corrections* (pp. 637–646). New York, NY: Wiley-Blackwell.

Pratt, J. (2008). When penal populism stops: Legitimacy, scandal and the power to punish in New Zealand. *Australian and New Zealand Journal of Criminology, 41*(3), 364–383. doi:10.1375/acri.41.3.364

Robinson, G., & McNeill, F. (2017). Punishment in the community: Evolution, expansion, and moderation. In A. Liebling, S. Maruna, & L. McAra (Eds.), *Oxford handbook of criminology* (pp. 868–888). Oxford, UK: Oxford University Press. doi:10.1093/he/9780198719441.003.0039

Safe and Effective Justice. (2018). *Hāpaitia te Oranga Tangata. Safe and Effective Justice.* Retrieved from https://safeandeffectivejustice.govt.nz/

Te Piki Oranga Māori Wellness Services. (n.d.). Retrieved from https://www.tpo.org.nz/

20

Restorative Justice
The 'Land of the Long White Lie'

Juan Marcellus Tauri

Arising in the late 1970s, the restorative justice (RJ) movement appeared to offer a new response to crime in jurisdictions like Aotearoa New Zealand. Its antecedents are debatable, but influential to the movement's development in the early days were the work of community justice practitioners in San Francisco (Engle Merry & Milner, 1993), and a probation officer in Kitchener, Ontario, who some RJ advocates argue *invented* modern RJ when he began facilitating victim–offender meetings for youth offenders (Richards, 2007). The movement gathered significant momentum in the late 1980s and early 1990s through the intellectual endeavours of John Braithwaite (1989), Howard Zehr (1990), and others. RJ advocates claim to have been driven to develop alternative practices because of their deep dissatisfaction with the formal justice system, and through a belief that more communitarian responses were required to reduce social harm (for examples of this argument, see Albrecht, 2011; Bazemore & Schiff, 2001; Weitekamp, 1999; see Richards, 2014, for a critique of this position).

As the literature clearly demonstrates, New Zealand holds a special place among RJ advocates and practitioners internationally. This is largely the result of the introduction of the family group conference (FGC) forum through the Children's, Young Persons, and Their Families Act (CYPFA) 1989 (now Oranga Tamariki Act 1989). The importance of the FGC to the RJ movement internationally cannot be overstated, as evidenced by the fact that a significant amount of RJ literature and research is dedicated to the forum (see Dijkstra et al., 2018; Hollinshead et al., 2017; Schmid & Morgenshtern, 2017). The introduction of the FGC has proven invaluable for the RJ movement in two ways: firstly, it significantly aided

RJ entrepreneurs when they began marketing their programmes on an increasingly globalised crime-control market (Tauri, 2016; also see discussion below). Secondly, it provided a valuable resource for settler-colonial governments who were grappling with high rates of Indigenous people's 'over-representation' in offending and imprisonment statistics (Blagg, 2016; Cunneen, 2002), and who were also seeking to recuperate control over the *narrative of justice* after decades of sustained Indigenous critique of the criminal justice system (Tauri, 2018).

In the next section, a detailed definition of RJ and an overview of its practice is offered. This is followed by a discussion of the development of RJ in New Zealand (it will be brief, as this issue has been covered extensively elsewhere: see Consedine, 1995; Henwood, 1997; Henwood & Stratford, 2014; Schmid, 2002). The final section offers a challenge to the prevailing narrative found in the RJ lexicon that sustains, and at times invigorates, the fiction that New Zealand is a *restorative paradise* that empowers Māori. It will be argued that the FGC, much lauded by RJ advocates everywhere, has thus far done little to empower Māori. However, before we discuss the key issues outlined above, we must first clarify what we mean when we talk about RJ policies and practices, and how they are distinguished from state practices.

WHAT IS RESTORATIVE JUSTICE?

While advocates offer a range of definitions of RJ, most contain common elements. For example, RJ is often described as a system or process of justice involving all parties affected by an act of social harm (including the offender, victim[s], and their mutual supporters), who meet to discuss ways to heal the hurt resulting from the harm, reconcile the victim and offender, and reintegrate each of them back into the community (Schmid, 2002; Zehr, 1990). Luna (2003) identifies three basic *principles* that guide RJ practice, namely:

> [1] [C]rime is not just an act against the state but against particular victims and the community in general, with [2] offending viewed primarily as a breach of social relationships and only secondarily as a violation of the law. [3] The community, family members, and supporters, rather than the state and its justice machinery, are considered the locus of crime control and sanctioning, with the restorative model seeking the active participation of victims, families, and community representatives to address the causes and consequences of offending (pp. 228–229).

Richards (2014) summarises the differences between RJ and state responses to crime and social harm, at least from the perspective of RJ advocates. She identifies that the formal justice system is *adversarial* to the point that consideration of wrongdoing often becomes an aggressive competition between two sides seeking to have their version of a criminal event accepted in order to win a conviction, or an acquittal. In comparison, restorative justice practitioners prefer an *inquisitorial* process that generates dialogue between all who are impacted by criminal conduct. Furthermore, while the formal system sidelines the victim, calling upon them to provide evidence for the state, the victim and their family are significant participants in the RJ process. And lastly, the focus of the state's justice system is to hold offenders to account for their actions by punishing them for their misdeeds. In comparison a process based on RJ principles, while also concerned with holding offenders accountable, is less obsessed with punishment and more concerned with facilitating reconciliation with the victim and supporting an offender's reintegration back into the community.

Restorative justice in practice
Since the conception of RJ, a range of programmes have stemmed from the intellectual labour of the founding scholars, including various forms of victim–offender mediation and iconic

processes such as sentencing circles, developed by judges in Canada in the 1990s, and various forms of conferencing forums including New Zealand's FGC.

According to McElrea (2002), the typical New Zealand restorative conference involves the prior admission of responsibility by the offender, the voluntary attendance of all participants, the assistance of a neutral facilitator, and the presence of a police officer. The process itself provides the opportunity for explanations to be given for offending behaviour, questions answered as to why it occurred, apologies offered, the drawing up of a plan to address the wrong done, and an agreement as to how that plan will be implemented and monitored post-conference.

Zedner (2007) notes that, despite diversity in RJ practices, what they 'have in common is that they involve a participatory process whereby all people with a stake in a particular offence ... come together to resolve collectively how to deal with the aftermath of the offence and its implications for the future' (p. 2). Other core practice values shared by RJ practitioners include a focus on victim empowerment and healing, offender accountability, reconciliation between victim and offender, and reparations made for the harm done (Zedner, 2007). Furthermore, RJ processes need to be community-centred, informal, de-professionalised, and focused on consensual decision-making and inclusiveness.

Having established the core principles and practices of RJ, identified how these are expressed in practice, and articulated the types of outcomes RJ practitioners seek to achieve, we now turn to the development of RJ in the New Zealand context.

Wiremu in Wonderland: The restorative justice landscape in Aotearoa New Zealand

When, or at what point in time, RJ developed as a recognisable justice practice in Aotearoa New Zealand is difficult to establish. Some would argue that RJ-type processes and principles were long practised by Māori, so the insertion of RJ policies and interventions in the early 1990s was simply a contemporary Pākehā manifestation of old justice practices (Hakiaha, 1999). However, in terms of contemporary manifestations, recognisable RJ policies and programmes began to formulate here in the late 1980s, and continued to develop throughout the 1990s and 2000s (McElrea, 2002; Suzuki & Wood, 2017).

According to McElrea (2002), a few years before the term 'restorative justice' became known and widespread throughout the country, New Zealand introduced the FGC forum through the CYPFA 1989. In so doing, the legislature began what some refer to as New Zealand's RJ revolution (Consedine, 1995; Shriver & Shriver, 2012). McElrea (2002) contends that '[o]ne of the primary objectives of the legislation was to strengthen the ability of families to hold their young people accountable and encourage them to develop in law-abiding and socially productive ways' (p. 2). He goes on to detail the early evolution of RJ across New Zealand via the FGC forum thus:

> Those like myself working with the Act soon saw it, talked about it and wrote about the FGC concept as a new model of justice. When I later returned to Cambridge on sabbatical leave and read Howard Zehr's *Changing Lenses* it seemed he was describing a very similar approach. In early 1994 I wrote two papers, the first assessing our youth justice model as a restorative model and the second arguing for the application of its central principles to adults through *community group conferences* (p. 2, italics in original).

While it started out as a youth justice initiative, the FGC has since expanded into other sections of the criminal justice system and across into other social policy portfolios. For example, in 1995, three pilot restorative community panels were implemented to divert adult offenders from the court system (Bowen et al., 2012). Thereafter the use of RJ forums for adult offenders was expanded through legislation, including the Sentencing Act 2002, the Parole Act 2002, and the Victims' Rights Act 2002 (Ministry of Justice, 2004). Furthermore, since the mid-2000s, New Zealand has pursued the development of RJ processes in educational institutions. Driven by concern at the rising rate of student exclusions (most especially Māori youth) from secondary schools, education practitioners turned to RJ in an attempt to move schools away from a retributive approach to problematic behaviour (Restorative Practices Development Team, 2003; Wearmouth et al., 2007).

If one is to believe the literature, the really interesting aspect of the development of RJ in New Zealand is the importance of Māori justice philosophies and practices to the movement's evolution. Advocates regularly inform us that Māori critique of the formal justice system was in large part responsible for the development of the FGC, which in time morphed into one of *the* leading RJ programmes in the world. There is some truth to these claims: Yes, the FGC forum was constructed partly in response to Māori critique of the justice system, especially of youth justice and childcare and protection practices (see Jackson, 1988; Ministerial Advisory Committee, 1988). And, if we look closely enough, we see elements within it that are comparable to traditional Māori approaches to social harm (McElrea, 2002), albeit not in practice (Olsen et al., 1995; Tauri, 2016). However, a closer reading of the legislation, the policy framework, and what little actual research has been done exposes the exaggerated, mythological nature of the claims-making of RJ advocates and entrepreneurs and the policy sector (Moyle & Tauri, 2016). To paraphrase Daly (2002), it is time to tell the real story about the supposed *Māoriness* of the FGC forum.

THE 'MĀORINESS' OF THE FAMILY GROUP CONFERENCING FORUM: THE REAL STORY

In her ground-breaking article 'Restorative Justice: The Real Story', Kathleen Daly (2002, p. 55) identifies four myths associated with the RJ movement, namely that:

1. restorative justice is the opposite of retributive justice;
2. restorative justice is a 'care' (or feminine) response to crime in comparison to a 'justice' (or masculine) response;
3. restorative justice can be expected to produce major changes in people; and
4. restorative justice uses Indigenous justice practices and was the dominant form of pre-modern justice.

For the remainder of this chapter I will focus on the last myth, that RJ uses components of Indigenous justice practice or, perhaps more accurately, that it can produce interventions that incorporate Indigenous justice processes and in turn empower those involved. This focus is necessary because that particular myth has been central to the successful globalisation of the FGC.

The range of myths, or perhaps more accurately *purposeful misrepresentations*, associated with the FGC forum are legion, beginning with the oft-repeated claim that the forum was one of the first truly restorative, state-sponsored interventions in the Western world (for examples of this [mis]representation, see Maxwell & Morris, 1993; McElrea, 2002; Wearmouth et al., 2007). In fact, as stated earlier, the FGC was never intended as an RJ forum that provided significant empowerment to Māori. Indeed, one of the key architects of both the forum and the legislation, Doolan (2002), has since stated categorically that it was never intended to be an RJ process or to empower 'the community', including Māori, to the extent that advocates have claimed (see Fox, 2018). As Suzuki and Wood (2017) write:

[W]hile New Zealand is often set forth in the literature as the first country to implement RJ systemically, none of the architects of the *Children, Young Persons, and Their Families Act 1989* (CYPFA) had ever heard of RJ when they included Family Group Conferencing (FGC) as part of this Act. Rather, FGC was only part of a larger diversionary framework of the CYPFA, such that its influence and notability as a 'restorative justice' paradigm was only retrospectively understood (p. 393).

Nor has the process empowered Māori, as advocates have claimed in the past (see Maxwell & Morris, 1993), and continue to do so today despite evidence to the contrary (see Henwood & Stratford, 2014, for an example of this type of claims-making, and see Bradley et al., 2006; Moyle, 2013, 2014; Moyle & Tauri, 2016 for a critique). This claim is largely a fiction manufactured by RJ advocates and perpetuated by policy workers tasked with recuperating governmental control of the justice narrative in order to offset the dual (political) threats of Māori over-representation in crime statistics and their ongoing critique of crime control practice.

Of late, advocates' assertions that the forum empowers Māori have been exposed by the author's own research and that of the social worker and activist Paora Moyle. Moyle's work (2013, 2014; Moyle & Tauri, 2016) in particular reveals wide-ranging dissatisfaction among Māori with the way in which the FGC forum has been run. Most especially problematic for her research participants – who included Māori social workers, youth offenders, and family members – were the glaring contradictions between the supposedly *Indigenous foundations* of the forum and their lived experience of it. Practitioners and participants alike expressed disquiet at the tokenistic approach to Māori cultural philosophy and practice they experienced during the FGC. This perspective is effectively summarised in comments from research participants, such as one who stated that '[t]he family group conference is about as restorative as it is culturally sensitive . . . in the same way Pākehā [European] social workers believe they are competent enough to work with our people . . . Pākehā think they're the natural ordinary community against which all other ethnicities are measured'. And another who argued that '*whakapapa* is intrinsically linked to the development of *tamariki* [children] but unfortunately it's something that this system does not recognise let alone value . . . I've seen FGCs run without any *whānau* showing up and then it's their fault for not caring enough . . . and that's what the Court report will show' (Moyle & Tauri, 2016, pp. 95–96, italics in original). The experiences of Moyle's research participants demonstrate that the FGC forum does not always deliver the restorative process or outcomes that advocates claim it does.

I contend that the forum has thus far failed to match the rhetoric of its advocates, and of their claims that it provides more culturally appropriate justice practice and a measure of jurisdictional empowerment to Māori. When that failure is considered alongside evidence that some of its members are purposefully and strategically using elements of Indigenous life-worlds to enhance the marketability of their RJ products (see the later discussion on the globalisation of RJ), then one quickly comes to the realisation that, right now, RJ works more to support the settler-colonial than it does for disempowered communities. The state's enthusiasm – and perhaps also the rationale – for claiming RJ and Indigenous-like status for interventions which, like the FGC, offer little in the way of empowerment is beautifully captured in the following quote from Love (2000), who wrote 'that the apparent state commitment to a culturally appropriate and empowering process [like the FGC forum] . . . may in fact serve only to provide a brown veneer for a white system that has historically contributed to state-run programs of cultural genocide and whanau dismemberment' (p. 29).

The case study of the FGC as mythologised RJ artefact reveals the political nature of crime control policy. In particular, it demonstrates how the state is able to capture projects, such as RJ, that often start out as community-led but which are then drawn into the ambit of the state.

Furthermore, it demonstrates the ease with which the mythologising process can proceed; in the case of the FGC, the exaggerated claims of academics responsible for initial evaluations (see Maxwell & Morris, 1993; Maxwell et al., 2004), and other early advocates (see Consedine, 1995; McElrea, 2002) of the *Māoriness* and *restorativeness* of the forum, led to it developing into a *cause célèbre* of the new justice movement. The exaggerated representation of the forum meant that, in time, it became instrumental in RJ becoming an essential part of the New Zealand state's justice processes, and in becoming a key component of its ongoing project to portray itself as a good Treaty partner for Māori (Tauri, 2016). Perhaps most significantly, the success of advocates and policy workers in portraying the forum as both Indigenous-inspired and restorative led to it becoming a popular response to *the Indigenous problem* in other settler-colonial jurisdictions, with significant consequences for their Indigenous peoples.

LEAVING WONDERLAND: EXPORTING THE FAMILY GROUP CONFERENCE TO THE WORLD

It is evident that over the past 20 years the FGC forum has been unrooted and globalised to such an extent that it is one of the most popular commodities on the international crime-control policy market (see Barnsdale & Walker, 2007; Deukmedjian, 2008; House of Commons Justice Committee, 2016; Scuro, 2013; Tauri, 2017). While the forum has proved popular in many Western jurisdictions, it has proved especially so in the settler-colonial jurisdictions of Canada, Australia, and the US, each of which has high rates of Indigenous offending and imprisonment.

In this section it will be argued, firstly, that what has been exported and globalised, the FGC in particular, is not RJ as such, but rather a state-centred (or at least 'supportive') *responsibilisation* forum that has been stripped over time of any true restorativeness. This has occurred as a result of the increasing standardisation of the forum, which has increasingly sidelined the communitarian ethos that underpinned the principles of RJ outlined earlier. I will also argue that much of the marketing of New Zealand RJ has exaggerated the restorativeness of interventions, and most especially the indigenousness of the various forums marketed on the globalised crime-control market.

The extent and impact of the globalisation of the family group conferencing forum

There is growing anecdotal evidence that the global transfer of crime control policy is negatively impacting Indigenous peoples (see Tauri, 2004, on New Zealand, and Victor, 2007, on Canada). This is particularly evident in the restorative and youth justice contexts. From a distance it appears that the process is impacting Indigenous peoples in a number of ways, including:

- containment of Indigenous critique of the formal justice systems of neocolonial states through the production of state-centred indigenised policies and programmes (Tauri, 2013); and
- blocking Indigenous activities aimed at enhancing their jurisdictional autonomy and ability to develop their own responses to social harm, via the importation of 'culturally appropriate' crime control products (Victor, 2007).

It is evident that New Zealand's FGC forum was purposefully marketed in other settler-colonial jurisdictions, especially Canada (Tauri, 2016). It is also evident that the marketing of these products was aided by academic literature which promoted the 'Māori origin myths' discussed earlier (for contemporary manifestations of the myth, see Maxwell, 2008; Ross, 2009; Waites et al., 2004). At an early stage in the process of globalisation, Indigenous scholars signalled disquiet with the importation of the FGC forum. For example, in 1997 Gloria Lee, a member of the Cree First Nation in Canada, published an article titled 'The Newest Old Gem: Family Group Conferencing'. In this work Lee expressed concerns about the recently imported forum being forced upon Canadian Indigenous peoples at the expense of the development and implementation of their own justice processes. She argued that 'First Nation communities are vigorously encouraged to adopt and implement the Māori process and to make alterations to fit the specific community needs, customs and traditions of people who will make use of the new process' (Lee, 1997, p. 1). Lee's concerns with the nature of the importation of the FGC process into the Canadian jurisdiction, and the impact it might have on Indigenous peoples' justice aspirations in that country, have since been shown to be valid.

In the 20-plus years since the publication of Lee's article, many Canadian Indigenous peoples are still struggling to gain state support for the implementation of their own justice processes (Tauri, 2016). We can demonstrate the potential negative impact of this process by citing just one case study, that of the Stó:lō First Nation of British Columbia and their experience of the importation of the supposedly *Māori justice process*, the FGC, by the Royal Canadian Mounted Police (RCMP) in the mid-1990s. Katz and Bonham (2006) relate that, in 1997, the RCMP adopted a policy which gave the police the discretion to use restorative justice. Based on the New Zealand-style conferencing format, as presented around Canada by advocates such as Moore and O'Connell (Rudin, personal communication, 2012), the RCMP subsequently developed guidelines for community justice forums, and over time the forum spread across Canada (Chatterjee & Elliott, 2003).

Dr Wenona Victor, a criminologist and activist from the Stó:lō Nation of the Fraser Valley in British Columbia, underlines the negative impact the importation of FGCs to Canada had on First Nation justice aspirations in that jurisdiction, thus not only demonstrating the effectiveness of the marketing process, but also confirming the concerns Lee expressed in the late 1990s. Dr Victor describes receiving training on implementing FGC within Stó:lō territory, a process that had been sold to them as having been developed by Māori, the Indigenous people of New Zealand:

> On the first day [of FGC-related training] we all eagerly awaited her [the trainer's] arrival. We were somewhat surprised to see an extremely 'White' looking lady enter the room; however, we have blonde blue-eyed, even red-headed Stó:lō among us, and so, too, we presumed, must the Māori. However, it did not take us long to come to realise this lady was not Māori and was in fact Xwelitem [European]. Ah, the Māori had sent a Xwelitem; okay, we do that too, on occasion. It is one of the many ironies of colonisation whereby Xwelitem often become our teachers ... [t]here are times when it is a Xwelitem who is recognised as the Stó:lō 'expert' and therefore, is the one talking even when there are Elders present. But by the end of the three-day training course I was convinced the Māori had lost their minds! There was absolutely nothing Indigenous about this [FGC] model of justice whatsoever! (in Palys & Victor, 2007, p. 6).

The global spread of the forum, especially across settler-colonial jurisdictions, is testament to the power of the marketing arm of the RJ movement and its swift incorporation into the formal justice system. The constant, erroneous, and exaggerated claims of the Māoriness of the forum, and of the extent to which it works as a restorative process, have been instrumental to the globalisation of the forum, but that has brought real negative consequences: for both Māori, who have seen their activism for a true measure of jurisdictional autonomy (Jackson, 1988) diverted into a centralised, heavily bureaucratic and scripted forum, and for other Indigenous peoples like the Stó:lō, who were forced to undertake training for the process at the expense of developing one based on their own philosophies and practices.

CONCLUSION

Without question RJ policy and practice has become an important part of the criminal justice landscape across most Western jurisdictions, including New Zealand. That the movement developed due to profound concerns by justice advocates for the perceived failings of the formal system is unquestionable. For that reason the early manifestations of RJ programmes were influenced by values that were at odds with state crime control, such as the meaningful participation for victims of crime, a focus on inquisitorial mediation and dialogue, and concern for the meaningful reintegration of both offenders and victims back into the community.

However, along the way something interesting happened: restorative justice in New Zealand and elsewhere became consumed by the state so that today it is a significant part of the formal justice landscape. The envelopment of the movement by the state was in large part the result of three interrelated developments that coalesced in the late 1980s and throughout the 1990s. There were: (1) the passing into law of the CYPFA 1989, including the FGC forum; (2) RJ advocates and criminologists 'discovering' and promoting the restorative elements of the forum; and (3) the development of the myth of the forum's 'Māoriness'. Since then the forum has come to signify RJ practice in this country and has become New Zealand's most successful crime control export.

While the mythologising associated with the forum has made New Zealand RJ well regarded throughout the world, it has not been without its negative consequences, especially for Māori and Indigenous peoples residing in other settler-colonial jurisdictions, such as the Stó:lō people reported earlier. In New Zealand, empirical research carried out by Māori scholars is challenging the continued portrayal of the forum as both a restorative process and an empowering one for Māori participants. Instead, the research demonstrates that participants are often well aware of the tokenistic treatment of their cultural values and practices by the officials who dominate the forum. Furthermore, research by Indigenous scholars, such as Dr Wenona Victor, highlights the nefarious impact that the misleading marketing of the FGC has had on Indigenous peoples who are attempting to reinvigorate their own traditional justice institutions.

STUDY QUESTIONS

- What were some of the factors that led advocates to take up RJ as an alternative way of dealing with crime and social harm?
- What are the key differences between RJ and the formal justice system?
- What are the key myths associated with the RJ movement, and what impact has the mythologising of restorative programmes (like the family group conferences) had on Indigenous peoples?

FURTHER READING

Monchalin, L. (2016). *The colonial problem: An Indigenous perspective on crime and injustice in Canada.* Toronto, Canada: University of Toronto Press.

Sylvester, D. (2003). Interdisciplinary perspectives on restorative justice: Myth in restorative justice history. *Utah Law Review, 1,* 471–522.

Wood, W. (2015). Why restorative justice will not reduce incarceration. *British Journal of Criminology, 55*(5), 883–900. doi:10.1093/bjc/azu108

REFERENCES

Albrecht, B. (2011). The limits of restorative justice in prison. *Peace Review: A Journal of Social Justice*, 23(3), 327–334. doi:10.1080/10402659.2011.596059

Barnsdale, L., & Walker, M. (2007). *Examining the use and impact of family group conferencing*. Stirling, Scotland: Social Work Research Centre, University of Stirling. Retrieved from https://www.iirp.edu/images/pdf/2007_FGC_Scotland_Research.pdf

Bazemore, G., & Schiff, M. (2001). Understanding restorative community justice: What and why now? In G. Bazemore & M. Schiff (Eds.), *Restorative community justice: Repairing harm and transforming communities* (pp. 21–46). Cincinnati, OH: Anderson Publishing Co.

Blagg, H. (2016). *Crime, aboriginality and the decolonisation of justice* (2nd ed.). Sydney, Australia: Federation Press.

Bowen, H., Boyack, J., & Calder-Watson, J. (2012). Recent developments within restorative justice in Aotearoa/New Zealand. In J. Bolitho, J. Bruce, & G. Mason (Eds.), *Restorative justice: Adults and emerging practice* (pp. 121–141). Sydney, Australia: Federation Press.

Bradley, T., Tauri, J. M., & Walters, R. (2006). Demythologising youth justice in Aotearoa/New Zealand. In J. Muncie & B. Goldson (Eds.), *Comparative youth justice* (pp. 79–95). London, UK: Sage Publications.

Braithwaite, J. (1989). *Crime, shame and reintegration*. Cambridge, UK: Cambridge University Press.

Chatterjee, J., & Elliott, E. (2003). Restorative policing in Canada: The Royal Canadian Mounted Police community justice forums and the Youth Justice Act. *Police Practice and Research: An International Journal*, 4(4), 347–359. doi:10.1080/15614260310001631253

Consedine, J. (1995). *Restorative justice: Healing the effects of crime*. Wellington, New Zealand: Ploughshares Publications.

Cunneen, C. (2002). Restorative justice and the politics of decolonization. In E. Weitekamp & H. Kerner (Eds.), *Restorative justice: Theoretical foundations* (pp. 32–49). Cullompton, UK: Willan Publishing.

Daly, K. (2002). Restorative justice: The real story. *Punishment and Society*, 4(1), 55–79.

Deukmedjian, J. (2008). The rise and fall of RCMP community justice forums: Restorative justice and public safety interoperability in Canada. *Canadian Journal of Criminology and Criminal Justice*, 50(2), 117–151. doi:10.3138/cjccj.50.2.117

Dijkstra, S., Creemers, H. E., van Steensel, F. J. A., Deković, M., Stams, G. J. J. M., & Asscher, J. J. (2018). Cost-effectiveness of family group conferencing in child welfare: A controlled study. *BMC Public Health*, 18(1), 1–14. doi:10.1186/s12889-018-5770-5

Doolan, M. (2002). Family group conferences – a partnership model. In B. Riepl, L. Wilk, & Y. Barman (Eds.), *Policies and services for children at risk* (pp. 107–119). Vienna, Austria: European Centre.

Engle Merry, S., & Milner, N. (1993). *The possibility of popular justice: A case study of community mediation in the United States*. Ann Arbor, MI: University of Michigan Press.

Fox, D. (2018). *Family group conferencing with children and young people: Advocacy approaches variations and impacts*. Cham, Switzerland: Palgrave Macmillan.

Hakiaha, M. (1999). Resolving conflict from a Māori perspective. In H. Bowen & J. Consedine (Eds.), *Restorative justice: Contemporary themes and practice* (pp. 90–94). Lyttelton, New Zealand: Ploughshares Publications.

Henwood, C. (1997). *The Children, Young Persons, and Their Families Act 1989: The New Zealand situation 1997 – A judicial perspective*. Paper presented to the Australian Law Commission.

Henwood, C., & Stratford, S. (2014). *New Zealand's gift to the world: The youth justice family group conference*. Wellington, New Zealand: The Henwood Trust.

Hollinshead, D., Corwin, T., Maher, E., Merkel-Holguin, L., Allan, H., & Fluke, J. (2017). Effectiveness of family group conferencing in preventing repeat referrals to child protective services and out-of-home placements. *Child Abuse and Neglect*, 69, 285–294. doi:10.1016/j.chiabu.2017.04.022

House of Commons – Justice Committee (2016). *Restorative justice: Fourth report of session 2016–17*. London, UK: House of Commons. Retrieved from https://www.basw.co.uk/system/files/resources/basw_62635-2_0.pdf

Jackson, M. (1988). *The Maori and the criminal justice system: A new perspective: He whaipaanga hou: Part 2*. Wellington, New Zealand: Policy and Research Division, Department of Justice. Retrieved from https://www2.justice.govt.nz/website-documents/maori-and-the-criminal-justice-system-a-new-perspective-p2.pdf

Katz, J., & Bonham, G. (2006). Restorative justice in Canada and the United States: A comparative analysis. *Journal of the Institute of Justice Studies, 6*, 187–196.

Lee, G. (1997). The newest old gem: Family group conferencing. *Justice as Healing, 2*(2), 1–3.

Love, C. (2000). Family group conferencing: Cultural origins, sharing and appropriation – a Māori reflection. In G. Burford & J. Hudson (Eds.), *Family group conferencing: New directions in child and family practice* (pp. 15–30). New York, NY: Walter de Gruyter Inc.

Luna, E. (2003). Punishment theory, holism, and the procedural conception of restorative justice. *Utah Law Review, 1*, 205–302.

Maxwell, G. (2008). Crossing cultural boundaries: Implementing restorative justice in international and Indigenous contexts. *Sociology of Crime, Law and Deviance, 11*, 81–95. doi:10.1016/s1521-6136(08)00404-1

Maxwell, G., & Morris, A. (1993). *Family, victims and culture: Youth justice in New Zealand*. Wellington, New Zealand: Social Policy Agency Rōpū Here Kaupapa & the Institute of Criminology, Victoria University of Wellington. Retrieved from https://www.msd.govt.nz/about-msd-and-our-work/publications-resources/research/family-victims-culture/index.html

Maxwell, G., Robertson, J., Kingi, V., Morris, A., & Cunningham, C. (2004). *Achieving effective outcomes in youth justice*. Wellington, New Zealand: Ministry of Social Development. Retrieved from https://www.msd.govt.nz/documents/about-msd-and-our-work/publications-resources/research/youth-justice/achieving-effective-outcomes-youth-justice-full-report.pdf

McElrea, F. (2002). *Restorative justice – a New Zealand perspective*. Paper presented at the Modernising Criminal Justice – New World Challenges conference, London, 16–20 June. Retrieved from http://restorativejustice.org/am-site/media/restorative-justice---a-new-zealand-perspective.pdf

Ministerial Advisory Committee. (1988). *Puao-Te-Ata-Tu (daybreak): The report of the Ministerial Advisory Committee on a Māori Perspective for the Department of Social Welfare*. Wellington, New Zealand: Department of Social Welfare. Retrieved from https://www.msd.govt.nz/documents/about-msd-and-our-work/publications-resources/archive/1988-puaoteatatu.pdf

Ministry of Justice. (2004). *Restorative justice: Best practice in New Zealand*. Wellington, New Zealand: Ministry of Justice. Retrieved from https://www.justice.govt.nz/assets/Documents/Publications/RJ-Best-practice.pdf

Moyle, P. (2013). *From family group conferencing to Whanau Ora: Māori Social Workers talk about their experiences*. Unpublished master's thesis, Massey University.

Moyle, P. (2014). Māori social workers' experiences of care and protection: A selection of findings. *Te Komako, Social Work Review, 26*(1), 5–64. doi:10.11157/anzswj-vol26iss1id55

Moyle, P., & Tauri, J. M. (2016). Māori, family group conferencing and the mystifications of restorative justice. *Victims and Offenders: Special Issue: The Future of Restorative Justice? 11*(1), 87–106. doi:10.1080/15564886.2015.1135496

Olsen, T., Maxwell, G., & Morris, A. (1995). Māori and youth justice in New Zealand. In K. Hazlehurst (Ed.), *Popular justice and community regeneration: Pathways to Indigenous reform* (pp. 45–66). Westport, CT: Praeger Publishers.

Palys, T., & Victor, W. (2007). Getting to a better place: Qwi:qwelstóm, the Stó:lō and self-determination. In Law Commission of Canada (Ed.), *Indigenous legal traditions* (pp. 12–39). Vancouver, Canada: UBC Press.

Restorative Practices Development Team. (2003). *Restorative practices for schools: A resource*. Hamilton, New Zealand: School of Education, University of Waikato. Retrieved from https://www.waikato.ac.nz/__data/assets/pdf_file/0018/240903/Restorative_Practices_for_Schools_A_Resource–1.pdf

Richards, K. (2007). *Rewriting history: Towards a genealogy of 'restorative justice'*. Unpublished PhD thesis, University of Western Sydney, Sydney, Australia.

Richards, K. (2014). A promise and a possibility: The limitations of the traditional criminal justice system as an explanation for the emergence of restorative justice. *Restorative Justice: An International Journal, 2*(2), 124–141. doi:10.5235/20504721.2.2.124

Ross, R. (2009). Searching for the roots of conferencing. In G. Burford & J. Hudson (Eds.), *Family group conferencing: New directions in community-centered child and family practice* (pp. 5–14). Piscataway, NJ: Transaction Publishers.

Schmid, D. (2002). Restorative justice: A new paradigm for criminal justice policy. *Victoria University Law Review, 34*(1), 91–133.

Schmid, J., & Morgenshtern, M. (2017). Successful, sustainable? Facilitating the growth of family group conferencing in Canada. *Journal of Family Social Work, 20*(4), 322–339. doi:10.1080/10522158.2017.1348109

Scuro, P. (2013). Latin America. In G. Johnstone & D. Van Ness (Eds.), *Handbook of restorative justice* (pp. 500–510). Cullompton, UK: Willan Publishing.

Shriver, D., & Shriver, P. (2012). Law, religion, and restorative justice in New Zealand. *Journal of Law and Religion, 28*(1), 143–177. doi:10.1017/s0748081400000266

Suzuki, M., & Wood, W. (2017). Restorative justice. In A. Deckert & R. Sarre (Eds.), *The Palgrave handbook of Australian and New Zealand criminology, crime and justice* (pp. 393–406). Cham, Switzerland: Palgrave Macmillan.

Tauri, J. (2013, September 10). Globalisation of crime control: Restorative justice and indigenous justice. *The Indigenous Criminologist* [Blog post]. Retrieved from http://juantauri.blogspot.com/2013/09/

Tauri, J. M. (2004). *Conferencing, indigenisation and orientalism: A critical commentary on recent state responses to Indigenous offending*. Paper presented at the Qwi:Qwelstom gathering: 'Bringing justice back to the people', Mission, BC, Canada, 22–24 March.

Tauri, J. M. (2016). *The state, the academy and Indigenous justice: A counter-colonial critique*. Unpublished PhD thesis, University of Wollongong, Wollongong, Australia.

Tauri, J. M. (2017). Indigenous peoples and the globalisation of crime control. *Social Justice: A Journal of Crime, Conflict and World Order, 43*(3), 46–57.

Tauri, J. M. (2018). Restorative justice as a colonial project in the disempowerment of Indigenous peoples. In T. Gavrielides (Ed.), *Routledge international handbook of restorative justice* (pp. 342–358). London, UK: Routledge.

Victor, W. (2007). *Indigenous justice: Clearing space and place for Indigenous epistemologies*. Research paper for the National Centre for First Nations Governance. Retrieved from http://www.fngovernance.org/ncfng_research/wenona_victor.pdf

Waites, C., MacGowan, M., Pennell, J., Carlton-LaNey, I., & Weil, M. (2004). Increasing the cultural responsiveness of family group conferencing. *Social Work, 49*(2), 291–300. doi:10.1093/sw/49.2.291

Wearmouth, J., McKinney, R., & Glynn, T. (2007). Restorative justice: Two examples from New Zealand schools. *British Journal of Special Education, 34*(4), 196–203. doi:10.1111/j.1467-8578.2007.00479.x

Weitekamp, E. (1999). The history of restorative justice. In G. Bazemore & L. Walgrave (Eds.), *Restorative juvenile justice: Repairing the harm of youth crime* (pp. 75–102). New York, NY: Criminal Justice Press.

Zedner, M. (2007). *Restorative justice: Ideals and realities*. Aldershot, UK: Ashgate Publishing.

Zehr, H. (1990). *Changing lenses: A new focus for crime and justice*. Scottsdale, PA: Herald Press.

21

Hyper-incarceration
Inequality and Imprisonment

Liam Martin

When Jacinda Ardern addressed a crowd gathered for Waitangi Day in 2018, becoming the first woman prime minister to speak at the upper marae on the grounds where Te Tiriti was signed, she named Māori imprisonment as a core issue in contemporary inequality (Ardern, 2018). Using both hands, Ardern gestured from Te Whare Rūnanga, where she stood, to the nearby cottage where James Busby had lived and drafted the Treaty more than 150 years before. She said:

> If you ask me the distance between this whare and the old homestead is the difference between us as people, the inequality we still have. The distance between here and here is unemployment, is rangatahi who don't have hope for their future, it's the poverty that exists among whānau, it's rangatahi who don't have access to mental health services who take their lives, it's the fact that not everyone has a decent home. And it's the incarceration of the Māori people disproportionately to everyone else. That is the distance between us, and so long as that exists, we have failed in our partnership (para. 17).

Māori scholars have long argued Māori imprisonment is rooted in social inequality and the legacies of colonisation (Jackson, 1988; McIntosh & Workman, 2017; Tauri, 2014). But the prime minister making these connections in a formal state ceremony signalled a possible shift in the prevailing politics of incarceration in Aotearoa New Zealand. In contrast to the penal populism which has dominated public discussion of prisons for three decades (Pratt, 2006;

Pratt & Clark, 2005) – centred on common-sense tropes demonising prisoners and espousing the need to 'get tough' on crime – the Labour government had announced controversial plans to reduce the prison population by 30 per cent (Labour Party, 2017). And at Waitangi, Ardern linked the goal of decarceration to broader aspirations for Treaty partnership and addressing social disadvantage.

This chapter locates current debates over the future of prisons in New Zealand in the context of a system strained by record expansion – or what I will call *hyper-incarceration* (Wacquant, 2010). It examines how rapid increases in prison numbers have transformed prison life on the ground and fuelled growing public concern over poor conditions and chronic overcrowding. It pulls together findings from prisoner surveys to highlight problems of widespread idleness and high levels of violence, and then draws on a series of written accounts from prisoners themselves to develop a more textured picture of the lived experience of harsh prison environments. But opening with the prime minister's words at Waitangi – which are yet to be matched with more tangible changes in government policy – is a way to centre the relationship between the problems unfolding inside prison and a larger social history of inequality and political struggle. The next step is sketching the rise of hyper-incarceration and the changing landscape of prisons in New Zealand.

HYPER-INCARCERATION AND THE SHIFTING POLITICS OF IMPRISONMENT

In the 30 years between 1986 and 2016, the number of people in New Zealand prisons went from 2690 to 9914, an increase of more than 365 per cent. The prison population peaked at 10,645 in 2018 and, even after falling slightly to 9969 in the middle of 2019, remains historically unprecedented. In the half-century between 1935 and 1985, the nation's incarceration rate – the number of prisoners per 100,000 in the national population – hovered in a narrow band between a low of 50 and a high of 91. It now sits at around 204. And in the most recent analysis of prison levels in the OECD (2016), New Zealand ranked ninth of 35 member states, with an incarceration rate well above comparable countries like Australia (152), the United Kingdom (146), Canada (106), and Ireland (82).

Incarceration on a scale outstripping historical and comparative norms is sometimes described as mass imprisonment (see Garland, 2001). But this implies a form of penal confinement with broad and indiscriminate reach across entire populations – like mass media or mass culture. In contrast, the term hyper-incarceration is meant to convey that prison growth in New Zealand has been finely targeted, concentrated among Māori and those living on the social margins, like those who are homeless and people experiencing various forms of mental illness or drug and alcohol dependency. Māori make up 15 per cent of the general population but more than half of all prisoners. And the disparities are even greater for women, with Māori comprising 62 per cent of all women serving custodial sentences.

Tracing the social roots of concentrated hyper-incarceration opens out to a broader discussion of deep inequalities in the structure of New Zealand society. It requires a long-term view: there were no prisons in Māori society before colonisation, and the state used the imported criminal justice system as an instrument of land dispossession, creating intergenerational impacts which place Māori at increased risk of imprisonment today (Jackson, 1990; McIntosh & Radojkovic, 2011). The more recent period of prison growth took place in the context of neoliberal restructuring and steep rises in inequality in the 1980s and 1990s (Poata-Smith, 2004; Roper, 2015). As the social safety net was slashed, those discarded from the post-industrial economy were increasingly pulled into the booming prison system (Cavadino & Dignan, 2006; Workman & McIntosh, 2013).

Hyper-incarceration in the wake of neoliberal reform involved not only a rapid rise in prison numbers but also deteriorating prison conditions – with the two closely connected (see Pratt & Erickson, 2014, pp. 9–21). The size of New Zealand prisons almost quadrupled between 1988 and 2019 – the average population at each facility jumping from 142 to 558 – with increasingly large institutions leaving staff and prisoners more often anonymous to one another and undermining the development of rapport and trusting relationships.[1] Record expansion spread scarce resources over a growing pool of prisoners, shrinking the availability of work and programmes, and leaving more prisoners idle for longer periods of time (Devine, 2007; Newbold, 2013). The same populist forces that pushed for lengthening sentences called for prison regimes emphasising discipline and harsh punishment. Garth McVicar, then head of the Sensible Sentencing Trust, visited the notorious tent prisons of Arizona and returned calling for the introduction of chain gangs in New Zealand (*New Zealand Herald*, 2007).

The most recent period of hyper-incarceration has been marked by important shifts in public discourse and government policy. Where media reporting on incarceration once focused on the perceived leniency of prisons operating like 'holiday camps' – under newspaper headlines like 'Prisoners Better Off than Many' in Wellington and 'Inmates Get KFC after Cell Searches' – there is now a growing sense of scandal about the problems caused by rapid growth and widespread overcrowding (Pratt, 2008). Accounts in major media outlets have described, for example, prisoners filling emergency beds meant for disaster readiness (Weekes, 2016), a prison gym being converted into a custodial unit (Pennington, 2016), and plans for prisoners to sleep on mattresses on the floor (Dunlop, 2018) or in police holding cells (Stewart, 2018). Other reports have highlighted links between overcrowding and suicide (Fisher, 2018), violence (Block, 2018), and rioting (Moorby, 2017).

The Labour-led government elected in 2017 committed to reducing prison numbers substantially – raising the question of whether the era of hyper-incarceration could be coming to an end. Yet the impact has so far been limited: the prison population has fallen only slightly from 10,394 shortly after the election to 10,040 at the most recent count released in September 2019. The public emphasis on decarceration has also been coupled with further spending on expansion, including large additions to capacity at Waikeria and Mount Eden prisons and plans to install eight 122-bed units at five other prisons around New Zealand (Department of Corrections, 2019, p. 40). The level of imprisonment remains well above historical norms, and, for now at least, the kinds of degrading conditions characteristic of hyper-incarceration appear firmly entrenched.

PRISON CONDITIONS UNDER HYPER-INCARCERATION

When New Zealand ratified the main United Nations convention against the mistreatment of people in detention in 2007, the Office of the Ombudsman became the government agency responsible for monitoring prisons (McGregor, 2017). It adopted a focus on prevention, launching regular unscheduled prison inspections and releasing public reports of its findings. Over time, the Ombudsman developed a survey instrument asking prisoners a range of questions about basic conditions, and, since 2015, has released the results of these exercises carried out with around 2490 prisoners at eight prisons across the country.[2] These surveys are an important contribution to the scarce literature on prison life in New Zealand – there has likely never been such a comprehensive effort to gather prisoner views on prison conditions (see Appendix).

At all eight prisons, survey participants were asked how many hours they spend outside their cell on a typical weekday. The results suggest that *prison life is characterised by the intensive control of movement through long periods of cell confinement*. At four of six men's prisons, over two-thirds of respondents described being out less than six hours of a typical 24-hour daily cycle: Spring Hill (69 per cent), Auckland South (71 per cent), Invercargill (71 per cent), and Manawatu (76 per cent). Even at the prison with the most open regime, Hawke's Bay, 40 per cent of prisoners said they were out of their cells less than six hours. And a smaller number of prisoners described being released from their cell less than two hours on a typical weekday: 6 per cent at Manawatu and Invercargill prisons, 8 per cent at Spring Hill, 13 per cent at Christchurch, and 16 per cent at Hawke's Bay and Auckland South.

The Ombudsman surveys also reveal *widespread idleness and high levels of disengagement from work and education*. Respondents were consistently asked if they participated in any of these activities: prison job, vocational or skills training, education (including basic skills), offending behaviour programmes, and release to work. At five of the six men's prisons, between 40 and 48 per cent of those surveyed reported no involvement in any activity on the list, and, at Hawke's Bay, 30 per cent of prisoners reported no activity. At no men's facility did more than 26 per cent of prisoners describe involvement in education (including basic skills), and, similarly, no more than 42 per cent reported having a prison job – the most common activity at every facility except Manawatu.

In the Ombudsman survey at Arohata women's prison, participants described lower levels of idleness than were reported in men's prisons. Yet around a quarter (23 per cent) of the women still described no involvement in work or education, and, similar to men's prisons, around 46 per cent reported spending less than six hours outside their cells on a typical weekday. Problems of overcrowding have been particularly severe at Arohata, with many women moved into previously closed buildings on the grounds of Rimutaka men's prison around 30 kilometres away. An Ombudsman survey carried out at the new site, Arohata Upper, which now holds more women than the original prison, revealed higher levels of idleness and confinement: 40 per cent of participants described no involvement in work or education, with 50 per cent being out of their cells for six hours or less each day.

The Ombudsman surveys asked prisoners to report on their experiences of interpersonal violence. All eight exercises included a question about whether the participant had been assaulted during their sentence – with the results suggesting *violent victimisation is a routine feature of the prison experience*. At four of the six men's prisons, a little under around half of the participants described being assaulted during their current sentence: Christchurch (49 per cent), Manawatu (47 per cent), Hawke's Bay (46 per cent), and Invercargill (44 per cent). A similar level of assault was found among women at Arohata Upper prison (47 per cent), but at the original Arohata site the level (20 per cent) was lower than at any other prison surveyed. At Spring Hill, a little more than one-third of prisoners (37 per cent) described having been assaulted, and even at the men's institution with the lowest levels of reported victimisation – South Auckland prison – a quarter of respondents said they had been assaulted at the prison. At the main Arohata site, 27 per cent of those assaulted said they did not report, and at the other seven prisons, rates of non-reporting ranged from 59 per cent at South Auckland to 84 per cent at Invercargill. These results suggest most prison violence is never brought to the attention of authorities and, as a result, that official estimates are likely to substantially undercount victimisation.

These three features of contemporary prison conditions – widespread idleness, long periods of cell confinement, and high levels of violence – are related in circular and mutually reinforcing ways (see Haney, 2006). When large numbers of prisoners are bored and lack meaningful ways to spend their time, this generates frustration and increases the likelihood of violence. Prison staff struggling to control unrest often resort to using long cell lockdowns and disciplinary segregation. Exposure to these socially isolating measures further separates prisoners from work and education, and can jeopardise well-being and mental health, creating even more disruptive behaviour later on, both inside prison and outside after release.

The Ombudsman surveys suggest the rehabilitative goals of correctional managers are being undermined by the basic conditions of prison life under hyper-incarceration. Not that rehabilitative ideals have been abandoned (Brown & Young, 2000, pp. 11–14): the Department of Corrections' high-level commitments to rehabilitation have spurred a wide range of innovations – for example, the opening of specialist drug treatment, Māori focus, and violence prevention units at prisons around the country (Johnston, 2015; Ward et al., 2006). But it appears many prisoners are unable to access these programmes and, more generally, are held in settings fundamentally opposed to positive change and healthy development.

A growing number of prisoners and former prisoners have produced written work grounded in personal experience of these institutions (e.g., Coster, 2013; Luff, 2018; Payne, 1994; Richards, 2014; Selwyn, 2006; Wood, 2019). Their firsthand accounts are an important complement to the broad quantitative snapshot provided by the Ombudsman surveys, opening a window on the lived experience of usually closed prison environments. And they provide an opportunity to bring often ignored inside voices to the discussion of imprisonment.

PRISONER AGENCY AND THE DILEMMAS OF PRISONISATION

Daniel Luff (2018) is completing a psychology doctorate while incarcerated at Paremoremo prison. The site of the research is significant: Paremoremo was opened in 1965 as a model of correctional liberalism emphasising training and rehabilitation, but has been increasingly transformed by American 'supermax' principles to a facility on permanent lockdown, with prisoners in their cells upward of 21 hours a day and escorted by staff whenever they leave cell landings (Newbold, 2013). Drawing on a mix of literature and personal experience, Luff argues these heavy-handed security measures provoke the very behaviours they are intended to control:

> Decades of research have established that carceral regimes involving prolonged inactivity and cell-confinement produce mental health problems and contribute to aggression. A key consequence of this is, I believe, increased aggression towards staff. The harsh routines we endure make us feel dangerous, as though we are animals. The officers become the face of the system; it is them we see locking us up each day for hours on end, enforcing policies made in the distant boardrooms of managers and head-office bureaucrats. Tragically, the anger this produces often prevents us from seeing the people behind the uniforms and, wound taut by intense boredom, some prisoners are like armed grenades by the time unlock comes. Indeed, such is the desire to get out of those cells that if the officers are late unlocking, by even five minutes, you're sure to hear men bash their doors in sheer frustration (p. 3).

Stan Coster describes a different kind of response to his confinement at Paremoremo: prison tattooing (Andrae et al., 2017a). As authorities attempted to control his body and suppress his use of gang symbolism, Coster turned to covert strategies to cover his face and neck with Mongrel Mob imagery. He converted everyday prison objects into tools of resistance, using cassette player motors to power tattoo guns made from ballpoint pens and sewing needles, and creating ink from boot rubber crushed to powder and mixed with water or even urine. The tattoos became a self-inscribed expression of autonomy from the prison that controlled so much of his life.

Tattooing is forbidden but common in New Zealand prisons: few who spend any length of time inside exit without some form of tattooed inscription on their bodies (Andrae et al., 2017a). And tattooing fulfils a range of important functions inside: providing an artistic outlet in dull and boring environments, forging connections to people and places outside, and asserting individual identity in prisons that replace names with numbers and clothes with uniforms (Phillips, 2001). Yet after release, these tattoos become lasting marks of prison history that can leave former prisoners branded dangerous or threatening. Since getting out, Stan Coster has grown his hair and cultivated a thick beard, camouflaging some tattoos, but many are still 'full frontal' and continue to dominate his face. The stigma they bring points to a paradox: his strategies for surviving in prison created hurdles when trying to leave that world behind.

Paul Wood (2019) was also released with lasting marks from prison time. He spent 11 years behind bars, working towards a doctoral degree in psychology, and, after release, gained employment with a long-time mentor. Despite his advantages over many released prisoners, he says the transition was rocky, with his prison history continuing to shape his routine experience of the outside world:

> For most of my adult life, I had been practising the adaptive behaviours you develop in prison, and those were – are – hard habits to break. It took a long time before I wouldn't feel my nostrils flare and a quickening of my pulse if I entered a space where there were unstructured groups of people. Or if I couldn't find a seat in a corner of a crowded room, I would find myself ill at ease, and seek to have a clear view of entrances and exits at all times. I still occasionally find that if someone comes and sits close to where I'm sitting when there are other options available, it puts me on alert. I don't like conversations I'm having to be overheard by strangers. . . . Sometimes it takes an active effort of will to overcome such impulses, but they are the exception rather than the rule these days. It has got progressively easier since my first days of liberty (p. 304).

The narratives of Paul Wood and Stan Coster might be understood in terms of *prisonisation* (Clemmer, 1940). This theoretical concept is used to describe the lasting impacts of doing time, as prisoners are transformed in deep and lasting ways by the experience – from simple habits to tattoos inscribed on the body. But Wood and Coster also point to the possibilities for agency in the experience of prisonisation: they not only undergo prisonisation as a disabling process happening to them, but also understand it analytically. As they learned particular ways of living in prison, they also developed an awareness of the transformative process involved, helping them take constructive steps to deal with their problems after release.

Tim Selwyn's (2006) writing while incarcerated at Hawke's Bay prison also emphasises the learning involved – it is framed as a step-by-step guide to the new prisoner. Selwyn describes, for example, a range of practical strategies for making use of scarce space during long periods in a cell: using toothpaste as adhesive, cardboard as shelving, and empty milk containers for storage. And his work points to the way prisonisation is often disconnected from the rehabilitative goals of official correctional programmes – which Selwyn barely mentions – and instead hinges on the more informal sharing of norms and customs among prisoners. As he writes:

> You might be out of your comfort zone but there's some things you'll end up doing just to fit in. You will find yourself mimicking the routines of other prisoners, whether conscious of it or not. You'll find yourself tapping on the pipes to warn your neighbors that the crews are making their rounds, playing touch with fully tattooed gang members and swapping dirty anecdotes with a cell full of giggling drug dealers – it's all part of normal life now (p. C4).

Richards (2014) describes the process of adapting to what is normal in prison as an ongoing dilemma and 'delicate dance'. Based on research carried out while incarcerated at Arohata and Christchurch prisons – using a combination of auto-ethnography, surveys, and interviews –

she argues the identity changes involved can lead to 'institutionalisation' and disrupt re-entry to the world outside. For example, she says prisoners are forced to be manipulative with staff to create the impression they are making progress and earn transfer from higher to lower security settings, and more generally, to be hyper-vigilant and suspicious of the people around them. At the same time, they need to always keep one eye to the very different expectations they will face after release:

> Doing a successful prison sentence is a state of mind. It is being able to live with oneself comfortably for long periods of time locked in a small cell. It is learning to keep emotions in check and, above all else, it is learning how to survive in the prison world while at the same time keeping a part of oneself locked away so that, when released, the inmate is able to re-enter the outside world, the other world, and have some chance of fitting in. It is being able to put on the mantle of 'inmate' while simultaneously retaining and identifying with the outside persona and being comfortable with that dichotomy. It is a delicate dance between fitting in and becoming institutionalised – fit in too well and the outside becomes too strange; not fit in enough and prison is an unbearable hell (p. 78).

Richards vividly describes the impossible choices involved in imprisonment: adapt, but not too much; learn to spend long periods alone in a cell, but also prepare for a world outside the cell after release. And even as she worries that adapting to prison may leave her institutionalised, she nonetheless feels compelled to do so, fearing the sentence may otherwise become an 'unbearable hell'. She describes the need to keep part of herself 'locked away' in the process – a kind of personal prison within the prison. These are the dilemmas of prisonisation in the era of hyper-incarceration.

CYCLES OF CONFINEMENT

Moana Jackson (1988) headed the first and only large-scale empirical research project into Māori experiences in the criminal justice system: travelling the country with a team of researchers holding hui and interviewing or surveying around 2800 people. Drawing on this work, Jackson described the social confinement of whole Māori communities through cultural deprivation and economic inequality – tracing the 'social forces [which] confine young Māori' and 'trap many young Māori in a limbo of cultural shame and uncertainty' (p. 100). A survey of 943 Māori offenders found none were fluent in te reo and only 41 per cent had knowledge of two-generation whakapapa (p. 295). Jackson argued a symbiotic relationship had emerged between this cultural deprivation and their poverty and imprisonment, and in making these connections he located the prison experience in a broader *cycle of confinement* extending outside beyond the walls (pp. 100–103).

After three decades of hyper-incarceration, record numbers of Māori leaving prison each year also experience confinement to the social margins (see McIntosh, 2011). Consider the steep obstacles former prisoners face gaining employment. A survey of 229 employers – organisations that together employ almost 10 per cent of the entire New Zealand labour force – found around two-thirds include a question about criminal records on job applications (Harcourt & Harcourt, 2003). And the Clean Slate Act 2004, which allows some people to seal their records after seven years, is not accessible to anyone who has served prison time. Incarceration remains a permanent driver of social exclusion long after people leave the institution and formally complete their sentences.

A recent study tracking employment among former prisoners – interviewing 97 people recently released – paints a picture of a group largely disconnected from the labour market altogether (Morrison & Bowman, 2017). Just 28 per cent of participants were employed when they were interviewed between four and six months after release, and more broadly, only 41 per cent described having worked even a single day since getting out. Among those who did gain employment, most entered various forms of casual or temporary work, which paid low wages and offered volatile hours that were seasonal or weather-dependent. Only a small minority were in stable jobs: just 12 per cent said they had always or almost always worked since release.

The research participants described finding a place to live as their biggest challenge (Morrison & Bowman, 2017). Around 47 per cent did not have stable housing immediately after getting out: they stayed in hostels or shelters, lived on the street, or were taken in temporarily by family and friends. In focus groups with former prisoners run by the Salvation Army (Johnstone, 2016, pp. 39–41), participants described the $350 Steps to Freedom grant as inadequate for even basic lodging at a boarding house. And when they tried to apply for the accommodation supplement, they were told they needed proof of rental payments, which without housing they could not provide. Other participants described difficulties getting a photo ID and bank account, with this becoming a significant hurdle to applying for accommodation in the weeks after release.

The experience of being denied work and housing is not only itself a form of confinement – trapping people in social exclusion – but also amplifies the chances of return to prison. Around 61 per cent of all people released from prison are convicted of new crimes within two years (Department of Corrections, 2019). This systemic reoffending is rooted in the links between chronic marginality and crime (Elizabeth, 2017) and the invasive state surveillance both of people leaving prison (Opie, 2012) and the poor and Māori communities to which they typically return (Tauri, 2014). There are even a small number of former prisoners who describe intentionally offending and getting caught to be returned to prison because the institution provides a better housing option than anything available to them outside (Block, 2019).

Cycles of confinement can become intergenerational through the ripple effects of imprisonment on families and children. As McIntosh and Radojkovic (2011) describe:

> The impact of incarceration is not purely limited to the individual who is imprisoned. Rather, there are collateral effects and consequences which spread from the individual outwards, reverberating along the radiating threads of social relationships and connections. There is also evidence to suggest that once set in motion, these reverberations can persist through time, increasing in resonance, generating long lasting and potentially intergenerational effects. One of the clearest examples is the impact of imprisonment on families. Individual incarceration is a collective experience. Prisoners come from families, they will return to families, and their imprisonment has a marked impact upon their families (p. 43).

Consider the results of a survey with 368 prisoners carried out by Gordon (2011): around 53 per cent described as a child having lived with someone who went to prison. And there were already flow-on effects from their own incarceration: more than a third of participants with children described their kids witnessing the arrest. Often the police were attempting to catch them off-guard, so launched arrests early in the morning, using verbal aggression and bringing dogs or brandishing weapons. In follow-up interviews with caregivers, participants described this exposure to police force and parental disempowerment as traumatising some children.

There are no reliable national counts of the number of children with parents in prison – the Department of Corrections does not systematically collect this data – and the impact of hyper-incarceration on children remains a largely hidden phenomenon. But the longitudinal Christchurch Health and Development Study, which has been tracking a cohort of New Zealanders for 40 years, provides some suggestive results. Around 1.6 per cent of study participants had spent time in prison by age 25, but among the subset of people who had a parent go to prison this jumped to 15.6 per cent (see Gordon, 2009, p. 64). The relatively small number involved makes the comparison tentative and uncertain – only 33 study participants had an incarcerated parent. Yet even as a baseline estimate it remains striking, suggesting those with histories of parental incarceration were almost 10 times as likely to be incarcerated by 25 years old.

Hyper-incarceration in New Zealand has drawn into its orbit families and whole communities. The ripple effects are concentrated in neighbourhoods where large numbers of Māori live under conditions of scarcity and disadvantage; and as young men are removed and returned repeatedly, the process threatens to become self-sustaining. Marginalisation and imprisonment in the current generation undermines the stability of families and economic supports for children and, as adults, these children are themselves at greater risk of social exclusion and incarceration. In this context, decisions over prison policy have social consequences well beyond the realm of criminal justice.

PROBLEMS OF PRISON REFORM

The confinement experienced by Stan Coster began long before imprisonment (Andrae et al., 2017b). Child welfare agencies were already monitoring his family when he was born. At nine years old, Coster was made a ward of the state and put in foster care when his mother died of cancer, and at 13 years-old he was sent to the notorious Epuni Boys' Home in Lower Hutt after incidents of petty theft and alcohol-related offending. He went on to serve more than two decades in prison.

At 55 years old, Coster has established a new life on the outside. He has been involved in several programmes supporting young people and collaborates with university researchers writing about his experience in the hope it might help others. Yet things are more complicated than a simple 'rags to riches' story of emancipation from prison (Andrae et al., 2017b, p. 133):

> Stan has been out of prison for over 15 years. He continues to navigate life outside the wire with what he refers to as his prison mind. His is not the redemptive story of the life turned around. It remains the bare life. For him, prison and the 'free' world are all part of the same social landscape that has systematically denied, at an individual and collective level, the right to self-determination and a legitimate part of the social.

Coster has come to understand inside and outside prison as not so different from one another – they are interconnected parts of a social order in which the right to self-determination is denied not only to him as an individual but to many Māori.

CONCLUSION

At a historical moment when public debate over prisons centres on controversial efforts to reduce the prison population, Stan Coster's autobiographical reflection draws attention to confinements left untouched by this kind of reform. It raises hard questions about the politics of trying to reverse hyper-incarceration by simply reducing the number of men and women behind bars. Even if the prison population is cut by 30 per cent, what about the other forms of confinement experienced by people like Coster?

This chapter has located the problems unfolding in New Zealand prisons (including widespread idleness and violence) as part of cycles of confinement fuelled by deeply entrenched inequalities in the wider society. Among state officials, there seems to be a growing willingness to recognise the relationship between problems in the prison system and broader inequalities in healthcare, employment, and housing – as shown by the prime minister in the Waitangi Day speech that opened this chapter. But addressing the social roots of hyper-incarceration will require more fundamental shifts in public spending and government priorities. After all, as the writing of those with lived experience of imprisonment makes clear, patterns of marginality have intergenerational consequences.

APPENDIX

Ombudsman Prisoner Surveys: Assault, Activity, Cell Time

	Released	Prisoners at facility	Surveyed	Assault[1] (%)	No activity[2] (%)	Out cell < 6 hours[3] (%)
Arohata Prison	Nov. 2015	62	56	20	23	46
Manawatu Prison	Jan. 2016	270	140	47	48	76
Invercargill Prison	May 2016	158	126	44	40	71
Hawke's Bay Regional Prison	Jul. 2017	676	442	46	30	40
Spring Hill Corrections Facility	Aug. 2017	969	562	37	48	69
Arohata Upper Prison	Mar. 2018	96	75	47	40	50
Christchurch Men's Prison	Dec. 2018	897	534	49	42	59
Auckland South Corrections Facility	Feb. 2019	909	555	25	48	71

1. Assault measured with one of the following questions: 'Have you been assaulted while in prison here?', 'Have you been assaulted in this prison?', or 'Have you been assaulted while in this prison?' The response categories were 'yes' and 'no'.
2. Activity measured with the question: 'Are you currently involved in any of the following activities? (please tick all that apply),' with the following list of responses: 'Vocational or skills training,' 'Education (including basic skills),' 'Offending behaviour programmes,' 'CIE employment,' 'Release to work', and 'Not involved in any of these.' At Hawke's Bay, the 'CIE employment' category was instead listed as 'Offender employment'.
3. Cell time measured with the question: 'On average how many hours do you spend out of your cell on a weekday? (Please include hours at education, at work, showers, etc.).' The response categories were 'Less than 2 hours,' '2 to less than 4 hours,' '4 to less than 6 hours,' '6 to less than 8 hours', and '8 hours +.' The '8 hours +' category was not included in the Arohata, Invercargill, or Manawatu surveys.

STUDY QUESTIONS

- Why might 'hyper-incarceration' be a more useful concept for describing the development of prisons in New Zealand than 'mass imprisonment'? What are some important features of hyper-incarceration?

- Since 2015, the Ombudsman has been releasing the results of surveys carried out with prisoners around New Zealand. What are some key findings?

- How would you define prisonisation? What dilemma is Richards (2014) pointing to when she describes the 'delicate dance' involved in adapting to imprisonment?

FURTHER READING

Jackson, M. (1988). *The Maori and the criminal justice system: A new perspective: He whaipaanga hou: Part 2*. Wellington, New Zealand: Policy and Research Division, Department of Justice. Retrieved from https://www2.justice.govt.nz/website-documents/maori-and-the-criminal-justice-system-a-new-perspective-p2.pdf

McIntosh, T., & Workman, K. (2017). Māori and prison. In A. Deckert & R. Sarre (Eds.), *The Palgrave handbook of Australian and New Zealand criminology, crime and justice* (pp. 725–735). Cham, Switzerland: Palgrave Macmillan.

Pratt, J. (2006). The dark side of paradise: Explaining New Zealand's history of high imprisonment. *British Journal of Criminology, 46*(4), 541–560. doi:10.1093/bjc/azi095

NOTES

1   Average prison size based on institution-level population counts from the *New Zealand Yearbook* (Department of Statistics, 1989) and the most recent edition of *Prison Facts and Statistics* (Department of Corrections, 2019).

2   The full Ombudsman inspection reports, including survey results, can be found at https://www.ombudsman.parliament.nz/whtat-we-can-help/monitoring-places-detention. The results of the survey conducted at Whanganui prison, released in September 2018, are excluded from the analysis in this chapter because of significant variation between the format of this survey and those used at other facilities.

REFERENCES

Andrae, D., McIntosh, T., & Coster, S. (2017a). 'You can't take my face': A personal narrative of self-modification through tattooing in the Aotearoa/New Zealand prison system. *New Zealand Sociology, 32*(2), 5–27.

Andrae, D., McIntosh, T., & Coster, S. (2017b). Marginalised: An insider's view of the state, state policies in New Zealand and gang formation. *Critical Criminology, 25*(1), 119–135. doi:10.1007/s10612-016-9325-8

Ardern, J. (2018, February 5). *Prime minister's Waitangi powhiri speech*. Retrieved from https://www.beehive.govt.nz/speech/prime-ministers-waitangi-powhiri-speech

Block, G. (2018, February 2). Otago prison 'more hostile'. *Otago Daily Times*. Retrieved from https://www.odt.co.nz/news/dunedin/otago-prison-%E2%80%98more-hostile%E2%80%99

Block, G. (2019, June 4). Desire to return to prison behind homeless man's alleged crime spree. *Otago Daily Times*. Retrieved from https://www.odt.co.nz/news/dunedin/crime/desire-return-prison-behind-homeless-mans-alleged-crime-spree

Brown, M., & Young, W. (2000). Recent trends in sentencing and penal policy in New Zealand. *International Criminal Justice Review, 10*(1), 1–31. doi:10.1177/105756770001000102

Cavadino, M., & Dignan, J. (2006). Penal policy and political economy. *Criminology and Criminal Justice, 6*(4), 435–456. doi:10.1177/1748895806068581

Clemmer, D. (1940). *The prison community*. New York, NY: Holt, Rinehart & Winston.

Coster, S. (2013). The state as parent and warden: Stan's story. In M. Rashbrooke (Ed.), *Inequality: A New Zealand crisis* (pp. 132–133). Wellington, New Zealand: Bridget Williams Books.

Department of Corrections. (2019). *Annual report 2018/19*. Wellington, New Zealand: Department of Corrections. Retrieved from https://www.corrections.govt.nz/resources/strategic_reports/annual-reports/annual_report_201819

Department of Statistics. (1989). *New Zealand official yearbook 1988–1989*. Wellington, New Zealand: Department of Statistics.

Devine, N. (2007). Prison education in Aotearoa New Zealand: From justice to corrections. *The New Zealand Annual Review of Education, 16*(1), 55–72. doi:10.26686/nzaroe.v0i16.1511

Dunlop, R. (2018, June 13). Corrections minister: Prisoners could sleep on mattresses on ground if prison population continues to grow. *New Zealand Herald*. Retrieved from https://www.nzherald.co.nz/nz/news/article.cfm?c_id=1&objectid=12070140

Elizabeth, V. (2017). No promised land: Domestic violence, marginalisation and masculinity. In A. Bell, V. Elizabeth, T. McIntosh, & M. Wynyard (Eds.), *A land of milk and honey? Making sense of Aotearoa New Zealand* (pp. 160–167). Auckland, New Zealand: Auckland University Press.

Fisher, D. (2018, June 6). The number of people taking their own lives while in prison has surged during the inmate boom. *New Zealand Herald*. Retrieved from https://www.nzherald.co.nz/nz/news/article.cfm?c_id=1&objectid=12065044

Garland, D. (2001). Introduction: The meaning of mass imprisonment. *Punishment and Society, 3*(1), 5–7. doi:10.1177/14624740122228203

Gordon, L. (2009). *Invisible children: First year research report: 'A study of the children of prisoners'*. Christchurch, New Zealand: Pillars. Retrieved from https://www.pillars.org.nz/wp-content/uploads/2019/05/A-study-of-the-children-of-prisoners-year–1-report–2009.pdf

Gordon, L. (2011). *Causes of and solutions to inter-generational crime: The final report of the study of the children of prisoners*. Christchurch, New Zealand: Pillars. Retrieved from https://www.pillars.org.nz/wp-content/uploads/2019/05/Year–2-report–2011.pdf

Haney, C. (2006). The wages of prison overcrowding: Harmful psychological consequences and dysfunctional correctional reactions. *Washington University Journal of Law Policy, 22*, 265–294. Retrieved from https://openscholarship.wustl.edu/cgi/viewcontent.cgi?article=1360&context=law_journal_law_policy

Harcourt, M., & Harcourt, S. (2003). The importance of full legal protection from discrimination on the basis of a criminal record. *Human Rights Law and Practice, 6*(3), 23–33.

Jackson, M. (1988). *The Maori and the criminal justice system: A new perspective: He whaipaanga hou: Part 2*. Wellington, New Zealand: Policy and Research Division, Department of Justice. Retrieved from https://www2.justice.govt.nz/website-documents/maori-and-the-criminal-justice-system-a-new-perspective-p2.pdf

Jackson, M. (1990). Criminality and the exclusion of Māori: Essays on criminal law in New Zealand: Towards reform? *Victoria University Law Review, 20*(2), 23–34.

Johnston, P. (2015). Twenty years of Corrections – the evolution of offender rehabilitation. *Practice: The New Zealand Corrections Journal, 3*(2). Retrieved from https://www.corrections.govt.nz/resources/newsletters_and_brochures/journal/volume_3_issue_2_december_2015_-_evidence_based_practice/twenty_years_of_corrections_the_evolution_of_offender_rehabilitation

Johnstone, A. (2016). *Beyond the prison gate: Reoffending and reintegration in Aotearoa New Zealand*. Auckland, New Zealand: Salvation Army. Retrieved from https://www.salvationarmy.org.nz/sites/default/files/uploads/20161207spputsa-prison-gate–2016_report.pdf

Labour Party. (2017). *New Zealand Labour Party manifesto: Justice*. Wellington, New Zealand: Labour Party. Retrieved from https://d3n8a8pro7vhmx.cloudfront.net/nzlabour/pages/8485/attachments/original/1505175899/Justice_Manifesto.pdf?1505175899

Luff, D. (2018, December 2). Paremoremo prison: An inmate's view from the inside. *North & South*. Retrieved from https://www.noted.co.nz/currently/currently-crime/aucklands-paremoremo-prison-an-inmates-view-from-the-inside

McGregor, J. (2017). The challenges and limitations of OPCAT national preventive mechanisms: Lessons from New Zealand. *Australian Journal of Human Rights, 23*(3), 351–367. doi:10.1080/1323238X.2017.1392477

McIntosh, T. (2011). Marginalisation: A case study: Confinement. In T. McIntosh & M. Mulholland (Eds.), *Māori and social issues* (pp. 262–283). Wellington, New Zealand: Huia Publishers.

McIntosh, T., & Radojkovic, L. (2011). Exploring the nature of the intergenerational transfer of inequalities experienced by young Māori in the criminal justice system. In D. Brown (Ed.), *Indigenising knowledge for current and future generations* (pp. 38–48). Auckland, New Zealand: Te Whare Kura: Indigenous Knowledges, Peoples and Identities Thematic Research Initiative; The University of Auckland; and Ngā Pae o te Māramatanga New Zealand's Indigenous Centre of Research Excellence.

McIntosh, T., & Workman, K. (2017). Māori and prison. In A. Deckert & R. Sarre (Eds.), *The Palgrave handbook of Australian and New Zealand criminology, crime and justice* (pp. 725–735). Cham, Switzerland: Palgrave Macmillan.

Moorby, C. (2017, April 9). Extended lock-up regime potentially caused 2013 Spring Hill Corrections Facility riot. *Dominion Post*. Retrieved from https://www.stuff.co.nz/national/91118676/tight-lockup-regime-potentially-led-to–2013-spring-hill-corrections-facility-riot

Morrison, B., & Bowman, J. (2017). What happens beyond the gate? Findings from the post-release employment study. *Practice: The New Zealand Corrections Journal, 5*(1), 41–50. Retrieved from https://www.corrections.govt.nz/resources/research_and_statistics/journal/volume_5_issue_1_july_2017/what_happens_beyond_the_gate_findings_from_the_post-release_employment_study

Newbold, G. (2013). Emergence of the supermax in New Zealand. In J. Ross (Ed.), *The globalization of supermax prisons* (pp. 111–128). New Brunswick, NJ: Rutgers University Press.

New Zealand Herald. (2007, August 21). We need chain gangs, say justice campaigners. Retrieved from https://www.nzherald.co.nz/nz/news/article.cfm?c_id=1&objectid=10459009

Organisation for Economic Co-operation and Development (OECD). (2016). *Society at a glance 2016: OECD social indicators*. Paris, France: OECD Publishing. doi:10.1787/9789264261488-en

Opie, A. (2012). *From outlaw to citizen: Making the transition from prison in New Zealand*. Palmerston North, New Zealand: Dunmore Press.

Payne, B. (1994). *Poor behaviour*. Auckland, New Zealand: Secker & Warburg.

Pennington, P. (2016, April 14). NZ's prison population booming. *Radio New Zealand*. Retrieved from https://www.rnz.co.nz/news/national/301436/nz's-prison-population-booming

Phillips, S. A. (2001). Gallo's body: Decoration and damnation in the life of a Chicano gang member. *Ethnography 2*(3), 357–388. doi:10.1177/14661380122230966

Poata-Smith, E. (2004). Ka tika a muri, ka tika a mua? Māori protest politics and the Treaty of Waitangi settlement process. In C. Macpherson, D. Pearson, & P. Spoonley (Eds.), *Tangata tangata: The changing ethnic contours of New Zealand* (pp. 59–88). Palmerston North, New Zealand: Dunmore Press.

Pratt, J. (2006). The dark side of paradise: Explaining New Zealand's history of high imprisonment. *British Journal of Criminology, 46*(4), 541–560. doi:10.1093/bjc/azi095

Pratt, J. (2008). When penal populism stops: Legitimacy, scandal and the power to punish in New Zealand. *Australian and New Zealand Journal of Criminology, 41*(3), 364–383. doi:10.1375/acri.41.3.364

Pratt, J., & Clark, M. (2005). Penal populism in New Zealand. *Punishment and Society, 7*(1), 303–322. doi:10.1177/1462474505053831

Pratt, J., & Erickson, A. (2014). *Contrasts in punishment: An explanation of Anglophone excess and Nordic exceptionalism*. London, UK: Routledge.

Richards, M. (2014). *Property of corrections: The experience of incarceration for female inmates in a New Zealand prison*. Unpublished master's thesis, Victoria University of Wellington, Wellington, New Zealand. Retrieved from https://pdfs.semanticscholar.org/a37b/eb61c9ac83152d0ba1883ed1162f03f665e6.pdf

Roper, B. (2015). New Zealand politics post-1984. In J. Hayward (Ed.), *New Zealand government and politics* (6th ed., pp. 25–36). Melbourne, Australia: Oxford University Press.

Selwyn, T. (2006, October 8). Surviving on the inside. *Sunday Star-Times*.

Stewart, M. (2018, February 21). Prisons under 'immense pressure' with only enough space for 300 more inmates. *Dominion Post*. Retrieved from https://www.stuff.co.nz/national/crime/101634611/prisons-under-immense-pressure-with-only-enough-space-for-300-more-inmates

Tauri, J. M. (2014). Criminal justice as a colonial project in contemporary settler colonialism. *African Journal of Criminology and Justice Studies, 8*(1), 20–37. Retrieved from https://pdfs.semanticscholar.org/22e5/7e02974530a069ff8c5868b99f527230a65d.pdf

Wacquant, L. (2010). Class, race and hyperincarceration in revanchist America. *Daedalus, 139*(3), 35–56. doi:10.1080/08854300.2014.954926

Ward, T., Day, A., & Casey, S. (2006). Offender rehabilitation down under. *Journal of Offender Rehabilitation, 43*(3), 73–83. doi:10.1300/J076v43n03_05

Weekes, J. (2016, May 1). Surplus Rimutaka inmates occupying 'critical' emergency beds. *Dominion Post*. Retrieved from https://www.stuff.co.nz/national/crime/79465288/surplus-rimutaka-inmates-occupying-critical-emergency-beds

Wood, P. (2019). *How to escape from prison*. Auckland, New Zealand: HarperCollins.

Workman, K., & McIntosh, T. (2013). Crime, imprisonment and poverty. In M. Rashbrooke (Ed.), *Inequality: A New Zealand crisis* (pp. 120–133). Wellington, New Zealand: Bridget Williams Books.

22

Rehabilitation
Risks, Needs, and Building Good Lives

Russil Durrant and Joanne Riley

Reoffending is a significant problem for the criminal justice system. In Aotearoa New Zealand, research indicates that around half of all offenders who are released from prison are reconvicted and reimprisoned within a five-year period (Nadesu, 2009). These findings clearly indicate that the experience of incarceration does very little to deter individuals who have committed crimes – indeed, imprisonment in and of itself may actually *increase* the risk of reoffending (Cullen et al., 2011). That being the case, how then might we intervene in individuals' lives to promote better outcomes – not only for society, but also for those who have been punished by the state? One potentially attractive idea is that we can utilise the criminal justice system to *rehabilitate* offenders. That is, we can intervene in the lives of offenders in ways that make reoffending less likely. The aim of this chapter is to provide a review of the concept of rehabilitation with a focus on how it is practised, especially within a New Zealand context.

We begin with a brief overview, before turning to a more in-depth look at specific approaches to offender rehabilitation with a focus on cognitive-behavioural programmes. The two main models of offender rehabilitation – the risk need-responsivity model and the good lives model – are then introduced. Here, we argue for the importance of having a comprehensive theory of desistance for guiding efforts to rehabilitate offenders. We then turn to an overview of rehabilitation within a New Zealand context, noting the range of programmes that are currently being delivered by the Department of Corrections. We conclude by addressing the all-important question of whether these programmes actually *work*. It will be argued that such programmes can be effective, but there is substantial scope for improvement in the nature and range of rehabilitation services offered to offenders in order to assist them in leading lives free from crime.

APPROACHES TO REHABILITATION

The idea that prisons or correctional facilities are places where individuals convicted of offences might in some sense be changed or reformed has a long and somewhat controversial history (McNeill, 2012). In the nineteenth century, the process of reform was supposed to follow from the opportunity provided to offenders to reflect on their wrongful behaviours, typically aided by a regimen of hard work and a liberal dose of religious instruction. After the Second World War, and the rise of psychology as a discipline, this model of reform was effectively replaced with approaches grounded in a more scientific understanding of behaviour and behaviour change. Here the emphasis was less on encouraging offenders to repent for their sinful ways and more on the development of techniques for treating or correcting behavioural problems. This focus on addressing flaws or problems in the way that offenders think and behave has continued to dominate most approaches to rehabilitation in the criminal justice system (Ward & Maruna, 2007).

There remains nonetheless substantial disagreement concerning just what such programmes should involve, and thus exactly what we mean by the term 'rehabilitation'. Importantly, as McNeill (2012, p. 31) notes, 'rehabilitation is a social project as well as a personal one', and thus it needs to address not only the psychological aspects of offenders (the way they think and behave), but also the broader social and cultural contexts of their lives. Internationally, there is a huge diversity of programmes that fall loosely under the rubric of 'offender rehabilitation' (Wilson, 2016). These vary in terms of their intensity (from short, motivational interventions to six-month residential programmes), approach (from mindfulness meditation to structured cognitive-behavioural therapy), location (prison or community), and target population, with many programmes specifically developed for particular 'types' of offender (e.g., sex offender programmes). Here we focus primarily on cognitive-behavioural rehabilitation programmes, while also considering a range of other approaches.

One important challenge that many offenders face when they have been released from prison is finding employment. There is generally good evidence that participation in meaningful employment is a protective factor against offending (Kazemian, 2015). It seems reasonable, therefore, to provide programmes that furnish offenders with opportunities to further their education and to develop specific skills that improve employment outcomes once they have completed their sentence. Many criminal justice systems offer such programmes. In New Zealand, for example, the Department of Corrections provides a range of educational and vocational services that include courses to improve numeracy and literacy skills, access to opportunities to obtain formal qualifications, and partnerships with industry to develop specific vocational skills (Department of Corrections, 2019).

Cognitive-behavioural therapy (CBT) focuses on how changing patterns of thinking (cognition) and affect (emotion) can result in changes to target behaviours. Widely employed for a diverse range of psychological problems, CBT in the context of offender rehabilitation is based on the idea that criminal offending is related in important ways to offender cognition — the way that offenders think, reason, and process social information (Casey et al., 2013; Wilson, 2016). Moreover, it is assumed that these patterns of thinking are essentially learned and hence are amenable to change. According to the CBT approach, psychological and behavioural problems (including criminal offending) arise through a combination of distorted thinking, cognitive biases, or 'deficits' in cognitive skills and capacities (Wilson, 2016). For example, some violent offenders demonstrate hostile attribution biases (Dodge, 2006) that result in a tendency to attribute hostile intent to others' (ambiguous or neutral) social behaviour. This, in turn, increases the risk of aggressive or violent responses. Examples of cognitive deficits may include a tendency to act impulsively without thinking through the consequences of behaviour and a failure to consider alternative response options.

CBT programmes for offenders thus focus on addressing distorted thinking patterns through cognitive restructuring and social skills training, and providing resources to improve cognitive skills and capacities (e.g., by learning to consider alternative response options and by improving self-regulatory capacities). Although the content and specific suite of strategies vary, CBT programmes tend to be manual-based (that is, they follow established guidelines in a structured fashion), are run in small groups, and facilitated by someone who is likely to have had formal training in clinical psychology.

Realising changes in thinking patterns and improving cognitive resources within a treatment context is one thing, but sustaining these over an extended time remains an ongoing challenge for all forms of rehabilitation or treatment. Many CBT programmes, therefore, incorporate the core ideas of *relapse prevention* (RP). Initially developed in the context of treating individuals with substance use problems, the idea of relapse prevention has been transferred to various offender rehabilitation programmes, such as the Kia Marama programme for child sex offenders in New Zealand (Hudson et al., 1998). In order to prevent relapse to problem behaviours, it is essential for individuals to recognise the factors that lead to offending. By understanding these 'offence chains' it is easier to ensure that high-risk situations are avoided and that clear plans are in place to negotiate contexts in which individuals may be motivated to offend.

The term 'alternative programmes' captures a diverse group of initiatives that fall outside of more mainstream rehabilitative efforts (e.g., CBT) (Joseph & Crichlow, 2015). In the United States, faith-based programmes have a long history within the correctional system and are predicated on the idea that if individuals embrace religion (typically Christianity), then they are more likely to turn away from offending lifestyles (Johnson, 2013). More recently, there has been growing interest in the potential role of mindfulness meditation and yoga in helping to improve psychological well-being and reduce reoffending (Auty et al., 2017; Muirhead & Fortune, 2016). Other programmes include those that are based on art, music, and drama; physical education and sporting practices; military style training; and even 'equine based psychotherapy' (Joseph & Crichlow, 2015). Although some of these approaches are promising (e.g., mindfulness meditation – Auty et al., 2017), many have been clearly shown to have no impact on reoffending (e.g., boot camps – MacKenzie et al., 2001); moreover, many alternative programmes have not been subject to rigorous evaluations.

MODELS OF OFFENDER REHABILITATION

The two most prominent theories or models of rehabilitation are the risk-need-responsivity (RNR) model developed by Andrews and Bonta (2010) and the good lives model (GLM) developed by Ward and colleagues (Ward, 2002; Ward & Maruna, 2007). Here we outline the core features of each model.

As its name suggests, the RNR model is based on three core principles: risk, need, and responsivity (see Figure 22.1). Some individuals are more likely to reoffend than others. A substantial body of research has identified risk factors that statistically predict the likelihood that someone will reoffend. Some of the risk factors are static – they are unable to be changed. Age, gender, and number of prior convictions are important static risk factors that predict offending. Others, however, are potentially amenable to change (e.g., antisocial cognition, antisocial associates, alcohol and drug problems), and hence are referred to as *dynamic risk factors*. Understanding the factors that predict reoffending is central to the RNR approach. The 'risk principle' guides decisions about who should participate in rehabilitation programmes and the intensity of treatment that they should receive. In short, based on self-explanatory logic, high-risk offenders should be the main target of treatment services and they should receive the most intense treatment programmes; low-risk offenders, in contrast, should receive minimal or no treatment services.

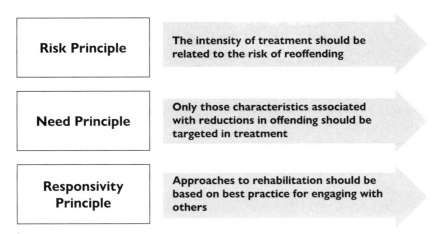

Figure 22.1.
The Risk-Need-Responsivity Model

The need principle is concerned with *what* should be targeted in a rehabilitation programme. For advocates of the RNR model the answer is straightforward: rehabilitation programmes should focus largely, if not exclusively, on those characteristics of individuals that best predict reoffending and are potentially amenable to change. In short, programmes should focus on addressing dynamic risk factors, or what Andrews and Bonta (2010) call *criminogenic needs*. Again, the logic behind this principle is clear: if a given characteristic (say, the tendency to associate with antisocial peers) predicts the likelihood that someone will reoffend, then if a programme can change that characteristic (make it less likely that they will associate with antisocial peers), this should result in a reduced likelihood of that individual committing crimes in the future.

The final component of the RNR model is the responsivity principle. This refers to the way that rehabilitation should be implemented. General responsivity concerns the use of best practice in the development and implementation of rehabilitation programmes which, for Andrews and Bonta (2010), entails CBT approaches delivered in a structured fashion by suitably qualified staff. Specific responsivity relates to the matching of programmes and programme elements to the specific characteristics of offenders – their cognitive ability, personality, gender, learning style, and level of motivation. In sum, the RNR model provides a framework that specifies *who* should be the main target of rehabilitation (the risk principle), what the main *targets* of treatment should be (the need principle), and how the rehabilitation programme should be implemented (the responsivity principle).

Despite the widespread implementation of the RNR model (including in New Zealand), it has not gone without criticism, in particular by Ward and colleagues (Casey et al., 2013; Ward, 2002, 2016; Ward & Maruna, 2007). Perhaps most importantly, it is argued that the RNR approach fails to adequately engage and motivate offenders. This is reflected in the very high attrition rate that is found with most offender rehabilitation programmes – internationally, over a quarter of individuals fail to complete their rehabilitation programme (Olver et al., 2011). By focusing almost exclusively on offenders' risks, their other needs, interests, and motivations are neglected, and hence they may see little benefit to themselves in completing the programme. This tight focus is potentially problematic for other reasons: it downplays the complex process of re-entry and reintegration into the social environment, and neglects the role of agency and the wider social and cultural context in the rehabilitation process. Finally, the emphasis on dynamic risk factors is based largely on their statistical relationship with reoffending, rather than their demonstrated causal role. As such, it is unclear that these factors should play a key role in guiding the kinds of things that should be addressed within a rehabilitation context (Ward, 2016).

An alternative rehabilitation framework which has been developed to address some of these issues with the RNR model is the GLM (Casey et al., 2013; Ward, 2002; Ward & Maruna, 2007). Whereas the RNR model is largely focused on eliminating risk, the GLM is a strength-based approach that emphasises the importance of harnessing offenders' specific interests, strengths, and motivations to develop treatment plans that are personally meaningful to them. A primary assumption of the GLM is that all individuals (including those who commit crimes) are goal-directed and motivated to achieve a number of primary goods, such as agency, knowledge, and happiness. Individuals who commit offences, it is argued, pursue these same primary goods, but do so in ways that may be individually and socially destructive. For example, an individual who sexually offends against children may be seeking the primary good of relatedness, but clearly does so in ways that are inappropriate and harmful to others.

One critical component of offender rehabilitation from a GLM perspective, therefore, is to provide offenders with the appropriate internal (e.g., psychological) and external (e.g., social and cultural) resources that will enable them to realise primary goods in a non-harmful manner and which will ultimately promote psychological well-being. As Ward and Brown (2004) summarise: 'We propose that the best way to lower offender recidivism rates is to equip individuals with the tools to live more fulfilling lives rather than to simply use increasingly sophisticated risk management measures and strategies' (p. 244).

Within the scholarly literature there remains an ongoing debate about the relative merits of the RNR and GLM approaches, which ranges across a number of fundamental issues, from the underlying aims of rehabilitation to the best way to reduce reoffending (Andrews et al., 2011; Willis & Ward, 2013). Regardless of how these issues are ultimately resolved, it is important to be clear about the theoretical underpinnings of specific rehabilitation programmes, as this will allow for a clearer understanding of how they work (if they do) and how they might be modified to improve outcomes for offenders and for society.

REHABILITATION PROGRAMMES IN AOTEAROA NEW ZEALAND

As illustrated in Table 22.1, diverse rehabilitation programmes are available in the New Zealand correctional system. A number of motivational programmes have been designed to enhance offenders' motivation to participate in rehabilitation (Grace et al., 2017). The Short Motivational Programme (SMP) was designed for this purpose and consists of five individual or group-based sessions. It aims to increase offenders' motivation to participate through motivational interviewing techniques (Grace et al., 2017). Tikanga Māori motivational programmes use Māori philosophy, values, knowledge, and practices to change the thinking and behaviour of Māori offenders (Byers, 2002). For example, the Mau Rākau programme focuses on developing a participant's understanding of traditional Māori values and spiritual concepts. Programme components include speech-making, and learning the traditional Māori wero (challenge).

These skills and knowledge are designed to help Māori offenders concentrate on issues related to their offending, and to increase their motivation to bring about individual change (Byers, 2002).

Table 22.1.
Rehabilitation Programmes Currently Available in New Zealand: A Selective Overview

Type of Programmes/ Units	Description	Examples
Motivational	These are for all offenders. They include programmes designed to encourage engagement in other interventions to reduce reoffending.	Tikanga Māori programmes Short Motivational Programme
Offence-focused	These programmes are for specific offenders, such as sex offenders, female offenders, and youth offenders. They involve teaching new skills about how to change attitudes and behaviours.	Medium Intensity Rehabilitation Programme Kowhiritanga
Special Treatment Units	These are specialised treatment units, for groups such as high-risk violent offenders and sex offenders. They involve group-based interventions utilising cognitive behavioural principles.	Kia Marama Special Treatment Unit
Culture-specific	These are designed for offenders of specific cultural backgrounds, such as Māori and Pasifika. They focus on culture, identity, and addressing reintegrative needs such as employment and whānau relationships.	Māori Focus Units
Drug and Alcohol	These are for offenders with a dependence on alcohol and other drugs. They build participant skills in relapse prevention, and teach about addiction, change, and the effects of their actions upon others.	Drug Treatment Units Intensive Treatment Programmes

In accordance with Andrews and Bonta's (2010) RNR framework, current rehabilitation programmes in New Zealand vary in intensity dependent upon the specific risk and offence of the observed offender. Male offenders at the moderate-risk level (excluding sex offenders) are often placed in the Medium Intensity Rehabilitation Programme (MIRP) (Grace et al., 2017). MIRP generally consists of four 2.5-hour sessions per week over a three-month period and addresses management of emotions, substance abuse, criminal associates, and the development of self-control skills and relationship skills (Grace et al., 2017). A similar programme has been developed for female offenders called Kowhiritanga. Kowhiritanga takes into account the New Zealand female offender profile and places more emphasis on relational aspects of group processes. Understandably, effective treatment of high-risk offenders is of extreme importance, and Wilson et al. (2013) developed an Adult Sex Offender Treatment Programme (ASOTP) based on RNR and CBT principles. A pilot study of this programme showed improved personality function and treatment responsivity in offenders, in addition to a clinically meaningful amount of risk-related change, as measured by post-treatment reductions in dynamic risk scores (Wilson et al., 2013). This programme has subsequently been incorporated across prison specialist unit sites in New Zealand.

New Zealand also has a number of special treatment units (STUs) that have enabled psychologists to address specific types of criminal behaviour (Polaschek & Kilgour, 2013).

Te Piriti and the aforementioned Kia Marama are two specialised units for adults imprisoned for sexual offences against children. Treatment at Kia Marama is delivered in a group-based setting, and the programme incorporates CBT and social learning theory elements. These range from victim impact and empathy, arousal conditioning, mood management, and relapse prevention (Hudson et al., 1998). An evaluation of this programme demonstrated significant reductions in recidivism, with 10 per cent of individuals who participated in the treatment sexually reoffending within four years of release compared to 21 per cent of the control group (Bakker et al., 1998). Te Piriti was subsequently developed to address the treatment of both Indigenous and non-Indigenous child sex offenders, combining Western perspectives with traditional Māori concepts and approaches (Thakker, 2014). Te Piriti incorporates the same CBT treatment methods employed at Kia Marama, although these are combined with practices based on a Māori world view. An evaluation of this programme has demonstrated a positive impact on treatment outcomes, with only 4.4 per cent of Māori offenders reoffending (compared to 13.6 per cent of Māori offenders who participated in the Kia Marama programme) (Nathan et al., 2003).

There are a variety of culturally specific treatment units in New Zealand. In addition to Te Piriti, a number of Māori Focus Units (MFUs) have been developed as residential therapeutic communities that emphasise Māori language and cultural practices (Thakker, 2014). Some of the MFUs offer culture-focused treatment programmes, such as the Māori Therapeutic Programme (MTP). The MTP is a 10-week, group-based programme that uses cognitive-behavioural and relapse prevention models, in addition to focusing on Māori concepts and values. International research suggests that 'culturally relevant programmes' can result in lower rates of reoffending for Indigenous offenders (Gutierrez et al., 2018). However, a number of scholars have challenged both the value and legitimacy of such programmes within a New Zealand context (McIntosh & Workman, 2017; Mihaere, 2015; Stanley & Mihaere, 2018; Thakker, 2014).

Mihaere (2015) argues that culture-specific approaches to Māori offenders have focused on Māori cultural identity as the key factor that can contribute to reductions in recidivism at the neglect of other more relevant factors and processes, such as socio-economic disadvantage arising from generations of Pākehā colonisation, and ongoing systemic discrimination within the criminal justice system. Moreover, Mihaere (2015) questions the *authenticity* of culture-specific programmes in New Zealand, arguing that they largely follow Western models of treatment with 'Maori cultural identity grafts' (Stanley & Mihaere, 2018, p. 113). Despite some positive outcomes of these programmes, as noted above, Thakker (2014) points out that the methodological rigour of this literature is less than satisfactory, with many studies having small sample sizes, lacking control groups, and being conducted 'in-house' by government departments, rather than subject to a more vigorous peer-review process. McIntosh and Workman (2017) concisely summarise these concerns: 'What has emerged over the last 20 years is a corrections-led approach to the reduction of Māori offending, which has been largely ineffective and alien to Māori thinking' (p. 732). Leaming and Willis (2016) argue that the incorporation of Māori models of health and well-being is often incompatible with an RNR framework, with its narrow focus on risk factors, and that a GLM framework, with its more holistic approach to understanding offending, is likely to provide better guidance. Although a GLM approach may well be a promising avenue to explore, more wide-ranging changes are probably necessary to address Māori reimprisonment rates (Stanley & Mihaere, 2018).

In addition to programmes that are based in prison, there are a number of community-based services for offenders that are operated by the Department of Corrections along with other providers. For example, Tai Aroha is a community-based treatment programme delivered in a therapeutic community setting (Thakker, 2014). In this programme, participants generally reside at the Tai Aroha house for 14–16 weeks and attend treatment sessions four days a week.

The treatment includes addressing issues such as relationship difficulties, self-regulation, and offence-related cognitions (Thakker, 2014). Preliminary evaluations of the first two years of the programme indicate that participation led to improvements in responsivity and treatment readiness, and reductions in personality problems (King, 2012). Community-based programmes are also available for individuals with alcohol and drug problems. A study by Wheeler et al. (2011) examined the effectiveness of a community alcohol and other drug (AOD) treatment programme for offenders serving community sentences. The authors found at three-month follow-up a significant reduction in alcohol and cannabis use and improved physical health in participants. In addition, the participants reported the AOD programme helped them reduce subsequent offending behaviour (Wheeler et al., 2011). Community programmes are important in reducing the likelihood of recidivism in both paroled offenders and those who have received non-custodial sentences.

Obtaining a clear picture of the relative effectiveness of the many different types of programme that are available in the New Zealand correctional landscape is a difficult task because relatively few such programmes have been subject to methodologically rigorous evaluations and published in peer-reviewed outlets. An examination of international research is therefore necessary to address the question of whether offenders, in general, can be rehabilitated.

DOES REHABILITATION WORK?

In a crushing review of rehabilitation programmes up until the late 1960s, Martinson (1974) influentially concluded that 'with few and isolated exceptions, the rehabilitative efforts that have been reported so far have had no appreciable effect on recidivism' (p. 25). Given the widespread use of rehabilitation programmes in New Zealand and overseas, it is clearly important to evaluate whether they are effective. As we shall see, since Martinson's review a substantial body of evidence has accumulated to support the idea that rehabilitation programmes can be effective (McGuire, 2013; Wilson, 2016). However, the task of evaluating the effectiveness of such programmes is far from straightforward, and it is important to develop appropriate methodologies that allow us to make robust claims about whether rehabilitation programmes can lead to reductions in offending, or improvements in other outcomes. Perhaps most importantly, evaluations need to either *randomly assign* participants to treatment and control groups – or, if this is not possible, then participants in control groups should be matched to those in the treatment group in terms of the characteristics that may predict reoffending (e.g., age, gender, number of prior convictions). If (and only if) participants in the treatment group are statistically less likely to reoffend than those in the control group when followed up after a reasonable amount of time (e.g., three to five years), we can claim – provisionally at least – that the rehabilitation programme 'worked'.

Although the results of well-designed individual studies are valuable, a better overall picture of the effectiveness of rehabilitation programmes can be obtained via systematic reviews and meta-analyses. Systematic reviews aim, as they suggest, to systematically review all studies in a particular area. Meta-analyses proceed in a similar fashion, but take the further step of statistically integrating the findings from multiple studies to provide a single overall statistical metric (the effect size), which indicates how effective such programmes are in reducing reoffending. Space precludes anything like a thorough review of the many systematic reviews and meta-analyses that have been conducted in this area; nonetheless, in summary, offender rehabilitation programmes – especially those based on CBT principles – *are* effective, although the overall effect size (how *much* they reduce reoffending) tends to be small to moderate (McGuire, 2013; Wilson, 2016). In other words, there is good evidence to support the continued use of rehabilitation programmes in the criminal justice sector, but there is also scope for improvement.

CONCLUSION

There are four key 'take home' messages from this overview of offender rehabilitation. First, rehabilitation is important. Criminal justice sanctions – that is, the sentences handed down to offenders – do not by themselves result in reductions in reoffending, so attempts to rehabilitate individuals who have committed crime should be strongly supported. Second, approaches to rehabilitation should be evidence-based; that is, they should be based – wherever possible – on what we know works to reduce reoffending. Third, rehabilitation programmes should be guided by clearly articulated rehabilitation theories or models because this allows us to identify *why* they work and how they might be improved. And, fourth, the fairly modest success of rehabilitation programmes and the generally high attrition rate should encourage efforts to develop new programmes (or add to old approaches) that better engage offenders and can more effectively improve outcomes for both the community and for the participants themselves.

We conclude by briefly considering several underexplored areas in the rehabilitation landscape. Although quantitative evaluations (and their associated systematic reviews and meta-analyses) are essential for providing evidence on the effectiveness of rehabilitation programmes, they are less informative about how rehabilitation is actually experienced by the individuals involved. For this, it is important to complement quantitative evaluations with more in-depth qualitative research that offers information about the lived reality of participation in rehabilitation programmes (e.g., Ashdown et al., 2019). This information, in turn, may be able to offer valuable insights into addressing some of the outstanding problems with many offender rehabilitation programmes, including the high attrition rate. Because of the over-representation of males in the criminal justice system it is perhaps unsurprising that most programmes (either implicitly or explicitly) are based on our understanding of male offending. However, given research that suggests that the pathways into (and out from) offending may be different for women, there is a need for more research on how best to develop programmes that can most effectively assist female offenders in desisting from offending (Bevan & Wehipeihana, 2015). Finally, there is also an ongoing need to address the wider social, cultural, and historical context in which rehabilitation takes place – a need that is particularly relevant in the context of post-colonial Aotearoa New Zealand.

STUDY QUESTIONS

- How does the good lives model differ from the risk-need-responsivity model of offender rehabilitation? Which model do you prefer, and why?
- What does the research evidence tell us about the effectiveness of offender rehabilitation programmes?
- What do you think are the most important issues facing the rehabilitation of offenders within the context of Aotearoa New Zealand?

FURTHER READING

Andrews, D. A., & Bonta, J. (2010). *The psychology of criminal conduct* (5th ed.). Newark, NJ: Anderson Publishing.

McGuire, J. (2013). 'What works' to reduce reoffending: 18 years on. In L. A. Craig, T. A. Gannon, & L. Dixon (Eds.), *What works in offender rehabilitation: An evidence-based approach to assessment and treatment* (pp. 20–49). Chichester, UK: Wiley & Sons.

Ward, T., & Maruna, S. (2007). *Rehabilitation*. London, UK: Routledge.

REFERENCES

Andrews, D. A., & Bonta, J. (2010). *The psychology of criminal conduct* (5th ed.). Newark, NJ: Anderson Publishing.

Andrews, D. A., Bonta, J., & Wormith, J. S. (2011). The risk-need-responsivity (RNR) model: Does adding the good lives model contribute to effective crime prevention? *Criminal Justice and Behavior, 38*(7), 735–755. doi:10.1177/0093854811406356

Ashdown, J. D., Treharne, G. J., Neha, T., Dixon, B., & Aitken, C. (2019). Māori men's experiences of rehabilitation in the Moana House therapeutic community in Aotearoa/New Zealand: A qualitative enquiry. *International Journal of Offender Therapy and Comparative Criminology, 63*(5), 734–751. doi:10.1177/0306624X18808675

Auty, K. M., Cope, A., & Liebling, A. (2017). A systematic review and meta-analysis of yoga and mindfulness meditation in prison: Effects on psychological well-being and behavioural functioning. *International Journal of Offender Therapy and Comparative Criminology, 61*(6), 689–710. doi:10.1177/0306624X15602514

Bakker, L., Hudson, S., Wales, D., & Riley, D. (1998). *And there was light . . . : Evaluating the Kia Marama treatment programme for New Zealand sex offenders against children*. Retrieved from https://www.corrections.govt.nz/__data/assets/pdf_file/0018/10647/kiamarama.pdf

Bevan, M., & Wehipeihana, N. (2015). *Women's experiences of reoffending and rehabilitation*. Retrieved from https://www.corrections.govt.nz/resources/research/womens_experiences_of_reoffending_and_rehabilitation

Byers, M. (2002). Correctional initiatives for Māori in New Zealand. *Corrections Today, 64*(1), 25–29.

Casey, S., Day, A., Vess, J., & Ward, T. (2013). *Foundations of offender rehabilitation*. London, UK: Routledge.

Cullen, F. T., Jonson, C. L., & Nagin, D. S. (2011). Prisons do not reduce recidivism: The high cost of ignoring science. *The Prison Journal, 91*(3, Suppl.), 48S–65S. doi:10.1177/0032885511415224

Department of Corrections. (2019). *Employment and support programmes*. Retrieved from https://www.corrections.govt.nz/working_with_offenders/prison_sentences/employment_and_support_programmes.html

Dodge, K. A. (2006). Translational science in action: Hostile attribution style and the development of aggressive behaviour problems. *Development and Psychopathology, 18*(3), 791–814. doi:10.1017/S0954579406060391

Grace, R. C., McLean, A., & Beggs Christofferson, S. (2017). Psychology and criminal justice. In J. Gilbert & G. Newbold (Eds.), *Criminal justice: A New Zealand introduction* (pp. 209–225). Auckland, New Zealand: Auckland University Press.

Gutierrez, L., Chadwick, N., & Wanamaker, K. A. (2018). Culturally relevant programming versus the status quo: A meta-analytic review of the effectiveness of treatment of Indigenous offenders. *Canadian Journal of Criminology and Criminal Justice, 60*(3), 321–353. doi:10.3138/cjccj.2017-0020.r2

Hudson, S. M., Wales, D. S., & Ward, T. (1998). Kia Marama. In W. L. Marshall, Y. M. Fernandez, S. M. Hudson, & T. Ward (Eds.), *Sourcebook of treatment programs for sexual offenders* (pp. 17–28). New York, NY: Springer.

Johnson, B. R. (2013). Religious participation and criminal behaviour. In J. A. Humphrey & P. Cordella (Eds.), *Effective interventions in the lives of criminal offenders* (pp. 3–18). New York, NY: Springer.

Joseph, J., & Crichlow, W. (Eds.) (2015). *Alternative offender rehabilitation and social justice: Arts and physical engagement in criminal justice and community settings.* New York, NY: Springer.

Kazemian, L. (2015). Desistance from crime and antisocial behavior. In J. Morizot & L. Kazemian (Eds.), *The development of criminal and antisocial behavior* (pp. 295–312). New York, NY: Springer.

King, L. (2012). *Tai Aroha – the first two years: A formative evaluation of a residential community based programme for offenders.* Retrieved from https://www.corrections.govt.nz/__data/assets/pdf_file/0017/10772/COR_Tai_Aroha_WEB.pdf

Leaming, N., & Willis, G. M. (2016). The good lives model: New avenues for Māori rehabilitation? *Sexual Abuse in Australia and New Zealand, 7*(1), 59–69. Retrieved from https://search.informit.com.au/documentSummary;dn=201588560268063;res=IELHEA

MacKenzie, D. L., Wilson, D. B., & Kider, S. B. (2001). Effects of correctional boot camps on offending. *The Annals of the American Academy of Political and Social Science, 578*(1), 126–143. doi:10.1177/000271620157800108

Martinson, R. (1974). What works? – Questions and answers about prison reform. *The Public Interest, 35,* 22. Retrieved from https://www.gwern.net/docs/sociology/1974-martinson.pdf

McGuire, J. (2013). 'What works' to reduce reoffending: 18 years on. In L. A. Craig, T. A. Gannon, & L. Dixon (Eds.), *What works in offender rehabilitation: An evidence-based approach to assessment and treatment* (pp. 20–49). Chichester, UK: Wiley & Sons.

McIntosh, T., & Workman, K. (2017). Māori and prison. In A. Deckert & R. Sarre (Eds.), *The Palgrave handbook of Australian and New Zealand criminology, crime and justice* (pp. 725–735). Cham, Switzerland: Palgrave Macmillan.

McNeill, F. (2012). Four forms of 'offender' rehabilitation: Towards an interdisciplinary perspective. *Legal and Criminological Psychology, 17*(1), 18–36. doi:10.1111/j.2044-8333.2011.02039.x

Mihaere, R. (2015). *A kaupapa Māori analysis of the use of Māori cultural identity in the prison system.* Unpublished PhD dissertation, Victoria University of Wellington, Wellington, New Zealand. Retrieved from https://researcharchive.vuw.ac.nz/xmlui/handle/10063/4185

Muirhead, J., & Fortune, C. (2016). Yoga in prisons: A review of the literature. *Aggression and Violent Behavior, 28,* 57–63. doi:10.1016/j.avb.2016.03.013

Nadesu, A. (2009). *Reconviction patterns of released prisoners: A 60 month follow-up analysis.* Retrieved from https://www.corrections.govt.nz/resources/research_and_statistics/reconviction-patterns-of-released-prisoners-a-60-months-follow-up-analysis2.html

Nathan, L., Wilson, N. J., & Hillman, D. (2003). *Te Whakakotahitanga: An evaluation of the Te Piriti special treatment programme.* Christchurch, New Zealand: Department of Corrections. Retrieved from https://www.corrections.govt.nz/resources/research_and_statistics/te-whakakotahitanga-an-evaluation-of-the-te-piriti-special-treatment-programme

Olver, M. E., Stockdale, K. C., & Wormith, J. S. (2011). A meta-analysis of predictors of offender treatment attrition and its relationship with recidivism. *Journal of Consulting and Clinical Psychology, 79*(1), 6–21. doi:10.1037/a0022200

Polaschek, D. L. L., & Kilgour, T. G. (2013). New Zealand's special treatment units: The development and implementation of intensive treatment for high-risk male prisoners. *Psychology, Crime and Law, 19*(5–6), 511–526. doi:10.1080/1068316X.2013.759004

Stanley, E., & Mihaere, R. (2018). Managing ignorance about Māori imprisonment. In A. Barton & H. Davis (Eds.), *Ignorance, power and harm: Agnotology and the criminological imagination* (pp. 113–138). Cham, Switzerland: Palgrave Macmillan.

Thakker, J. (2014). Cultural factors in offender treatment: Current approaches in New Zealand. *Procedia – Social and Behavioral Sciences, 113,* 213–223. doi:10.1016/j.sbspro.2014.01.028

Ward, T. (2002). Good lives and the rehabilitation of offenders: Promises and problems. *Aggression and Violent Behavior, 7*(5), 513–528. doi:10.1016/S1359-1789(01)00076-3

Ward, T. (2016). Dynamic risk factors: Scientific kinds or predictive constructs. *Psychology, Crime & Law, 22*(1–2), 2–16. doi:10.1080/1068316X.2015.1109094

Ward, T., & Brown, M. (2004). The good lives model and conceptual issues in offender rehabilitation. *Psychology, Crime and Law, 10*(3), 243–257. doi:10.1080/10683160410001662744

Ward, T., & Maruna, S. (2007). *Rehabilitation*. London, UK: Routledge.

Wheeler, A., Websdell, P., Wilson, P., Pulford, J., Galea, S., & Robinson, E. (2011). Outcome evaluation of a community alcohol and other drug intervention programme for offenders serving community sentences in Auckland, New Zealand. *New Zealand Journal of Psychology, 40*(3), 120–128. Retrieved from https://search.proquest.com/docview/1025744876?pq-origsite=gscholar

Willis, G. M., & Ward, T. (2013). The good lives model: Does it work? Preliminary evidence. In L. A. Craig, T. A. Gannon, & L. Dixon (Eds.), *What works in offender rehabilitation: An evidence-based approach to assessment and treatment* (pp. 305–317). Chichester, UK: Wiley & Sons.

Wilson, D. B. (2016). Correctional programs. In D. Weisburd, D. P. Farrington, & C. Gill (Eds.), *What works in crime prevention and rehabilitation* (pp. 193–217). New York, NY: Springer.

Wilson, N., Kilgour, G., & Polaschek, D. (2013). Treating high-risk rapists in a New Zealand intensive prison programme. *Psychology, Crime and Law, 19*(5–6), 527–547.

23

(Re)Integration
Recentring Strengths in Communities

Alice Mills and Cinnamon Lindsay Latimer

Just under ten thousand people are currently incarcerated in New Zealand prisons (Department of Corrections, 2019a), and approximately sixteen thousand releases are made each year (Department of Corrections, 2018). While much has been written about those imprisoned, there has been surprisingly little discussion of life after prison. In Aotearoa New Zealand the term 'reintegration' is commonly used to describe the process of being released from prison and moving back into the community. Reintegration is also associated with various initiatives and services to facilitate this process, and is broadly equivalent to the concepts of 're-entry' (commonly employed in the US and Canada) and 'resettlement' (often used in the UK). A somewhat contentious term, reintegration is rarely an uncomplicated or linear process. The limited discussion of reintegration in New Zealand has been dominated by the needs-based support narrative (Maruna & LeBel, 2003) and service provision, which suggests that in order to reduce crime the multiple 'deficits' or needs of people leaving prison must be addressed.

This chapter will discuss the need for reintegration policy and services within the New Zealand context, and will highlight key theoretical approaches behind reintegration initiatives. It then briefly examines several schemes designed to support reintegration, before critically discussing the concept of reintegration and its application in New Zealand. It argues that reintegration policy and provision should better align with the literature on desistance, adopt strengths-based approaches, and consider structural inequalities, to ensure community integration.[1]

In considering (re)integration practices it is necessary to recognise how New Zealand's colonial backdrop informs the experiences of those both in prison and on release. Historically, colonial processes of land theft, cultural subjugation, and political dominance – premised on European superiority – functioned to marginalise, other, and control Māori through cultural violence and assimilation (Tauri, 2014). Such processes set the foundations for institutional racism and inequalities to flourish in New Zealand (Waretini-Karena, 2017), reflected in our largely monocultural policing and justice systems, where Māori are more likely to be arrested, prosecuted, and convicted than non-Māori, in addition to experiencing high rates of victimisation (Quince, 2007). Discussions of imprisonment and reintegration that ignore this history and contemporary reality decontextualise Māori experiences from relevant socio-political contexts of intergenerational trauma and colonial legacy (Groot et al., 2019; Waretini-Karena, 2017). For Māori, reintegration involves not just reintegration into society but also (re)integration into a colonial society.

REINTEGRATION IN THE NEW ZEALAND CONTEXT

The Department of Corrections (2016) defines reintegration as 'the process for successfully transitioning offenders back into the wider community following the end of their sentences. An offender is said to have successfully transitioned when they remain crime-free and settle into the wider community with prosocial constructive attitudes and behaviours' (p. 57). Many people do not successfully transition back into the wider community or remain crime-free. Of those released from prison in 2016/17, 46.8 per cent were reconvicted and 32.2 per cent were reimprisoned within 12 months of being released, with men and those aged under 20 being more likely to reoffend than women and those over 40 (Department of Corrections, 2018).[2]

Various barriers to successful reintegration have been identified, including the absence of housing or employment, continued involvement with gangs or other antisocial peers, absent or strained whānau/family relationships, material deprivations, and the absence of marketable skills amongst those released from prisons (Ganapathy, 2018). The experience of imprisonment is likely to exacerbate many of these challenges, and not all individuals will experience these multiple and interlinked barriers equally. Sixty-two per cent of prisoners have experienced a mental health or substance use disorder in the previous 12 months (Indig et al., 2016), which, along with physical health problems, is likely to create further difficulties in obtaining work or accommodation and accessing appropriate and affordable treatment (Western, 2018). Additionally, women are less likely to be able to find work on release, as they tend to have more limited work histories, a narrower range of vocational skills, and smaller existing employment networks to leverage for potential opportunities (Morrison et al., 2018).

Within the criminological literature, there has been a growing shift from examining individualised aspects of reintegration (such as relationships and employment) to considering these factors within wider structural systems that complicate successful transitions into society (Farrall, 2009). Prison populations disproportionately come from disadvantaged social and economic positions. They are likely to have faced societal exclusion throughout their lifetimes (McIntosh & Workman, 2017; Workman, 2014), and have limited opportunities to participate in mainstream society. The process of reintegration is further complicated for minority groups who must navigate these contexts alongside other institutional structures such as racism and/or homophobia. Sixty-eight percent of Māori released from prison are reconvicted within 24 months, compared to 52 per cent of non-Māori, and 50 per cent of Māori are reimprisoned compared to 35 per cent of non-Māori (Department of Corrections, 2019b). This is likely to be a consequence of the racism and discrimination they face both in the criminal justice system and in obtaining employment, housing, and basic services in wider society (Harris et al., 2012; McIntosh & Workman, 2017).

Corrections and reintegration services

According to section 6(h) of the Corrections Act 2004, 'offenders must, so far as is reasonable and practicable in the circumstances within the resources available, be given access to activities that may contribute to their rehabilitation and reintegration into the community' (as cited in Salvation Army, 2016, p. 46). In recent years, increasing efforts have been made by Corrections to promote reintegration amongst people leaving prison. These efforts can at least partly be attributed to the 2012 Better Public Services Goal to reduce the rate of reoffending by 25 per cent by 2017 (an unmet goal that was abolished in 2017) (Ministry of Justice, 2012). Corrections' current approach is based around six 'pillars of reintegration': accommodation, oranga (health and well-being), family/whānau/community support, education and training, employment, and skills for life (Tissera, 2019). Broadly, Corrections' approach is needs-based, whereby reintegration is promoted by tackling the needs or challenges faced by individuals on release from prison (Dorne, 2016). Every prisoner serving over 28 days should be assigned a case manager who assesses their reintegration needs, creates an offender plan (Office of the Auditor General, 2013), and provides support from the beginning of the sentence to co-ordinating release (Salvation Army, 2016).

The 'implicit criminology' (Maguire & Raynor, 2006) of this approach is therefore largely a positivist 'opportunity-deficit model' (Raynor, 2007, p. 36), which reflects the idea that crime (in this case reoffending) is caused by economic and social challenges faced by individuals, and that people leaving prison are likely to reoffend due to a lack of access to resources (Raynor, 2007, p. 36). In this model, the broader societal stigma and systemic structural challenges that people leaving prison often experience are not acknowledged. This approach to reintegration also appears to be influenced by the risk-need-responsivity model (Andrews & Bonta, 1998; see also Durrant & Riley, chapter 22 this volume), which has dominated correctional practice in New Zealand. Under this model, work with prisoners is based on their risk of reoffending, their level of 'criminogenic' needs, and how well they respond to services (Fox, 2014). 'Criminogenic needs' are those that are associated with changes in the risk of reoffending, rather than being linked to the individual's perception of what they require (Fox, 2014; Hannah-Moffatt, 2005; Workman, 2012). They include various factors relevant to reintegration, including employment, education, family, peers, and substance misuse (Hannah-Moffatt, 2005).

Corrections funds a variety of different initiatives that aim to meet the perceived needs of people leaving prison and promote successful reintegration, most of which are provided by non-governmental organisations (NGOs), such as PARS, Salvation Army, Presbyterian Support, Anglican Action, and other local and faith-based organisations. Services include intensive programmes to teach literacy/numeracy and work-ready skills, and navigational services such as the Out of Gate programme for those serving under two years or on remand for more than 60 days. Under this programme, contracted NGOs provide support including travel from prisons to home areas, and assistance to attend appointments, open bank accounts, and find employment and accommodation (Department of Corrections, 2016; Office of the Auditor General, 2013). Corrections research suggests that Out of Gate programmes can reduce the rate of reimprisonment by 4.5 per cent (Department of Corrections, 2018). However, officially they only provide support for up to one month after release, raising questions about their effectiveness in encouraging long-term reintegration (Salvation Army, 2016). A range of services operate for long-term prisoners (serving over two years or more) including the Guided Release Programme, which aims to promote a gradual transition from prison to the community, including support for whānau members. People leaving prison identify social support as critical to help them meet the challenges of reintegration (Bevan, 2015; Fox, 2014; Moore, 2011). Corrections therefore also works with a variety of different partners, including whānau, iwi/marae-based groups, community, and faith-based organisations, to develop positive relationships to improve the chances of successful reintegration (Department of Corrections, 2016).

However, reintegration services provided by both Corrections and NGOs have been historically dominated by Pākehā values and approaches that undermine Māori cultural resources. In response to this, Corrections has begun to adopt kaupapa Māori approaches in an effort to engage with, and be relevant for, Māori. For example, Tiaki Tangata provides whānau-centric services and support for long-serving offenders, including transitional accommodation and help to connect with iwi, hapū, whānau, and others (Campbell, 2016). Whare Oranga Ake units located outside the prison walls at Hawke's Bay and Spring Hill prisons provide a kaupapa Māori environment and are operated by iwi-based Māori community service providers to form or maintain supportive networks with iwi, hapū, and community organisations (Campbell, 2016).

Housing and employment

Overseas research has discovered that, alongside strong family support, stable housing and meaningful employment are likely to increase the chances of successful reintegration (Baldry et al., 2006; Fox, 2015, 2016; Laub & Sampson, 2001; Social Exclusion Unit, 2002; Walsh et al., 2011). Despite the growing recognition in the academic literature that housing is the 'lynchpin that holds the reintegration process together' (Bradley et al., 2001, p. 7), until recently it has been somewhat neglected in reintegration policy and provision. Stable housing may enable individuals to maintain or create strong whānau or community relationships, gain employment, and access a range of other services such as health, welfare, or addictions assistance (Mills et al., 2013). Housing can be of particular importance for women, who may need accommodation to regain custody of their children. International studies indicate that stable housing can reduce the risk of reoffending after prison by between 11 and 62 per cent (Baldry et al., 2006; Ellison et al., 2013; Williams et al., 2012). For example, Baldry et al. (2006) found that 59 per cent of those who moved twice or more in a three-month post-release period were reincarcerated after nine months compared to 22 per cent of those who moved just once.

Unfortunately, many people leaving prison will face homelessness on release (Salvation Army, 2016). Only around half are able to settle into long-term accommodation (Johnston, 2018). Those released from prison face a number of barriers in finding accommodation, including a lack of suitable references, limited finances for rent and/or bond, and restrictions due to supervision/ parole conditions, as well as landlord reluctance to house them due to the stigma of imprisonment (Faure, 2019; Hallot & Patterson, 2017; Parhar & Wormwith, 2013). These difficulties are likely to be intensified by New Zealand's lack of halfway houses for released prisoners (Faure, 2019), rising rents, and a serious shortage of both social and private rental housing, which are substantially more likely to affect Māori and Pasifika (Johnson et al., 2018) than Pākehā. The opposition shown by some sections of the community to housing and (re)integrating released prisoners in their neighbourhoods (Sharpe, 2019) also demonstrates punitive societal attitudes towards offenders (Pratt, 2007). Consequently, many people leaving prison will move in with whānau members or friends (Lindsay et al., 2019). Although this may provide a source of support, living with others is unlikely to turn an ex-prisoner away from crime, particularly if relations are strained (Halsey, 2006).

Corrections funds almost 1000 accommodation places annually for people released from prison (usually provided by NGOs), but most initiatives are limited to fairly short-term, transitional accommodation (Faure, 2019). For example, the Supported Accommodation for Long-Servers scheme provides housing and wraparound support services for 13 weeks to those who have served over two years and are deemed to be at high risk of reoffending (Hallot & Patterson, 2017). Clients are then expected to progress into independent accommodation, with a further 13 weeks of individual case management support (Hallot & Patterson, 2017). The scheme provides accommodation for approximately 640 people each year (Department of Corrections, 2018), but the limit of 13 weeks' accommodation has been described as too inflexible to meet the needs of many ex-prisoners (Mills, 2014). In 2016, fewer than half of prisoners on the scheme were supported into longer-term accommodation (Treasury, 2017).

Creating Positive Pathways provides longer-term housing places for those who are eligible for social housing and unable to source sustainable housing after completing a Corrections reintegration programme. It involves placement in public housing, funded by the Ministry of Housing and Urban Development, and access to tailored wraparound support services until the individual is ready to transition to greater independence (Johnston, 2018). This scheme marks a change in the attitude of public housing agencies to those involved in the criminal justice system. Housing New Zealand, for example, has previously refused permission for people released from prison and those on bail to live with whānau members in their properties (Mills, 2014; Pennington, 2016).

Employment has long been perceived as vital for successful reintegration and to prevent further reoffending. Ex-offenders who are employed are substantially less likely to be rearrested and reincarcerated (Baldry et al., 2006; Growns et al., 2018; Robson, 2015). Paid employment not only may diminish the motivation for offending, but also can provide a degree of informal social control (Christofferson, 2014). However, people leaving prisons are likely to face various barriers to stable employment. In addition to the stigma of a criminal record and the lack of training, employment-related skills, and finances to pay for transport or work clothing (Cunningham, 2017), just over 60 per cent of prisoners have literacy and numeracy levels below Level 1 NZQA (Lishman, 2018). Access to some professions may be barred to anyone with a criminal conviction (Salvation Army, 2016).

Various New Zealand employers and community organisations work with Corrections to improve the employment prospects of people leaving prison. For example, under the Release to Work scheme participants leave prison on daily release to work in paid positions in the community, and over 50 per cent of participants retain their positions with the same employer post-release (Christofferson, 2014; Dorne, 2016). Supporting Offenders into Employment uses intensive client support managers (ICSMs), employed by the Ministry of Social Development, to work with prisoners pre- and post-release to secure employment and reduce barriers to employment including work-related costs and the lack of education and training and identification documents. By September 2018, just over 50 per cent of the clients assisted by ICSMs had secured employment (Lishman, 2018). However, it should be noted that not all people leaving prison will be able to work, due to illness, age, caring responsibilities, and the need to fulfil post-release conditions. This varies across gender lines, with women being less likely to be employed post-release (Morrison et al., 2018).

CRITICAL ISSUES IN REINTEGRATION IN NEW ZEALAND

Despite recent efforts to improve experiences of reintegration, a number of critical issues remain. The first relates to the significant difficulties of reintegration itself.

The problem of (re)integration

The concept of reintegration (or re-entry/resettlement) has been the subject of substantial criticism. It is often unclear what reintegration refers to, particularly when many incarcerated persons have never been or felt integrated into the community prior to prison, and this may explain why they came into contact with the criminal justice system in the first place (Social Exclusion Unit, 2002). Inherent in the concept of reintegration is the expectation that people leaving prison will be entering prosocial communities. Yet, many prisoners hail from highly socially and economically marginalised communities, with high rates of addiction and mental health problems, poor physical health, and low levels of literacy and employment (Indig et al., 2016; Ministry of Justice, 2012). Such environments may not have the structural capabilities to foster attitudes and resources to encourage successful reintegration or support desistance from crime (Bevan 2015; Moore 2011; Wacquant 2010). Consequently, as Wacquant (2010, p. 605) notes, 'most released convicts experience not re-entry but ongoing circulation between the prison and their dispossessed neighbourhoods'. It may therefore be more appropriate to discuss the need for 'integration' rather than 'reintegration'.

The impact of the criminal justice system

The challenges of reintegration can be substantially compounded by the negative effects of contact with the criminal justice system, including stigma and the difficulties of leaving the highly regulated prison environment (Salvation Army, 2016). Imprisonment may cause people to lose their homes, jobs, and family relationships, and can have negative effects on their mental health (Social Exclusion Unit, 2002), therefore potentially intensifying the conditions that lead to offending (Workman & McIntosh, 2013). Parole and release conditions that prohibit people from certain geographical areas can isolate people from whānau, employment opportunities, and other sources of support (Pogrebin et al., 2014). Requirements to complete post-release programmes may also hinder opportunities to establish prosocial routines (Salvation Army, 2016). Such conditions serve as reminders that people leaving prison remain outsiders, and that the path to becoming an insider is 'long, frustrating and sometimes downright impossible to contemplate let alone ensure' (Halsey, 2010, p. 550), meaning that true community reintegration remains highly elusive (Fox, 2015). As such, prisons become a major cause of the very problems that reintegration services seek to redress (Workman, 2014).

Lack of connections to desistance and the need for strengths-based approaches

The deficit-focused model of reintegration has been criticised for failing to align with research on desistance (Moore, 2011). Much research finds that the chances of desisting from crime typically hinge 'on the ability to develop social capital' (Fox, 2016, p. 69). Social capital can be seen as the resources available to members of social networks through their social connections (Bourdieu, 1986), and can be provided through various mechanisms. For example, stable employment and strong whānau ties can increase social capital and the chances of desistance because people do not want to risk their job or relationships through engagement in criminal behaviour (Laub & Sampson, 2001; Mills & Codd, 2008). Social capital may be of particular importance for secondary desistance, which develops after the initial cessation of offending (primary desistance) and involves the reassessment and restructuring of self-identity whereby individuals start to see themselves as non-offenders (Maruna et al., 2004).

Several commentators have argued that reintegration should therefore be based on more inclusive strengths-based models, such as the good lives model (GLM), which focus on a shared humanity and the development and maintenance of social capital rather than purely meeting practical needs (Fox, 2014; Moore, 2011; Workman, 2012; see also Durrant & Riley, chapter 22 this volume). The GLM assumes that offenders share the same human needs and aspirations as everyone else, and that by providing people with the conditions to meet these needs, including social support, skills, and opportunities, they will be less likely to act in harmful ways (Ward & Stewart, 2003). This approach is likely to be preferred by Māori, for whom whānau and community are key cultural institutions and are likely to be the locus for the reduction of offending (Workman, 2012). In Te Ao Māori, restitution is prioritised over punishment. Approaches that offer opportunities to take responsibility and restore the mana of individuals, whānau, and communities through service and relationship-building are valued, and ensure that former offenders can access the same social goods and resources as the rest of the community (Workman, 2012, 2014).

Holistic, strengths-based approaches are currently limited in New Zealand. One example of a strengths-based programme, underpinned by the GLM and desistance theory, is the Pathway Total Reintegration Programme run by the Pathway Charitable Group in Canterbury. In addition to providing regular one-on-one social work support and help with practical needs, this eight-month programme aims to enable 'restorative reintegration', including measures to repair relationships with victims, whānau, and the community at large (Gilbert & Elley, 2015). Clients have a community mentor and participate in 'community days' where they engage in work alongside the wider community, which enables them to widen their social circle (Gilbert & Elley, 2015). This can serve as a ritual of reintegration to remove their exclusion from the community created by imprisonment (Maruna, 2011). This process may help to lead to tertiary desistance: a more cemented state of desistance which results from feelings of genuine belonging or integration into a prosocial community (Fox, 2016). Although the longer-term effects of the Pathway programme are as yet unknown, people on the programme were 33.3 per cent less likely to be reconvicted within a year after release than would be expected if they were not involved in the programme (Gilbert & Elley, 2015).

However, while strengths-based approaches to reintegration may show substantial promise, it should be noted that not all communities will be in a position to offer such assistance to those leaving prison. The process of acquiring social capital is constrained by social structures, including racism and poverty, and imprisonment can erode social cohesion among individuals, their families, and communities – with disproportionate effects within our most economically vulnerable communities (Workman & McIntosh, 2013). As such, strengths-based models need to be accompanied by the restructuring of access to resources and dismantling of institutional barriers to effect change for those who wish to reintegrate back into their wider communities.

Lack of provision for Māori

Perhaps the most significant criticism of reintegration policy and provision in New Zealand is that it does not provide appropriate help for Māori. Historically, approaches to reintegration have been predominantly premised on Westernised, colonial values and processes (Workman, 2014), as have the operations of major social institutions, such as education and healthcare, which function to marginalise Māori and exacerbate the conditions that make offending more likely. The disparity between recidivism rates for Māori and non-Māori, and the lack of specialist provision for Māori or specific targets to reduce reoffending by Māori, were the subject of a successful claim to the Waitangi Tribunal in 2016, brought by a former senior probation officer, Tom Hemopo, and his iwi, Ngāti Kahungunu.[3] The tribunal found that the Crown, through Corrections, had breached the Treaty principles of equity and active protection of Māori interests (Waitangi Tribunal, 2017).

In 2019 a new strategy to address the over-representation of Māori in prison was announced. Hōkai Rangi is co-designed with Māori, and recognises the importance of working in partnership with Māori and prioritising mātauranga Māori to reduce the devastating effects of imprisonment on whānau, hapū, iwi, and hapori Māori. It aims to utilise tikanga Māori by recognising and upholding the mana of people in prison, supporting whānau, and fostering a shift away from punitive cultures within Corrections. Initiatives under this strategy include a new resettlement centre for wāhine Māori and the creation of Māori pathways at Hawke's Bay and Northland prisons. Crucially for reintegration, Hōkai Rangi represents a shift from focusing on the individual prisoner to focusing on the collective, including whānau and the wider community (Department of Corrections, 2019b). However, although promising, its success will depend largely on its implementation. Prior research on Māori cultural programmes within Corrections has found that, in practice, they are reduced to an individualised focus, and obscured by penal institutional philosophies (Mihaere, 2015). Historically, Māori community-centred approaches have been dominated by the priorities of the state, rather than leading to any significant structural or relational changes in criminal justice processes (Tauri & Webb, 2012). Furthermore, incorporating mātauranga Māori within the prison system may seem like a noble goal, but does little to acknowledge that prison systems are incompatible with mātauranga Māori. Hōkai Rangi accepts Māori imprisonment as a fact, with little emphasis on decolonisation and liberation. Māori remain overwhelmingly subject to the coloniser's criminal justice system as the state has ignored calls for increased Māori jurisdictional authority (Jackson, 1988). Therefore, a stronger shift is needed towards meaningful engagement with mātauranga Māori and tino rangatiratanga across *all* social institutions in order to promote decolonisation and facilitate reintegration for Māori leaving prison.

CONCLUSION

Although academic literature and discussion on prisoner reintegration in New Zealand is somewhat sparse, reintegration has received increasing attention and resources from Corrections in recent years. This has largely been justified by the need to reduce the risk of reoffending, rather than being characterised by inclusionary principles and humanitarian concern for those leaving prison. The dominant approach has therefore focused on addressing the multiple perceived social and economic deficits or needs of people leaving prison. While this is undoubtedly an improvement on the purely psychological paradigm that has dominated Corrections practice in recent years, there are two reasons why such an approach is unlikely to be wholly successful in promoting reintegration. Firstly, it overlooks the lessons from desistance research and strengths-based approaches, which suggest that for reintegration to be achieved, people leaving prison need to be accepted into the community. As McNeill (2006) has noted, Corrections and other professionals cannot reintegrate individuals; only communities can, and this may be highly challenging in the punitive public culture of New Zealand (Pratt, 2007). Secondly, it neglects to consider the social and structural context of those communities in which reintegration may take place, and how the experiences of people leaving prisons are affected by issues such as colonialism, racism, and sexism.

The approach to reintegration proposed in Corrections' recent Hōkai Rangi strategy shows some promise in acknowledging the harm caused by the over-representation of Māori in prison and improving reintegration for Māori and others by adopting a collective rather than an individualised approach. However, the long-term effectiveness of this strategy in keeping people out of prison remains to be seen. Corrections alone cannot be held responsible either for reducing reoffending or successful reintegration. Reintegration needs to be a shared goal across government departments, with the input of different agencies to improve the social conditions to which people leaving prison return. Some government departments (such as the Ministries of Social Development and of Housing and Urban Development) have now recognised this and have begun to work with Corrections (Faure, 2019). Without better state infrastructure to provide frameworks of social agency and whānau/family support in which ex-prisoners can work to establish and integrate themselves in their community, the majority of people leaving prison are likely to be locked into the reincarceration cycle (Baldry et al., 2006).

STUDY QUESTIONS

- What is meant by reintegration? Is reintegration ever a realistic possibility?
- How does reintegration differ for Māori? What are important things to consider that are unique to their experiences?
- What are the dangers of 'deficit-focused' approaches to reintegration? What other approaches could be used instead?

FURTHER READING

Fox, K. (2014). Restoring the social: Offender reintegration in a risky world. *International Journal of Comparative and Applied Criminal Justice, 38*(3), 235–256. doi:10.1080/01924036.2013.848221

Moore, R. (2011). Beyond the prison walls: Some thoughts on prisoner 'resettlement' in England and Wales. *Criminology and Criminal Justice, 12*(2), 129–147. doi:10.1177/1748895811425445

Workman, K. (2014). The social integration of Māori prisoners. *Aotearoa New Zealand Social Work, 26*(1), 39–46. doi:10.11157/anzswj-vol26iss1id53

NOTES

1. The 'continued state of non-offending' (Maruna et al. 2004, p. 18).
2. Reconviction figures include only those people who receive a Corrections-administered sentence (e.g., imprisonment or probation, intensive supervision, community work). They do not include those who were reconvicted and received financial penalties or discharges. Moreover, these reconviction figures are the sole available indicators of successful reintegration; no other measures are routinely collected.
3. The tribunal is able to determine whether matters are inconsistent with the principles of the Treaty of Waitangi and to make recommendations on claims relating to the practical application of the Treaty (Waitangi Tribunal 2017).

REFERENCES

Andrews, D., & Bonta, J. (1998). *The psychology of criminal conduct.* Cincinnati, OH: Anderson Publishing.

Baldry, E., McDonnell. D., Maplestone, P., & Peeters, M. (2006). Ex-prisoners, homelessness and the state in Australia. *Australian and New Zealand Journal of Criminology, 39*(1), 20–23. doi:10.1375/acri.39.1.20

Bevan, M. (2015). Women's experiences of rehabilitation and re-offending summary of findings. *Practice: The New Zealand Corrections Journal, 3*(1), 5–9.

Bourdieu, P. (1986). The forms of social capital. In J. G. Richardson (Ed.), *Handbook of theory and research for the sociology of education* (pp. 241–258). New York, NY: Greenwood.

Bradley, K. H., Oliver, R. B., Richardson, N. C., & Slayter, E. M. (2001). *No place like home: Housing and the ex-prisoner* [Policy brief]. Boston, MA: Community Resources for Justice. Retrieved from https://www.academia.edu/2419311/NO_PLACE_LIKE_HOME_Housing_and_the_Ex-prisoner

Campbell, N. (2016). The Department of Corrections' tikanga-based programmes. *Practice: The New Zealand Corrections Journal, 4*(2), 5–8. Retrieved from https://www.corrections.govt.nz/resources/newsletters_and_brochures/journal/volume_4_issue_2_december_2016/the_department_of_corrections_tikanga-based_programmes

Christofferson, S. B. (2014). Prison-based employment interventions: Effects on recidivism. *Practice:*

The New Zealand Corrections Journal, 2(1), 28–31. Retrieved from https://www.corrections.govt.nz/resources/newsletters_and_brochures/journal/volume_2_issue_1_april_2014

Cunningham, S. (2017). Targeting recidivism of ex-offenders through the use of employment. *Practice: The New Zealand Corrections Journal, 5*(1), 57–60. Retrieved from https://www.corrections.govt.nz/resources/newsletters_and_brochures/journal/volume_5_issue_1_july_2017/targeting_recidivism_of_ex-offenders_through_the_use_of_employment

Department of Corrections. (2016). *Annual report 2015/16*. Retrieved from https://www.corrections.govt.nz/__data/assets/pdf_file/0010/857737/Annual_report_201516.pdf

Department of Corrections. (2018). *Annual report 2017/18*. Retrieved from https://www.corrections.govt.nz/resources/strategic_reports/annual-reports/annual_report_201718

Department of Corrections. (2019a). *Prison facts and statistics – June 2019*. Retrieved from https://www.corrections.govt.nz/resources/research_and_statistics/quarterly_prison_statistics/prison_stats_june_2019.html

Department of Corrections. (2019b). *Hōkai Rangi: Ara Poutama Aotearoa strategy 2019–2024*. Retrieved from: https://www.corrections.govt.nz/resources/strategic_reports/corrections_strategic_plans/hokai_rangi

Dorne, S. (2016). *Reintegration services: Evidence brief*. Wellington, New Zealand: Ministry of Justice. Retrieved from https://www.justice.govt.nz/assets/Documents/Publications/Reintegration-services.pdf

Ellison, M., Fox, C., Gains, A., & Pollock, G. (2013). An evaluation of the effect of housing provision on re-offending. *Safer Communities, 12*(1), 27–37. doi:10.1108/17578041311293125

Farrall, S. (2009). Explorations in theories of desistance: Societal-level approaches to reform – an introduction. *Theoretical Criminology, 13*(1), 5–8. doi:10.1177/1362480608100170

Faure, J. (2019). Housing supports and services in New Zealand: A cross-agency response. *Practice: The New Zealand Corrections Journal, 7*(1), 71–74. Retrieved from https://www.corrections.govt.nz/resources/research_and_statistics/journal/volume_7_issue_1_july_2019/housing_supports_and_services_in_new_zealand_a_cross-agency_response

Fox, K. (2014). Restoring the social: Offender reintegration in a risky world. *International Journal of Comparative and Applied Criminal Justice, 38*(3), 235–256. doi:10.1080/01924036.2013.848221

Fox. K. (2015). Theorizing community integration as desistance-promotion. *Criminal Justice and Behavior, 42*(1), 82–94. doi:10.1177/0093854814550028

Fox, K. (2016). Civic commitment: Promoting desistance through community integration. *Punishment and Society, 18*(1), 68–94. doi:10.1177/1462474515623102

Ganapathy, N. (2018). Rehabilitation, reintegration and recidivism: A theoretical and methodological reflection. *Asia Pacific Journal of Social Work and Development, 28*(3), 154–167. doi:10.1080/02185385.2018.1501416

Gilbert, J., & Elley. B. (2015). Reducing recidivism: An evaluation of the Pathway Total Reintegration Programme. *New Zealand Sociology, 30*(4), 15–37. Retrieved from https://www.semanticscholar.org/paper/Reducing-recidivism%3A-An-evaluation-of-the-pathway-Gilbert-Elley/5425cbef6b84a60077c08ced3c9ff257a6212d92

Groot, S., Le Grice, J., & Nikora, L. (2019). Indigenous psychology in New Zealand. In W. Li, D. Hodgetts, & K. Foo (Eds.), *Asia-Pacific perspectives on intercultural psychology* (pp. 198–217). London, UK: Routledge.

Growns, B., Kinner, S. A., Conroy, E., Baldry, E., & Larney, S. (2018). A systematic review of supported accommodation programs for people released from custody. *International Journal of Offender Therapy and Comparative Criminology, 62*(8), 2174–2194. doi:10.1177/0306624X17714108

Hallot, D., & Patterson, M. (2017). Supported accommodation services for released offenders in New Zealand – a review. *Practice: The New Zealand Corrections Journal, 5*(2), 62–65. Retrieved from https://www.corrections.govt.nz/resources/research_and_statistics/journal/volume_5_issue_2_november_2017/supported_accommodation_services_for_released_offenders_in_new_zealand_-_a_review

Halsey, M. (2006). Assembling recidivism: The promise and contingencies of post-release life. *Journal of Criminal Law and Criminology, 97*(4), 1209–1260. Retrieved from https://pdfs.semanticscholar.org/7baf/28737c10f64e45c0e32556dec3010651abf2.pdf

Halsey, M. (2010). Imprisonment and prisoner re-entry in Australia. *Dialectical Anthropology, 34*(4), 545–554. doi:10.1007/s10624-010-9173-y

Hannah-Moffatt, K. (2005). Criminogenic needs and the transformative risk subject. *Punishment and Society, 7*(1), 29–51. doi:10.1177/1462474505048132

Harris, R., Cormack, D., Tobias, M., Yeh, L. C., Talamaivao, N., Minster, J., & Timutimu, R. (2012). The pervasive effects of racism: Experiences of racial discrimination in New Zealand over time and associations with multiple health domains. *Social Science and Medicine, 74*(3), 408–415. doi:10.1016/j.socscimed.2011.11.004

Indig, D., Gear, C., & Wilhelm, K. (2016). *Comorbid substance use disorders and mental health disorders among New Zealand prisoners.* Retrieved from https://www.corrections.govt.nz/resources/newsletters_and_brochures/journal/volume_4_issue_1_august_2016/comorbid_substance_use_disorders_and_mental_health_disorders_among_new_zealand_prisoners

Jackson, M. (1988). *The Maori and the criminal justice: A new perspective: He whaipaanga hou: Part 2.* Wellington, New Zealand: Policy and Research Division, Department of Justice. Retrieved from https://www2.justice.govt.nz/website-documents/maori-and-the-criminal-justice-system-a-new-perspective-p2.pdf

Johnson, A., Howden-Chapman, P., & Eaqub, S. (2018). *A stocktake of New Zealand's housing.* Wellington, New Zealand: Ministry of Business Innovation and Employment. Retrieved from https://www.beehive.govt.nz/sites/default/files/2018-02/A%20Stocktake%20Of%20New%20Zealand%27s%20Housing.pdf

Johnston, H. (2018). Creating positive pathways: A long-term housing initiative for people released from prison. *Practice: The New Zealand Corrections Journal, 6*(2), 8–10. Retrieved from https://www.corrections.govt.nz/resources/newsletters_and_brochures/journal/volume_6_issue_2_november_2018/creating_positive_pathways_a_long-term_housing_initiative_for_people_released_from_prison

Laub, J. H., & Sampson, R. J. (2001). Understanding desistance from crime. *Crime and Justice: A Review of the Research, 28*, 1–70. doi:10.1086/652208

Lindsay, C., Mills, A., Milne, B., & Groot, S. (2019). *Stable housing and reintegration in Aotearoa New Zealand.* Paper presented to the 15th Reintegration Puzzle Conference, Darwin, Australia, 26–28 June 2019.

Lishman, R. (2018). Supporting offenders into employment. *Practice: The New Zealand Corrections Journal, 6*(2), 74–76. Retrieved from https://www.corrections.govt.nz/resources/newsletters_and_brochures/journal/volume_6_issue_2_november_2018/supporting_offenders_into_employment

Maguire, M., & Raynor, P. (2006). How the resettlement of prisoners promotes desistance from crime: Or does it? *Criminology and Criminal Justice, 6*(1), 19–38. doi:10.1177/1748895806060665

Maruna, S. (2011). Reentry as a rite of passage. *Punishment and Society, 13*(1), 3–28. doi:10.1177/1462474510385641

Maruna, S., Immarigeon, R., & LeBel, T. (2004). Ex-offender reintegration: Theory and practice. In S. Maruna & R. Immarigeon (Eds.), *After crime and punishment: Pathways to offender reintegration* (pp. 3–16). Cullompton, UK: Willan Publishing.

Maruna, S., & LeBel, T. (2003). Welcome home? Examining the 'reentry court' concept from a strengths-based perspective. *Western Criminology Review, 4*(2): 91–107. Retrieved from http://westerncriminology.org/documents/WCR/v04n2/article_pdfs/marunalebel.pdf

McIntosh, T., & Workman, K. (2017). Māori and prison. In A. Deckert & R. Sarre (Eds.), *The Palgrave handbook of Australian and New Zealand criminology, crime and justice* (pp. 725–736). Cham, Switzerland: Palgrave Macmillan.

McNeill, F. (2006). A desistance paradigm for offender management. *Criminology and Criminal Justice, 6*(1), 39–62. doi:10.1177/1748895806060666

Mihaere, R. (2015). *A kaupapa Māori analysis of the use of Māori cultural identity in the prison system.* Unpublished PhD dissertation, Victoria University of Wellington, Wellington, New Zealand. Retrieved from https://researcharchive.vuw.ac.nz/xmlui/handle/10063/4185

Mills, A. (2014). *Housing ex-prisoners in New Zealand: An intractable problem?* Paper presented at the Australian and New Zealand Society of Criminology, University of Sydney, 30 September – 3 October 2014.

Mills, A., & Codd, H. (2008). Prisoners' families and offender management: Mobilizing social capital. *Probation Journal, 55*(1), 9–24. doi:10.1177/0264550507085675

Mills, A., Gojkovic, D., Meek, R., & Mullins, D. (2013). Housing ex-prisoners: The role of the third sector. *Safer Communities, 12*(1), 38–49. doi:10.1108/17578041311293134

Ministry of Justice. (2012). *Delivering better public services: Reducing crime and re-offending result action plan.* Wellington, New Zealand: Ministry of Justice. Retrieved from http://gdsindexnz.org/wp-content/uploads/2015/10/Delivering-Better-Public-Services-Reducing-Crime-and-Reoffending-Result-Action-Plan.pdf

Moore, R. (2011). Beyond the prison walls: Some thoughts on prisoner 'resettlement' in England and Wales. *Criminology and Criminal Justice, 12*(2), 129–147. doi:10.1177/1748895811425445

Morrison, B., Bevan, M., & Bowman, J. (2018). Employment needs post-prison: A gendered analysis of expectations, outcomes and service effectiveness. *Practice: The New Zealand Corrections Journal, 6*(1), 42–48. Retrieved from https://www.corrections.govt.nz/resources/newsletters_and_brochures/journal/volume_6_issue_1_july_2018/employment_needs_post-prison_a_gendered_analysis_of_expectations,_outcomes_and_service_effectiveness

Office of the Auditor General. (2013). *Department of Corrections: Managing offenders to reduce reoffending.* Wellington, New Zealand: Office of the Auditor General. Retrieved from https://www.oag.govt.nz/2016/reoffending

Parhar, K., & Wormwith, J. S. (2013). Risk factors for homelessness among recently released offenders. *Journal of Forensic Social Work, 3*(1), 16–33. doi:10.1080/1936928X.2013.826610

Pennington, P. (2016, February 29). Bail requests to state houses 'blocked'. *Radio New Zealand.* Retrieved from https://www.rnz.co.nz/news/national/297686/bail-requests-to-state-houses-%27blocked%27

Pogrebin, M., West-Smith, M., Walker, A., & Unnithan, N. P. (2014). Employment isn't enough: Financial obstacles experienced by ex-prisoners during the re-entry process. *Criminal Justice Review, 36*(4), 394–410. doi:10.1177/0734016814540303

Pratt, J. (2007). *Penal populism.* London, UK: Routledge.

Quince, K. (2007). Māori and the criminal justice system in New Zealand. In J. Tolmie & W. Brookbanks (Eds.), *Criminal justice in New Zealand* (pp. 333–358). Wellington, New Zealand: LexisNexis.

Raynor, P. (2007). Theoretical perspectives in resettlement: What it is and how it might work. In A. Hucklesby & L. Hagley-Dickinson (Eds.), *Prisoner resettlement* (pp. 26–42). Cullompton, UK: Willan Publishing.

Robson, S. (2015). *Location, location, location? Comparing release plan quality, community experience, and recidivism rate of high-risk offenders released to a fresh start or returning to the devil they know.* Unpublished master's thesis, Victoria University of Wellington, Wellington, New Zealand. Retrieved from https://pdfs.semanticscholar.org/84fa/cfc334364d3e485b5f99c5c965f2ae1bb54d.pdf?_ga=2.34279397.516564140.1580685902–1154062498.1580103073

Salvation Army. (2016). *Beyond the prison gate.* Auckland, New Zealand: Salvation Army. Retrieved from https://www.salvationarmy.org.nz/article/beyond-prison-gate

Sharpe, M. (2019, October 29). Residents told that backpackers likely to become ex-prisoner accommodation. *Stuff.* Retrieved from https://www.stuff.co.nz/national/116881351/residents-told-that-backpackers-likely-to-become-exprisoner-accommodation#comments

Social Exclusion Unit. (2002). *Reducing re-offending by ex-prisoners.* London, UK: Social Exclusion Unit. Retrieved from https://www.bristol.ac.uk/poverty/downloads/keyofficialdocuments/Reducing%20Reoffending.pdf

Tauri, J. M. (2014). Criminal justice as a colonial project in settler-colonialism. *African Journal of Criminology and Justice Studies, 8*(1), 20–37. Retrieved from https://ro.uow.edu.au/cgi/viewcontent.cgi?referer=https://www.google.com/&httpsredir=1&article=4202&context=sspapers

Tauri, J. M., & Webb, R. (2012). A critical appraisal of responses to Māori offending. *The International Indigenous Policy Journal, 3*(4), 1–16. Retrieved from http://ir.lib.uwo.ca/iipj/vol3/iss4/5

Tissera. N. (2019). New Zealand's six pillar model of reintegration and international reintegrative models: A review of the literature. *Practice: The New Zealand Corrections Journal, 7*(1), 66–70. Retrieved from https://www.corrections.govt.nz/resources/research_and_statistics/journal/volume_7_issue_1_july_2019/new_zealands_six_pillar_model_of_reintegration_and_international_reintegrative_models_a_review_of_the_literature

Treasury. (2017). *Creating positive pathways for people with a corrections history*. Retrieved from https://treasury.govt.nz/sites/default/files/2017–11/b17–3658489.pdf

Wacquant. L. (2010). Prisoner re-entry as myth and ceremony. *Dialectical Anthropology, 34*(4), 605–620. doi:10.1007/s10624–010–9215–5

Waitangi Tribunal. (2017). *Tū mai Te Rangi! Report on the Crown and disproportionate reoffending rates*. Wellington, New Zealand: Waitangi Tribunal. Retrieved from https://forms.justice.govt.nz/search/Documents/WT/wt_DOC_121273708/Tu%20Mai%20Te%20Rangi%20W.pdf

Walsh, C. A., MacDonald, P., Rutherford, G. E., Moore, K., & Krieg, B. (2011). Homelessness and incarceration among Aboriginal women: An integrative literature review. *Pimatisiwin: A Journal of Aboriginal and Indigenous Community Health, 9*(2), 363–386. Retrieved from http://www.pimatisiwin.com/online/wp-content/uploads/2012/01/06WalshMacDonald.pdf

Ward, T., & Stewart, C. A. (2003). The treatment of sex offenders: Risk management and Good Lives. *Professional Psychology: Research and Practice, 34*(4), 353–360. doi:10.1037/0735-7028.34.4.353

Waretini-Karena, R. (2017). Colonial law, dominant discourses, and intergenerational trauma. In A. Deckert & R. Sarre (Eds), *The Palgrave handbook of Australian and New Zealand criminology, crime and justice* (pp. 697–709). Cham, Switzerland: Palgrave MacMillan.

Western, B. (2018). *Homeward: Life in the year after prison*. New York, NY: Russell Sage Foundation.

Williams, K., Poyser, J., & Hopkins, J. (2012). *Accommodation, homelessness and reoffending of prisoners*. London, UK: Ministry of Justice. Retrieved from https://assets.publishing.service.gov.uk/government/uploads/system/uploads/attachment_data/file/278806/homelessness-reoffending-prisoners.pdf

Workman, K. (2012). *How should we reintegrate prisoners?* Wellington, New Zealand: Rethinking Crime and Punishment. Retrieved from https://www.yumpu.com/en/document/view/41288971/how-should-we-reintegrate-prisoners-rethinking-crime-and-

Workman, K. (2014). The social integration of Māori prisoners. *Aotearoa New Zealand Social Work, 26*(1), 39–46. doi:10.11157/anzswj-vol26iss1id53

Workman, K., & McIntosh, T. (2013). Crime, imprisonment and poverty. In M. Rashbrooke (Ed.), *Inequality: A New Zealand crisis* (pp. 120–131). Wellington, New Zealand: Bridget Williams Books.

24

Prison Abolitionism
Philosophies, Politics, and Practices

Ti Lamusse and Tracey McIntosh

'What does prison take? Family, freedom and the future.' These words, from a woman who had spent much of her adult life churning through the prison system and far too much of her childhood within the state care system, speak to her personal legacy of devastation. While prison's corrective and rehabilitative objectives are hard to evidence, its damaging impacts at individual and societal levels are easier to document. Another young woman who had suffered high levels of social harm and violence as a child, followed by imprisonment as a teenager, wrote in a poem:

> The one thing that you will never see
> Is to be captured having never been free.[1]

The absence of prisons would not in itself create the conditions for individual or societal freedom. For that to happen, we would need to have societal structures which create the conditions that allow freedom from poverty, freedom from inequality, freedom from racism and practices of discrimination and marginalisation, and freedom from harms, including interpersonal harms. To have a just society, we must create just conditions. While prisons confine people, and institute forced associations between individuals who often share similar histories and social characteristics (Sharnock, 2016), they do not eradicate the conditions conducive to the production and reproduction of social harms. Indeed, they reproduce them.

This chapter gives an overview of prison abolitionist theory and activism in Aotearoa New Zealand. It first outlines why abolitionists posit the necessity of prison abolition, arguing that prisons fail to rehabilitate, deter crime, promote safety, and provide justice for victims. It then details political and moral justifications for prison abolition, including the incompatibility of imprisonment with tikanga Māori practices, the production of inequalities and injustice through prisons, and the pain that prisons cause. The third section provides a brief overview of prison abolitionism and current prison abolitionist organisations. Finally, the chapter summarises the key strategies that abolitionists use in pursuit of the goal of abolition.

A REVIEW OF ABOLITIONIST THEORY

For almost as long as there have been prisons, there have been calls for abolition (Knopp et al., 1976, pp. 13–15). However, understandings of abolition are varied and sometimes contradictory. According to the prison abolitionist theorist and activist Angela Davis, there are 'multiple histories of prison abolition' (Davis, as cited in Davis & Rodriguez, 2000, p. 215). Faith-based abolitionists base their opposition to prison on scriptural references, while anti-racist abolitionists point to chattel slavery and its subsequent abolition in the United States, as well as the colonisation of Indigenous lands, as starting points (Davis, 2003, 2005; Jackson, 1988; Lamusse et al., 2016). Others acknowledge the rise of critical criminology in the late 1960s and early 1970s, and the publication of key abolitionist texts such as Mathieson's (1974) *The Politics of Abolition* and Prison Research Education Action Project's *Instead of Prisons* (Knopp et al., 1976), as the start of the modern prison abolitionist movement.

From this history come various definitions of prison abolition. Prison abolition is usually seen as a long-term goal of a society without prisons. Most abolitionists also tie the need for prison abolition into a wider struggle for social justice. Abolition can also refer to the abolition of criminal justice practices (Folter, 1986), such as the death penalty or prisons, as dominant modes of punishment (Davis, 2003; Knopp et al., 1976). For others, it may mean the abolition of societies where prisons are possible (Davis, 2003, 2005, 2014; Knopp et al., 1976; Lamusse et al., 2016; Lee, 2008). In this sense, prison abolition is a long-term process in the struggle for structural changes to society according to an abolitionist ideal (Knopp et al., 1976; Mathiesen, 2015; Scott, 2013).

WHY ABOLITION?

While their goal may seem idealistic and even dangerous to some, prison abolitionists argue that decades of criminological evidence demonstrate the practical necessity of abolition. And they are not alone in their assessment that prisons are a fundamentally flawed way of dealing with harm. Even government departments and mainstream politicians concede that prisons do not work: they do not deter crime, rehabilitate ex-prisoners, or keep communities safe; moreover, they are economically unsustainable.

Highlighting the failures of prisons, abolitionists provide pragmatic reasons for abolition. They are pragmatic in that they demonstrate the failure of prisons to work according to their stated purposes – namely: prisons fail to rehabilitate people; prisons do not deter crime; prisons can undermine public safety; and prisons do not serve victims.

Rehabilitation

A stated core objective of the Department of Corrections is to rehabilitate. Indeed, the very name of Corrections implies that the purpose of imprisonment is to 'correct' harmful behaviour. However, prisons are poor at helping people change, or (re)habilitating them, as the New Zealand government has known for decades (Roper et al., 1989).

The failure to rehabilitate is due to a number of reasons. First, prisons are often volatile places where a heightened level of vigilance and anxiety is normalised and where violence can be used as a regulatory tool. Prisons are non-therapeutic environments. They exacerbate prisoners' existing health problems and can introduce new health problems (National Health Committee, 2010). Second, prison-based rehabilitation is undermined by the process of institutionalisation or 'prisonisation' (Goffman, 1961; see Martin, chapter 21 this volume; Sykes & Messinger, 1960), through which the culture, routines, practices, and specialised lexicon of the prison are normalised. Institutionalisation 'speaks not only to the deleterious effects of confinement but [also] to the embedded quality that remains even once the institution is no longer present' (McIntosh & Coster, 2017, p. 78). Prisons are

> institutions that in their architecture, systems and policies articulate the power of the state over the individual and within them prisoners are likely to experience a profound unfreedom. They may also have further developed patterns of behaviour and a way of viewing and being in the world which, while perhaps useful within prison walls, are perhaps potentially maladaptive and harmful outside of this specialised environment (McIntosh, 2011, p. 273).

In its *Case Against Prisons* report, JustSpeak argues that rehabilitation programmes in the community 'are more effective, cheaper, and have fewer negative effects' (Anderson et al., 2018, p. 14). Following this logic, abolitionists argue that if the aim is to rehabilitate people who have caused harm, the most effective environment in which to do so would be in the community, not the prison.

Deterrence
It is often posited as fact that prisons are necessary in order to deter people from committing crimes. However, there is little evidence to demonstrate that prisons succeed in this objective. Reported and actual crime rates (including non-reported crimes) have no causal relationship to the rate of imprisonment. Prisoner numbers are governed more by criminal justice policy and prison capacity (Armstrong, 2013). In Aotearoa New Zealand, recent large increases in the prison population have been primarily attributed to 2013 changes to bail laws and judicial practices that made it harder for people to be held in the community before trial (Black et al., 2017).

With this in mind, the deterrence theory assumes that people will be deterred if they (1) realise their actions are criminalised, (2) believe they are likely to be caught, (3) believe they are likely to be punished, (4) take this likely outcome into account and (5) can change their behaviour in response to this assessment. In practice, however, prisons fail to deter 'criminal' behaviour. In fact, 60.9 per cent of people released from prison are reconvicted, while 43.2 per cent are reimprisoned, within two years (Department of Corrections, 2018).

Studies have shown that, compared to community-based alternatives, imprisonment can cause a slight increase in reoffending (Mitchell et al., 2017) and lengthier prison sentences can also increase risks of reoffending (Cochran et al., 2014). Because very few instances of criminal behaviour actually result in imprisonment, and because people engaging in criminalised behaviour do not always think 'rationally' according to a deterrence model, abolitionists argue that prisons are ineffective at deterring harmful behaviour.

Safety
In the short term, prisons offer safety through *containment*. This assumes that while people who are presumed to be dangerous are in prison, they are prevented from harming others in the community. Proposals to reduce the size of the prison population elicit alarmist responses

from the Sensible Sentencing Trust (2017), a 'tough-on-crime' lobbyist group who stoke public anxieties at the prospect of criminals at large. Despite these fears, there is little evidence to suggest that prisons actually keep the public safe. Although an incarcerated individual imprisoned person is separated from broader society, they are still capable of harming others, and being violently victimised themselves, while in prison. Prison itself can be a site of intensified violence. As a seminal New Zealand report found, the 'prison system has not only failed to confront the criminal with the crime but it has also provided an environment which supports the distorting of the individual's offending' (Roper et al., 1989, p. 3).

The idea that prisons keep society safe is dependent on the erroneous assumption that there is a clear link between harmful behaviour and imprisonment. However, according to the latest Crime Victimisation Survey, there were an estimated 1,777,000 victimisations in 2017–18, with 29 per cent of New Zealanders experiencing victimisation (Ministry of Justice, 2019). Over three-quarters (77 per cent) of those victimisations were never reported to the police (Ministry of Justice, 2019). By contrast, 7378 people were sentenced to imprisonment in 2018 (Shannon, 2019), some of whom were imprisoned for victimless crimes, such as breach of parole or bail conditions. Given the vast disparity between the number of imprisonments and the number of victimisations, safety through containment is structurally unable to have more than a marginal effect. If containment were a serious attempt to ensure safety, it would require imprisoning hundreds of thousands of people. In practice, only a very small subset of those who commit 'crimes' ever see the inside of a cell. Therefore, containment is simply not an effective way of ensuring safety.

Victims of crime
There is one point on which tough-on-crime lobbyists and prison abolitionists tend to agree, which is that the current criminal justice system fails victims of crime. Under New Zealand's common law system, for example, victims traditionally had no formal role in the criminal justice system. Decisions about how harmful acts will be addressed are almost exclusively in the hands of parties other than the victim. The advisory group set up by the Labour government in 2018 found that 'too many people who have been harmed by crime feel unheard, misunderstood and re-victimised' (Te Uepū Hāpai i te Ora, 2019, p. 14). The current structure of the criminal justice system offers little to victims by way of restitution, support, or participation in the criminal justice process (Anderson et al., 2018). In addition, the distinction between victims and offenders is often blurred, with many people caught up in the justice system having experienced victimisation themselves.

THE POLITICS OF ABOLITION
Beyond pragmatic reasons, abolitionists also provide a range of political, moral, and ethical justifications for abolition. For the sake of clarity, we have made a distinction between pragmatic and political reasons for abolition. However, they are not entirely distinct. As many abolitionists argue, the prison is entirely political, and the argument in favour of or against its existence has political inflexions and implications.

Incompatibility with tikanga Māori
The key claim from Māori prison abolitionist scholars (Jackson, 2017; McIntosh, 2018) and activists (Kopeke-Te Aho et al., 2017) is that the criminal justice system is incompatible with tikanga Māori (customary practices and law). Mead (2003) notes that there have been discussions about whether tikanga Māori can be regarded as a system of rules which could have courts where offenders could be formally tried:

Obviously tikanga Māori has not worked this way in the past. But there is some force and power in tikanga Māori. Transgressions can hurt the offenders and result in some punishment. Tikanga Māori is supported by a social and ritual force which does not need to be monitored by a police force. People who are committed to being Māori generally regard themselves as being bound to uphold tikanga Māori (p. 7).

Before colonisation, tikanga guided behaviour and practices, including how to respond to harmful behaviour. However, the current New Zealand criminal justice system is the product and legacy of the colonial imposition of the British system on Māori (Jackson, 1988; Mikaere, 2011; Quince, 2007). This claim has been recognised by the Crown, with the government-commissioned *Te Ara Hou* report acknowledging that the concepts of justice and punishment that lay the foundation for prisons are based entirely on Pākehā principles (Roper et al., 1989). Where tikanga Māori attempts to understand the collective and individual causes and responsibilities for harm, tikanga Pākehā tends to attribute blame to individuals. Further, where tikanga Māori stresses the need to address imbalance and restore relationships, tikanga Pākehā stresses punishment and isolation (Jackson, 1988).

In its *Abolitionist Demands* (described below), the New Zealand prison abolitionist organisation No Pride in Prisons (NPIP), known since 2017 as People Against Prisons Aotearoa (PAPA) argues that imprisonment itself is 'fundamentally incompatible' with tikanga Māori (Lamusse et al., 2016, p. 92), and that prisons make the restoration of the imbalance of a relationship impossible by removing people who have harmed from their communities. This removal ends the possibility of restoring relationships. Moana Jackson (2017, para. 6), a leading scholar in prison abolition and Māori legal systems, further notes that 'the idea of confining a wrongdoer in something like a prison would have been culturally incomprehensible' in pre-colonial Aotearoa. For these scholars and activists, prison abolition is necessary in order to ensure that Māori can express tino rangatiratanga, as guaranteed under Te Tiriti o Waitangi.

Inequalities and injustice
In his landmark report into Māori offending, *He Whaipaanga Hou*, Jackson (1988) makes a clear link between the colonial subjugation of tikanga and mātauranga Māori and the disproportionate imprisonment of Māori: the 'correlation between offending and the cycle of confinement in which many Maori exist is a real and almost inevitable consequence of the racial and economic inequalities' (p. 100). In the 30 years since his report, Māori have continued to represent more than 50 per cent of the prison population, while the total number of prisoners has increased from around 3000 prisoners to more than 10,000 (Department of Corrections, 2019a). Māori are disproportionately more likely to be arrested, charged, prosecuted, convicted, and sentenced to imprisonment than non-Māori (Te Uepū Hāpai i te Ora, 2019). In 2019 the disaggregated incarceration rate for non-Māori and Māori makes clear the differences in whom we incarcerate. The non-Māori incarceration rate is 119 per 100,000, and the Māori incarceration rate is 685 per 100,000 (Tanielu et al., 2020).

The effect of the mass imprisonment of Māori is stark, with one in five Māori men being imprisoned before the age of 35 compared to one in 12 non-Māori men (Te Uepū Hāpai i te Ora, 2019). In this context, the criminal justice system generally, and prisons in particular, are increasingly labelled as racist (Jackson, 1988, 2017; Lamusse et al., 2016; Te Ohu Whakatika, 2019; Te Uepū Hāpai i te Ora, 2019). This is something the Sixth Labour Government has also started to acknowledge with the launch of Hōkai Rangi, the Department of Corrections' (2019b) strategy for reducing Māori reoffending. Hōkai Rangi recognises that the government has failed Māori in the past and fundamentally needs to change its approach to Māori offending.

While Māori and the poor are much more likely to be imprisoned, imprisonment also entrenches inequalities experienced by these communities. Imprisonment, even if brief, has long-term effects beyond just the incarcerated person: it can lead to the loss of jobs, income, housing, and security. The children of incarcerated people also bear the brunt of prisons, sometimes experiencing long-lasting emotional and psychological effects and being much more likely to themselves be imprisoned in adulthood (Gordon & MacGibbon, 2011; McIntosh, 2011; Mlinac, 2016). In this way, people leaving prison *and* their whānau often face worse living standards and prospects as a consequence of imprisonment. Prison, therefore, helps to reproduce cycles of poverty which entrench structural racism and undermine the futures of incarcerated communities.

Pain

Prison abolitionists also argue against imprisonment on moral grounds because it requires the deliberate and unnecessary infliction of pain, and it does not undo the suffering caused by that person or change their behaviour. Prison simply adds to the total amount of pain experienced in society (Martinot, 2014; Mathiesen, 2015; Morris, 1995; Scott, 2013).

This pain is not an abstract concept, but a concrete practice embedded in the structure of imprisonment. At a fundamental level, imprisonment creates pain by separating people from their communities, significant others, friends, and whānau. This separation and distance can undermine relationships and the well-being of both the imprisoned person and their whānau, with imprisonment often leading to relationship breakdown and further isolation.

In addition, the social and physical environment of imprisonment can cause substantial harm to incarcerated people. At its most extreme, people in prison are regularly placed in solitary confinement, experiencing inhumane and degrading treatment that can have serious long-term implications for their well-being (Lamusse, 2018a; Shalev, 2017). For some people, the pains of imprisonment can be so overwhelming that they take their own life; the suicide rate among incarcerated people is six times that in the general population (Lamusse, 2017).

PRISON ABOLITIONISM IN AOTEAROA NEW ZEALAND

As Māori did not have prisons prior to colonisation, there was strong Māori resistance to official attempts to imprison Māori in the period following the signing of Te Tiriti in 1840. While Māori accepted that their whānau should take responsibility for their actions, many refused to hand over their whānau for imprisonment, as it was seen as 'degrading', 'pointless', and an 'inappropriate method of punishment' (Roper et al., 1989, p. 10). In the wake of Te Tiriti, Māori even won a concession through the Native Exemption Ordinance 1844, which reinforced the principle of utu as a substitute for imprisonment of all offences other than rape and murder. It is important to understand the whakapapa of Māori resistance to prisons and its connection to contemporary forms of abolition.

Abolitionism in twentieth-century Aotearoa New Zealand can be traced back to the Movement for Alternatives to Prison (MAP), which was established in the 1970s by a mixture of community workers, ex-prisoners, faith groups, and academics (McNeill et al., 2008). Its newsletters and documentation demonstrate that its objectives were clearly abolitionist as opposed to reformist. MAP claimed that prison reforms prop up 'an expiring system' and that reforms could not combat the deleterious effects of institutionalisation. They further argued that 'prisons wherever they be situated, constitute a failure industry and are based on the public's desire for revenge and retribution rather than providing workable habilitation opportunities to assist offenders with reintegration into the community' (McNeill et al., 2008, p. 12). MAP was active until well into the 2000s.

Groups such as Rethinking Crime and Punishment (which operated 2005 to 2015) and JustSpeak (operating from 2011) have advocated for reductions to the prison system and support alternatives to prison. Outwardly, these projects, while not explicitly abolitionist, had and have a membership range of views from penal and legislative reform to prison abolition (Campbell, 2017). In 2015, a self-described queer and transgender prison abolitionist organisation called No Pride in Prisons (NPIP) was established. Inspired by the work of Angela Davis and similar queer and trans prison abolitionist organisations in the US, such as Black and Pink, NPIP started organising the LGBTIQ community in opposition to prisons (Lamusse, 2016). In 2016, NPIP published the *Abolitionist Demands*, which contains 50 demands on the government that would, if enacted, lead to the abolition of prisons. This book, collectively written by more than 20 people, refocused NPIP's attention on its abolitionist strategy and structure. From late 2016 to 2017, NPIP determined to become a prison abolitionist organisation for everyone, not just queer and transgender people. It changed its name to People Against Prisons Aotearoa (PAPA) and restructured to be a more inclusive and effective volunteer-run organisation (Lamusse, 2018b).

ABOLITIONIST STRATEGIES AOTEAROA IN NEW ZEALAND

Most abolitionists accept that prison abolition can be achieved through a long process of reforms and replacement of the current criminal justice system. What, then, distinguishes a prison abolitionist from a prison reformer? Prison reformers believe that prisons must play a key role in the criminal justice system, and that they can be reformed to be more humane and effective. Abolitionists, however, can see the strategic use of certain types of reform as a tool to achieve a different end goal: the abolition of prisons. This means that while the strategies of reformers and abolitionists sometimes overlap, they also diverge. Abolitionists distinguish between reforms that bolster the prison system and abolitionist reforms 'which do not legitimize the prevailing system, but gradually diminish its power and functions' (Knopp et al., 1976, p. 24). The strategies for abolition include some of the following reforms.

Constitutional transformation

In the settler-colonial context, the most politically important strategy for prison abolition in Aotearoa New Zealand is constitutional transformation. In this context, constitutional transformation refers to a restructuring of power relations between the Crown and tangata whenua in line with Te Tiriti o Waitangi. The *Matike Mai* (2016) report outlines various frameworks that would ensure partnership and power-sharing between tangata whenua and tangata tiriti (non-Māori New Zealanders) by 2040. Constitutional transformation as outlined in *Matike Mai* would, importantly, enshrine a true expression of tino rangatiratanga for Māori, including full authority to engage in tikanga Māori practices for addressing harm.

In this respect, constitutional transformation has been a key component of recommendations to address the failures of the criminal justice system over the past 30 years (Jackson, 1988; Roper et al., 1989). In 2019 alone, two government reports found that constitutional reform is essential to addressing issues of systemic racism in the criminal justice system (Te Ohu Whakatika, 2019; Te Uepū Hāpai i te Ora, 2019).

Excarceration

A key plank of abolitionist strategy is excarceration. This refers to the reduction in the size and scope of the prison system over time, by sending fewer people to prison in the first place (Knopp, 1994; Knopp et al., 1976; Scott, 2013). Scott (2013) highlights three main tactics of excarceration: decriminalisation, diversion, and minimisation. Decriminalisation refers to the removal of criminal sanctions for criminalised actions. Knopp et al. (1976) suggest prioritising the decriminalisation of victimless crimes, which PAPA echoes in its call to end the drug war and decriminalise all drugs (Lamusse et al., 2016). In diversion, certain people (because of their background, for instance, or age) are routed away from the formal justice system 'on the grounds of responsibility or vulnerability' (Scott, 2013, p. 108). Minimisation refers to limiting the ability of the formal legal system to intervene. Taken as a whole, the intended effect of excarceration strategies would be to reduce the number of people sentenced to imprisonment.

Decarceration
Whereas excarceration aims to prevent people from being sent to prison, decarceration refers to getting people out of prison (Knopp, 1994; Knopp et al., 1976; Scott, 2013). Decarceral tactics aim to reduce the current prison population in a safe and sustainable way. These tactics can include: eliminating the practice of remanding people in prison awaiting trial (Knopp, 1994); presumptive early parole or release practices (Knopp et al., 1976; Scott, 2013); restitution to victims in lieu of serving further time (Knopp et al., 1976); retroactive decriminalisation of victimless crimes (Knopp et al., 1976); amnesties or pardons (Scott, 2013); and the review and reduction of current long-term sentences (Knopp et al., 1976; Scott, 2013). In New Zealand, the strategy of decarceration has been implicitly supported by government as 'it can be concluded that existing prisons are of limited use to society and for the future we must plan for a continuing reduction in prison numbers by other more effective means of responding to crime' (Roper et al., 1989, p. 22).

Moratorium
A key part of the abolitionist strategy has been the call for a moratorium on all new prison construction (Armstrong, 2013; Knopp et al., 1976; Scott, 2013). Armstrong's (2013) study suggests that the number of incarcerated people is largely determined by the total capacity for incarceration:

> More prison capacity means more prisoners. When judges get tough and send more people to prison, unless new prisons are built the prison system is forced to create safety valves – house arrest, parole adjustments, early release, suspended sentences. When judges sentence fewer people to prison, the people already in prison get to stay longer. Whatever judges do, prison capacity acts as a limiting factor on the total population size. Outside of the forecasting model, a new explanation becomes possible: prisons cause prisoners (p. 155).

In this sense, stopping the expansion of prison capacity through new prison construction or the expansion of double-bunking is a core element of an abolitionist strategy to combat incarceration (Lamusse et al., 2016). For example, a proposed new mega-prison in Waikeria was met with significant opposition in 2017 and 2018 by activists, academics, and faith-based organisations, and from civil society. Although the prison construction went ahead, it did so on a much smaller scale than originally intended.

Negative reforms
In addition to excarceration and decarceration, abolitionists advocate for reforms that not only reduce inmate numbers but also shrink the system by abolishing some of its most extreme elements. Abolitionist scholars and activists have different names for this kind of reform. Here, we will refer to what Mathiesen (2015, p. 223) calls *negative reforms*: those 'changes which abolish or remove greater or smaller parts on which the system in general is more or less dependent'.

A prime example of a negative reform would be PAPA's campaign to end solitary confinement.[2] In solitary confinement, a person is held in their cell for 22–24 hours a day without any meaningful human contact, as defined by the United Nation's 'Mandela Rules' (United Nations General Assembly, 2015). PAPA argues that solitary 'is the harshest form of punishment available in the New Zealand prison system' (Lamusse, 2018a, p. 1). PAPA's campaign to abolish solitary confinement aims to take away the state's power to inflict its most painful form of punishment, abolishing a core part of the prison system. Similar negative reforms include PAPA's calls to abolish double-bunking and strip searches (Lamusse et al., 2016).

Alternatives to imprisonment

The question of alternatives to prison is hotly contested within abolitionism. This contestation varies, with some abolitionists completely rejecting the need to propose alternatives to prison (Folter, 1986; Hulsman, 1997; Mathiesen, 2015; Ruggiero, 2010) and others laying out concrete plans for what could be done instead (Knopp et al., 1976; Morris, 1995; Scott, 2013; Scott & Gosling, 2016).

Mathieson (1986) argues that the experience of the implementation of early 'alternatives' was poor. Rather than serving as an alternative method of justice, potentially transformational alternatives, such as probation, community detention, and community service, ended up causing a 'net-widening' effect, in which policy change simply increased the number of people swept into the formal justice system. For this reason, many thinkers are highly critical of alternatives that increase, rather than decrease, the reach of the justice system (Cohen, 1985; Mathiesen, 1986; Morris, 1995).

As a result, a critical approach to alternatives is required to ensure that their implementation occurs alongside real reductions in the prison population (Cohen, 1998; Knopp et al., 1976; Scott, 2013). Contrary to those abolitionists who argue that outlining alternatives is not politically necessary (Folter, 1986; Mathiesen, 2015), other abolitionists argue that the goal of prison abolition is fundamentally undermined if abolitionists do not offer clear, rational, and realistic alternatives to prisons (Cohen, 1998; Malloch, 2013; Scott, 2013).

Indeed, the unwillingness of abolitionists to propose alternatives has been criticised by sympathetic but critical scholars (Greenberg, 1983; Scheerer, 1986). This criticism is made more powerful by the seemingly automatic reply from people outside the abolitionist milieu when first introduced to the idea of prison abolition: 'But what do we do instead?' An inadequate response to this question can make abolitionists seem naïve and utopian. In this sense, proposing alternatives to prison is also about capturing the imagination of ordinary people who understand that prisons do not work but cannot see any better options.

So what are the abolitionist alternatives to imprisonment? Davis (2003) argues there is not a singular, all-encompassing alternative institution to prisons but a 'constellation of alternative strategies and institutions' (p. 106). This 'constellation' is required because abolitionists like Davis are seeking not simply to tear down prison walls, but further to abolish the conditions that enable imprisonment in the first place. Prison abolition without attending to the drivers of harm would not reduce injustice. Alternatives, then, differ depending on what is seen as the injustice. For example, if we take the founding injustice of settler colonisation, Jackson (1988) has proposed constitutional transformation with Māori-led alternatives to imprisonment for Māori. Under Jackson's model, the injustice of colonisation would be addressed, alongside the injustice of the racist criminal justice system, while allowing for alternative ways of dealing with interpersonal harm drawing on tikanga Māori.

Alongside Māori alternatives, under the constitutional transformation envisioned by *Matike Mai*, tangata tiriti could work in partnership with tangata whenua to implement other prison alternatives. These could include restorative justice, transformative justice, community service, reparations, fines, supervision, therapeutic communities, and community detention (for more, see Knopp et al., 1976; Scott, 2013; see also Tauri, chapter 20, Durrant & Riley, chapter 22, and Mills & Latimer, chapter 23 this volume). This is by no means an exhaustive list, and not all prison abolitionists would argue that all of these are even *abolitionist* alternatives. Abolitionists who do argue for these kinds of alternatives also argue that in order to avoid net-widening and to ensure these represent abolitionist alternatives, their implementation would need to occur simultaneously alongside rapid decarceration and excarceration (Knopp et al., 1976).

CONCLUSION

Regardless of the reasoning and strategies for prison abolition, many people simply see prison abolition as impossible. It is unfathomable to some that there could ever be enough public support for abolitionism when tough-on-crime approaches are rampant. For many abolitionists, the inevitability of the prison is intimately linked to its social function within capitalism. Davis (2003, 2014) argues prisons play a crucial role in hiding social problems, while at the same time reproducing inequality and oppression. As a result, the beneficiaries of the current economic system can maintain their place in the social order through mass imprisonment (Reiman, 2004). In this sense, one of the most important barriers to the achievement of abolition is the capitalist economic system (Davis, 1998, 2003, 2014).

However, it is important to remember that social change can seem impossible right up until it happens. This has been the case for such profound social changes as the abolition of slavery, the dismantling of apartheid in South Africa, and the decriminalisation of homosexuality and introduction of marriage equality in Aotearoa New Zealand. Politics and criminal justice policy also vary greatly over time. In the 1970s, many abolitionists and policy-makers believed we were on the verge of the end of prisons altogether (Mathiesen, 2015). Although these predictions were undermined by the global economic and social restructuring known as neoliberalism in the 1980s, they demonstrate that there have been times when an abolitionist justice system seemed likely.

We may be approaching such an era again. A recent government expert advisory group report found that 'transformative change to our criminal justice system is urgent' (Te Uepū Hāpai i te Ora, 2019, p. 69), while another government-supported report called for the abolition of prisons (Te Ohu Whakatika, 2019). To end imprisonment as a primary means of addressing social, economic, and political problems requires new social institutions and conceptual frameworks that would render incarceration unnecessary. Although there is still much to do before prison abolition can be achieved, there are promising signs that we may be able to achieve this seemingly impossible goal.

STUDY QUESTIONS

- Why is prison abolition necessary?
- Why do we need to understand the history of colonialism, tikanga Māori, and Māori incarceration rates in thinking about prison abolition?
- What are the differences between excarceration, decarceration, prison reform, and prison abolition? And what strategies are used by prison abolitionists to achieve prison abolition in Aotearoa New Zealand?

FURTHER READING

Anderson, J., Brooks, B., Black, A., Grose, S., Heffernan, M., Lindsay, A., . . . Schuman, K. (2018). *The case against prisons*. Wellington, New Zealand: JustSpeak. Retrieved from https://www.justspeak.org.nz/ourwork/the-case-against-prisons-report

Davis, A. Y. (2003). *Are prisons obsolete?* New York, NY: Seven Stories.

Lamusse, T., Morgan, S., & Rākete, E. (Eds.). (2016). *Abolitionist demands: Toward the end of prisons in Aotearoa*. Auckland, New Zealand: No Pride in Prisons Press.

NOTES

1. This excerpt is from a poem by a young incarcerated wāhine Māori who writes her poetry under the pseudonym Maia. Poems that Maia has written can be found at https://www.radionz.co.nz/news/national/321773/poetry-brings-peace-behind-bars

2. See https://endsolitary.papa.org.nz

REFERENCES

Anderson, J., Brooks, B., Black, A., Grose, S., Heffernan, M., Lindsay, A., . . . Schuman, K. (2018). *The case against prisons*. Wellington, New Zealand: JustSpeak. Retrieved from https://www.justspeak.org.nz/ourwork/the-case-against-prisons-report

Armstrong, S. (2013). Using the future to predict the past: Prison population projections and the colonisation of penal imagination. In M. Malloch & B. Munro (Eds.), *Crime, critique and utopia* (pp. 136–164). London, UK: Palgrave Macmillan.

Black, A., Lindsay, A., Jeremich, A., Anderson, F., Anderson, J., Bruce, K., . . . Heffernan, M. (2017). *Bailing out the justice system: Reopening the window of opportunity*. Wellington, New Zealand: JustSpeak. Retrieved from https://d3n8a8pro7vhmx.cloudfront.net/justspeak/pages/129/attachments/original/1493195153/Bailing_out_the_Justice_System.pdf?1493195153

Campbell, M. (2017). *Foucauldian analysis of campaigns for prison abolition and decarceration in New Zealand*. Unpublished bachelor of arts honours thesis, Victoria University of Wellington, Wellington, New Zealand.

Cochran, J. C., Mears, D. P., & Bales, W. D. (2014). Assessing the effectiveness of correctional sanctions. *Journal of Quantitative Criminology, 30*(2), 317–347. doi:10.1007/s10940-013-9205-2

Cohen, S. (1985). *Visions of social control: Crime, punishment, and classification*. Cambridge, UK: Polity Press.

Cohen, S. (1998). Intellectual scepticism and political commitment: The case of radical criminology. In P. Walton & J. Young (Eds.), *The new criminology revisited* (pp. 98–129). London, UK: Macmillan.

Davis, A. Y. (1998). Racialised punishment and prison abolition. In J. James (Ed.), *The Angela Y. Davis reader* (pp. 96–110). Malden, MA: Blackwell Publishing.

Davis, A. Y. (2003). *Are prisons obsolete?* New York, NY: Seven Stories.

Davis, A. Y. (2005). *Abolition democracy: Beyond empire, prisons, and torture*. New York, NY: Seven Stories.

Davis, A. Y. (2014). Deepening the debate over mass incarceration. *Socialism and Democracy, 28*(3), 15–23. doi:10.1080/08854300.2014.963945

Davis, A. Y., & Rodriguez, D. (2000). The challenge of prison abolition: A conversation. *Social Justice, 27*(3), 212–218.

Department of Corrections. (2018). *Annual report 1 July 2017 – 30 June 2018*. Wellington, New Zealand: Department of Corrections. Retrieved from https://www.corrections.govt.nz/__data/assets/pdf_file/0005/33809/Department_of_Corrections_Annual_Report_2017_2018.pdf

Department of Corrections. (2019a, June 4). *Prison statistics*. Retrieved from http://www.corrections.govt.nz/resources/research_and_statistics/quarterly_prison_statistics.html

Department of Corrections. (2019b). *Hōkai rangi: Ara poutama Aotearoa strategy | 2019–2024*. Wellington, New Zealand: Department of Corrections. Retrieved from https://www.corrections.govt.nz/resources/strategic_reports/corrections_strategic_plans/hkai_rangi

Folter, R. S. (1986). On the methodological foundation of the abolitionist approach to the criminal justice system. A comparison of the ideas of Hulsman, Mathiesen and Foucault. *Contemporary Crises, 10*(1), 39–62. doi:10.1007/BF00728495

Goffman, E. (1961). *Asylums: Essays on the social situation of mental patients and other inmates*. Harmondsworth, UK: Penguin.

Gordon, L., & MacGibbon, L. (2011). *A study of the children of prisoners: Findings from Māori data June 2011*. Wellington, New Zealand: Te Puni Kōkiri. Retrieved from https://www.tpk.govt.nz/en/a-matou-mohiotanga/criminal-justice/a-study-of-the-children-of-prisoners-findings-from

Greenberg, D. F. (1983). Reflections on the justice model debate. *Contemporary Crises, 7*(4), 313–327.

Hulsman, L. (1997). *Themes and concepts in an abolitionist approach to criminal justice*. Retrieved from https://hulsmanfoundation.org/wp-content/uploads/2014/07/abolitionistapproach.pdf

Jackson, M. (1988). *The Maori and the criminal justice system: A new perspective: He whaipaanga hou: Part 2*. Wellington, New Zealand: Policy and Research Division, Department of Justice. Retrieved from https://www2.justice.govt.nz/website-documents/maori-and-the-criminal-justice-system-a-new-perspective-p2.pdf

Jackson, M. (2017, October 14). Moana Jackson: Prison should never be the only answer. *E-Tangata*. Retrieved from https://e-tangata.co.nz/comment-and-analysis/moana-jackson-prison-should-never-be-the-only-answer/

Knopp, F. H. (1994). On radical feminism and abolition. *Peace Review, 6*(2), 203–208. doi:10.1080/10402659408425796

Knopp, F. H., Boward, B., Brach, M. J., Christianson, S., Largen, M. A., Lewin, J., . . . Newton, W. (1976). *Instead of prisons: A handbook for abolitionists* (Ed. M. Morris). Syracuse, NY: Prison Research Education Action Project.

Kopeke-Te Aho, H., Morgan, S., Pickering, D., Rākete, E., & Zionov, A. (2017, June). Prison abolition is a Māori issue: The whakapapa of prisons in Aotearoa. *Mana Magazine, 135*, 30–31.

Lamusse, T. (2016). Politics at pride? *New Zealand Sociology, 31*(6), 49–70. Retrieved from https://search.informit.com.au/documentSummary;dn=507933240724129;res=IELHSS

Lamusse, T. (2017). *Grieving prison death*. Unpublished master's thesis, University of Auckland, Auckland, New Zealand.

Lamusse, T. (2018a). *Solitary confinement in New Zealand prisons*. Wellington, New Zealand: Economic and Social Research Aotearoa. Retrieved from https://esra.nz/wp-content/uploads/2018/01/Solitary-Confinement-in-New-Zealand-Prisons.pdf

Lamusse, T. (2018b). Strategies for building the revolutionary left: A case study of prison abolitionism in Aotearoa. *Counterfutures: Left Thought and Practice Aotearoa, 6*, 120–138. Retrieved from http://counterfutures.nz/6/LAMUSSE.pdf

Lamusse, T., Morgan, S., & Rākete, E. (Eds.). (2016). *Abolitionist demands: Toward the end of prisons in Aotearoa*. Auckland, New Zealand: No Pride in Prisons Press. Retrieved from https://papa-site-assets.ams3.cdn.digitaloceanspaces.com/publications/abolitionist-demands.pdf

Lee, A. (2008). Prickly coalitions: Moving prison abolitionism forward. In B. Goldstein, B. Richie, C. Gilmore, D. Stein, D. Rodriguez, I. Ontiveros, . . . Y. Omowale (Eds.), *Abolition now! Ten years of strategy and struggle against the prison industrial complex* (pp. 109–113). Oakland, CA: AK Press.

Malloch, M. (2013). Crime, critique and utopian alternatives. In M. Malloch & B. Munro (Eds.), *Crime, critique and utopia* (pp. 21–43). London, UK: Palgrave Macmillan.

Martinot, S. (2014). Toward the abolition of the prison system. *Socialism and Democracy, 28*(3), 189–198. doi:10.1080/08854300.2014.954922

Mathiesen, T. (1974). *The politics of abolition*. New York, NY: Wiley Publishing.

Mathiesen, T. (1986). The politics of abolition. *Contemporary Crises, 10*(1), 81–94. doi:10.1007/BF00728497

Mathiesen, T. (2015). *The politics of abolition revisited*. Abingdon, UK: Routledge.

Matike Mai Aotearoa. (2016). *He whakaaro here whakaumu mō Aotearoa: The report of Matike Mai Aotearoa – The independent working group on constitutional transformation*. Auckland, New Zealand: Matike Mai Aotearoa. Retrieved from https://nwo.org.nz/wp-content/uploads/2018/06/MatikeMaiAotearoa25Jan16.pdf

McIntosh, T. (2011). Marginalisation: A case study: Confinement. In T. McIntosh & M. Mulholland (Eds.), *Maori and social issues* (pp. 263–282). Wellington, New Zealand: Huia Publishers.

McIntosh, T. (2018). Indigenous rights, poetry and decarceration. In E. Stanley (Ed.), *Human rights and incarceration: Critical explorations* (pp. 285–301). Cham, Switzerland: Palgrave Macmillan. doi:10.1007/978-3-319-95399-1

McIntosh, T., & Coster, S. (2017). Indigenous insider knowledge and prison identity. *Counterfutures: Left Thought and Practice Aotearoa, 3*, 69–100.

McNeill, R., Magill, P., & Kitione, K. (2008, May). What is the kaupapa of MAP? *Movement for Alternatives to Prison Newsletter, 103*. Retrieved from http://www.mentor.kiwi.nz/wp-content/uploads/2012/02/MAP_May_2008.pdf

Mead, H. M. (2003). *Tikanga Māori: Living by Māori values*. Wellington, New Zealand: Huia Publishers.

Mikaere, A. (2011). *Colonising myths – Māori realities: He rukuruku whakaaro*. Wellington, New Zealand: Huia Publishers.

Ministry of Justice. (2019). *New Zealand Crime and Victims Survey (NZCVS) 2018*. Wellington, New Zealand: Ministry of Justice. Retrieved from https://www.justice.govt.nz/justice-sector-policy/research-data/nzcvs/

Mitchell, O., Cochran, J. C., Mears, D. P., & Bales, W. D. (2017). Examining prison effects on recidivism: A regression discontinuity approach. *Justice Quarterly, 34*(4), 571–596. doi:10.1080/07418825.2016.1219762

Mlinac, I. (2016). *Exclusion, over-regulation and complexities: The effects of parental incarceration on prisoners' children and their families*. Unpublished master's thesis, University of Auckland, Auckland, New Zealand. Retrieved from http://hdl.handle.net/2292/31496

Morris, R. (1995). *Penal abolition, the practical choice: A practical manual on penal abolition*. Toronto, Canada: Canadian Scholars' Press.

National Health Committee. (2010). *Health in justice: Kia piki te ora, kia tika! – Improving the health of prisoners and their families and whānau: He whakapiki i te ora o ngā mauhere me ō rātou whānau*. Wellington, New Zealand: Ministry of Health. Retrieved from https://www.moh.govt.nz/notebook/nbbooks.nsf/0/F403EA147E87922FCC25776C0080A46A/$file/health-in-justice2.pdf

Quince, K. (2007). Māori and the criminal justice system. In J. Tolmie & W. Brookbanks (Eds.), *Criminal justice in New Zealand* (pp. 333–358). Wellington, New Zealand: LexisNexis.

Reiman, J. (2004). *The rich get richer and the poor get prison*. Boston, MA: Pearson.

Roper, C., Dunstall, K., Biddle, R., Garrett, W. D., McCormick, I., Withers, T. A. F., & Thompson, M. (1989). *Te ara hou: The new way – Ministerial committee of inquiry into the prisons system*. Wellington, New Zealand: Crown.

Ruggiero, V. (2010). *Penal abolitionism: A celebration*. New York, NY: Oxford University Press.

Scheerer, S. (1986). Towards abolitionism. *Contemporary Crises, 10*(1), 5–20. doi:10.1007/BF00728493

Scott, D. (2013). Visualising an abolitionist real utopia: Principles, policy and praxis. In M. Malloch & B. Munro (Eds.), *Crime, critique and utopia* (pp. 90–113). London, UK: Palgrave Macmillan.

Scott, D., & Gosling, H. (2016). Before prison, instead of prison, better than prison: Therapeutic communities as an abolitionist real utopia? *International Journal for Crime, Justice and Social Democracy, 5*(1), 52. doi:10.5204/ijcjsd.v5i1.282

Sensible Sentencing Trust. (2017, September 17). Labour weakness on bail law a dangerous back-flip – McVicar. *Scoop*. Retrieved from http://www.scoop.co.nz/stories/PO1709/S00306/labour-weakness-on-bail-law-a-dangerous-back-flip-mcvicar.htm

Shalev, S. (2017). *Thinking outside the box? A review of seclusion and restraint practices in New Zealand*. Auckland, New Zealand: Human Rights Commission. Retrieved from https://www.seclusionandrestraint.co.nz/

Shannon, J. (2019, May 6). *Outcomes of people held on remand*. [Official Information Act response to Ti Lamusse]. Retrieved from https://fyi.org.nz/request/10017/response/34193/attach/4/74667%20Ti%20Lamusse%20final.pdf

Sharnock, J. (2016). *A sense of reason: Revealing the greatest political lie in human history*. Christchurch, New Zealand: Lincoln Digital Print.

Sykes, G. E., & Messinger, S. E. (1960). The inmate social system. In R. A. Cloward, D. R. Cressey, G. H. Grosser, R. McCleery, L. E. Ohlin, G. E. Sykes, & S. E. Messinger (Eds.), *Theoretical studies in social organization of the prison* (pp. 5–19). New York, NY: Social Science Research Council.

Tanielu, R., Barber, P., & Wijeysingha, V. (2020). *Tangata whenua, tangata tiriti, huia tangata kotahi – People of the land, people of the treaty, bring everyone together: State of the nation report*. Auckland, New Zealand: Salvation Army Social Policy & Parliamentary Unit. Retrieved from https://www.salvationarmy.org.nz/sites/default/files/files/%5Bfile_field%3Atype%5D/tsa_sotn_2020.pdf

Te Ohu Whakatika. (2019). *Ināia tonu nei – Now is the time: We lead, you follow, hui Māori report*. Retrieved from https://safeandeffectivejustice.govt.nz/news/latest-news/maoriperspectives-on-justice-report-released/

Te Uepū Hāpai i te Ora. (2019). *He waka roimata: Transforming our criminal justice system, 1*. Wellington, New Zealand: Te Uepū Hāpai i te Ora: Safe and Effective Justice Advisory Group. Retrieved from https://www.safeandeffectivejustice.govt.nz/assets/Uploads/fa55462d44/teuepureport_hewakaroimata.pdf

United Nations General Assembly. (2015, December 17). *Resolution 70/175: The United Nations standard minimum rules for the treatment of prisoners*. Retrieved from https://www.unodc.org/documents/justice-and-prison-reform/Nelson_Mandela_Rules-E-ebook.pdf

Part Four

Differential Experiences

The eight chapters in Part Four cover further crucial debates for criminology in Aotearoa New Zealand. Focused largely around the treatment of specific populations – including Māori, Pasifika, children and young people, women, those with mental health problems, those with disabilities, gang members, sex workers, and 'non-citizens' – these chapters illustrate how responses to 'crime' sustain ongoing racist, sexist, ableist, and economic power relations. At the same time, these chapters are future-focused and help us reimagine how we can view crime or engage in justice.

The first chapter reflects on how victims have been managed at the margins of criminological thought. Detailing the emergence of victimology, along with its guiding frameworks and concepts, Rebecca Stringer illustrates how early scholars built their contributions around victim-blame as they cast victims as culpable, dishonest, and even potentially guilty of the crimes against them. She provides a searing analysis of how these foundations continue to frame criminal justice reporting, policy, practice, and social perceptions. These elements are especially resonant in the treatment of women and children who have been victimised through violence. However, victim-blaming and silencing are selectively directed towards those victims with least social power. The implications, as critical and radical scholars have shown, are widespread, including a silencing of harms, and the moving of attention away from offenders as well as from the wider backdrops of structural disadvantages, institutional failings, and sociocultural conditions that legitimise violence.

With its emphasis on institutionalised racism and systemic bias, Kim Workman's chapter returns us to the issue of policing. Given New Zealand's colonial context, policing has been a key indicator of the embedded nature of racism and discrimination through the justice sector (a situation exacerbated by the structural realities of neoliberalism and penal populism). Workman shows how law and punishments have been continually used to assert colonial controls and to assimilate Māori, not least by removing opportunities for punishments according to Māori traditions and tikanga. More recent culturally responsive strategies have failed to materialise into improved conditions or outcomes for Māori. Indeed, they have often normalised discriminatory criminal justice operations, diverted attention from addressing the root causes of discrimination, suppressed the full expression of rangatiratanga, and re-emphasised Māori as *the* targets of criminal justice attention. Workman argues that culturally appropriate programmes and services can sometimes make a valuable contribution to the organisational culture, but they do not, on their own, address the underlying presence of personal racism and structural bias within organisations like the police. He concludes that police leadership (which is so central to the cultures that underpin officers' decision-making, discretion, and organisational socialisation) has to take affirmative action.

These realities are reasserted in the chapter – by Tamasailau Suaalii-Sauni, Juan Marcellus Tauri, Robert Webb, Arapera Blank-Penetito, Naomi Fuamatu, Fa'afete Taito, and Salevao Faauuga Manase – that considers Māori and Samoan experiences of youth justice. Beginning with a discussion on the need for community-based research with Māori rangatahi, Samoan talavou, and their families, they draw on recent research to provide a critical examination of government responses to the disproportionate representation of Māori and Pasifika youth in the justice system. They show how key policy responses – such as family group conferences and new policing initiatives, as well as Rangatahi and Pasifika Courts – have regularly failed to divert Māori or Pasifika young people, and have not de-professionalised justice, shaken government power, or empowered Māori or Pasifika victims, offenders, and their whānau. They argue that these policies and processes expand the state's reach into Māori and Pasifika communities by a dual process of co-option and indigenisation. And they conclude with an assertion for ethical and Indigenous-led community justice alternatives that can decolonise justice and enhance the well-being and aspirations of the community.

The next chapter, by Bruce Cohen, provides an encompassing critique of the ways in which criminologists, practitioners, and New Zealand society more broadly have perceived, labelled, and responded to mental health in relation to crime and criminal justice. Unpacking the definitions of 'crime' and 'mental illness', he challenges the dominant scholarship that relies on pathological deficit models as explanations for contact with criminal justice agencies. In New Zealand, people with mental illness have increasingly been criminalised and imprisoned. This has resulted from penal populism, a growing public intolerance of eccentric behaviour, the closure of mental health facilities, the rise of mental health industries, as well as deeply entrenched (false) narratives that equate mental health problems with violence, unpredictability, or dangerousness. Tracing dominant theories, Cohen argues that increasingly popular rationalities of 'faulty' biology or genetic degeneracy are fuelling racist discourses – particularly in relation to Māori, who are inevitably captured by these models – while downplaying the intrinsically political nature of criminal justice that serves powerful interests in a capitalist, settler society.

Anita Gibbs's chapter on neuro-disabilities highlights an emerging area for criminological research, advocacy, and intervention. Neuro-disabilities affect a significant number of people who encounter the criminal justice system. Identifying the prevalence of neuro-disabilities, internationally and in New Zealand, Gibbs highlights how these hidden disabilities regularly coalesce with structural disadvantage and sociocultural marginalisation. People with neuro-disabilities have long-term impairments that impact on their daily life; these can lead to them acting in ways that are quickly criminalised. Once in the criminal justice arena, those with neuro-disabilities are heavily disadvantaged by system approaches, such as those that demand offenders demonstrate guilt or which strengthen punishments for recidivist offenders. Adequate responses to neuro-disability are yet to be developed in New Zealand. International 'best practices' indicate some ideas on how we might respond, but any initiatives have to be culturally conscious, age-appropriate, gender-relevant, and directed towards non-punitive approaches that centralise Dis/Abled perspectives.

Jarrod Gilbert's chapter provides a case study of the long-term political responses to gangs in New Zealand. Critiquing some of the key moments and events when gangs and politics have intersected, he shows the contradictory approaches to gang members and associates over decades. At times, politicians have acknowledged how structural disadvantages, marginalisation, and inequalities have underpinned the development and consolidation of gang membership and any related offending. From this position, actions such as employment schemes or welfare support programmes have often reduced offending behaviours among gang members and had broader positive impacts for them and their wider communities. And yet a dominant political strategy to gangs has also involved recourse to moral panic, exclusion, containment, and punishment. Politicians' claims of offending by gang members have often been exaggerated, and unsubstantiated through data, yet 'crackdowns' have regularly found popular support. Gilbert concludes with an assertion of the importance of more sophisticated approaches to one of New Zealand's sustaining social concerns.

Reflecting on the need for more nuanced, and socially just, approaches, Lynzi Armstrong considers in her chapter the potential for decriminalisation to reduce harms within society. Whilst there are several decriminalisation, or legalisation, debates ongoing in New Zealand – for example, in relation to the 2020 cannabis referendum – she explores the decriminalisation of sex work, an industry that has historically been treated in deeply stigmatising ways. New Zealand is currently the only country in the world to have decriminalised sex work. Armstrong explores the activism and collaborations required to change the law (the Prostitution Reform Act 2003), and shows the diverse ways in which decriminalisation has minimised harms: allowing workers to manage the risks of violence; improving police attitudes; giving workers the ability to refuse clients; and building stronger employment, health and safety, and legal rights. While there are limitations to the Act, and exploitative employment conditions and stigma can remain, decriminalisation has reduced violence and harms for sex workers in New Zealand communities. This is an important consideration when common responses to violence often involve a ramping up of criminalising and punitive responses.

Borders between communities are always sites of tension, and many developed countries have vigorously policed and securitised their borders, engaging new technologies and carceral sites to ensure the exclusion of 'risky' populations and to deport those found unpalatable or threatening. The final chapter in the collection, by Elizabeth Stanley, places recent debates on deportations in a broader historical context. She considers the role of border controls in the deployment of state power, and highlights how the economic, political, and racialised sorting of populations has been developed through a tightening and contractualising of citizenship. Stanley focuses on two case examples from New Zealand: first, the shameful practice of 'dawn raids' from the mid-1970s, alongside contemporary practices of deporting 'overstayers' (including those fleeing significant environmental risks); and second, the ongoing detention and expulsion of New Zealand citizens from Australia. The chapter demonstrates that deportation processes have significantly expanded in scope, and are reproducing structural inequalities and discrimination, with those affected enduring multiple state harms.

25

Victimology
From Criminality to 'Victimity' and the Problem of Victim Blame

Rebecca Stringer

Is criminology missing something? Some have argued 'yes'. For much of its history criminology has focused on offenders and criminal justice. As such it is 'missing one third of the crime triangle': victims of crime (Growette Bostaph et al., 2014). Instead of being a point of focus, victims have been at the margins of criminological thought, featuring as unspecified 'points of impact of crime into society' (Drapkin & Viano, 1974, p. xi). As Karmen (2016, p. 18) describes, 'Criminology is the older parent discipline and victimology is the recent offshoot.' In the 1940s, the founders of victimology set out to show that by focusing on victims we can 'obtain a better understanding of crime and its origins and implications' (Drapkin & Viano, 1974, p. xi). They created victimology, the 'science of the victim', and studied victimisation systematically for the first time. Where criminology had focused on 'criminality', they focused on 'victimity', using the tools of logical positivism (explained below) to probe 'the victim as a living being' (Mendelsohn, 1956, p. 26). Their work succeeded in establishing victimology as a significant subdiscipline, but the foundation they laid for 'positivist victimology' was fraught with problems, not least as the founders 'introduced a victim-blaming orientation into the new discipline' (Karmen, 2016, p. 12). In other words, these scholars wanted to study victims because they thought victims were often to blame for crimes committed against them. Determined to shift legal, political, and social attitudes, they created a science of victim culpability focused on distinguishing between 'ideal'/blameless victims and 'guilty'/

blameworthy victims. In this way, victims went from being absent from the study of crime to being visible as potentially guilty suspects in crimes committed against them.

Later generations of radical and critical victimologists rejected these victim-blaming orientations, and forged new approaches to the study of criminal victimisation. They viewed victim-blaming as a profoundly harmful social response to victims. Rejecting the founders' approach on moral grounds, they also saw that victim-blaming explanations of crime are beset with intractable definitional and logical problems. Despite these problems and critiques, the founders' positivist framework and victim-blaming approach are by no means things of the past. Their view of the victim has become the normative view, affecting 'our very conceptualization of crime and victimization' (Eigenberg & Garland, 2008, p. 34). Their influence continues to be strong within victimology and, more importantly, in the contexts of criminal justice policy and practice, the media, and everyday perceptions.[1] In the contemporary era of neoliberalism, where personal responsibility is prized, many popularly resonant and culturally shared perceptions of victimisation – from the idea that some victims 'ask' to be victimised, through to the apparently more benign belief that everyday practices of personal vigilance are 'common sense' to avoid victimisation – rehearse victim-blaming concepts of positivist victimology, redrawing their moral and conceptual problems seemingly without awareness.

Knowing the story of positivist victimology – its framework and key concepts, the critique that has been made of it, and the concerns arising from its enduring influence – is essential, not only for understanding the field of victimology, but also for critically decoding dominant ways of talking about and responding to victims in society, including in Aotearoa New Zealand. Accordingly, this chapter sets out the story of positivist victimology. The opening sections explore the work of the founders and the key concepts of 'victimity', the 'penal couple', 'ideal-versus-guilty' victim types, and victimisation prevention. It then clarifies the conceptual problems with positivist victimology and victim-blaming, before exploring their continued influence today. Having thus worked through the story of positivist victimology, the chapter draws upon Christie (1986) to summarise the different way critical victimology approaches the study of victimisation.

POSITIVIST VICTIMOLOGY: FROM 'CRIMINALITY' TO 'VICTIMITY'

Hans von Hentig (1887–1974) and Benjamin Mendelsohn (1900–1998) are the founders of victimology and their early writings launched the field (Mendelsohn, 1956; von Hentig, 1940, 1948a). Both voiced complaint that criminology was dominated by 'the static unidimensional study of the offender' (Fattah, 2000, p. 22) and needed to study the victim. Their early work was produced in the onset, duration, and aftermath of the Second World War, which loomed large in the lives of both men. In 1936, von Hentig emigrated from Germany to the United States, having lost his criminology professorship for 'failing to engage in the Hitler salute' (Dupont-Morales, 2009, p. 307), and, in the McCarthy era, his left-wing political sympathies drew negative attention. Mendelsohn, a Jewish Romanian criminal defence attorney, coined the term 'victimology' in 1947, a decade after he began analysing the victims encountered in his legal practice. During the Nazi occupation of Romania, Mendelsohn 'personally experienced the severe results of anti-Semitism' (Hoffman, 1992, p. 91), and after the war emigrated to Jerusalem.

The founders' biographies feature events we can arguably regard as victimisation, from unfair dismissal to political and religio-ethnic discrimination. Their work, however, shows little trace of either man's personal experience of victimisation. This is because they adopted the scientific method, where the researcher strives to occupy a position of objectivity in relation to the phenomenon under investigation, transcending subjective bias. In the context of victimology, the scientific method encourages a view of personal accounts of victimisation as untrustworthy data. Perspectives voiced by victims are seen as inevitably entangled in subjective bias, thus largely invalid. It is thought that clear observation and valid knowledge of the 'victim-being' can be achieved only from the remote, dispassionate position of the victimologist working to identify patterns and regularities in bodies of verifiable aggregate data. In this way, von Hentig and Mendelsohn set themselves apart from the victims they would analyse, like doctors to patients. In this respect their work bears the marks not of the world events taking place, but of the intellectual trends of the time, namely the dominance of logical positivism in social science from the 1920s to the 1950s.

Grounded in the belief that society, like the physical world, operates on the basis of universal laws that are discoverable through application of the scientific method, logical positivism was first developed by Auguste Comte (1798–1857) and achieved prominence with the 'functionalist' approach developed by Émile Durkheim (1858–1917). The logical positivists argued that knowledge about society – human psychology and behaviour, morality, social structures, and forms of organisation – had so far been dominated by 'the unverifiable claims of metaphysics and religion' (Keat & Urry, 1975, p. 3). They applied methodologies forged in the natural sciences to the study of society, in hope of discovering verifiable facts that could help to explain social problems. Mendelsohn (1956, p. 26) commended criminology for following Comte's 'revolution in thought'. Positivist criminology was already under way, with efforts to explain the 'crime problem' by studying scientifically 'the personality of the delinquent'. But positivist criminology had mistakenly ignored the 'equally interesting personality' of the victim, separating the delinquent 'from his partner, his adversary: the victim, without whose existence there is no delinquent' (p. 27). Mendelsohn considers that most victims are not innocent and instead share guilt with the offender, and for this reason he dubbed the delinquent–victim pair the 'penal couple'.

As a new science both 'parallel' to criminology and the 'reverse' of it (Mendelsohn, 1956, p. 35), positivist victimology sought to show that crime is brought about not only by criminality, but also by 'victimity', or the victim's degree of 'receptiveness to' or 'precipitation of' the crime, understood to be the portion of victim *responsibility* for the crime. Criminology asks why the criminal has committed the crime, whereas victimology asks: 'Why do some individuals [show] an inclination to sufferance?' (Mendelsohn, 1956, p. 4). Von Hentig (1940) shared Mendelsohn's concern that 'victimity' had escaped scrutiny in criminology and law: 'Looking into the genesis of the situation in a considerable number of cases, we meet a victim who consents tacitly, co-operates, conspires or provokes. The victim is one of the causative elements' (p. 303). Mendelsohn (1956), referring to the victim as a 'cardinal point in the fight against criminality' (p. 36), goes so far as to claim that '[i]n the 20th century a right sentence is given by . . . error' (p. 27), suggesting that a vast number of legal convictions would be overturned if the victim's role in 'soliciting' the crime were known: 'It often happens that the condemned persons are the victims of the claimants.'

Mendelsohn (1956, p. 4) hoped positivist victimology would successfully identify 'the common elements peculiar to all victims', thought to be a mix of biologically inherited and socially acquired traits, that 'inclined' them towards victimisation. Once the essential traits of victimity were discovered, victimologists, lawyers, and doctors would together usher in 'another attitude in social life, in science and in Justice towards the victim' and embark on programmes of 'earnest preventive education' to help citizens 'towards the discovery of their deficiencies in order to prevent and remediate their victimity' (p. 36). The end goal was to prevent crime by addressing the problem of 'victimity'. For this reason, Mendelsohn is credited with having influenced the broad shift from 'crime prevention', which focuses on curbing would-be offenders' 'deviant' behaviours, to 'victimization prevention', which focuses on curbing would-be victims' 'risky' behaviour (Mawby & Walklate, 1994). After reviewing the founders' victim typologies, we will see that positivist victimology's 'attempt to explain "victimization" by an examination of those held to be victims' (Miers, 1989, pp. 3–4) soon ran into serious moral and epistemological problems.

IDEAL AND GUILTY VICTIMS: THE FOUNDERS' VICTIM TYPOLOGIES

Like botanists cataloguing flora, von Hentig and Mendelsohn created typologies that classified victims according to their perceived degree of 'victimity' – their perceived susceptibility, proneness, or receptiveness to, precipitation or provocation of, and degree of culpability for, the victimising event. They examined only a small patch of the forest, however. The positivist criteria for verifiable data restricted them to cases known through police and the courts, and Mendelsohn drew upon cases from his own legal practice. Hence they worked within the criminal justice system, instead of examining the way 'crime' is constructed by that system. As a result, their typologies ignored a wide array of forms of victimisation, focusing narrowly on reported crimes against the person (such as confidence fraud, sexual assault, and homicide) occurring between individuals in their private lives. In relation to homicide, for example, they focused on uxoricide (murder of one's wife) or parricide (murder of one's father), ignoring more prevalent and no less distressing forms of homicide involving entities such as corporations, the state, and the military, in the form of 'deaths at work, on the roads, following industrial accidents or pollution' or during military conflict (Miers, 1989, p. 8). Von Hentig (1940, p. 304) identified four types of 'perfect murder victim' who in different ways display 'an inclination to be victimized'.[2] He later identified 13 types of victim, who by some trait of susceptibility (including youth, femaleness, old age, 'mental derangement', recent immigration, membership of a minority group, depression, acquisitiveness, and 'wantonness') consciously or unconsciously solicit victimisation, causing crime to occur (von Hentig, 1948a).

Mendelsohn's (1956, p. 33) victim typology begins with the 'ideal victim', who is for example unconscious, or a child, and therefore 'completely innocent' (though as we will see, he does not regard all children as 'innocent'). Mendelsohn then progresses through degrees of victim guilt. The 'less guilty' victim was fully ignorant of what would befall them, and the victim who is 'as guilty as the delinquent' has, for example, voluntarily requested euthanasia. The 'more guilty' victim has acted as the 'provocator', and finally the 'most guilty' victim, who bears most or all of the guilt, acted as the initial aggressor, or is a 'simulating' or 'imaginary' victim – as Eigenberg and Garland (2008, p. 30) explain, these are 'not victims but offenders posing as victims for some ulterior motive'.

Routinely depicted as depraved and dishonest, women and children victimised through violence occupy a special place in the founders' typologies as the 'most guilty' victims. The founders display the kinds of attitudes towards women and children victimised through violence that, although still present today, have since been thoroughly critiqued by the feminist anti-violence movement. For example, von Hentig (1940, p. 307) warns courts hearing cases of rape and incest to beware of 'the incredible depravity of many half-grownup girls', and claimed, as *Time* magazine records, 'the nagging wife is flirting with murder' (von Hentig, 1948b, p. 85).

As an attorney, Mendelsohn specialised in criminal defence of clients accused of violence against women and children, and the idea for victimology first came to him when he was defending a man who 'had, with premeditation, killed his wife and her lover' – crimes Mendelsohn (1963, p. 241) blamed on the 'perversity' of the murdered wife. Mendelsohn was influenced by the Freudian denial of child sexual abuse (Masson, 1992), and saw women's and children's allegations of rape and incest as inherently untrustworthy. From the perspective of the feminist anti-violence movement and later generations of victimologists, the founders' typologies are best regarded as vehicles of existing social biases against certain groups of victims, rather than windows onto the eternal traits of 'victimity'.

PROBLEMS WITH POSITIVIST VICTIMOLOGY: VICTIM-BLAMING AND TAUTOLOGY

At this point we can see why the founders earned a reputation for blaming the victim. The term 'victim-blaming' was coined by William Ryan (1969, p. xiii), who defines it as 'justifying inequality by finding defects in the victims of inequality', such as when poverty is blamed upon the poor's lack of striving, instead of being recognised as an effect of the unequal distribution of wealth and resources within class-stratified society. Positivist victimology is an especially clear example of victim-blaming, for its explicit mission is to explain crime by finding defects in victims of crime. The very concept of 'victimity' – the idea that there is a distinct population of defective victims out there, causing crime – is steeped in victim-blame. The founders regarded their victim-blaming stance (the mission to find and fix 'victimity') as both scientifically necessary and morally beneficial. For them, readiness to blame the victim signals the scientist's position of 'dispassionate neutrality' – and it is only from this value-free position that we can gain valid knowledge about victims that will serve 'the interests of humanity' by preventing crime (Mendelsohn, 1956, p. 26).

As Ryan (1969) suggests, however, victim-blaming is neither a morally nor a scientifically neutral activity. Victim-blaming tends to be selectively directed towards victims with the least social power. It has the effect of silencing and scapegoating victims, and shifts the blame for social problems onto those most severely affected by them. It ushers attention away from the offender and, most importantly for Ryan, the wider backdrop of eliminable but persistent forms of structural disadvantage in society. Instead of leading away from bias and conferring scientific neutrality, victim-blaming grounded the founders in 'the perspective of the offender' (Weis & Weis, 1973, p. 4), leading to a position of bias *against* victims, particularly women and children victimised through violence. Mendelsohn's position as a criminal defender hardly afforded him a neutral viewpoint, and his victimological research was designed to serve his legal practice, according scientific authority to his approach of 'defending suspects by pointing out the victim's contribution to the criminal act' (Ben-David, 2000, p. 57). In their readiness to blame victims, the founders mistook transitory features of their cultural settings – dubious myths about 'nagging wives' and 'depraved' women and children – for unchanging traits of 'victimity'. This not only was unfair to victims, but also made for poor science.

The further scientific issue with the founders' victim-blaming is that it stalls on the problem of tautology, or 'circular logic' (Eigenberg & Garland, 2008, p. 29). The founders set out to identify the common characteristics that cause us to become victims, which theoretically would deliver a clear distinction between 'victims' (victimal traits or types) and 'non-victims' (people with traits that lead away from victimity). Yet, victims and non-victims 'exhibit similar behaviours' and, in fact, 'empirical research has failed to identify any common characteristics that cause one to become a victim other than the process of victimization. The only thing that causes one to be a victim is the process of being victimized, and the process of being victimized is the only thing that distinguishes victims from non-victims.' (Eigenberg & Garland, 2008, p. 29). Von Hentig sees the 'nagging wife' as 'flirting with murder', but a spouse can 'nag' without becoming a victim of uxoricide, and uxoricide can take place without 'nagging'. Hence it is the activity of uxoricide, and not 'nagging' (victim behaviour), that is necessary for uxoricide to occur, and it is not logically sound to say that avoiding 'nagging' can by itself prevent uxoricide.

The founders' typologies have also been criticised for imposing a 'qualitative disjunction' (Miers, 1989, p. 8) between victims and offenders, ignoring 'victim-offender overlap', or the fact that many offenders are victims (Fattah, 2000). This is a valid criticism, though it must be said the founders did encompass 'victim-offender overlap', albeit in another form. From the perspective of positivist victimology, most victims are also offenders, for their 'victimity' is wholly or partly responsible for the crime. Similarly, most offenders are victims of their own victims, for their offence was brought about by their victim's 'victimity', as much or more so than their own 'criminality'.

The numerous problems with positivist victimology prompted Mendelsohn to later reformulate his approach as 'general victimology', which recognised a wider array of victims (including victims of genocide and natural disasters), promoted rights and compensation for victims, and desisted from victim-blaming. Critical perspectives also began to flourish in victimology, forging new approaches that examine victimisation in its social context, interrogating instead of rehearsing the 'ideal-versus-guilty victim' construct, and including victims' insights and perspectives as worthy sources of data. As Walklate (1990, pp. 39–40) describes, instead of 'measuring patterns of victimization', critical victimology investigates 'the deeper order that produces and changes those patterns and the strategies people use to survive them'. Despite these developments, positivist victimology has lived on and, in many ways, Mendelsohn's (1956, p. 36) early wish to turn the 'attitude in social life, in science and in Justice towards the victim' in a more victim-blaming direction did come true. The following section will review the ongoing influence of positivist victimology, before moving on to explore critical victimology.

POSITIVIST VICTIMOLOGY TODAY

In the 'justice' context, Mendelsohn's strategy for defending clients accused of violence against women and children (blaming or 'prosecuting' the victim, under the guise of scientific neutrality) was subsequently developed in the influential work of Amir (1971). It remains a generic strategy of criminal defence. Legal victim-blaming in trials concerning rape and femicide already existed before Mendelsohn, but his advocacy helped elevate it to enduring scientific authority, contributing to a widespread belief that the ability to 'prosecute' the victim in court is essential to a 'fair' trial. Victim-blaming has been persistently challenged by feminists since the 1970s, but it is really only in recent years, with mobilisations such as SlutWalk and #MeToo, that its moral and logical problems have been fully and publicly exposed, affording feminist critiques more support within society.

In Aotearoa New Zealand this issue came to a head in 2019 when the Grace Millane murder trial caused public outcry. The defendant had strangled Millane to death following their Tinder date, later disposing of her body in the Waitākere Ranges. The defence promised not to 'blame' Millane, but did just that, drawing upon Millane's sexual history to characterise the murder as consensual erotic asphyxiation gone wrong, and using the pair's intoxication to shift blame from the defendant to the victim. Earlier high-profile cases, notably the police-perpetrated sexual assault and subsequent legal and media victim-blaming experienced by Louise Nicholas, have helped spark changes to policing and the legal system (McDonald & Tinsley, 2011) that may yet shift the legal culture in New Zealand away from the Mendelsohn style (see Jordan, chapter 6 this volume).

As observed earlier, in the context of criminal justice policy, positivist victimology and its 'associated concepts' influenced the broad shift from 'crime prevention' to 'victimization prevention' (Mawby & Walklate, 1994, pp. 7–8), and to the subsequently dominant 'situational approach' to governing crime (O'Malley, 1992), which gained prominence under neoliberalism in the 1980s. Resonating with positivist victimology's mission to reduce crime by addressing citizens' 'victimity', the 'situational approach' focuses on crime 'before it occurs' and makes prevention 'the responsibility of the victim' (O'Malley, 1992, p. 262). Mendelsohn's early vision of government-sponsored education encouraging citizens to remediate their victimal 'deficiencies' is realised in the neoliberal discourse of citizenship, which shifts the focus from citizens' rights to citizens' responsibilities, urging citizens to avoid 'victim mentality' and to assume 'personal responsibility' for calculating and reducing their vulnerability to crime, or else be regarded as the cause of crime should it occur. As Laster and Erez (2000, p. 249) observe, 'The ideal reasonable victim actively resists becoming a victim altogether, according to neoliberal ideology.' The idea that crime is caused by victimity is not logically sound, but this has been no impediment to the perception of victimisation as brought about by the would-be victim's failure to practice vigilance, maximise resilience, and adequately manage risks to personal safety, security, and well-being.

New Zealand became a neoliberal polity under the Fourth Labour Government in 1984. Here, as elsewhere, situational approaches are promoted as a 'common sense' response to crime and responsible citizenship, and they permeate state-sponsored and media depictions of crime. This can be seen in New Zealand Police signage found in public spaces all over New Zealand. At my local beach, for example, the police signage reads: 'Warning: Lock it or lose it. Car theft occurs when you encourage it. Always lock your car securely. Close all windows. Always lock your boot. Keep valuables with you or keep them out of sight.' On the surface, the sign merely provides apparently logical safety precautions to help secure property. At a deeper level, the sign perfectly rehearses the key concepts of positivist victimology. Foregrounding 'victimity', the sign bluntly blames the victim, who 'encourages' car theft. Distinguishing between 'ideal' and 'guilty' victims, the sign provides instructions for ideal victim behaviour, indicating that if the instructions are not observed and a crime occurs, it will be the victim's fault. The sign evokes the fear of an unknown stranger who may be lurking nearby, ready to commit crime. This lurking stranger, and the insufficiently wary property owner, constitute the 'penal couple'. Crimes of the sort targeted in the sign are typical 'crimes of survival' that provide subsistence income amidst conditions of hardship. But the sign does not warn about the negative effects of economic inequality, instead narrowly framing crime as brought about by the penal couple's bad choices. The sign targets theft and promotes vigilant theft avoidance, but, following positivist victimology, it does so in the narrowest of ways. This sign is also at a beach, and from the perspective of tangata whenua – as expressed, for example, in the twenty-thousand-strong hīkoi from Northland to Wellington to protest the Foreshore and Seabed legislation in 2004 – signage at beaches could just as feasibly warn local iwi about the threat of land theft by the Crown. As Pita Sharples (2007) documents, however, instead of being seen as applaudably vigilant theft avoidance, the hīkoi to defend customary rights to the seabed and foreshore area was derogated in the media as an example of 'victim mentality'. Sharples (2007) observes that 'the coupling of the two words, "Māori" and "Victim" have most frequently occurred in ways which have been pejorative'. The situational approach does not treat all crimes and victims equally, and does not celebrate all forms of victimisation prevention, specifically excluding collective political resistance from legitimacy.

CRITICAL VICTIMOLOGY AND THE 'IDEAL VICTIM' CONSTRUCT

Having followed the story of positivist victimology from the founders to today, this final section introduces the different way critical victimology conceptualises victimisation, drawing upon Norwegian criminologist Nils Christie's (1986) classic essay 'The Ideal Victim' and exploring further examples. Unlike victimology's founders, Christie did not set out to 'discover' the ideal victim; instead, he examined the way dominant cultural values shape our perceptions of who can and cannot qualify as an ideal victim. Christie (p. 18) conceived of the 'ideal victim' as a social construct rather than a fixed set of traits, asking, '[W]hat characterises – at the social level – the ideal victim?' He explained that by 'ideal victim' he meant *a person or a category of individuals who – when hit by crime – most readily are given the complete and legitimate status of being a victim*' (p. 18, original italics).

Christie enumerated the attributes of the 'ideal victim' in his social context, seeing these as derived from dominant cultural values, and as highly contestable and subject to political and historical change, rather than as unchanging and essential. The prevailing normative 'ideal victim' is seen as weak, respectable, and blameless, is victimised by a 'big and bad' (p. 19) stranger, and is 'powerful enough to make [their] case known' (p. 21). This narrow construct leaves many 'victims who are not seen as victims' (p. 27). Christie's much-cited example of the 'ideal victim' is 'the little old lady on her way home in the middle of the day after having cared for her sick sister', who is 'hit on the head by a big bad man who thereafter grabs her bag and uses the money for liquor or drugs' (pp. 18–19).

Christie's 'little old lady' is the kind of victim most likely to gain public sympathy and legal redress. While she certainly does deserve these things, Christie urged us to acknowledge the many other victims who, through no fault of their own, do not measure up to ideal victimhood, and therefore stand little chance of gaining these things in the absence of an organised struggle or focused campaign on their behalf. Christie indicated that typical non-ideal victims include women victimised by intimate partners, victims of structural violence or crimes of the powerful, and offenders who are victims. Where 'ideal victims' receive a sympathetic social response, 'non-ideal' victims are blamed and silenced in a perpetuation of the socially embedded inequalities that have rendered them non-ideal in the first place. In this way, the 'ideal victim' construct reflects and furthers power imbalances in society, doing tangible harm to victims who, in addition to victimisation, also have to endure the social and institutional hostilities directed at 'non-ideal' victims. By excluding so many victims from legitimacy, prevailing conceptions of the 'ideal victim' tend to obscure rather than clarify prevalent forms of victimisation, and the profile of those most commonly victimised, in the social context where they prevail. Critical victimology reveals the workings of the 'ideal victim' construct and its unequal treatment of victims in society, showing the way toward more ethical and equitable structures of recognition and responses to victimisation.

Importantly, Christie perceived problems not only for those who do not measure up to the ideal victim, but also for those who do. Ideal victims receive compassion but are restricted to a 'subordinated, weak position' (p. 27), from which they would deviate at their peril. Christie did not address the cultural origins of the 'ideal victim' problem, but Jan van Dijk's (2009) research suggests this problem is not an inevitable or universal state of affairs, instead having origins in late Christian theology. The treatment of victims in Western societies is shaped by 'unspoken but powerful Christian values' that are reproduced in the cultural expectation that victims align with 'Christ-like' traits of innocent, blameless suffering, or else become targets of communal hostility. Seen in this wider historical context, it becomes clear that positivist victimology worked with, rather than against, the reproduction of this cultural expectation, elevating it to a 'science', and playing a significant role in how the 'ideal victim' construct has been reproduced in the neoliberal era.

In New Zealand there is abundant evidence of Christie's 'ideal victim' construct. Christie's 'little old lady' is literally reflected in the story of Nan Withers who, in 1997 at the age of 70, while minding her son's shop, was brutally assaulted by an offender on parole. The assault took place in a wider context of rising incarceration rates and lengthening prison terms (Pratt & Clark, 2005). Despite this, Withers' story was mobilised in the formation of the Sensible

Sentencing Trust, validating its depiction of New Zealand as overrun by violent crime and judicial softness, and smoothing the path toward law reforms that toughened penalties for violent offenders. The swift and strong response an ideal victim can command in the context of a conservative victims' rights movement contrasts with the barriers to public empathy faced by non-ideal victims, such as the people populating New Zealand's prisons in the era of mass incarceration, a majority of whom have not been convicted of violence offences. Incarcerated people in New Zealand routinely face institutionalised violence in the form of 'dehumanising practices', such as regular strip-searches, 'being denied adequate medical care and being denied fundamental bodily autonomy' (No Pride in Prisons, 2016, p. 66), but convicted offenders are 'victims who are not seen as victims' (Christie, 1986, p. 27), and institutionalised violence in prisons does not typically ignite public sympathy, while calls for change run against the grain.

We would expect that cruelly mistreated children would stand a better chance of qualifying as ideal victims in New Zealand, but as Elizabeth Stanley's (2016) research on children in state care has shown, it depends upon the context of the offending. Many children in state-run residential care facilities between the 1950s and the 1980s faced 'a host of violent punishments, isolation techniques and damaging medical treatments', and yet, for decades, there was 'little social or state admonishment of this institutionalized violence' (Stanley, 2016, p. 8). As Christie (1986, p. 26) observed, the victim is ideal when the offender is ideal – when they align with the threatening image of the 'dangerous man coming from far away'. When, on the other hand, the offending is state-led, victims and advocates have to press hard against the grain to make their cases known, presenting them to the same entity that stands accused. After decades of struggle amidst persistent state denial, a Royal Commission of Inquiry into Abuse in Care was established in 2018. These examples clearly show the presence of Christie's 'ideal victim' construct, indicating the need and scope for critical victimology in New Zealand.

CONCLUSION

The founders of victimology promised to end criminology's neglect of the victim, but their victim-blaming orientation ensured that decades passed before victims' voices, insight, and perspectives, and the stories of non-ideal victims, were welcome within criminological and victimological inquiry. As we have seen, positivist victimology and its victim-blaming orientation persist in the spheres of law and policy, and in dominant conceptions of crime and victimisation. At the same time, victim-blaming is highly contested, and New Zealand examples such as McDonald and Tinsley's (2011) work on rape law reform, or Stanley's (2016) work on state violence against children, indicate that research propelled by critical criminological and victimological perspectives, coupled with victim activism and advocacy, can eventually have a progressive impact, suspending the rules of the 'ideal victim' construct, and countering victim-blame, at least for a time. Such research accords neglected victims much-needed recognition, and enables us to glimpse a social context in which victim-blaming is not the normative social response to all but a dubiously defined ideal victim.

STUDY QUESTIONS

- How does positivist victimology understand the victim's role in crime?
- What problems have critical victimologists discerned in the victim-blaming approach of positivist victimology?

- Outline an example of the 'ideal victim' construct in Aotearoa New Zealand, identifying a group of 'non-ideal' victims. What kind of victimological research would best support progressive efforts to make these victims' cases known?

FURTHER READING

Christie, N. (1986). The ideal victim. In E. A. Fattah (Ed.), *From crime policy to victim policy: Reorienting the justice system* (pp. 17–30). Basingstoke, UK: Macmillan.

Eigenberg, H., & Garland, T. (2008). Victim blaming. In L. J. Moriarty (Ed.), *Controversies in victimology* (pp. 21–36). Newark, NJ: LexisNexis.

Mawby, R. I., & Walklate, S. (1994). Perspectives on victimology. In R. I. Mawby & S. Walklate (Eds.), *Critical victimology: International perspectives* (pp. 7–22). London, UK: Sage Publications.

NOTES

1. As Walklate (1994) explains, positivist victimology lives on as 'conventional victimology', which persists in the search for patterns and regularities in verifiable aggregate data, nowadays gleaned from victimisation surveys more so than police and legal case files.
2. These are the 'depressive', 'greedy', 'wanton', and 'tormentor' types (von Hentig, 1940, pp. 304–307).

REFERENCES

Amir, M. (1971). *Patterns in forcible rape*. Chicago, IL: University of Chicago Press.

Ben-David, S. (2000). Needed: Victim's victimology. In P. C. Friday & G. F. Kirchhoff (Eds.), *Victimology at the transition from the 20th to the 21st century: Essays in honor of Hans Joachim Schneider* (pp. 55–72). Mönchengladbach, Germany: World Society of Victimology Publishing & Shaker Verlag.

Christie, N. (1986). The ideal victim. In E. A. Fattah (Ed.), *From crime policy to victim policy: Reorienting the justice system* (pp. 17–30). Basingstoke, UK: Macmillan.

Drapkin, I., & Viano, E. (1974). Preface. In I. Drapkin & E. Viano (Eds.), *Victimology* (pp. xi–xiii). Boston, MA: Lexington Books.

Dupont-Morales, T. (2009). Von Hentig, Hans. In J. K. Wilson (Ed.), *The Praegar handbook of victimology* (pp. 307–308). Santa Barbara, CA: Praegar Publishers.

Eigenberg, H., & Garland, T. (2008). Victim blaming. In L. J. Moriarty (Ed.), *Controversies in victimology* (pp. 21–36). Newark, NJ: LexisNexis.

Fattah, E. A. (2000). Victimology: Past, present and future. *Criminologie, 33*(1), 17–46. doi:10.7202/004720ar

Growette Bostaph, L., Brady, P., & Giacomazzi, A. (2014). Criminal justice education: Are we missing one-third of the crime triangle? *Journal of Criminal Justice Education, 25*(4), 468–485. doi:10.1080/10511253.2014.967507

Hoffman, H. (1992). What did Mendelsohn really say? In S. Ben-David & G. F. Kirchhoff (Eds.), *International faces of victimology* (pp. 89–104). Mönchengladbach, Germany: WSV Publishing.

Karmen, A. (2016). *Crime victims: An introduction*. Boston, MA: Cengage Learning.

Keat, R., & Urry, R. (1975). *Social theory as science*. London, UK: Routledge & Kegan Paul.

Laster, K., & Erez, E. (2000). The Oprah dilemma: The use and abuse of victims. In P. O'Malley (Ed.), *Crime and the criminal justice system in Australia: 2000 and beyond* (pp. 240–258). Sydney, Australia: Allen & Unwin.

Masson, J. (1992). *The assault on truth: Freud's suppression of the seduction theory* (2nd ed.). New York, NY: HarperCollins.

Mawby, R. I., & Walklate, S. (1994). Perspectives on victimology. In R. I. Mawby & S. Walklate (Eds.), *Critical victimology: International perspectives* (pp. 7–22). London, UK: Sage Publications.

McDonald, E., & Tinsley, Y. (2011). *From 'real rape' to real justice: Prosecuting rape in New Zealand*. Wellington, New Zealand: Victoria University Press.

Mendelsohn, B. (1956). The victimology. *Études Internationales de Psycho-Sociologie Criminelle, 10,* 4–36.

Mendelsohn, B. (1963). The origin of the doctrine of victimology. *Excerpta Criminologica, 3*(6), 239–244.

Miers, D. (1989). Positivist victimology: A critique. *International Review of Victimology, 1*(1), 3–22. doi:10.1177/026975808900100102

No Pride in Prisons (2016). *Abolitionist demands: Toward the end of prisons in Aotearoa*. Auckland, New Zealand: No Pride in Prisons Press. Retrieved from https://papa.org.nz/publications/

O'Malley, P. (1992). Risk, power and crime prevention. *Economy and Society, 21*(3), 252–275. doi:10.1080/03085149200000013

Pratt, J., & Clark, M. (2005). Penal populism in New Zealand. *Punishment in Society, 7*(3), 303–322. doi:10.1177/1462474505053831

Ryan, W. (1969). *Blaming the victim*. New York, NY: Vintage Books.

Sharples, P. (2007, October 14). *Pita Sharples: Victims' issues: Advancing practice, policy and research* [Press release: Victim support biennial conference]. *Scoop*. Retrieved from http://www.scoop.co.nz/stories/PA0710/S00267/pita-sharples-victims-issues.htm

Stanley, E. (2016). *The road to hell: State violence against children in postwar New Zealand*. Auckland, New Zealand: Auckland University Press.

van Dijk, J. (2009). Free the victim: A critique of the Western conception of victimhood. *International Review of Victimology, 16*(1), 1–33. doi:10.1177/026975800901600101

von Hentig, H. (1940). Remarks on the interaction of perpetrator and victim. *Journal of Criminal Law and Criminology, 31*(3), 303–309. doi:10.2307/1137415

von Hentig, H. (1948a). *The criminal and his victim: Studies in the socio-biology of crime*. New Haven, CT: Yale University Press.

von Hentig, H. (1948b). Go ahead, hit me. *Time, 52*(12), 85. Retrieved from http://content.time.com/time/magazine/article/0,9171,799202,00.html

Walklate, S. (1990). Researching victims of crime: Critical victimology. *Social Justice, 17*(3), 25–42.

Walklate, S. (1994). Can there be a progressive victimology? *International Review of Victimology, 3*(1–2), 1–15.

Weis, K., & Weis, S. (1973). Victimology and the justification of rape. In I. Drapkin & E. Viano (Eds.), *Victimology: A new focus. Volume V – exploiters and exploited: The dynamics of victimization*. Boston, MA: Lexington Books.

26

Police Racism
The Responsibilities of Police Leadership

Kim Workman

After Andrew Little was appointed minister of justice in November 2017, he openly acknowledged that institutional racism and bias existed within the criminal justice system (Little, 2019). In August 2018, he launched a strategy, Te Hāpaitia te Oranga Tangata: Safe and Effective Justice, and established an advisory group, Te Uepū Hāpai i te Ora, which consulted widely with the community, iwi, and Māori to develop a sector-wide criminal justice strategy for change. There followed reports from the group as well as other criminal justice agencies acknowledging and owning racism and bias within their organisations (Department of Corrections, 2019; Ināia Tonu Nei, 2019; Te Uepū Hāpai i te Ora, 2019a; 2019b). In December 2019, Te Uepū Hāpai i te Ora (2019a) released its second and final report, *Turuki! Turuki!*, concluding that:

> Racism is endemic throughout our society. Racism can manifest in overt acts of racial violence and abuse; in racist attitudes such as prejudice, stereotyping and profiling in beliefs that western ways of doing things are 'normal' or 'superior' to those of other cultures, and that others should assimilate or adapt; and in institutional and systemic racism, in which organisations and social systems systematically discriminate against some ethnicities or cultures (p. 45).

Any meaningful analysis of racist behaviour calls for a study of the specific environment in which people behave (Bronfenbrenner, 1979, p. 22). In the criminal justice environment, officers actively participate in shaping culture through a combination of individual decision-making, the exercise of discretion, and organisational socialisation (Chan, 2003; Crank, 2004). The link between organisational culture and leadership is strong. While all workers have the positional power and authority to control 'the way we do things around here', the leadership may either enable or be a barrier to the reduction of racism. This chapter considers these issues with a focus on one criminal justice organisation: New Zealand Police (NZP). It does so within the context of its colonial origins, the changing police culture, and its impact on both the personal and organisational behaviour of the police over time.

COLONISATION AND POLICE RACISM IN NEW ZEALAND

A close examination of police history in Aotearoa New Zealand shows primary reliance on a policing style common to all colonising nations. Colonial police forces were created by the state as agencies of social control, to impose the will of the state upon unwilling subjects (Hill, 1997, p. 3). The emergence of policing in New Zealand was no exception. First, the imposition of British law and penal policy on Māori expedited the process of assimilation by preparing Māori for British citizenship. Second, it denied Māori the right to punish and correct according to their own traditions and tikanga. Third, the imprisonment and arbitrary detention of entire whānau was a key strategy for dealing with Māori who resisted the *unlawful* actions of the state, and who were perceived by the state as comprising a 'dangerous underclass' or being 'in rebellion' to the state (Pratt, 1992, pp. 41–68). The trauma of colonial policing is fully described by Bradley et al. in chapter 14 this volume.

Post-colonial policing

By the 1880s New Zealand was an 'atomised' society, characterised by transient workers, interpersonal violence, and drunkenness (Fairburn, 1989). The settlers developed strong and mutually beneficial relationships within and beyond their immediate families, building a nation in which social solidarity and community cohesion were highly valued. But there was another, dark side to this apparent paradise. The state was there to bolster stability and security, and to fervently police morals and conduct. Outsiders were not welcome and dissent was frowned on; paradise had to be preserved at all costs (Pratt, 2006).

Following the First World War, the number of charges against Māori rose from 11 per 100,000 general population in 1910 to 40 in 1919, rising briefly above the non-Māori rate. The near 400 per cent increase in Māori offending rates in less than 10 years represented a turning point. The official Māori crime rate remained high, and the gap between Māori and Pākehā continued to increase (Dunstall, 1999, p. 206).

Police attitudes toward Māori were largely shaped by the policies of colonisation, and were reinforced by NZP leadership. In 1920, Police Commissioner O'Donovan broke the mould when, in an address to staff, he emphasised the need for police initiative and discretion: 'we keep a baton, but seldom use it, [and] when we do its application should be scrupulously proportioned to the need. Consistency and firmness without harshness was to be the guiding principle' (O'Donovan, 1920, p. 5). For him, the police had to stand above community and factional influence and to act out their part as impartial servants of an impartial law. The commissioner advocated for wise discretion, warnings where appropriate, and the use of force as a last resort. Policing by consent was about securing public support for police policies and strategies. Had it been applied to them in equal measure, Māori would have responded warmly to O'Donovan's focus.

Notwithstanding O'Donovan's leadership, the police were still under the direct control of the minister, and strategies of coercion were still employed as a means of protecting the middle class against an unruly working class; the 1951 waterside strike comes to mind (Bassett, 1972). Policing by consent came to mean providing the middle classes with visible, polite security symbols while refraining from trampling on their interests or encroaching too far on their daily lives. By the 1990s, the police were seen as protectors of the largely white middle class. As Das (1993) comments:

> Politicians in New Zealand defend the values implicit in the concept of law and order. The police have succeeded in identifying themselves with a whole range of sturdy, middle class values. More importantly, the climate of public opinion is such that anyone who does not support the police is likely to be called a stirrer, a protestor, a person who represents unacceptable and unrespectable segments of New Zealand society (p. 93).

Māori offending can be linked to economic disadvantage as well as to the ongoing effects of the colonising process. Durie (2005, p. 62) refers to the complex interaction between historical identity factors and socio-economic profiles and offending; loss of land, language, and tikanga. Moving into the cities after the Second World War, Māori shifted from 80 per cent rural in 1940 to some 80 per cent urban by 1986 (Pool, 1991). Though this was part of a worldwide drift in response to changing labour demands, for Māori it was not a drift but a demographic revolution. The impact was traumatising. In the words of Durie (2007):

> [Māori] shifted from extended to nuclear families (government pepper-potting prevented Māori aggregations), from support networks to relative isolation, from family bonds to bonds with disaffected others, from a secure place in a community to a place that could be hostile to brown faces, from a place where one was a leader to a place where one worked for 'the boss', from a place where community values were internalised to a place where all sanctions came from outside and were enforced by police.

Postwar policing

Toward the end of the Second World War, and over the ensuing decades, there was growing evidence that the police were harder on Māori than on Pākehā (Butterworth & Butterworth, 2008, pp. 30–31). They began to funnel significant numbers of Māori into the criminal justice system. Between 1954 and 1958, Māori youth offending rose by 50 per cent (Hunn, 1961, p. 64). The 1961 *Hunn Report*, the first government report to express concern about Māori involvement in criminal justice, confirmed that Māori were more likely to be arrested and imprisoned, sent to Borstal, or placed on probation; less likely to have court cases dismissed; and more likely to be committed to the Supreme Court for trial than non-Māori (Hunn, 1961). Most Māori came to court with no idea how to plead or defend themselves (Butterworth & Butterworth, 2008, pp. 32–33; O'Malley, 1973). More recent work (Bold-Wilson, 2018) has found that Māori continue to feel lost in the court environment, where 'the use of legal terminology and inadequate preparation time with their lawyer' meant 'defendants were left feeling powerless, unheard and disengaged in the justice' (p. 102).

One of the reasons for this policing approach related to police recruitment policies that reflected society's prevailing view of Māori as second-class citizens. In 1950, Inspector Bill Carran was the sole Māori officer in the NZP. In the same year, Commissioner J. B. Young canvassed his staff about recruiting Māori and found them 'almost unanimously opposed' to the idea (Butterworth & Butterworth, 2008, p. 16). Despite some external pressure to recruit Māori, by 1958 there were just 26 Māori police officers. In that same year, Commissioner Les Spencer declared that 'Chinese, Hindus [he probably meant Indians] and Pacific Islanders were unsuited to policing and would not be recruited. Apart from Māori, policing should be done only by the "white races"' (Butterworth & Butterworth, 2008, p. 20).

During the same period, NZP culture emphasised values of conformity, discipline, and order. The organisation had a clear and collective view of what constituted acceptable conduct, how officers should behave, and what they should think. The job of the 'policeman' (as female officers were few and far between) was to 'maintain order' and 'fight crime', and the most obvious, although flawed, measure of that was a high offender apprehension and conviction rate. This was a much more tangible outcome than exercising discretion in a way likely to reduce future offending (Reiner, 2010, pp. 118–119).

On these grounds, young Māori were labelled as criminals on the basis of police dealings with older siblings of the same whānau, or the reputation of the whānau itself. These youngsters were far more likely to be prosecuted at a young age than Pākehā, even though their offending was no more serious. Notwithstanding this focus on whānau for targeting purposes, the primary focus was then on the individual offender. Holding hui with whānau was anathema to most Pākehā police officers, who feared losing control of the process (Workman, 2018, p. 84). Youths who had been arrested for an offence were not eligible for diversion. Frontline staff and CIB staff arrested young Māori offenders more frequently, knowing that an arrest precluded diversion (Morris & Young, 1987, p. 35; Workman, 2018, pp. 84–85).

More generally, the high number of police on the streets, and the lack of efficient communication technology, also meant that police officers were largely unsupervised. It was not uncommon for a mobile patrol to pick up a couple of policemen off the street and, knowing there was safety in numbers, go looking for trouble. Young people, whether in cars or walking, would be routinely stopped and questioned, and sometimes searched. Any protest or resistance from the victims was likely to lead to confrontation and trumped-up charges of 'obstructing the police', 'obscene language', or 'resisting arrest'. Some police sergeants actively ramped up constables to make arrests, and policemen competed to see how many arrests they could make over an eight-hour shift; nor was there great interest in the quality of arrest. If hassling young people on the street was standard fare, then it was increasingly the case for young Māori, most of whom were relatively new to the urban environment. Young Māori were increasingly the target of police attention (Robinson & Hutton, 1989; Workman, 2018, pp. 48–49).

Police activities were also central to the rising numbers of Māori children going into state care environments. Māori children were often dealt with differently by way of supervision, or removal to an institution, rather than through constructive engagement with their whānau (Webb, 2011, p. 253). In 1971, more than 10,000 families were subject to official oversight from social welfare and Māori children were subject to increased scrutiny (Dalley, 1998, p. 188). Both the police and social workers lacked Māori networks, and sent Māori children to live with (often reluctant) Pākehā foster parents (Doolan, 1991). Māori children were also far more likely to be institutionalised (Ministerial Advisory Committee, 1988). By 1985, the department recorded a 78 per cent Māori population across six social welfare institutions in Auckland (Dalley, 1998). For many of the children, especially Māori, the institutions became a fertile breeding ground for the formation of gangs and involvement in the criminal justice system (Stanley, 2016; Webb, 2011).

NEOLIBERALISM AND ORDER-MAINTENANCE POLICING

The inequalities that stemmed from the general social and economic position of Māori through colonisation and urbanisation were seriously aggravated by the neoliberal policies pursued by both Labour and National governments from 1984. Increasingly, order-maintenance policing relied on the neoliberal logic of individual responsibility to criminalise disorderly behaviour; including the belief that individuals are alone responsible for their lack of success. It led to a punitive turn, with policing now deployed against poor communities

(Skogan, 1990, pp. 3–9) and an increasing reliance of the state on police power to address the consequences of poverty (Kaplan-Lyman, 2012). A 1989 study of Incident Car Patrolling in New Zealand showed that while official guidelines encouraged a community engagement role, many officers favoured a more aggressive, crime-fighting style of policing. There was no evidence that the police took time to improve relationships with local communities; rather, 'downtime' made it easier for them to identify and stop 'scroats, scumbags, shitheads and arse holes' (Robinson & Hutton, 1989, p. 92). While defending their turnover practices, a Samoan constable remarked, 'It's hard not to end up stereotyping old cars, blacks, woolly hair etc., when you know that's who is doing all the crime' (Robinson & Hutton, 1989, p. 65). The 2017 case of *Kearns v R* made it clear that being a dark-skinned male is not, in and of itself, sufficient grounds to search a car.[1]

New Zealand's experience from the mid-1990s highlights the impact of neoliberal policies on criminal justice expansion and imprisonment levels. While recorded crime rates have fallen significantly from the early 1990s – from 1308 recorded offences per 10,000 people in 1996 to 777 per 10,000 in 2014 (New Zealand Parliament, 2018, p. 3) – the rate of imprisonment has more than doubled in the same period. Gluckman (2018) demonstrated that if Māori had the same proportion of their population in prison as non-Māori, the New Zealand prison population would be 44 per cent smaller.

Workman and McIntosh (2013, p. 120) argued that this expansion of the criminal justice sector was not because New Zealand society was becoming more criminal, but rather because we had an increasingly divided and punitive society. In any society with large income gaps, trust and empathy between different groups tend to diminish, and those in power become increasingly concerned to punish, rather than help, those who offend. People in certain communities, especially ethnic minorities, are more likely to be stigmatised, blamed, and punished for their supposed failings. The ideology of neoliberalism normalised poverty, and subsequent disorder, as an individual responsibility; and members of poor, marginalised, and ethnic communities were redefined as 'dangerous' rather than disadvantaged, thereby justifying their increased incapacitation and incarceration. Moreover, perceptions of disorder and dangerousness were increasingly linked to the racial composition of communities (Sampson & Raudenbush, 2004).

While the place of neoliberalism, rising inequalities, and the increased marginalisation of Māori communities was not the only reason for Māori over-representation in the criminal justice system, the evidence shows that it aggravated and contributed to an already dire situation. By 1998, Māori were significantly over-represented in apprehension, prosecution, and conviction statistics (Doone, 2000, p. 18). By 2008, 19 per cent of children and young people in New Zealand were living in families in precarious economic circumstances, with constant financial stress and forced to economise on essential items, including food and healthcare. For Māori, the hardship rate was 32 per cent, and for Pasifika children and young people it was even higher at 40 per cent (Perry, 2009, pp. 54–55).

As the Dunedin life-course study of over 1000 New Zealanders (and other research) shows, people from low socio-economic backgrounds are three times more likely to commit crimes recorded by police than those from wealthy families (Department of Corrections, 2001, pp. 27–28.). As Workman and McIntosh (2013) comment:

> Unless one espouses the repugnant belief that those people are less 'good' than others, we must accept that growing up in poverty does damage individuals in ways that are not under their control and may predispose them to commit crime (p. 124).

POLICE AND MĀORI PERCEPTIONS

In the late 1990s, New Zealand Police and Te Puni Kōkiri contracted researchers to assess Māori perceptions of the police, and police perceptions of Māori. Māori research participants were unanimous in their perception that 'the police institution is a racist institution that perpetuates strong anti-Māori attitudes' (Te Whāiti & Roguski, 1998, p. 2). Participants related numerous examples of racial bias, including: being stopped and questioned on the pretext of criminal offending; verbal racist abuse; physical abuse during arrest; and disrespect for tikanga Māori (Te Whāiti & Roguski, 1998). Many respondents thought that police officers often provoked Māori into verbally and/or physically retaliating to justify arrests. Some stated a strong attitude of distrust towards the police, such that they would be hesitant in going to them for assistance, or in providing assistance to police if asked.

The parallel research on police perceptions of Māori mirrored some of the negative attitudes perceived in the Māori study (Maxwell & Smith, 1998). At least two-thirds of the 737 police respondents reported hearing colleagues use racist language about Māori. Many reported a greater tendency to suspect Māori of an offence, or to stop and query Māori driving 'flash' cars. Overall, the data suggested that about 25 per cent of police held negative attitudes towards Māori (Maxwell & Smith, 1998). Later research confirmed these findings (Cunningham et al., 2009; James, 2000; MM Research, 2002; Morrison et al., 2010). More recently, research by Nakhid et al. (2016) into the policing experiences of African youth in Auckland aired similar complaints about unfair and discriminatory police practice.

According to Tauri (2016), the police response to the research by Te Whāiti and Roguski (1998) and Nakhid et al. (2016) was remarkably similar. In both cases, NZP sought to deny the veracity of the findings by attacking the methodology, arguing that the complaints were unsubstantiated and should be handed over to the police for investigation. In 2020, NZP responded to the JustSpeak research on police racism by questioning its reliability (Johnson, 2020).

Societal and police attitudes have contributed to increases in both formal and informal profiling by police, and disproportionate rates of arrest and entry into the justice system for Māori as offenders. Māori are over-represented at every stage in the criminal justice system. In 2018, Māori were 38 per cent of people proceeded against by the police, 42 per cent of adults convicted, and 57 per cent of adults sentenced to prison. One in five Māori born in 1981 have spent time in prison, compared with one in 12 of all New Zealand men born in 1981. Of people in youth justice custody, 67 per cent are Māori. Another 13 per cent identify as Māori and Pacific, and 7 per cent as Pacific (Te Uepū Hāpai i te Ora, 2019b, p. 47).

FROM SILENCE TO SOME ACKNOWLEDGEMENT

Thirteen research reports between 1998 and 2009, including reports from government agencies, provided clear evidence of systemic bias against Māori within the criminal justice system (Workman, 2011). However, ministers of the Crown continued to deny the existence of racism. Between 2009 and 2017, the government did not commission any similarly focused research, and its agencies declined to support external research applications about Māori in the criminal justice system.

When the Hon. Dr Pita Sharples, co-leader of the Māori Party (and then associate minister of corrections), launched the party's justice policy in 2011, he noted the structural discrimination against Māori within the criminal justice system in general, and the police in particular (*New Zealand Herald*, 2011). Police Commissioner Peter Marshall denied his staff were racist (Marshall, 2011), and sent a newsletter to all staff confirming his view (Te Ao Māori, 2011). Then minister of police, the Hon. Judith Collins, publicly chastised Sharples for being 'out of line' (Reid, 2011, para. 9).

Under these conditions, criminal justice agencies have developed 'Responsiveness to Māori' strategies. These have become the conduit for the integration of acceptable elements of Māori culture into the state-dominated system, but they have failed to address the structural organisation or the power relations between the state and Māori (Tauri & Webb, 2012).

Such strategies have been criticised on several grounds. First, that in their presentation, they have perpetually represented Māori as *the* targets of criminal justice attention. Second, they have established a pervasive ritualism within reporting processes, such that they are used as window-dressing, or a subterfuge to convince external observers that the government agency is fully committed to a Crown–Māori partnership. Third, they have normalised discriminatory criminal justice operations, high imprisonment levels, and inequalities. Fourth, they have served to avoid addressing the root causes of discrimination within the criminal justice sector, and indeed of crime, against Māori and Pasifika peoples. Fifth, they are used as a tool to manage, control, and suppress the full expression of tino rangatiratanga (Stanley & Mihaere, 2019; Workman, 2017). Stanley and Mihaere (2018) argue that penal capture is underpinned by a combination of ideological, institutional, and structural forms of agnosis (or ignorance-making), including the deflection of responsibility from both the structural disadvantages and the state-institutionalised violence and discrimination endured by Māori over generations.

UNCONSCIOUS BIAS

In November 2015, Commissioner Mike Bush attributed the disparity in the way NZP exercised its discretion in relation to alternative resolutions not to systemic racism but to 'unconscious bias', thus shifting accountability for the exercise of bias from the institution to individual police officers (Owen, 2015). It was a step too far for some. Criminologist Juan Tauri (2016) referred to unconscious bias as 'bullshit', while Professor Judy McGregor referred to it as a 'fake term', because it 'implies that no one is actually responsible' (Parker, 2017, para. 21).

McGregor is both wrong and right. Unconscious bias is not a 'fake term'; it describes associations that we hold which, despite being outside our conscious awareness, can have a significant influence on our attitudes and behaviours. Regardless of how fair-minded we believe ourselves to be, all people have some degree of unconscious bias. We automatically respond to others (e.g., people from different racial or ethnic groups) in positive or negative ways, and our responses are deeply ingrained into our thinking and emotions (Cornish & Jones, 2013). There is a significant body of literature which addresses unconscious bias in the criminal justice system, and within the police (see, for example, Fridell, 2017).

In a recent publication, professor of psychology Jennifer Eberhardt (2019) explores her 15 years of working with law-enforcement agencies. In one experiment, Eberhardt (2019, pp. 64–66) describes a computer simulation 'shoot – don't shoot' scenario in which police officers were told to press a 'shoot' or 'don't shoot' button based on whether or not the figure was carrying a gun. If there was no gun present, police officers were quicker to respond to 'don't shoot' if the figure was white than if the figure was black. When a gun was present, they pressed the 'shoot' button more quickly if the figure was black, and were more likely to mistakenly shoot a black person. The same bias was found with college students and community members, and with both black and white participants. Mere exposure to black faces – even subliminal – facilitated the detection of crime objects.

The terms 'unconscious' and 'implicit' are often used interchangeably when describing bias. Cornish and Jones (2013) question 'the level to which [these] biases are unconscious especially as we are being made increasingly aware of them. Once we know that biases are not always explicit, we are responsible for them. We all need to recognise and acknowledge our biases and find ways to mitigate their impact on our behaviour and decisions' (p. 1).

This research bears some resemblance to the research of social psychologist Jonathan Haidt (2012), who explored the origins of difference. His starting point is moral intuition – the spontaneous perceptions that all humans have about other people and the things they do. He argues that these intuitions feel like self-evident truths, making us righteously certain that those who see things differently are wrong. He shows how these intuitions differ across political and ideological cultures, explaining that moral intuitions arise long before moral reasoning has a chance to get started, and that these intuitions tend to drive out later reasoning (Rethinking Crime and Punishment, 2014).

But McGregor was also right: labelling racism as 'unconscious bias' can be a convenient way for organisations to avoid responsibility, shifting responsibility from the state to the 'blameless' individual. In a recent example, JustSpeak's (2020) research used Statistics NZ data to compare similar groups of people who identified as Māori or European, and who had no prior interactions with the justice system. From their first interaction, police were 1.7 times more likely to take a legal action against a Māori person, and seven times more likely to charge a Māori person than their European counterparts. Police Deputy Commissioner Wally Haumaha told *Radio New Zealand* that the discrepancy may be due to Māori committing more serious crimes than Pākehā, which are ineligible for diversion programmes, adding that 'if they are being arrested at the lower end of the scale and those opportunities are not being provided, then I would be concerned'. He added that police undergo unconscious bias training, but 'we have yet to look at an evaluative process, to see whether it is working' (Johnson, 2020), thus implying that if there was a bias, it was 'unconscious'.

The assertion that variations in police discretion in applying alternative dispositions results from individual police officers exercising 'unconscious bias' does not align with the evidence. In 1998, the author conducted research into the low levels of Māori participation in the adult diversion process (Workman, 1998). What emerged was significant variations in the exercise of police discretion *at the institutional level*. In simple terms:

- Some districts were not interested in adult diversion, and referrals were almost non-existent.
- Some districts had a high level of referrals overall, with proportionate referrals for Māori and non-Māori.
- Some districts had high levels of Pākehā referrals, and low levels of Māori referrals.
- Some districts explained away low levels of Māori referrals as a misunderstanding around eligibility criteria.
- The accompanying language and behaviour of the police clearly demonstrated that there was nothing 'unconscious' or 'implicit' about the bias.

The existing research on police turnovers (Nakhid et al., 2016), pre-charge warnings (Independent Police Conduct Authority [IPCA], 2016), possession of cannabis (Fergusson et al., 2003), youth apprehensions (Becroft, 2005; Fergusson et al., 1994), and custodial remands (Workman, 2012) shows that the police behaviour is a product of both personal and institutional racism, rather than 'unconscious bias'.

The problem may lie deeper that we think. Because social psychologists tend to analyse and attribute racism as a problem of biased individuals (rather than a systemic force embedded in society), we can easily lose sight of the role played by institutions and wider society. This portrayal of racism as an individual – rather than systemic – phenomenon can blind Pākehā to racism and can guide policy attitudes and preferences in ways that perpetuate racial disparities. The individualistic portrayal is problematic because institutions and systems greatly contribute to reinforcing and reproducing inequality (Adams et al., 2008, p. 350).

Commissioner Bush has relied on unconscious bias training (UBT) as a means to unpick implicit associations that link Māori with crime, and which affect the personal perceptions, decision-making, and actions of police officers. However, a recent evaluation of UBT shows that, while it can be effective for reducing implicit bias, it is unlikely to eliminate it; nor will it reduce explicit bias. There is a potential for backfire when participants are exposed to information that suggests stereotypes and biases are unchangeable (Cornish & Jones, 2013). On the other hand, awareness of the power of institutions *can* be taught. Tutorials about structural or sociocultural racism have been shown to increase perceptions and acknowledgement of systemic racism and increase endorsement of policies designed to promote equality (Adams et al., 2008).

CONCLUSION

Police leadership is critical to modelling and developing a culture which actively lives out those values that mitigate racism. Police officers are, by necessity, drawn into a protective subculture where a group mentality prevails (Reiner, 2010). Through colonisation, NZP approaches employed a distinct 'us' (police) and 'them' (Māori) mindset. Officers may join the police with strong values around protecting people's rights and protecting individual freedoms, but their role frequently requires them to deprive people of those rights, and to psychologically violate these values in the performance of their duty. It is natural for them to rationalise that those on the receiving end deserve what they get (Prunkun, 1991, p. 12). It takes an 'authentic' leader in the mould of O'Donovan to influence cultural change; someone consistent in their words, actions, and values (Yukl, 2010).

Since 1996, NZP has done more than any other government agency to address its relationship with Māori (see Bradley et al., chapter 14 this volume); yet the outcomes for Māori have not greatly changed. Culturally appropriate programmes and services (in whatever guise) can make a valuable contribution to the organisational culture, but they do not, on their own, address the underlying presence of personal racism and structural bias. Rangatahi Courts, the Te Pae Oranga programme, and restorative justice conferences have the potential to affect reoffending rates, but if district commanders and operational management either resist or fail to promote staff awareness and participation in these alternative dispositions, nothing much will change.

Police culture is unique, and it has the potential to either create stress or support well-being. Police officers actively participate in shaping culture through a combination of individual dispositions and organisational socialisation (Chan, 2003; Crank, 2004). However, disparities can be affected by changing policy – for example, racial disparities can be enhanced through policies around the use of searches.

Police regularly exercise discretion in the discharge of their duties, and it is at this point that bias comes into play. Police stops or 'stop and search' procedures are one area that Māori and other ethnic groups complain about the most, an issue highlighted in the 2017 *Kearns v R* case. Discriminatory policing can be remedied – such as through changes in training, supervision, monitoring, recording processes, disciplinary procedures, the use of body-worn cameras, and new changes for officers to obtain written consent for searches (LaFraniere, 2015). Legal, policy, and institutional changes can lead to big reductions in police searches without increasing crime. Whether it is police turnovers, police bail decisions, prosecutorial decisions, plea bargaining, sentencing indication hearings, custodial remands, or alternative dispositions, focused research and evaluation into criminal justice practices can establish whether racism exists, and identify policies and practices to reduce the level of discrimination. This is the one area where police leadership must take affirmative action.

STUDY QUESTIONS

- How was the relationship between police and Māori shaped by colonisation? Does the legacy of colonisation continue to impact Māori–Police interactions?

- What has been the impact of neoliberalism on the ongoing disproportionate arrest, prosecution, and conviction of Māori and Pasifika peoples in New Zealand?

- What do 'unconscious' and/or 'implicit' bias refer to? Do these concepts supply a sufficient explanation for the hugely inflated rates of Māori incarceration? What else helps explain the criminal justice experience among Māori?

FURTHER READING

Carrington, K., Hogg, R., Scott, J., Sozzo, M., & Walters, R. (2019). Rethinking race and crime from the global south. In K. Carrington, R. Hogg, & M. Sozzo (Eds.), *Southern criminology*. Abingdon, UK: Routledge.

Cunneen, C., and Tauri, J. M. (2017). Indigenous criminology. In A. Brisman, E. Carrabine, & N. South (Eds.), *The Routledge companion to criminological theory and concepts*. Abingdon, UK: Routledge.

Hill, R. (2008). Māori, police and coercion in New Zealand history. In D. Keenan (Ed.), *Terror in our midst*. Wellington, New Zealand: Huia Publishers.

NOTES

1 The police approached Mr Kearns, described by a police officer as 'a large, dark-skinned male', questioned him, and searched his car without permission. The Court of Appeal held that Mr Kearns had the right not to be approached and inquired of by police officers, on the basis of his race or colour. See: *Kearns v R* (CA183/2016; [2017] NZCA 51).

REFERENCES

Adams, G., Edkins, V., Lacka, D., Pickett, K. M., & Cheryan, S. (2008). Teaching about racism: Pernicious implications of the standard portrayal. *Basic and Applied Social Psychology, 30*(4), 349–361. doi:10.1080/01973530802502309

Bassett, M. (1972). *Confrontation '51: The 1951 waterfront dispute*. Wellington, New Zealand: Reed Publishing.

Becroft, A. (2005, November). *Offending by Māori*. Paper presented at the New Zealand Police Management conference, Nelson, New Zealand.

Bold-Wilson, P. (2018). *'The injustice in justice': An examination of the quality of legal representation young Māori men receive in the criminal justice system*. Unpublished master's thesis, Unitec Institute of Technology, Auckland, New Zealand, p. 102.

Bronfenbrenner, U. (1979). *The ecology of human development: Experiments by nature and design*. Cambridge, MA: Harvard University Press.

Butterworth, G., & Butterworth, S. (2008). *Policing and the tangata whenua, 1935–85*. Rangatiratanga series number 16. Wellington, New Zealand: Treaty of Waitangi Research Unit, Stout Research Centre for New Zealand Studies, Victoria University of Wellington.

Chan, J. (2003). *Fair cop: Learning the art of policing*. Toronto, Canada: University of Toronto Press.

Cornish, T., & Jones, P. (2013). *Unconscious bias in higher education: Literature review*. London, UK: Equality Challenge Unit. Retrieved from https://www.ecu.ac.uk/publications/unconscious-bias-in-higher-education/

Crank, J. (2004). *Understanding police culture* (2nd ed.). Cincinnati, OH: Anderson Publishing.

Cunningham, C., Triggs, S., & Faisandier, S. (2009). *Analysis of the Māori experience: Findings from the New Zealand Crime and Safety Survey 2006*. Wellington, New Zealand: Ministry of Justice.

Dalley, B. (1998). *Family matters: Child welfare in twentieth-century New Zealand*. Auckland, New Zealand: Auckland University Press in association with the Historical Branch, Department of Internal Affairs.

Das, D. K. (1993). *Policing in six countries around the world: Organizational perspectives*. Chicago, IL: Office of International Criminal Justice, University of Illinois at Chicago.

Department of Corrections. (2001). *About time: Turning people away from a life of crime and reducing re-offending*. Wellington, New Zealand: Department of Corrections. Retrieved from https://www.corrections.govt.nz/__data/assets/pdf_file/0014/10652/abouttime.pdf

Department of Corrections. (2019). *Hōkai rangi: Ara poutama Aotearoa strategy 2019–2024*. Retrieved from https://www.corrections.govt.nz/resources/strategic_reports/corrections_strategic_plans/hkai_rangi

Doolan, M. (1991). Youth justice reform in New Zealand. In J. Vernon & S. McKillop (Eds.), *Preventing juvenile crime* (pp. 121–130). Conference proceeding series no. 9. Canberra, Australia: Australian Institute of Criminology.

Doone, P. (2000). *Report on preventing and combatting Māori crime: Hei whakarurutanga ma te aō*. Wellington, New Zealand: Crime Prevention Unit, Department of the Prime Minister and Cabinet.

Dunstall, G. (1999). *The history of policing in New Zealand: Vol. 4. A policeman's paradise? Policing a stable society 1918–45*. Palmerston North, New Zealand: Dunmore Press in association with the Historical Branch, Department of Internal Affairs.

Durie, E. T. (2007, July 27). *The study of Māori offending*. An address to the New Zealand Parole Board conference, Te Papa Tongawera, Wellington, New Zealand.

Durie, M. (2005). *Ngā tai matatū: Tides of Māori endurance*. Melbourne, Australia: Oxford University Press.

Eberhardt, J. L. (2019). *Biased: Uncovering the hidden prejudice that shapes what we see, think, and do*. New York, NY: Viking Press.

Fairburn, M. (1989). *The ideal society and its enemies*. Auckland, New Zealand: Auckland University Press.

Fergusson, D. M., Horwood, L. J., & Lynskey, M. (1994). The childhoods of multiple problem adolescents: A 15-year longitudinal study. *Journal of Child Psychology and Psychiatry and Allied Disciplines, 35*(6), 1123–1140. doi:10.1111/j.1469-7610.1994.tb01813.x

Fergusson, D. M., Swain-Campbell, N. R., & Horwood, L. J. (2003). Arrests and convictions for cannabis related offences in a New Zealand birth cohort. *Drug and Alcohol Dependence, 70*(1), 53–63. doi:10.1016/s0376-8716(02)00336-8

Fridell, L. A. (2017). *Producing bias-free policing: A science-based approach*. New York, NY: Springer Publishing.

Gluckman, P. (2018). *Using evidence to build a better justice system: The challenge of rising prison costs*. Auckland, New Zealand: Office of the Prime Minister's Chief Science Advisor.

Haidt, J. (2012). *The righteous mind: Why good people are divided by politics and religion*. New York, NY: Pantheon Books.

Hill, R. (1997). 'The control of both races': The policing of the Wellington settlement, 1840–1853. *Journal of New Zealand Studies, 7*(1), 3–13. doi:10.26686/jnzs.v7i1.394

Hunn, J. K. (1961). *Report on the Department of Māori Affairs*. Wellington, New Zealand: Government Printer.

Independent Police Conduct Authority (IPCA). (2016, September 14). *Review of pre-charge warnings*. Retrieved from https://www.ipca.govt.nz/Site/z-archive/2015-Template-Archive-/media/Media-2016/2016SEP14-Pre-Charge-Warnings.aspx

James, B. (2000). *Challenging perspectives: Police and Māori attitudes toward one another*. Wellington, New Zealand: Te Puni Kōkiri & New Zealand Police. Retrieved from https://www.police.govt.nz/resources/2000/challenging-perspectives--police-and-maori/challenging-perspectives--police-and-maori.pdf

Johnson, M. (2020, February 27). Justice system called 'fundamentally racist' – Māori more likely to go to court. *Radio New Zealand*. Retrieved from https://www.rnz.co.nz/news/te-manu-korihi/410466/justice-system-called-fundamentally-racist-new-study-shows-maori-more-likely-to-go-to-court

JustSpeak. (2020, February 26). *Justspeak IDI Research – A justice system for everyone*. Retrieved from https://www.justspeak.org.nz/ourwork/justspeak-idi-research-a-justice-system-for-everyone

Kaplan-Lyman, K. (2012). A punitive bind: Policing, poverty, and neoliberalism in New York City. *Yale Human Rights and Development Law Journal, 15*(1), 177. Retrieved from https://digitalcommons.law.yale.edu/yhrdlj/vol15/iss1/6/

LaFraniere, S. (2015, November 11). Greensboro puts focus on reducing racial bias. *New York Times*. Retrieved from https://www.nytimes.com/2015/11/12/us/greensboro-puts-focus-on-reducing-racial-bias.html

Little, A. (2019, January 21). *Andrew Little speech to United Nations Human Rights Council for the third universal periodic review – Delivered at the United Nations Geneva*. Retrieved from https://www.beehive.govt.nz/speech/andrew-little-speech-united-nations-human-rights-council-third-universal-periodic-review

Marshall, Commissioner P. (2011, October 12). Racism slur must be challenged [Blog post].

Maxwell, G., & Smith, G. (1998). *Police perceptions of Māori: A report*. Wellington, New Zealand: Institute of Criminology, Victoria University of Wellington, New Zealand Police, Te Puni Kōkiri, Victoria Link Ltd.

Ministerial Advisory Committee. (1988). *Puao-Te-Ata-Tu (Daybreak): The report of the Ministerial Advisory Committee on a Māori Perspective for the Department of Social Welfare*. Wellington, New Zealand: Department of Social Welfare. Retrieved from https://www.msd.govt.nz/documents/about-msd-and-our-work/publications-resources/archive/1988-puaoteatatu.pdf

MM Research. (2002, September). *Annual survey of public satisfaction with Police service*. Wellington, New Zealand.

Morris, A., & Young, W. (1987). *Juvenile justice in New Zealand: Policy and practice*. Wellington, New Zealand: Institute of Criminology, Victoria University of Wellington.

Morrison, B., Smith, M., & Gregg, L. (2010) *The New Zealand Crime and Safety Survey: 2009: Main findings report*. Wellington, New Zealand: Ministry of Justice. Retrieved from https://ndhadeliver.natlib.govt.nz/delivery/DeliveryManagerServlet?dps_pid=IE3338529

Nakhid, C., Azanaw, L., Essuman, K., Ghebremichael, N., Mukuhi Kimata Kamau, M., Kayitesi, T., . . . Mutamuliza, R. (2016). *African youth experiences with the police and the New Zealand justice system*. Auckland, New Zealand: Report commissioned by African Communities Forum Inc. (ACOFI). Retrieved from http://www.communityresearch.org.nz/research/african-youth-experiences-with-the-police-and-the-new-zealand-justice-system/

New Zealand Herald. (2011, October 1). Justice system discriminates against Māori – Sharples. Retrieved from http://www.nzherald.co.nz/politics/news/article.cfm?c_id=280&objectid=10755915

New Zealand Parliament (2018). *From offences to victimisations: Changing statistical presentations of crime in New Zealand 1994–2017*. Parliamentary Library Research Paper (July), Wellington.

O'Donovan, J. (1920). *Address to the New Zealand Police Force*. Wellington, New Zealand: Government Printer.

O'Malley, P. (1973). The amplification of Māori crime: Cultural and economic barriers to equal justice in New Zealand. *Race, 15*(1), 47–57. https://journals.sagepub.com/doi/pdf/10.1177/030639687301500103

Owen, L. (2015, November 28). Lisa Owen interviews Police Commissioner Mike Bush. *Scoop*. Retrieved from https://www.scoop.co.nz/stories/PO1511/S00456/lisa-owen-interviews-police-commissioner-mike-bush.htm

Parker, T. (2017, December 5). Why NZ is missing out on a $900m per year economic boost. *New Zealand Herald*. Retrieved from https://www.nzherald.co.nz/personal-finance/news/article.cfm?c_id=12&objectid=11952725

Perry, B. (2009). *Non-income measures of material wellbeing and hardship: First results from the 2008 New Zealand Living Standards Survey, with international comparisons*. Wellington, New Zealand: Ministry of Social Development. Retrieved from https://www.msd.govt.nz/about-msd-and-our-work/publications-resources/monitoring/living-standards/living-standards–2008.html

Pool, I. (1991). *Te iwi Māori: A New Zealand population, past, present and projected*. Auckland, New Zealand: Auckland University Press.

Pratt, J. (1992). *Punishment in a perfect society: The New Zealand penal system, 1840–1939*. Wellington, New Zealand: Victoria University Press.

Pratt, J. (2006). The dark side of paradise: Explaining New Zealand's history of high imprisonment. *British Journal of Criminology, 46*(4), 541–560. doi:10.1093/bjc/azi095

Prunckun, H. W. (1991). Police culture and stress. *Criminology Australia, 2*(4), 10–13. Retrieved from https://www.ncjrs.gov/App/Publications/abstract.aspx?ID=133217

Reid, N. (2011, October 3). Māori cop raw deal – Sharples. *Stuff*. Retrieved from https://www.stuff.co.nz/national/politics/5717522/Maori-cop-raw-deal-Sharples

Reiner, R. (2010). *The politics of the police* (4th ed.). Oxford, UK: Oxford University Press.

Rethinking Crime and Punishment. (2014). *What do I have to do to change your mind? Changing public attitudes to crime and punishment*. Smart on Crime & Robson Hanan Trust. Retrieved from https://www.academia.edu/search?utf8=%E2%9C%93&q=Changing+public+attitudes+to+crime+and+punishment

Robinson, J., & Hutton, N. (1989). Police on patrol: A study of incident car patrolling. In W. Young & N. Cameron (Eds.), *Effectiveness and change in policing*. Wellington, New Zealand: Institute of Criminology, Victoria University of Wellington.

Sampson, R., & Raudenbush, S. (2004). Seeing disorder: Neighbourhood stigma and the social construction of 'broken windows'. *Social Psychology Quarterly, 67*(4), 319–342. doi:10.1177/019027250406700401

Skogan, W. G. (1990). *Disorder and decline: Crime and the spiral of decay in American neighborhoods*. New York, NY: Free Press.

Stanley, E. (2016). *The road to hell: State violence against children in postwar New Zealand*. Auckland, New Zealand: Auckland University Press.

Stanley, E., & Mihaere, R. (2018). Managing ignorance: About Māori imprisonment. In A. Barton & H. Davis (Eds.), *Ignorance, power and harm: Agnotology and the criminological imagination* (pp. 113–138). Cham, Switzerland: Palgrave Macmillan.

Stanley, E., & Mihaere, R. (2019). The problems and promise of international rights in the challenge to Māori imprisonment. *International Journal for Crime, Justice and Social Democracy, 8*(1), 1–17. doi:10.5204/ijcjsd.v8i1.1045

Tauri, J. (2016, March 16). NZ Police national headquarters – the gift that keeps on giving [Blog post]. Retrieved from http://juantauri.blogspot.co.nz/2016/03/nz-police-national-headquarters-gift.html

Tauri, J. M., & Webb, R. (2012). A critical appraisal of responses to Māori offending. *The International Indigenous Policy Journal, 3*(4), 1–16. doi:10.18584/iipj.2012.3.4.5

Te Ao Māori. (2011, October 13). Top officer rejects Māori party's attack on police. *Radio New Zealand*. Retrieved from https://www.rnz.co.nz/news/te-manu-korihi/88223/top-officer-rejects-maori-party's-attack-on-police

Te Ohu Whakatika. (2019). *Ināia tonu nei – Now is the time: We lead, you follow, hui Māori report.* Retrieved from https://safeandeffectivejustice.govt.nz/news/latest-news/maori-perspectives-on-justice-report-released/

Te Uepū Hāpai i te Ora – Safe and Effective Justice Programme Advisory Group. (2019a). *He waka roimata: Transforming our criminal justice system.* Wellington, New Zealand. Retrieved from https://www.safeandeffectivejustice.govt.nz/assets/Uploads/7efb12cccb/teuepureport_hewakaroimata2.pdf

Te Uepū Hāpai i te Ora – Safe and Effective Justice Programme Advisory Group. (2019b). *Turuki! Turuki! Moving together.* Wellington, New Zealand. Retrieved from https://www.safeandeffectivejustice.govt.nz/about-this-work/te-uepu-report/

Te Whāiti, P., & Roguski, M. (1998). *Māori perceptions of the police.* Wellington, New Zealand: He Pārekereke/Victoria Link Ltd. Retrieved from https://www.police.govt.nz/sites/default/files/publications/maori-perceptions-of-police.pdf

Webb, R. (2011). Incarceration. In T. McIntosh & M. Mulholland (Eds.), *Māori and social issues* (pp. 249–262). Wellington, New Zealand: Huia Publishers.

Workman, K. (1998). *Police adult diversion: Increasing Māori participation.* New Zealand: Kim Workman & Associates.

Workman, K. (2011). *Māori over-representation in the criminal justice system – Does structural discrimination have anything to do with it?* Discussion paper. Available at rethinking.org.nz

Workman, K. (2012). *Submission to the Law and Order Select Committee on the Bail Amendment Bill 2011.* Wellington, New Zealand: Robson Hanan Trust & Rethinking Crime and Punishment.

Workman, K. (2017). *Brief of Evidence to Wai 2450: Claim to Waitangi Tribunal by Tom Hemopo against the Department of Corrections.*

Workman, K. (2018). *Journey towards justice.* Wellington, New Zealand: Bridget Williams Books.

Workman, K., & McIntosh, T. (2013). Crime, imprisonment and poverty. In M. Rashbrooke (Ed.), *Inequality: A New Zealand crisis* (pp. 120–133). Wellington, New Zealand: Bridget Williams Books.

Yukl, G. A. (2010). *Leadership in organisations* (6th ed.). Upper Saddle River, NJ: Prentice Hall.

27

Rangatahi Māori, Samoan Talavou, and Youth Justice
Challenging the Monoculture through Decolonising Practices

Tamasailau Suaalii-Sauni, Juan Marcellus Tauri, Robert Webb, Arapera Blank-Penetito, Naomi Fuamatu, Faʻafete Taito, and Salevao Faauuga Manase

This chapter provides an overview of Māori and Samoan experiences of youth justice in Aotearoa New Zealand. It explores previous research studies, and incorporates some of the findings from a recent Marsden-funded project involving participants in five regions across the country. Past and current data on Māori and Pasifika rangatahi and talavou (youth or young person) and their participation in youth justice, coupled with the dearth of in-depth research since the early 1990s, provide a clear rationale for why the research, and this chapter, were necessary.[1] Whilst Māori and Pasifika communities and youth (especially those defined by the policy sector and media as 'gang-affiliated') are commonly portrayed as a 'problem population' (Beals, 2006; McCreanor et al., 2014), little empirical research that details their experiences of criminal justice has been carried out with them (despite other key policy areas, such as education and health, where informed engagement is prioritised; see Kidman, 2014; Williams et al., 2018).

We begin this chapter with a discussion of the rationale for engaging community-based research with Māori rangatahi and Samoan talavou, and their families. This is followed by an overview of previous studies, and then a critique of government responses to the problem of

Māori and Pacific youth over-representation since the late 1980s, all designed (according to government rhetoric) to alleviate the problem and enhance the 'cultural appropriateness' of the justice system. Finally, we draw upon and examine some of the preliminary themes from our three-year study into youth justice in settler-colonial jurisdictions. We detail the objectives of the research with Māori and Pasifika communities, and offer some preliminary analyses of crime control experiences as articulated by our participants. This data provides a community-level critique of the efficacy of state responses to youth offending and victimisation. It is used to provide an analysis of the state's policies and interventions supposedly designed to meet the specific sociocultural 'needs' of Māori and Samoan youth and their whānau/aiga caught up in the criminal justice system.

WHY RESEARCH MĀORI AND SAMOAN YOUTH AND CRIMINAL JUSTICE?

The decision to research Māori rangatahi and Samoan talavou experiences of criminal justice was predicated on several rationales. The first was the extent to which predominantly Māori and Pasifika young people continue to be arrested and processed into the formal justice system, despite overall declining numbers of young offenders in recent years. Official statistics on New Zealand's youth justice system from the Ministry of Justice (for 2018) demonstrate that this is a well-founded concern. Rangatahi Māori are 48 per cent and Pasifika are 8 per cent of all youth recorded as distinct offenders; and the proportion of young people who had a family group conference or court action were predominantly Māori (40 per cent) or Pasifika (30 per cent). For those 12–17-year-olds who appeared in the Youth Court, 36 per cent of Māori and 36 per cent of Pasifika were remanded in custody (Ministry of Justice, 2019). This is not simply an issue of offending, but also reflects the ways in which these populations are disproportionately subject to formal state crime-control measures (see Morrison, 2009; Quince, 2017). Statistics like these give only a partial insight into the youth justice system, and demonstrate the necessity for expanding research to understand the specific concerns of populations, Māori and Samoan for example, that have high involvement proportionally in the system.[2]

The second rationale was the nature and impact of government responses to this situation, minus any significant independent research with rangatahi or talavou, and their whānau/aiga, and those who work with them in their communities, about their experiences of and responses to the criminal and youth justice systems. The third rationale is to engage with knowledge and understandings of justice from the communities themselves, to recognise the importance of these to a meaningful and critical criminological enterprise. When young people experience youth justice, they experience not only the Youth Court system but also a multiplicity of state agencies, community services, and culturally focused interventions, and exploring these has been the aim of our project, detailed further below (see Suaalii-Sauni et al., 2018).

STATE RESPONSES TO THE MĀORI RANGATAHI AND SAMOAN TALAVOU 'PROBLEM'

The importance of dealing with Māori and Pasifika youth justice issues has long been on the agenda for policy-makers in Aotearoa New Zealand, especially since the late 1980s (Williams, 2001). At this time, policy changes occurred as a result of criticisms of criminal justice (including youth-related) and social welfare systems from significant reports, most especially from the John Rangihau-led *Puao-Te-Ata-Tu (Daybreak)* report on Māori perspectives on the Department of Social Welfare (Ministerial Advisory Committee, 1988), and Moana Jackson's

(1988) landmark research into Māori experiences of the criminal justice system, *The Maori and the Criminal Justice System: A new perspective: He whaipaanga hou*.

Jackson's report identified a number of key ideas on the operation of the criminal justice system in regard to Māori. Firstly, as a consequence of colonisation, the legal and criminal justice system is a cultural system derived from settler-colonial institutions of law. Secondly, state assimilation policies have undermined ngā ture a te Māori, Māori social control and authority. In turn, there needs to be an understanding of the way interpretations of law and crime, and subsequent state responses, contribute to descriptions and analyses of crime rates. In the youth justice system, rangatahi Māori became alienated not only from both Māori traditional authority and conceptions of behaviour, but also from Pākehā systems of justice.

Speaking to solutions, Jackson identified the need to decolonise the state justice system, and to have Māori-led justice that recognised self-determination and Te Tiriti o Waitangi. Moreover, he argued for the decolonisation of the ways in which Māori had been constituted in criminological thought, to move away from pathologising individuals. He sought understanding of the collective social structures of Māori, and the interactions between the different cultural elements of our criminal and youth justice systems and wider society. These ideas were also reflected in the *Puao-Te-Ata-Tu* report, which identified Māori community concern over monocultural and institutionalised racism in social policy, and made recommendations for changes to legislation and policies to recognise the social, cultural, and economic values of all cultural groups. The report identified that children and young persons were members of a wider kin group or hapū that exercised collective responsibility for children's care, and that community programmes should strengthen this (Ministerial Advisory Committee, 1988).[3]

As a result of these reported critiques, criminal justice agencies went through a period of focused policy and strategic work designed to enhance their responses to the needs of Māori and Pasifika offenders, victims, their whānau, and wider communities. Tauri (2019), commenting on Māori-targeted policy and legislative directives, contends that ensuing official responses were introduced with one or more of the following outcomes in mind:

- to reduce Māori and Pasifika offending;
- to make the justice system generally more 'responsive' to Māori and Pasifika offenders, victims, and their families; and/or
- to increase the 'positive participation' of Māori and Pasifika in the criminal justice system.

Table 27.1 (overleaf) provides an indication of the types of responses that resulted from Māori critiques of justice practices, and how state agencies sought to enhance the cultural responsiveness of the sector, including responsivity to Pasifika.

In the following sections we offer an overview of some of the key policy responses to the Māori and Samoan youth offending 'problem', starting with the most well-known intervention, the family group conference (FGC). This is followed by an overview of police initiatives, and of the Rangatahi and Pasifika Courts, all of which are argued to enhance responsiveness to the needs of specific ethnic communities.

Family group conferencing

The FGC forum is the most well-known (internationally speaking) response to youth offending developed in New Zealand. The forum was introduced into the justice system with the passing of the Children, Young Persons, and Their Families Act 1989 (later renamed the Oranga Tamariki Act 1989). This legal development was heavily influenced by Māori criticisms (as noted above) that brought a need for government to be seen to be doing something constructive, particularly

Table 27.1.

Selected State Responses to Māori and Pasifika Over-Representation in the Criminal Justice System Post–1980s

Corrections	Police	Courts	Youth Justice
'Blended' psychological and cultural therapeutic interventions (e.g., Saili Matagi programme; Te Tirohanga) Māori and Pasifika focus units Māori and Pasifika cultural assessment tools	Māori and Pasifika responsiveness strategies Iwi liaison officers Joint police and Te Puni Kōkiri youth gang liaison project	Cultural sensitivity training for judges District Court restorative justice Rangatahi and Pasifika Courts	Family group conferencing Youth rehabilitation programmes with cultural 'add-ons' South Auckland youth (gang) project

Source: Adapted from Tauri, 2019

in response to perceived rises in youth offending within Māori and Pasifika communities (Tauri, 2019).

According to advocates (see Hassall, 1996; Henwood, 1998), the FGC forum was designed to address the number of Māori youth appearing in court, by enhancing the *cultural appropriateness* of the youth justice system. Becroft (2002) argued that two specific components were included to promote participation by young Māori offenders and increase the likelihood of positive outcomes, namely: (1) the inclusion of whānau, hapū, and iwi in repairing the harm caused by offending behaviour; and (2) the opportunity to have the conference in chosen, familiar surroundings, including the marae.

Advocates of the FGC forum made a number of claims about the relationship between the conferencing format, Māori justice practices, and the role the forum played in satisfying Māori concerns with the criminal justice system. For example, it was often claimed that because the conferencing process and Māori justice practice have restorative elements, the conferencing process therefore provides Māori with a culturally appropriate avenue for addressing their justice needs (Olsen et al., 1995). Similarly, the conferencing process was cast as an example of the system's ability to culturally sensitise itself and to empower Māori to deal with their youth offenders in culturally appropriate ways (Maxwell & Morris, 1993; Olsen et al., 1995). The same claims have often been made for Pasifika.

Yet, empirical research has failed to confirm that it replicates Māori and Pasifika 'justice practices', or empowers Māori (or Pasifika) victims, offenders, and their whānau, to the extent claimed by advocates (Chief Victims Advisor to Government, 2019, pp. 54–58; see also Tauri, chapter 20 this volume). What research has demonstrated is that:

- promises to 'de-professionalise' youth justice, and empower Māori (or Pasifika) whānau to have more say in how youth offending is dealt with, have failed to materialise, with the forum dominated by justice functionaries (Tauri, 2014);
- few if any forums are held on non-government sites (Moyle & Tauri, 2016; Nga Kaiwhakamarama i Nga Ture, 1999);
- the FGC process is often described by Māori (and Pasifika) as both culturally inappropriate and disempowering; and
- forum-related practices sometimes undermine, and even at times exclude, Māori (or Pasifika) cultural expertise (Moyle, 2013, 2014; Moyle & Tauri, 2016).

Responsive policing

From the 1990s, New Zealand Police has followed a wider inter-agency responsiveness policy to address Māori and Pasifika community concerns over the policing of their young people (Te Whaiti & Roguski, 1998). Attempts to address this can be seen in the first 1997 police Responsiveness to Māori strategy, Te Urupare Whītiki, which had a goal to gain a greater understanding and acceptance of the significance and role of Te Tiriti o Waitangi to Māori, New Zealand, and police. New initiatives developed, including designated iwi liaison officer roles to support iwi-led crime prevention initiatives. In 2002, NZP released the Pacific People's Responsiveness Strategy 2002–2006, which established a Māori and ethnic (minority) services team (including Pasifika) in Police National Headquarters under the Office of Māori, Pacific and Ethnic Services (OMPES). The strategy focused recruitment efforts to increase Māori, Pasifika, and other ethnic minority staff, and led to the establishment of Māori and Pasifika responsiveness managers, and advisory boards like the Commissioner's National Pacific Advisory Forum, formed in 2015. In 2012, the police initiated the Turning of the Tide strategy, which gave strategic-level focus to longer-term crime prevention. Amongst these strategic developments have been iwi and community justice panels that were implemented from 2014 in Manukau, Gisborne, and Hutt Valley, later extended to Hastings, Northland, Papakura, Rotorua, and Waikato. These community justice panels are an alternative to prosecution for low-level offending for people aged 17 years and older, and involve police, iwi or Māori service providers, and lay community members in panel hearings with offenders (Walton et al., 2019). The most recent police responsiveness strategies for Māori and Pasifika are the 2018 O Le Taeao Fou – Dawn of a New Day: Pasifika National Strategy and the 2019 Te Huringa o Te Tai strategy, both established to further promote community-led crime prevention.

Within this policy background sits the public acknowledgement by Police Commissioner Mike Bush, in 2015, of unconscious bias in the policing of Māori, and the need to improve community relationships (Harley, 2015). The explanation of bias as individually motivated, rather than institutionally structured, downplays the explanations of systemic bias in policing and other criminal justice practices over a lengthy period, and its role in shaping the distrust that underpins Indigenous and ethnic minority relationships with the state (Hill, 2008; Workman, chapter 26 this volume). Police acknowledgement that they were less likely to use other warnings or alternatives to arrest when dealing with Māori compounds the situation. For ethnic minority young people this use of discretion is of particular significance, as police are the primary gatekeepers to the youth justice system.

Rangatahi and Pasifika Courts

Since 2008 a number of targeted court alternatives for Māori and Pasifika youth have been established, including Ngā Kōti Rangatahi (Rangatahi Youth Courts) that are held on marae (across 15 sites nationally), and two Pasifika Youth Courts introduced in Auckland (Tuimavave, 2017).[4] These courts are stated to be a contemporary solution that immerses rangatahi in Te Ao Māori and tikanga, and Pasifika in Pasifika values, processes, and protocols, throughout the duration of the court process. A central aim is to help rangatahi and whānau reconnect and strengthen their understanding of who they are and where they are from. Both rangatahi and Pasifika youth are encouraged to explore their individual and cultural identities (Youth Court, 2020). Although the Rangatahi and Pasifika Courts are aimed at Māori and Pasifika youth, they are open to all young people.

The Pasifika Youth Courts, first established in 2010, emerged as a judge-led initiative to reduce the offending and recidivism of Pasifika youth, and as a specific forum to recognise the distinct values and needs of Pasifika communities (Suaalii-Sauni et al., 2018; Tuimavave, 2017; Tunufaʻi, 2017). The stated aim of the Pasifika Youth Court is to have court proceedings conducted in an environment conducive to Pasifika needs, being inclusive and supportive of Pasifika culture, and encouraging the involvement of the Pasifika community (Urale-Baker, 2016).

The literature on the Pasifika Youth Court is limited, and no formal evaluation has yet been conducted on the outcomes and participation rates for Pasifika youth. However, some scholars have demonstrated the distinctiveness of Pasifika youth offender identities and the need for a focused response by the youth justice system to Pasifika youth who come to system attention (see Ioane, 2017; Ioane et al., 2013; Suaalii-Sauni, 2006; Tunufa'i, 2017). Most of this research has focused on the Samoan experience.

Samoan communities have settled and raised families in New Zealand for some decades, a large number since the 1950s. Ioane (2017) argues that a New Zealand-born youth experience of being Samoan includes a growing sense of disconnection between themselves and their Island-born parents or caregivers. There are perceived and real disconnections between traditional Samoan values, languages, and customs and their own. At the same time, these young people often experience a disconnection with the dominant Pākehā culture of New Zealand. Ioane (2017) suggests that, as a result of these multiple and layered disconnections, Samoan and other Pasifika youth report feelings of confusion around defining their Pasifika identities. Tunufa'i (2017) underlines the importance of understanding Pasifika youth perceptions of ethnic identity and how these are imported into offending identities or gang cultures. Pasifika youth offender narratives are confirmed when Pasifika youth use ethnic-specific symbols, language terms, or motifs to name who they are or want to be as Pasifika gang members – for example, he argues that Samoan talavou involved in youth gangs draw on ethnic markers and stereotypes of prowess to link Samoan and gangster identities to garner respect from rival groups. What Ioane (2017), Tunufa'i (2017), and others (e.g., Ravulo et al., 2019; Suaalii-Sauni, 2006, 2010; Urale-Baker, 2016) have found is that ethnic identity values are important to Pasifika youth, notwithstanding engagement in youth offending activities. Any responsive criminal justice approach has to be attentive to these different identities and cultural forms and their associations with individualised and group behaviours, cultures, and accountability systems. Whether or not this has been made possible through police Pacific strategies or Pasifika Courts remains to be seen.

The policy response in perspective

As noted above, Māori have long criticised the broad spectrum of crime control policies and practices, from the lack of Māori working in the system, to concerns with racial profiling and aggressive police practices, to the apparent inequity of sentencing decisions in the courts. As detailed above, the criminal justice system response has been significant in terms of the range of policies, strategies, and interventions (see Williams, 2001). What has not been gauged thus far is the impact this body of policy work has had on Māori in terms of any reductions in offending or victimisation, or general feelings of safety and well-being. This can be attributed to the lack of outcome evaluation activity undertaken by the sector, and to what Tauri (2019) considers to be the tokenistic nature of the justice sector's response.

In the main, the sector's work can be grouped into two forms of response: (1) indigenisation, such as the recruitment drives aimed at increasing the number of Māori (and Pasifika) peoples working in the system, and the adoption of Māori names for organisations/institutions/strategies; and (2) co-option, which includes adding select components of Māori and Pasifika cultural practices onto mainstream interventions, such as the FGC and Rangatahi and Pasifika Courts (see Tauri, 2019, pp. 193–198). Both Tauri (2019) and Williams (2001) argue that the system's dual response of indigenisation and co-option has largely been focused on enhancing responsiveness to Māori (and to a lesser extent Pasifika people), while at the same time ensuring that the response did not impact on the state's domination of the system itself. As noted above, the seeming reluctance of the policy sector to entertain significant changes to the process of criminal justice and its associated theory of crime and justice, along with the dearth of research (by both the policy sector and members of the academy) on Māori rangatahi and Pasifika youth and their whānau, and their experiences of youth justice over the past 30 years, prompted the authors to undertake research of their own. This is discussed through the remainder of this chapter.

THE MARSDEN PROJECT

In 2017 we started an international comparative qualitative study involving community hui, talanoa, and interviews of Māori and Samoan experiences of youth justice systems operating in New Zealand, Australia (Brisbane and Gold Coast), and the US (California). The project explores how contemporary youth justice institutions, organisations, professions, and persons interact with the communities and cultural values and practices of Māori rangatahi and Samoan talavou, Māori whānau, and Samoan aiga across the three jurisdictions. The Aotearoa New Zealand part of the study involves six sites: West and South Auckland, Porirua, Gisborne, Taranaki, and Christchurch. In each site we have included community hui and fono, building towards separate interviews with Māori and Samoan young people, and with whānau and aiga members.

Importantly, while we acknowledge that there are distinct social histories for these communities in New Zealand, for Māori as tangata whenua there is also a recognition of a shared cultural heritage with Samoans as tangata Pasifika. The contemporary situation is often one of living in areas with similar social conditions, and seeking to engage community-level responses that are informed by Indigenous knowledge which reflects collective, rather than individual, world views and identities. We attempt to recognise both the similarities and the differences in their understandings and experiences of the youth justice system, and also the knowledge that their communities and social service organisations draw upon as they work in this area. Concomitant with the colonising process, academic research has often discounted or dismissed Māori and Pasifika knowledges as simply 'perspectives', and has favoured research methods that are 'non-engaging' – that is, they do not privilege the need for face-to-face (kanohi ki te kanohi or faaaloalo) research approaches and active researcher engagement in the process of gathering research or data (see Tauri, 2013). In this project we have sought to acknowledge the importance of Māori and Samoan Indigenous methodologies, and to use their approaches and/or methods (Suaalii-Sauni et al., 2018).

There are sizeable Māori and Samoan communities living in Australia, and a significant Samoan community living in the US. As in New Zealand, they are experiencing concerns over their youths' experiences with their respective criminal justice systems. Very little documented evidence exists of the youth justice experiences of Māori and Samoan youth living in these other settler-colonial jurisdictions outside of New Zealand, or indeed within it. Of particular concern to these communities is the impact that the system has on the wellbeing and futures of young Māori and Samoan people (Tauri, 2019; Tunufa'i, 2017). Māori and Samoan communities are not simply the passive recipients of state interventions. They actively work towards community advancement and development (Durie, 2003; Macpherson, 2012), and Māori and Pasifika non-governmental organisations and groups have made significant contributions to building community-based responses to offending and victimisation.

Community voices

From analysis of preliminary themes in New Zealand, two pertinent areas have emerged. First, that the contemporary youth justice system continues to be seen as monocultural in practice and, second, that Indigenous values can inform Māori and Samoan community-based responses to decolonise state justice.

Despite Moana Jackson's research from 1988, and the programmatic reforms that have ensued to meet cultural needs over several decades, community participants still raised concerns about the monocultural responses of the state justice system. For example, from the research interviews one community worker observed that:

> The system is a system of power . . . it doesn't love us . . . it will never show us alofa [love, compassion], it does not know what faaaloalo [reciprocal respect] is . . . It doesn't know what tautua [the principle of service] and feagaiga [the principle of sacred covenants] is. It will never know that. It will never know manaakitanga, whanaungatanga, all the tangas. It won't. Because it doesn't want to know it (Community worker).

Many participants raised concerns that the system remained exclusive of meaningful community control or engagement. Despite advocating for de-professionalisation, the system continues to use professionalised legal language in monocultural ways that actively and 'unconsciously' deny Māori or Samoan voices:

> So, I don't wanna enter into that space any more, and I don't want my young people going into that space any more. Because why? Because it's unsafe. You don't even listen to us, you can't even see us. So yeah I think, there's the languaging in terms of that, but then there's also the tone of, um, and I'm gonna say, it's a racist discourse. It's a discourse that does not acknowledge a Samoan tone, a Samoan voice, or a Māori voice (Community worker).

There was recognition given to the work of those in the system who have worked closely to help youth and families. Some recognised the importance of justice developments, such as the Rangatahi Courts, but also spoke of the need for community-led justice alternatives to move away from the court system. As one community worker reflected: 'I know there's lots of individuals, lots of judges who are awesome with our rangatahi in court, but do they need to get to court to know the judge is awesome? . . . does it need to get to that stage?'

A dominant concern was that officials sought to process young people into the justice system with a goal of arrest and court appearances, while ignoring other community approaches. Nonetheless, there was some reflection of potential change to this practice, with the introduction of iwi panels: 'Iwi panels are having more of a significant difference because they're not in court. It's a community. Even though it's a police initiative; but it's not new for the community to be sorting out their own things within the community' (community worker). For some participants, the iwi community panels held a clearer connection to the community. Like the Rangatahi Youth Court, the panels seemingly involve tikanga and have community members involved in the process. Further independent research may yet work to uncover whether this police-led approach has led to a drop in the number of rangatahi entering the formal court system.

Community responses

As can be seen from the above, participants spoke about the operation of community-based programmes for youth outside of the formal justice system. Community organisations identified ways in which they were proactively supporting youth in the justice system, and how they took a wider approach beyond punishment to focus on well-being and the aspirations of the community. Community workers spoke of the way they could provide holistic and aspirational lenses. For example, one community worker noted that their marae-based approach involved tikanga that had a strength-based focus on long-term well-being:

> Māori providers . . . probably have a more aspirational view about working with the kids rather than sticking to what they've been told the kids need . . . they probably think long-term, though, where is this heading for the kids? . . . how will this benefit the kid? And what does this rangatahi actually wanna do? And that might be why you can see a change . . . because they're probably working from a more aspirational viewpoint than 'this kid is all bad and they need to tick these things off' (Community worker).

Some solutions were framed in opposition to the dominant system, being located in the community and with a focus upon the family. This approach can be interpreted as following a decolonisation agenda, to find solutions in communities:

> I think there's a growing collective of us who are actually, yes, disrupting the system but also actually choosing not to engage. And by choosing not to engage, that choice is actually about not becoming the invisible people in a Palagi system that continues to punish us for kind of, yeah, making mistakes like every other human person makes mistakes. But that's the other thing that I've seen. There's no acknowledgement of the value of – that this family may actually have the solution themselves (Community worker).

Overall, these comments speak to the aim of decolonising state justice through community empowerment, and the prioritisation of Indigenous values and voices in this endeavour. They continue to reflect the sentiments made by Jackson (1988) for the development of a justice system based upon tikanga that reflects self-determination from Te Tiriti o Waitangi, and the more recent United Nations Declaration on the Rights of Indigenous Peoples.

In his address to the 2013 He Manawa Whenua Indigenous Research Conference, Moana Jackson raised 10 ethical points that are important for transforming policy-making, law-making, and service delivery in ways that are responsive to Indigenous peoples, Pasifika included.[5] These are the ethics of: (1) prior thought; (2) moral or right choice; (3) the imagination; (4) change; (5) time; (6) power; (7) courage; (8) honesty; (9) modesty; and (10) celebration (Jackson, 2015). These 10 points inform Jackson's proposition for a Māori philosophy of ethics. Inherent in this are principles of self-determination; of doing transformative research in ways that honour the values of faaaloalo and tika (of what is respectful, right, moral, and just); of celebrating with modesty, honesty, and courage, the wisdom and whakapapa of prior knowledge ('of manaakitanga . . . all the tangas'); of the interconnectedness of people through time and place (whanaungatanga and whakapapa); and of respecting both the immutability and fluidity of change. These principles also recognise the critical culture-bound role that the imagination plays in all our searches, Indigenous and otherwise. For Māori, Pasifika, and other Indigenous peoples, this must include the legitimisation, not co-option, of their prior knowledge, ethics, and values. Jackson's 10 ethics of research offer a barometer for testing systemic legitimacy and recognition.

The community voices from our Marsden research, gathered with Māori and Pasifika communities, echo the voices of our experts (including our kaumātua or elders). They indicate concerns about the monoculturalism persisting in the youth justice system. They express the desire and aspiration to support community well-being through alternatives to the formal system, to draw upon community knowledge and strengths, and to address bias that is as much systemically as it is individually nurtured and located. A critical step to decolonising the youth justice system is the task of making visible and audible the voices, stories, and experiences of those who are so devastatingly affected by it.

DECOLONISING JUSTICE

In response to criticisms raised by earlier reports (Jackson, 1988), various responsiveness policies have been introduced into the youth justice system in a belated effort to achieve more direct community control over, involvement in, and recruitment into the formal justice system. Despite these efforts, significant concerns remain. Processes like those adopted by family group conferences in youth justice have fallen short of empowering communities to address the issues of rangatahi and talavou and the underlying causes of their offending. In addition, we argue that these policies and processes actually expand the state's ideological and systemic reach into Māori and Pasifika communities through using a dual process of co-option and indigenisation. One specific criticism to this end is that, as the theoretical basis of the criminal justice system remains unchanged, these policies both wittingly and unwittingly implement co-optive strategies in the attempt to address rangatahi Māori or Pasifika talavou engagement with the youth justice system. One important finding of our work is that Māori and Samoan organisations that work alongside the justice system, and the members who are recruited into state agencies, often face the dual pressure of navigating and facilitating both community-based values/expectations and the frameworks of state directives. The pressure is compounded by the restrictions imposed by contractual obligations to deliver outcomes specified by government.

Notwithstanding the intent behind the development of state responsiveness strategies and legislation, the ongoing complexity of neocolonial justice policies and practices, and the ways in which they are experienced by communities on the ground, is illuminated by the preliminary analysis of the narratives of Māori and Samoan respondents. Their responses continue to illustrate that the justice system does not fully address or recognise community values or needs in empowering ways. Such criticisms are not new, and it is with some frustration that we find ourselves once again reporting similar findings to those contained in Jackson's seminal report (1988). Their narratives speak to a need to expose the blatant and subtle subjugations of the state over Indigenous or community values if there are to be (1) a decolonisation of the justice system and (2) aspirations for self-determination in community-led and -operated justice.

While participant experiences can be and are susceptible to reinterpretation through monocultural systemic criminal justice filters and practices in ways that shape and frame Māori and Pasifika offending in deficit terms, continued assertions of tikanga frameworks – such as Moana Jackson's 10 ethical principles – can help reorient and reframe the narrative and its analysis to a place of empowerment and cultural integrity rather than of apologia. This supports shifting the problem as one resulting from cultural disconnection leading to pathological or dysfunctional individuals to one of disconnection resulting from systemic, institutional, cultural, and collective bias, discrimination, and/or racism.

Both tikanga Māori and Fa'a Samoa foundations for addressing wrongdoing emphasise the collective or community, rather than individually focused rights, responsibilities, or healing processes. The frameworks of aiga or whānau and iwi – including elder, kaumātua and/or matai – frame the responsibilities of youth through collective forgiveness-seeking practices, such as with the Samoan ifoga (Jackson 1988; Suaalii-Sauni 2006, 2010). Echoing earlier work, our Marsden research identifies the need for criminology, especially in New Zealand, to further engage with Māori and Pasifika knowledge frameworks, to ask questions with an ethical mind, to know the historical capability of these frameworks to produce a justice system that has maintained law and order for centuries, and to make these frameworks accessible and comprehensible to all throughout New Zealand.

CONCLUSION

This chapter has explored the ways that various responsiveness policies in the youth justice system have sought to introduce more direct community involvement in a formal centralised justice system. Drawing on a recent Marsden-funded project, it outlined Māori and Samoan experiences of youth justice in Aotearoa New Zealand while highlighting the dearth of in-depth, independent research with rangatahi or talavou and their whānau/aiga, and those who work with them in their communities. The chapter identified ongoing concerns regarding the failure to adequately empower communities to address the issues of rangatahi and talavou and the underlying causes of their offending. More broadly, the chapter gives much-needed voice to community-level critiques of the efficacy of extant state responses to youth offending and victimisation. It recognises the importance of these to a meaningful and critical criminological enterprise, and provides researchers with a template for how to engage with knowledge and understandings of justice from the communities themselves.

STUDY QUESTIONS

- What benefits might accrue from research on Māori and Pasifika peoples' experiences of criminal justice in Aotearoa New Zealand?
- Identify some of the key policy and strategic responses developed by government into Māori and Pasifika experiences of criminal justice. What specific practices have emerged from these policies and strategies? And what impact have they had?
- Can you suggest any other policies or interventions that might enhance the criminal justice sector's response to these communities?

FURTHER READING

Jackson, M. (1988). *The Maori and the criminal justice system: A new perspective: He whaipaanga hou: Part 2*. Wellington, New Zealand: Policy and Research Division, Department of Justice. Retrieved from https://www2.justice.govt.nz/website-documents/maori-and-the-criminal-justice-system-a-new-perspective-p2.pdf

Smith, L. T. (1999). *Decolonising research methodologies: Research and Indigenous peoples.* Dunedin, New Zealand: Otago University Press.

Tunufa'i, L. (2017). Samoan youth crime. In A. Deckert & R. Sarre (Eds.), *The Palgrave handbook of Australian and New Zealand criminology, crime and justice* (pp. 175–189). Cham, Switzerland: Palgrave Macmillan.

NOTES

1. The terms 'Pasifika' and 'Pacific' are used interchangeably in this chapter to refer to the Indigenous peoples of Pacific nations, such as Samoa, Tonga, Cook Islands, Niue, Tokelau, and Fiji, who have migrated and settled in Aotearoa New Zealand. The term 'Pasifika' is widely used in New Zealand, by the state in policy and official data, and by society at large, to describe Pacific migrants.

2   The Samoan population of New Zealand makes up just under half of Aotearoa's Pacific population at 48.7 per cent. Cook Islanders make up 20.9 per cent, Tongans 20.4 per cent, and Niueans 8.1 per cent (Statistics New Zealand, 2014).

3   This need for strengthening remains a significant issue. For example, the Oranga Tamariki Act 1989 allows for Māori and iwi services to provide accommodation for rangatahi with a supervision with residence order. These services also cater for non-Māori youth, including Pasifika. However, Henwood et al. (2018, p. 51) observe that section 238(1)(d), which provides for young offenders to be delivered into the custody of an approved iwi social service or approved cultural service, has remained largely unused and dormant for most of the past 25 years.

4   In 2018 there were 1486 appearances in Rangatahi Courts and 337 in Pasifika Courts (Youth Court, 2020).

5   This can be seen at: https://www.youtube.com/watch?v=lajTGQN8aAU.

REFERENCES

Beals, F. (2006). *Reading between the lines: Representations and constructions of youth and crime in Aotearoa/New Zealand*. Unpublished doctoral thesis, Victoria University of Wellington, Wellington, New Zealand.

Becroft, A. (2002). *Family group conferencing a New Zealand model for young persons' participation in youth justice processes*. Paper presented at the XVI Youth and Family World Congress, Melbourne, Australia.

Chief Victims Advisor to Government. (2019). *Strengthening the criminal justice system for victims: Workshop playback report*. Wellington, New Zealand: Ministry of Justice. Retrieved from https://chiefvictimsadvisor.justice.govt.nz/resources/

Durie, M. (2003). *Ngā kāhui pou: Launching Māori futures*. Wellington, New Zealand: Huia Publishers.

Harley, A. (2015). Commissioner: Police addressing bias in Maori relations. *Newshub*. Retrieved from https://www.newshub.co.nz/home/new-zealand/2015/11/commissioner-police-addressing-bias-in-maori-relations.html

Hassall, I. (1996). Origin and development of family group conferences. In J. Hudson, A. Morris, G. Maxwell, & B. Galaway (Eds.), *Family group conferences: Perspectives on policy and practice* (pp 17–36). Leichardt, NSW, Australia: Federation Press.

Henwood, C. (1998). Children, Young Persons, and Their Families Act 1989 (NZ): A judicial perspective in 1997. *Judicial Review, 3*(4), 215–249.

Henwood, C., George, J., Cram, F., & Waititi, H. (2018). *Rangatahi Māori and youth justice: Oranga rangatahi*. Research undertaken for the Iwi Chairs with the support of the Henwood Trust and the Law Foundation. Retrieved from https://iwichairs.maori.nz/wp-content/uploads/2018/02/RESEARCH-Rangatahi-Maori-and-Youth-Justice-Oranga-Rangatahi.pdf

Hill, R. (2008). Māori, police and coercion in New Zealand history. In D. Keenan (Ed.), *Terror in our midst? Searching for terror in Aotearoa New Zealand* (pp. 39–62). Wellington, New Zealand: Huia Publishers.

Ioane, J. (2017). Talanoa with Pasifika youth and their families. *New Zealand Journal of Psychology, 46*(3), 38–45. Retrieved from https://www.psychology.org.nz/journal-archive/Talanoa-with-Pasifika-youth-and-their-families-private.pdf

Ioane, J., Lambie, I., & Percival, T. (2013). A review of literature on Pacific Island youth offending in New Zealand. *Aggression and Violent Behavior, 18*(4), 426–433. doi:10.1016/j.avb.2013.05.002

Jackson, M. (1988). *The Maori and the criminal justice system: A new perspective: He whaipaanga hou: Part 2*. Wellington, New Zealand: Policy and Research Division, Department of Justice. Retrieved from https://www2.justice.govt.nz/website-documents/maori-and-the-criminal-justice-system-a-new-perspective-p2.pdf

Jackson, M. (2015). He manawa whenua. In L. Pihama, H. Skipper, & J. Tipene (Eds.), *He manawa whenua, e kore e mimiti: Indigenous centred knowledge – unlimited potential* (pp. 59–63). Waikato, New Zealand: Te Kotahi Research Institute.

Kidman, J. (2014). Representing Māori youth voices in community education research. *New Zealand Journal of Educational Studies, 49*(2), 205–218.

Macpherson, C. (2012). Empowering Pacific peoples: Community organisations in New Zealand. In S. Mallon, K. Mahina-Tuai, & D. Salesa (Eds.), *Tangata o le moana: New Zealand and the people of the Pacific* (pp. 179–200). Wellington, New Zealand: Te Papa Press.

Maxwell, G., & Morris, A. (1993). Juvenile justice in New Zealand: A new paradigm. *Australia and New Zealand Journal of Criminology, 26*(1), 72–90. doi:10.1177/000486589302600108

McCreanor, T., Rankinem, J., Moewaka-Barnes, A., Borell, B., Nairn, R., & McManus, A. (2014). The association of crime stories and Māori in Aotearoa New Zealand print media. *Sites, 11*(1), 121–144. doi:10.11157/sites-vol1iss2id240

Ministerial Advisory Committee. (1988). *Puao-Te-Ata-Tu (Daybreak): The report of the Ministerial Advisory Committee on a Māori Perspective for the Department of Social Welfare.* Wellington, New Zealand: Department of Social Welfare. Retrieved from https://www.msd.govt.nz/documents/about-msd-and-our-work/publications-resources/archive/1988-puaoteatatu.pdf

Ministry of Justice. (2019). *Youth justice indicators summary report – August 2019.* Wellington, New Zealand: Ministry of Justice. Retrieved from https://www.justice.govt.nz/assets/Documents/Publications/E4NOUP-Youth-Justice-Indicators-Summary-Report-August-2019.pdf

Morrison, B. (2009). *Identifying and responding to bias in the criminal justice system: A review of international and New Zealand research.* Wellington, New Zealand: Ministry of Justice. Retrieved from https://www.justice.govt.nz/assets/Documents/Publications/Identifying-and-responding-to-bias-in-the-criminal-justice-system.pdf

Moyle, P. (2013). From family group conferencing to Whānau Ora: Māori social workers talk about their experiences. Unpublished master's thesis, Massey University, Wellington, New Zealand.

Moyle, P. (2014). Māori social workers' experiences of care and protection: A selection of findings. *Te Komako, Social Work Review, 26*(1), 55–64. doi:10.11157/anzswj-vol26iss1id55

Moyle, P., & Tauri, J. M. (2016). Māori, family group conferencing and the mystifications of restorative justice. *Victims and Offenders: Special Issue: The Future of Restorative Justice?, 11*(1), 87–106. doi:10.1080/15564886.2015.1135496

Nga Kaiwhakamarama i Nga Ture. (1999). *Māori and the criminal justice system: Ten years on.* Conference proceedings from the Māori and the Criminal Justice System Hui, July 1998, Wellington. Wellington, New Zealand: Nga Kaiwhakamarama I Nga Ture.

Olsen, T., Maxwell, G., & Morris, A. (1995). Māori and youth justice in New Zealand. In K. Hazelhurst (Ed.), *Popular justice and community regeneration* (pp. 89–102). London, UK: Praeger Publishers.

Quince, K. (2017). Rangatahi Courts. In A. Deckert & R. Sarre (Eds.), *The Palgrave handbook of Australian and New Zealand criminology, crime and justice* (pp. 711–723). Cham, Switzerland: Palgrave Macmillan.

Ravulo, J., Scanlan, J., & Koster, V. (2019). Delivering youth justice for Pacific young people and their families. In J. Ravulo, T. Mafile'o, & D. Yeates (Eds.), *Pacific social work: Navigating practice, policy and research* (pp. 47–57). London, UK & New York, NY: Routledge.

Statistics New Zealand. (2014). *2013 Census QuickStats about culture and identity.* Retrieved from http://archive.stats.govt.nz/Census/2013-census-profile-and-summary-reports/quickstats-culture-identity/pacific-peoples.aspx

Suaalii-Sauni, T. (2006). *Le Matuamoepo: Competing 'spirits of governing' and the management of New Zealand-based Samoan youth offender cases.* Unpublished doctoral thesis, University of Auckland, Auckland, New Zealand.

Suaalii-Sauni, T. (2010). New Zealand-based Samoan youth offender subjectivities: Working the 'spaces between'. In M. O'Loughlin & R. Johnson (Eds.), *Imagining children otherwise: Theoretical* and critical perspectives and childhood subjectivity (pp. 87–110). New York, NY: Peter Lang Publishing.

Suaalii-Sauni, S., Tauri, J. M., & Webb, R. (2018). Exploring Māori and Samoan youth justice: Aims of an international research study. *Journal of Applied Youth Studies, 2*(5), 29–40.

Tauri, J. M. (2013). Indigenous critique of authoritarian criminology. In K. Carrington, M. Ball, E. O'Brien, & J. M. Tauri (Eds.), *Crime, justice and social democracy: International perspectives* (pp. 217–233). London, UK: Palgrave Macmillan.

Tauri, J. M. (2014). An Indigenous, critical commentary on the globalisation of restorative justice. *British Journal of Community Justice, 12*(2), 35–55. Retrieved from https://ro.uow.edu.au/cgi/viewcontent.cgi?article=4203&context=sspapers

Tauri, J. M. (2019). Indigenous perspectives and experience: Māori and the criminal justice system. In T. Bradley & R. Walters (Eds.), *Introduction to criminological thought* (3rd ed., pp. 183–204). Auckland, New Zealand: Edify.

Te Whaiti, P., & Roguski, M. (1998). *Māori perceptions of the police*. Wellington, New Zealand: He Pārekereke, Victoria Link Ltd. Retrieved from https://www.police.govt.nz/sites/default/files/publications/maori-perceptions-of-police.pdf

Tuimavave, L. (2017). *The Pasifika Youth Court: A discussion of the features and whether they can be transferred*. Unpublished LAWS523 dissertation, Faculty of Law, Victoria University of Wellington, Wellington, New Zealand.

Tunufa'i, L. (2017). Samoan youth crime. In A. Deckert & R. Sarre (Eds.), *The Palgrave handbook of Australian and New Zealand criminology, crime and justice* (pp. 175–189). Cham, Switzerland: Palgrave Macmillan.

Urale-Baker, N. (2016). *Aua le limatētē ina ne'i ola pala'ai fanau: Samoan youths' views on their experience in the Pasifika Youth Court*. Unpublished master's thesis, University of Auckland, Auckland, New Zealand. Retrieved from https://researchspace.auckland.ac.nz/handle/2292/28454

Walton, D., Martin, S., & Li, J. (2019). Iwi community justice panels reduce harm from re-offending. *Kōtuitui: New Zealand Journal of Social Sciences Online*, 1–18. doi:10.1080/1177083X.2019.1642921

Williams, C. (2001). *The too-hard basket: Māori and criminal justice since 1980*. Wellington, New Zealand: Institute of Policy Studies, Victoria University of Wellington.

Williams, A., Clark, T., & Lewycka, S. (2018). The associations between cultural identity and mental health outcomes for Indigenous Māori youth in New Zealand. *Frontiers in Public Health, 6*, 319. doi:10.3389/fpubh.2018.00319

Youth Court. (2020). *The Rangatahi Courts' newsletter – Ngā Kōti Rangatahi o Aotearoa, 11*. Wellington, New Zealand: District Court of New Zealand.

28

Mental Health and Crime
A Critical Review

Bruce M. Z. Cohen

Following two separate mass shootings in August 2019 in El Paso, Texas, and Dayton, Ohio, where a total of 31 mainly black and Latino people were killed by white gunmen, a USA Today/Ipsos poll found that, above all other factors – including racism and loose gun laws – the US public held the mental health system most responsible for the atrocities (Page, 2019). The widespread perception of people who commit such acts of violence as mentally unwell was also reflected by the US president, who commented at the time that '[t]hese are people that are very, very seriously mentally ill' (Kimball, 2019). Similar speculations were also made earlier in the year regarding the lone gunman of the Christchurch mosque shootings in which 51 people were murdered (Williams, 2019). When we think of the issue of mental health in relation to crime, it is often such images of the insane, violent perpetrator which come most readily to mind. The reality, however, is strikingly different: those with mental health problems commit less violent crime than the rest of us and, in fact, are more likely to be victims of crime than are the general population.

This chapter investigates the complexities involved in understanding mental health issues in relation to crime, criminal behaviour, and the criminal justice system. In doing so it necessarily questions the simplistic and often false ideas on what 'crime' and 'mental illness' are, along with the many problems in drawing any direct causal relationship between the two. The first section offers an overview of the current context, highlighting key issues criminologists need to consider when engaging with the topic of mental health. It includes a discussion of the latest crime figures as well as Aotearoa New Zealand's rising rates of mental illness in prison. What might appear to be contradictory findings arising from the first section are illuminated in more detail through consideration of both conservative and critical scholarship on crime and mental health in the two sections that follow. Biological and conservative sociological ideas have utilised accepted measures in the field to contend that there are marked patterns of pathological behaviour – within either the individual or the environment – which can effectively account for why some groups are over-represented in both the criminal justice and psychiatric systems. These 'deficit' models, however, do not account for the culturally and historically fluid nature of both crime and mental illness designations; something that is acknowledged by labelling and social constructionist scholars in the discussion of critical ideas in the penultimate section. Through applying a relativist approach, where the less powerful are labelled 'criminal' and 'mentally ill' deviants by those with power, it will be demonstrated that current carceral systems in New Zealand operate as effective systems of (neo)colonial social control which increasingly medicalise criminal behaviour. The final section returns to reflect both on the contradiction between dominant understandings of crime and mental health and on the research evidence to suggest some fruitful pathways for future work on the topic.

CURRENT CONTEXT AND KEY ISSUES

The 1954 murder of Honorah Parker in Christchurch at the hands of her 16-year-old daughter Pauline Parker and the daughter's best friend, 15-year-old Juliet Hulme, remains one of New Zealand's most notorious murder cases. Parker was killed by blows to the head from a brick in a stocking. The ensuing court case and media frenzy often suggested the girls were 'mentally touched' (*Star-Sun*, 1954). The insinuation of such crimes is that offenders are not only acting unlawfully but have also lost their minds; the popular implication that follows is that those with mental illness are more likely to commit (especially) violent crime than those who are mentally healthy. This image of the 'mad' as also potentially 'very bad' has endured over time. Indeed, in a recent review of research on public attitudes towards people with mental illness in the US, Markowitz (2011b) found that, despite perceptions becoming more nuanced since the 1950s, there is an increasing association of mental health problems with ideas of 'dangerousness, violence, and unpredictability' (p. 39).

Such perceptions endure despite overwhelming evidence to the contrary. As Keshavan and Shah (2013) point out, '[w]hile about a quarter of the population experience a mental disorder in any given year in the US, mentally ill individuals constitute only a very small percentage of those who commit serious violence' (p. 1). For example, recent research in the UK demonstrated that only 11 per cent of homicides between 1997 and 2016 were committed by people with mental disorders (Appleby et al., 2018, p. 31). The same study revealed that people with mental illness are 2.6 times more likely to be a victim of a homicide than the general population (p. 31), a finding supported by a host of other studies on criminal victimisation (see, for example, Dean et al., 2018; Khalifeh et al., 2015; Maniglio, 2009; Teplin et al., 2005).

The above picture is further complicated when considering the very high rates of mental illness among prison populations. As a recent survey from the New Zealand Department of Corrections found, 91 per cent of prisoners 'had a lifetime diagnosis of a mental health or substance use disorder', and 62 per cent had suffered a mental health problem in the past 12 months (compared to 21 per cent within the general population) (Indig et al., 2016, pp. v, ix). Female prisoners had an even higher rate of 12-month diagnosis at 75 per cent, with over half experiencing a lifetime post-traumatic stress disorder diagnosis (Department of Corrections, n.d., p. 11). Similar figures have been found in other countries (see, for example, Brandt, 2012; Coleborne & MacKinnon, 2006; Mills & Kendall, 2018). Moreover, rates of mental illness among the prison population in New Zealand have increased over time (Indig et al., 2016, pp. v–vi).

If mental illness is not criminogenic and if people with mental health issues commit less crime than others, how do so many end up at the wrong end of the criminal justice system? A popular explanation has pointed to 'transinstitutionalisation', whereby those previously cared for in psychiatric institutions have migrated to the prison system, leading to the suggestion that contemporary society has effectively criminalised people with mental illness (Erickson & Erickson, 2008). Scholars have argued that there is a direct correlation between the decrease in the institutionalised psychiatric populations across Western societies from the 1960s onwards (under the guise of a shift towards 'care in the community') and the increased proportion of prison populations categorised as 'mentally ill'. As the chief executive of the Department of Corrections has pointed out, the prison system is now 'managing more people with mental illness than any other institution in New Zealand' (Department of Corrections, n.d., p. 11). A similar picture elsewhere has led commentators to describe modern prisons as the 'new asylums' (Peter Norden, policy director of Jesuit Social Services, as cited in Coleborne & MacKinnon, 2006, p. 376), and a 'recreation of Bedlam' where people with mental illness are once again incarcerated and subjected to punishment rather than treatment (*The Guardian*, as cited in Cox & Marland, 2018). Researchers have certainly suggested that this 're-institutionalisation' (Burrell & Trip, 2011, p. 180) is a major contributing factor in the increasing prevalence of mental disorder in prison, meaning prisons have become 'de facto mental health treatment centers, even though adequate care is not provided' (Brandt, 2012, p. 554; see also Markowitz, 2011a).

While figures demonstrate that prison populations rose roughly around the same time as psychiatric hospital populations began to decrease (Harcourt, 2011; Markowitz, 2011a; Primeau et al., 2013; Yoon, 2011), the precise nature of this relationship remains unclear and the numbers migrating from hospital to prison are contested. For instance, an investigation of the period 1968 to 1978, when the state mental hospital population in the US decreased by two-thirds, found that less than 3 per cent of former patients were admitted to state prisons (Monahan & Steadman, as cited in Curran & Renzetti, 2001, p. 85). Further, in a recent review of the research assessing the transinstitutional relationship, Kim (2016) reflected that it remained 'uncertain whether and how much an effect [psychiatric] deinstitutionalization had on the U.S. prison growth' (p. 11).

Given these ongoing issues with the transinstitutional argument, some scholars have instead focused on the increasingly punitive policing practices in Western society since the 1980s. It is argued that due to the heightened surveillance of the public by the police, a diminished public tolerance for eccentric behaviour, the expanding prison–industrial complex, increased policing powers, and political policies such as the war on drugs, people with mental illness have become an increasing target for the criminal justice system (Brandt, 2012). The US Bureau of Justice Statistics (1999), for instance, has recorded that between 1980 and 1998, those arrested for public order offences – a category that typically includes many people with mental health problems – rose more than threefold. Turner (2007) has argued that people with mental illness are more likely to be victims of the criminal justice system due to discriminatory practices which lead to increased police harassment, a greater likelihood of being arrested, and longer prison sentences. Other research, however, has suggested that the police may in fact be performing 'mercy bookings' in which arrests for misdemeanour offences are made to protect people with mental health issues from victimisation on the street (Brandt, 2012, p. 546). In the context of New Zealand, Holman et al. (2018) have noted a significant increase in recent years in police contact with people with mental health issues, as well as a tendency to more regularly use force (most often handcuffing) against them.

This issue of linking mental health to crime can be further problematised when considering the social production of official measures. For a long time, criminologists have recognised the reliability and validity issues of crime statistics that are subject to social, cultural, and political processes both within the criminal justice system as well as in the wider state apparatus. There is a marked over-focus on blue-collar crime and crimes of the powerless in the policing and recording of crimes at the expense of white-collar and corporate crime; the crimes that qualitatively cause society the most social harm are, contrarily, the least policed and the least represented in official figures (see Brownstein, 2000). Likewise, classifications of mental illness remain highly unreliable (psychiatrists regularly disagree on what form of mental pathology a person has, or if they even have a mental illness at all), leaving the validity of psychiatric science still very much in doubt (see Burstow, 2015; Cohen, 2016, pp. 9–17; Whitaker & Cosgrove, 2015). Most recently, research on major diagnostic categories in the latest edition of the American Psychiatric Association's (APA) *Diagnostic and Statistical Manual of Mental Disorders* (DSM–5) by Allsopp et al. (2019) concluded that labels of mental illness such as 'schizophrenia,' 'bipolar disorder', 'depressive disorders', and 'anxiety disorders' were heavily subjective and 'scientifically meaningless'. As with criminal statistics, while figures for mental illness tell us little about the true incidence of the phenomenon, they may be more useful as indicators of changing professional priorities and practices.

CONSERVATIVE THEORISING

Despite the serious questions raised in the previous section regarding the linkage between mental illness and criminal offending, there has long been a tradition within both criminology and psychiatry of theorising just such a relationship. Answering why such theories have been promoted in Western society will be returned to below. Here, however, I will outline what I refer to as conservative sets of ideas, highlighting both biologically and socially oriented theories which have sought to cement ideas within the public imagination of criminals as victims of either their own internal pathology or an external, pathological environment.

The birth of psychiatry and criminology as modern disciplines in the nineteenth century coincided with the emergence of biological theories on criminal behaviour as signs of mental pathology. The 'father of modern psychiatry', Philippe Pinel, used the term *manie sans délire* (the origins of the DSM–5's antisocial personality disorder [APA, 2013, pp. 659–663], commonly understood as the 'psychopath') to describe a person who was abnormal yet not mentally ill, while the 'father of American psychiatry', Benjamin Rush, suggested that some patients had an 'innate preternatural moral depravity' (Siegel, 2007, p. 8). Similarly, the pioneering British psychiatrist Henry Maudsley felt there had to be a strong association between crime and insanity, and that irrational emotions caused by brain functioning or the person's personality were bound to lead to irrational behaviour, some of which would be criminal in nature (Siegel, 2007, p. 8). These early psychiatric ideas on the insane as inclined towards criminality were in turn echoed in the 1860s by the 'father of criminology', Cesare Lombroso, who theorised the criminal as a victim of internal psychological traits which predisposed him or her to violent and immoral acts (Lombroso, 1911/2006). For Lombroso, these traits were marked physically on the body through irregular head size and various facial features; signs that for him marked the criminal as 'atavist', an evolutionary throwback to an earlier stage of human development.

Similar theories linking criminal activity to a faulty or defective biology, and as a manifestation of degeneracy, followed Lombroso's work into the twentieth century, including Ernest A. Hooton's longitudinal study of American prisoners in the 1930s. Focusing almost exclusively on racial and physical features, Hooton argued that criminals were biologically inferior and that types of criminality such as burglary or sex offences paralleled different physical body and racial schema; the criminal was generally of inferior stock and in some cases 'perverted in body as in mind' (as cited in Moran, 1992, p. 220). Research that suggested criminals were genetically inferior and mentally abnormal led to the increased engagement of the mental health system over time, with Moran noting that in the name of offering a supposed 'more humane approach' to dealing with criminality, psychiatry promoted the use of forced sterilisations against those labelled as 'degenerate', 'syphilitic', and 'hereditary criminal' (p. 222). 'Lobotomy, electric shock, and preventive incarceration of the "dangerous classes"', comments Moran (p. 222), 'were likewise practiced as preferable penal substitutes.'

Moran (1992) reminds us that both criminology and psychiatry have remained surprisingly attached to biological theory in the contemporary setting. Despite the serious deficiencies and dangers in such research, the search for the biological causes of crime and mental illness continue with some enthusiasm. A recent study in China by Wu and Zhang (2016) specifically channelled Lombroso and Hooton when they argued that their research on the faces of criminals and 'non-criminals' proved that while non-criminals have very similar facial features, the faces of criminals tended to show significant deviations. More usually, though, biological criminology has attempted to appear more sophisticated through performing research that makes connections between crime, intelligence (see for example, Oleson, 2016, pp. 39–72), and genetics (see for example, Tiihonen et al., 2015). New Zealand has not been spared such 'scientific' research; in 2006, genetic epidemiologist Rod Lea claimed that he had found a 'warrior gene' in Māori. Based on a sample of 17 Māori males, Lea stated that the genetic variance he found 'goes a long way to explaining some of the problems Māori have . . . they are going to be more aggressive and violent and more likely to get involved in risk taking behaviour like gambling' (as cited in Crampton & Parkin, 2007, p. 2439; for current examples of neuroscientific research in New Zealand connecting criminality with 'neuro-disabilities', see Gibbs & Sherwood 2017; Lambie et al., 2016; Lynch, 2016).

Such a racialised discourse within biological research on criminality and potential mental abnormalities is perhaps less surprising when considering the mental health system's active involvement in urban crime and violence initiatives in the twentieth century. In 1967, at the height of US civil rights protests, a psychiatrist and two neurosurgeons (Mark et al., as cited in Moran, 1992, p. 225) suggested in the *Journal of the American Medical Association* that black urban rioters probably had brain dysfunctions that led to such violent behaviour, recommending in turn that early screening, detection, and treatment (including brain surgery) would lead to 'a better and safer world for all of us'. Such recommendations came closer to practice in the early 1990s – at the peak of a 20-year growth in the US crime rate – when, backed by senior psychiatrists, the federal government proposed a 'violence initiative' involving the mass screening of inner-city children across America to determine those biologically or genetically predisposed towards antisocial or violent behaviour. As a vaccine against criminality, medical researchers argued at the time that once the 'conduct-disordered' children were identified they could then be administrated psychotropic drugs (Breggin & Breggin, 1998).

These reductionist ideas of biological criminology and psychiatry have been questioned by sociology since the early decades of the twentieth century, especially following the Chicago School studies on crime and mental illness in the 1930s and 1940s. Faris and Dunham's (1939) study on the urban distribution of schizophrenia demonstrated high levels of mental pathology in the city centre, which remained unchanged over time as populations migrated in and out of the central areas of multiple deprivation. This therefore suggested a problem within the *environment*, rather than the *individual*, which could lead to a greater chance of criminal behaviour and mental abnormalities (among other issues). Theorising the city as a microcosm of society, such scholars argued that 'social strains' within the structures of society created 'socially disorganised' neighbourhoods with a lack of social cohesion, where poor-quality housing and living conditions could lead to multiple social problems, including crime and mental pathology.

Contemporary versions of this 'strain theory' have tended to emphasise both criminal and mental illness-related behaviour as rooted within the socio-economic environment; those groups most likely to experience multiple indicators of deprivation are also those most likely to experience mental health problems and to be subject to the criminal justice system (for a useful summation, see Wilkinson & Pickett, 2010). This argument can explain, for example, why working-class Māori living in poor neighbourhoods are much more likely to be subject to the criminal justice system and be designated as 'mentally ill' compared to middle-class Pākehā living in wealthy areas. Thus, the cause and the solution to both crime and mental illness are fundamentally located in the socio-economic inequalities that have been produced by society; it is forwarded that there needs to be a reallocation of resources and services in order to address the conditions that produce (and reproduce) criminality and poor mental health in such communities. This consideration of environmentally caused, multidimensional socio-economic issues has led Curran and Renzetti (2001) to state that forwarding a direct causal 'relationship between mental illness and crime may be spurious' (p. 86). Siegel (2007, p. 152) agrees, suggesting that both mental illness and criminal behaviour may be the result of independent factors, such as social problems, living in disadvantaged neighbourhoods, and negative policing practices. Typically, research has found that both crime and mental disorder have a stronger relationship to the variable of lower social class than they do to each other (see Monahan & Steadman, in Curran & Renzetti, 2001, p. 86).

What the above conservative theories have in common is a belief in crime and mental illness as static and objective categories of pathology. There is a focus on a deficit in character or environment, which fails to consider issues of social deviance and professional power in the process of designating certain groups as 'criminal' and 'mentally ill' while others escape such labels. The following section broadens the discussion to consider ways in which the criminal justice and mental health systems align to perform specific social control functions in New Zealand.

CRITICAL THEORISING

Critical scholars of crime and mental health, including labelling, social constructionist, Marxist, and post-colonial theorists, question whose knowledge becomes dominant on these subjects in a given time period, and to what ends. As noted above, the 'crime' and 'mental illness' concepts continue to be subject to professional bias and measurement issues; both have a historical and cultural fluidity to them; and thus there are serious ongoing reliability and validity problems. Taking a critical approach, however, we can make sense of this situation when we understand mental illness and crime as social constructs that have been produced for specific reasons, and are subject to social, cultural, and political negotiation. Markers of criminality or mental pathology can then be understood as labels applied to certain groups or individuals designated as 'socially deviant'. According to labelling theorists, the criminal justice and mental health systems are institutions of social control which serve the powerful in labelling and confining those who threaten the social order due to their perceived dangerous and non-conforming behaviour (Becker, 1963; Scheff, 1966). Such institutions are serving a fundamentally moral purpose in society; the professionals within them are understood as 'moral entrepreneurs' responsible for reinforcing and reproducing dominant social norms and values while punishing deviations from these.

As we have clearly seen, immorality has been conceptualised as pathology by criminologists and psychiatrists since the beginning of their professions. As conduits for the powerful, these professions have supported the status quo through incarcerating and labelling 'problem' populations as criminal and/or mentally disordered. Through such analysis we can then understand why those in the suffragette movement, for example, were typically labelled by psychiatry as suffering from the biological condition of 'hysteria', and often confined in one institution or another and 'treated' predominantly by physicians (Showalter, 1985, p. 145). As one of the symptoms for antisocial personality disorder in the DSM-5 makes clear, you may have this mental illness if you fail 'to conform to social norms with respect to lawful behaviors, as indicated by repeatedly performing acts that are grounds for arrest' (APA, 2013, p. 659).

As with the criminal justice system, the mental health system plays an obvious social control role here, labelling acts of social deviance (including the committing of unlawful acts) as 'mad' as well as 'bad'. Where we see the two institutions working together more frequently is when the social deviance is perceived as being particularly 'dangerous' in some way (as the suffragettes were to patriarchal society). Yet as Foucault (1988, p. 191, original emphasis) reminds us, '[t]o be dangerous *is not an offense*. To be dangerous *is not an illness*. It is not a symptom. And yet we have come, as if it is self-evident, and for over a century now, to use the notion of danger, by a perpetual movement backwards and forwards between the penal and the medical.'

According to Conrad and Schneider (1992), over time we have seen a change in the lead institutions responsible for designations of social deviance in Western society, from the religious in feudal society, to the criminal in industrial society, and more recently the medical in the modern, scientific era. Thus, understandings of deviant behaviour have likewise shifted from sin to crime and then sickness. For example, once considered a sin against God and then a crime, alcoholism is now considered a disease ('alcoholic use disorder' is a current mental illness in the DSM-5 [APA, 2013, pp. 490–497]). Previously subject to religious and criminal sanctions, homosexuality was more recently considered a mental illness by Western psychiatry (Kutchins & Kirk, 1997, pp. 55–99). The implication from Conrad and Schneider's (1992) work is that designations of social deviance increasingly fall under the purview of medicine; significant to this discussion, behaviour that was previously criminalised is now more likely to be medicalised (more precisely here, we might say 'psychiatrised' or 'psychologised') and falls under the jurisdiction of such medical authorities. Acts of juvenile delinquency, for example, are increasingly being seen by mental health experts as symptoms of a 'neuro-disability' (such as attention deficit hyperactivity disorder [ADHD] or autism spectrum disorder [ASD]); in New Zealand, medical professionals are now estimating that between 60 and 90 per cent of youth offenders may be affected by such a disorder (Lynch, 2016, p. 7). This analysis helps us to understand how designations of mental illness are generally increasing in society (Cohen, 2016, pp. 2–3), including within the criminal justice system (Brandt, 2012; Indig et al., 2016, pp. v–vii).

As noted, since its modern beginnings psychiatry has been interested in theorising aspects of criminal behaviour as symptoms of mental illness, and labels associated with criminal pathology such as antisocial personality disorder, oppositional defiance disorder, and conduct disorder have become increasingly common over time. Since deinstitutionalisation, however, the mental health system has been forced to expand its practices into arenas outside of the psychiatric hospital, including the work, home, and school environments (for a full discussion, see Cohen, 2016). Similarly, the criminal justice system can be understood as another arena where this medical expansion has taken place, hence the increased number of psychiatric and related professionals working in courts and prisons, the increased labelling of the accused and convicted as 'mentally ill,' and the constant call for more mental health services to fill perceived gaps, especially in prisons. This medical expansionism serves the interests of not only mental health professionals themselves, but also the criminal justice system, the capitalist economy, and the ruling elites.

Scholars such as Moran (1992, p. 222) have previously noted that the increasing medicalisation of the criminal justice system has the advantage of attempting to 'humanise' what remains a fundamentally punitive system of 'justice', with psychiatric treatment measures also being useful management tools for staff dealing with 'difficult' prisoners. Claims that prisons are the largest institutions housing people with mental health issues today suggests that such institutions should be seen by the public as places of health rehabilitation rather than punishment, despite the reality to the contrary. The increased profile of mental health issues in prison has led not only to the deployment of more medical professionals in this environment, but also to increased revenue streams for associated mental health industries, most obviously the sales of anti-psychotics and antidepressants, which benefit the bottom line of pharmaceutical corporations.

Yet perhaps of most significance here is the successful labelling of nearly the entire prison population with some form of mental illness, while similar claims have been made about the extraordinarily high prevalence of neuro-disabilities and other 'syndromes' and 'disorders' in the youth offender population (see Gibbs, chapter 29 this volume). Marxist scholars argue that the successful application of these labels serves the interests of economic elites in society by pathologising criminals, thereby neutralising the fundamentally political nature of the criminal justice system in capitalist society (Cohen, 2016; Wacquant, 2009). As Moran (1992) has stated of the medicalisation of crime:

> To conceive of crime in medical terms is to depoliticize and remove moral judgment from the behavior in question. Much as the label 'crime' allows no attention to the social environment, 'sickness' removes the offending act and actor even farther from any political and ethical context. Under this definition, crime becomes a question of the individual's ability to 'adjust' ultimately to the status quo (p. 222).

Further, the reduction of criminal behaviour to disease by mental health professionals also offers continuing justification for the expansion of the prison–industrial complex in countries like New Zealand in the face of falling crime rates; now that psychiatric hospital beds are scarce, it is implied through this discourse that the incarcerated have become a greater threat to the community and require extended 'rehabilitation' in such facilities.

Using these critical arguments in the context of New Zealand, we can then understand the historical and contemporary over-representation of working-class people within the criminal justice and mental health systems as the continued social control of the 'dangerous classes'. Under-represented in the local criminal justice system, we nevertheless find that local working-class women in prisons are more likely to be victims of 'double deviance' (Busfield, 1996), not only criminalised but more likely to also be labelled with mental illnesses in comparison to men. Of most concern, however, has been the way in which Māori have been marked through these systems of social control as violent, dangerous, criminal, and mentally ill since the cultural renaissance and political struggles against New Zealand's colonial hegemony in the 1960s and 1970s (Cohen, 2014). While only 15 per cent of the total population of New Zealand, Māori make up over half the prison population (Stanley & Mihaere, 2019, p. 3). They are also twice as likely to be incarcerated in a psychiatric facility, and more than three times more likely to be labelled as 'schizophrenic' compared to any other ethnic group (Baxter, 2008, pp. 108, 130). As Harcourt (2011) points out, deinstitutionalisation was a heavily racialised process, with the proportion of minority and Indigenous groups incarcerated increasing over time, based 'heavily on predictions of future dangerousness' (p. 85). Anticolonial and civil rights struggles across the globe saw young black men particularly targeted with such labels of 'dangerousness' by both the criminal justice and mental health systems during this period (see for example, Fernando, 2010; Metzl, 2009). New Zealand has produced a similar response, with a dramatic increase in the criminalisation and medicalisation of a politically conscious Indigenous population (Walker, 1990) since the 1970s (Cohen, 2014).

CONCLUSION

Giving criminological consideration to the issue of mental health means not only engaging with the research evidence and range of theoretical ideas available, but also critically reflecting upon these in the light of the present structures of society through which some ideas become dominant while others are overlooked or invalidated. Typically, in a settler society such as Aotearoa New Zealand, we witness the dominance of positivist criminology, which ignores its own history as part of the colonial project and instead believes that the causes (as well as the remedies) for crime are almost within our reach. It is believed that crime is a 'fact' of our society, that it can be accurately measured, and, as we have seen, that mental pathology has considerable and substantive linkage to such criminal behaviour. Yet careful reflection of the topic reveals not only the spurious nature of such a linkage but also serious validity issues with both concepts. As a result, students of criminology cannot avoid consideration of critical scholarship that reflects upon the important questions of why such inaccurate knowledge continues to dominate. That being said, it is noticeable how sparse critical research on the topic remains. Criminologists may be reticent to follow biological models, but they are still prone to reproducing conservative, sociological argumentation which inevitably concludes with a call for more mental health services for those 'at risk' of committing crime. Rectifying this obvious research gap within the literature is crucial for progressing our knowledge of the ongoing dynamics that place criminality and mental illness in similar analytical spaces.

Used to pathologise Indigenous peoples in the colonial space, labels of social deviance have been a very effective means by which Pākehā have silenced political and social change in New Zealand. While the cultural renaissance achieved some notable successes in acknowledging and seeking redress for colonial violence and European land occupation, Māori have paid an especially heavy price through the fragmentation of whānau, hapū, and iwi due to victimisation at the hands of both the criminal justice and mental health systems. These systems are (neo) colonial institutions, they serve the needs of the powerful, they forward an ideology of 'dangerousness' of the working classes and minority communities, they promote and protect professional interests, and they also produce surplus value for capitalism. A decolonisation of New Zealand would, therefore, necessarily involve the reduction and ultimate abolition of these systems of social control. The state has normalised such institutions as necessary for society (Cohen, 2016; Stanley & Mihaere, 2019), and yet, as we have discussed here, the dominant practices of mental health and criminal justice workers are not based on any accurate 'science' of their profession, but rather are oriented towards labelling and confining the least powerful (and the least dangerous) in the protection of the interests of the powerful. These colonial institutions have existed on this soil for only two hundred years, yet have inflicted great damage on our communities. As critical criminologists we must debate, challenge, and protest the continuing existence of such places which turn social and political action into criminality and mental illness.

STUDY QUESTIONS

- What are the key limitations of conservative theories (both biological and social) on crime and mental illness?

- Why should professionals in both the criminal justice and mental health systems be considered as moral entrepreneurs?

- Who benefits from the increasing medicalisation of criminal behaviour and in what ways?

FURTHER READING

Conrad, P., & Schneider, J. (1992). *Deviance and medicalization: From badness to sickness* (rev. ed.). Philadelphia, PA: Temple University Press.

Kutchins, H., & Kirk, S. A. (1997). *Making us crazy: DSM: The psychiatric bible and the creation of mental disorders*. New York, NY: Free Press.

Scull, A. (2015). *Madness in civilization: A cultural history of insanity, from the Bible to Freud, from the madhouse to modern medicine*. Princeton, NJ: Princeton University Press.

REFERENCES

Allsopp, K., Read, J., Corcoran, R., & Kinderman, P. (2019). Heterogeneity in psychiatric diagnostic classification. *Psychiatry Research, 279*, 15–22. doi:10.1016/j.psychres.2019.07.005

American Psychiatric Association (APA). (2013). *Diagnostic and statistical manual of mental disorders* (5th ed.) (DSM–5). Arlington, VA: American Psychiatric Association.

Appleby, L., Kapur, N., Shaw, J., Hunt, I. M., Ibrahim, S., Gianatsi, M., . . . Burns, J. (2018). *The National Confidential Inquiry into Suicide and Safety in Mental Health: Annual report: England, Northern Ireland, Scotland, Wales*. Manchester, UK: University of Manchester. Retrieved from http://documents.manchester.ac.uk/display.aspx?DocID=38469

Baxter, J. (2008). *Māori mental health needs profile: A review of the evidence*. Palmerston North, New Zealand: Te Rau Matatini. Retrieved from https://www.mentalhealth.org.nz/assets/ResourceFinder/Maori-Mental-Health-Need-Profile-full.pdf

Becker, H. S. (1963). *Outsiders: Studies in the sociology of deviance*. New York, NY: Free Press.

Brandt, A. L. S. (2012). Treatment of persons with mental illness in the criminal justice system: A literature review. *Journal of Offender Rehabilitation, 51*(8), 541–558. doi:10.1080/10509674.2012.693902

Breggin, P. R., & Breggin, G. R. (1998). *The war against children of color: Psychiatry targets inner city youth*. Monroe, MO: Common Courage Press.

Brownstein, H. H. (2000). The social production of crime statistics. *Justice Research and Policy, 2*(2), 73–89. doi:10.3818/JRP.2.2.2000.73

Burrell, B., & Trip, H. (2011). Reform and community care: Has de-institutionalisation delivered for people with intellectual disability? *Nursing Inquiry, 18*(2), 174–183. doi:10.1111/j.1440-1800.2011.00522.x

Burstow, B. (2015). *Psychiatry and the business of madness: An ethical and epistemological accounting*. New York, NY: Palgrave Macmillan.

Busfield, J. (1996). *Men, women and madness: Understanding gender and mental disorder*. Houndmills, UK: Macmillan Press.

Cohen, B. M. Z. (2014). Passive-aggressive: Māori resistance and the continuance of colonial psychiatry in Aotearoa New Zealand. *Disability and the Global South: An International Journal, 1*(2), 319–339. Retrieved from https://disabilityglobalsouth.files.wordpress.com/2012/06/dgs-01-02-07.pdf

Cohen, B. M. Z. (2016). *Psychiatric hegemony: A Marxist theory of mental illness.* London, UK: Palgrave Macmillan.

Coleborne, C., & MacKinnon, D. (2006). Psychiatry and its institutions in Australia and New Zealand: An overview. *International Review of Psychiatry, 18*(4), 371–380. doi:10.1080/09540260600813248

Conrad, P., & Schneider, J. (1992). *Deviance and medicalization: From badness to sickness* (rev. ed.). Philadelphia, PA: Temple University Press.

Cox, C., & Marland, H. (2018). 'We are recreating Bedlam': A history of mental illness and prison systems in England and Ireland. In A. Mills & K. Kendall (Eds.), *Mental health in prisons: Critical perspectives on treatment and confinement* (pp. 25–47). Cham, Switzerland: Springer Nature.

Crampton, P., & Parkin, C. (2007). Warrior genes and risk-taking science. *Aotearoa New Zealand Medical Journal, 120*(1250). Retrieved from http://citeseerx.ist.psu.edu/viewdoc/download?doi=10.1.1.499.5774&rep=rep1&type=pdf

Curran, D. J., & Renzetti, C. M. (2001). *Theories of crime* (2nd ed.). Needham Heights, MA: Allyn & Bacon.

Dean, K., Laursen, T. M., Pedersen, C. B., Webb, R. T., Mortensen, P. B., & Agerbo, E. (2018). Risk of being subjected to crime, including violent crime, after onset of mental illness: A Danish national registry study using police data. *JAMA Psychiatry, 75*(7), 689–696. doi:10.1001/jamapsychiatry.2018.0534

Department of Corrections. (n.d.). *Change lives shape futures: Investing in better mental health for offenders.* Wellington, New Zealand: Department of Corrections. Retrieved from https://www.corrections.govt.nz/__data/assets/pdf_file/0018/30528/Corrections_Womens_Strategy_August_2017_web.pdf

Erickson, P. E., & Erickson, S. K. (2008). *Crime, punishment, and mental illness: Law and the behavioral sciences in conflict.* New Brunswick, NJ: Rutgers University Press.

Faris, R. E. L., & Dunham, H. W. (1939). *Mental disorders in urban areas: An ecological study of schizophrenia and other psychoses.* Chicago, IL: University of Chicago Press.

Fernando, S. (2010). *Mental health, race and culture* (3rd ed.). Houndmills, UK: Palgrave Macmillan.

Foucault, M. (1988). *Politics, philosophy, culture: Interviews and other writings, 1977–1984.* New York, NY: Routledge.

Gibbs, A., & Sherwood, K. (2017). Putting fetal alcohol spectrum disorder (FASD) on the map in New Zealand: A review of health, social, political, justice and cultural developments. *Psychiatry, Psychology and Law, 24*(6), 825–842. doi:10.1080/13218719.2017.1315784

Harcourt, B. E. (2011). Reducing mass incarceration: Lessons from the deinstitutionalization of mental hospitals in the 1960s. *Ohio State Journal of Criminal Law, 9*(1), 53–88. doi:10.2139/ssrn.1748796

Holman, G., O'Brien, A. J., & Thom, K. (2018). Police and mental health responses to mental health crisis in the Waikato region of New Zealand. *International Journal of Mental Health Nursing, 27*(5), 1411–1419. doi:10.1111/inm.12440

Indig, D., Gear, C., & Wilhelm, K. (2016). *Comorbid substance use disorders and mental health disorders among New Zealand prisoners.* Wellington, New Zealand: Department of Corrections. Retrieved from https://www.corrections.govt.nz/resources/research_and_statistics/comorbid_substance_use_disorders_and_mental_health_disorders_among_new_zealand_prisoners

Keshavan, M. S., & Shah, J. L. (2013). Violence and mental illness. *Asian Journal of Psychiatry, 6*(1), 1–2. doi:10.1016/j.ajp.2013.01.001

Khalifeh, H., Johnson, S., Howard, L. M., Borschmann, R., Osborn, D., Dean, K., . . . Moran, P. (2015). Violent and non-violent crime against adults with severe mental illness. *The British Journal of Psychiatry, 206*(4), 275–282. doi:10.1192/bjp.bp.114.147843

Kim, D. Y. (2016). Psychiatric deinstitutionalization and prison population growth: A critical literature review and its implications. *Criminal Justice Policy Review, 27*(1), 3–21. doi:10.1177/0887403414547043

Kimball, S. (2019, August 4). Trump says mass shootings in El Paso and Dayton are a 'mental illness problem'. *CNBC.* Retrieved from https://www.cnbc.com/2019/08/04/trump-says-hate-has-no-place-in-our-country-after-shootings-in-dayton-and-el-paso.html

Kutchins, H., & Kirk, S. A. (1997). *Making us crazy: DSM: The psychiatric bible and the creation of mental disorders.* New York, NY: Free Press.

Lambie, I., Best, C., Ioane, J., Becroft, A., & Polaschek, C. (2016). What every judge and lawyer needs to know about s.333 psychiatric/psychological court reports. *New Zealand Law Journal, 1,* 24–37.

Lombroso, C. (2006/1911). *Criminal man.* (M. Gibson & N. H. Rafter, Trans.). Durham, NC: Duke University Press.

Lynch, N. (2016). *Neurodisability in the youth justice system in New Zealand: How vulnerability intersects with justice.* Dyslexia Foundation of New Zealand: Summarising the contributions of participants at the 2016 Neurodisabilities Forum, hosted by DFNZ in Wellington. Retrieved from http://neurodisabilitiesforum.org.nz/wp-content/uploads/2016/05/Neurodisabilities-Forum–2016-Report–1.pdf

Maniglio, R. (2009). Severe mental illness and criminal victimization: A systematic review. *Acta Psychiatrica Scandinavica, 119*(3), 180–191. doi:10.1111/j.1600–0447.2008.01300.x

Markowitz, F. E. (2011a). Dysfunctional social control of mental illness: A commentary on Yoon. *Social Science and Medicine, 72*(4), 456–459. doi:10.1016/j.socscimed.2010.11.013

Markowitz, F. E. (2011b). Mental illness, crime, and violence: Risk, context, and social control. *Aggression and Violent Behavior, 16*(1), 36–44. doi:10.1016/j.avb.2010.10.003

Metzl, J. M. (2009). *The protest psychosis: How schizophrenia became a black disease.* Boston, MA: Beacon Press.

Mills, A., & Kendall, K. (2018). Introduction. In A. Mills & K. Kendall (Eds.), *Mental health in prisons: Critical perspectives on treatment and confinement* (pp. 1–22). Cham, Switzerland: Springer Nature.

Moran, R. (1992). Medicine and crime: The search for the born criminal and the medical control of criminality. In P. Conrad & J. Schneider (Eds.), *Deviance and medicalization: From badness to sickness* (pp. 215–240). Philadelphia, PA: Temple University Press.

Oleson, J. C. (2016). *Criminal genius: A portrait of high-IQ offenders.* Oakland, CA: University of California.

Page, S. (2019, August 8). Americans dig at roots of violence. *USA Today.* Retrieved from https://www.pressreader.com/usa/usa-today-international-edition/20190808/281535112614551

Primeau, A., Bowers, T. G., Harrison, M. A., & Xu, X. (2013). Deinstitutionalization of the mentally ill: Evidence for transinstitutionalization from psychiatric hospitals to penal institutions. *Comprehensive Psychology, 2*(2), 1–10. doi:10.2466/16.02.13.CP.2.2

Scheff, T. J. (1966). *Being mentally ill: A sociological theory.* Chicago, IL: Aldine Transaction.

Showalter, E. (1985). *The female malady: Women, madness, and English culture, 1830–1980.* New York, NY: Penguin.

Siegel, L. J. (2007). *Criminology: The core* (5th ed.). Stamford, CT: Cengage.

Stanley, E., & Mihaere, R. (2019). The problems and promise of international rights in the challenge to Māori imprisonment. *International Journal for Crime, Justice and Social Democracy, 8*(1), 1–17. doi:10.5204/ijcjsd.v8i1.1045

Star-Sun. (1954, August 28, p. 3). Symptoms enumerated. Retrieved from http://christchurchcitylibraries.com/Heritage/Digitised/ParkerHulme/pdf/page12.pdf

Teplin, L. A., McClelland, G. M., Abram, K. M., & Weiner, D. A. (2005). Crime victimization in adults with severe mental illness: Comparison with the National Crime Victimization Survey. *Archives of Genral Psychiatry, 62*(8), 911–921. doi:10.1001/archpsyc.62.8.911

Tiihonen, J., Rautiainen, M-R., Ollila, H. M., Repo-Tiihonen, E., Virkkunen, M., Palotie, A., . . . Paunio, T. (2015). Genetic background of extreme violent behavior. *Molecular Psychiatry, 20*(6), 786–792. doi:10.1038/mp.2014.130

Turner, C. (2007). Ethical issues in criminal justice administration. *American Jails, 20*(6), 49–53.

US Bureau of Justice Statistics. (1999). *Correctional populations in the United States, 1996*. Washington, DC: U.S. Department of Justice. Retrieved from https://www.bjs.gov/index.cfm?ty=pbse&sid=5

Wacquant, L. J. D. (2009). *Punishing the poor: The neoliberal government of social insecurity*. Durham, NC: Duke University Press.

Walker, R. (1990). *Ka whawhai tonu matou: Struggle without end*. Auckland, New Zealand: Penguin.

Whitaker, R., & Cosgrove, L. (2015). *Psychiatry under the influence: Institutional corruption, social injury, and prescriptions for reform*. New York, NY: Palgrave Macmillan.

Wilkinson, R., & Pickett, K. (2010). *The spirit level: Why equality is better for everyone* (rev. ed.) London, UK: Penguin.

Williams, C. (2019, March 20). Mental illness no excuse for Christchurch mosque shooting, says Mental Health Foundation. *Stuff*. Retrieved from https://www.stuff.co.nz/national/christchurch-shooting/111422166/mental-illness-no-excuse-for-christchurch-mosque-shooting-says-mental-health-foundation

Wu, X., & Zhang, X. (2016). Automated inference on criminality using face images. *arXiv*. Retrieved from https://www.semanticscholar.org/paper/Automated-Inference-on-Criminality-using-Face-Wu-Zhang/1cd357b675a659413e8abf2eafad2a463272a85f

Yoon, J. (2011). Effect of increased private share of inpatient psychiatric resources on jail population growth: Evidence from the United States. *Social Science and Medicine, 72*(4), 447–455. doi:10.1016/j.socscimed.2010.07.023

29

Neuro-disabilities and Criminal Justice
Time for a Radical Rethink

Anita Gibbs

Over the past 20 years in Aotearoa New Zealand, there has been a growing awareness of how having a neuro-disability – from an acquired brain injury, or being prenatally exposed to alcohol (leading to foetal alcohol spectrum disorder, FASD), or having autism spectrum disorder (ASD) or attention deficit hyperactivity disorder (ADHD) – increases the vulnerability of children, youth, and adults to both victimisation and criminalisation. For example, Lynch (2016) reported on a Wellington gathering of 60 key stakeholders who explored neuro-disability in the New Zealand youth justice system. Lynch noted the significant vulnerability of people with neuro-disabilities at all stages of the justice system, pointing out that some form of neuro-impairment could affect more than 60 per cent of youth offenders. Recent studies from Australia and Canada have reiterated these numbers (Bower et al., 2018; McLachlan et al., 2019).

Several notable Youth Court judges, including former principal Youth Court judge Andrew Becroft (now Children's Commissioner), have been particularly vocal in highlighting the need for New Zealand to ascertain the prevalence rates of neuro-disabilities and provide neuro-informed criminal justice policies and practices (Gibbs & Sherwood, 2017; Lambie et al., 2016; Lynch, 2016). Yet, due to a lack of research both internationally and here in New Zealand, the vast majority of the criminal justice population remains unscreened, misdiagnosed, or 'hidden' from a diagnosis (Fast & Conroy, 2009; Flannigan et al., 2018; Gibbs & Sherwood, 2017; McLachlan et al., 2019).

Against this backdrop, this chapter explores neuro-disabilities in the criminal justice system, which are as common as mental health issues but are often 'hidden' due to a lack of diagnoses as well as an inability of justice professionals to believe that offenders, in particular, might have a disability that requires accommodations rather than punishment. This chapter considers the prevalence of neuro-disabilities, the main impairments as they relate to criminal justice involvement, and the impacts of having neuro-disabilities ignored or discounted. It identifies the practices that can ameliorate or improve the lives of those with neuro-disabilities, and ends with a critical discussion on how the acceptance of neuro-disabilities establishes a need to radically rethink how we view offenders.

THE PREVALENCE OF NEURO-DISABILITIES IN CRIMINAL JUSTICE

In a ground-breaking international study, Hughes and colleagues identified the prevalence of neuro-disabilities in the youth criminal justice population (Hughes et al., 2012). They noted significant prevalence rates for: traumatic/acquired brain injury (TBI) (more than 65 per cent); FASD (10.9–11.7 per cent); ASD (15 per cent); ADHD (12 per cent); and a range of other neuro-impairments. In New Zealand, we have recent data on TBI prevalence in the prison population, showing that 64 per cent of prisoners have had at least one TBI, and 32.5 per cent have had multiple TBIs (Mitchell et al., 2017). However, for most neuro-disabilities we are reliant on the international evidence.

Two recent international studies have identified high rates of FASD in offending populations, namely, 17.5 per cent in Canada and 36 per cent in Australia (Bower et al., 2018; McLachlan et al., 2019). These rates are extremely high given the accepted prevalence of FASD as being 2–5 per cent of the general population (McLachlan et al., 2019). These studies also reported that 89–93 per cent of the criminal justice populations had at least one severe neuro-cognitive impairment. Alongside this impairment, criminal justice populations have more than a 90 per cent chance of a co-occurring mental health disorder, as well as substance misuse disorders, and a host of other serious challenges (Brown et al., 2014; Fast & Conroy, 2009; Streissguth et al., 1996; Streissguth et al., 2004; Wozniak et al., 2019). Indeed, as discussed below, it is hard to separate the cognitive impairment from additional co-morbid conditions.

The Banksia study in Western Australia (Bower et al., 2018) is perhaps the most 'local' compelling study of neuro-impairments in an incarcerated population to date. The Banksia study noted that 65 per cent of incarcerated youth had at least three areas of neuro-impairment, including impairments in memory, executive function, and attention. Of the study population, 25 per cent would have met the criteria for an intellectual disability, and 73 per cent were Indigenous. These worrying statistics mirror data from other criminal justice studies, and confirm that vulnerable groups are likely to have higher rates of neuro-disability and TBI (Fast & Conroy, 2009; Flannigan et al., 2018; Lynch, 2016; McLachlan et al., 2019; Mitchell et al., 2017).

Vulnerable populations are also more likely to come from groups that have experienced social deprivation, oppression, colonisation, intergenerational trauma, and racialised practices of discrimination (Bower et al., 2018; Flannigan et al., 2018; Gibbs & Sherwood, 2017; McLachlan et al., 2019; Stewart & Glowatski, 2018). Prevalence rates for neuro-disabilities are notably much higher in populations that have been in state care, those with backgrounds of neglect and abuse, and those with parental substance misuse (Flannigan et al., 2018; McLachlan et al., 2019). In the New Zealand study on TBI prevalence, adults with a TBI history were more likely to be sent to prison than their siblings without such a history (Mitchell et al., 2017). We lack robust or detailed data on the kinds of offences that offenders with neuro-disabilities may commit, but a few studies have shown that crimes including theft, burglary, and verbal or physical assaults are common (Flannigan et al., 2018; Mitchell et al., 2017; Streissguth et al., 1996; Young et al., 2011).

PRIMARY IMPAIRMENTS AND SECONDARY CHALLENGES

Neuro-disabilities are likely to be lifelong, with a range of physical, cognitive, emotional, and behavioural impairments (Rutman, 2016; Streissguth et al., 1996; Wozniak et al., 2019). Functional deficits or primary lifelong impairments will directly affect day-to-day functioning, and secondary challenges are those conditions arising from a lack of services, supports, or accommodations to help individuals flourish with their primary impairments (Streissguth et al., 1996). Typical primary impairments include: executive functioning challenges; poor working memory; impulsiveness; attention and concentration issues; difficulty with abstraction and generalising information; slower cognitive processing; problems understanding cause and effect; poor adaptive and social skills; poor self-regulation; and communication difficulties (Fast & Conroy, 2009; Lambie et al., 2016; Wozniak et al., 2019; Young et al., 2011). Other issues that can impact those with neuro-disabilities might be sleep disorders, feeding difficulties, motor control impairments, ear and eye problems, a higher risk of autoimmune diseases, and a range of other physical conditions which are higher than that expected in general populations (Wozniak et al., 2019; Young et al., 2011).

The helpful mnemonic ALARMERS, based on the work of Fast and Conroy (2009), is used by educators to summarise the main neuro-impairments of FASD, but it applies also to impairments faced by those with ASD, ADHD, TBI, and a range of other neuro-disabilities.[1]

- **Attention**. People with neuro-disabilities are likely to struggle with short attention spans, or they become easily distracted by events that draw their attention and focus away from the task at hand. They might find it hard to concentrate. However, they might also be able to devote an inordinate amount of attention to one particular task, which can be a strength and a weakness. People with attention issues (most notably ADHD) are also highly likely to have challenges with impulsiveness and reasoning capacity (see 'Reasoning' below). This can lead to all sorts of difficulties in relationships with others.
- **Language**. Often people with neuro-disabilities can have strengths in expressive language, yet really struggle with comprehension and receptive language. They might appear articulate, but then struggle with instructions, if such instructions are overly complicated. Communication skill impairments are estimated to affect 60–90 per cent of the youth justice population (Hughes et al., 2012). Dyslexia affects at least 50 per cent of the prison population (Lynch, 2016).
- **Adaptive behaviours** (life skills). Adaptive functioning is a key issue for those people struggling with neuro-disabilities, affecting them at all stages of early childhood and on through the life course to adulthood. Adaptive challenges may include: dressing, showering and feeding oneself; keeping to a timetable or maintaining attendance at school or employment; managing money; finding and keeping accommodation; and many other daily tasks that those without neuro-disabilities take for granted.
- **Reasoning**. This is a crucial primary impairment. If a young person has a neuro-disability it is quite likely that their ability to ascertain cause and effect, or to weigh up the consequences of actions, or simply learn to be safe over time, will be substantially impaired. Often this is where a young person may be described as behaving at a much younger level (having dysmaturity) than their chronological age would suggest. When reasoning is impaired, young people are far more likely to take risks. For some young people it is as if, like a much

younger toddler, they do not have a 'stop' button. They will act before they think. When reasoning is impacted it is also likely that the person will appear unable to empathise or understand when they may have upset someone.
- **Memory**. Memory impairments can lead to distress and confusion, as well as endless repetition and confabulation or 'filling in the gaps' to make a story sound convincing. Memory issues will affect learning in a range of areas: basic life and academic skills, learning to get on with others, learning about ownership, and following instructions.
- **Executive functioning**. This is another significant brain domain where impairments impact a person's overall capabilities. People have problems with judgement, planning, problem-solving, completion of tasks, regulating and controlling behaviour, and decision-making, and they may be disinhibited or unable to keep their thoughts to themselves. They might also be rigid in their thinking, such that attempts to reason with them are unlikely to succeed. This rigid thinking is also known as 'cognitive rigidity' or 'perseveration'.
- **Regulation of body functions**. People with neuro-impairments are likely to have issues recognising aspects of bodily signals, such as when they are hot or cold, or full or hungry, or tired.
- **Sensory issues**. People might be hyper- or hyposensitive to all sorts of noises, sights, sounds, and a range of other sensory stimuli, to a far greater degree than neuro-typical people. Sensory overload can lead to emotional outbursts or extreme anxiety, leading to 'meltdowns', which in turn may lead to verbal or physical aggression. If people with sensory processing issues are hyposensitive, they might actively seek risky sensory experiences and become distressed.

None of these primary impairments in themselves should necessarily lead to outcomes that severely disadvantage those who have them, yet they often do lead to what can be described as problematic or secondary challenges. The interactions between a person's primary impairments and the social, educational, and cultural environments they engage with often lead to stigma, misunderstanding, negative reactions and a lack of accommodations, exclusion, rejection, distress, and chaos. Sadly, in the FASD field in particular, where most research has been undertaken, the impacts include: problems at school or low academic achievement; misuse of substances; experience of care placements; getting into trouble with the law; prison experiences; victimisation; mental health issues; suicide attempts; problems with accommodation and employment; and problems with sexual behaviours or high risk of teen pregnancy (Fast & Conroy, 2009; Flannigan et al., 2018; Pei et al., 2016; Streissguth et al., 1996, 2004).

Protective factors

A number of protective factors outlined by Streissguth et al. (1996, 2004) have offered those with neuro-impairments better outcomes than those without protective factors. The protective factors are: living in stable, nurturing homes; not having been a victim of violence; having early intervention because of an early diagnosis; remaining in education; and not having problems with substance misuse. A number of these protective factors point to significant environmental supports that mitigate the negative impacts of primary impairments, and ameliorate the entitlement to services and funding. For example, having an IQ of less than 70 is a protective factor, as it is an official indicator for intellectual disability and therefore leads to funded support and services (Fast & Conroy, 2009). Studies of FASD subjects show that about 30 per cent or less have an IQ of below 70, and therefore only those people would qualify for extra financial and service support for having a neuro-disability, regardless of the scale of their impairments or cognitive functional capacity (Bower at al., 2018; McLachlan et al., 2019; Streissguth et al., 1996).

WHERE PRIMARY IMPAIRMENTS INTERSECT WITH CRIMINAL JUSTICE

There is a growing literature detailing the vulnerability to both criminal justice involvement and victimisation among people with neuro-disabilities (Brown et al., 2014; Fast & Conroy, 2009; Flannigan et al., 2018; Lambie et al., 2016; Pei at al., 2016). If a person (child, youth, or adult) struggles to comprehend concepts of ownership, then stealing might become an issue. They might not be aware that an item which appears to be available to take belongs to someone else. The tendency of those with neuro-impairments to repeat the same mistakes over and over because of an inability to learn from mistakes or read social cues can also lead to trouble with the law. The poor self-regulation capacity of many of those with neuro-impairments means they may be less able to resist temptation or control their emotional responses, hence they can easily and suddenly lash out, damage things, use verbally aggressive language, or agree to participate in events that sound like a lot of fun but are likely to get them arrested (e.g., stealing clothes or alcohol from shops). Young people with neuro-impairments are likely to be easily led and swayed by their peers, or by older adults who promise them rewards.

ADHD symptoms can lead to conduct disorder, impulse responding, and chaotic behaviour (Fast & Conroy, 2009; Young et al., 2011), often with serious and unintended consequences. One recent example of spontaneous, high-risk, opportunistic behaviour was that of three Christchurch boys who stole a vehicle. Following a high-speed chase by the police, the driver lost control and crashed, killing all three boys, one of whom had ADHD and mental health issues (I. Stewart, 2019). Another example of tragic impulsiveness is that of Haami Hanara who, aged only 14 years, stabbed and killed 40-year-old Kelly Donner (*New Zealand Herald*, 2019). It was an impulsive and violent crime for which Haami was sentenced to life imprisonment, with a minimum of eight years in youth custody and prison. Haami had FASD and ADHD, additional learning challenges, and a background of disrupted education and a difficult childhood.

The suggestibility of those with neuro-impairments might also lead them to admit to crimes they did not commit. A classic example here is that of Teina Pora, a 17-year-old Māori male who was wrongfully convicted of rape and murder in 1994, and who went on to serve 21 years in prison (Gibbs, 2018; Gibbs & Sherwood, 2017). Teina was born with FASD, but this was not diagnosed until 2014, when an experienced neuro-psychologist assessed and diagnosed his FASD as part of the reviews into his case. Teina exhibited extensive confabulation during his police interviews. He filled gaps in his memory with material that, on investigation (many years later), was proven false. His 'storytelling' and confessions to serious offending were a crucial part of his original conviction. That Teina spent so long in prison is an example of a missed diagnosis leading to extremely serious consequences. Teina's reasoning age was assessed to be that of a nine-year-old. With hindsight it is easy to see how he ended up in prison; yet one wonders whether, if his FASD had been picked up as a child, his life might have been different (Gibbs, 2018).

The impact of neuro-disabilities on people, particularly in reasoning and cognitive functioning, can thus have far-reaching consequences. A person with memory issues will probably forget details of an incident and therefore may be unreliable as a witness or defendant, and may also become confused about arrest, legal, or court procedures. They are likely to have problems organising themselves and keeping appointments. Such adaptive challenges may mean that many of those with neuro-disabilities will leave school early, and will struggle to keep employment or stable accommodation, or manage money. All of which makes them vulnerable to becoming offenders or victims. Repeating the same mistakes over and over, and approaching tasks chaotically, means that offenders with neuro-impairments will struggle to learn from their mistakes or co-operate with consequence- or reasoning-based punishments.

Fast and Conroy (2009) noted the reality of dysmaturity as a feature of neuro-disability, where young people or adults present as much younger than their chronological age in some, but not all, areas of functioning. A classic example might be an 18-year-old who verbally communicates well or reads at an older age than their chronological age but, when assessed thoroughly, are found to have a social reasoning age of seven years and are thus unable to reason at an adult level. Linked to dysmaturity issues might be inappropriate sexual behaviour (Brown et al., 2014); this might include touching, advances, compulsions, and sexual assaults. Some of these may well lead to charges of sexual offending or becoming a victim of sexual assault, due to exploitation. Dysmaturity, alongside a failure to read social and visual clues as well as misreading them, can lead to adolescents in particular getting into trouble (Brown et al., 2014).

Perseveration – typified by demanding, 'bullying' or 'pushy', obsessive-compulsive, demand-avoidance, or oppositional behaviours – can lead to criminal justice charges. An individual with perseveration issues can appear to be stuck in their own concrete thinking and communication patterns, and cannot be persuaded to empathise or see another perspective. They appear to be very self-focused (or egocentric), and are often unable to take personal responsibility for actions, or to comply with instructions. This can give the misleading impression that the person is choosing to be difficult (Brown et al., 2014; Fast & Conroy, 2009); it may seem that individuals cannot be bothered to keep to court conditions or orders, for instance, and they may end up in jail for multiple breaches of bail and other conditions.

Offenders with neuro-disabilities are particularly vulnerable to becoming victims of the negative aspects of the criminal justice and mental health systems. Suicide rates for those in Corrections are higher than in the general population (McLachlan et al., 2019), and it has been estimated that as many as 23 per cent of people with FASD will attempt suicide at some point in their lives (Streissguth et al., 1996, 2004). The story of Tamaki Heke, a young man with FASD who died by suicide, was highlighted in 2019 as an example of how New Zealand systems fail to support those with neuro-disabilities in the community and in the mental health and criminal justice systems (Rosenburg, 2019).

It is important to note that is not inevitable that those with neuro-disabilities will end up in the criminal justice system; and even if they do, they may not become entrenched on a justice pathway. In fact, many of those with neuro-impairments have great strengths and qualities that, once supported and encouraged, can help them to flourish (Carel, 2017; Pei et al., 2016). Strengths might include creative and artistic flair, confidence in communication skills, or willingness to explore new opportunities. Often the same people can have incredible talents and significant challenges. It is important that those who express a neuro-diverse approach to life have the right accommodations and supports, combined with strength-based responses from others.

Two studies with offenders (Currie et al., 2016; Pei et al., 2016) noted that where early diagnosis, structure, supervision, and support were provided, contact with the criminal justice system reduced. In both studies, a strengths-based approach by human service and Corrections professionals was valued, as was ongoing support for caregivers by professionals. Offenders with FASD noted their strengths as being kind, resilient, artistic, interested, and good at hands-on and physical activities. Accordingly, we now turn to criminal justice responses and interventions that can promote systemic best practice to support the well-being of those with neuro-disabilities.

CRIMINAL JUSTICE RESPONSES AND INTERVENTIONS TO NEURO-DISABILITY

Due to a lack of recognition, as well as research, criminal justice responses and interventions for neuro-disability have been somewhat non-existent in Aotearoa New Zealand (Gibbs & Sherwood, 2017; Lynch, 2016). There are, however, some promising projects under way. For example, the Benchmark project is an online initiative, funded with support from the Law Foundation and IHC, that provides a range of evidence-based resources to help legal and other professionals provide the best possible advice and care towards vulnerable people, especially those with intellectual and neurological disabilities.[2] Judges have also called for the increased use of psychiatric and psychological reports in courts to identify neuro-disabilities, and to implement FASD-informed criminal justice practices (Gibbs & Sherwood, 2017; Lambie et al., 2016). The work of the New Zealand youth justice system has also improved to better cater for the needs of youth with neuro-disabilities. For example, communication assistants are now more regularly provided for young people with communication challenges at court appearances, while neuro-disabilities are often now assessed through the use of the section 333 reports (Gibbs & Sherwood, 2017; Lambie et al., 2016).[3]

From international best evidence, responses to individuals with neuro-disabilities should be focused on accommodating impairments, building strengths, and reducing contact with criminal justice professionals and systems. Hence, best practice involves prevention from the earliest opportunity, and on through the provision of early diagnosis and intervention (Brown et al., 2014; Currie et al., 2016; Pei et al., 2016). Ideally, this should occur during primary school years. It may depend on whether or not a child is already struggling with communication, educational, and social and behavioural issues. Responses to the individual can be based on a range of options. It might include being consistent, giving simple and specific instructions, ensuring structure and adequate supervision, and having a focus on the strengths of a person (Evensen & Lutke, 1997; Gibbs et al., 2018; Pei et al., 2016; Rutman, 2016). Specific educational and social interventions – maths, social skills, and learning self-regulation – have had promising results, as have interventions involving advocacy, peer mentoring, and family or caregiver support (Gibbs et al., 2018; Rutman, 2016). An overall wraparound approach, involving case managers, has also been shown to be successful. There is also a need to recognise that some of those with neuro-disabilities need both targeted and lifelong supports (Gibbs et al., 2018; Pei et al., 2016; Rutman, 2016).

Increased awareness of the prevalence and impact of neuro-disabilities in the criminal justice system, and more training to help criminal justice professionals to be neuro-disability-informed, are necessary (Brown et al., 2014; Gibbs & Sherwood, 2017; Lambie et al., 2016; Lynch, 2016; McLachlan et al., 2019; Pei et al., 2016). Overseas, there are examples of specialist police officers with knowledge of neuro-impairments, and examples of using ID cards or medical alert systems to inform police that they are dealing with someone who has a neuro-disability (Fast & Conroy, 2009; Gibbs, 2018). There are also examples of neuro-disability courts which have recently been considered in New Zealand (Doogue & Walker, 2019), and a recent judgment in Wellington by Judge Hastings highlighted the importance of considering FASD as a mitigating factor.[4]

At every stage of the criminal system a neuro-informed approach is critical (Fast & Conroy, 2009; Young et al., 2011). During arrest and police interviewing, and at court, is it likely that someone with a neuro-disability will need help either from well-trained lawyers or lay advocates or communication assistants, as well as having social workers, probation staff, police, and judges who understand their complex needs and co-occurring problems. If judges are to give bail conditions or impose orders of any kind, then realistic bail support is required for those with neuro-disabilities, particularly because they are more likely to lead chaotic lives and will need extra support and supervision. Business-as-usual approaches will not work (Fast

& Conroy, 2009; District Court of New Zealand, 2019). Similarly, sentencing these offenders to reasoning programmes will not work. While structured employment, substance misuse, and other intervention programmes might help, it is the provision of facilitated or scaffolded support that will make such programmes successful (Stewart & Glowatski, 2018). There can be no substitute for extra assistance, advocacy, and communication help at all times. A report prepared by competent psychologists and other social and health professionals in both youth and adult criminal justice settings, and screening for neuro-impairments, must become far more typical in courts than is currently seen (Fast & Conroy, 2009; Lambie et al., 2016; Lynch, 2016). Multi-agency co-operation of the kind operating in the Youth Courts also now needs to increase in the adult courts, as those coming into criminal justice have multiple, cross-cutting, and complex needs that require ongoing assistance with compliance, accommodation, managing work and money, dealing with mental health needs, and accessing disability support services (District Court of New Zealand, 2019).

An important consideration is the potential over-representation of Māori in the population of those assessed and diagnosed with neuro-disabilities (Crawford, 2018; Gibbs & Sherwood, 2017). In Canada, the government has been called upon to undertake reforms in the criminal justice system to address the needs of offenders with FASD in particular (Stewart & Glowatski, 2018). There, the legacy of systemic racism and the residential school care system have deeply impacted the Canadian Indigenous people, and the call to action has focused on efforts to improve all aspects of the criminal justice system for those with FASD. Alternatives to mainstream sentences and imprisonment are suggested, alongside increased supports for community, corrections, and parole options (Stewart & Glowatski, 2018). In New Zealand, Crawford (2018) has proposed using Indigenous models based on building connectedness, belonging, and identity (that are already in use with kaupapa Māori practices) to help those with FASD.

PATHWAYS TO THE FUTURE

As noted above, in Aotearoa New Zealand there have been limited studies of the prevalence of neuro-disabilities, or best practices and interventions with the criminal justice population. There are, nonetheless, some new initiatives under way, including: a Corrections study of dyslexia; a social work dissertation exploring youth justice social work and FASD; plans to help young offenders with emotional regulation programmes; and ongoing training initiatives for criminal justice and health personnel (K. Katene, personal communication, 15 October 2019; Oatley, 2019; M. Stewart, 2019).[5] We clearly need a raft of robust research initiatives to develop strategies and practices that will ensure those with neuro-impairments are identified early and supported to live successful lives without, or with reduced, criminal justice involvement (Pei et al., 2016). We also need pathways out of offending that incorporate positive and inclusive options for disabled people.

A positive approach is to take the position that those with neuro-disabilities need extra support, and that they require the provision of opportunities to flourish in the same way as those who are not disabled (Carel, 2017; Gibbs et al., 2018; Goodley & Runswick-Cole, 2016; Young et al., 2011). This requires a radical rethink of how we view deviant behaviour and actions, and for the criminal justice system to seek disability-oriented supports and alternatives to justice interventions. Such supports will facilitate disability-based strategies that ameliorate and mitigate the worst excesses of punishment from standard criminal justice responses (Fast & Conroy, 2009; District Court of New Zealand, 2019). This is challenging, but small interventions can make a big difference towards achieving radical change (Gibbs et al., 2018; Stewart & Glowatski, 2018).

It is important to screen those with neuro-impairments as early as possible and ensure that disability rights dictate action. From a rights-based perspective it must be understood that those born with neuro-disabilities, and most of those acquiring brain injuries, did not choose the pathway of exclusion, stigmatisation, offending, or victimisation. Systemic, societal, and individual responses to those with neuro-disabilities often make a challenging life much more difficult. A helpful way of thinking about these issues comes from the work of Goodley and Runswick-Cole (2016) and Carel (2017). These authors discuss the view that people with disabilities need to have social barriers removed and to be able to participate in all aspects of society without discrimination. Carel (2017) especially notes that people with neuro-impairments should be able to flourish in spite of their 'deficits'. Goodley and Runswick-Cole (2016) discuss the concept of being 'Dis/Abled', giving people the right to present themselves as both able and disabled if they so choose. A DisAbled perspective allows those with neuro-disabilities to be empowered to be fully human and yet accepted as being fully diverse or different, and it also allows them to be fully included rather than excluded. A DisAbled perspective also allows those with a disability to educate those around them who are 'Able', as well as to occupy leadership positions and become positive role models of success. People with a DisAbled voice will be further encouraged by allies to become the 'new' teachers about their neuro-disability, and in doing so they will be able to 'Dis' (or challenge and reshape) normative assumptions and attitudes about neuro-disability.

Finally, alongside providing a voice to those with neuro-disabilities, we also need pathways aimed at systemic and political change. In New Zealand, some neuro-disabilities, such as ASD, qualify for funded disability supports, but notable others (e.g., FASD and ADHD) do not. This needs to change to ensure that all of those with neuro-disabilities have equitable access to funded services, and lifelong supports. To exclude some groups over others makes little sense and denies many of those in our prisons and corrections services the help they need.

CONCLUSION

This chapter has explored the extent of neuro-disability in Aotearoa New Zealand, and the impact it is likely to have when intersecting with the criminal justice system. People with neuro-disabilities have lifelong impairments, and many of these impairments make them vulnerable to arrest, conviction, and imprisonment. The lack of New Zealand research on prevalence or interventions hampers our understanding of the needs of both offenders and victims with a range of neuro-disabilities. In New Zealand, we also lack mechanisms or capacity for screening and diagnosing those with neuro-disabilities, especially before they engage with criminal justice agencies. Early action on these fronts is required. Few would argue that we should punish individuals for having a disability. We need radical alternatives to punishment for people born with neuro-disabilities and those acquiring brain injuries. By acknowledging and accommodating their impairments at early stages, in the same way as we accommodate those with obvious physical disabilities, and by supporting them fully and appropriately if/when they encounter the criminal justice system, we can start to prevent exclusion, stigma, and societal disapproval, while providing tangible supports aimed at inclusion, tolerance, and positive outcomes for all.

STUDY QUESTIONS

- What evidence-based strategies should criminal justice officials implement to help those with neuro-disabilities?
- What needs to be done to provide alternative pathways for people with neuro-disabilities to avoid criminal justice involvement?
- How would having DisAbled rights or neuro-diversity perspectives change peoples' experiences of criminal justice?

FURTHER READING

Carel, H. (2017). Virtue in deficit: The 9-year-old hero. *The Lancet, 389*(10074), 1094–1095. doi:10.1016/S0140–6736(17)30709–2

District Court of New Zealand (2019). *New Zealand Police v Morrison* 2019, NZDC 13977, per Hastings J. Retrieved from www.districtcourts.govt.nz/all-judgments/new-zealand-police-v-morrison–2019-nzdc–13977/

Gibbs, A., & Sherwood, K. (2017). Putting fetal alcohol spectrum disorder (FASD) on the map in New Zealand: A review of health, social, political, justice and cultural developments. *Psychiatry, Psychology and Law, 24*(6), 825–842. doi:10.1080/13218719.2017.1315784

NOTES

1. From http://neafan.ca/
2. See https://www.benchmark.org.nz/
3. Section 333 reports from the Oranga Tamariki Act 1989 are written to assist judges in their decision-making in the Youth Courts. Section 333 reports focus on medical, psychiatric, and psychological factors that are relevant to a young person's fitness to stand trial, as well as their impact on a young person's offending (Lambie et al., 2016).
4. See *New Zealand Police v Morrison* 2019, NZDC 13977.
5. See https://www.tepou.co.nz/disability-workforce/fetal-alcohol-spectrum-disorder-fasd/239 and https://www.health.govt.nz/our-work/diseases-and-conditions/fetal-alcohol-spectrum-disorder/summary-progress-fetal-alcohol-spectrum-disorder-fasd-action-plan

REFERENCES

Bower, C., Watkins, R., Mutch, R., Marriott, R., Freeman, J., Kippin, N., . . . Giglia, R. (2018). Fetal alcohol spectrum disorder and youth justice: A prevalence study among young people sentenced to detention in Western Australia. *BMJ Open, 8*(2), 1–10. doi:10.1136/bmjopen–2017–019605

Brown, J., Long-McGie, J., Wartnik, A., Oberoi, P., Wresh, J., Weinkauf, E., Falconer, G., & Kerr, A. (2014). Fetal alcohol spectrum disorders in the criminal justice system: A review. *The Journal of Law Enforcement, 3*(6), 1–10. Retrieved from https://canfasd.ca/wp-content/uploads/2018/01/Brown–2014-FASD-in-the-criminal-justice-system.pdf

Carel, H. (2017). Virtue in deficit: The 9-year-old hero. *The Lancet, 389*(10074), 1094–1095. doi:10.1016/S0140–6736(17)30709–2

Crawford, A. (2018). *Social cognition, executive functioning and IQ. What are the important influences on adaptive functioning in children with fetal alcohol spectrum disorder?* Unpublished doctoral thesis, University of Auckland, Auckland, New Zealand.

Currie, B. A., Hoy, J., Legge, L., Temple, V. K., & Tahir, M. (2016). Adults with fetal alcohol spectrum disorder: Factors associated with positive outcomes and contact with the criminal justice system. *Journal of Population Therapeutics and Clinical Pharmacology, 23*(1), E37–E52.

District Court of New Zealand (2019). *New Zealand Police v Morrison* NZDC 13977, per Hastings J. Retrieved from www.districtcourts.govt.nz/all-judgments/new-zealand-police-v-morrison–2019-nzdc–13977/

Doogue, J., & Walker, J. (2019). *Proposal for a trial of young adult list in Porirua District Court*. Wellington, New Zealand: District Courts of New Zealand. Retrieved from https://www.districtcourts.govt.nz/assets/Uploads/Proposal-for-a-trial-of-Young-Adult-List-in-Porirua-District-Court-pdf.pdf

Evensen, D., & Lutke, J. (1997). *Eight magic keys: Developing successful interventions for students with FAS*. Retrieved from: http://www.come-over.to/FAS/brochures/EightMagicKeysBroch.pdf

Fast, D., & Conroy, J. (2009). Fetal alcohol spectrum disorders and the criminal justice system. *Developmental Disabilities Research Reviews, 15*(3), 250–257. doi:10.1002/ddrr.66

Flannigan, K., Pei, J., Stewart, M., & Johnson, A. (2018). Fetal alcohol spectrum disorder and the criminal justice system: A systematic literature review. *International Journal of Law and Psychiatry, 57*, 42–52. doi:10.1016/j.ijlp.2017.12.008

Gibbs, A. (2018). If only Teina Pora had a MedicAlert bracelet. *New Zealand Medical Journal, 131*(1473), 85–87. Retrieved from https://pdfs.semanticscholar.org/0151/933441aa2830d608fa4de7451631685edcf7.pdf?_ga=2.131549903.1364657202.1580103073–1154062498.1580103073

Gibbs, A., Bagley, K., Badry, D., & Gollner, V. (2018). Foetal alcohol spectrum disorder: Effective helping responses from social workers. *International Social Work, 63*(4), 496–509. Retrieved from: https://journals.sagepub.com/doi/pdf/10.1177/0020872818804032

Gibbs, A., & Sherwood, K. (2017). Putting fetal alcohol spectrum disorder (FASD) on the map in New Zealand: A review of health, social, political, justice and cultural developments. *Psychiatry, Psychology and Law, 24*(6), 825–842. doi:10.1080/13218719.2017.1315784

Goodley, D., & Runswick-Cole, K. (2016). Becoming dishuman: Thinking about the human through dis/ability. *Discourse: Studies in the Cultural Politics of Education, 37*(1), 1–15. doi:10.1080/01596306.2014.930021

Hughes, N., Williams, H., Chitsabean, P., Davies, R., & Mounce, L. (2012). *Nobody made the connection: The prevalence of neurodisability in young people who offend*. London, UK: Office of the Children's Commissioner. Retrieved from https://yjlc.uk/wp-content/uploads/2015/03/Neurodisability_Report_FINAL_UPDATED__01_11_12.pdf

Lambie, I., Best, C., Ioane, J., Becroft, A., & Polaschek, C. (2016). What every judge and lawyer needs to know about s.333 psychiatric/psychological court reports. *New Zealand Law Journal, 1*, 24–37.

Lynch, N. (2016). *Neurodisability in the youth justice system in New Zealand: How vulnerability intersects with justice*. Dyslexia Foundation of New Zealand: Summarising the contributions of participants at the 2016 Neurodisabilities Forum, hosted by DFNZ in Wellington. Retrieved from http://neurodisabilitiesforum.org.nz/wp-content/uploads/2016/05/Neurodisabilities-Forum–2016-Report–1.pdf

McLachlan, K., McNeil, A., Pei, J., Brain, U., Andrew, G., & Oberlander, T. F. (2019). Prevalence and characteristics of adults with fetal alcohol spectrum disorder in corrections: A Canadian case ascertainment study. *BMC Public Health, 19*(43), 1–10. doi:10.1186/s12889–018–6292-x

Mitchell, T., Theadom, A., & du Preez, E. (2017). Prevalence of traumatic brain injury in a male adult prison population and its association with the offence type. *Neuroepidemiology, 48*(3–4), 164–170. doi:10.1159/000479520

New Zealand Herald. (2019, February 5). Haami Hanara sentenced to life imprisonment for murder of Hastings man Kelly Donner. Retrieved from https://www.nzherald.co.nz/nz/news/article.cfm?c_id=1&objectid=12200890

Oatley, V. (2019). *Fetal alcohol spectrum disorder, the youth justice system and social work*. Unpublished dissertation, University of Otago, Dunedin, New Zealand.

Pei, J., Leung, W. S., Jampolsky, F., & Alsbury, B. (2016). Experiences in the Canadian criminal justice system for individuals with fetal alcohol spectrum disorders: Double jeopardy? *Canadian Journal of Criminology and Criminal Justice, 58*(1), 56–86. doi:10.3138/cjccj.2014.E25

Rosenburg, M. (2019, February 24). An inconvenient truth: The commonly misunderstood disorder filling our prisons. *Stuff*. Retrieved from https://www.stuff.co.nz/national/health/110502282/an-inconvenient-truth-the-commonly-misunderstood-disorder-filling-our-prisons?rm=m

Rutman, D. (2016). Becoming FASD informed: Strengthening practice and programs working with women with FASD. *Substance Abuse: Research and Treatment, 10*(S1), 13–20. doi:10.4137/SaRt.S34543

Stewart, I. (2019, May 6). Crash victims' mother: 'I had extreme fears that Craig was going to die'. *Radio New Zealand*. Retrieved from https://www.rnz.co.nz/news/national/388536/crash-victims-mother-i-had-extreme-fears-that-craig-was-going-to-die

Stewart, M. (2019). Supporting neurodiverse learners in New Zealand prisons. *Practice: The New Zealand Corrections Journal, 7*(1), 45–47. Retrieved from: https://www.corrections.govt.nz/resources/newsletters_and_brochures/journal/volume_7_issue_1_july_2019/supporting_neurodiverse_learners_in_new_zealand_prisons

Stewart, M., & Glowatski, K. (2018). *Truth and reconciliation call to action #34: A framework for action*. Canada FASD Research Network, Regina, Saskatchewan, Canada. Retrieved from https://canfasd.ca/trc34/

Streissguth, A. P., Barr, H. M., Kogan, J., & Bookstein, F. L. (1996). *Final report: Understanding the occurrence of secondary disabilities in clients with fetal alcohol syndrome (FAS) and fetal alcohol effects (FAE)*. Seattle, WA: University of Washington Publication Services. Retrieved from http://lib.adai.uw.edu/pubs/bk2698.pdf

Streissguth, A. P., Bookstein, F. L., Barr, H. M., Sampson, P. D., O'Malley, K., & Young, J. K. (2004). Risk factors for adverse life outcomes in fetal alcohol syndrome and fetal alcohol effects. *Journal of Developmental and Behavioral Pediatrics, 25*(4), 228–238. doi:10.1097/00004703-200408000-00002

Wozniak, J., Riley, E., & Charness, M. (2019). Clinical presentation, diagnosis, and management of fetal alcohol spectrum disorder. *Lancet Neurology, 18*(8), 760–770. doi:10.1016/S1474-4422(19)30150-4

Young, S., Adamou, M., Bolea, B., Gudjonsson, G., Muller, U., Pitts, M., . . . Asherson, P. (2011). The identification and management of ADHD offenders within the criminal justice system. *BMC Psychiatry, 11*(32), 1–14. doi:10.1186/1471-244X-11-32

30

Gangs
The Politics and Political Management of the 'Gang Problem'

Jarrod Gilbert

It is sensible (though far from simple) to precisely define what a gang is. Klein (1971) noted that '[p]ractitioners, researchers, and theoreticians alike have used the "gang" sometimes inconsistently, sometimes loosely, and sometimes in direct opposition to each other, but never in concert' (p. 8). In more recent times, a standardised definition has been sought so that gangs can be studied comparatively and internationally (Klein et al., 2001). This has met with mixed success at best. One researcher has even argued whether a definition is necessary or possible (Horowitz, 1990, p. 47), and certainly there is benefit in multiple definitions (Gilbert, 2013, p. viii).

In Aotearoa New Zealand, the majority of gangs have worn back patches and so have self-identified.[1] But even this is not foolproof, as some social motorcycle groups – including those made entirely of firefighters – wear back patches but are not gangs, while other groups (notably LA-style street gangs) do not wear patches at all. For the purposes of this chapter, a gang will be defined as: a structured group (of five or more people) that maintains an exclusive membership marked by common identifiers and formal rules that supersede the rules of the state.

This neutral identification of gangs is somewhat at odds with the political and media attention to them. Since their earliest formation, patched gangs in New Zealand have sparked acute media commentary and significant legislative efforts aimed at control. This commentary has tended to be sensational and populist, and, at best, the success of ensuing gang legislation has been marginal. This chapter looks at the New Zealand history of political responses to gangs. It examines and critiques key moments and events when gangs and politics have intersected.

The chapter highlights the way that governments, often without evidence and spurred by moral panic, have changed views around gangs so that any explanations of the social and economic drivers of gang membership and activity have been replaced by a discourse of 'law and order'.

THE BEGINNINGS

What can be seen as the beginning of the modern wave of gangs can perhaps be placed on a specific date: 1 July 1961 is recognised as the official start of the Hells Angels in New Zealand.[2] That 'chapter' was the first outside of California, and its establishment fundamentally changed the gang scene in New Zealand (Gilbert, 2013). By following the example provided by the Hells Angels, the loosely structured incipient gangs evident in New Zealand's town and cities of the 1950s were transformed into organised groups with hierarchical leaders and sets of rules. They also became much more visible because they wore back patches. Initially these developments were the preserve of the motorcycle-riding groups, but by the late 1960s the far bigger, predominately Māori street gangs began to adopt them. By the early 1970s gangs were ubiquitous.

Following an exposé by the *Gallery* television programme, highlighting the 1970 violence from a group called the Stormtroopers in Ōtara, New Zealand gangs were the subject of a multi-agency governmental investigation. Despite public and police concerns, the group's report suggested that the formation of gangs was not a new thing, 'nor is it necessarily an unhealthy or anti-social one' (Investigating Committee, 1970, p. 1). Furthermore, the report concluded that the high proportion of Polynesian youths involved in gangs was a 'cultural response to their urban environment' (p. 1). They were not emotionally disturbed, but were rather a product of 'inadequate socialisation' and a 'cultural void', and the gangs provided them with an identity that their homes and school life did not (p. 21). Moreover, the young gang members were typically from state housing areas where poorer (often large) families were concentrated, creating an '"unbalanced" type of community with an over-representation of unskilled, young adults and families, and the "casualties" of society' (p. 21). In short, the gangs were symptoms of community problems as much as they were causes. This type of thinking conforms to academic literature (see, for example, Klein, 1995; Shaw & McKay, 1942/1969; Thrasher, 1927; Vigil & Yun, 1990), but, as we will see, it would in time fade from public and political thinking.

In the 1970s there was an acceptance that youthful gang members just needed to be moved in a more positive direction. The Labour MP for Māngere, Colin Moyle, said he had talked to some gang leaders and they demonstrated 'leadership qualities and a certain attitude of responsibility that could be built on' (Moyle, 1970). The minister of police, David Thomson, agreed, saying they 'would provide good leaders in the future' (Thomson, 1970). In December of that year, the minister of Māori and Island affairs, Duncan MacIntyre, visited a music festival and met members of the Stormtroopers, and was taken for a 'hair raising' ride by one of the youths who owned a motorcycle (*New Zealand Herald*, 7 December 1970, as cited in Gilbert, 2013). It clearly made an impression. In Parliament in June 1971, he said: 'I am not singing the praises of the gangs but I think some gangs have been unduly criticised. I instance the case of the Stormtroopers from Otara,' who, he said, had run dances and other social activities (MacIntyre, 1971). While this rather ambivalent attitude to the young gangs is striking by today's standards, exactly what came of the multi-agency report recommendations is unclear. What is clear, however, is that the gangs continued to grow and cause concern, and, without any obvious social polices targeting them, were simply left as an issue of law and order to be dealt with by police as they saw fit.

The most significant political development of this period, then, occurred in the lead-up to the 1972 election when opposition Labour leader Norman Kirk responded to growing concern around gangs by promising to 'take the bikes off the bikies' (as cited in Gilbert, 2013, p. 68). Kirk never did this – in fact, the idea proved to be so legally impractical that he never even tried – but he did get elected, and the idea of gangs as an issue to garner electoral advantage was born.

EARLY 'CRACKDOWNS'

While Kirk failed to tackle the bikies, violence between gangs became increasingly commonplace as the groups sought to carve out territory. The overwhelming police response was to crack down, an approach obvious as early as the late 1950s when police were keen to 'keep on their tails' (Green, 1959, p. 25). But the strength of the police response increased dramatically. This was best highlighted by Christchurch police superintendent Gideon Tait, an 'old-school' cop frustrated by 'liberals' who ignored the troubles created by such groups but who were quick to call 'fascism' if police 'resort to violent measures' (Tait & Berry, 1978, p. 69). In 1973, Tait raided a gang's New Year's Eve party. It was the first time tear gas had been used in New Zealand in a situation not involving firearms. Eighty-one people were charged, mostly with 'unlawful assembly'; a newly enacted offence that did not come into effect until the start of 1974, which meant that all charges were subsequently dismissed (Gilbert, 2013, p. 69). That failure did nothing to stop Tait being transferred to Auckland to take over the Police Task Force, perhaps the most notorious tool used against the gangs at that time.

The Police Task Force was established in 1974 to curb public drunkenness and violence, which was often associated with the growing number of street gangs. Numbering some 200 specially trained officers, it became highly controversial after complaints of racism and provocative behaviour began to surface. Critics pointed out their hardline tactics were creating more harm than good. Research by one lobby group, the Auckland Committee on Racism and Discrimination, concluded that the task force was a failure in law enforcement and a disaster in community relations (as cited in Gilbert, 2013, p. 70). The official police view was dismissive of such criticisms (Appendix to the Journals of the House of Representatives [AJHR], 1975). Notwithstanding that, the task force was renamed Team Policing Units, but controversy over the approach toward gangs did not end there. By the end of the decade there was a chorus of questions asking publicly whether hardline tactics were, in fact, counter-productive. Gangs would once again become a highly political issue, sparked by events in the small Northland town of Moerewa.

A RIOT AND A RETHINK

Tensions in South Auckland between the Stormtroopers and Black Power led to tit-for-tat skirmishes over a number of months in 1979 until an assault by a Northland Black Power member on an Auckland Stormtrooper ignited a showdown (Kelsey & Young, 1982, p. 27). On 3 August 1979, carloads of Stormtroopers set about smashing up the Okaihau Hotel before turning their attention to police. In Moerewa they destroyed a police car and forced the officers to retreat, despite the police firing warning shots into the air. More violence ensued, and police reinforcements became involved in a pitched battle. Several police officers were beaten, a police van was set alight (Kelsey & Young, 1982, p. 28), and gang members raided a fire truck and stole a number of axes to use as weapons. During the melee, a police officer fired several warning shots from a pistol before shooting a gang member in the thigh (Gilbert, 2013, p. 101).

While there was a good deal of breast-beating on both sides of Parliament after the riot, in a remarkable pivot, both National and Labour MPs acknowledged that long-term solutions were not to be found in law-and-order legislation or suppressive police tactics. The leader of the Labour opposition, Bill Rowling, said that a 'sudden whiplash reaction of bashing back is not going to solve the problem' (Rowling, 1979). Furthermore:

Parliament must examine closely the social, economic, and community climate that breeds and fosters the kind of alienation and brutal desperation – one cannot describe it any other way – that we saw last weekend. I stress that I am not talking about apportioning blame. I suppose that, in some ways, we can all take a share of that (Rowling, 1979).

He saluted work co-operatives being undertaken by some gangs and, like other MPs, identified the problem of burgeoning unemployment: 'They must have work. We will never get decent citizens from an element of young people who feel that they have no stake in the country' (Rowling, 1979). The idea that the gang problem required social policies survived the Moerewa incident.

The police hierarchy had come to a similar conclusion. In the 1979 police annual report, tabled several days after the Moerewa incident, Commissioner Bob Walton said: '[A]s advocated by some, the gang problem cannot be eliminated by force. Whatever short-term gains that may accrue, the long-term results would be greater disorder' (AJHR, 1979). In the wake of Moerewa, Parliament passed two pieces of legislation that gave police more power to search for gang weapons (Police Offences Amendment Act) and allowed publicans to ban gang patches (Sale of Liquor Amendment Act). The most significant move, however, came from the realisation that tough police action wasn't working, and that gangs were now not only battling each other but also turning on police; this led politicians to adopt a new social policy approach to counter the gang problem.

THE SOCIAL POLICY AGENDA

The formal plan came out of the 1981 Comber Report published by the Committee on Gangs. It reached a number of conclusions – for instance, that gangs 'will probably always exist since they arise from a particular set of social and economic conditions' (Committee on Gangs, 1981, p. 6). Echoing the findings of the 1970 multi-agency committee, among the conditions identified in the Comber Report were housing problems, unemployment, cultural change, education failure, and family breakdown (Committee on Gangs, 1981, pp. 1, 10, 12).

As a direct result, the government established the Group Employment Liaison Scheme (GELS). GELS, an independent agency funded by the Department of Labour, was set up to work with gangs and link them with existing social services, primarily the Project Employment Programme (PEP). This was a make-work scheme that had been designed by government to mop up what they thought would be temporary unemployment in the late 1970s.

Prime Minister Muldoon had previously articulated his goal to turn each rebellious group 'into a club, rather than a gang' (Muldoon, 1976), and the social policy agenda was based on that approach. The fact that Muldoon was prepared to work with the predominantly Māori gangs was remarkable given he was said to be at his least sympathetic when it came to race relations. Just a few years earlier he had called for the banishment of young 'Māori louts' to the countryside (Kelsey & Young, 1982, p. 102). But Muldoon was fostering a relationship with the gangs – notably Black Power – that was unique in the political history of this country (Gustafson, 2000, p. 206). This relationship between Muldoon and the gangs, and subsequently his social policy agenda, was in large part influenced by Black Power's Denis O'Reilly, who was one of a number of gang members employed as field workers by GELS, and would later head the organisation. O'Reilly had helped Black Power arrange work co-operatives in the past and was part of a drive to push his gang in a more prosocial direction from within.

Initially, Muldoon's approach was seen as successful. Numerous media stories appeared about the positive impact of putting the gangs to work (see Gilbert, 2013, pp. 112–114). Muldoon was pleased with the outcomes of the work by GELS, and claimed work trusts established by the gangs to gain government funding had calmed them down and decreased gang conflict (Gilbert, 2013, p. 113). Senior police also acknowledged the benefits of putting the gangs to work: Commissioner Bob Walton told MPs in 1983 that, while gang violence (particularly the use of firearms) remained a serious concern, work schemes were having some success in turning members away from antisocial behaviour. He said:

> Several larger gangs, notably Black Power 'chapters' in Auckland and Wellington, have become committed to work schemes and as a result some decrease in the level of offending by their members is apparent (as cited in Gilbert, 2013, p. 113).

Despite such positive reports, however, the tide quickly turned against the social policy approach. A change to a Labour government in 1984 meant not only the removal of Muldoon, but also a dramatically changing economic and political environment based on free-market ideas (see, for example, Boston et al., 1999; Kelsey, 1993). Under this new neoliberal ideology, the make-work schemes at the heart of the social policy agenda were an anathema. Ongoing concerns around gangs profiteering from the work schemes (Gilbert, 2013, pp. 116, 119–122) came to a head via a high-profile gang rape in Auckland's Ambury Park in November 1986 (see Du Chateau & Roger, 1987, p. 136; Jones, 1987, p. 24). The social policy approach was ostensibly dead from that moment and replaced with a stringent law-and-order agenda. Over time, this was widely normalised through the penal-populist approach that developed through New Zealand, in which harsher punishments escalated and prison populations increased (see Pratt & Anderson, chapter 13 this volume).

THE EMPHASIS ON LAW AND ORDER

Government reports from the 1970s and 1980s suggested that gangs were a consequence of negative social and economic conditions, but into the 1990s these ideas were forgotten or ignored. In the new paradigm, gangs were not to be funded, supported, or worked with – they were now deemed a policing, law-and-order problem.

Following a number of serious incidents of gang violence in 1996, Aotearoa New Zealand's largest legislative drive against gangs was launched, just months out from the first MMP election. But while it was violence that sparked the legal thrust, the political rhetoric changed dramatically as, for the first time, gangs became framed as organised crime groups; a label that largely defines them to this day. Opposition justice spokesperson Mike Moore summed up the new threat. Gangs, he said, 'are no longer groups of hoons who smash the occasional pub. They have graduated into serious organised crime' (Gilbert, 2013, p. 214). Similarly, newly appointed police commissioner Peter Doone claimed New Zealand had just five years to destroy gangs or they would grow so large and powerful that they would be completely beyond control, comments that Moore described as a 'powerful wake-up call' (as cited in Gilbert, 2013, p. 214). The claim that gangs had become the primary manifestation of organised crime in New Zealand has since been described as a moral panic (Gilbert, 2013, p. 217).

The term 'moral panic' was devised by sociologist and criminologist Stanley Cohen to describe the response to battles between youth groups in the English seaside community of Brighton in the mid-1960s. Cohen believed the conflict was a part of a broader phenomenon whereby events or people are defined as a threat, hyped by the media, and defined by the danger they pose to societal values. Community leaders and other 'right-thinking people' call for action, often resulting in new laws or policies (Cohen, 1972, p. 9). Following immense public and political pressure in New Zealand, the government proposed (before the 1996 election) and then passed (after the election) a swathe of new measures via the Harassment Act 1997, as well as amendments to the Crimes Act 1961, Criminal Justice Act 1985, Local Government Act 1974, Misuse of Drugs Act 1975, Summary Offences Act 1981, and Telecommunications Act 1987. Some of the measures were uncontroversial, such as those that increased fines which had not been adjusted for years. Others, however, were more contentious and were criticised on the basis of perceived efficacy, their negative human rights implications, and the fact that they were actually general law-enforcement provisions, and 'gang laws' in name only.

Despite these criticisms, the laws passed comfortably. And notwithstanding the dire threat that gangs were said to pose, and the great urgency in dealing with them, much of the resulting legislation has been rarely applied or has proven superfluous; in fact, if a clearer breakdown of many of the provisions was available, it would almost certainly find that the laws have overwhelmingly been used against people not in gangs. Even ignoring that assertion, it is difficult to avoid the conclusion that the laws had little or no effect on New Zealand's gang scene. They did, however, have an indirect effect via the process of their establishment, in which officials created a discourse that gangs were the country's foremost organised crime problem and existed solely for reasons of profit-driven crime. As will be highlighted below, these ideas continued to be promulgated by police and politicians, particularly in relation to organised criminal activity. No longer seen as the product of social and economic conditions, gangs were now seen as quasi-mafia groups – and with that there is no need for social policies: just firmer enforcement and control.

PATCH BANS AND YOUTH GANGS

In the 2000s, as the law-enforcement approach to gang control continued, one of the most significant developments originated not from national politics but from the council of Whanganui, and more specifically its mayor, Michael Laws.[3] Following a violent clash between the Hells Angels and the Mongrel Mob at a service station in February 2006, Laws said it was 'high time that central government equipped local police with the staff and resources to deal with them once and for all' (as cited in Gilbert, 2013, p. 275). Laws struck on the idea of banning gang patches. It was not the first time the idea had been suggested, but in this instance it was given greater impetus with a May 2007 drive-by shooting, in which shots fired by Mongrel Mob members at a rival Black Power house missed their mark and instead killed a young girl, Jhia Te Tua, as she slept on a couch. Before her death, Whanganui Council had drafted a bylaw banning gang regalia in the city, but lawyers for the city deemed that it would need parliamentary approval to ensure it was not in breach of the Bill of Rights Act (Gilbert, 2013, p. 276). Following the killing, the political debate changed and Jhia Te Tua became the symbol for the ban's necessity.

It was never made clear by the ban's supporters, indeed nobody even tried to articulate, how the patch ban would have saved Te Tua's life. A lack of evidence or consistency had not stopped anti-gang laws in the past, but this proposal was subjected to closer critical scrutiny than previous measures. A number of current and former police officers argued against the proposed ban. In a 14 March 2006 letter to the *New Zealand Herald* (Gilbert, 2013, p. 278), the head of the police Organised Crime Unit, Sergeant Daryl Brazier, wrote that while Laws and his council might 'mean well', the proposal to ban patches was misguided. For him, patches were a way that gangs 'could be identified and policed', and removing them would drive such groups underground. These ideas were echoed by Steve Plowman, editor of *Police News* (April 2006), who suggested that by giving gangs a lower profile the bylaw may 'inadvertently . . . advantage' them (as cited in Gilbert, 2013, p. 278).

The government was unmoved and Whanganui was granted the power to create bylaws banning patches in certain public areas. Michael Laws believed the wording of the legislation gave him greater power than it actually did, and he banned patches in all public places, a move that would ultimately be the ban's undoing. The ban was legally challenged by a member of the Hells Angels, Phil Schubert – with funding from a number of different groups – and was struck out by the High Court (*Schubert v Wanganui District Council,* 2011).[4] Another populist suppressive approach had fallen flat.

THE YOUTH ACTION PLAN

At the same time as these developments that would render gangs less visible, a new form of gang was proving problematic, in part because of the difficulty in identifying them from the crowd. LA-style street gangs – based on the look and style of the American Bloods and Crips – first gained media attention in 1990, when a small article in the *New Zealand Herald* reported concerns about a group of youths in South Auckland who were wearing 'colours' (bandanas), dressing like 'violent American street gangs', and calling themselves the 'Tongan Crip Gang' or 'TCG' (Gilbert, 2013, p. 256). (This form of gang was so unfamiliar that the media source incorrectly spelt 'Crip' as 'Crypt'.) Reflecting the assumption that gangs wear patches, police told the *Herald* that they were not a 'gang' and were 'nothing more than five teenage thugs' (as cited in Gilbert, 2013, p. 256). While that may have been true at the time, by the mid-2000s these groups had grown in size and number, the most significant of which was the Killer Beez, founded by a member of the Tribesmen in 2003.

A spotlight focused on South Auckland after a spate of murders was linked to these young groups in 2006. The police established a youth gang suppression unit to patrol the streets at night. But the fact that there was such a crossover in the style of the new gangs – *sans* patches – and wider fashion led to blanket-style policing. South Auckland police quickly amassed a database of some 850 names of people they believed were gang members, and police estimated that there were as many as 1000 in the region, and perhaps twice that number in all of Auckland, a point that was later conceded by police as regrettable (Gilbert, 2013, p. 263). In their early attempts to come to grips with the problem, police had identified any likely-looking youth as a gang member. Also, the police quickly became aware that many of the gangs came and went 'in the blink of an eye' (Detective Inspector Hewett, personal communication, 2009). Consequently, the numbers were grossly overstated.

Nevertheless, a political response was inevitable. Following work undertaken by the Ministry of Social Development (MSD, 2008) in light of the killings, the government provided $10 million over four years to the Auckland Youth Support Network, which was charged with implementing the Plan of Action – Improving the Outcome for Young People in Counties Manukau. Although the additional money was limited, the change in approach was significant. The plan signalled a return to thinking about (youth) gangs as a social problem and not simply one of law and order. Linked with a number of different government agencies, Auckland Youth Support Network sought to implement 26 actions 'as a first step to addressing the underlying factors to social disadvantage and youth gang and youth crime issues' (Auckland Youth Support Network, 2006, p. 6).

In January 2010, the MSD published a review of the Plan of Action, which outlined the range of work being undertaken (including parenting programmes, youth events, advocacy, and intensive individualised support), and reported on a reduction in youth gang activity (MSD, 2010, p. 16). Although this reduction was based on stakeholder perceptions rather than objective data, one major US study (involving 21 cities) found that 'perceptions [of gang improvements by key stakeholders] correlated perfectly with empirical indicators' (Howell, 1998, p. 296). Moreover, encouraging signs in relation to youth offending were captured by other objective indices. Following a peak in 2006, the year the plan was devised and implemented, overall youth apprehensions dropped in Counties Manukau. Between 2007 and 2008, apprehensions among people aged 20 years and under fell by 9 per cent, while the nationwide average saw an overall increase of 3 per cent (MSD, 2010).

Furthermore, positive results were found in Manukau City Council's annual perceptions survey with regard to questions on crime and safety. Between 2006 and 2009, residents who felt 'safe' or 'very safe' in their homes, in their neighbourhoods, and in their local town centres (both during the day and after dark), increased among all categories (MSD, 2010, p. 18), as shown in Table 30.1.

Table 30.1.
Percentage of Residents Who Feel Safe, by Place, 2006–2009

% of residents who feel 'very safe'/'safe' in their:	2006	2007	2008	2009
Home during the day	90	92	91	95
Home after dark	80	82	84	89
Local neighbourhood during the day	88	90	91	94
Neighbourhood after dark	61	55	58	77
Local town centre during the day	80	86	84	94
Local town centre after dark	37	40	37	55

Source: (MSD, 2010, p. 18)

To what degree the improvements are linked directly or indirectly to the Youth Action Plan is impossible to gauge, but the more important point is that the plan signalled at least a limited and temporary return to a social policy approach.

FALSE DATA AND FEWER RIGHTS . . . WHERE TO FROM HERE?

While youth gangs elicited a policy approach that stretched beyond law and order, it was more of the same when it came to the political approach to patched gangs. This was nowhere more evident than in the lead-up to the 2014 general election when the government released a comprehensive gang strategy, much of which focused on organised crime. The basis for the approach was data provided by New Zealand Police (NZP) to the minister of police, Anne Tolley. Tolley's data claimed that the country's 4000 adult gang members were responsible for 34 per cent of class A and B drug offences, 25 per cent of homicide-related offences, and large proportions of offending in a range of other categories (Tolley, 2014). Although shocking, these numbers were presented and reported as being uncontroversial because they confirmed a state of affairs aligned with public perception. Upon close examination, however, this data was found to contain significant errors that vastly overestimated the contribution of gang members to a range of major crimes, including organised criminal activity. Upon obtaining the correct data, it was discovered that the true figures were 4 per cent of class A and B drug offences, and the homicide figure (over the period Tolley had used) was actually zero (Gilbert, 2015). The figures had been artificially inflated because the police had included as 'gang members' not only prospective members, but also:

- those charged together with a gang member for the same offence;
- those with an identified familial tie with a gang member; and
- those with an identified connection to a gang member.

Whether the use of the data was a cynical political ploy or an honest error is unknown, but certainly the real figures revealed a dearth of data that might underpin a need for 'crackdowns', and could not sustain the claim that gangs monopolise the drug trade, a view commonly expressed since the 1990s. Indeed, the episode showed how panic and criminalisation had no underpinning evidence.

This trend toward attacking gangs as an election-year scapegoat grew even sharper in the lead-up to the 2017 election. In launching tough measures on organised crime, including searching gang members' homes without warrants, then Police Minister Paula Bennett attempted to justify the proposal by claiming some people 'have fewer human rights than others' (Leslie, 2017, para. 1). A number of academics, lawyers, and newspaper editorials condemned the statement, and Prime Minister Bill English was forced to backtrack on her behalf (Walters, 2017). On a topic rife with hyperbole and claims-making, the incident indicated that there are limits on what politicians can say about gangs.

But perhaps the most interesting contemporary development around the political management of and response to gangs is one that may not materialise. Within some criminal justice jurisdictions, there are tentative conversations happening once again around the idea of working with gangs. Not since the days of Muldoon and the social policy agenda of the 1980s has the idea been given oxygen. In part, it has been spurred by concerns around the burgeoning prison population, which after steep growth had ballooned to over 10,000 in 2018 (see Martin, chapter 21 this volume). Solving the problem of imprisonment necessarily meant finding a solution to the problems posed by gangs: a significant portion of the prison population are gang members, they have higher recidivism rates, and their reoffending is on average more serious than those people without gang associations (Ong, 2015).

In 2019, Corrections minister Kelvin Davis met with delegates from the Hamilton base of the Mongrel Mob Kingdom to discuss ideas for solving the problems associated with gangs. This represented a remarkable political turnaround. Just three years earlier Ngapari Nui, a prosocial Black Power president, was banned from volunteering in Whanganui prison based on his gang membership (Ngawhare, 2016). He has since been reinstated in the role, reflecting a change in some political thinking. The idea behind these developments is to harness the power of prosocial members to help reach those who create the most problems, particularly around methamphetamine use and family violence. To what degree working with gangs will become more common or formalised is unclear. Certainly, such a strategy carries political risks, something that has recently become evident. The National Party has changed tack and returned to a more populist approach to law and order, and to gangs specifically. In response to a rise in gang numbers, and some high-profile gang incidents, National promised to bring in policies that 'harass and disrupt gangs every single day' (McCulloch, 2019, para. 7).[5] And while this 'zero tolerance' echoes past approaches (such as the Police Task Force), they have looked to Australia for inspiration.

In the new millennium, various Australian states have taken a hard-line approach to outlaw motorcycle clubs. The Queensland government, for example, passed the Vicious Lawless Association Disestablishment Act in 2013. Under the provisions of that Act, patched clubs were declared illegal by political decree, and they had no right to challenge that ruling. Members of listed clubs could not go to their clubhouse or meet in groups of three or more. If caught, bail was forbidden, and those convicted would serve a mandatory term of six months in prison. If a single member wore any regalia denoting membership in a drinking establishment the same regime applied. Furthermore, if a club member committed certain crimes they were to receive the punishment imposed by that crime plus an additional 15 years in prison or, if an office-holder in the club, an additional 25 years. Club members were also banned from working in certain industries, notably tattooing.

In New South Wales, the state government relied on consorting laws that forbid people from associating after two warnings. These came into effect in 2012, and were one of the tools employed by a militarised police unit called Strike Force Raptor. In 2017 the National Party announced that if re-elected it would establish a similar Raptor-style 'strike force' within NZP.

The hard-line Australian approach, as exemplified in Queensland and New South Wales, has not been without its critics for its draconian nature. In Queensland, prominent QC Tony Fitzgerald, who famously headed the inquiry into state corruption in the 1980s, said: 'History teaches us that claims that repressive laws will reduce serious crime are usually hollow and that laws which erode individual freedom and expand a state's power over its citizens are fraught with peril' (*Brisbane Times*, 2013, para. 6). Such concerns began to materialise when non-gang members were caught up in the laws, including those with friendship or familial relationships, such as librarian Sally Kuether, who was arrested and jailed for having a drink with her partner and an outlaw club member in a bar (Goldsworthy, 2014).

As in Queensland, the New South Wales laws have impacted on the visible presence of the outlaw clubs. From this, police have heralded the success of Strike Force Raptor, but it too has attracted controversy, notably for heavy-handed tactics. Terry Goldsworthy, a professor at Bond University and a former police officer, pointed out that there is little evidence to show it has had any real effect on overall crime rates (Personal communication, 2020). Mike Kennedy, a senior lecturer at the University of Western Australia and another former police officer, said the laws have simply moved gangs underground, and in that sense they have been a 'disaster' (*Radio New Zealand Checkpoint*, 2019, para. 1; see also Bradley et al., chapter 14 this volume).

If history has taught us anything in New Zealand, it is that a lack of data and the absence of evidence are unlikely to affect the political will to implement laws against gangs, nor the public appetite to accept them. With this in mind, it is likely the heavy politicisation of gangs is set to continue.

CONCLUSION

In the early years of patched gang formation in New Zealand, the political response acknowledged their social and economic causes, but, as gangs became framed as organised crime groups, this was replaced with stiff suppressive measures. Often these changes occurred due to isolated sensational incidents and moral panics that had little basis in sound data. From the 1990s anti-gang measures formed part of a broader 'populist', tough-on-crime approach. The impact of specific anti-gang measures have been marginal at best, but the approach to youth gangs in South Auckland in the early 2000s demonstrates that more sophisticated strategies are available and do show promise. In recent times, with an eye on tackling broader problems in the criminal justice sector, there have been limited progressive moves to exploring work with prosocial gang members, an approach not seen since the 1980s. However, given the political risks that these pose, and the ubiquitous appeal of 'getting tough' on crime, it will not take much for tentative steps in that direction to be removed from the political agenda. And, for some, the hard-line approach of Australia offers a politically tantalising template.

STUDY QUESTIONS

- What could explain the development of gang membership in New Zealand?
- In other countries, like Scotland, the formal response to gangs is driven by a public health approach. What does this mean, and could it be applied in New Zealand?
- Is it important to differentiate between gang membership and the criminal activity of gang members?

FURTHER READING

Bradley, C. (2020). Outlaw bikers and patched street gangs: The nexus between violence and shadow economy. *National Security Journal*. Centre for Defence and Security Studies, Massey University. doi.org/10.36878/nsj20200201.02

Hallsworth, S. (2013). *The gang and beyond*. Basingstoke, UK: Palgrave Macmillan.

Ministry of Social Development (MSD). (2008). *From wannabes to youth offenders: Youth gangs in Counties Manukau – research report*. Wellington, New Zealand: Centre for Social Research and Evaluation Te Pokapū Rangahau Arotake Hapori, Ministry of Social Development. Retrieved from https://www.msd.govt.nz/about-msd-and-our-work/publications-resources/research/youth-gangs-counties-manukau/index.html

NOTES

1. Back patches are usually in three pieces, with the gang name and chapter on the top and bottom rockers, and the gang's symbol – like a logo – in the centre.
2. The 'Hells' in Hells Angels is spelled without an apostrophe.
3. Whanganui was spelled Wanganui at the time, hence that spelling in references.
4. *Schubert v Wanganui District Council* [2011] NZAR 233 (HC).
5. These included Tauranga, where a house was fired upon and a business set ablaze, and Hawke's Bay, where a number of shots were fired during a clash between two gangs outside a restaurant.

REFERENCES

Appendix to the Journals of the House of Representatives (AJHR). (1975), G.6 at pp. 11–12.

Appendix to the Journals of the House of Representatives (AJHR). (1979), G.6, at p. 4.

Auckland Youth Support Network. (2006). *Improving outcomes for young people in Counties Manukau: Plan of Action 2006*. Wellington, New Zealand: Ministry of Social Develeopment. Retrieved from https://www.msd.govt.nz/documents/about-msd-and-our-work/publications-resources/planning-strategy/improving-outcomes-young-people/improving-outcomes-action-plan.pdf

Boston, J., Dalziel, P., & St John, S. (1999). *Redesigning the welfare state in New Zealand: Problems, policies and prospects*. Auckland, New Zealand: Oxford University Press.

Brisbane Times. (2013, October 28). New Queensland government laws dangerous: Fitzgerald. Retrieved from https://www.brisbanetimes.com.au/national/queensland/new-queensland-government-laws-dangerous-fitzgerald-20131028-2wafc.html

Cohen, S. (1972). *Folk devils and moral panics: The creation of the mods and rockers*. London, UK: MacGibbon & Kee.

Committee on Gangs. (1981). *Report of the Committee on Gangs*. Wellington, New Zealand: Government Printer.

Du Chateau, C., & Roger, W. (1987, August). The present. *Metro*, pp. 132–156.

Gilbert, J. (2013). *Patched: The history of gangs in New Zealand*. Auckland, New Zealand: Auckland University Press.

Gilbert, J. (2015, September, 29). Jarrod Gilbert: Govt stats on gangs 'wildly inaccurate'. *New Zealand Herald*. Retrieved from https://www.nzherald.co.nz/nz/jarrod-gilbert-govt-stats-on-gangs-wildly-inaccurate/X5KDX33HBMKX6V2LMFFNDPWEYU/

Goldsworthy, T. (2014, February 21). The battle to win hearts and minds in Queensland's bikie war. *The Conversation*. Retrieved from http://theconversation.com/the-battle-to-win-hearts-and-minds-in-queenslands-bikie-war–23283

Green, J. G. (1959). *Gang misbehaviour in Wellington*. Wellington, New Zealand: Inter-departmental Committee on Adolescent Offenders.

Gustafson, B. (2000). *His way: A biography of Robert Muldoon*. Auckland, New Zealand: Auckland University Press.

Horowitz, R. (1990). Sociological perspectives on gangs: Conflicting definitions and concepts. In C. R. Huff (Ed.), *Gangs in America* (pp. 37–54). Thousand Oaks, CA: Sage Publications.

Howell, J. C. (1998, August). Youth gangs: An overview. *OJJDP: Juvenile Justice Bulletin, NCJ 167249*. Washington DC: U.S. Department of Justice. Retrieved from https://secure.ce-credit.com/articles/101181/167249.pdf

Investigating Committee. (1970). *Report by the investigating committee into juvenile gangs*. [Unpublished report]. Auckland, New Zealand: Sub Committee of the Joint Committee on Young Offenders.

Jones, L. (1987, August 1). Sour grape at Ambury Farm Park. *New Zealand Listener*, pp. 22–29.

Kelsey, J. (1993). *Rolling back the state: Privatisation of power in Aotearoa/New Zealand*. Wellington, New Zealand: Bridget Williams Books.

Kelsey, J., & Young, W. (1982). *The gangs: Moral panic as social control*. Wellington, New Zealand: Institute of Criminology, Victoria University of Wellington.

Klein, M. W. (1971). *Street gangs and street workers*. Englewood Cliffs, NJ: Prentice Hall Publishing.

Klein, M. W. (1995). *The American street gang: Its nature prevalence and control*. New York, NY: Oxford University Press.

Klein, M. W., Kerner, H. J., Maxson, C., & Weitekamp, G. M. (2001). *The Eurogang paradox: Street gangs and youth groups in the U.S. and Europe*. Dordrecht, Netherlands: Kluwer Academic Publishers.

Leslie, D. (2017, September 3). Serious criminals 'have fewer human rights' – National. *Radio New Zealand*. Retrieved from https://www.rnz.co.nz/news/election–2017/338588/serious-criminals-have-fewer-human-rights-national

MacIntyre, D. (1971). Imprest Supply Bill. *New Zealand Parliamentary Debates, 372*, 836.

McCulloch, C. (2019, November 26). National Party wants elite police force to target gangs. *Radio New Zealand*. Retrieved from https://www.rnz.co.nz/news/political/404154/national-party-wants-elite-police-force-to-target-gangs

Ministry of Social Development (MSD). (2008). *From wannabes to youth offenders: Youth gangs in Counties Manukau – research report*. Wellington, New Zealand: Centre for Social Research and Evaluation Te Pokapū Rangahau Arotake Hapori, Ministry of Social Development. Retrieved from https://www.msd.govt.nz/about-msd-and-our-work/publications-resources/research/youth-gangs-counties-manukau/index.html

Ministry of Social Development (MSD). (2010). *Review of the Plan of Action: Improving outcomes for the young people in Counties Manukau, summary report*. Wellington, New Zealand: Centre for Social Research and Evaluation, Ministry of Social Development. Retrieved from https://www.msd.govt.nz/documents/about-msd-and-our-work/publications-resources/planning-strategy/improving-outcomes-young-people/youth-gangs-review-of-the-plan-of-action-january–2010.pdf

Moyle, C. (1970). Appropriation Bill – Estimates. *New Zealand Parliamentary Debates, 368*, 3441.

Muldoon, R. D. (1976). Oral Answers to Questions. *New Zealand Parliamentary Debates, 407*, 3764.

Ngawhare, D. (2016, July 15). Ngapari Nui should have been treasured by Corrections, not stood down. *Stuff*. Retieved from https://www.stuff.co.nz/taranaki-daily-news/opinion/82165493/ngapari-nui-should-have-been-treasured-by-corrections-not-stood-down

Ong, S. (2015, January 21). *Improving effectiveness of rehabilitation programmes with gang members: Research phase 2 findings* [Unpublished internal memorandum, service development]. New Zealand: New Zealand Department of Corrections.

Radio New Zealand Checkpoint. (2019, Novermber 27). Australian ex-cop blasts National's 'Strike Force Raptor' plan. *Radio New Zealand*. Retrieved from https://www.rnz.co.nz/national/programmes/checkpoint/audio/2018724382/australian-ex-cop-blasts-national-s-strike-force-raptor-plan

Rowling, W. E. (1979). Adjournment – Gang Violence, Northland. *New Zealand Parliamentary Debates, 424*, 2072–2073.

Shaw, C. R., & McKay, H. D. (1942/1969). *Juvenile delinquency and urban areas*. Chicago, IL: University of Chicago Press.

Tait, G., & Berry, J. W. (1978). *Never back down*. Christchurch, New Zealand: Whitcoulls.

Thomson, D. (1970). Appropriation Bill – Estimates. *New Zealand Parliamentary Debates, 368*, 3443.

Thrasher, F. M. (1927). *The gang: A study of 1,313 gangs in Chicago*. Chicago, IL: University of Chicago Press.

Tolley, A. (2014, August 5). *Whole of government action plan on tackling gangs* [Press release]. Retrieved from https://www.beehive.govt.nz/release/whole-government-action-plan-tackling-gangs

Vigil, J. D., & Yun, S. C. (1990). Vietnamese youth gangs in southern California. In C. R. Huff (Ed.), *Gangs in America* (pp. 146–162). Thousand Oaks, CA: Sage Publications.

Walters, L. (2017, September 4). Bill English says everyone in New Zealand has human rights. *Stuff*. Retrieved from https://www.stuff.co.nz/national/politics/96456807/bill-english-says-everyone-in-nz-has-human-rights

31

Decriminalising Crimes
The Case of Sex Work

Lynzi Armstrong

Aotearoa New Zealand's penal policy is largely oriented towards criminalisation. While this has become particularly visible in recent decades, state responses to offending in New Zealand have been characterised by punitiveness since the inception of colonisation (Pratt, 2017). New Zealand's rate of imprisonment is one of the highest of all developed countries (Boomen, 2018), the prison population having increased significantly over the past four decades (Pratt, 2017). This growth has been attributed to 'penal populism', where the state's conceptualisation and responses to crime are shaped by assumptions about 'public mood or sentiments' (Pratt & Clarke, 2005, p. 304).

At the same time, however, the harms of criminalisation have increasingly been acknowledged, and calls to decriminalise or legalise some acts defined as crimes have gathered momentum. For example, since 2019 two shifts to legalisation stand out: the End of Life Choice Act (2019), which legalised assisted dying,[1] and the Abortion Legalisation Act (2020). In 2020 a non-binding referendum on the legalisation of cannabis failed to gain the necessary public support, but calls have since been made to switch the focus from legalisation to decriminalisation. Despite these examples, liberalising approaches such as decriminalisation and legalisation are still relatively uncharted territory in New Zealand.

This chapter examines the issue of decriminalisation through a case study on sex work in New Zealand. It begins by introducing the concept of decriminalisation, briefly explaining the differences between it and the related concept of legalisation, before providing an overview of the criminalisation of sex work. It then turns to overarching debates regarding the decriminalisation of sex work before introducing the New Zealand case study. The chapter concludes with a summary of the key issues canvassed, considering the lessons this may offer for policy debates in New Zealand and further afield.

WHAT IS DECRIMINALISATION?

Before engaging with the specific case of sex work, it is important to note that, while decriminalisation is commonly linked with legalisation, these terms have different meanings (Armstrong, 2010). A very basic definition of decriminalisation is that it involves the repeal of legislation that made a specific act a crime. Thus, when an act is decriminalised it is no longer subject to criminal law. Legalisation differs in bringing an act that was previously criminalised into the strict control of the government via new laws and state-imposed regulations (Mossman, 2007). Decriminalisation and legalisation are therefore, to some extent, terms that overlap in that they both involve the repeal of laws that specifically criminalised an act. However, legalisation typically involves more intensive state control. Sex work, for example, is legalised in places such as Germany, the Netherlands, the state of Victoria in Australia, and the state of Nevada in the US. Those working in these jurisdictions must comply with numerous sex work-specific regulations, such as mandatory sexual health checks, and registration with police or other government authorities; in Germany all sex workers are required by law to carry a sex-worker identification card (Herter et al., 2017; Mossman, 2007).

While decriminalisation does *not* mean an absence of regulation, regulatory requirements are typically comparable to other commercial businesses (Abel, 2010). For example, in New Zealand, where sex work is decriminalised, sex work businesses must comply with health and safety laws, just like other commercial businesses. However, there are no cumbersome regulations for sex workers to comply with as there are in jurisdictions where sex work is legalised (Mossman, 2007).

SEX WORK AND THE CRIMINALISATION OF PROSTITUTION

When discussing the decriminalisation of sex work, it is important to be clear as to what is meant by sex work, and to outline the nature and prevalence of its criminalisation. Sex work can encompass a range of activities, but for the purpose of this chapter it will be used to describe the exchange of physical sexual services for money – which has historically been termed 'prostitution' (Overs, 2002). While 'prostitution' and 'prostitute' will still be used in the chapter to authentically capture historical debates, 'sex worker' is primarily used, in recognition that 'prostitute' has become a pejorative term and because 'sex worker' is commonly preferred by those working in the sex industry (Lister, 2017).

In 2019, New Zealand was the only country to have decriminalised sex work.[2] The significance of this is underlined by a deeply ingrained global history of criminalisation. Criminalisation is, and has long been, the norm, while decriminalisation remains the exception within most countries.[3] Although criminalised frameworks dominate the legal landscape, approaches differ between jurisdictions. In Scotland, England, and Wales, for example, working as a sex worker or paying for sex are not technically crimes, but surrounding activities are illegal, such as soliciting (offering money in exchange for sex), brothel-keeping (running a premises in which sex work occurs), procuring (arranging for sex work to take place), and living on the earnings of prostitution (Sanders et al., 2009; Smith, 2015). In some countries both the sale and purchase of sex and its organisation (what has historically and colloquially been termed 'pimping') are criminalised (for example, in the US, China, South Africa, and Argentina). In other countries (for example, Sweden, Iceland, Canada, the Republic of Ireland, France, and

Norway), only the purchase of sex and the organisation of sex work are directly criminalised, in what is known as the Nordic model.

Thus, while the criminalisation of sex work remains the most common approach, precisely what (and who) is criminalised, and how this is implemented, differs considerably throughout the world. What also differs is *why* aspects of sex work are criminalised, and an appreciation of these rationales is essential to understanding subsequent arguments for and against decriminalisation.

THE UNDERPINNINGS OF CRIMINALISATION

Wagenaar and Altink (2012, p. 281) have stated that prostitution policy-making has been driven by 'morality politics', a type of political argument pertaining to issues which 'concern central, often embodied, aspects of personal life'. Such morally driven arguments in favour of criminalisation are historically anchored in patriarchal beliefs regarding women's sexuality (Jordan, 2010). Specifically, the patriarchal notion that women who are sexual are 'bad', while women who repress their sexuality are 'good', meant that prostitution came to be viewed as threatening the moral fabric of society.

Alongside patriarchal mores, other factors have also influenced the criminalising of sex work. Historically, sex workers were constructed as a threat to public health. For example, in the late nineteenth century, contagious diseases Acts were passed in New Zealand, Britain, and Australia in response to concerns about the possible impacts of prostitution on public health through the spread of syphilis (Ryan, 2005). Under this legislation, any woman suspected of being 'a common prostitute' could be apprehended by a justice of the peace and taken to a lock hospital for examination, and could be forcibly detained there for up to three months (Ryan, 2005). This framing of prostitution as a threat to public health did not languish in history. The presumption that sex workers are complicit in spreading disease is still alive. Yet, while stigmatising, this has also served as a rationale for decriminalisation in more recent times.

While the whole sex industry has historically been framed as a threat to moral order, varying degrees of tolerance have been afforded to the indoor sector, while street-based sex workers bore the brunt of criminalisation (Bartley, 2000). The vilification of street-based sex workers, targeted for defying societal expectations that prostitution should remain behind closed doors, was cemented in legislation such as New Zealand's Vagrancy Act 1866. Under this legislation, 'common prostitutes' who were deemed to be behaving in a 'riotous or indecent manner' could be labelled 'idle and disorderly' and subsequently imprisoned (Eldred-Grigg, 1984, p. 31). This singling out of street-based sex workers through policy and law has endured, and they remain the most criminalised population of sex workers globally (Scoular & O'Neill, 2007).

The idea that sex workers are deviant and threatening to moral values is therefore a fundamental strand underpinning the history of criminalising sex work in New Zealand and similar societies. However, by the mid-twentieth century sex workers were viewed in a contradictory way. On the one hand, they posed a threat to moral order, but on the other they were regarded as victims: 'fallen women' who were thought to be trapped in the sex industry due to financial desperation. In the same period, the judgement of men who paid for sex also changed, and clients came to be viewed as abnormal and incapable of accessing sex in other, morally accepted, ways (Scott, 2005).

Contemporary rationales for criminalising sex work link to arguments relating to the acceptability of prostitution and the safety of sex workers, with such debates becoming particularly heated among feminists. While some feminists conceptualise prostitution as a form of work, and support full decriminalisation because this is most conducive to workers' rights and occupational health and safety (see, for example, Frances & Gray, 2007; Krüsi et al., 2014; Laurie, 2010), others campaign for a model of criminalisation focused on 'tackling demand' for sex workers' services (see, for example, Bindel, 2018; Farley, 2004; Raymond, 2003). This latter perspective, commonly referred to as the 'radical', 'abolitionist' (or more recently 'neo-abolitionist') feminist perspective, is based on a framing of women who sell sex as victims (Vuolajärvi, 2019; Ward & Wylie, 2017). While this to some extent echoes the historical positioning of sex workers as 'fallen women', the abolitionist perspective conceptualises those who sell sex as victims of not only circumstance, but also male violence. Specifically, proponents of this perspective posit that there is no such thing as sex 'work', and prostitution is in itself a form of violence against women (Farley, 2004; Jeffreys, 1997; Raymond, 1998). Furthermore, they argue that the sex industry must be abolished as it is symbolic of gender inequality and has negative implications for all women (Bindel, 2018). They do not advocate for the direct criminalisation of those who sell sex, but rather for the criminalisation of clients and other third parties (e.g., brothel and agency managers), which as previously noted is known as the Nordic model. However, sex workers working under the Nordic model can still be criminalised indirectly through brothel-keeping laws or other associated legislation. For example, in 2019 two migrant sex workers were imprisoned in Ireland for brothel-keeping after they were apprehended by police while working together (Lynott, 2019). The endorsement of criminalisation among some feminists in the name of gender equality has led to a 'carceral feminism' in which police powers and wider criminal justice system activities are used to repress the sex industry (Bernstein, 2012, p. 240; Mac & Smith, 2018). However, while criminalisation of the sex industry remains the norm globally, calls to decriminalise sex work have been growing louder.

THE CASE FOR DECRIMINALISATION

The campaign to decriminalise sex work has gathered momentum over the past 30 years, with successful sex worker-driven campaigns in New South Wales in Australia (1999) and Aotearoa New Zealand (2003) (Aroney & Crofts, 2019). An increasingly diverse group of allies (such as Amnesty International, the World Health Organization, and the United Nations) have joined sex workers in their call for decriminalisation (Abel, 2018; Amnesty International, 2016). This diversity is mirrored by myriad rationales for decriminalising sex work. To some extent, rationales are based on the harms of criminalisation, which have been well documented. For example, the criminalisation of sex workers and/or their clients has been associated with increasing risks of violence, through sex workers having to work more covertly so that they avoid detection by police (Brooks-Gordon, 2006; Krüsi et al., 2014; Wotton, 2005). Thus, it is argued that the decriminalisation of sex work will help to minimise risk by ensuring that sex workers can work more visibly (Armstrong, 2014). Some arguments in favour of decriminalisation are based on an understanding that criminalisation itself is what underpins and sustains many of the harms of sex work (Graham, 2017).

While some decriminalisation rationales are focused almost exclusively on what harms a legislative approach would reduce or eliminate, others focus on what value decriminalisation would add. For example, sex worker-led organisations have often centred on the issue of rights, arguing that decriminalisation is important because it would afford sex workers rights that they do not have access to when their work is criminalised (Mac & Smith, 2018). Access to rights would better place sex workers to challenge exploitative working practices, violence, and discrimination (Lopez-Embury & Sanders, 2009).

However, while the language of harm reduction and rights has provided a strong platform for advocates of decriminalisation, such arguments have been contested. Opposition is typically grounded in perceptions of the acceptability of sex work. For example, as noted earlier, those holding abolitionist feminist perspectives reject the concept of sex work, and view the sex industry as a fundamental site of women's oppression. From this perspective, full decriminalisation (where it is not against the law to sell, purchase, or facilitate and profit from sex work) is castigated on the basis that sex work is intrinsically harmful (Bindel, 2018). Other opponents continue to draw on arguments pertaining to morality, objecting on the basis that decriminalisation would normalise sex work and send a message to society that it is legitimate. These stances are clearly persuasive, since the decriminalisation of sex work remains a rare legislative approach despite long-standing campaigns for it. Thus, understanding how decriminalisation has been achieved in the few contexts it has is very important. This chapter will now turn to examine a successful case study in New Zealand, where sex work was decriminalised in 2003.

CASE STUDY: THE DECRIMINALISATION OF SEX WORK IN AOTEAROA NEW ZEALAND

As the only country in which sex work is decriminalised, Aotearoa New Zealand is now central to international debates on sex work laws. Before 2003, however, New Zealand was not 'on the map' in relation to its prostitution policy; and as a colonised country, its laws historically mirrored those of Britain. Section 26 of the Summary Offences Act 1981 made it an offence to offer money in exchange for sex in a public place, meaning that sex workers could be convicted for soliciting. Section 147 of the Crimes Act 1961 made it an offence to manage a brothel, section 148 made it illegal to live on the earnings of prostitution of another person, and section 149 prohibited procuring sex for another person. Thus, the range of offences essentially made it impossible for sex workers to work without breaking laws (Healy et al., 2010).

The campaign for decriminalisation was initiated by sex workers who were dissatisfied with these laws and their impact on their work and broader lives. The establishment of the New Zealand Prostitutes Collective (NZPC) in 1987 marked the start of this campaign (Healy et al., 2010). While the NZPC is now a government-funded organisation with several community bases throughout the country, the organisation emerged following informal meetings between a diverse group of sex workers – including Māori, transgender, and street-based sex workers – who wanted to challenge their criminalisation (Wilton, 2019). Although the core focus underpinning the organisation was realising rights for sex workers, under the leadership of Catherine Healy the group organised strategically and practically around the issue of sexual health in the context of the AIDS epidemic. This enabled funding to be secured through the Department of Health in 1988 to provide sexual health services to sex workers for the purpose of harm reduction. This strategic focus would prove crucially important to the eventual decriminalisation of sex work as the campaign developed (Jordan, forthcoming 2021).

The path to decriminalisation was steadfastly pursued by the NZPC over a 15-year period. The Bill that led to the passing of the Prostitution Reform Act (PRA) was initially drafted by the NZPC along with Labour MP Tim Barnett, who sponsored and introduced it as a Private Members' Bill on 21 September 2000 (Barnett et al., 2010).[4] The harm reduction rationale underpinning the legislation inferred that decriminalisation could mitigate some of the harms associated with sex work, such as violence and exploitation. This rationale was important since it could reasonably appeal to a diverse range of people regardless of their moral position on sex work (Abel, 2017).

When the PRA was eventually passed on 25 June 2003, a diverse range of allies had joined in support of it, including the New Zealand AIDS Foundation, the Young Women's Christian Association, and the New Zealand Council of Women, in addition to several churches and

Catholic nuns. This meant that the voices of sex workers were far from isolated (Armstrong, 2018a; Barnett et al., 2010). However, the passing of the Act was still tenuous. There was considerable resistance to the proposed change in law from some corners, particularly among conservative Christian groups and some feminists (Barnett et al., 2010). Given that prostitution is imbued with stigma and stereotypes, owing to a long history of being deemed immoral, such resistance to decriminalisation is far from surprising. Opposition was often based on speculation regarding what might happen post-decriminalisation. A particularly important feature of the legislation was therefore a requirement that its impacts be reviewed three years after it was passed.

The PRA and the impacts of decriminalisation

The harm minimisation rationale underpinning the passage of the Prostitution Reform Act is evident in the wording of the legislation. As stated in section 3:

> The purpose of this Act is to decriminalise prostitution (while not endorsing or morally sanctioning prostitution or its use) and to create a framework that –
> (a) safeguards the human rights of sex workers and protects them from exploitation:
> (b) promotes the welfare and occupational health and safety of sex workers:
> (c) is conducive to public health:
> (d) prohibits the use in prostitution of persons under 18 years of age:
> (e) implements certain other related reforms.

The legislation focused on shifting power to sex workers through the provision of rights. The Act reduces the scope for exploitation by brothel operators and affords sex workers more control in interactions with their clients (Abel et al., 2007). This is evident in specific provisions of the Act. For example, section 16 makes it an offence to induce or compel a person to provide or continue to provide sexual services, meaning that it is against the law to coerce or force another person to do sex work. Section 17 states that sex workers have a right to refuse to provide sexual services at any time, meaning that they can refuse to see a client at any point. In recognition of the difference in maturity needed to provide commercial sex versus engaging in non-commercial sex, sections 20–23 of the PRA prohibit paying for sex with anyone under the age of 18, assisting a person under 18 to do sex work, or living on the earnings of a person under 18 (while the age of consent in New Zealand is 16). Importantly, though, young people themselves cannot be criminalised if they are found to be working in the sex industry (Abel et al., 2010).

As previously noted, a particularly important feature of the Act is a requirement that its impacts be evaluated within three years of its enactment. To this end, research was conducted by public health researchers from the Christchurch School of Medicine (see Abel et al., 2007). The research involved qualitative interviews with 58 sex workers and a quantitative survey, which was completed by 772 sex workers throughout New Zealand. The evaluation found numerous positive impacts of decriminalisation. For example, over half of survey participants who had worked prior to the enactment of the PRA felt that police attitudes had improved significantly towards sex workers since the law had changed (Abel et al., 2007). The research also indicated an increased willingness among sex workers to refuse to see clients they did not want to see, with 68 per cent of survey participants reporting that they had refused to see a client in the previous 12 months, compared with 47 per cent before the law changed. This highlights the value of the rights afforded by the Act in shifting power in favour of sex workers (Abel et al., 2007; Abel, 2014). Over 90 per cent of survey participants felt that they had stronger employment, occupational health and safety, and legal rights under the PRA. In-depth interviews also indicated that sex workers felt more in control of their interactions with clients (Abel et al., 2007).

The overall review of the Act was presided over by the Prostitution Law Review Committee (PLRC). Members of the PLRC were appointed by the Ministry of Justice and comprised a diverse range of people, including sex workers, academics, a former police officer, a city counsellor, a public health official, a brothel operator, representatives of NGOs, a general practitioner, a social worker, and a nun. The committee met regularly for five years following the PRA's enactment to monitor and discuss the impacts, and was required to produce a report after the five years to conclude on its findings. The report concluded that, overall, the PRA had been a success, as the vast majority of those working in the sex industry were in a better situation than they had been prior to the law change (PLRC, 2008).

Subsequent studies have built on this evidence and have indicated that decriminalisation has helped sex workers – particularly on the street – to manage the risks of violence, and has significantly improved relationships between police and street-based sex workers (Armstrong, 2014, 2016). Several examples reported by the media have also illustrated the impacts of decriminalisation in recent years. In 2014, a sex worker won a sexual harassment case against a brothel operator that she had pursued through the Human Rights Review Tribunal (Duff, 2014). In the same year, it was reported that when a client refused to pay a street-based sex worker for the services she had provided, police escorted the client to an ATM to ensure payment (Wynn, 2014). And in 2018, the founder of the NZPC – Catherine Healy – was made a Dame in recognition of her services to the rights of sex workers (Davison, 2018). Such occurrences would not have been possible when sex workers were defined in law as criminals, and while the police operated to enforce the laws that criminalised aspects of their work.

LIMITATIONS OF DECRIMINALISATION

While there have been several important benefits of decriminalising sex work, there are also limitations. One is the fact that access to the rights afforded by the PRA is restricted to citizens and permanent residents of New Zealand. Section 19 of the PRA prohibits holders of temporary visas from engaging in sex work. Thus, temporary migrants are not able to access the protections of the PRA and can be deported if they come to the attention of authorities. Such sex workers are therefore still vulnerable to exploitation, and their access to justice is limited by their status as illegal workers(Armstrong, 2018b).

The PLRC report also highlighted limitations, noting that the official review of the Act found that many sex workers were still vulnerable to exploitative employment conditions and that stigma remained a problem (PLRC, 2008). This is to be expected. Exploitative labour practices occur across all forms of work, and thus it cannot be expected that decriminalisation will eliminate them. What decriminalisation has provided is a context in which sex workers have increased scope to challenge those who seek to exploit them, and have clear expectations of what constitutes unacceptable treatment in sex work businesses. The continued influence of stigma is, similarly, to be expected, given the long history that connects sex work to criminalisation and to the patriarchal legacies in which women's sexuality is subject to harsh societal judgement. In time, it will become clearer whether decriminalisation has made more substantial progress in reducing exploitation and gradually eroding stigma.

CONCLUSION

Decriminalisation is the process through which acts which were previously against the law become legally permissible. The decriminalisation of certain acts may be sought for several reasons, not least because criminalisation is profoundly discriminatory and/or because it is clearly causing harm. In the case of sex work, decriminalisation was sought by sex workers for decades, on the grounds that criminalisation denied sex workers their fundamental labour rights. The passage of the Prostitution Reform Act 2003, marking Aotearoa New Zealand as the first country to decriminalise sex work, brought about a landmark change in protecting sex workers' rights. It was also unique within New Zealand's broader approach to crime and justice, which has historically been punitive in many respects.

The decriminalisation of sex work was achieved largely due to the advocacy of sex workers themselves. However, the language of harm minimisation proved essential to the successful campaign since it was a rationale that a diverse range of people could relate to and support, regardless of their moral stance on the sex industry. Research conducted since decriminalisation indicates that the intention to minimise harm has largely been realised, particularly in terms of improved access to justice for sex workers through removing the risk of arrest and providing rights they can harness to challenge those who seek to exploit them.

The decriminalisation of sex work was a contentious change that some feared would have grave social consequences, mirroring concerns commonly raised regarding the proposed decriminalisation of other acts defined as crimes, such as abortion and drug use. The case of sex work decriminalisation in New Zealand provides crucial insights to inform these broader debates about liberalising laws, demonstrating that decriminalisation has improved the situation of sex workers, and there is no evidence of a widespread 'moral decline' some may have imagined prior to the law reform. Thus, the case highlights how the harms of criminalisation often far outweigh any advantages, and while decriminalisation is not a panacea it has clear benefits in terms of harm reduction and human rights. These are crucial lessons not only in New Zealand but also globally, offering a more fruitful pathway to overcome the futility of criminalisation.

STUDY QUESTIONS

- What are the differences between decriminalisation and legalisation?
- What are the key arguments for and against decriminalising sex work?
- What was the rationale for decriminalising sex work in New Zealand, and why was it successful?

FURTHER READING

Abel, G. M. (2014). A decade of decriminalization: Sex work 'down under' but not underground. *Criminology and Criminal Justice, 14*(5), 580–592. doi:10.1177/1748895814523024

Armstrong, L., & Abel, G. (Eds.). (2019). *Sex work and the New Zealand model: Decriminalisation and social change*. Bristol, UK: University of Bristol Press.

Mac, J., & Smith, M. (2018). *Revolting prostitutes: The fight for sex workers' rights*. London, UK: Verso Books.

NOTES

1 In the public referendum held in 2020, there was a majority vote in favour of passing the End of Life Choice Bill.

2 Sex work was first decriminalised in the Australian state of New South Wales in 1995 (Aroney & Crofts, 2019).

3 See https://www.nswp.org/sex-work-laws-map for a concise overview of the various approaches to sex work law globally.

4   Private Members' Bills (now known only as Members' Bills) can be put forward in a ballot system by any New Zealand MP who is not a minister. See New Zealand Parliament (2017).

REFERENCES

Abel, G. (2010). *Decriminalisation: A harm minimisation and human rights approach to regulating sex work*. Unpublished doctor of philosophy dissertation, Otago University, Dunedin, New Zealand.

Abel, G. (2017). In search of a free and fair society: The regulation of sex work in New Zealand. In E. E. Ward & G. Wylie (Eds.), *Feminism, prostitution and the state: The politics of neo-abolitionism* (pp. 140–155). Abingdon, UK: Routledge.

Abel, G. (2018). Decriminalisation of sex work protects human rights. *The British Medical Journal, 362*, k3630. doi:10.1136/bmj.k3630

Abel, G., Fitzgerald, L., & Brunton, C. (2007). *The impact of the Prostitution Reform Act on the health and safety practices of sex workers: Report to the Prostitution Law Review Committee*. Retrieved from https://www.otago.ac.nz/christchurch/otago018607.pdf

Abel, G., Healy, C., Bennachie, C., & Reed, A. (2010). The Prostitution Reform Act. In G. Abel, L. Fitzgerald, & C. Healy (Eds.), with A. Taylor, *Taking the crime out of sex work: New Zealand sex workers' fight for decriminalisation*. Bristol, UK: Policy Press.

Abel, G. M. (2014). A decade of decriminalization: Sex work 'down under' but not underground. *Criminology and Criminal Justice, 14*(5), 580–592. doi:10.1177/1748895814523024

Abortion Legislation Bill, 164–1 (2019).

Amnesty International. (2016). *Resolution on state obligations to respect, protect and fulfil the human rights of sex workers*. Retrieved from https://www.amnesty.org/en/policy-on-state-obligations-to-respect-protect-and-fulfil-the-human-rights-of-sex-workers/

Armstrong, L. (2010). Out of the shadows (and into a bit of light): Decriminalisation, human rights and street-based sex work in New Zealand. In K. Hardy, S. Kingston, & T. Sanders (Eds.), *New sociologies of sex work*. Farnham, UK: Ashgate.

Armstrong, L. (2014). Screening clients in a decriminalised street-based sex industry: Insights into the experiences of New Zealand sex workers. *Australian and New Zealand Journal of Criminology, 47*(2), 207–222. doi:10.1177/0004865813510921

Armstrong, L. (2016). From law enforcement to protection? Interactions between sex workers and police in a decriminalized street-based sex industry. *British Journal of Criminology, 57*(3), 570–588. doi:10.1093/bjc/azw019

Armstrong, L. (2018a). New Zealand. In B. Gerasimov & M. Stacey (Eds.), *Sex workers organising for change: Self-representation, community mobilisation, and working conditions*. Bangkok, Thailand: Global Alliance Against Traffic in Women.

Armstrong, L. (2018b). Sex worker activism and the decriminalisation of sex work in New Zealand. In S. Dewey, I. Crowhurst, & C. Izugbara (Eds.), *The Routledge international handbook of sex industry research*. London, UK: Routledge.

Aroney, E., & Crofts, P. (2019). How sex worker activism influenced the decriminalisation of sex work in NSW, Australia. *International Journal for Crime, Justice and Social Democracy, 8*(2), 50–67.

Barnett, T., Healy, C., Reed, A., & Bennachie, C. (2010). Lobbying for decriminalisation. In G. Abel, L. Fitzgerald, & C. Healy (Eds.), with A. Taylor, *Taking the crime out of sex work: New Zealand sex workers' fight for decriminalisation*. Bristol, UK: Policy Press.

Bartley, P. (2000). *Prostitution: Prevention and reform in England, 1860–1914*. London, UK: Routledge.

Bernstein, E. (2012). Carceral politics as gender justice? The 'traffic in women' and neoliberal circuits of crime, sex, and rights. *Theory and Society, 41*(3), 233–259.

Bindel, J. (2018). *The pimping of prostitution: Abolishing the sex work myth*. London, UK: Palgrave Macmillan.

Boomen, M. (2018). Where New Zealand stands internationally: A comparison of offence profiles and recidivism rates. *Practice: The New Zealand Corrections Journal, 6*(1). Retrieved from https://www.corrections.govt.nz/resources/research_and_statistics/journal/volume_6_issue_1_july_2018/where_new_zealand_stands_internationally_a_comparison_of_offence_profiles_and_recidivism_rates.

Brooks-Gordon, B. (2006). *The price of sex: Prostitution, policy and society*. Cullompton, UK: Willan.

Davison, I. (2018). Queen's Birthday Honours: Dame Catherine Healy – Sex workers 'brought into the fold'. *New Zealand Herald*. Retrieved from https://www.nzherald.co.nz/nz/news/article.cfm?c_id=1&objectid=12062840

Duff, M. (2014). Sex worker gets $25,000 over harassment. *Dominion Post*. Retrieved from https://www.stuff.co.nz/business/industries/9777879/Sex-worker-gets–25–000-over-harassment

Eldred-Grigg, S. (1984). *Pleasures of the flesh: Sex and drugs in colonial New Zealand, 1840–1915*. Wellington, New Zealand: Reed.

End of Life Choice Bill 269–3 (2019).

Farley, M. (2004). 'Bad for the body, bad for the heart': Prostitution harms women even if legalised or decriminalised. *Violence Against Women, 10*(10), 1087–1125.

Frances, R., & Gray, A. (2007). Unsatisfactory, discriminatory, unjust and inviting corruption: Feminists and the decriminalisation of street prostitution in New South Wales. *Australian Feminist Studies, 22*(53), 307–324.

Graham, L. (2017). Governing sex work through crime: Creating the context for violence and exploitation. *The Journal of Criminal Law, 81*(3), 201–216. doi:10.1177/0022018317702802

Healy, C., Bennachie, C., & Reed, A. (2010). History of the New Zealand Prostitutes Collective. In G. Abel, L. Fitzgerald, & C. Healy (Eds.), with A. Taylor, *Taking the crime out of sex work: New Zealand sex workers' fight for decriminalisation*. Bristol, UK: Policy Press.

Herter, A., Fem, E., & Lehmann, M. (2017). *Professed protection, pointless provisions: Overview of the German Prostitutes Protection Act*. Retrieved from http://www.sexworkeurope.org/news/general-news/germany-sex-workers-rights-day-icrse-launches-briefing-paper-germanys-new

Jeffreys, S. (1997). *The idea of prostitution*. North Melbourne, Victoria, Australia: Spinifex.

Jordan, J. (2010). Of whalers, diggers and 'soiled doves': A history of the sex industry in New Zealand. In G. Abel, L. Fitzgerald, & C. Healy (Eds.), with A. Taylor, *Taking the crime out of sex work: New Zealand sex workers' fight for decriminalisation*. Bristol: Policy Press.

Jordan, J. (forthcoming, 2021). 'On the clients' terms': Sex work in New Zealand before decriminalisation. In L. Armstrong & G. Abel (Eds.), *Sex work and the New Zealand model: Decriminalisation and social change*. Bristol, UK: Bristol University Press.

Krüsi, A., Pacey, K., Bird, L., Taylor, C., Chettiar, J., Allan, S., . . . Shannon, K. (2014). Criminalisation of clients: Reproducing vulnerabilities for violence and poor health among street-based sex workers in Canada – a qualitative study. *The British Medical Journal Open, 4*(6). doi:10.1136/bmjopen–2014–005191

Laurie, A. (2010). Several sides to this story: Feminist views of prostitution reform. In G. Abel, L. Fitzgerald, & C. Healy (Eds.), with A. Taylor, *Taking the crime out of sex work: New Zealand sex workers' fight for decriminalisation*. Bristol, UK: Policy Press.

Lister, K. (2017). Sex workers or prostitutes? Why words matter. *INews*. Retrieved from https://inews.co.uk/opinion/columnists/sex-workers-prostitutes-words-matter–95447

Little, A. (2019). *New Zealanders to make the decision in cannabis referendum* [Press release]. Retrieved from https://www.beehive.govt.nz/release/new-zealanders-make-decision-cannabis-referendum

Lopez-Embury, S., & Sanders, T. (2009). Sex workers, labour rights and unionization. In T. Sanders, M. O'Neill, & J. Pitcher (Eds.), *Prostitution: Sex work, policy and politics*. London, UK: Sage.

Lynott, L. (2019, June 10). Disgust as jail sentences are handed to sex workers, one of them pregnant. *Irish Independent*. Retrieved from https://www.independent.ie/irish-news/courts/disgust-as-jail-sentences-are-handed-to-sex-workers-one-of-them-pregnant–38197205.html

Mac, J., & Smith, M. (2018). *Revolting prostitutes: The fight for sex workers' rights*. London, UK: Verso Books.

Mossman, E. (2007). *International approaches to decriminalising or legalising prostitution.* Prepared for the Ministry of Justice. Wellington, New Zealand: Crime and Justice Research Centre, Victoria University of Wellington. Retrieved from https://www.procon.org/wp-content/uploads/newzealandreport.pdf

New Zealand Parliament. (2017, February 15). *Members' Bills* [Research paper]. Retrieved from https://www.parliament.nz/en/pb/research-papers/document/00PLLawRP2017011/members-bills

Overs, C. (2002). *Sex workers: Part of the solution. An analysis of HIV prevention programming to prevent HIV transmission during commercial sex in developing countries.* Retrieved from https://www.who.int/hiv/topics/vct/sw_toolkit/115solution.pdf

Prostitution Law Review Committee (PLRC). (2008). *Report of the Prostitution Law Review Committee on the operation of the Prostitution Reform Act 2003.* Retrieved from http://prostitutescollective.net/wp-content/uploads/2016/10/report-of-the-nz-prostitution-law-committee-2008.pdf

Pratt, J. (2017). New Zealand penal policy in the twenty-first century. In A. Deckert & R. Sarre (Eds.), *The Palgrave handbook of Australian and New Zealand criminology, crime and justice* (pp. 347–361). Cham, Switzerland: Palgrave Macmillan.

Pratt, J., and Clarke, M. (2005). Penal populism in New Zealand. *Punishment and Society, 7,* 303–322.

Raymond, J. (2003). Ten reasons for not legalizing prostitution and a legal response to the demand for prostitution. In M. Farely (Ed.), *Prostitution, trafficking and traumatic stress.* New York, NY: The Haworth Press.

Raymond, J. G. (1998). Prostitution as violence against women: NGO stonewalling in Beijing and elsewhere. *Women's Studies International Forum, 21*(1), 1–9.

Ryan, A. (2005). From dangerous sexualities to risky sex: Regulating sexuality in the name of public health. In G. Hawkes & J. Scott (Eds.), *Perspectives in human sexuality.* South Melbourne, Victoria, Australia: Oxford University Press.

Sanders, T., O'Neill, M., & Pitcher, J. (2009). *Prostitution: Sex work, policy and politics.* London, UK: Sage.

Scott, J. (2005). A labour of sex? Female and male prostitution. In G. Hawkes & J. Scott (Eds.), *Perspectives in human sexuality.* South Melbourne, Victoria, Australia: Oxford University Press.

Scoular, J., & O'Neill, M. (2007). Regulating prostitution: Social inclusion, responsibilization and the politics of prostitution reform. *British Journal of Criminology, 47*(5), 764–778. doi:10.1093/bjc/azm014

Smith, E. (2015). The changing landscape of Scottish responses to sex work: Addressing violence against sex workers. *Graduate Journal of Social Science, 11*(2), 101–128.

Vuolajärvi, N. (2019). Governing in the name of caring – the Nordic model of prostitution and its punitive consequences for migrants who sell sex. *Sexuality Research and Social Policy, 16*(2), 151–165. doi:10.1007/s13178-018-0338-9

Wagenaar, H., & Altink, S. (2012). Prostitution as morality politics or why it is exceedingly difficult to design and sustain effective prostitution policy. *Sexuality Research and Social Policy, 9*(3), 279–292. doi:10.1007/s13178-012-0095-0

Ward, E., & Wylie, G. (2017). Introducing neo-abolitionism: Definition, drivers and debates. In E. E. Ward & G. Wylie (Eds.), *Feminism, prostitution and the state: The politics of neo-abolitionism.* London, UK: Routledge.

Wilton, K. (2019). *My body, my business: New Zealand sex workers in an era of change.* Dunedin, New Zealand: Otago University Press.

Wotton, R. (2005). The relationship between street-based sex workers and the police in the effectiveness of HIV prevention strategies *Research for Sex Work, 8,* 11–13.

Wynn, K. (2014). Police help short-changed sex worker. *New Zealand Herald.* Retrieved from https://www.nzherald.co.nz/nz/news/article.cfm?c_id=1&objectid=11292537

32

Deportations
Sorting Citizens across Borders

Elizabeth Stanley

Borders have always been sites of tension. However, border closures and controls have taken increased social and political prominence in recent years. From former US president Donald Trump's endeavours to 'build a wall' or his government's 'zero tolerance' separation of young migrant children from their parents to the Australian government's continued reliance on inhumane immigration prisons, many Western states have reasserted their power through populist border controls. These controls 'function theatrically', as they 'present an image' of a strong and 'sovereign state power' (Aas, 2011, p. 333) able to fortify boundaries and protect citizens from real and imagined threats (Malloch & Stanley, 2005). Of course, such performances are established at a time when most states do not protect people from significant harms, including global economic inequalities and the escalating devastations of climate crises emerging from advanced capitalism that tend to force population movements.

Borders illustrate the 'capture' not only of territory but also of power, people, state force, and taxation (Mbembe, 2018). For these reasons, Western states spend inordinate resources on controlling borders, often through highly technical processes. For example, airport scanners, biometric passports, sensors, drones, and other surveillance technologies work to track and prevent entry, control movement, screen arrivals, or identify those to be deported. At the same time, border work is also primitive. Western states frequently refuse protections to those attempting to travel to safer or more prosperous destinations. In 2018, over two thousand people were allowed to drown in the Mediterranean Sea (United Nations High Commissioner for Refugees, 2018), while, in 2016, European states detained over 47,000 people in 'camps' on the basis that they were 'ineligible' for protection, transit, or entry (Mbembe, 2019).

We might imagine that most border activities occur at the edge of physical territories (for example, at local ports), but border work is often 'carried out remotely, far away from us' (Mbembe, 2019, para. 18). Many Western states send military ships to patrol distant coastlines to prevent the movement of those who might reach 'our' shores, and they compel airlines to prohibit transit for visa-less travellers, especially those from designated 'risky' countries. This border work signifies belonging, and it makes whole populations 'potential illegal migrant[s], unable to move' without state approval (Mbembe, 2018, para. 17). It determines who must be territorially excluded, often on the constructions of racialised, economic, political, and gendered differences (Bosworth & Guild, 2008). Thus, those who cross borders are marked, assessed, digitised, and sorted, and only certain populations may travel freely around this planet that 'rightfully belongs' to all (Mbembe, 2019).

Across many Western states, such preventive exclusions are dovetailed with an expanding deployment of deportations for those who are found unpalatable or threatening. Here, the official agenda is interpreted towards a state duty to reduce 'risks' and provide a sense of community protection, whatever the costs (Weber & Pickering, 2013). Under these remits, deportations are 'a governmental device for the exporting of risk' (Weber & Pickering, 2013, p. 112). While state agencies can be preoccupied with integration and community cohesion for those who may belong (seen, for example, in New Zealand's Migrant Settlement and Integration Strategy), they are increasingly concerned with exclusion and the banishment of those found not to fit.

This chapter reflects on the nature and expansion of deportations. It charts the rise of deportations among Western states, but also focuses on two case examples from Aotearoa New Zealand: first, the shameful former practice of 'dawn raids' that has deeply affected Pasifika populations; and, second, the more recent use of detention and expulsion from New Zealand, and also with regard to New Zealand citizens expelled from Australia. The chapter demonstrates that these deportation processes have reproduced structural inequalities and discrimination, with those affected enduring significant stigmatisation and state harms.

DEPORTATIONS AND CITIZENSHIP

Territorial banishment has a long history, from the exile of foreigners or offenders from Roman territories to the transportation of British 'criminals' to the Australian colony during the eighteenth and nineteenth centuries (Grewcock, 2014). However, more recently, banishment practices have gained renewed significance within Western states.

While these exclusionary practices may appear to be administratively and technically neutral, applied to all non-citizens in a reasonable way, deportation practices are opaque and highly politicised (Bigo, 2007). The criteria for the revocation of visas and the rationale for deportations are ever-shifting (Grewcock, 2014), so much so that individuals who devote their whole lives and families to a country can find that they are deemed 'illegal' and deported on the grounds of incomplete paper trails or incorrect records. This experience was repeatedly demonstrated in the UK's recent Windrush scandal,[1] in which Afro-Caribbean British people were targeted as illegal immigrants and deported. Their family ties, employment records, community relationships, home ownership, and civic contributions counted for little in their appeals against deportation.

The system for identifying who is deportable has often been based on stereotypical assumptions of 'race, poverty [and] inequality' (Bigo, 2007, p. 31). During the twentieth century, most deportations were targeted towards people from developing countries (Grewcock, 2014).

However, the grounds for deportations are changing and expanding in new ways, such that the risks of actual or potential conduct, and even a person's associations, have also come to be grounds for expulsion. At the heart of the issue for most is a lack or loss of citizenship.

The contingent nature of citizenship

There is a hierarchy between foreigners that is determined by Otherness – whether the 'Other' is regarded as suspicious or threatening, but also whether they might seamlessly integrate, assimilate, and overtly contribute to the mainstream economy and culture. Some foreigners, especially the global elites who promise finances, connections, skills, or status, regularly enjoy a hyper-hospitality from receiving governments. With mobility and privilege, they travel freely across the globe and glide through border processing. They also enjoy fast-track citizenship processes, sometimes outside the usual rules. For example, in 2011, National minister Nathan Guy granted New Zealand citizenship to a US billionaire, Peter Thiel. Ordinarily, permanent residents must reside in New Zealand for at least 1350 days over five years to gain citizenship status, yet Thiel had spent just 12 days in New Zealand and never planned to live in the country.

While citizenship is often presented as a 'natural order', then, it is profoundly discretionary and reflects a process of economic, racialised, and political sorting (Stumpf, 2014). In Western states, citizenship has long been linked to state calculations of how an individual might contribute to the economy and the market. Migrants must prove they will optimise opportunities and engage in entrepreneurship and self-investment towards a nation's economic growth (Epstein, 2007). In an era of neoliberal responsibilisation, there is also an expectation that non-citizens will not require financial safety nets. Neoliberal states (such as New Zealand, Australia, and the UK) have continued to roll back welfare supports for non-citizens, placing these individuals in ever-precarious positions. Those without citizenship are subsequently more likely to face high levels of financial hardship and employment insecurity, and they are vulnerable to exploitation, family stress, ill-health, and violence (Stringer, 2016; Tazreiter et al., 2016). Such conditions make non-citizens increasingly susceptible to behaviours that can lead to their official identification as criminal or immigration risks (Tazreiter et al., 2016). However, when non-citizens fail to thrive, they are blamed for their perceived lack of resilience and their perceived resource claims (Aas, 2014; Brown, 2016).

Citizenship in Western states has also been tightened and contractualised (Somers, 2008), so that non-citizens have to prove their conformity and 'their ability to perform citizenship, through acts of speech, demeanour, gesture, consumption and display' (Perera, 2009, p. 649). These performances often mean that non-citizens must prove their national belonging and commitment in ways not expected of citizens. Beyond economic utility and self-sufficiency, they are often propelled to demonstrate their national knowledge (e.g., through citizenship tests) and overtly show allegiance to mainstream social and political norms (Brown, 2016; Stanley, 2017).

At the same time, historical stereotypes presenting foreigners as 'dangerous' have also found renewed favour across multiple political and policy settings. Western politicians frequently propound concerns that outsiders are societal threats, such that a 'culture of fear' exists about non-citizens and their presumed propensities for lawlessness (Stumpf, 2014, p. 237). Authorities increasingly attempt to monitor and disrupt 'potential danger[s]' among non-citizens (Bigo, 2007, p. 30). These strategies dismiss established legal principles – such as the presumption of innocence – in favour of disrupting 'risky' associations or pre-empting potential future criminality (McCulloch & Wilson, 2015). Increasingly, non-citizens can be deported for who they are, how they act, or what they may become. These interventions allow crime and immigration control authorities to demarcate a border between citizens to be protected and suspect communities, with those produced as deportable being permanently excluded from society.

It is also useful to acknowledge that while citizenship is meant to be absolute, this legal standing can also be contingent on conformity (Bosworth et al., 2012). Citizens who espouse contentious views, are deemed disloyal, or are seen to pose a danger, increasingly face the removal of citizenship. In the UK, for example, the home secretary can remove citizenship if they believe that 'it is conducive to the public good' (Bosworth & Guild, 2008, p. 710). On this basis, over 100 people were stripped of British citizenship in 2017 alone (Dearden, 2019). In 2019, British Home Secretary Sajid Javid cancelled the citizenship of a young British woman, Shamima Begum, who had never committed a crime but was groomed as a 15-year-old to leave the UK to join Islamic State.[2]

Ideologically driven treatments mean that many non-citizens (and even demonised citizens) occupy an insecure status that is perpetually threatened. For those targeted as 'illegals', the border is always in operation and it is everywhere, across physical spaces and social interactions (Bigo, 2007). Border policing can be undertaken in homes, workplaces, and community settings, as demonstrated in the 2019 multi-city sweeps by US Federal Immigration and Customs Enforcement (ICE) to arrest thousands of 'undocumented migrants'. Living under a threat of deportation creates many insecurities – those cast as 'outsiders' continually fear being caught out, they do not want to engage with state agencies, they are nervous about claiming social supports, and they can often endure exploitative working conditions and treatments (Doering-White et al., 2016; Harris, 2013). It is an 'eternal probation' (Newstead & Frisso, 2013, p. 387).

This ambiguous position can be lifelong. That is, while many non-citizens hold a deep sense of belonging to their country of residence (and claim social citizenship on the basis of their family ties, employment, and contributions), they may be perennially excluded. As populist rhetoric has become increasingly intolerant of difference, a hierarchy of justice is beginning to develop across Western states (Bosworth et al., 2012). Those without formal membership now endure a host of different procedural treatments, protections, rights standards, and rule of law (Aas, 2014, p. 521).

NEW ZEALAND AS A DEPORTING STATE

The New Zealand state has not been immune to these border management activities. In many ways, the New Zealand image is one of openness – stridently neoliberal, the country has opened up borders for the movement of goods, finance, tourism, education, and so on. Those who are wealthy or who hold international sociocultural capital enjoy a hospitable welcome from authorities. Geographically isolated, the country also has few border pressures. Aotearoa New Zealand has accommodated relatively few refugees compared to other Western states – for a long time, New Zealand took up to 750 UN-mandated refugees each year, but, following prolonged campaigning from civil society groups, from 2020 the annual quota increased to 1500. The vast majority of non-citizens who arrive at the border are travelling as short-term tourists or hold visas to work or study for longer periods. Some Pacific Island populations (for example, from Samoa, Kiribati, Tuvalu, Tonga, and Fiji) may also apply for ballot-determined residence visas, on account of the historical relationships between New Zealand and their states.

Notwithstanding the country's reputation as a progressive, rights-conscious country, New Zealand authorities have also operated in harmful ways towards non-citizens. This has been most apparent in narratives and actions towards those determined to be 'overstayers', a category that has been heavily racialised and directed especially to Pasifika populations. This has contemporary resonance, but has longer roots in the dawn raids.

The dawn raids

Aotearoa New Zealand has an established history of restricting immigration to white populations (Beaglehole, 2013). Through most of the nineteenth and twentieth centuries, immigration regulations established criteria that favoured groups aligned with mainstream Pākehā society. British, Australians, North Americans, and Europeans were prioritised, with restrictions imposed on Indians, Chinese, Pacific populations, and other 'race aliens' deemed less able to assimilate into mainstream New Zealand society (Beaglehole, 2013). Even in 1953, a memo from the Department of External Affairs noted that 'we are and intend to remain a country of European development . . . Whereas we have done much to encourage immigration from Europe, we do everything to discourage it from Asia' (Beaglehole, 2015, para. 30; see also Botha & Poynting, chapter 9 this volume).

Yet, following the Second World War, labour was in short supply around New Zealand. To kick-start the economy, political parties openly encouraged immigration from Pacific islands (Macpherson, 2004), and diverse Pasifika communities settled in the 1950s, especially around Auckland and Wellington. Any welcome was short-lived, however, as Pasifika populations were soon economically and politically marginalised; they were poorly paid in 'unwanted' work and faced endemic sociocultural discrimination. New Zealand's economic recession during the 1970s (which emerged from the oil crisis and worsening trade conditions) provided fertile ground for racist rhetoric to develop. Pasifika people were increasingly blamed for a host of social problems – from urban decline, or unemployment, to violent crime (Krishnan et al., 1994; Spoonley & Bedford, 2012).

The scapegoat of the 'overstayer' began to take hold, fuelled first by the Labour government and then with more vigour by the National government (McFadden, 2015). Despite the fact that most overstayers were actually from Britain and Australia, the term was overwhelmingly directed to Pasifika people (Spoonley & Bedford, 2012). In the mid-1970s, the police developed an initiative called Operation Pot Black where officers undertook 'random' checks on residency documentation on the street, at workplaces, and in local bars. In 1974, this escalated into dawn raids on the homes of those 'who looked like Pacific Islanders or potential overstayers, regardless of their status as citizens' (Anae, 2012, p. 222). During the raids, immigration and police officers forcibly entered homes with demands for proof of passports and visas. For the Pasifika families involved, these were violent, terrifying, and humiliating experiences. Some families completely lost contact with those deported. The raids also led to some Pasifika children being placed into institutional state care, leading them to sites of abuse (Stanley, 2016).[3]

The raids were vehemently resisted, not least by 'highly incensed' members of the Polynesian Panthers, a group that formed in 1971 as a response to the racist state repression (McFadden, 2015; Reid, 2010). The Panthers undertook all kinds of community activities. They organised to protect those targeted by distributing pamphlets that informed people of their rights when interacting with police (one written by a well-known Māngere lawyer, and future New Zealand prime minister, David Lange), established activity records of police and immigration officials, and provided legal supports to those fighting deportation (Tahana, 2019). They also organised food co-operatives, ran bus services, and created safe homework spaces for Pasifika children to study (Anae, 2012; Tahana, 2019). However, their main role was to disrupt racist actions to Pasifika communities. They targeted discriminatory landlords with direct action (such as piling rubbish at their houses), and followed police officers going about their work, as part of so-called Police Investigation Group (P.I.G.) patrols (Tahana, 2019). They even performed dawn raids on the homes of the minister of immigration, Bill Birch, and National MP George Gair. Arriving at 3 a.m., with loudspeakers and spotlights, the Panthers demanded to view their passports (McFadden, 2015; Pacific Media Centre, 2019). The police raids ended soon afterwards (Reid, 2010).

The raids and deportations, as well as the broader treatment of Pasifika populations during this time, have been regarded as a significant trauma in New Zealand–Pacific relationships.[4] While the work of the Panthers has continued to inspire Polynesian music, community actions, and struggles against injustice, the raids have also left legacies of intergenerational trauma.

Contemporary 'overstayers'

From 1 July 2018 to 30 June 2019, Immigration New Zealand deported 453 people, with another 1321 choosing to voluntarily leave during this period. Deportations are directed to those who are 'overstayers', who have 'character issues', or who have been convicted of criminal offences (Immigration New Zealand, 2019). An estimated 13,895 'overstayers' resided in New Zealand at December 2017, with identified populations mostly coming from Tonga, Samoa, China, India, Malaysia, and the UK. These numbers have dropped significantly from the early 2000s, when estimates tended to sit at between 18,000 and 20,000 people (Immigration New Zealand, 2018).

Despite a declining problem, there has been something of a resurgent media and political discourse on overstayers in New Zealand. Commentaries often revolve around the presumed economic burdens of those who 'overstay' (often without empirical evidence and with a focus on Pasifika peoples), and the costs faced by immigration authorities in policing this concern (*One News*, 2018). Dovetailing with this escalated reporting, there has been continued debate on who belongs in New Zealand, as well as whether New Zealand should assist Pacific neighbours who face specific economic and environmental risks. For example, in 2018, the journalist Heather du Plessis-Allan reiterated 'dawn raids' themes in her comments that Pacific peoples were 'sponging off New Zealand'; she added, 'The Pacific Islands don't matter. They are nothing but leeches on us' (Peacock, 2018, para. 1, 28). The Broadcasting Standards Authority later ruled that her comments were 'inflammatory' and 'had the potential to cause widespread offence and distress' (Broadcasting Standards Authority, 2019).

At the same time, Immigration New Zealand has increasingly engaged risk-profiling to guide immigration and deportation decisions (Campbell, 2018). Guided by questions of who might pose a burden in the future – on the grounds of health, employment, welfare, or crime – it is anticipated that Pasifika populations will find that their genetic predispositions to long-term health concerns (such as diabetes or obesity) could make them more vulnerable to exclusion, at entry or via deportation (Campbell, 2018). Inequalities and even ethnicity are increasingly being 'scientifically' reproduced as 'risks' to New Zealand society. But for Pasifika people, who often have family members in New Zealand and who are now coping with increasingly precarious and risky conditions – from the Western depletion of their natural resources to climate crises or the global advanced capitalist trade routes that mark island homelands – the ability to secure employment in New Zealand can be a strategy of both belonging and survival. For those who live beyond their visa, there is a significant sense of shame and fear (Anae, 2012).

DEPORTING NEW ZEALANDERS

New Zealanders have not been immune to the practice of deportations, as Kiwis are increasingly targeted in neighbouring Australia (see Stanley, 2017). Following the 1973 Trans-Tasman Travel Arrangement, New Zealanders readily moved 'across the ditch' to reside and work in Australia. At the 2016 Australian Census, almost 520,000 New Zealand citizens lived in Australia, with over 200,000 in Queensland alone; almost 65 per cent had been in Australia for over a decade (Department of Home Affairs, 2018).

Historically, New Zealanders were treated as permanent residents in Australia (with reciprocal agreements in place for Australians in New Zealand). Over time, however, these hospitalities retracted in Australia, as a stigmatising discourse of New Zealand 'bludgers . . .

soaking up the sun on Bondi beach' consolidated (Nolan, 2015, p. 262). Only Australian citizens now enjoy the full range of welfare safety nets and services. Gaining citizenship is, however, difficult, especially for those who do not work in a skills-shortage industry or do not have a long-term Australian partner. Even those born in Australia, to long-resident New Zealand parents, have no automatic right (Nolan, 2015, p. 260). It is estimated that less than 10 per cent of New Zealanders who arrived between 2006 and 2012 have gained permanent status (Tazreiter et al., 2016, p. 114).

While New Zealanders contribute an estimated A$5 billion in taxes each year, they are not able to fully access services and opportunities (Chenery, 2016). As one example, children of New Zealand citizens are half as likely as their Australian counterparts to attend university (Chenery, 2016; Tazreiter et al., 2016). New Zealanders of Māori and Pasifika descent have been particularly hard-hit by retractions. Māori rarely hold resident visas, and their children 'stand little chance' of gaining Australian citizenship or enjoying the educational, health, or social advantages of full civic membership (Hamer, 2012, p. 14). Australia has also sought to limit pathways to Australia from Pasifika peoples who first gain citizenship to New Zealand (Tazreiter et al., 2016, p. 106). As in New Zealand, then, hospitality is made conditional on racialised and economic grounds. Australian authorities regularly assert demonising rhetoric about 'foreigners' who are culturally unsuitable to the Australian dream or who pose risks of 'drug smuggling, terrorism and the displacement of Australian workers' (Tazreiter et al., 2016, p. 107).

In December 2014, amendments to Australia's Migration Act expanded conditions for the cancellation of visas. Under section 501 of the amended Act, some non-citizens were destined for mandatory visa cancellations. These included those who: received a prison sentence of a year or more (or had received cumulative sentences for this time); had been detained in a mental health institution after acquittal on the grounds of unsound mind or insanity; or had been convicted of any offence within immigration detention. The minister or their delegate may also cancel a visa in the 'national interest', if they 'reasonably suspect' that a person would not pass a character test – for example, that a person poses a significant risk of engaging in criminal conduct or inciting discord or representing a danger to the Australian community. Further, a visa cancellation can occur if the person 'may be, or would or might be, a risk' to the 'health, safety or good order of the Australian community or a segment of the Australian community' or to 'the health or safety of an individual' (s 116(1)(e)).[5]

These legal provisions have significantly expanded the discretionary capacity of the Australian government to remove anyone, based on the opaque language of reasonableness, seriousness, association, risk, or safety (Stanley, 2017). This pre-emptive expansion has shifted usual legal norms in favour of civil-administrative measures of suspicion and pre-punishments (Zedner, 2015). The result has been a significant escalation of visa cancellations and, of the 943 cancellations over 2018–19, close to half ($n=435$) involved New Zealand citizens (Department of Home Affairs, 2019a).

Upon visa cancellation, most non-citizens are detained to await deportation or (if there is a revocation in decision) their release. New Zealanders are now commonly held in immigration detention facilities. At 30 June 2019, 146 detainees (135 men, 11 women) – over 10 per cent of the 1352 people within immigration detention – held New Zealand citizenship.[6] Detainees spend on average 485 days in detention, across multiple sites (Department of Home Affairs, 2019b). About half of detained New Zealanders have lived in Australia for more than a decade (Anderson, 2015) and some for much longer; despite their lack of legal citizenship, they are 'effectively Australian' (Grewcock, 2011, p. 61).

Detention

Immigration detention centres in Australia have faced sustained criticism from UN agencies, human rights organisations, medics, academics, and others. Detainees report punitive treatments, lack of access to their families or legal representation, arbitrary rules, extensive searches, harsh conditions, and sexual and physical assaults by hostile staff (Coffey et al., 2010; Poulsen, 2015; Refugee Council of Australia, 2016; Sachdeva, 2016). Depression, self-harm, and suicide attempts by detainees are common (Coffey et al., 2010; Grewcock, 2011; McLoughlin & Warin, 2008), and dozens have died in detention, often in unclear circumstances (Powell et al., 2013). For survivors, the long-term impacts of detention are extensive: many ex-detainees experience relationship difficulties, poor mental health, depression, memory problems, anxiety, and post-traumatic stress disorder (PTSD). They often feel isolated and stigmatised, and they hold a deep sense of injustice about their treatment (Coffey et al., 2010; Steel et al., 2006).

Despite these treatments, there are no clear processes for complaints (Grewcock, 2011). Immigration centres are often isolated and are not monitored like criminal justice institutions (McLoughlin & Warin, 2008, pp. 254–260). Staff are also compelled into silence – the Australian Border Force Act 2015 forbids employees from reporting on conditions or the treatment of detainees; those who contravene the Act can face two-year prison sentences (Stanley, 2017). Under these conditions, detainees have protested against their treatment, and sought solidarity with others through hunger strikes, riots, and escapes (see Boochani, 2018; Grewcock, 2012). In January 2019, for example, New Zealanders performed a haka in support of hunger-striking detainees at Yonga Hill who protested against a 'failed' system that prioritised the use of indefinite detention (Whitten, 2019).

A continuum of punitiveness

The numbers of those deported to New Zealand has steadily grown – from January 2015 to 22 February 2019, Australia deported 1664 New Zealanders (Walters, 2019). Those deported immediately lose their connections with family members, friends, workplaces, and communities in Australia. People who have lived most of their lives in Australia also experience New Zealand as an alien country; they struggle to 'fit in' and have high levels of isolation and economic hardship. For example, in 2015, a 56-year-old tetraplegic, 'Paul', was deported after a 13-month sentence 'for self-medicating with controlled painkillers'. Having spent most of his life in Australia, he had been 'dumped' in Auckland with 'a voucher for a week's accommodation' (Plumb, 2015; Oz Kiwi, 2015, paras 2, 4).

In response, New Zealand authorities have largely sustained a punitive approach towards arrivals (Stanley, 2017). New legislation – the Returning Offenders (Management and Information) Act 2015 – was passed, under urgency. The law focuses on those convicted for imprisonable offences overseas who return to New Zealand within six months of release. Returning offenders must comply with police requests for personal details, photographs, fingerprints, and DNA, and they are subject to release conditions. This entails regular reporting to probation as well as possible conditions on work, housing, or associations. Added to this, courts can also impose special conditions (such as electronic monitoring, programme attendance, or geographical restrictions). Any breaches may result in a one-year sentence or a fine of $2000 (Stanley, 2017). In short, there are multiple layers of punishment in operation as individuals receive a prison sentence, indefinite immigration detention, deportation, and community-based controls (Stanley, 2017), often for relatively minor offending.

CONCLUSION

In an era where advanced global capitalism has exacerbated insecurities for increased numbers of people, Western political authorities have asserted the control of borders as a central aspect of state power. Borders are heavily militarised, and degrading treatments towards non-citizens deemed to be unwanted, illegal, criminal, or potentially threatening are increasingly normalised and can be stridently supported by voting publics. At the same time, these authorities have been consistently met with resistance from those affected, as well as from activist allies who reiterate values of human rights, compassion, and solidarity.

The drive of Western states to sort and deport also appears to be intensifying as global challenges – such as climate change – create new anxieties, not just for those who need to migrate to safer places but also for polluting states who may be expected to provide protections. In the future, we should expect that countries like New Zealand will need to answer significant questions about how our borders will be operationalised and how our responses to non-citizens can be developed and sustained. The application of criminological knowledge – that attends to issues such as the treatment of 'outsiders', conflict resolutions, the reparation of harms, 'crimmigration', borders, and state crimes – will be vitally important in ensuring that any responses are sustained by values of human rights, non-discrimination, and social justice.

STUDY QUESTIONS

- How might we explain the ongoing securitisation of borders and the increasing state use of deportations?
- Find and examine a case of an individual targeted for removal in the dawn raids. What have been the short- and long-term impacts of this experience on them and their community?
- What particular problems might those deported from Australia to New Zealand face, and how might New Zealand agencies respond to these?

FURTHER READING

Bhatia, M. (2019). Crimmigration, imprisonment and racist violence: Narratives of people seeking asylum in Great Britain. *Journal of Sociology, 56*(1), 36–52. doi:10.1177/1440783319882533

Boochani, B. (2018). *No friend but the mountains: Writing from Manus Prison.* London, UK: Picador.

Walia, H. (2013). *Undoing border imperialism.* Oakland, CA: AK Press.

NOTES

1. People from the Caribbean who took up British government invitations to migrate and assist with labour shortages in the UK between 1948 and the early 1970s are known as the 'Windrush Generation'. The name refers to the first ship, MV *Empire Windrush*, on which the first of these Commonwealth workers and their families arrived. In 2018, by which time the Caribbean immigrants and their families had lived and worked in the UK for decades, many were detained and deported (or threatened with such action) on the grounds that they lacked documentation to prove their 'right to remain' (after the Home Office destroyed landing cards and other records).

2. In July 2020, the Court of Appeal ruled that Shamima Begum should be able to return to the UK to have a fair appeal against the removal of her citizenship at the Supreme Court. However, some months later the UK government successfully appealed that decision in the Supreme Court, ruling that the government had the right to prevent Ms Begum's return to the UK.

3   The author would link to thank Jade Gifford for her great work in collating material on the dawn raids.

4   In 2019, a travelling exhibition toured around New Zealand cities, featuring art, photographs, testimonies, and other Panthers memorabilia on the dawn raids. Featuring a 1970s New Zealand lounge, the exhibition was derived from an award-winning book for young people, *Dawn Raid*, written by Pauline (Vaeluaga) Smith, which charts a teenager's growing engagement with her activism and sense of identity. The Polynesian Panthers celebrated their 50th anniversary in February 2021.

5   In July 2019, the Australian government introduced the Migration Amendment (Strengthening the Character Test) Bill, which would further extend conditions for visa cancellations. This would amend section 501 of the Migration Act to assert that those convicted of 'designated offences' would not pass the character test. The list of offences includes threats of violence, violence offences, burglary, non-consensual sexual conduct, using or possessing a weapon, or breaching an order made by a court or tribunal for another's personal protection. Visa cancellations would occur even in cases where a jail term was not imposed by the court. It is anticipated that this new law, if passed, will significantly increase the number of people deported from Australia.

6   Detainees also came from Iran (148 detainees), Vietnam (95), Sri Lanka (78), India (66), Sudan (61), UK (60), Iraq (56), and Afghanistan (55), among other countries. Immigrant detainees include those with cancelled visas as well as 'illegal arrivals' and 'overstayers' (Department of Home Affairs, 2019b).

REFERENCES

Aas, K. (2011). 'Crimmigrant' bodies and bona fide travelers. *Theoretical Criminology, 15*(3), 331–346. doi:10.1177/1362480610396643

Aas, K. (2014). Bordered penality: Precarious membership and abnormal justice. *Punishment and Society, 16*(5), 520–541. doi:10.1177/1462474514548807

Anae, M. (2012). All power to the people: Overstayers, dawn raids and the Polynesian Panthers. In D. Salesa, K. Māhina-Tuai, & S. Mallon (Eds.), *Tangata o le moana: New Zealand and the people of the Pacific* (pp. 220–239). Wellington, New Zealand: Te Papa Press.

Anderson, M. (2015, November 14–20). The plight of New Zealand '501' detainees on Christmas Island. *Saturday Paper*. Retrieved from https://www.thesaturdaypaper.com.au/news/politics/2015/11/14/the-plight-new-zealand–501-detainees-christmas-island/14474196002628

Beaglehole, A. (2013). *Refuge New Zealand: A nation's response to refugees and asylum seekers*. Dunedin, New Zealand: Otago University Press.

Beaglehole, A. (2015, August 18). Immigration regulation. *Te Ara: The Encyclopedia of New Zealand*. Wellington, New Zealand: Ministry for Culture and Heritage. Retrieved from https://teara.govt.nz/en/immigration-regulation/print

Bigo, D. (2007). Detention of foreigners, states of exception, and the social practices of control of the banopticon. In P. Rajaram & C. Grundy-Warr (Eds.), *Borderscapes: Hidden geographies and politics at territory's edge* (pp. 3–34). Minneapolis, MN: University of Minneapolis Press.

Boochani, B. (2018). *No friend but the mountains: Writing from Manus Prison*. London, UK: Picador.

Bosworth, M., & Guild, M. (2008). Governing through migration control. *British Journal of Criminology, 48*(6), 703–719. doi:10.1093/bjc/azn059

Bosworth, M., Hannah-Moffat, K., & Lynch, M. (2012). Subjectivity and identity in detention: Punishment and society in a global age. *Theoretical Criminology, 16*(2), 123–140. doi:10.1177/1362480612441116

Broadcasting Standards Authority. (2019). *BSA decisions: Day & Moss and NZME Radio Ltd, 2018–090(2 April 2019)*. Retrieved from https://bsa.govt.nz/decisions/all-decisions/day-and-moss-and-nzme-radio-ltd–2018–090–2-april–2019/

Brown, W. (2016). Sacrificial citizenship: Neoliberalism, human capital, and austerity politics. *Constellations, 23*(1), 3–14. doi:10.1111/1467–8675.12166

Campbell, G. (2018, April 6). Gordon Campbell on racial profiling at Immigration NZ. *Pacific Scoop Media*. Retrieved from http://pacific.scoop.co.nz/2018/04/gordon-campbell-on-racial-profiling-at-immigration-nz/

Chenery, S. (2016, April 16). New Zealanders in Australia are still treated like second-class citizens. *Stuff*. Retrieved from https://www.stuff.co.nz/world/australia/78998518/new-zealanders-in-australia-are-still-treated-like-secondclass-citizens

Coffey, G., Kaplan, I., Sampson, R., & Tucci, M. (2010). The meaning and mental health consequences of long-term immigration detention for people seeking asylum. *Social Science and Medicine, 70*(12), 2070–2079. doi:10.1016/j.socscimed.2010.02.042

Dearden, L. (2019, February 20). Shamima Begum: Number of people stripped of UK citizenship soars by 600% in a year. *Independent*. Retrieved from https://www.independent.co.uk/news/uk/home-news/shamima-begum-uk-citizenship-stripped-home-office-sajid-javid-a8788301.html

Department of Home Affairs. (2018). *New Zealand-born community information summary*. Retrieved from https://www.homeaffairs.gov.au/mca/files/2016-cis-new-zealand.pdf

Department of Home Affairs. (2019a). *Visa cancellation statistics*. Retrieved from https://www.homeaffairs.gov.au/research-and-statistics/statistics/visa-statistics/visa-cancellation

Department of Home Affairs. (2019b). *Immigration detention and community statistics summary, 30 June 2019*. Retrieved from https://www.homeaffairs.gov.au/research-and-stats/files/immigration-detention-statistics-30-june-2019.pdf

Doering-White, J., Horner, P., Sanders, L., Martinez, R., Lopez, W., & Delva, J. (2016). Testimonial engagement: Undocumented Latina mothers navigating a gendered deportation regime. *International Migration and Integration, 17*(2), 325–340. doi:10.1007/s12134-014-0408-7

Epstein, C. (2007). Guilty bodies, productive bodies, destructive bodies: Crossing the biometric. *International Political Sociology, 1*(2), 149–164. doi:10.1111/j.1749-5687.2007.00010.x

Grewcock, M. (2011). Punishment, deportation and parole: The detention and removal of former prisoners under section 501 Migration Act 1958. *Australian and New Zealand Journal of Criminology, 44*(1), 56–73. doi:10.1177/0004865810392866

Grewcock, M. (2012). The great escape: Refugees, detention and resistance. In E. Stanley & J. McCulloch (Eds.), *State crime and resistance* (pp. 54–67). London, UK: Routledge.

Grewcock, M. (2014). Reinventing 'the stain': Bad character and criminal deportation in contemporary Australia. In S. Pickering & J. Ham (Eds.), *The Routledge handbook on crime and international migration* (pp. 121–137). London, UK: Routledge.

Hamer, P. (2012). *Māori in Australia: An update from the 2011 Australian census and the 2011 general election*. Wellington, New Zealand: Victoria University of Wellington. doi:10.2139/ssrn.2167613

Harris, P. (2013, March 28). Undocumented workers' grim reality: Speak out on abuse and risk deportation. *Guardian*. Retrieved from https://www.theguardian.com/world/2013/mar/28/undocumented-migrants-worker-abuse-deportation

Immigration New Zealand. (2018, October 18). *Overstayers*. Retrieved from https://www.immigration.govt.nz/documents/statistics/immigration-new-zealand-overstayers-factsheet.pdf

Immigration New Zealand. (2019, July 19). *Immigration factsheets: Deportations*. Retrieved from https://www.immigration.govt.nz/documents/media/deportations-factsheet.pdf

Krishnan, V., Schoeffel, P. S., & Warren, J. A. N. (1994). *The challenge of change: Pacific Island communities in New Zealand 1986–1993*. Wellington, New Zealand: NZ Institute for Social Research and Development.

Macpherson, C. (2004). From Pacific Islanders to Pacific people and beyond. In P. Spoonley, C. Macpherson, & D. Pearson (Eds.), *Tangata tangata: The changing ethnic contours of New Zealand* (pp. 135–156). Southbank, Victoria, Australia: Thomson Dunmore Press.

Malloch, M., & Stanley, E. (2005). The detention of asylum seekers in the UK: Representing risk, managing the dangerous. *Punishment and Society, 7*(1), 53–71. doi:10.1177/1462474505048133

Mbembe, A. (2018, November 11). *The idea of a borderless world*. Retrieved from https://africasacountry.com/2018/11/the-idea-of-a-borderless-world

Mbembe, A. (2019, February 18). Deglobalization. *Eurozine*. Retrieved from https://www.eurozine.com/deglobalization/

McCulloch, J., & Wilson, D. (2015). *Pre-crime, pre-emption, precaution and the future*. London, UK: Routledge.

McFadden, S. (2015, March 7). When Pacific Islanders were raided in their beds. *New Zealand Herald*. Retrieved from https://www.nzherald.co.nz/nz/news/article.cfm?c_id=1&objectid=11413079

McLoughlin, P., & Warin, M. (2008). Corrosive places, inhuman spaces: Mental health in Australian immigration detention. *Health and Place, 14*(2), 254–264. doi:10.1016/j.healthplace.2007.06.008

Newstead, C., & Frisso, G. (2013). Asserting criminality and denying migrant belonging. *Theoretical Criminology, 17*(3), 377–395. doi:10.1177/1362480613481488

Nolan, M. (2015). Welfare limbo? Social welfare and citizenship debates about New Zealanders living in Australia. *Commonwealth and Comparative Politics, 53*(3), 253–273. doi:10.1080/14662043.2015.1043689

One News. (2018, March 26). Over 10,000 overstayers in NZ, Immigration not actively looking for most. *One News*. Retrieved from https://www.tvnz.co.nz/one-news/new-zealand/most-read-story-over-10-000-overstayers-in-nz-immigration-not-actively-looking

Oz Kiwi. (2015, October 18). Quadriplegic New Zealander reportedly deported by Australia. *Oz Kiwi*. Retrieved from http://www.ozkiwi2001.org/2015/10/quadriplegic-new-zealander-reportedly-deported-by-australia-theguardian/

Pacific Media Centre. (2019, April 10). Dawn raids – Pasifika 'liberated' to talk about painful past. *Evening Report*. Retrieved from https://eveningreport.nz/2019/04/10/dawn-raids-pasifika-liberated-to-talk-about-painful-past/

Peacock, C. (2018, September 16). Broadcaster Heather du Plessis-Allan under fire for Pacific Island 'leeches' claim. *Radio New Zealand*. Retrieved from https://www.rnz.co.nz/national/programmes/mediawatch/audio/2018662440/broadcaster-heather-du-plessis-allan-under-fire-for-pacific-islands-leeches-claim

Perera, S. (2009). White shores of longing: 'Impossible subjects' and the frontiers of citizenship. *Continuum, 23*(5), 647–662. doi:10.1080/10304310903154693

Plumb, S. (2015, October 18). Anger after tetraplegic 'dumped' in NZ. *New Zealand Herald*. Retrieved from https://www.nzherald.co.nz/nz/news/article.cfm?c_id=1&objectid=11530899

Poulsen, J. (2015, November 30). Anguish for mum of woman who was detained in Darwin's Wickham Point detention centre. *NT News*. Retrieved from http://www.ntnews.com.au/news/northern-territory/anguish-for-mum-of-woman-who-was-detained-in-darwins-wickham-point-detention-centre/news-story/29411a431ac649cb5475b7487938fdaa?=

Powell, R., Weber, L., & Pickering, S. (2013). Counting and accounting for deaths in Australian immigration custody. *Homicide Studies, 17*(4), 391–417. doi:10.1177/1088767913501078

Refugee Council of Australia (RCA). (2016). *Submission to Senate Legal and Constitutional Affairs Committee, Migration Amendment (Character Cancellation Consequential Provisions) Bill 2016*. Sydney/Melbourne, Australia: RCA.

Reid, Z. (2010, May 31). How the Polynesian Panthers changed our world. *Salient*. Retrieved from https://web.archive.org/web/20171201083703/http://salient.org.nz/2010/05/how-the-polynesian-panthers-changed-our-world/

Sachdeva, S. (2016, January 15). Kiwi detainees being moved to Christmas Island again. *Stuff*. Retrieved from http://www.stuff.co.nz/national/politics/75924244/kiwi-detainees-being-moved-to-christmas-island-again-advocacy-group

Somers, M. R. (2008). *Genealogies of citizenship: Markets, statelessness, and the right to have rights*. Cambridge, UK: Cambridge University Press.

Spoonley, P., & Bedford, R. (2012). *Welcome to our world? Immigration and the reshaping of New Zealand*. Auckland, New Zealand: Dunmore Publishing.

Stanley, E. (2016). *The road to hell: State violence against children in postwar New Zealand*. Auckland, New Zealand: Auckland University Press.

Stanley, E. (2017). Expanding crimmigration: The detention and deportation of New Zealanders from Australia. *Australian and New Zealand Journal of Criminology, 51*(4), 519–536. doi:10.1177/0004865817730858

Steel, Z., Silove, D., Brooks, R., Momartin, B., & Susljik, I. (2006). Impact of immigration detention and temporary protection on the mental health of refugees. *British Journal of Psychiatry, 188*(1), 58–64. doi:10.1192/bjp.bp.104.007864

Stringer, C. (2016). *Worker exploitation in New Zealand: A troubling landscape.* Auckland, New Zealand: Human Trafficking Research Coalition. Retrieved from https://img.scoop.co.nz/media/pdfs/1612/Worker_Exploitation_in_New_Zealand_Stringer.pdf

Stumpf, J. (2014). Crimmigration: Encountering the Leviathan. In S. Pickering & J. Ham (Eds.). *The Routledge handbook on crime and international migration* (pp. 237–250). London, UK: Routledge.

Tahana, J. (2019, September 12). Melanie Anae: 'We said we weren't going to take it anymore'. *Radio New Zealand.* Retrieved from https://www.rnz.co.nz/national/programmes/eyewitness/audio/2018712603/melani-anae-we-said-we-weren-t-going-to-take-it-anymore

Tazreiter, C., Weber, L., Pickering, S., Segrave, M., & McKernan, H. (2016). *Fluid security in the Asia Pacific: Transnational lives, human rights and state control.* London, UK: Palgrave Macmillan.

United Nations High Commissioner for Refugees. (2018, November 6). *2,000 Lives and counting: Mediterranean death toll in 2018.* [Briefing Notes]. Retrieved from https://www.unhcr.org/news/briefing/2018/11/5be15cf34/2000-lives-counting-mediterranean-death-toll—2018.html

Walters, L. (2019, March 4). Aust committee seeks deportation changes. *Newsroom.* Retrieved from https://www.newsroom.co.nz/2019/03/04/467962/australian-committee-calls-for-changes-to-deportation-policy

Weber, L. & Pickering, S. (2013). Exporting risk, deporting non-citizens. In F. Pakes (Ed.), *Globalisation and the challenge to criminology* (pp. 110–128). London, UK: Routledge.

Whitten, C. (2019, January 19). Kiwis at Australian detention centre claim hunger strike could affect chances of release. *Newshub.* Retrieved from https://www.newshub.co.nz/home/world/2019/01/kiwis-at-australian-detention-centre-claim-hunger-strike-could-affect-chances-of-release.html

Zedner, L. (2015). Pre-crime and pre-punishment. *Criminal Justice Matters, 102*(1), 23–24. doi:10.1080/09627251.2015.1143629

Contributors

Jordan Anderson is currently completing her PhD in criminology at the Institute of Criminology, Te Herenga Waka – Victoria University of Wellington. Her research focuses on risk and dangerousness in modern society, with particular attention to the post-sentence regulation of sex offenders in Aotearoa New Zealand. Jordan's research interests include risk, post-sentence regulation, sentencing, and youth justice.

Lynzi Armstrong is a senior lecturer in criminology at Victoria University of Wellington. She is a feminist criminologist, and her research is broadly focused on gender, sexuality, and justice. She has a strong interest in sex workers' rights, sexual violence, anti-trafficking discourses, stigma, and the impacts of laws on marginalised populations.

Arapera Blank-Penetito (Ngāti Hauā, Ngāti Porou) is a graduate of the University of Auckland's criminology programme. Her 2019 master's thesis explored whānau Māori, community workers, and some state agents' experiences of youth justice systems operating in Aotearoa, with a specific focus on Ngā Kōti Rangatahi (marae-based Youth Courts).

Daniel Botha is a postgraduate student and tutor in criminology at Victoria University of Wellington. His research interests include hate crime, far-right terrorism, voter disenfranchisement, digital harm, and the politicisation of criminal justice. Outside of academia, Daniel can occasionally be seen performing in local theatre productions in Wellington.

Trevor Bradley is a senior lecturer at the Institute of Criminology, Victoria University of Wellington, where he teaches courses on policing and crime prevention. He has an ongoing programme of research focused on plural policing in New Zealand that incorporates private policing, security, and various citizen-led policing bodies. Recent projects have included an international research collaboration on intelligence-led policing, as well as work on volunteer community policing in New Zealand. His recent publications include a third edition of the book *Introduction to Criminological Thought* (Edify, 2019), as well as various articles on governance failures and poor standards in the New Zealand private security industry. In 2020, he co-authored articles on policing during the Covid-19 pandemic.

Bruce M. Z. Cohen is an associate professor in sociology at the University of Auckland. He teaches courses on the sociologies of mental health, cultural studies, and education, and his publications include the critically acclaimed monographs *Mental Health User Narratives: New perspectives on illness and recovery* (Palgrave Macmillan, 2008) and *Psychiatric Hegemony: A Marxist theory of mental illness* (Palgrave Macmillan, 2016).

Sally Day is a PhD candidate at the Institute of Criminology, Victoria University of Wellington. Her thesis explores resistance strategies to state–corporate harms, analysing the 2010 Pike River mine disaster as a case study.

Antje Deckert, formerly a German defence lawyer, is a senior lecturer in criminology at Auckland University of Technology. She is co-editor in chief of the journal *Decolonization of Criminology and Justice*, and co-editor of the *Palgrave Handbook of Australian and New Zealand Criminology, Crime and Justice* (Palgrave, 2017) and *Decolonising Our Futures: Neo-colonial criminal justice and the mass imprisonment of Indigenous women* (Palgrave, 2020). Her primary research interest concerns the sociology of criminological knowledge. More specifically, she examines mainstream academic and media criminological discourses and their interactions with Indigenous peoples and epistemologies to determine whether these discourses contribute to the marginalisation of Indigenous peoples in academia and in wider society.

Russil Durrant is a senior lecturer at the Institute of Criminology, Victoria University of Wellington. His research interests lie broadly within the field of criminal and forensic psychology, with a particular focus on the application of evolutionary theory to our understanding of crime and crime-related phenomena.

Naomi Fuamatu is a doctoral candidate with the University of Auckland's criminology programme. Her research and professional interests include Pacific equity policy and practice, and Pacific youth and youth culture. Her doctoral thesis focuses on the interactions between youth justice systems and different models of family.

Anita Gibbs is an associate professor at the University of Otago, teaching criminology and social work. Her research interests include mental health and neuro-disabilities, notably fetal alcohol spectrum disorder (FASD). Anita is a qualified social worker, and her passion for advocacy for those with disabilities in the criminal justice system stems from her own lived experience as a parent of children living with FASD.

Jarrod Gilbert is a sociologist and the director of criminal justice at the University of Canterbury. He is the author of the award-winning book *Patched: The history of gangs in New Zealand*, and the co-editor of *Criminal Justice: A New Zealand introduction*, and *A Rebel in Exile*. He advises a number of government agencies on policy matters, and was a member of Te Uepū Hāpai i te Ora – the Safe and Effective Justice Advisory Group, which investigated changes to the criminal justice system in New Zealand.

Fairleigh Gilmour is a lecturer in criminology and gender studies at the University of Otago. Their teaching and research interests include sex work governance, media representations of crime, incarceration, and surveillance.

Fiona Hutton is an associate professor (reader) at the Institute of Criminology, Victoria University of Wellington. Her teaching and research cover a number of criminological topics, including criminological theory, youth crime and cultures, gender, drug policy, harm reduction, and alcohol and other drugs. She is the author of *Risky Pleasures? Club cultures* *and feminine identities* (Ashgate, 2006), and the edited collection *Cultures of Intoxication: Key issues and debates* (Palgrave Macmillan, 2020). Current research projects include: documenting the experiences of those with a drug-related conviction; critically exploring the concept of intoxication; and how the intoxication practices of diverse groups are experienced and responded to.

Jan Jordan is adjunct professor of criminology at Victoria University of Wellington. For the past three decades she has been active in sexual violence research, with a particular focus on how women victims/survivors are impacted by rape and their reporting experiences. She has also spent much of that time working alongside police to improve sexual assault investigations, as well as researching girls' and women's feminist self-defence strategies. Jan is currently completing a book that seeks to understand what sustains rape culture and keeps our rates of sexual violence so high.

Ang Jury is the chief executive of the National Collective of Independent Women's Refuges, the umbrella organisation comprising 40 women's refuges. She has been involved in the family violence and community services sector for over 20 years. Her PhD is in sociology, and both this and her subsequent research interests focus on gender and domestic violence.

Ti Lamusse is a PhD candidate in sociology at the University of Auckland. His research explores the possibilities for a justice system in Aotearoa without prisons. Ti is also a founding member and national secretary of the prison abolitionist organisation People Against Prisons Aotearoa.

Cinnamon Lindsay Latimer (Ngāti Porou, Ngāpuhi, Ngā ti Whatua) is an early career researcher who holds an MSc in psychology. She is passionate about community work, and her research interests include housing, mana wāhine, racism, and Māori health.

Angus Lindsay is a PhD candidate at the Institute of Criminology, Victoria University of Wellington, where he is investigating narratives that drive far/extreme right-wing violence. His recent master's research critically examined the far-right adjacent online subculture of incels (involuntary celibates). His academic research interests also include intelligence-led policing, online misogyny and hate-speech, and far/extreme right terrorism.

Nessa Lynch is an associate professor at the Faculty of Law, Victoria University of Wellington. She teaches and researches in youth justice, child rights, data ethics, and biometrics.

Simon Mackenzie is a professor of criminology at Victoria University of Wellington and head of the School of Social and Cultural Studies. His research is in the fields of white-collar crime and organised crime, and especially the confluence of these two types of crime in global criminal markets. His latest books on these topics are *Trafficking Culture* (Routledge, 2019) and *Transnational Criminology* (Bristol University Press, New Horizons in Criminology Series, 2020).

Salevao Faauuga Manase is a retired psychiatric nurse in Porirua, Wellington. He is a faufautua or senior cultural advisor to a Marsden-funded research team at Waikato University, and helped to facilitate its project fono. Salevao was part of the foundation team that set up the first Pacific mental health services (Health Pasifika) in Wellington.

In October 2015 he received a civic award from Porirua City for his services to mental health nursing and for his leadership in the Pasifika community.

Liam Martin is a criminology lecturer at Victoria University of Wellington. He has a forthcoming book based on ethnographic research at a halfway house in Greater Boston: *Halfway Home: Carceral care on the frontier of mass incarceration* (New York University Press). This work is part of a broader set of research interests focused on the causes and consequences of rising prison populations and alternatives to imprisonment.

Tracey McIntosh (Ngāi Tūhoe) is a professor of Indigenous studies and co-head of Wānanga o Waipapa at the University of Auckland. Her teaching and research interests include the politics of incarceration and strategies of decarceration, with a particular focus on wāhine Māori.

Claire Meehan is a lecturer in criminology at the University of Auckland. She is interested in co-constructed, youth-centred research with young people to understand their digital sexual lives and relationships.

Alice Mills is a senior lecturer in criminology at the University of Auckland. Her research interests include: post-prison housing; prisoner reintegration; the role of community and voluntary organisations in criminal justice; specialist courts; and mental health in prisons. She is co-editor of *Mental Health in Prisons: Critical perspectives in treatment and confinement* (Palgrave Macmillan, 2018), and is currently leading a study examining the role of stable housing in reducing reoffending amongst those who have left prison.

Sarah Monod de Froideville is a lecturer at the Institute of Criminology, Victoria University of Wellington. Her current research is broadly centred on harms to the New Zealand environment, with a specific focus on: water-related harms and water security; historical pollution; and exploitative human–animal relations. She also has an ongoing interest in the intersections between media representations, crime, and youth justice, stemming from her past work on moral panics in relation to young people. Early papers and her monograph *Making Sense of Moral Panic: A framework for research* (Palgrave, 2017) paid close attention to the changing shape of panics in neoliberal societies focused on preventing risk.

James Oleson is an associate professor of criminology at the University of Auckland. With a background in law and psychological criminology, his research interests include criminal law and procedure, criminal justice policy, criminological theory, risk assessment, and sentencing.

Scott Poynting is adjunct professor in the School of Justice at Queensland University of Technology and at the Centre for Islamic Studies and Civilisation at Charles Sturt University. He is co-author of *Bin Laden in the Suburbs: Criminalising the Arab other*, and co-editor of *Global Islamophobia: Muslims and moral panic in the West* (Routledge, 2016) and *Media, Crime and Racism* (Palgrave Macmillan, 2018).

John Pratt is a professor of criminology at Victoria University of Wellington and a Fellow of the Royal Society of New Zealand. He has been invited to lecture at universities in Europe, Asia, and North and South America. He has published extensively, including *Punishment and Civilization* (Sage, 2002), *Penal Populism* (co-author Anna Eriksson,

Routledge, 2007), *Contrasts in Punishment* (Routledge, 2013), and *Law, Insecurity and Risk Control* (Springer Nature, 2020). His writings have been translated into 11 languages and earned him national and international awards.

Khylee Quince (Ngāpuhi, Ngāti Porou, Ngāti Kahungunu) is an associate professor of law at Auckland University of Technology. Her teaching and research interests focus on Māori engagement in criminal justice, including offending by women and young people. Khylee has a legal practice background in criminal and family law, and continues to prepare cultural reports for sentencing in criminal courts.

Joanne Riley is a master's student in forensic psychology at Victoria University of Wellington. Her research interests include the application of theories from evolutionary psychology and health psychology to offender rehabilitation.

Moorea Smithline graduated from Victoria University of Wellington in 2018 with a bachelor of arts (honours) degree in criminology. As part of her research within the field of green criminology, Moorea's final dissertation examines New Zealand's horse-racing industry from a speciesist criminological perspective. In addition to animal rights, her other areas of interest include social re-entry following incarceration, homelessness, and community-based reintegrative programmes. Moorea is currently working as a researcher for the Royal Commission of Inquiry into Abuse in Care.

Elizabeth Stanley is a professor in criminology who works in the areas of state crime, human rights, incarceration, and social justice. Her books include: *Human Rights and Incarceration* (Palgrave, 2018); *State Crime and Resistance* (Routledge, 2013); and *Torture, Truth and Justice* (Routledge, 2009). Her monograph *The Road to Hell* (Auckland University Press, 2016) contributed to the 2018 establishment of the Royal Commission of Inquiry into Abuse in Care. She held a prestigious Rutherford Discovery Fellowship from 2014 to 2019, and is director of the Institute of Criminology, and deputy head of the School of Social and Cultural Studies, at Victoria University of Wellington.

Rebecca Stringer teaches feminist theory and critical victimology at the University of Otago, and is the author of *Knowing Victims: Feminism, agency and victim politics in neoliberal times* (Routledge, 2014). Her current research projects investigate early victimology and visual victimology.

Tamasailau Suaalii-Sauni is an associate professor in criminology at the University of Auckland. Her research and teaching interests include Pacific Indigenous jurisprudence and Pacific Indigenous research methodologies.

Fa'afete Taito is a graduate of the University of Auckland's sociology and Māori studies programmes. He is currently working as a community engagement advisor to the Royal Commission of Inquiry into Abuse in Care. As a former ward of the state he is a critic of justice reforms, and advocates for state accountability and improving reintegration outcomes for prisoners upon release.

Juan Marcellus Tauri (Ngāti Porou) is a senior lecturer in criminology at the University of Waikato. Juan has carried out a number of research projects on a diverse range of topics, including youth gangs, gendered violence, Indigenous experiences of prison and policing, and the globalisation of restorative justice. Juan co-edited a special issue of the *African Journal of Criminology and Justice Studies* on 'Indigenous Perspectives and Counter Colonial Criminology' (2014), and his book *Indigenous Criminology*, co-authored with Professor Chris Cunneen from the University of Technology, Sydney, was the first of its kind in exploring Indigenous peoples' contact with criminal justice systems.

Natalie Thorburn is a registered social worker with a practice and research background spanning various forms of gendered violence. The principal policy advisor for the National Collective of Independent Women's Refuges (NCIWR), she leads NCIWR's research programme, with a particular focus on researching sensitive topics safely.

Robert Webb (Ngāpuhi) is a senior lecturer in criminology at the University of Auckland. His research and teaching interests include criminal justice policies and Māori, youth justice, Indigenous criminology, and Māori and organ donation.

Ruth Weatherall is a lecturer in not-for-profit and social enterprise management at the University of Technology, Sydney. Her research uses feminist, queer, and ethical perspectives, and is concerned with how social justice, particularly related to gender inequality, is achieved in and through not-for-profit organisations.

Kim Workman (Ngāti Kahungunu ki Wairarapa, Rangitāne) KNZM, QSO is a retired public servant whose career spanned roles in New Zealand Police, the Office of the Ombudsman, the State Services Commission, and the Department of Māori Affairs. He was head of the Prison Service from 1989 to 1993. In 2006 Kim joined with the Salvation Army to launch the Rethinking Crime and Punishment (RCP) project. In 2011 he formed JustSpeak, a movement that involves youth in criminal justice advocacy and reform. He was recently appointed to the Human Rights Review Tribunal and the New Zealand Parole Board. He represents the Kingitanga as co-chair on the Kawenata Governance Board, which manages a Memorandum of Understanding between the Kingitanga and the Department of Corrections.

Index

Entries in **bold** denote tables, entries in *italics* denote figures. Entries of the form 'XnY' refer to endnote Y on page X. The word 'Te' has been ignored in alphabetisation of terms in te reo, as with English 'The'.

A

ableism 3, 75, 80, 303
abolition *see* prison abolition; sex work, abolitionist perspectives on
Abortion Legalisation Act 2020 383
ABS (Australian Bureau of Statistics) 26
abusive behaviour, non-criminalised 77
academic criminology 35, 37–39
ACC (Accident Compensation Corporation) 121, 133, 155
accidents: responsibility for 4, 49, 122; white-collar crime as 127, 133
accountability 4; corporate actors evading 138; of public institutions 15; in sexual abuse 88; in therapeutic jurisprudence 193; for unconscious bias 323; and white-collar crime 49; in youth justice 215, 219, 233, 336
acquaintance rape 70
ACT party 155
adaptive behaviours 255, 360
addiction 54; to the internet 84; receiving help for 228; and sentencing 192–93, 208
ADHD (attention deficit hyperactivity disorder) 351, 358–60, 362, 366
Adult Sex Offender Treatment Programme (ASOTP) 269
age: of criminal responsibility 215–16; of penal majority 216, 219; *see also* youth offending
agnosis 49, 131–34, 138–39, 323

alcohol: and crime prevention 179, 183; dependency on 251; local government powers to ban 14; Māori consumption of 51, 161; *see also* alcoholism; binge-drinking; foetal alcohol spectrum disorder
alcohol and other drug (AOD) treatment 271
Alcohol and Other Drug Treatment Court *see* Te Whare Whakapiki Wairua
alcohol–crime link 50, 53, 55–57
alcoholism 351
Alexander, Michelle 41
algorithmic justice 206; *see also* evidence-based sentencing
alternative programmes 266
animal welfare 107, 111
Animal Welfare Act 1999 111
anthropocentrism 49, 108–9, 111, 114
antisocial behaviour 179, 181, 374
antisocial peers 180, 267, 277
antisocial personality disorder 348, 351
anti-violence services 79
ANZSOC (Australian and New Zealand Standard Offence Classification) 29n6
te ao Māori: dispute resolution in 188; and environmental harms 113; restitution in 282; and youth justice 215, 335
AODTCs (Alcohol and Other Drug Treatment Courts) *see* Te Whare Whakapiki Wairua
Te Ara Hou 2

413

Ardern, Jacinda 48, 95–96, 101, 103n1, 135, 250–51
Armed Offender Squad 165
Armed Police Force 161
armed policing, tactical options 165–66, 169n11, 169–70n13
Armed Response Teams 144, 160, 163–66
ASD (autism spectrum disorder) 351, 358–60, 366
assaults: prison-based 35; sentencing for 203; as volume crime 22–23, **24**, 28
atomisation of society 318
Auckland Committee on Racism and Discrimination 372
Auckland Youth Support Network 376, 380
Australia: gangs in 378–79; New Zealand migrants to 399–401
authoritarian populism 149
Te Awa Tupua Act 2017 113–14

B

Barnett, Tim 100, 387
Bastion Point 41, 161, 169n3
Baxter, James K. 64
Bazley, Margaret 68
Bazley Report (Commission of Inquiry into Police Conduct) 68, 159
Begum, Shamima 397, 402n2
Benchmark project 364
Better Public Services Goal 278
bias: conscious 163; hostile attribution 266; implicit 325; structural 304, 325; subjective 307–8; systemic 303, 322, 335; unconscious 163, 323–24, 335
'Big Data' 184
Bill of Rights Act 375
binge-drinking 51, 56, 57n2
biocentrism 109, 114
Black Power 372–75, 378
blue-collar crime 119, 127, 348
borders: control of 2–3, 6, 305, 394–97, 402; rhetoric of 397–98, 400; technology of 394
Borrin Foundation 37
boundary crises 14
brain development 215–16, 219, 221
brain trauma *see* traumatic brain injury
Bridgecorp 121
brothel-keeping 67, 386–89
bullying 88, 138, 180, 363
burglaries, as volume crime 8, 22–23, **24**, 28
Bush, Mike 163, 323, 325, 335

C

Canadian Indigenous peoples 245, 365
cannabis: crimes related to 52–53, 324; legalisation of 52, 383; *see also* synthetic cannabis
capitalism: and environmental harms 112; and mental health 353; and prisons 298; and state-corporate crimes 133, 139; and white-collar crimes 121, 125
cartel conduct 126
Cartwright Inquiry 40, 42n2
case management 194, 207, 229, 278, 280, 364
CCJ (crime and criminal justice) research 8, 34–38; decolonial 41–42; funding of 36–37; and policy-making 35–36
CCTV 182–84
CERT (Computer Emergency Response Team) 27
chain gangs 252
child abuse: and intimate partner violence 75; racialised representations of 14; as risk factor for future offending 177, 179
child exploitation 86, 89–90
child maltreatment 74
child pornography *see* child exploitation
child sex offenders 266, 270
children: cybercrime against 85; detention of 218; as guilty victims 309–11, 314; news value of 12; and young persons 216
Children, Young Persons, and Their Families Act 1989 213–14, 239, 243, 246; *see also* Oranga Tamariki Act 1989
children's rights 219
Christchurch earthquakes of 2011–12 122; *see also* CTV Building
Christchurch mosque massacres of 2019 4, 48, 94–98, 101–2; and Armed Response Teams 165–66; and digital technology 15–16; and mental health 345; shooter's manifesto 103n4
Christian Heritage Party 150
Christianity: and rehabilitation 266; and victimology 313
Christie, Nils 307, 312–14
citizen journalism 15

citizen-initiated referendum on law and order 1999 150
citizenship: as contract 305, 396; and deportations 395; neoliberal discourse of 312; and non-citizens 397; removal of 397, 402n2; restrictions on 3, 396–97
civil rights movements 41, 349, 352
civil society 11, 132–33, 397
climate crises 5, 49, 394, 399
climate change criminology 108
coercive control, and intimate partner violence 30, 72, 75, 77–78, 80
cognitive distortions 193
cognitive skills 178, 265–66
cognitive-behavioural therapy 265–67, 269–71
colonial violence, Māori resistance to 353
colonialism 39; and decolonisation 41; and Islamophobia 98; *see also* settler colonialism
colonisation: and bias 303, 318, 325; colonial law 288; and criminal justice system 196, 333; and decline of deference 151; and environmental harms 113–14; impacts on Māori 74–75, 225, 270, 277; and institutionalised discrimination 303, 333; inter-generational impacts of 5, 75, 161–62, 277; media discussion of 11; and neuro-disabilities 359; and policing 144, 160–62; and prisons 293; and white-collar crime 120
Comber Report, Committee on Gangs 1981 373
Commerce (Criminalisation of Cartels) Amendment Act 2019 126
Commissioner's Māori Focus Forum 162
common sense 98, 307
community detention 203, 227, 229–32, 234, 297–98
community justice courts 208
community programmes 226–28, 271, 333
community sentences 3, 35, 145, 203, 225; compliance and breaches 232; costs 232; effectiveness of 232, 234–35; and ethnicity 233; hierarchy of 229; history of 226–28; management of 229; and Māori 233; and mass surveillance 234; rationales for 228–29; rehabilitation programmes for Māori 268–70; reintegration programmes for Māori 279, 282; types of 230–31; and youth 233
community service 226–28, 230–31, 297, 332
community work 203, 216, 227–32, 234
computer-dependent crimes 26

computer-enabled crimes 26
Comte, Auguste 308
confinement: cycles of 256–58, 293; solitary 294, 297
conformity 124, 320, 396–97
consent: policing by 164, 318; and sexual violence 65
consequentialism 201
constitutional transformation 295, 297
consumer fraud 126
contagious diseases Acts 385
corporate crime: disasters as 122; and the media 11; statistics on 348; *see also* state–corporate crimes
corporate harms 132–33
corporate scandals and collapses 120–21; *see also* Bridgecorp; Enron; Equiticorp; South Canterbury Finance; Viaduct Capital and Mutual Finance; Youi
Corrections Act 2004 278
Coster, Stan 254–55, 258
counter-colonial criminology 37, 39, 43
counter-publics 16
Court of Appeal 138, 189, 206, 326n1
Court of Special Circumstances 193
courts: cultural sensitivity training in 334; divisions of 189; ethnicity and gender in 189–90; hierarchy of 144, 188–89; Māori-focused initiatives 190–92, 195; solution-focused 144, 190, 192–94, 197; solution-focused, *see also* problem-solving courts; state of flux in 197
'Creating Positive Pathways' 280
crime: against animals and ecosystems 4, 108–9, 112–14; black-letter-law definition of 38–39; definitions of 22; differential experiences of 3; displacement 52, 75; framing 312; knowledge 3, 7; news 7, 9–12, 15–16, 154; pattern theory 181–82; proximal causes 177; risk factors for 14, 144, 177–81; types 3
crime and victim surveys *see* NZCVS
crime control policies, global transfer of 243–44
crime prevention 3–4, 144, 176; community 177–78, 180, **181**, 335; definition of 177; developmental 177–80, **181**, 183; effectiveness of 177–78; situational 177, 181–82, **183**; and victimology 311–12
crime problem 4–7; and CCJ research 34; and police operations 167–68; and police statistics 22, 28; public perception of 9, 149, 152–54

Crime Survey of England and Wales 26
Crimes Act 1961 22, 77; and gangs 375; and hate crime 100; sentencing provisions 203; and sex work 387
Crimes Amendment Act 2019 122
criminal justice 3–4; risk-focused approaches 3; *see also* CCJ
Criminal Justice Act 1985 226, 375
criminal justice prevention 177
criminal justice system 143–46; and decline of deference 151–52; expansion under neoliberalism 321; and family violence 77; Māori over-representation in 162–63, 190, 197, 214, 220, 243, 282–83, 321–22, **334**; medicalisation of 352; negative consequences of contact with 281; racism and bias within 317–18; role of victims in 292; and white-collar crime 125, 133
criminal other 34, 37–38
criminalisation 383–85, 389; of gangs 378; harms of 383, 386, 390; hyper-criminalisation 5
criminality: and insanity 348–50, 353; and victimity 306–7
criminogenic needs 267, 278
criminological perspectives, transformation of 1
criminology: biological theories of 348–49, 352; implicit 278; legitimacy turn in 160; orthodox and counter-colonial 37–39; positivist 308, 353; victims in 306
'crimmigration' 402
'critic and conscience' role of research 36
CTV Building, collapse of 122, 128
cultural appropriateness 218, 332, 334
cultural deprivation 256
cultural identity 191, 195–96, 270, 335
curfew 193, 201, 203, 229, 231
custodial remands 324–25
cybercrime 89–90; defining 26, 30n13, 85–86; and gender 48; misunderstanding of harms of 88; in New Zealand 86; police responses to 8, 144, 160, 167–68; and volume crime 21–22, 25–27; young people and 217
cyber-harm 48, 86, 89–90
cyber-security 27, 170n14
cyber-victimology 89
cycles of confinement 256–58, 293

D
dangerous classes 52, 349, 352
dangerousness 209, 304, 321, 346, 352–53
Davis, Angela 290, 295
Davis, Greg 190–91
dawn raids 305, 395, 397–99, 403n4
DDoS (distributed denial of service) 26
death penalty *see* punishment, capital
decarceration 42, 251–52, 296, 298
Deckert, Antje 41
decolonisation 5; approaches to 34, 41–42; decolonising criminology 39, 41–42; decolonising justice 3, 5–6, 114, 304, 333, 338–40; decolonising perspectives 1–2; decolonising research methodologies 8
decriminalisation 6, 295–96, 305, 389–90; limitations of 389; of sex work 4, 305, 383–84, 386–87, 390; use of term 384
Defence Act 1886 161
deference, decline of 143, 151
deficit-focused models 281, 284, 304, 346
degeneracy 304, 348
dehumanising practices 314
deinstitutionalisation 347, 351–52
Department of Conservation 109, 135–36
Department of Corrections, and CCJ research 35–36
deportations 305, 394–402
deprivation: multiple indicators of 350; and neuro-disabilities 359
desistance 146; comprehensive theory of 264; and reintegration 281–83; resources in prisons for 155; strengths-based models 282–83
deterrence: as goal of sentencing 144, 201–2; prison failing to attain 291
deviance, double 352
deviant behaviour 12, 86, 308, 351, 365
Diagnostic and Statistical Manual of Mental Disorders (DSM-5) 348, 351
difference, origins of 324
differential association 124
digital crime 4; *see also* cybercrime
digital media 5, 9, 15–17
disability: caused by white-collar crime 119, 122; discrimination and 100; hidden 304; and IPV 75; students with 37; *see also* neuro-disabilities
disability rights 366
disability support services 365–66

dis/abled perspectives 305, 366
disadvantages: social and economic 54, 145, 270, 319, 376; structural 75, 303–5, 310, 323
disasters: responsibility for 4, 49, 122; white-collar crimes as 127
discourse, Foucault on 38
discretion 4; police use of 163, 168, 216, 245, 304, 317–18, 320, 323, 325; in sentencing 204–6
discrimination 2–3; and hate crime 100; racial 101, 133, 169n9, 225; religio-ethnic 307
distorted thinking 265–66
District Court 189; appointments to 189–90
District Courts Act 2016 191
diversion 4, 214–16, 295–96, 320, 324
DNA 184, 219, 401
doli incapax 216
Domestic Protection Act 1982 76
domestic violence: and substance use 55–56; *see also* IPV
Domestic Violence Act 1995 76
Donner, Kelly 362
double-bunking 296–97
DRAOR (Dynamic Risk Assessment for Offender Re-entry) 38
drug courts 207–8, 209n4
drug laws 52, 55
drug–crime relationship 47, 50–52, 54–57; substance-/drug-defined crimes 52–53; substance-/drug-influenced crimes 53; substance-/drug-related crimes 52–53
drugs: consumption of 51; decriminalisation of 296; illegal 50–54, 56–57, 60, 201; normalisation thesis 51; recreational use of 52–53
due process 195, 209, 216
Durie, Mason 319
Durkheim, Émile 308
dynamic risk factors 267–68, 275
dysmaturity 360, 363

E
Early Start programme 179
ecocentrism 109, 114
ecocide 108
eco-justice 107–9, 113–14
economic abuse 74, 77
economic crime 121; *see also* white-collar crime
eco-philosophies 109

education: and community sentences 226, 228, 230, 235; and crime prevention 144, 178–79, **181**; and deference 151; feminist 16; for FGCs 217; and gangs 373; and institutionalisation 162; and IPV 75, 79; and migration 397; and neuro-disabilities 361–62; of prisoners 145, 253, 259; and rehabilitation 265–66; and reintegration 278, 280, 282; and victimology 308, 312; and youth justice 233
Education Act 1989 36
Effective Interventions strategy 227
elder abuse 74
electronic monitoring (EM) 203, 227, 229–32, 234–36, 401
ELLA (Electronic Lifelike Assistant) 167
emotion, as news value 12, 14
empathy, low 177–78
employment: access for victims to 79; loss of 88; in neoliberal era 153; and reintegration 277, 279–80; and reoffending 265; of white-collar offenders 125
Employment Court 189
empowerment 67, 79–80, 242–43, 340
End of Life Choice Act 2019 383, 390n1
Enron 124
Environment Court 189
environmental design 122
environmental harms 39, 49, 107–8; and criminology 39; and industry 112–13; and mātauranga Māori 113–14; as state–corporate crimes 132
environmental justice 109
environmental victimisation 108, 116
EPMU (Engineering, Printing and Manufacturing Union) 138
Equiticorp 120–21
ethnic cleansing 98–99
Ethnic Strategy 169n6
evaluation: of crime prevention programmes 177–82; of FGCs 217; of rehabilitation programmes 270–72; of sex work decriminalisation 388; of special-purpose courts 193–95; of UBT 325; of youth justice 221–22
evidence: collecting 26, 135, 219; dismissing 2; DNA 184, 219, 401; fingerprints 219, 401
evidence-based sentencing 144, 201, 206–8
excarceration 295–96, 298

expressive theory of punishment 202
extended supervision orders 154, 227

F

Fa'a Samoa 340
Facebook, and Christchurch mosque massacres 15–16
face-to-face relationships 85, 167, 337
facial recognition systems 184
Fair Trading Act 1986 126
Fairfax 10
faith-based programmes 266
family conflict 48, 179
Family Court 78, 189
family environment, risk factors for future offending in 179–80
Family Group Conferences 145, 191, 215–18, 220, 333; and community sentences 233; 'Māoriness' of 242–44, 246, 334, 336; and Ngā Kōti Rangatahi 191; and restorative justice 239–42; standardisation and globalisation 244–45
family violence 2, 4, 73–74; and act of possession 64; contemporary issues 77; costs 75; empowerment model 79–80; and image-based sexual abuse 88; impacts of 75; legislation 76–78; *see also* IPV; child abuse
Family Violence Court 196, 198n3, 208
FASD *see* foetal alcohol spectrum disorder
fear, culture of 396
femininity, and alcohol 56, 58n9
feminism 6, 42; carceral 386; and rape 61–62, 67, 69
feminist criminology 39
field officers 231
financial abuse 30n11
financial crime 86, 120–21, 126; *see also* white-collar crime
Financial Markets Authority 126
fines 111, 229, 232, 234, 298, 375
fingerprints 219, 401
First Offenders' Probation Act 1886 226
foetal alcohol spectrum disorder (FASD) 220, 358, 363, 366; impairments 360–61; links to offending 359, 362, 364–65; strengths-based approach 363; and suicide 363
folk devils 13–14
followership, engaged 125

forfeiture orders 203
Foucault, Michel 38, 351
fraud: corporate 176; in NZCVS 30n13; NZP statistics on 27–28; online 25–26; welfare *see* welfare fraud; as white-collar crime 119, 126
freshwater ecosystems 109, 112–13
Functional Family Therapy 180
functionalist approach 308
FVDRC (Family Violence Death Review Committee) 74–76, 79

G

gangs 305; ban on regalia of 254, 375–76; and colonisation 162; definitions of 370; Gilbert's research on 36; legislation on 373–75; media commentary on 371, 376; offending by 376–77, 380n5; and Pasifika youth 336; police responses to 166, 372; political discourse on 370–74, 377–78; and reintegration 277; types of 376; youth gang liaison 334; youth 336, 375–77, 379
gangs strategy: Strike Force Raptor 166, 379; zero tolerance 378
gender, gendered harms 4
gender equality 62, 69, 75, 386
gender stereotypes, and family violence 74–75, 77–78, 80
Gilbert, Jarrod 36, 305
girls: forming counter-publics 16; and rape culture 66; and sexting 87; in youth justice 145, 220
global crimes 5
Global Economic Crime and Fraud Survey 121
global financial crisis (GFC) 121, 134
global insecurities 143, 153
globalisation, and white-collar crime 123
good lives model (GLM) 146, 264, 266, 268, 270, 281–82
Gotingco, Blesilda 154
GPS (global positioning system) 227, 231
graduated liability 215
Great Strike of 1913 164, 169n7
green criminology 49, 107–8, 114
Green Party 156
Group Employment Liaison Scheme 373
group norms, internalisation of 124
Guided Release Programme 278

H

Habitual Criminals Act 1906 205
HAIL (Hazardous Activities and Industries List) 113
halfway houses 279
Hāpaitia te Oranga Tangata 317
Harassment Act 1997 374
harm 53, 291–92; *see also* environmental harms; social harm
harm reduction 207, 386–87, 390
harmful behaviours 134, 139, 290–93
Harmful Digital Communications Act 2015 76–77, 88–89
hate crimes 4, 47–48; anti-Muslim 95, 97; legislation on 99–101; New Zealand state's denial of 102; 'permission to hate' 48, 101–3; punishments for 99–100; statistics on 97
hate speech 16, 69, 100–1
Havelock North, gastroenteritis and drinking water crisis in 112–13
He whaipaanga hou see *The Maori and the criminal justice system: A new perspective*
healing 192, 225, 241
health and safety, corporate infringements on 119, 124, 133, 137
Health and Safety at Work Act 2015 126, 138
Health and Safety in Employment Amendment Act 2013 138
Healy, Catherine 387, 389
hegemonic masculinity 66
hegemony 7, 9–11, 99, 352
Heke, Tamaki 363
Hells Angels 371, 375–76, 380n2
heroin 50–51, 54
heterosexual binary 69
hierarchy, social 38, 102
High Court 138, 189–90, 219, 376
Hōkai Rangi 282–83, 293
home detention 145, 203, 227, 229–32, 234
home visitation 179
homelessness 144; for released prisoners 279; and solution-focused courts 193, 208
homicides 189, 214, 216–17, 309, 346, 377
homophobia 48, 100, 102, 277
horses: betting on 111; harms against 110–11; Kaimanawa 109–10; racing industry 107, 109–12
'hot spots' 182

house arrest 203, 296; *see also* home detention
housing: stable 257, 279; supported accommodation 228; *see also* homelessness
HRC (Human Rights Commission), and hate crime 97, 100
human rights: and crime prevention 183; and gangs 378; and water pollution 112
Human Rights Act 1993 100
Human Rights Review Tribunal 389
Hunn Report 1961 319
Te Huringa o Te Tai 162, 335
hyper-incarceration 144–45, 252; and children 257; cycles of confinement 256–58, 293; definition of 251; features of 252–54; of Māori 3, 5, 144, 197, 256–58; reversing 258–59

I

identity theft 8, 22, 26–27
idleness, in prisons 145, 251, 253, 258
ignorance 131, 133–34, 136, 138–39; organised *see* agnosis
Ihumātao occupation 161, 164
immigration: and penal populism 152–53, 156; and white supremacy 98
Immigration and Customs Enforcement (US) 397
immigration detention centres 400–1
impact evaluations 177–78
impairments, primary 360–61
imprisonment: adaptation to 255; alternatives to 226, 231, 235, 297–98; as colonial control 2, 293; conditions of 148, 252–53; experiences of 145–46, 252–56; impacts of 294; rates of 147–48, 155–56, 204, 291, 250–51, 321, 352; and rehabilitation 283; and reintegration 277, 281; release from 256–57; repeated 277; scandals in 155, 252; stigma of 279; targeting of 251; treatment in 254; and violence *see* prisons, violence in; of young people 218; *see also* hyper-incarceration
Ināia Tonu Nei 156, 220
incapacitation, as goal of sentencing 144, 201–3
incarcerated people *see* prisoners
incarceration: of racialised minorities 41; and social exclusion 256–57
incarceration rates 200, 235, 251, 313; in New Zealand 200, 202, 250–51
incest 309–10

incidence, use of term 29n4
Incredible Years Parenting Programme 179
Independent Police Conduct Authority (IPCA) 163, 324
indigecentric eco-philosophy 49, 114
indigenisation 5, 304, 336, 340
Indigenous models: for justice reform 297; for mental health 365
Indigenous peoples: and alcohol 51; co-option of culture 5, 196, 304, 336, 339–40; incarceration of 39, 352–53; justice of 145, 242; knowledges 337; life-worlds 243; and research ethics 40–41; and restorative justice 240, 244–45; trauma of colonisation 162; values 338–39
industrial pollution 5, 49, 107
inequalities 2, 4–5; in academia 37; and drug–crime link 55; media discussion of 11; and sexual violence 62
informal sanctions 207, 216
Inland Revenue Department 126
insider trading 120, 124, 126
Institute of Criminology, Victoria University of Wellington 1, 34
institutional racism 161, 163, 277, 303, 317, 324, 333
institutionalisation 256, 291, 294
intensive supervision 145, 203, 227, 229–30, 232, 234
intergenerational trauma and disadvantage: and colonisation 5, 75, 161–62, 277; and criminal justice system 143; and dawn raids 399; of imprisonment 146, 251, 257, 259; and institutional racism 161; and neuro-disabilities 359
internet access 84
intersectionality 56–57
intimate images, sharing 76, 84–89
intimate partner violence *see* IPV
intoxication: crimes of 47, 50–51, 53; cultures of 51, 55
IPV (intimate partner violence) 8, 48, 73; causes of 74; grassroots responses to 75–76; impacts of 75; social attitudes to 77; victims of 74–75, 78–79; and volume crime 22, 24–25
Islamic Women's Council of New Zealand (IWCNZ) 97
Islamophobia 48, 95–97, 101–2; as racism 97–99
iwi panels 338

J
Jackson, Moana 2, 35, 41, 256; on constitutional transformation 297; and criminal justice system 333, 340; funding for research of 37; government rejection of conclusions 38; on prisons 293; on specialist courts 196; on transforming policy-making 339; *see also The Maori and the criminal justice system: A new perspective: He whaipaanga hou*
JBL 120
journalism, investigative 9
judicial discretion 144, 205, 207–8
judiciary 189–90, 196; diversity of 5, 144, 189–90, 197; Māori 190
jurisdictional autonomy 244–45
justice: cultural dynamics of 6, 144; differential experiences of 3; Māori systems of 225
JustSpeak 295; funding of 36; and penal populism 156; and prisons 291; research on police racism 322, 324

K
kaitiakitanga 114
kaupapa Māori, and reintegration 279
Kearns v. R 321, 325, 326n1
Kia Marama programme 266, **269**–70
Killer Beez 376
knowledge-making, control of 133–34
Te Kooti o Timatanga Hou 193
Ngā Kōti Rangatahi 1, 5, 144, 191–92, 218, 236n6, 304, 325, 333–36, 338; appearances in 342n4; expansion of 220; Māori critique of 196
Kowhiritanga programme 269
Kuggeleijn, Scott 65–66

L
labelling effects 181, 216
labelling theory 350
Labour Party: criminal justice initiatives 2; and neoliberalism 120, 151; and prison population 145, 148, 150, 156; and three-strikes law 42n1
Land Wars *see* New Zealand Wars
Law Foundation 37, 364
law and order 11, 149, 153, 155–56, 166, 319, 371, 374
Laws, Michael 375
legalisation 305, 383–84, 390

legitimacy: and effective policing 15, 144, 160, 166, 168; and law and order 149
Lex Aotearoa 197
Little, Andrew 101, 122, 135, 140n9, 208, 317
lobby groups 148–49, 156, 226, 372
Local Government Act 1974 375
logical positivism 306, 308
Lombroso, Cesare 38, 348–49
longitudinal research 98, 178–79, 257, 348
Luff, Daniel 254

M
macro-level analysis 123
male entitlement 4, 62
'male gaze' 67
males, over-representation of 272
mana 188, 225, 235n1; restoring 282
Te Mana o Ngāpuhi Kowhao Rau 191
mana tamaiti 215
manaakitanga 338–39
mandatory sentences 144, 201, 205, 208
Mandela Rules *see* UN Standard Minimum Rules for the Treatment of Prisoners
manslaughter, corporate 140n9
Māori: colonisation and violence 75; and community sentences 232–33, 235; co-option of 5, 196, 304, 336, 339–40; and criminal justice system 144–46, 283; disproportionate sentencing of 145; and gangs 373; and homelessness 193–94; incarceration of 293, 298 (*see also* imprisonment); justice practices 245, 334; migrants to Australia 400; and neuro-disabilities 365; in news media 14; as offenders 7; pathologisation of 349–50, 352–53; police perceptions of 322–25; policing of 144, 160–65, 304, 318–21, 335; punishment of 282, 293–94, 304, 318; self-determination and sovereignty *see* tino rangatiratanga; and substance-linked crimes 54; theft of land 96; as victims 161, 312; women 14, 48, 75; and women's organisations 75–76
The Maori and the criminal justice system: A new perspective. He whaipaanga hou 2, 35, 333; and co-option of Māori 196; funding for 37; and imprisonment 293
Māori Appellate Court 189
Māori children 14, 145, 162, 221, 320

Māori communities: colonisation and violence in 74–75; consultation with 156–57; contemporary stresses on 162; social exclusion of 256–57
Māori Focus Units **269**–70
Māori Land Court 189
marae 188, 191, 196, 218, 250, 334–35
marae-based approach 339
marginalisation: and hyper-incarceration 258; of Māori 163; media discussion of 11; and moral panics 13; and neuro-disabilities 304; and penal populism 149
marginalised populations 3–4
masculine entitlement 48, 66
masculinity: and alcohol 56; and rape 65–66; under patriarchy 67, 69
mass imprisonment 251, 260, 293, 298
mass shootings 345
mass surveillance 233–34
Matariki Court 5, 144, 190–91
mātauranga Māori 113–14, 282–83, 293
Matike Mai report 295, 297
'Mau Rākau' programme 268
maximum penalties 100, 108, 203, 205
MBIE (Ministry for Business, Innovation and Employment) 37, 126, 135
McGregor, Judy 323
McIntosh, Tracey 41
McVicar, Garth 150, 252
media: deregulation of 10, 15, 17, 153; *see also* digital media; social media
media–crime nexus 7, 9
medical expansionism 351
Medium Intensity Rehabilitation Programme 269
Mendelsohn, Benjamin 306–12
mental health 304, 345, 353; and community sentences 233; and crime prevention 183; and homeless people 193; police responses to 165–66, 348; stereotypes 345; and substance use 56–57; supporting offenders with 228
mental health courts 208
mental health detention 161
mental health theories: conservative 348–50; critical 350–52
mental health units 304

mental illness 5, 345; classifications of 348; criminalisation of 159, 304, 347; Indigenous groups 352–53; pathologies 346, 348–53; and racism 348–49; relation to crime 346–51; relation to imprisonment 251, 346, 352; and use of police force 165; women's 352; working class 352–53; and youth justice 220
'mercy bookings' 347
meso-level analysis 123–24
methamphetamine 50–54, 56, 57n3, 166, 378
micro-level analysis 123–24
Migrant Settlement and Integration Strategy 395
migrants: controls over 389, 396; 'illegal' 395, 397; legislation on 398, 401, 403n5; Pacific quota 397
Migration Act (Australia) 400, 403n5
Mihaere, Riki 41
Mikaere, Ani 41
Millane, Grace 7, 12, 311
mindfulness meditation 265–66
minimisation 295–96
mining 120, 132, 134, 136, 139
Ministry of Justice (MoJ): and NZCVS 21; research agenda of 35
Ministry of Social Development (MSD), funding research 37
misogyny 62–63, 65
mission creep 165
Misuse of Drugs Act 1975 51–52, 375
MMP (Mixed Member Proportional) electoral system 152, 156
Moerewa incident 372–73
money laundering 120
Mongrel Mob 254, 375, 378
monoculturalism 197, 225, 333, 338–40
moral entrepreneurs 13, 350
moral intuitions 324
moral panics 7, 9; and gangs 305, 371, 374; in New Zealand press 13–14
morality politics 385
motivational programmes, *see also* Mau Rākau programme; Medium Intensity Rehabilitation Programme; Kowhiritanga
Movement for Alternatives to Prison 294
multisystemic therapy 180
muru 225, 235n1

N

National Network for Ending Sexual Violence Together 76
National Party 102, 166, 227, 378–79
Native Exemption Ordinance 1844 294
navigators 233
negative reforms 296–97
neocolonialism 39, 41, 139, 244, 340, 346, 353
neoliberalism 303; and authoritarian populism 149; and corporate harms 132–34, 137–39; and criminology 1–2; and gangs 374; and incarceration 251–52; and migration 396–97; and NTE 56; and penal populism 5, 151; and policing 320–21; and social change 298; and victimology 307, 311–12
net widening 86, 207
Netsafe 27, 86–88
neuro-disabilities 304–5; and community sentences 233; criminal justice engagement with those with 359, 362–66; impairments and challenges 360–61; incarceration of those with 352; links to offending 349; perseveration 363; prevalence of 304, 359–60, 365; protective factors 361; and vulnerability 358–59, 362–63; and youth justice 220–21, 358
neuro-disability courts 364
neuro-informed criminal justice practices 358
neutralisation, techniques of 124, 127
New Public Management 137, 140n4
New Zealand: continuation of colonialism in 39; criminal justice apparatus of 4; decolonial criminology in 42; features of criminal justice system 1–2; gun laws of 95; inequalities in 251, 277; migration policy 397–98; news media political economy in 10–11, 17; penal policy in 44, 147–48; self-image as clean and green 107; self-image as non-racist 96, 101–2
New Zealand Armed Constabulary 161
New Zealand Attitudes and Values Study 98–99
New Zealand Crime and Victims Survey *see* NZCVS
New Zealand First party 23, 101, 152, 156
New Zealand Prostitutes Collective (NZPC) 387, 389
New Zealand Wars 96
news: anti-establishment 15; citizen journalism 15; clickbait approach to 15
news media: political economy of production 10–11; race in 14; reporting on crime 1, 3, 9

news values 11–13; the extraordinary as 12
newsworthiness 11–12, 153
NGOs (non-governmental organisations) 36, 85, 278–79, 337, 389
Nicholas, Louise 68, 311
night-time economy (NTE) 51, 55–56
non-association orders 193, 203–4
non-molestation orders 76
non-silencing research methods 39
Nordic model 385–86
normalisation thesis 51
NPIP (No Pride in Prisons) see PAPA
NTE (night-time economy) 51, 55–56
NZ ADUM (Arrestee Drug Use Monitoring) 47, 53–55, 57
NZCASS (New Zealand Crime and Safety Survey) 21–25, **24**, 29n1
NZCVS (New Zealand Crime and Victims Survey) 21–22, 28–29, 29n1 30n10, 30n13, 35, 69, 176; burglaries and assaults in **24**, 25; and cybercrime 27; and imprisonment 292; sexual violence in 69
NZME 10
NZP (New Zealand Police): and CCJ research 35–36; colonial history of 161; and crime prevention 183; Māori officers 162, 164, 319; Māori perceptions of 322; operational priorities of 166–67; over-policing 161, 168; paramilitarisation of 144, 160, 165; relationship with Māori 162–63, 318–20, 325, 335; statistics collated by 7–8, 21–25, 27–29, 30n11; transformation of 159, 168; under-policing 161, 168; and volume crime 22–23

O

obedience, crimes of 125
objectification 37, 66–68; see also 'male gaze'
'offender-centric' approaches 228
offenders: backgrounds 269, 296, 321; community-based services for 270–71; female 219, 269, 272; high-risk 227, 267, 269; low-risk 207, 267; programmes 253, **269**; supporting 228, 235; treatments 254, 266–71, victims as 311
Office of Māori, Pacific and Ethnic Services (OMPES) 335
Te Ohaaki-a-Hine 76
the Ombudsman, Office of 35, 252–54, **259**, 260n2
online crime: fraud 8, 22, 25–28, 30n13; harassment 15, 76, 89; police responses to 167

Operation Pot Black 398
opportunity-deficit model 278
Oranga Tamariki 169n5, 214
Oranga Tamariki Act 1989 214, 221, 233, 239, 333, 342n3, 367n3
'ordinary people' 149, 151, 155, 297
O'Reilly, Denis 373
organisational culture 124, 304, 318, 325
organisational deviance 123–24
organised crime 166, 183, 203, 374, 377–78
Osborne, Anna 138, 140n7
othering 37, 98, 101–2
Otherness 396
'Out of Gate' programme 278
over-stayers 305, 397–99, 403n6

P

Pacific People's Responsiveness Strategy 335
Te Pae Oranga – Iwi/Community Panels 162, 216, 325
pain, and imprisonment 294
PAPA (People Against Prisons Aotearoa) 293, 295–97
parallel justice system 197
paramilitarism 144, 160, 169
Paremoremo prison 254
parenting 77, 179
parenting programmes 179, 376
Parihaka 161, 168n1, 169n2
Parker, Honorah 346
Parole Act 2002 155, 242
participation: positive 333–34; principle of 40; in rehabilitation 271–72; in restorative justice 240, 246; in Youth Court 215, 217
Pasifika, use of term 341n1
Pasifika Court 218, 304, 333, 335–36, 342n4
Pasifika peoples 3; co-option of 5, 339–40; and criminal justice system 200, 205, 233, 303–4, 333, **334**; hardship rate 321; and housing 279; as judges 190; migration to Aotearoa New Zealand 395, 397–400; police attitudes to 160, 163, 165, 323; see also dawn raids; Samoan talavou
Pasifika students 3, 37, 304, 335
Pasifika youth 14, 37, 304, 331–32, 335–37
Pasifika Youth Courts 335–36
patches 370–71, 373, 375–76, 380n1
pathological behaviour 346
pathologisation of populations 196, 333, 352–53

'Pathway Total Reintegration' Programme 282
patriarchy 47–48, 61–63, 69
penal couple 307–8, 312
Penal Policy Review Committee 148
penal populism 5, 143–45, 303; causes 150–55; and community sentences 226–29; consequences of 155; and criminalisation 383; decline of 156–57; definition of 148–49; and prisons 250–52
penal power, axis of 148
penology 37–38; new 207
People Against Prisons Aotearoa *see* PAPA
periodic detention 147, 226–28, 231
Perry Preschool Project 178
personification, as news value 12–13
pharmaceutical corporations 352
Pike River Coal company 136–38
Pike River Mine: disaster at 49, 131–32, 134–35, 139; recovery of bodies 135, 138; Royal Commission on 126, 135–36; unsafe practices at 124
Pike River Recovery Agency 135
Te Piki Oranga 228, 233
pimping 384
Pinel, Philippe 348
Te Piriti 270
Plan of Action – Improving the Outcome for Young People in Counties Manukau 376
plea bargaining 4, 144, 204–5, 207, 325
police: accountability 15, 159; armed patrols 165; culture 318, 325; and cybercrime 8, 144, 160, 167–68; discrimination by 317, 322–23, 325; diversion 213, 216; and gangs 166, 372; legitimacy of 144, 160, 163–64, 166–68; and the media 10–11; militarisation of 165–66; preventative patrolling 165; at protests 41, 169n9; and racism 317–25; reporting on abuses by 15; and sex workers 384, 386, 388–89; statistics 21–22, 25–26, 28–29; 'tactical options' 165–66; turnovers 324–25; unarmed 1; *see also* NZP (New Zealand Police)
Police Force Act 1886 161
Police Offences Amendment Act 373
police strategies: Te Huringa o Te Tai 2019 162, 335; Pacific People's Responsiveness Strategy 2002, O Le Taeao Fou 335; punitive 125, 166
Police Task Force 372, 378
policing: coercive 160, 163; colonial 144, 161, 164, 168, 303–4, 318; and mental illness 347; order-maintenance 320–1; responsive 335; 'special powers' 2, 169n8; unconscious bias in 323–24
policing models 164
policy setting 396
policy transformation 148
politics: morality 385, 393; populist 157
pollution: contaminated land 107, 113; freshwater 109, 112–13; industrial 5, 49, 107; landfill emissions 113
Polynesian Panthers 398, 403n4
populism: and criminal justice 1; use of term 149; and volume crime 23; *see also* penal populism
populist punitiveness 100–1, 143, 149
Pora, Teina 362
pornography: child pornography 86, 89–90; and rape 66, 68
positivist 314
postcode justice 195
post-colonial policing 318
post-colonialism 39, 160
post-detention conditions 227, 234
post-release programmes 281
Pou Oranga 194
poverty, normalisation of 321
power differentials 4, 40
power relations: and corporate harms 133; and criminal justice system 143; settler-colonial 4, 6
the powerful, crimes of 5, 11, 49, 56, 127, 131, 134, 313
pre-charge warnings 163, 324
presumptive penalties 205
prevalence, use of term 29n4
Prevention First model 166, 183
preventive detention 147–48, 200, 203–4
primary goods 268
prison abolition 42, 146, 289–90, 298; arguments for 290–92; definition of 290; history of 294–95; implementation of 297–98; politics of 292–94; theory of 290
prison conditions *see* imprisonment, conditions of
prison construction 148; moratorium on 296
prison jobs 253
prison pipeline 218
prison population: and bail laws 291; and community sentences 231, 234; demography of 204–5, 277; mental illness in 346–47, 352;

neuro-disability in 359; reducing 145, 156, 227, 251–52; statistics on 35
prison rates 235; *see also* incarceration rates
prison reform 258, 295; negative 296–97
prisoners: agency of 254–56; children of 257–58, 294; experiences of 145–46, 252–56; surveys of 252–54, 257, 259; violence against 314
Prisoners' and Victims' Claims Act 2005 155
prison-industrial complex 347, 352
prisonisation 146, 254–56, 291
prisons 145–46; cell confinement 145, 252–54; culture of 255–56; drug offences in 54; failings of 290–92; inhumane treatment in 2; Māori in *see* Māori, incarceration of; Māori resistance to 294; Māori Therapeutic Programme 270; overcrowding in 148, 155, 251–53; rehabilitation programmes for Māori 268–70; reintegration programmes for Māori 279, 282; researcher access to 36; scandals 252; size of 252, 260n1; statistics on 35–36; and tough-on-crime approach 11; violence in 253, 292; yoga in 266; *see also* imprisonment; Māori Focus Units
private security 169, 183, 227, 229, 234
probation 204, 206, 226, 228–29, 284n2, 297, 319, 401; eternal 397; staff 36, 203, 226, 229–30
problem behaviours 143, 179, 266
problem-solving courts 5–6, 144–45, 190, 201, 207–8, 217
procedural justice 160, 207, 209n3
profitability, threats to 123–24
profit-seeking 112, 127, 136–37
Project Employment Programme (PEP) 373
property crime: online 167; as volume crime 8, 23
prosocial communities 281–82
prostitution 66, 384–88; *see also* sex work
Prostitution Law Review Committee 389
Prostitution Reform Act 2003 305, 387–90
protection orders 73, 76–79, 148, 204, 221
protest, policing of 160, 164
proximity, as news value 12
psychiatry 348–49, 351
psychological abuse 74, 76–77
PTSD (post-traumatic stress disorder) 233, 346, 401
Puao-Te-Ata-Tu 2, 332–33
public discourse, and social media 16
public order policing 18, 164

public safety 22, 35, 230; and community sentences 228–31; and cybercrime 167; and paramilitary policing 166; and prisons 146, 290; and sentencing 206, 209; and youth justice 219–20
Public Safety Act 2014 148
public sphere 10, 15–16
Te Puni Kōkiri (TPK) 35–36, 322
punishment: capital 200–1, 290; consequentialist and non-consequentialist theories of 201; corporal 147, 200; expressive 154, 202
punitiveness 226–27, 229, 383, 401
PWUD (people who use drugs) 51, 54
pyramidal system of control 126

Q

Quince, Khylee 41, 96, 144

R

racial profiling 163, 336
racism 2; denial of 95–96, 98, 102; embedded nature of 303; and hate crimes 48; institutional 161, 163, 277, 303, 317, 324, 333; personal 304, 325; responses to 94–96, 100, 102; systemic 295, 317, 323, 325, 365; as unconscious bias 323–24
racist violence 96–98
Rangatahi Courts *see* Kōti Rangatahi
rape: and gangs 374; history of 47–48, 62–69; legal definition of 61; marital 64; and patriarchal thinking 63; research on 37; sentencing for 203; and victim-blaming 309–11
Rape Crisis 75
rape culture 48, 63, 69; and image-based sexual abuse 89; and social media 16
rational choice theory 123, 181
RCOS (Recorded Crime Offender Statistics) 27
RCVS (Recorded Crime Victim Statistics) 27
recidivism 264; and community sentences 226–28, 230–31, 233; in criminology 38; and Māori offenders 282; and neuro-disabilities 304; prisons leading to 146; and rehabilitation programmes 266–72; and sentencing 205–7; and social exclusion 257; and solution-focused courts 191, 193, 195; in white-collar crime 120
reciprocity 40, 229

reconciliation 225, 229, 240–41
reconvictions: and community sentences 230–32, 234; failure of prisons to prevent 291; and rehabilitation 264; and reintegration 277, 282, 284n2
recorded crime 21–22, **24**, 26–27, 321
re-entry 256, 268, 276, 280–81
referendum on law and order *see* citizen-initiated referendum on law and order 1999
refugees 397
regulation: corporate self-regulation 137; limits of 3; minimisation of 49, 132
rehabilitation 144, 146, 264; approaches to 265–66; and community sentences 227–30, 233–35; critiques of: evaluations of 271–72; failure of prison to attain 290–91; and gender: as goal of sentencing 201–2; good lives model: Māori: models of 266–68, 272
rehabilitation programmes: attendance at 230; attrition rates 267–68; cognitive-behavioural 264–65; diversity in 146; effectiveness of 271–72; in New Zealand 268–70, **269**; in RNR model 267
rehabilitative practice, and therapeutic jurisprudence 192
reincarceration cycle 146, 283
re-institutionalisation 347
reintegration 4, 37, 146, 276–77; barriers to 277, 279–80, 282; community organisations involved in 278–79; deficit-focused model 281; definitions of 277; differential experiences of 280–82; housing and employment 279–80; intensive client support managers (ICSMs) 280; lack of provision for Māori 277, 282–83; and media coverage 218; New Zealand context of 277; pillars of 278; problem of 280–81; programmes 278; and punishment 192; and rehabilitation 228, 268; and restorative justice 240, 246, 282; and sentencing 202
relapse prevention 266, 269–70
release from prison 256–57
Release to Work scheme 280
remand: number of prisoners on 155; young people on 215, 218
te reo Māori 190–91, 256
reoffending *see* recidivism
reparation 97, 143, 202–3, 228–29; as alternative to prison 298

representations 3; class-based 10–13; of crime in the media 9–12; of crime picture 10, 22; of drug users 47; of New Zealand 14; racialised 14; sexist 3
research: ethics in 34, 39–41; funding of 36–37; kaupapa Māori research 38, 40; Māori and Samoan Indigenous methodologies 337; Partnership, Participation, Protection 40; scholarships 37
research power 38
researcher access 34
resettlement 276, 287
resistance: Māori 161, 163, 294, 312; in prison 254; social movements 132
responsibilisation 145, 244, 396
responsibility, personal 307, 312, 320–21, 363
responsiveness policies 333, 336, 340–41
Responsiveness to Māori (RTM) 162, 323, 335–36
responsivity principle 267
restoration 143, 203, 229, 233–34, 293
restorative conferences 229, 241
restorative justice: as alternative to prison 297; definitions of 240; emergence of 240–41; and family group conferences 217, 239–40; and Indigenous peoples 242–43, 245; Māori criticisms of 145, 241–44, 246; myths of 242; in New Zealand 241–42; policy transfer of 244–46; practice of 240–41; and therapeutic jurisprudence 192; and youth justice 215
Rethinking Crime and Punishment (RCP) 156, 295, 324
retribution, as goal of sentencing 144, 201–2
retributivism 201–2
Returning Offenders (Management and Information) Act 2015 401
revenge porn 89; *see also* sexual abuse, image-based
rights: animal 116; children's 223–24; citizens' 312; collective 40; customary 312; democratic 164; disability 366; ecosystem 112; gay 100; individual 147, 183; international 329, 356; legal 305, 388
rights movements 63, 226, 314
rights standards 216, 221, 397
right-wing terrorism 94–95, 97, 102
risk: as news value 12; predicting 206; profiling 206, 212; to society 399

risk assessment: and environmental harm 108; and sentencing 144, 206

risk factors: dynamic 267–68, 275; for offending 14, 144, 177–81; for reoffending 266, 270; static 266

risk rationalities 3

risk-management approach 145

risk-need-responsivity model 146, 202, 227, 264; components of 266, *267*; critiques of 267–68; and Māori models 270; and reintegration 278

risk-profiling 399

risky populations 3, 207, 305

RNR *see* risk-need-responsivity model

Roast Busters 66, 71, 88

Rockhouse, Sonya 138, 140n7

Rogernomics 120

Roguski, Michael 41

romance scams 26, 86

routine activities theory 123, 181

Rūātoki 161, 169n4

Ryan, William 310

S

safety: failure of prison to achieve 291–92; perceptions survey **377**; risks to 135–36

safety crimes 129, 133

Saili Matagi programme **334**

Sale of Liquor Amendment Act 373

Samoan population of New Zealand 342n2

Samoan talavou 304, 331–33, 336–37, 340–41

scams: online 26–27; as white-collar crime 119

scandal: policy driven by 155; and white-collar crime 49, 119–20, 124–25

schizophrenia 348–49, 352

scholar-activism 34, 41–42

school performance, as risk factor 178

school-based programmes 180

section 282 discharge 218

self-determination 40, 75, 228, 248, 258, 339–40; *see also* tino rangatiratanga

self-harm 218, 401

self-regulation: corporate 137; and neuro-disabilities 360, 362, 364; personal 178

Selwyn, Tim 255

Sensible Sentencing Trust 148, 150–51, 155–56, 205, 252, 292, 313–14

sentences: community detention 203; community work 203; discharge 145, 203; fine or reparation 203; home detention 203; imprisonment 203, 232; intensive supervision 203; length of 100, 147–48; supervision 203, 226, 228–30, 232; suspended 296

sentencing: aggravating factors 100; and class 204; discrimination in 204; disparities 144, 201, 204–7; goals of 144, 201–4; grid 206; guidelines 144, 201, 206–8; hierarchy of 229; inequity of 336; Māori 145, 205, 225; mitigating factors 364; Pasifika 205; for young people 219

Sentencing Act 2002 202–4; children under 219; and community sentences 227; and hate crime 99–100; and Māori-focused initiatives 191; restorative justice in 242

Sentencing Amendment Act 2007 234

Sentencing and Parole Reform Act 2010 148, 150

sentencing circles 241

serious offences 25, 61, 216, 218–19, 222, 362

seriousness, victim perceptions of 25

settler colonialism 1, 4, 6, 145; impacts on law 333; and Islamophobia 95; nature of 161; and restorative justice 240, 244; and youth justice 332, 337

sex offences: Adult Sex Offender Treatment Programme 269; *see also* sexual assault

sex offenders: civil detention of 148; and penal populism 150, 154

sex work 383–84; abolitionist perspectives on 386–87; control and policing of 384–86; criminalising 383–86; decriminalising 305, 384, 386, 389–90, 390n2; history of 385; legalisation of 384; organisation of 386

sex workers 305; campaign for decriminalisation 387–90; denigration and imprisonment of 385; Māori 387; rights of 386–88; street-based 385, 387, 389; transgender 387

sexism 62, 64, 80, 283, 303

sexting 48, 86–89

sextortion 26

sexual abuse: Freud's denial of 309; image-based 48, 86–88

sexual assault: and neuro-disabilities 363; police responses to 159, 168; police-perpetrated 311; prison-based 35; teenage girls and 89; victims of 309

sexual harassment 16, 66

sexual violence 2; and alcohol 58n9; prevalence of 69; and rape 62; representations of 4; and volume crime 22, 25; *see also* IPV
Sexual Violence Court 194–96
sexuality, control of women's 385, 389
SFO (Serious Fraud Office) 121–22, 126
shareability 12, 15
Sharples, Pita 194, 312, 322
Short Motivational Programme (SMP) 268–69
significant harms 3, 56, 112, 139, 394
silencing: and victimology 303, 310; of women 48, 62–63, 68
situational approaches 144, 182, **183**, 311–12
situational prevention 177
SlutWalk 311
social capital 153, 192, 281–82
social class 56, 125, 204, 350; and mental illness 350; and policing 318–19, 321
social cohesion 156, 180, 282, 349
social constructionism 346, 350
social control: and colonisation 333; informal 220, 280; and mass incarceration 41; and mental health 346, 350–53
social deviance 350–51, 353
social entrapment 48, 75, 79–80
social exclusion 256–58, 277
social harm 2; and crime 39, 348; of cybercrime 85; of IPV 76; kaupapa Māori approach to 38; Māori approaches to 242; prisons causing 289; and restorative justice 239–40; and state–corporate crimes 132–33
social injuries 133
social justice 146, 290, 402
social learning theory 270
social media 7, 84–85; and crime news 12, 15; and online counter-publics 16; and online fraud 25; and penal populism 149, 153
social problems, criminalisation of 6, 145
social skills 177, 179, 266, 360, 364
social support 278, 281
social workers 78, 233; and restorative justice 243
solitary confinement 294, 297
South Canterbury Finance 121
sovereignty 41, 188
Space Shuttle disaster 122, 124, 132
Special Circumstances, Court of 193
special treatment units (STUs) 269–70; *see also* Kia Marama; Te Piriti

specialised access, crimes of 123
specialist courts 1, 190–95, 217; criticisms of 195–96; experience of 193–95; nature of 190; values 192–93
species: harms 5; justice 107, 109–12
spectacle, as news value 12
Springbok tour 14, 41, 164, 169n9
stare decisis 189, 198n1
state care 289, 314, 320, 359, 398
state crime 11, 120, 131, 402
state–corporate crimes 4, 49, 131–32, 139; justice following 138; and management of ignorance 133–34; nature of harms 133; Pike River as 135; state-facilitated 132; state-initiated 132; structural basis of 137–38
statistics: tier 1 29n5; *see also* crime problem, and police statistics
Statistics New Zealand 207, 324
Steps to Freedom grant 257
stereotypes: ethnic 325, 336, 396; gender 75, 78; of sex work 388
stigma 3; of drug use 54; of imprisonment 279; and youth justice 214, 216
Stó:lō nation 245–46
stock market crash of 1987 152
Stormtroopers gang 371–72
strain theory 350
strangulation 76
street crimes 11, 131
street lighting 182–83
strength-based focus 339
strengths-based approaches 146, 268, 276, 281–83, 363
structural inequalities 4, 146, 276, 305, 395
Sturm, Jacquie 64
substance misuse: among prisoners 277–78, 346; parental 359; and rehabilitation 269; as risk factor 14; and solution-focused courts 144, 193, 196, *see also* drug courts; treatment programmes 230, 365
substances: substance-defined crime 52–53; substance-influenced crime 53; substance-related crime 53; *see also* drugs
suicide: and cybercrime 88; in prisons 252, 294, 363
Summary Offences Act 1981 97, 375, 387
supervision 203, 226, 228–30, 232; as alternative to prison 298; excessive 206; *see also* intensive supervision

supervision with residence orders 214, 218
Supported Accommodation for Long-Servers scheme 279–80
Supreme Court 140n8, 189, 197
surveillance 3–4, 143, 145; in community sentences 203, 225–27, 229–32, 234; and crime prevention 182, 217; and criminology 38; invasive 227, 257; of Māori 161; online 16; of the police by the public 347; softer and harder forms of 163–64; technologies of 3, 226, 394
surveys: of children of prisoners 257; of crime 21–22, 25–27, 29, 377; of Māori offenders 256; of prison experience 145, 251–52, 255, 346; of racist ideas 98; of sex workers 388; of white-collar crime 120, 127
survival, crimes of 312
synthetic cannabis 51

T
Tai Aroha 270
talkback radio 154
tangata whenua *see* Māori
tapu 225, 235n1
target hardening 182
Tarrant, Brenton 95
tattooing: gangs excluded from work in 378; in prison 254–55
Taumaunu, Heemi 190–91
Tauri, Juan Marcellus 41, 145, 323
tautology 310
Team Policing Units 372
technologies, new 5, 7, 84, 305
Telecommunications Act 1987 375
terrestrial crime 25, 27–28, 167; and cybercrime 85–86, 90
terror, war on 98
therapeutic communities 270, 298
therapeutic jurisprudence 144, 188, 193, 209n2; and solution-focused courts 192; and Youth Court 217
third systems 221
Thompson and Clark 169n10
three-strikes law 23, 42n1, 148, 150, 155, 200, 205
Tiaki Tangata programme 228, 279
tikanga Māori: and alternatives to imprisonment 297; and courts 188, 190–91, 195, 197; motivational programmes 268; and prisons 146, 290, 292–93; and reintegration 282; and youth justice 215, 340
tino rangatiratanga 196, 283, 293, 295, 323
Te Tiriti o Waitangi (Treaty of Waitangi) 5, 8; and decolonisation 333; and green criminology 114; and justice system 188, 196–97, 215, 339; and New Zealand Police 168; and policing 335; and prisons 293; and research ethics 39–40; research obligations under 34; and women's organisations 75
Tolley, Anne 377
Tongan Crips 376
'tough-on-crime' approach 11, 100, 226, 292, 298, 379
TPF (Tripartite Framework) 50, 57n1
transformative justice 297
transformative responses to crime 6, 143
transgender people 75, 295, 387
transinstitutionalisation 347
transnational crimes 5, 48, 86
Transparency International 122
transphobia 48, 102
Trans-Tasman Travel Arrangement 1973 399
trauma: of colonial policing 161–62, 318; of dawn raids 399; in racehorses 110; of victims 154
traumatic brain injury 220–21, 233, 359–60
treatment programmes 180, 227, 267, 270–71
treatment units 269–70
Trembath, Jason 67
tribunals 189
Triple P programme 179–80, 183
Trump, Donald 95, 394
trust, decline of 152–53
Te Tua, Jhia 375
Turning of the Tide strategy 162, 335

U
Te Uepū Hāpai i te Ora – the Safe and Effective Justice Advisory Group 2, 156, 317
UN Committee on the Rights of the Child 216, 221
UN Convention on the Rights of the Child 215, 219
UN Declaration on the Rights of Indigenous Peoples 339
UN Standard Minimum Rules for the Treatment of Prisoners 297
unconscious bias training (UBT) 163, 324–25

unemployment 11
urbanisation 108, 320
Te Urewera 161
Urupare Whītiki *see* Responsiveness to Māori
utilitarianism 201
utu 225, 235n1, 294
uxoricide 309–10

V

Valley Longwall International 138, 140n5
Viaduct Capital and Mutual Finance 121
Vicious Lawless Association Disestablishment Act 2013 (Queensland) 378
victim empowerment 241
victim mentality 312
victim responsibility 308
victim self-blame 69
victim-blaming 4, 48; and image-based sexual abuse 88; and intoxication 58; and safety crimes 133; and victimology 303, 307, 310, 314
victimisation 4–5; barriers created by 78–79; and cybercrime 85; environment-related 108; of Māori 277; media representations of 12; normalising 3–4; in NZCVS 21; personal accounts of 307–8; prevention of 308–9, 311; in prisons 145; of racehorses 109; violent 12, 253
'victimity' 306–12
victimless crimes 292, 296
victimology 303, 306; conventional 315n1; critical 311–13; general 311; and the 'penal couple' 307–8, 312; positivist 306–14; radical 307
victims: bias against 310; courts' engagement with 190, 196; guilty victims 306–7, 313–14; ideal 306–7, 309, 312–14; and imprisonment 292; and penal populism 148–50, 154–55; sex workers as 386; support for 79–80; surveys 22, 25; types of 309, 311
Victims' Rights Act 2002 76, 154, 242
victims' rights movement 314
violence: against Muslims 94–97; impulsive 362; institutionalised 142, 314; racialised explanations of 349; not reporting 78; 'senseless' 11; structural 313; *see also* violent crime
violent crime: and alcohol 50, 56; in the news 9, 11
visa cancellations 400, 403n5

volume crimes 8, 21–28, 29n7, 30n9; and drug–crime link 52
von Hentig, Hans 307–10

W

Waitangi Day 41, 250, 259
Waitangi Tribunal 282, 284n3
Wall Walk 162
Walton, Bob 373–74
warrior gene 349
water safety 109, 112–13
waterside strike 1951 318
Webb, Robert 41
welfare fraud 125–26
welfarism 148, 213
well-being 6; children's 145–46; environmental 108–9, 112, 114; Māori models of 270; of Māori youth 336–37, 339; in Oranga Tamariki Act 215; and police culture 325; of prisoners 294; in rehabilitation 266, 268; of victims 75, 149, 312; *see also* Pou Oranga
whakapapa 114, 339; knowledge of 256; of Māori resistance 294; and Māori-focused courts 190–91, 197; and youth justice 215, 243
whanaungatanga 215, 338–39
Whanganui River rights and Te Awa Tupua Act 2017 113–14
Te Whare Whakapiki Wairua 194–96, 201, 208
whenua 279
white supremacy 95, 98, 102
white-collar crime 4, 25, 49, 119–20, 131; controlling 125–27; costs of 121; and criminology 38; and the media 11; in New Zealand 120–22; police responses to 168; relationship to colonisation 120; statistics on 348; theories of 123–24, 126
Whittall, Peter 138, 140n8
Windrush scandal 395, 402n2
Withers, Nan 313
Withers, Norm 150, 157n1
women: as judges 190; as offenders 14, 220; racialised representations of 14; as victims 2, 309–11, 313; working-class 352; *see also* sexuality; silencing
women's bodies, male possession of 4, 48, 62, 66–69
Women's Refuge 75–79
Wood, Paul 255
working class 318, 352–53

Workman, Kim 41
workplace injuries 133, 140n2
WorkSafe 138
WorkSafe New Zealand Act 2013 126, 138

Y

Youi 125
young adults 88, 221, 371
young people: adverse life events 220; alienation of 14, 333; in custody 35, 218; moral panics about 13; and Ngā Kōti Rangatahi 191; as offenders 145, 319–20, 334; prolonged detention of 159; research on 337; student exclusions of 242; and youth justice 37, 214–15, 220, 304, 331–32, 338–41
young persons: definition of 216; in Ngā Kōti Rangatahi 191
young women, and intoxicating substances 51
Youth Action Plan 183, 376–77
Youth Court 144–45, 332; and 1989 Act 213; in courts hierarchy 189; and neuro-disabilities 358, 365; offences out of the jurisdiction of 219; procedures of 217–18; Section 333 reports in 367n3; sentencing powers 214, 218; *see also* Kōti Rangatahi
Youth Crime Action Plan 191
youth justice: contemporary challenges 219–20; de-professionalising 334; future of 221–22; and gender 145, 220; informal nature of 213, 216–17; key features of 215–19; Māori and Pasifika in 304, 331–32, 335–37, 340–41; Māori critique of 242; New Zealand model of 1, 213–14; participation in 215, 217; reforms to 214–15; residences 218
youth offending 145; by children with neuro-disabilities 217, 358–60, 365; by girls 145, 220; Māori and Pasifika 332, 342n3; moral panics about 7; sentences for 219; serious 218
youth subcultures 13

Z

Zehr, Howard 239, 241
zemiology 39